Educational Psychology
The Teaching-Learning Process

Educational Psychology
The Teaching-Learning Process

by
Daniel L. Barlow

TechBooks

First published in 1985 by Moody Bible Institute of Chicago

Copyright © 1992 by TechBooks
ISBN 1-878907-50-6

All rights reserved. No part of this book may be reproduced in any form without permission in writing from the publisher, except in the case of brief quotations embodied in critical articles or reviews.

Every reasonable effort has been made to trace owners of copyrighted materials used in this book, but in some instances this has proved impossible.

The publisher will be glad to receive information leading to more complete acknowledgements in subsequent printings and in the meantime extends apologies for any ommisions.

Printed in the United States of America.

TechBooks
2600 Seskey Glen Court
Herndon, VA 22071
Phone: (703) 758-1518

To
Wilma Mae, Dana Scott, Brett Robin, Douglas Lee, Forest Lee,
my wife and sons, and
Walter Joseph, Ruth Lenox, Walter Lenox, Betty Skidmore,
my father, mother, brother, and sister:
my two families, without whom the writing of this book would not
have been possible

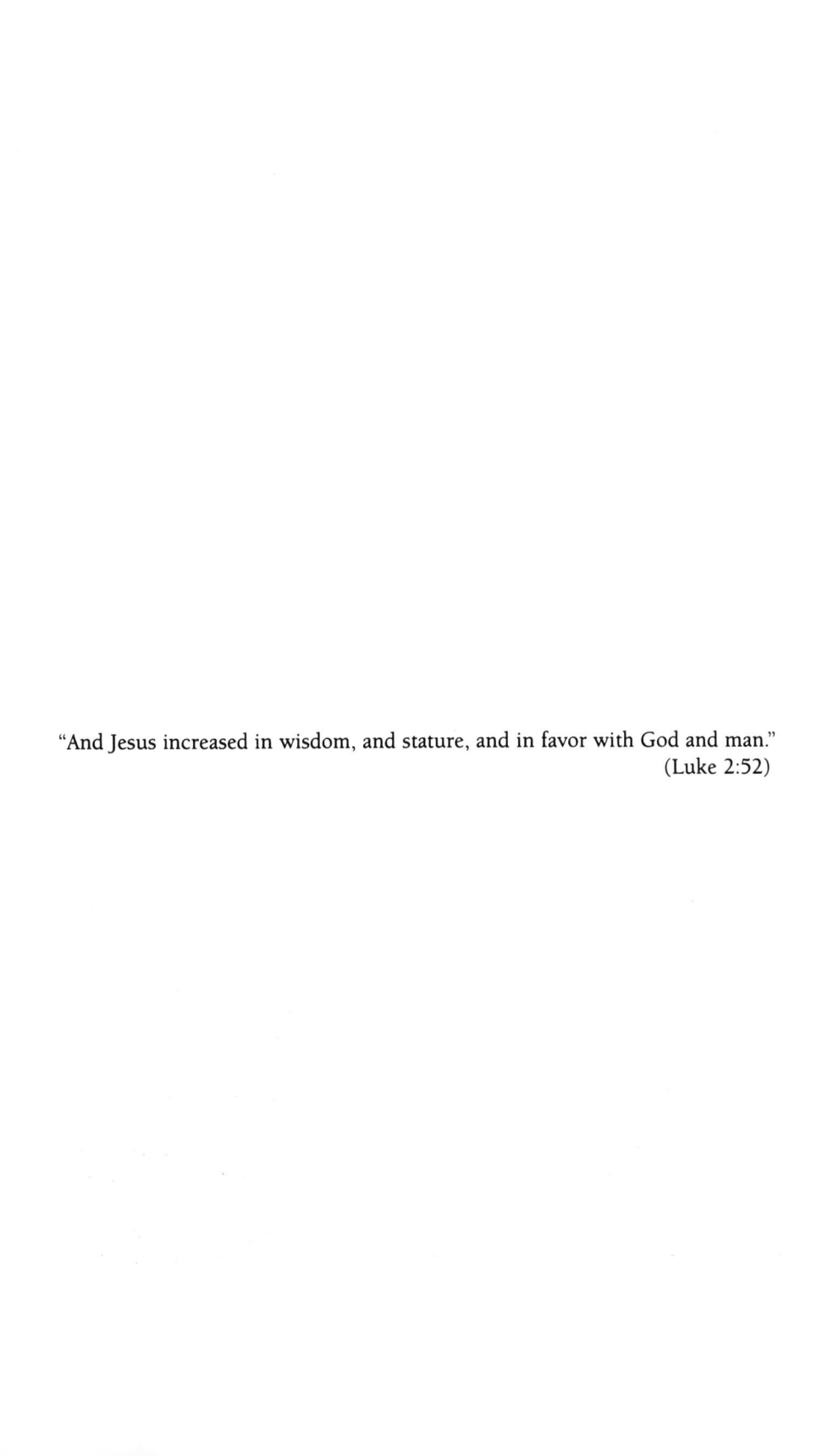

"And Jesus increased in wisdom, and stature, and in favor with God and man."
(Luke 2:52)

CONTENTS

CHAPTER		PAGE
	Preface	ix
	Part 1: The Dimensions of the Teaching-Learning Process	
1.	Educational Psychology and the Teaching-Learning Process	3
2.	Teaching at the Schoolhouse—What's It Like?	40
	Part 2: The Developmental Process	
3.	Concepts and Theories	69
4.	Characteristics and Sequences	105
	Part 3: The Learning Process	
5.	The Behavioristic Approach	131
6.	The Cognitive-Discovery Approach	157
7.	The Humanistic Approach	183
8.	The Christian Approach	205
9.	Varieties, Conditions, and Designs	226
10.	Remembering, Forgetting, and Transferring	254
	Part 4: The Teaching-Learning Process	
11.	Management—Classroom Control	277

12.	Management—Classroom Climate	299
13.	Classroom Methodology	322
14.	Student Motivation	348
15.	Student Multipotentiality	372
16.	Mainstreaming Students—Exceptionality	398
17.	Measurement—Student Performance	418
18.	Measurement—Student Feedback	449

Part 5: The Teacher in the Teaching-Learning Process

19.	Personal and Professional Development	467
20.	Future Changes in the Teaching-Learning Process	487
	Glossary	505
	Subject Index	521
	Person Index	528

Preface

This book is intended for use as an introductory college-level text in educational psychology, human development and learning, or other courses in which the central concern is with how people develop and learn.

Most colleges and universities require their education majors to take this kind of course. Increasingly, preprofessional students in law, medicine, nursing, religion, counseling, and other helping professions are required or elect to enroll as well. Still others who may find this book helpful are parents interested in understanding the teaching-learning process better, or the clergyman whose church is interested in establishing a school.

There are a substantial number of excellent texts in this area already, but this book is written from the *Christian perspective*. It is for those who desire a text that presents various approaches fairly, yet frankly espouses the Christian viewpoint.

The organization of this book is clearly explained in chapter 1. I believe it is important for the organizational structure of a textbook to be made part of the teaching-learning process, in order to help the student develop his or her own cognitive structure for the course. The table of contents reflects, of course, the topical structure.

Special aids for the teaching-learning process are included in chapter 1 also, under the heading of "Handles on Your Learning." Those "handles" should become part of the material learned within the formal instructional process, rather than added-on pieces of material. Just as the effective elementary teacher includes rules and regulations as a part of the teaching-learning process in the classroom, so organizational structure and special aids should be included at the college level in similar fashion. They should be *taught as part of the course.*

This book grew out of my conviction that Christian scholarship should combine the finest in academic excellence with unswerving commitment to biblical Christianity. Although the book does not have references for Bible verses scattered throughout, the Christian perspective is made clear at appropriate places.

Many people have, knowingly and unknowingly, been part of the making of this book over the years—professors, parishioners, colleagues, students. Space precludes my listing so many of them by name but in no way lessens my gratitude for their contributions.

For advice, guidance, aid, and encouragement on the manuscript itself, there are many I must thank. Dr. Ann McFarland contributed chapters 4 and 13; Dr. Maurice Stone contributed chapters 17 and 18. Both are esteemed colleagues at Liberty Baptist College. Mildred Livesay went far beyond the call of duty many times in typing and otherwise readying the final manuscript; the great patience and encouragement of Dr. George Livesay, her husband and my colleague, must be noted. Marlene Evans came to my rescue at several critical points with her excellent secretarial skills and willingness to be a "crisis" helper. Laura Champe worked faithfully and thoroughly during the final summer of preparation as a student editorial assistant. Robert DeVaul of the photography department at Liberty and his staff were of inestimable value with their cheerful advice and practical help with photographs. Judy Trenary worked diligently to prepare the glossary. Jeanne Palacios, Debbie Barton, Cheryl Cook, Cheryl Harris, and Sharon Snodgrass contributed secretarial and clerical help at important points along the way.

I am indebted for the encouragement of the administration at Liberty Baptist College, as reflected through the office of President Pierre Guillermin, Vice-President for Academic Affairs Russell Fitzgerald, and Dean Garth Runion of the School of Education.

This is my first book, and no one could have better introduced me to the "trade" than the editors and staff of Moody Press. I am especially grateful for the expertise and good humor of Managing Editor Ella Lindvall and Senior Academic Editor Gary Knussman, and I must thank as well the Moody Press staff, who transformed the final manuscript into printed book.

I have dedicated this book to two families—the one I grew up with, who introduced me to and nurtured me through the first twenty years of the human development and learning process; and the second, my wife of thirty-seven years and four sons, who through their love, patience, honesty, and endurance have refined my understanding of the teaching-learning process and made the writing of this book possible.

I thank God for my two families and for the family of God, without whom, in the profoundest sense, this book could not have been written.

Part 1

The Dimensions of the Teaching-Learning Process

1
Educational Psychology and the Teaching-Learning Process

CONTENTS

	PAGE
Key Terms	3
That's Debatable!	4
Foresight	6
Some Honest Questions About You and Teaching	6
How This Book Can Help You	13
Educational Psychology: What It Is—How It Helps	15
What Competent Teachers Need to Know	23
The Competent Teacher: Philosopher-Clinician	27
Hindsight	31
Chalkboard Challenges	32
Want to Know More?	33

KEY TERMS

Clinician
  The teacher as a person who can perform competently in the teaching-learning process
Communication skills
  Listening, writing, speaking, and the ability to present your ideas in such a manner your listeners will readily understand them
Competent
  Responsibly able to perform appropriate duties

Computation skills
: The ability to know, understand, and recognize how and when to apply the techniques of mathematics, computers, and statistics to the solutions of real-life problems

Educational psychology
: A body of knowledge grounded in psychological research, which provides a scientific approach to the teaching-learning process

Educational services professional
: A person prepared to work effectively in an educational setting other than the schoolhouse classroom

Educational setting
: The particular place/environment in which the teaching-learning process occurs

Effects
: Influences, expected or unexpected, that can occur during scientific studies of behavior and can "contaminate" the outcomes

Glossary
: A group of words and their definitions

"Handles" on your learning
: Features to help you take hold of and understand clearly the meanings of concepts

Learning society
: Characteristic of our own society, where the explosion of new ideas and techniques has created the need for many people to learn many things

Philosopher
: The teacher as a person who brings a philosophic perspective—fed by experiences, knowledge, and reflective commitment—to his performance as a clinician in the teaching-learning process

Repertoire of responses
: A "stored supply" of information (concepts, skills, techniques, and the like) from which the teacher can draw as they are needed in order to perform competently in the teaching-learning process; educational psychology a major contributor to the repertoire for the teacher

Schoolhouse environment
: All components (people, responsibilities, expectations, smells, etc.) that are found at the schoolhouse and which affect the individuals working there

Textbook "blues"
: The discouraged feelings students frequently experience because they perceive the textbook as boring, drudgery, something they "have to read"

THAT'S DEBATABLE!

IS PREPARATION FOR TEACHING ADEQUATE?

Affirmative. Student teachers perceive that their cooperating teacher and university supervisor share similar views on education.[1] Over 90 percent of the professors of education have had classroom teaching experience.[2] Over two-thirds of teacher-education students sampled reported "very satisfied" in relation to their professional education courses.[3] From a national survey of teacher-preparation programs, it was calculated that 54 percent of the credits were in liberal arts and 46 percent in education: of the 46 percent, one-third of the credits are in clinical experiences.[4] There is a satisfactory articulation between the clinical and course-based experiences.[5] Many of the teacher preparation programs begin clinical experiences in the student's freshman year.[6] Two-thirds of the teacher-education programs report students can elect to or are required to work with poor and/or minority children.[7] Graduating students believe they are adequately prepared to begin teaching and believe they are capable of organizing and managing a classroom.[8]

Negative. Enrollment criteria in more than 80 percent of the programs were based on the student's decision to enter rather than stringent criteria established by the programs in education.[9] The provincialism of education students is reflected by the fact that 83 percent of the students attend a college or university in their home states; more than two-thirds of the students attend a school within 100 miles of their homes; and only 4 percent can speak a second language.[10] Only five percent of the programs have a preassessment technique to measure those skills that are lacking or have been achieved previously by the individual student.[11] Professors of education teach with technology of the eighteenth and nineteenth centuries and avoid the technologies of the twentieth century. There is a lack of interaction among the student teacher, the cooperating teacher, and the university supervisor. Often, observations by the university supervisor are cursory at best. Secondary teachers become substantially more bureaucratic in orientation as a result of student teaching.[12] The typical graduate of a teacher-preparation program desires clients with the smallest risks: middle-class students in suburban and rural areas.[13]

---

1. Sam Yarger, Kenneth Howey, and Bruce Joyce, "Reflections on Preservice Preparation: Impressions from the National Survey, Part II: Students and Faculty," *Journal of Teacher Education* 28 (November-December 1977):35.
2. Ibid.
3. Sam Yarger and Bruce Joyce, "Going Beyond the Data: Reconstructing Teacher Education," *Journal of Teacher Education* 28 (November-December 1977):21.
4. Kenneth Howey, Sam Yarger, and Bruce Joyce, "Reflections on Preservice Preparation: Impressions from the National Survey, Part III: Institutions and Programs," *Journal of Teacher Education* 29 (January-February 1978):39.
5. Ibid.
6. Ibid.
7. Ibid.
8. Ibid.
9. Ibid.
10. Yarger, Howey, and Joyce, p. 35.
11. Ibid.
12. Wayne K. Hoy and Richard Rees, "The Bureaucratic Socialization of Student Teachers," *Journal of Teacher Education* 28 (January-February 1977):25.
13. Yarger and Joyce, p. 21.

Why is it they want to avoid those students who are in need of the greatest help: urban and rural poor, racial and cultural minorities?[14]

FORESIGHT

We live in a "learning society." Demands for educational services are increasing at an unprecedented rate. Education is developing many new dimensions, the vast majority of which require a knowledge of the teaching-learning process.

As you begin this book it is highly probable you have in mind the teaching-learning process as it relates to the classroom of the school. And it is that particular educational setting to which this book addresses itself primarily. But keep your mind open to the many educational possibilities becoming available in a wide variety of situations and institutions, for which your training as a teacher will be invaluable.

Educational psychology is a body of knowledge grounded in psychological research, which provides a repertoire of resources to aid you in functioning more effectively as a teacher in the teaching-learning process. In this chapter, you will read about educational psychology—what it is, how it works, and some of the problems scientists face in studying behavior; you will explore some of the honest questions you have about *you* and teaching; you will learn how to get some helpful handles on *your* learning and how to use this book effectively; you will be exposed to a model of the competent teacher as the philosopher-clinician, combining the use of scientific findings with the individual's professional judgment to produce the teacher who can significantly impact the way students develop and learn.

Regardless of the educational setting in which you may become involved, we wish you well as you explore the fascinating world of educational psychology and the teaching-learning process.

"Everything you've always wanted to know about teaching and were afraid to ask?" That might not be a bad title for a book, but it is dubious whether any book could answer *all* the questions any person has about teaching. The following section deals with some of the most frequent questions students ask as they think about careers in education. You will probably find yourself speculating about some of these. It is hoped you will begin to find answers.

SOME HONEST QUESTIONS ABOUT YOU AND TEACHING

AM I REALLY SURE THIS IS WHAT I WANT TO DO?

How did I get this far? You already have experienced twelve or more years of

---

14. This section was adapted from Leo W. Anglin, Jr., Richard M. Goldman, and Joyce S. Anglin, *Teaching: What It's All About* (New York: Harper & Row, 1982), pp. 327-30.

education, and from that experience some facets have been attractive enough to cause you to give serious thought to becoming a teacher. You may find it helpful to list those facets as a starting point for your consideration.

Will I fit? As you read about what it's like teaching at the schoolhouse (chapter 2), you may find it helpful to reflect upon "the schoolhouse environment" with *you* in the midst of it. How do you think you would respond or react to the situations and responsibilities described?

What age level should I teach? Perhaps you find yourself in the company of many other students who wonder about what age or grade level they should teach. You will be able to gain additional insights into the characteristics of students at different age levels as you read chapters 3 and 4, and that knowledge may help you toward a decision to teach at a particular grade level.

How do people learn? Learning can and should be an exciting process. You will be able to understand better how people learn as you study chapters 5 through

---

Insight: Teaching as an Art

Gilbert Highet, a distinguished professor of literature, comments in his book *The Art of Teaching*:

I believe that teaching is an art, not a science. It seems to me very dangerous to apply the aims and methods of science to human beings as individuals, although a statistical principle can often be used to explain their behavior in large groups and a scientific diagnosis of their physical structure is always valuable. But a "scientific" relationship between human beings is bound to be inadequate and perhaps distorted. Of course it is necessary for any teacher to be orderly in planning his work and precise in his dealing with facts. But that does not make his teaching "scientific." Teaching involves emotions, which cannot be systemically appraised and employed, and human values, which are quite outside the grasp of science.... "Scientific" teaching, even of scientific subjects, will be inadequate as long as both teachers and pupils are human beings. Teaching is not like inducing a chemical reaction: it is much more like painting a picture or making a piece of music, ... like planting a garden or writing a friendly letter. You must throw your heart into it, you must realize that it cannot all be done by formulas, or you will spoil your work, and your pupils, and yourself. From *Teaching as an Art* (New York: Vintage, 1957), pp. vii-viii. Used by permission.

Fig. 1.1

10, and you can speculate as to which approach(es) to learning you might use, and why.

Will I be satisfied? Will you enjoy teaching? No one can completely answer that question until he has actually taught, but as you reflect upon the teacher's role and responsibility in the teaching-learning process (chapters 11-18), you can form a realistic picture of what you will do if you become a teacher, and whether you will find satisfaction in it.

What about my future as a teacher? The remaining chapters (19-20) enable you to look more deeply into the personal and professional aspects of being a teacher and to gain a perspective as to what the future holds for the teacher in the teaching-learning process.

WHAT DO I HAVE TO LEARN TO BECOME A TEACHER?

Can I make a difference? Teachers can have a major influence on the development and learning of students. And the really effective instructors (parents, classroom teachers, instructors in industry, etc.) combine teaching skills with an active conviction that the teacher can make a difference in learning.[15]

What do I need to know? The competent teacher needs to know how people develop, how they learn, how teaching relates to learning, how to become personally effective in the classroom, how to develop personally and professionally, and how to prepare for future changes in the teaching-learning process.

Obviously, these areas require that the teacher possess skills and knowledge. These are derived largely, though not exclusively, from the discoveries of psychologists. Psychologists use the methods of science to study behavior and on the basis of their findings have established principles and theories to summarize their conclusions. Educational psychology uses those conclusions and applies them in particular to the teaching-learning process. Therefore, the answer to your question, "What do I have to learn to become a teacher?" is that you will need to acquire insights into the teaching-learning process based primarily on scientific discoveries by psychologists.

What do I need to emphasize? Biehler and Snowman stress the teacher as theorist and the teacher as practitioner.[16] An approach, a point of view, is exceedingly important in determining how you will operate in the classroom or other educational setting. Of course, there will always be the restrictions of the particular setting, but we believe it is important to develop the philosophical (theoretical) background as a framework in which to operate as a practitioner

---

15. T.L. Good and J.E. Brophy, *Educational Psychology: A Realistic Approach*, 2d ed. (New York: Holt, Rinehart, & Winston, 1980).
16. R.F. Biehler and J. Snowman, *Psychology Applied to Teaching*, 4th ed. (Boston: Houghton Mifflin, 1982).

Educational Psychology and the Teaching-Learning Process 9

Insight: Teaching as a Science

J. M. Stephens, an educational psychologist, presents a scientist's point of view concerning teaching:
The professional educator must have considerable faith in the educational process. . . . He must hope and believe that it will accomplish great things. . . . Teaching is often such a warm, emotional, enthusiastic process. It calls for devotion and commitment to a given course of action. It is possible that a cold analytic attitude of suspended judgment would prevent the teacher from stimulating students and would make for poor rapport.

These convictions and emotional commitments which may be so necessary in the practice of education are obvious handicaps in the careful and precise study of education. Enthusiastic feelings or warm hopes should not influence our decisions as to what is so. . . .

To understand a process, we must try to put our feelings and wishes in cold storage for a time, and having done so, we must try to face the facts with an open mind. But although we must face facts, we need not become the slaves of facts.

From *Educational Psychology,* 2d ed. (New York: Holt, Rinehart, and Winston, 1956), pp. 21-22. Used by permission.

Fig. 1.2

(clinician). At the same time, we place heavy emphasis on the applications of theories to the practical operations in the educational setting. Farther along in this chapter, a model of the teacher as a philosopher-clinician will be presented.

WILL THE JOB OPPORTUNITIES BE THERE?

There are at least three basic considerations that can help you answer this question: assessing the situation in the traditional K-12 public schools; exploring the job possibilities in other educational settings; and considering whether *any* kind of career preparation guarantees obtaining a particular kind of job in our rapidly changing society.

Job opportunities in the traditional K-12 public schools. At this writing there are more people seeking jobs in teaching than the number of jobs available. There is considerable disagreement as to how long and in what areas this overabundance of teacher supply will last. Some estimate there will be an adequate supply of teachers

A Comparison of Education-Related Careers

	Preparation Required	Experiences	Salary Range	Role Description	Job Possibilities
In-school, teaching	Bachelor's Degree* Specialization* Student Teaching*	Volunteer work with children† Camp counselor† Babysitter†	$10-26,000 for nine months	Instructional responsibilities completed by certified classroom teacher in formal school organization.	Improvement over 1970s in all areas. Better possibilities in rural areas and Sun Belt. Needs exist in special education, mathematics, science, and vocational education.
In-school, nonteaching	Bachelor's (except for nurses)* Specialization* Postbachelors and Masters-Counselor, Psychologist, Principal*	Extensive experiences with children† Teaching experience†	$10-35,000	Educational support provided in emotional, physical, and cognitive areas. Responsibilities carried out within formal school organization.	Among the best rapid-growth areas in the last decade.
Teaching, nonschool	Bachelor's Degree* Area of specialization outside education*	Teaching experience† Acquire specialized content knowledge*	$8-20,000	Conveying specialized school-related knowledge in formal organization outside school.	An emerging area for jobs in 1980s.
Community, youth, and family services	Bachelor's Degree* Specialized training outside education*†	Teaching experience† Volunteer work with groups†	$8-35,000	Conveying specialized knowledge usually not related to school curriculum, with	An emerging area because of increased leisure time. Long-term employment not guaranteed because of problems with funding sources.

			emphasis on the psychomotor and affective areas.	
Higher education	Master's Degree* Doctorate†	Teaching experience with children* Experience with school organizations†	$12-42,000	Expert in specific school-related area. Some offer direct service (e.g., teacher preparation); others offer indirect service (e.g., educational researcher)	The shrinking job market of the 1970s will improve in the 1980s.
School support	Bachelor's Degree* Specialized training*	Teaching experience†	$15-75,000	Concern with all aspects of education; do not have direct involvement with teaching/learning process.	Many positions in area are new since the 1960s. With the demands currently being placed on schools by the public, additional support staff needed.
Government agencies	Bachelor's Degree* Master's and Doctorate†	Teaching experience†	$15-50,000	Individuals responsible for developing and implementing policy and programs mandated by legislative bodies.	Legislatures have mandated that specified groups receive improved education (e.g., handicapped and the disadvantaged). These mandates have opened additional occupational possibilities in government agencies.

*Required
†Recommended

From Leo W. Anglin, Jr., Richard M. Goldman, and Joyce Shanahan Anglin, *Teaching, What It's All About* (New York: Harper & Row, 1982), pp. 352–53. © 1982 by Harper & Row, Publishers, Inc. Reprinted by permission of Harper & Row, Publishers, Inc.

Fig. 1.3

for the public schools throughout the 1980s.[17] Others believe we will witness a teacher shortage of varying proportions, particularly in the large urban areas, beginning in the mid-1980s.[18]

It would appear that toward the end of the 1980s, the supply-demand situation will at least level off, but another aspect becomes increasingly important. During this decade, the technological revolution is becoming institutionalized in the public schools. Standards for admission to teacher education programs are becoming increasingly rigorous, and the teacher who completes a degree and certification will need to be proficient in communication and computation skills. The teacher who is not proficient in the advancing technology will find it difficult, if not impossible, to compete for a job.

So the answer to your question regarding job opportunities in the K-12 public schools is probably a guarded "yes." Yes, there will be jobs for those who are well prepared, not only in a "subject area," but as well in the communication and computation skills areas (especially the video- and computer-related forms of technology). Additionally, the teacher will need to have had experiences in providing educational opportunities for *exceptional* people, in order to compete successfully for available jobs.

Job opportunities in nontraditional educational settings. Job opportunities for those thoroughly skilled in the teaching-learning process are available in many educational settings other than schools. Demands for educational services are increasing rapidly in the changing social context of our society.

> Teaching, counseling, developing and administrating educational programs, and analyzing education processes and issues are performed in many settings other than schools. Hospitals, recreation agencies, nursing homes, libraries, health care agencies, correctional institutions, museums, community centers, churches, businesses and many other agencies and institutions are performing educational functions. Publishers of education books and media need editors and other staff knowledgeable about education. Legislative offices, legal firms, judicial staffs, architectural firms, and government planning offices often need educators' expertise on their staffs or as consultants. Education affairs offices are being developed and expanded in many professional, business and government organizations. Television and the developing communication and information exchange systems are increasingly involved in education functions and issues.[19]

Persons trained for and engaged in these nontraditional education settings are usually referred to as *educational services professionals.* They play a critical role

---

17. B.G. Burch, "New Missions for Colleges of Education," *Action In Teacher Education* 2, no. 3 (1980):1-11.
18. J.R. Applegate, D.E. Black, and R.K. Carlton, "The Preparation of Educational Personnel in the 1980s," *Action in Teacher Education* 2, no. 3 (1980):13-16.
19. Dean Corrigan, "Undergraduate Major in Educational Studies in Multiple Settings" (University of Maryland, College of Education, April 1979). Cited in Burch, p. 1. Used by permission of the author.

Educational Psychology and the Teaching-Learning Process

in the education of citizens in our modern urban and multicultural society. Burch in her article cited above, calls for colleges of education to broaden the dimensions of their training to meet these nontraditional needs, and provides some excellent recommendations for the procedures involved.[20] For further information and resources regarding nontraditional education settings, see suggestions in "Want to Know More?" at the end of this chapter.

In the nontraditional education setting, the answer to your question about job opportunities will be found in carefully assessing your interests and abilities, gathering appropriate information, and acquiring appropriate education and training for the opportunities involved in becoming an educational services professional.

Guaranteeing a particular kind of job. The rapidly changing economic, political, and social conditions in our own nation, and indeed throughout the world, make it impossible to guarantee that *any* kind of career preparation will result in obtaining a particular kind of job.

Biehler makes an excellent point in this regard:

> Even if you do not seek or secure a job as a teacher, it is likely that what you learn in education courses will benefit you as much as, if not more than, what you might have learned in a different degree program. The knowledge you acquire of learning, teaching, and human behavior, for example, may contribute to success in finding many kinds of jobs not directly related to education. In addition, you may be able to use information presented . . . to improve your learning ability. If you become aware of a career possibility that necessitates acquiring a new set of skills in a short period of time, you may be able to use information provided . . . to facilitate self-instruction. Furthermore, if you have children, you should be able to understand better the kind of education they receive and also to serve as an effective tutor in school-related and other learning situations.[21]

Although your training as a teacher will not guarantee a particular kind of teaching position or a particular job, nevertheless it will benefit you in many ways: to help find jobs not directly related to education, or in nontraditional educational settings; to learn new skills quickly; to understand better the education of your children; and to intelligently participate in many aspects of school, community, and national life.

How This Book Can Help You

If you are like many other students, you are well supplied with textbooks and other learning materials. At the beginning of the term, there may be that day or even week of excitement, seriousness about reading every assignment, and then the

---

20. Burch, pp. 1-11.
21. R.F. Biehler, *Psychology Applied to Teaching,* 3d ed. (Boston: Houghton-Mifflin, 1978), p. 8. Used by permission.

excitement fades. I am convinced that part of the reason for the fading is the student's not understanding how to use the textbook (and other materials) in valuable and exciting ways. To help prevent "textbook blues" with this book, you are urged to read carefully about the features of this book that will put "handles" on your learning, and the further suggestions for using this book effectively.

FEATURES: HANDLES ON YOUR LEARNING

Gallery of Greats. Pictures and brief biographies of outstanding psychologists and educators.

Brief Table of Contents. A brief outline is provided at the beginning of each chapter to help you structure that chapter's contents in your mind. These items can act as pegs on which to hang information.

Key Terms and Alphabetical Glossary. Look for the key terms at the beginning of each chapter, crisply defined, and the alphabetical glossary of key terms from all of the chapters at the back of the book.

Foresight. At the beginning of each chapter is a clearly written preorganizer geared to arouse your curiosity about the topics to be discussed in that chapter.

That's Debatable! Just one to a chapter, a summary of pros and cons of a controversial issue related to that chapter's discussion.

Insight. Boxed in, clearly formulated key information relevant to the highlights of that particular chapter. You will find one or more of these in each chapter.

Hindsight. At the end of each chapter a summary of major areas covered in that chapter.

Chalkboard Challenges. Immediately following "Hindsight" in each chapter are questions and activities designed to get you actively involved with the issues of that chapter. These include practical applications to help you develop specific skills and learn how you can use those skills in the teaching-learning process.

Want to Know More? The final segment of each chapter contains suggestions for further reading and study in areas that interest you or may be assigned. These have been selected carefully to help you get to target areas quickly.

SUGGESTIONS FOR USING THIS BOOK EFFECTIVELY

Make the book your friend. The attitude you have toward any text is extremely important. If you think of a text as "something I've *got* to read" (because it is assigned and may not be your *favorite* pastime), your attitude will probably affect both your receptiveness to and enthusiasm for the material contained in the text. This book has been written to help you learn appropriate information and develop insights and specific skills as a teacher.

Get a "feel" for the book. Don't let it be a stranger to you! Look at the table of contents to get the sweep of the text. Then look through the more detailed table of

Educational Psychology and the Teaching-Learning Process

contents at the beginning of each chapter. Note carefully how your instructor suggests you use the book—this will vary with instructors and educational settings.

Use this text to help you develop a teacher's notebook. A notebook containing your own ideas and suggestions will be one of the most valuable outcomes of this course. This text can help, along with your instructor and your experiences, to develop the kind of notebook you will turn to frequently during your student teaching and early teaching career days, especially.

Plan to keep this book as a reference work. While you are busy during college days with many courses and activities, during your student teaching time, and even perhaps the first year or so of your teaching career, you probably will have neither the time nor inclination to carry out a great deal of independent study beyond what you have to do to survive. But once you become established, feeling more at ease in the teaching-learning process, you may decide or be assigned to carry out some independent research in a particular, or several, areas. In this book are many valuable references, guidelines, and pieces of solid information related to educational psychology and the teaching-learning process that will be greatly helpful to you in your independent research. It is a book you may well want to keep.

By thinking of this text in a friendly manner, getting a "feel" for its direction and contents, using it to help you develop your *teacher's notebook,* and remembering its value as a reference book—it is probable you will pick it up much more frequently and read it more carefully. At least give these suggestions a try, and see if they don't help you get rid of some of those textbook blues!

What Is Educational Psychology?

A body of knowledge grounded in psychological research.

A "repertoire of resources" containing systematized information about the theories and practices of the teaching-learning process: a repertoire to be used under the guidance of the principled, professional judgment of the teacher to produce appropriate learning in the lives of students.

A scientific approach to the teaching-learning process.

Fig. 1.4

EDUCATIONAL PSYCHOLOGY: WHAT IT IS—HOW IT HELPS

At the center of our educational system is the teaching-learning process, and at the center of that process is the teacher, regardless of what the educational setting may be. At the center of the resources geared to help the teacher perform competently is a body of knowledge known as *educational psychology*. There are countless other resources, of course, but it is crucial for the competent teacher to understand and be able to appropriate selectively for his own use the knowledge and techniques of educational psychology. The remainder of this chapter, therefore, presents briefly the facets of educational psychology and relates those facets to the model of the competent teacher as a *philosopher-clinician*.

A BODY OF KNOWLEDGE GROUNDED IN PSYCHOLOGICAL RESEARCH

Psychologists study behavior based on scientific methodology. They draw conclusions and formulate theories based on their results. Those conclusions and theories frequently are not in harmony with each other. There are inconsistencies and downright contradictions. The teacher should not look to the field of educational psychology as a storehouse packed with all the right answers about all the situations he or she will face, but educational psychology does contain a substantial array of vital theories and practices upon which the teacher can draw.

Educational psychology can be viewed best as a repertoire of resources containing systematized information about the theories and practices of the teaching-learning process. That repertoire is to be used under the guidance of the principled, professional judgment of the teacher to produce appropriate learning in the lives of students.

Three outstanding contributors—and their quite different contributions to the historical development of educational psychology—are William James, Edward Thorndike, and John Dewey (described briefly in the Gallery of Greats). It is important for you to become knowledgeable about them, for their insights are being debated (and used) to this very moment.

A SCIENTIFIC APPROACH TO THE TEACHING-LEARNING PROCESS

One of the leading influences insisting that scientific knowledge can and should be used to improve human behavior—including behavior in the teaching-learning process—is B. F. Skinner, a leading American psychologist of this century. He has urged psychologists and educators to develop what he calls a "technology of teaching."[22] He lists some of the characteristics of science: "It is a disposition to deal with the facts rather than what someone has said about them . . . a willingness to accept facts even when they are opposed to wishes . . . [an awareness] of the value of remaining without an answer until a satisfactory one can be found . . . a search for order, for uniformities, for lawful relations among events in nature."[23]

Skinner's approach and contributions will be summarized and critiqued at a

---

22. B.F. Skinner, *The Behavior of Organisms: An Experimental Analysis* (New York: Appleton, 1968). Used by permission of the author.
23. B.F. Skinner, *Science and Human Behavior* (London: Macmillan, 1953), pp. 12-13. Used by permission.

number of places in this text, especially in chapter 5. But at this point his emphasis on a scientific approach to the teaching-learning process serves to warn us against drawing false conclusions because of unsystematic observations of and approaches to that process. The scientific approach possesses many strengths.

People who follow this approach are more apt to come up with accurate information than those who observe only casually. Likewise, it is probable that scientific observers will use what they learn more effectively because of the procedures they follow:

Usually, they study a *representative sample of subjects* so that highly individual characteristics are eliminated.

They strive to *remain objective* and not allow themselves to be misled by preconceived ideas or wishful thinking unsupported by solid evidence.

They *make observations* in a meticulously prescribed manner, so that all observers can compare results.

They strive to *maintain control*. They consciously look at all possible/plausible hypotheses to explain any particular behavior and then test each of those hypotheses in a controlled environment.

They seek, usually, to *hold constant all factors but one* in the experiment, so as to trace the impact of a given circumstance or condition on subjects who have been and those who have not been exposed to it.

They strive to *report and publish their results accurately,* usually in professional journals. Typically, the report contains descriptions of the subjects (persons) studied, methods used, results obtained, and conclusions drawn.

They encourage others to *replicate their experiments,* speculate upon the results, and engage in further experimentation to help make progress in the area being investigated.

Obviously, there are many advantages to a scientific approach to the teaching-learning process. Certainly, this approach is far superior to unscientific observation and corrects many of its limitations (false generalizations, jumping to conclusions, ignorance of what others have discovered, and similar weaknesses.) But the "rub" comes when people begin to interpret and *apply* the scientifically acquired knowledge.

A COMPLICATED PROCESS—THE TROUBLES WITH STUDYING BEHAVIOR

In the film *The Trouble with Harry,* Harry's trouble is that he is a corpse, and because of complication after complication, he has to be buried and dug up a number of times. To the audience, the silhouette of Harry's being carried back and forth becomes highly humorous, but to those involved in the plot itself, it is serious business until the problem is finally resolved.

I have often drawn the analogy between *The Trouble with Harry* and the Trouble with Studying Behavior. To all of us involved in the educational process, it is serious business. Yet, we—and others, watching—have had to chuckle at the theories and practices that just won't "stay put." Sometimes we think we have buried a theory or practice, but later it is dragged out again. Or we bury something that perhaps should not be buried. At least we may think so while others differ sharply with us. Studying behavior is a complicated process and presents some genuine difficulties. It can help you as a teacher to understand the varying conclusions of studies and the disagreements among educational psychologists (and others) if you are aware of at least some of the major complicating factors. Most of all, it can help you to make more appropriate decisions in applying the results of studies to your own practice in the teaching-learning process.

We have grouped the "troubles" into seven major areas (not intended to be exhaustive). Each area is labeled as an *effect*—because we are referring to the kinds of effects that can occur in studying behavior and that account at least in part for conflicts in the way scientific information may be interpreted and why the techniques of teaching may change so rapidly. The effects are listed alphabetically, not necessarily in order of importance or influence.

Assortment effect. This has to do with the selection and interpretation of data. There is so much information available on behavior it is extremely difficult—really impossible—for any one individual to examine or interpret all of it. Because scientists must usually restrict themselves to examining one facet of behavior at a time (due to its complexity), most research reports on a particular facet. Therefore, if we are to gain more comprehensive understanding of behavior, we must combine and interrelate separate studies.

Because of the enormous amount of data available and the need to combine separate studies on particular facets of behavior, descriptions of behavior are necessarily based on information selected and interpreted in the writer's own way. To put it differently, there is a huge *assortment* of separate studies on behavior—and even if we assume that each study is based on solid scientific evidence, when different individuals choose and explain the results of what they have chosen, we may quite literally be locked at opposing points of view.

The assortment effect results in differences of opinion due to the selection and interpretation of data.

Bandwagon effect. We are using the term *bandwagon* here in its everyday meaning: "It works—jump on!" This effect is not difficult to translate into the realm of the study of behavior. A series of studies results in the development of a new concept or practice that meets with high success when it is first tested. The news spreads rapidly, and many people "jump on the bandwagon." Enthusiasm is great. Then, further studies reveal some flaws: perhaps there were "holes" in the original research, or results were due to novelty rather than to the merit of the concept or practice.

Biehler lists teacher expectations, programmed instruction, and open education as examples he would include among concepts and practices initially engaged in with enthusiasm and later shown to have limitations.[24] We would add a

24. Biehler, 3d ed.

more recent major example that conceivably could fit this category—computer instruction for *all* students. The professional, while remaining open-minded, must check carefully the actual merits of an idea or practice as against being caught up in enthusiasm merely because of its novelty.

Dissonance effect. Usually referred to as *cognitive dissonance,* this effect describes an individual who has made up his mind about something and therefore tends to reject (or ignore) any ideas that are dissonant (in conflict with) his own.[25] Can this happen to scientists (educational psychologists) who are seeking to be as objective as possible in their thinking and practice? Unfortunately, it can—and does.

The dissonance effect leads to sharp disagreement among psychologists and other scientists. All of us have to watch out for this effect in our own research, reading, writing, and practice. For example, if you are strongly convinced through reading, observation, and experience that every student needs to take computer programming, you probably will tend to reject evidence (should it come along) that this is not necessarily a good idea. You will tend to reject the new evidence because it is dissonant with your present strong convictions.

It is important for each of us to be patient and open-minded as we consider concepts and practices. As an antidote to the dissonance effect, I make a practice of deliberately reading at least monthly a substantial amount of material written by those with whom I know I have been in disagreement. I encourage you to find deliberate ways to help counteract the dissonance effect with which all of us must contend.

Experimenter bias effect. This effect refers to something the experimenter does subtly and unintentionally: communicating his expectations to the subjects of a study. It is important to distinguish this from the Pygmalion effect described below, where there is intentional and open communication of expectations to the subjects. The experimenter bias effect, frequently abbreviated EBE, was first described by psychologist Robert Rosenthal.[26] What happens, according to Rosenthal, is that one experimenter might expect his hypothesis to be supported, while another experimenter expects the same hypothesis to be rejected. During the course of the experimentation, the experimenters unintentionally communicate their expectations to the subjects, and this influences the outcome. Such expectations may be unintentionally communicated through a nod of the head or a tone in the voice, or in many other verbal and nonverbal ways. It may have been such effects that caused Theodore X. Barber and five colleagues to come up with results which did *not* support the EBE hypothesis when they replicated Rosenthal's experiments.[27] Anytime you read about inconsistent results of scientific studies, those inconsistencies may be due to the EBE impact.

Hawthorne effect. This is one of the better-known effects, and you may well

---

25. L. Festinger, *Theory of Cognitive Dissonance* (Evanston, Ill.: Row, 1957).
26. Robert Rosenthal, *Experimenter Effects in Behavioral Research* (New York: Appleton, 1966).
27. Theodore X. Barber, *Hypnosis, A Scientific Approach* (New York: Van Nostrand-Reinhold, 1969).

have read about it in other contexts. We like to refer to it as the "Attention, please!" effect, because it may be defined as people responding to a change just because they appreciate the attention being paid to them.

This effect was first noticed in a study made at the Hawthorne, Illinois, plant of Western Electric. Investigators discovered that the subjects of their study of working conditions there did indeed respond to almost any change of conditions, because they were grateful for the attention they were receiving.[28]

Translated into a teaching-learning process situation, suppose we are seeking to improve the attendance of a group of high school students with a record of high absenteeism. We may visit their homes, hold special individual or small group meetings with them, and engage in a number of processes to encourage them to improve their attendance at school. Let us assume their attendance increases by an average of one day per week at the end of the first two months of our treatment. That improvement might be due to the techniques involved, or it might be due simply to the fact that these students appreciate somebody's paying special attention to them. If it is the latter, it is possible that over a period of time the improvement might disappear as the novelty of the attention wears off.

Educational psychologists must guard against the Hawthorne effect in their research and reporting, and teachers must be aware of it when applying a new technique in their educational setting.

Pygmalion effect. The mythical Greek sculptor Pygmalion caused a statue he had carved to become endowed with life through his expectations. George Bernard Shaw's *Pygmalion* (1973; or the film *My Fair Lady*) has as a heroine the cockney flower girl Eliza Doolittle, who becomes a "lady" and makes a grand entrance at a ball because of the expectations of Colonel Pickering. Eliza explains this effect to Pickering: "The difference between a lady and a flower girl is the way she is treated. I shall always be a flower girl to Professor Higgins, because he treats me as a flower girl, and always will; but I know I can be a lady to you, because you treat me as a lady, and always will."

In 1968, Rosenthal and Jacobson picked up this same theme in a book entitled *Pygmalion in the Classroom*. As a result of his earlier research on the EBE, Rosenthal reasoned that if experimenters had an influence (even though unintentional) on their subjects' behavior, because of their expectations, how much more might it be true that teachers could influence their students' behavior by communicating to them *intentionally* their expectations of them.

Rosenthal and Jacobson picked at random elementary students to whom they had administered tests and told their teachers these children were "superior," when in fact there was no difference between the test results of these children and those of the nondesignated children. They reported in their book that the students who were labeled "superior" showed significant gains in IQ and that the reason for these

---

28. F.J. Roethlisberger and W.J. Dickson, *Management and Morale* (Cambridge: Harvard U., 1939).

gains was the fact that the teachers expected more of them.[29]

This Pygmalion effect is also known as the "self-fulfilling prophecy," since a prophecy made about the student's behavior may become fulfilled. If teachers intentionally communicate their expectations to students that they will behave intelligently and improve in achievement, those students may behave in the expected manner.

It will come as no surprise to anyone to learn of the enthusiasm and controversy that followed the publication of *Pygmalion in the Classroom*. On the enthusiasm side were pronouncements that it could revolutionize the education of disadvantaged children and others from poor backgrounds. All teachers needed to do was to let the students know of their high expectations for them, and performance would improve. Initial enthusiasm soon faded, however, as doubts and further qualifications came into the picture. Psychologists pointed out the weaknesses of the Rosenthal and Jacobson study.[30] They replicated the study but failed to find supportive evidence for the Pygmalion effect in the classroom.[31] Rosenthal then pointed out that many of these studies were not exact replications of his work.[32] Other researchers found evidence that supported at least some aspects of Rosenthal's study.[33]

A significant publication on this effect, *Pygmalion Reconsidered,* contains a lengthy critique by the editors, a review of studies on teacher expectancy, six reviews of *Pygmalion in the Classroom,* a reply to the editors' critique by Rosenthal ("Pygmalion Reaffirmed"), and a reply to Rosenthal by the editors.[34] Carl Braun reviewed seventy-eight articles on the impact of teacher expectations and concluded that the conflicting results of the many studies could possibly be explained on the basis of so many variables involved, and that some teachers

---

29. R. Rosenthal and L.F. Jacobson, *Pygmalion in the Classroom: Teacher Expectations and Pupils' Intellectual Development* (New York: Holt, 1968).
30. R.E. Snow, "Unfinished Pygmalion," *Contemporary Psychology* 14, no. 4 (April 1969):197-99. Robert L. Thorndike, Book review of *Pygmalion in the Classroom, Teachers College Record* 70 (1969):805-7.
31. W. Clairborn, "Expectancy Efforts in the Classroom: A Failure to Replicate," *Journal of Educational Psychology* 60 (1969):377-83. H. Jose, and J. Cody, "Teacher-Pupil Interaction as It Relates to Attempted Changes in Teacher Expectancy of Academic Ability and Achievement," *American Educational Research Journal* 8, no. 1 (January 1971):39-49. E.S. Fleming and R.G. Anttonene, "Teacher Expectancy or My Fair Lady," *American Educational Research Journal* 8, no. 2 (March 1971):241-52.
32. Robert Rosenthal, "On Not So Replicated Experiments and Not So Null Results," *Journal of Consulting and Clinical Psychology,* 33:7-10.
33. E.B. Leacock, *Teaching and Learning in City Schools: A Comparative Study* (New York: Basic, 1969). Alfred L. Shaw, "Confirmation of Expectancy and Change in Teacher's Evaluations of Student Behavior," *Dissertation Abstracts Journal* 30, no. 5-A (1969):1878-79. D.H. Meichenbaum, K.S. Bowers, and R.R. Ross, "Modification of Behavior of Institutionalized Female Adolescent Offenders," *Behavior Research and Therapy* 6, no. 3 (1968):343-53.
34. J.D. Elashoff and R.E. Snow, *Pygmalion Reconsidered* (Worthington, Ohio: Jones, 1971).

communicate expectations to some students in some situations.[35]

The Pygmalion effect is an outstanding illustration of how an effect can create both enthusiasm and controversy and numerous studies with conflicting results. These results do cause sometimes rapid changes in teacher and student behavior. The competent teacher needs to be aware of what he or she is communicating to students in the teaching-learning process. For although most educators agree that teachers probably cannot cause *all* their students to function as scholars simply by communicating their expectations that they do so, many agree that teacher expectations may influence student performance under some circumstances.

SPEC effect. We have coined the "SPEC" label to represent the effect of social, political, economic, and cultural change on teachers and the teaching-learning process. Conditions changing in our society and throughout the world may necessitate a revision of our thinking about teaching, the teaching-learning process, and the application of knowledge to changing situations. Obviously, discussion of a topic of this magnitude could cover many volumes, so we have deliberately limited our treatment here to two illustrative instances.

In the later 1950s the Russians successfully launched the first humanly created object—Sputnik—to orbit the earth. Like a firecracker, this event exploded on the educational scene. Science and mathematics became the "important" subjects, and many enticements were offered to lure students into these areas, from science fairs to generous scholarships for those who would major in these vital pursuits. Many splendid young scientists were produced. In a short time a man was landed on the moon, and the United States had gained back her leadership role in the sciences.

In early 1983, the National Commission on Excellence in Education issued its report "Our Nation Is at Risk." Citing a "rising tide of mediocrity" that has undermined the quality of education in America over the last two decades, the commission called for tougher requirements for high school graduation, higher salaries for teachers, and new incentives to attract academically gifted students into the teaching profession. After offering a rather bleak picture of American schools, the report stated that the United States had lost its international preeminence in education after having "squandered the gains in student achievement made in the wake of the Sputnik challenge."[36]

Within days of the release of this report, educational leaders began calling for changes in curriculum at all levels, including teacher preparation programs. Politicians issued a call for billions more of federal monies to be appropriated to aid education. And so a significant SPEC effect is in process even as these words are being written. The impact of the commission's report will be discussed at several

---

35. Carl Braun, "Teacher Expectation: Sociopsychological Dynamics," *Review of Educational Research* 46, no. 2 (1976):185-213.
36. National Commission on Excellence in Education, "Our Nation Is at Risk," *Chronicle of Higher Education* 26 (4 May 1983):11-16.

points throughout this book. It is likely to bring about some major changes for teachers and the teaching-learning process.

In these last several pages, you have been asked to consider the values of educational psychology—what it is, how it helps, its scientific basis and some of the major effects that can lead to conflicting reports of scientific studies and impact the teacher and the teaching-learning process. We have suggested that the teacher can perhaps best view the field of educational psychology as a repertoire of resources containing systematized information about the theories and practices of the teaching-learning process, a repertoire to be used under the guidance of the professional judgment of the teacher to produce appropriate learning in the lives of students.

You will note we have stressed both the importance of *science* and the *judgment* of the teacher. We believe the competent teacher must incorporate both the benefits of science and a mature philosophical judgment if he is to be successful.

What Competent Teachers Need to Know

Competent as used in this book is defined as "being responsibly able to perform." The competent teacher, then, is the one who is able to perform responsibly in the teaching-learning process.

It is important to emphasize we are *not* advocating the kind of model that states that a teacher becomes competent by demonstrating an array of competencies. We *are* advocating a model that views the competent teacher as one who is familiar with a repertoire of systematized information provided largely by educational psychology and who exercises mature professional judgment in drawing from and using that information responsibly to help produce desired learning results in his or her students. We see educational psychology as the major, though not exclusive, source from which the competent teacher draws information. In spite of changes in specific concepts and interpretations brought about by the accumulation of scientific knowledge and the change forces of society, certain kinds of knowledge will always be essential for teachers, and those are the areas of knowledge with which this book concerns itself. Those areas contain the kinds of information that competent teachers need to know.

HOW PEOPLE DEVELOP

There seems to be little question that the age of an individual does make substantial differences in the ways that individual responds to instruction. Therefore, it is important for the teacher to understand how people develop and what characteristics may be reflected at various developmental levels. You might think of this area as a repertoire of the theories, concepts, and characteristics of human development, and as you read chapters 3 and 4, you may want to add your

What Competent Teachers Need to Know

Knowledge Areas:

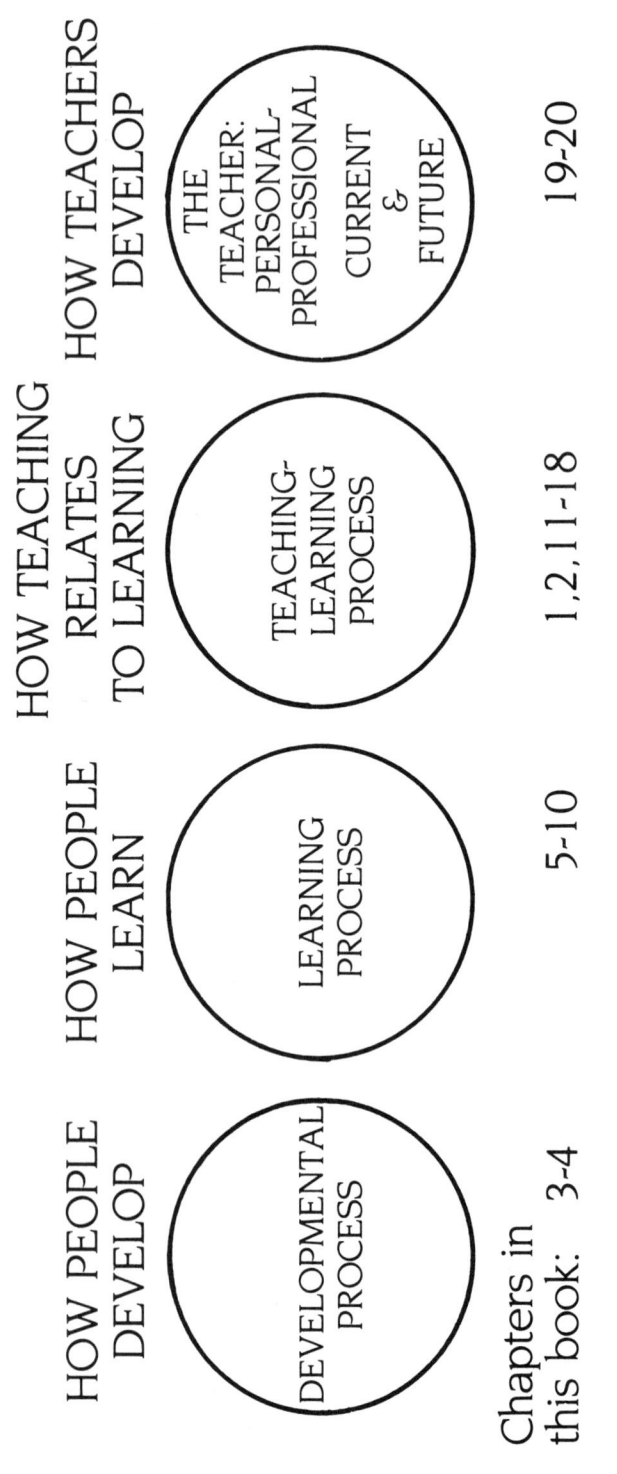

HOW PEOPLE DEVELOP	HOW PEOPLE LEARN	HOW TEACHING RELATES TO LEARNING	HOW TEACHERS DEVELOP
DEVELOPMENTAL PROCESS	LEARNING PROCESS	TEACHING-LEARNING PROCESS	THE TEACHER: PERSONAL-PROFESSIONAL CURRENT & FUTURE

Chapters in this book: 3-4   5-10   1,2,11-18   19-20

Fig. 1.5

own ideas and experiences to your *teacher's notebook* regarding the applications of developmental knowledge to the teaching-learning process.

HOW PEOPLE LEARN

No matter what the educational setting, the primary reason teachers are hired is to help students learn. It is essential for the teacher to understand the learning process. Four main approaches to the process are described in chapters 5, 6, 7, and 8. In each of these approaches, the background influences, current concepts, and key people associated with the particular approach are presented. The concepts then are applied to each of five key areas in the classroom: the teacher, the student, the curriculum, the methodology, and the social function of the school. A critique containing implications for the teaching-learning process concludes each chapter.

In chapter 9, the varieties, conditions, and designs of learning are discussed. The Mastery approach to learning is clarified, as are Bloom's Taxonomy of Educational Objectives and Mager's suggestions for preparing instructional objectives. Gagne's varieties of learning and Glaser's systematic instructional design are explained. At this point these names may not mean much to you, but you will discover them to be persons who have presented important concepts related to the learning process. Specific applications and examples will be included, and again you will want to keep your notebook close by to complete and add your own ideas.

We not only want to learn, we want to be able to remember what we learn and transfer what we learn from one situation to another. In chapter 10, you will be looking at the factors that cause us to remember (retain) information, factors that cause us to forget, a framework for information processing, and suggestions that will help you to teach in such a manner that there will be a higher probability of appropriate transfer for your students.

HOW TEACHING RELATES TO LEARNING

How teaching relates to learning, including how you can become personally effective in the classroom, is the focus for Part 4, The Teaching-Learning Process. This section of the book will become more meaningful if you imagine yourself in the center of an actual classroom. What happens now? What should have happened before this moment to help prepare for what should happen now? And what should happen after the instructional process is concluded?

How do you become an effective classroom manager? What procedures (methodology) should you use? How can you motivate your students? How do you relate to individual differences, including exceptional students? How can you measure student performance and give feedback effectively? You need to be able to make appropriate instructional decisions, implement effective teaching strategies, evaluate instructional outcomes, and adjust to different learning situations.

Chapters 11 through 18 cover these topics in detail, providing many specific examples and suggestions to help you become personally effective in the classroom.

Insight: The Teacher as Decision Maker

In order to be successful, a teacher must state goals explicitly, schedule class work around those goals, and use feedback to determine how well the goals are being achieved. Task analysis can help to sequence activities effectively, but one must also use cues about students, and constantly reexamine assumptions to be an effective decision-maker. Effective teachers see their roles as positive and worthwhile, while ineffective teachers see teaching as a dull job. Inner control, personal responsibility, realistic attitudes, and a problem-solving orientation further characterize effective teachers.

Factors restricting teacher decisions are lack of awareness of student problems, allegiance to unworkable ideas, limited resources, and inaccurate observations. Also, both student and teacher expectations, coupled with self-fulfilling prophecies and self-defeating strategies adopted by some students, can interfere with learning. Finally, external pressures impose constraints, especially those generated by parents, administrators, previous experiences, facilities, and the like. In spite of these, however, *evidence supports the conclusion that the teacher is the most powerful single factor affecting academic achievement* (emphasis added).

From Thomas L. Good and Jere E. Brophy, *Educational Psychology, A Realistic Approach,* 2d ed. (New York: Holt, Rinehart, Winston, 1980), p. 19.

Fig. 1.6

HOW TO DEVELOP PERSONALLY AND PROFESSIONALLY

Personal and professional development are vital aspects of any competent teacher's life and work. These should be in high, conscious view for each teacher, both for his mental health and for his responsible functioning in the teaching-learning process.

Part 5 of the book includes a significant discussion of the functioning of the competent teacher in a pluralistic society, both current and future, related to the philosopher-clinician model. We move now to a brief explanation of this model as we conclude chapter 1.

The Competent Teacher: Philosopher-Clinician

Limitations of Unsystematic Observations

1. One possible explanation (usually the first) may be treated as if it were the *only* explanation.
2. One incident may be mistakenly generalized to other similar incidents.
3. Idiosyncratic factors that may occur only for a specific person in a specific situation may not be treated in proper perspective.
4. Attention may be given only to evidence that fits the observer's point of view, while other evidence may be ignored.
5. Ignorance of the cumulative knowledge of the field may lead to repeated mistakes and faulty solutions.

Fig. 1.7

A preliminary comment is needed: Although we discuss these two concepts separately for learning reasons, in actuality they intermingle constantly, or should, in the life and work of the competent teacher.

THE COMPETENT TEACHER AS PHILOSOPHER

We define *philosophy* here as "the professional perspective of the teacher." The teacher's experiences, scientific knowledge, and reflective commitment combine to produce his or her professional perspective (philosophy). The conscious development of this *perspective* is essential to the effective *performance* of the teacher as a clinician.

The teacher's experiences obviously feed into and are a major source of the teacher's professional perspective. Early experiences may be modified by more recent ones, and more recent ones may help us view earlier ones differently—but all of them represent a major source of the teacher's professional perspective. As you think about your own experiences, which have led you at least to an interest in teaching, you probably will agree that both pleasant and unpleasant experiences affect not only an individual's becoming a teacher, but also his perception of how teaching ought to be done. Experiences make up one major component of the teacher's professional perspective (philosophy.)

The teacher's scientific knowledge is the second major component of the professional perspective. The more the teacher understands of especially that kind of knowledge with which the field of educational psychology deals, the more informed will be that individual's professional perspective. The scope of that knowledge is reflected by this and other texts in educational psychology.

It is important again to note that the teacher's knowledge should not be limited only to the field of educational psychology. The teacher's scientific knowledge should broaden to other areas such as sociology, anthropology, medicine, and related fields—a conscious, deliberate effort on the part of the teacher—so that he or she may be as well-informed as possible in developing a professional perspective in relation to the teaching-learning process.

The teacher needs to be cautious about extremes in viewpoints about the causes of behavior. At one extreme one is tempted to say, "I know the *exact* cause of that behavior," and at the other, "It's so complex, we'll never be able to understand it." There is no "supertheory" that can account for all aspects of behaviors.[37] The teacher needs to learn how to handle carefully and intelligently the scientific knowledge that comes from multiple sources. That knowledge is the second major component of the teacher's professional (philosophic) perspective.

The teacher's reflective commitment, not so easily defined as the first two components, nevertheless constitutes a third crucial component of the teacher's philosophic perspective. We are here referring to the teacher who consciously and deliberately reflects upon his or her experiences and scientific knowledge and seeks to arrive at a set of beliefs about who the students are, what the nature of the students is, and what ought to be happening as they interact in the teaching-learning process. It is the teacher's conviction that teaching is worthwhile, and he has committed himself to it. He is genuinely interested in his students, and the students know it. He has an optimistic approach to life, is convinced it is worthwhile, and wants to help students find personal fulfillment.

These are not teachers who are "pollyannish," or who are afraid to face the hard questions. Quite the opposite, their convictions have been hammered out of their own struggles as they have reflected with integrity upon their knowledge and experiences.

The reflective commitment of the teacher may limit the individual's actions at any given moment, but the commitment is not of the sort that closes his or her mind to new ideas, new experiences, and new insights. To the contrary, this teacher eagerly seeks new input upon which to reflect and improve.

This teacher, having sought to integrate scientific knowledge and experience through careful reflection, is a teacher from whom we would expect mature professional judgment. This teacher has a *philosophic perspective* to bring to the teaching-learning process.

THE COMPETENT TEACHER AS CLINICIAN

The label *clinician* may conjure up a picture of cold, calculating procedures being enacted upon someone, but that is certainly not the picture we are painting.

---

37. R.C. Sprinthall and N.A. Sprinthall, *Educational Psychology: A Developmental Approach,* 3d ed. (Reading, Mass.: Addison Wesley, 1981).

Gallery of Greats

William H. McGuffey
"The time has gone by, when any sensible man will be found to object to the Bible as a school book, in a Christian country."* (Courtesy American Book Company)

The curriculum of the early public schools was Bible-centered largely due to the efforts of one outstanding American educator, William Holmes McGuffey, compiler of the famous McGuffey readers. Born in 1800 along the Ohio frontier of Scottish Presbyterian parents, he came to be known in his day as "the schoolmaster of the nation." A popular minister of the gospel, a Christian college professor and president, he introduced a graded reading series (McGuffey Eclectic Readers—four levels), put pictures into elementary textbooks, added study questions to help students comprehend

---

*Preface to McGuffey's Third Eclectic Reader.

PHILOSOPHER Model: The Teacher as Philosopher-Clinician

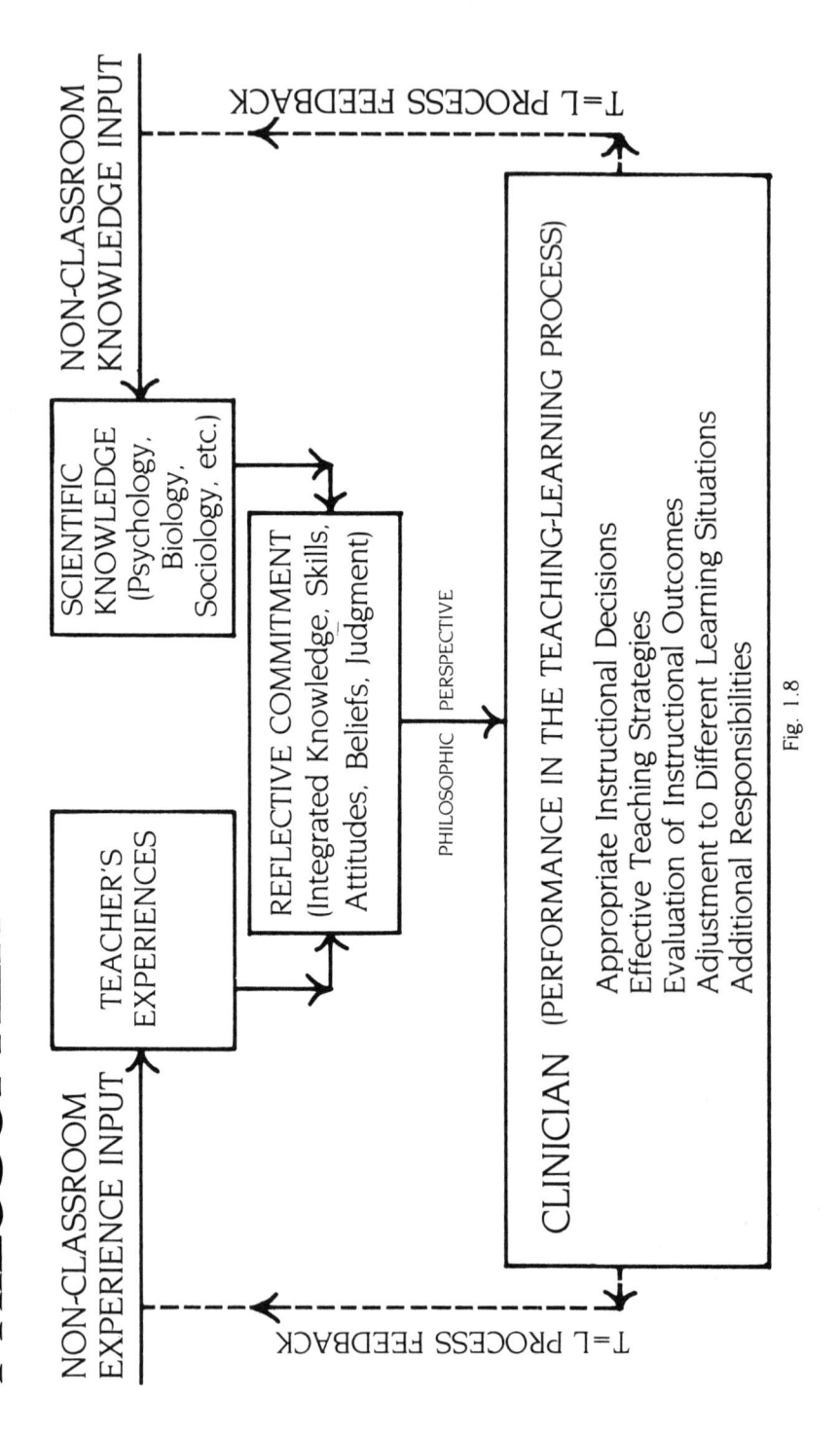

NON-CLASSROOM EXPERIENCE INPUT → TEACHER'S EXPERIENCES

NON-CLASSROOM KNOWLEDGE INPUT → SCIENTIFIC KNOWLEDGE (Psychology, Biology, Sociology, etc.)

REFLECTIVE COMMITMENT (Integrated Knowledge, Skills, Attitudes, Beliefs, Judgment)

PHILOSOPHIC PERSPECTIVE

CLINICIAN (PERFORMANCE IN THE TEACHING-LEARNING PROCESS)
- Appropriate Instructional Decisions
- Effective Teaching Strategies
- Evaluation of Instructional Outcomes
- Adjustment to Different Learning Situations
- Additional Responsibilities

T=L PROCESS FEEDBACK

Fig. 1.8

the material, and constantly urged more parent involvement in the education of children.

His readers were filled with stories that had moral lessons—some of them actual Bible stories. He strongly believed the Bible deserved a central place in American education.

John W. Westerhoff III on McGuffey readers: "It is estimated that at least 120 million copies of McGuffey Readers were sold between 1836 and 1920, placing their sales in a class with the Bible and Webster's Dictionary."†

Mark Sullivan, historian, (1929) on McGuffey: ". . . the most popular, most affectionately remembered person in the nineteenth century, a national giant to be ranked with George Washington and Abraham Lincoln."‡

For us, clinician refers to the actual performance of the teacher in the teaching-learning process. Whereas the key word for the philosopher (in our model) is *perspective,* the key word for the clinician is *performance.* The teaching-learning process is the clinical setting where the teacher performs, exercises skills to achieve objectives, and seeks to make genuine differences in students' lives.

The teacher who can bring a mature philosophic perspective to the clinical practice is one who has high probability of making appropriate instructional decisions, implementing effective teaching strategies, effectively evaluating instructional outcomes, and adjusting appropriately to different learning situations. As this teacher listens, observes, decides, acts, questions, and continues to reflect, it is likely he or she will perform in a more consistent, stable, and purposeful manner to enhance the appropriate learning and development of the students.

The teacher as philosopher is seeking always to integrate knowledge and experience, and to bring the resulting reflective commitment to the clinical setting of the teaching-learning process. As for the clinician's "deskside manner," we recommend warmth and enthusiasm combined with skill and mature judgment.

As you read this model and consider it, let me encourage you *not* to be discouraged because we have talked a great deal about "maturity," and you are just in the early stages of teacher preparation. Remember that a model seeks to represent the best workable set of principles and procedures. Look upon the model as a goal toward which you can develop. But as you do so, be sure to evaluate the model carefully, reflect upon it, test it out, talk to other educators or educators-to-be about it, find other models in other books and do the same with them. And all the while, keep your notebook handy to jot down your ideas for future reference.

Hindsight

We live in a learning society where demands for educational services are

---

†John W. Westerhoff III, *McGuffey and His Readers*
‡Mark Sullivan, *Our Times: The U.S. 1900-1925,* vol. 2, *America Finding Herself* (New York: Charles Scribner's Sons, 1927), p. 11.

increasing and the educational settings are becoming more varied. Although it is probable you have in mind the school classroom setting, you may wish to explore some of the more diverse teaching-learning situations.

Regardless of the setting, the competent teacher needs to understand the values of educational psychology—what it is, how it helps, its scientific basis, and some of the major effects that can lead to conflicting reports of scientific studies and which impact the teacher and the teaching-learning process. The teacher can perhaps best view the field of educational psychology as a repertoire of resources containing systematized information about the theories and practices of the teaching-learning process—a repertoire to be used under the guidance of the teacher's professional judgment to produce appropriate learning in the lives of students.

The competent teacher needs to know how people develop, how they learn, how teaching relates to learning, and how to become personally effective in the classroom. The competent teacher will be called upon to make appropriate instructional decisions, implement effective teaching strategies, evaluate instructional outcomes, and adjust to different learning situations. The competent teacher needs to hold in high conscious view his or her own personal and professional development and be prepared for future changes in the teaching-learning process.

The model of the competent teacher as philosopher (professional perspective fed by knowledge, experiences, and reflective commitment) and as clinician (effective performance in the clinical setting of the teaching-learning process) was presented. The teacher-to-be is urged to test out this and all other models and to begin the keeping of a careful *teacher's notebook*.

CHALKBOARD CHALLENGES

1. Look through some recent issues of one or two of the professional journals listed under *Want to Know More?* Find an article that interests you either because you agree or disagree. Then, taking a 4" × 6" or 5" × 7" card, use the following format: upper left corner—your name and date. Upper right corner—author's name (last name first), title of article in quotes, journal name underlined, volume, number, issue, date, pages of journal in which article is found. One-third of the way down on left hand side your summary of what the author is saying in the article (3 or 4 sentences); two-thirds of the way down write the word *Analysis,* and then in three or four sentences why you do or do not agree with the author. Always use the same size cards, and begin a file (alphabetically by author's last name or subject area such as "Teacher Behavior"). You can begin a file in an old shoe box and gather an enormous amount of information in this simple fashion. Those cards come in handy when you are ready to write a term paper or, later on, an article.

2. In the National Commission's report "Our Nation Is at Risk," five "New Basics" are listed: four years of English, three years of mathematics, three years of science, three years of social studies, and one-half year of computer science. These

basics, combined with work in the fine and performing arts and two years of foreign language should form the core for the receiving of a high school diploma. Do you agree? Why or why not? Develop your own list of basics and reasons for listing them, after reading the commission's report thoroughly. Discuss these with your peers and professors, parents and business people, to get responses and reactions. You may want to note these in your *teacher's notebook.*

3. In your *teacher's notebook,* make two columns. Head one up with the label "Items Favoring My Becoming a Teacher" and the other, "Items Favoring a Different Profession." List now, and as you proceed in this book and in this course (and other materials and courses), those items you believe appropriately belong in one column or the other. Be careful not to give too much weight to particular items in either column, for example, "teaching gives me summers and other frequent times off" or "they just don't pay teachers enough." We suggest you endeavor to balance the total impact of the lists in terms of satisfaction, motivation, and the like. To help you with this, you may want to get a peer discussion going on this topic and challenge each other to a deeper probing of these items.

4. In the philosopher-clinician model, you are translating your philosophic perspective (fed by experiences, a repertoire of knowledge, and reflective commitment) into your actual performance in the clinical setting of the teaching-learning process. Using the following situation, analyze (preferably in writing) how you would use this model as a competent teacher.

> You are showing a 16mm. sound film to a seventh-grade class. As the film begins to roll, the projector stops running. You have built up the class to this film as a highly important one to view. When the projector stops, laughter, groans, and cheers are heard from your students. The class period is just five minutes old, with forty-five minutes to go. What do you do?

Clues to help you: Will your experiences or repertoire of knowledge be of any service? What about your reflective commitment concerning what ought to be happening in the teaching-learning process? Do you have any clinical skills that can aid you? Test the model thoroughly to find out whether it is adequate for the classroom teacher.

Want to Know More?

PROFESSIONAL JOURNALS

If you are going to develop personally and professionally, it is essential to remain current on the latest information, experiments, trends, and techniques in psychology and education. One way to do this is to learn how to use professional journals and other information resources effectively. The professional journals in psychology and education listed below contain primarily reports of experiments. Each experiment might be thought of as one letter in a word. And of course these experimental results eventually combine into many "words" to become a principle or theory. These titles are not intended to form an exhaustive list but do represent some of the key professional journals in psychology. Most college libraries will have these available.

American Educational Research Journal
Behavioral Science
Child Development
Developmental Psychology
Educational and Psychological Measurement
Exceptional Child
Genetic Psychology Monographs
Harvard Educational Review
Journal of Abnormal and Social Psychology
Journal of Applied Behavior Analysis
Journal of Educational Psychology
Journal of Educational Research
Journal of Educational Sociology
Journal of Experimental Child Psychology
Journal of Experimental Education
Journal of Experimental Psychology
Journal of Teacher Education
Merrill-Palmer Quarterly of Behavior and Development
Mental Hygiene
Psychological Monographs
Psychological Review
Psychology in the Schools
Society for Research in Child Development Monographs

ABSTRACTS AND REVIEWS

After you have read about a particular experiment in one of the journals above, how do you relate the results to other research in a similar area so you can begin to formulate some conclusions? Obviously, you need to become familiar with this other research. A number of journals and reference works aid you by providing abstracts (brief summaries) and reviews of articles which have appeared in the type of journal listed above.

Journals of Abstracts.
    Child Development Abstracts and Bibliography
    Exceptional Child Education Abstracts
    Psychological Abstracts

Reviews and Research Analyses.
> *Encyclopedia of Educational Research* (1982), edited by Harold E. Mitzel
> *Encyclopedia of Education* (1971), edited by Lee C. Deighton
> *Review of Research in Education* (1978), edited by Lee S. Shulman
> *Second Handbook of Research on Teaching* (1973), edited by R. Travers
> *The Teacher's Handbook* (1971), edited by Dwight W. Allen and Eli Selfman
> *Annual Review of Psychology* (reviews of significant studies in special areas for a given year)
> *Contemporary Psychology* (reviews of new books in psychology)
> *Review of Educational Research* (descriptions and analyses of studies on a particular theme)

JOURNALS OF ISSUES AND TECHNIQUES

Some professional journals, while containing some reports of experiments, emphasize discussions of educational issues, current developments, and techniques. Many of these journals provide helpful tips for teachers and feature book reviews.

> *Change* (higher education)
> *Childhood Education*
> *Clearing House* (junior/senior high school teaching)
> *Education*
> *Education Forum*
> *Educational Leadership*
> *Educational Record* (college/university teaching)
> *Educational Technology*
> *Elementary School Journal*
> *Exceptional Children*
> *High School Journal*
> *Journal of Education*
> *Journal of General Education*
> *Journal of Higher Education*
> *Junior College Journal*
> *Phi Delta Kappan*
> *School Review*
> *Teachers College Journal*
> *Teachers College Record*
> *Theory Into Practice*
> See also *Educational Digest* (condensed articles from the types of journals above)

MAGAZINES AND NEWSPAPERS

Some publications employ an everyday writing style, feature many illustrations and attractive graphic designs. Others are published in newspaper style.

Chronicle of Higher Education
Grade Teacher
Instructor
Learning
Education Week (elementary through senior high)
Psychology Today
Today's Education

SUBJECT AREA JOURNALS FOR TEACHERS

The probability is high that you can find a journal related to your subject area in education. The following journals contain reports and reviews of research and experimental studies, as well as helpful teaching suggestions and practices, in specialized subject areas.

Action in Teacher Education
Agricultural Education Magazine
American Biology Teacher
American Business Education
American Music Teacher
American Speech
American String Teacher
American Vocational Journal
Arithmetic Teacher
Art Education
Athletic Journal
Audiovisual Instructor
Business Education World
Christian Teaching
Coach and Athlete
Coaching Clinic
Education and Training of the Mentally Retarded
Educational Theatre Journal
Elementary English
Elementary School Guidance and Counseling
English Language Teaching
English Studies
Forecast for Home Economics
French Review
Fundamentalist Journal

Geographical Teacher
German Review
Gifted Child Quarterly
Hearing and Speech News
History Today
Improving College and University Teaching
Industrial Arts and Vocational Education
Industrial Arts Teacher
Instrumentalist
Journal of Industrial Teacher Education
Journal of Negro Education
Journal of Nursing
Journal of Reading
Journal of Research on Science Teaching
Journal of School Health
Journal of Special Education
Reading Specialist
Marriage and Family Living
Mathematics Teacher
Music Education Journal
Music in Education
Music Journal
National Business Education Quarterly
National Elementary Principal
Physical Educator
Physics Teacher
Recreation
Safety Education
Scholastic Coach
School Arts
School Counselor
School Musician
School Musician Director and Teacher
School Science and Mathematics
School Shop
Science Educator
Science Teacher
Swimming Technique
Teaching Exceptional Children
Tennis
Theatre Arts
Theatre World
Today's Speech
Track Technique

ERIC:

Thousands of articles are produced each year on a wide variety of topics related to educational psychology and education as a whole. The Educational Resources Information Center (ERIC) was established by the US Office of Education to help you locate articles of interest. ERIC publishes three sources of information:

Current Index to Journals in Education—Annual Cumulation. Here you will find an index of articles in better than three hundred education-oriented journals published in a particular year. Included is a Subject Index, Author Index, Journal Contents Index, and Main Entry Section (title, author, journal reference, and brief abstract of articles published in many journals). If you want to discover what is available in journals, refer to this publication.

Research in Education. Here you will find important materials *not* published in journals (curriculm guides, catalogues, papers, reports, monographs, etc.). In the Document Resume section, descriptions of the documents can be found along with information about where you may obtain any document.

ERIC Educational Documents Index. Here you will find a listing of titles of important educational documents *not* contained in journals. Each document is classified under various general and specific categories. It is helpful to remember that the titles of articles listed in this publication are noted and abstracted in *Research in Education and Office of Educational Research Reports.*

How to Use ERIC Sources.

Question: What's available in journal articles on my topic?
Answer: Use Current Index to *Journals in Education*
Question: What's available outside journals on my topic?
Answer: Find titles of documents in *Educational Documents Index* and descriptions plus information on how to obtain those documents in *Research in Education.*

BOOKS IN PRINT

Books in Print, updated annually, contains virtually all available books, new and old, indexed by author and by title with full ordering information. If you know the author's name but not the book title, or vice versa; if you need to find books in a given subject area; if you need to find additional books by the same author—these are just a few of the many possible uses of this publication.

VIEWS ON PYGMALION EFFECT

You may wish to look at a variety of views on the Pygmalion effect. If so, read *Pygmalion Reconsidered,* edited by Janet D. Elashoff and Richard E. Snow,

(Worthington, Ohio: Jones, 1971). For an excellent review of research on teacher expectations in relation to behavior, look at the article "Teacher Expectations: Sociopsychological Dynamics," by Carl Braun, in *Review of Educational Research* 46, no. 2 (1976): 185-213.

NATIONAL COMMISSION REPORT ON EXCELLENCE

The National Commission on Excellence in Education issued a historic report entitled "Our Nation Is at Risk" early in 1983. It strongly criticized the "mediocrity" in the schools of our nation and called for strong action to correct the situation. Plaudits and criticisms immediately began appearing. It is a major report, and for easy access to its full text, see *The Chronicle of Higher Education* 26, no. 10 (4 May 1983): 11.

TEACHER BEHAVIOR AND STUDENT LEARNING

Interested in research linking teacher behavior to student learning? We recommend that you read "Teacher Behavior and Student Learning" in *Educational Leadership* 37, no. 1 (October 1979). Written by Jere E. Brophy, this article is a helpful review of the research on teacher effectiveness. A good number of further references are included at the end of the article.

Another helpful review in this same area is the article by William B. Martin, "Teacher Behaviors—Do They Make a Difference?" in the *Kappa Delta Pi Record* 16 (1979): 48-60, 63.

TEACHING AS AN ART

Psychologists encourage a scientific approach to teaching, while not ruling out artistic aspects. There are others who place great stress on the view that teaching is an art. Some stimulating reading representing the "art" point of view includes: Gilbert Highet's *The Art of Teaching* (New York: Vintage, 1957); Highet's *The Immortal Profession* (New York: Weybright and Talley, 1976); John E. Colman's *The Master Teachers and the Art of Teaching* (New York: Pitman, 1967); and Robert S. Ulich's *Three Thousand Years of Educational Wisdom* (Cambridge: Harvard U., 1954).

NONTRADITIONAL EDUCATIONAL SETTINGS

An excellent review of the evolving educational services professional for nontraditional educational settings can be found in Barbara C. Burch's article "New Mission for Colleges of Education," *Action in Teacher Education* 2, no. 3 (Summer 1980): 1-12.

2

Teaching at the Schoolhouse: What's It Like?

CONTENTS

	PAGE
Key Terms	40
That's Debatable!	41
Foresight	44
A *Gaze* at the Schoolhouse: A Teacher's-Eye View	44
The *Days* at the Schoolhouse: Typical Schedules	55
The *Ways* of the Schoolhouse: Requirements and Regulations	55
The *Waves* at the Schoolhouse: Criticisms and a Brief Critique	59
You in the Schoolhouse?	63
Hindsight	63
Chalkboard Challenges	64
Want to Know More?	65

KEY TERMS

Alternative school
  Any school other than a "typical" public school, usually characterized by more flexibility in procedures, a closer relationship among teachers and students, and extended responsibilities for students and faculty; refers to both private schools and to special programs set up within the public school domain; students and staff usually there by choice, so sometimes referred to as "choice" schools

Clinical setting
: The schoolhouse/classroom environment in which the teacher performs his or her responsibilities

Direct instruction
: Instruction in which the teacher does a great deal of the direction as opposed to the open classroom, where discovery learning may be the principal approach

Factual level question
: A question that requires a factual answer, not requiring a great amount of use of the cognitive processes such as reflecting, reasoning, and the like

Middle school
: The school between the elementary and secondary schools; often referred to as "junior high," but grades contained in middle schools vary substantially depending on the philosophy, space availability, and other factors in the local school district; originally developed to meet the special needs of children in this age range

Nonverbal communication
: The giving of a message without using words, such as through the nod of the head, facial expression, the pointing of a finger, etc.

Private schools
: Schools not in the public domain, financed and operated by private groups for special educational and/or religious purposes

Prospective teacher
: The student in the early stages of thinking about a career as a teacher

School autonomy
: The degree of independence with which a particular school is permitted to operate in relation to its governing body

Self-esteem
: The worth with which a person perceives himself or herself

Task-oriented
: Instruction designed and implemented with a view to spending a great amount of time on specific tasks

Typical
: That which occurs in the majority of instances in schools within the framework designated

THAT'S DEBATABLE!

WILL I FIT IN AT THE SCHOOLHOUSE?

Throughout this chapter we ask you to keep this question uppermost in your mind as you consider some samplings of what the schoolhouse is like. It is always

GALLERY OF GREATS

Horace Mann
"Let the next generation be my client."* (Courtesy Little, Brown & Co.)

Born in Franklin, Massachusetts, in 1796, Horace Mann did not attend school as a child, except briefly at his village school at the age of fourteen. Such were the beginnings of a man who became a successful lawyer, secretary of the Massachusetts State Board of Education, president of the state senate, and spent his last years before he died in 1859 as president of Antioch College in Yellow Springs, Ohio. He began the first public school in America (1837) and the first state normal school to educate teachers (1839).

*Quotations above are excerpted from Louise Tharp, *Until Victory: Horace Mann and Mary Peabody* (Boston: Little Brown, 1953), pp. 136, 143. Used by permission.

Teaching at the Schoolhouse—What's It Like?

Mann had a deep, persistent conviction that a new kind of school could create a new kind of teacher. "Select schools for select children should be discarded. Instead of the old order of nobility, a new order should be created—an order of teachers, wise, benevolent, filled with Christian enthusiasm and rewarded and honored by all." His burning, determined enthusiasm for the education of all children is reflected in an 1837 speech:

> The mobs, the riots, the burnings, and lynchings, perpetrated by the men of the present day, are perpetrated because of their tiger passions now, when they are full grown; but it was years ago when they were whelped and suckled. And so too, if we are derelict in our duty in this matter, our children in their turn will suffer. If we permit the vulture's eggs to be hatched, it will then be too late to take care of the lambs.

debatable whether a prospective teacher will fit in at the schoolhouse. In addition to other ways of helping you look at the schoolhouse in this chapter, may we suggest you debate this question with reference to the nature of the tasks you will be called on to perform. If Philip Jackson is right, elementary school teachers have as many as one thousand interpersonal interchanges each day.[1] Some of these you may perceive as very low-level, mundane, routine interchanges, such as:

Keeping attendance records
Getting equipment ready to use
Helping children on and off with coats, boots, etc.
Making sure children's toileting needs are met
Arranging attractive bulletin boards
Taking care of the classroom pet and plants
Collecting milk money
Patrolling the playground

The middle school teacher has many of the same kinds of tasks, with some variations—for example, checking on cigarette smokers in the cubby holes and restrooms. The secondary school teacher may be asked to enforce a dress code. According to Margaret Lay and John Dopyers, more than 30 percent of the major responsibilities of the teachers of young children fall into what might be called this "routine" category.[2] And we suspect the percentages are approximately the same for middle and secondary teachers.

Of course, there are the remaining 70 percent or so of the tasks and interchanges that might be perceived by teachers at a much higher level of responsibility: designing instructional concepts and activities, working with parents to build good relationships, and sharing from time to time with other

---

1. Philip Jackson, *Life in Classrooms* (New York: Holt, Rinehart, and Winston, 1968).
2. Margaret Lay and John Dopyers, *Becoming a Teacher of the Young Child* (Lexington, Mass.: D.C. Heath, 1977), p. 47.

professionals in assessment and counseling activities.

Usually these so-called higher level responsibilities represent no problem to the teacher in terms of how the teacher perceives what he or she is expected to do. The "routine" or "lower level" responsibilities are the ones that give many teachers difficulty, again in terms of their perceptions of what a professional ought to be expected to do.

How do you perceive yourself in relation to the performance of these routine tasks? Will you go to school each day resenting them? Or are they, in your perception, not so routine after all? Perhaps they are reasonable expectations. Think about them as you consider whether you will fit in at the schoolhouse.

FORESIGHT

What is the real world of teaching like? What about the teacher's professional roles, responsibilities, happy times, and frustrating times? What actually goes on in the classrooms of the schoolhouse? It would take many volumes to fully describe the answers to these questions. In this chapter we attempt to portray at least some of the answers by sampling activities and behaviors at the schoolhouse through the eyes of the teacher. "Biting the apple" from the teacher's side of the desk may bring some surprises to you, but better now than during your student teaching time or first year of teaching. Teaching is an exciting profession. We urge you to ask yourself whether you want to be part of that profession—can you picture yourself with reasonable satisfaction in the schoolhouse?—as we sample in this chapter the days, the ways, and the waves in the midst of which you must perform if you choose to become a teacher.

A GAZE AT THE SCHOOLHOUSE: A TEACHER'S-EYE VIEW

This is a *teacher-centered* chapter rather than a *student-centered* chapter, and intentionally so. It is important for you as a prospective teacher to take a realistic look at the schoolhouse to see what it is like. You have looked at it for many years through a student's eyes, but in this chapter you will step into the shoes of the teacher, sit behind the teacher's desk, take off your student eyeglasses and put on the teacher's spectacles to view the complex processes of the schoolhouse.

As you do so, we emphasize that teachers *do* make a difference. With so much criticism aimed at the schools in our society, we frequently discover prospective teachers who become discouraged upon hearing or reading the criticism. The discouragement translates into something like, "I guess teachers don't really make that much difference anyhow, so I'll think about a different career." But teachers *can* and *do* make a difference! For example, a major finding of one study (Project Follow Through) emphasized that the quality of interactions that occurred between the teacher and the students was of primary importance in determining both successful and unsuccessful classroom outcomes.[3] Good and Brophy state that teachers can have a major influence on the way students learn and develop.[4] As you take a careful look at the schoolhouse through these brief but representative samplings, do not allow yourself to be overwhelmed either by the complexity of the schoolhouse processes or the criticisms leveled at those processes. The outcome of your reading this chapter may be a decision *not* to become a teacher. But whatever the outcome, we urge you to keep one question uppermost in your thinking as you read: "Will I fit in at the schoolhouse?"

INSIGHT: NEA-AFT Comparison Sheet	
NEA	AFT
Historical Origins	
In 1875 a small group of educators met in Philadelphia to establish the National Teachers Association. This group was the forerunner of what is today known as the National Education Association (NEA).	The American Federation of Teachers (AFT) was founded in 1916 and affiliated itself with the American Federation of Labor. This group stayed small, and membership was limited to small groups located in urban centers until the early 1960s.
Purpose	
The purpose of the NEA, as stated by its charter, is to elevate the character and advance the interests of the profession of teaching and to promote the cause of education in the United States.	The primary purpose of the AFT is to promote collective bargaining for teachers and other education workers, to secure adequate funding for school programs, and to promote academic freedom and professional autonomy to enhance academic excellence.
Membership	
NEA is the largest teachers' association in the United States with more than 1.7 million members. Included in the NEA are more than 29 different departments and affiliated organizations. Throughout the country, NEA has more than 8000 affiliates. The members include teachers as well as administrative and supervisory personnel. The NEA was originally comprised of only school administrators.	AFT is the second largest teachers' organization in the United States with more than 500,000 members from approximately 2000 affiliates. AFT is an affiliate of the AFL-CIO. John Dewey took out the first membership in the AFT in 1916 and remained an active member all his life. He believed that it was important that there be an organization made up exclusively of teachers. To this day, only teachers are allowed to join the AFT.

---

3. L. Stebbins and R. St. Pierre, *Education as Experimentation: A Planned Model* (Cambridge, Mass.: Abt Associates, 1977), vol. 4-A.
4. Thomas Good and Jere E. Brophy, *Educational Psychology: A Realistic Approach*, 2d ed. (New York: Holt, Rinehart, and Winston, 1980).

Policy Making

The NEA employs more than 1500 full-time people. The NEA consists of an elaborate organization, with offices at the national and state levels. The local concerns of the membership are dealt with by full-time uniserve directors.

The AFT is governed by a convention of delegates. Every two years the convention elects a president and 30 vice presidents who constitute the National Executive Committee. An executive board consisting of five members and the president are selected from the National Executive Committee.

Affiliations

The NEA works closely with the Coalition of American Public Employees (CAPE), which includes fire, police, municipal, and other public employees.

The AFT is affiliated with the AFL-CIO, which operates on a principle of reciprocal support. That is, the AFT gets the support of other unions' 14 million members when an important piece of legislation is up for consideration.

Political Clout

The NEA is a very powerful political organization. Traditionally, its power has been at the state level, but it is rapidly becoming a powerful lobby in Congress as well. Recently, the NEA has begun to endorse political candidates who support educational measures. Political activities are coordinated by the Political Action Committee for Education (NEA-PAC). In a recent election year, the NEA sent 172 delegates to the Democratic convention and 55 delegates to the Republican convention.

The AFT's political strength is in Washington, D.C., and local districts. The Committee of Political Education (COPE) coordinates AFT political activities. The AFT, like the NEA, endorses political candidates, monitors voting records of politicians, and analyzes the positions of new candidates. Both organizations contribute to campaign funds, but their greatest strength lies in organizing their memberships to campaign for candidates. The AFT participates primarily through the Democratic Party.

Budget

NEA has an annual budget of approximately $48 million and a professional staff of approximately 280.

AFT has an annual budget of approximately $16 million and a professional staff of 66.

From Leo W. Anglin, Jr., Richard M. Goldman, and Joyce Shanahan Anglin, *Teaching: What It's All About* (New York: Harper & Row, 1982), pp. 298-99. © 1982 by Harper & Row, Publishers, Inc. Reprinted by permission of Harper & Row, Publishers, Inc.

Fig. 2.1

Along with the genuine excitement of teaching go many unglamorous, unpublicized daily routines and genuine frustrations, which can become traumatic experiences especially for the first-year teacher who has not looked and thought ahead. This chapter is designed to help you make enough sense out of the schoolhouse and its processes that you will be able to make a more intelligent decision as to whether teaching is for you.

Teaching at the Schoolhouse—What's It Like?

SOME TYPICAL CHARACTERISTICS OF TEACHING: PRESCHOOL THROUGH SENIOR HIGH SCHOOL

In his book *Life in Classrooms,* which many believe is becoming a classic, Philip Jackson provides a flavorful sampling of school life in the following passage:

> School is a place where tests are failed and passed, where amusing things happen, where new insights are stumbled upon, and skills acquired. But it is also a place in which people sit, and listen, and wait, and raise their hands, and pass out paper, and stand in line, and sharpen pencils. School is where we encounter both friends and foes, where imagination is unleashed and misunderstanding brought to ground. But it is also a place in which yawns are stifled and initials scratched on desktops, where milk money is collected, and recess lines are formed. Both aspects of school life, the celebrated and the unnoticed, are familiar to all of us, but the latter, if only because of its characteristic neglect, seems to deserve more attention than it has received to date from those who are interested in education.[5]

In another passage, Jackson describes the relatively stable framework of settings and routines in schools:

> Even the odors of the classroom are fairly standardized. Schools may use different brands of wax and cleaning fluid, but they all seem to contain similar ingredients, a sort of universal smell which creates an aromatic background that permeates the entire building. Added to this, in each classroom, is the slightly acrid scent of chalk dust and the faint hint of fresh wood from the pencil shavings. In some rooms, especially at lunch time, there is the familiar odor of orange peels and peanut butter sandwiches, a blend that mingles in the late afternoon (following recess) with the delicate pungency of children's perspiration. If a person stumbled into a classroom blindfolded, his nose alone, if he used it carefully, would tell him where he was. . . .
>
> Not only is the classroom a relatively stable physical environment, it also provides a fairly constant social context. Behind the same old desks sit the same old students, in front of the familiar blackboard stands the familiar teacher.[6]

These two descriptions alone remind us that schools are places filled with constant and variable activities and reasonably large groups of students for which the teacher is responsible. Although overall they are relatively stable places, the teacher must be prepared for delays, interruptions, frustrations, distractions, and misunderstandings.

Since schools represent the clinical setting in which the teacher must function, we reiterate here the necessity for the philosophic perspective, described in the previous chapter, to be brought to the clinical performance in order to deal effectively with the complicated drama of the schoolhouse.

---

5. Reprinted by permission of the publisher from Jackson, Philip, *Life in Classrooms.* (New York: Teachers College Press, © 1990 by Teachers College, Columbia University. All rights reserved. pp. 4-7.
6. Ibid., p. 7.

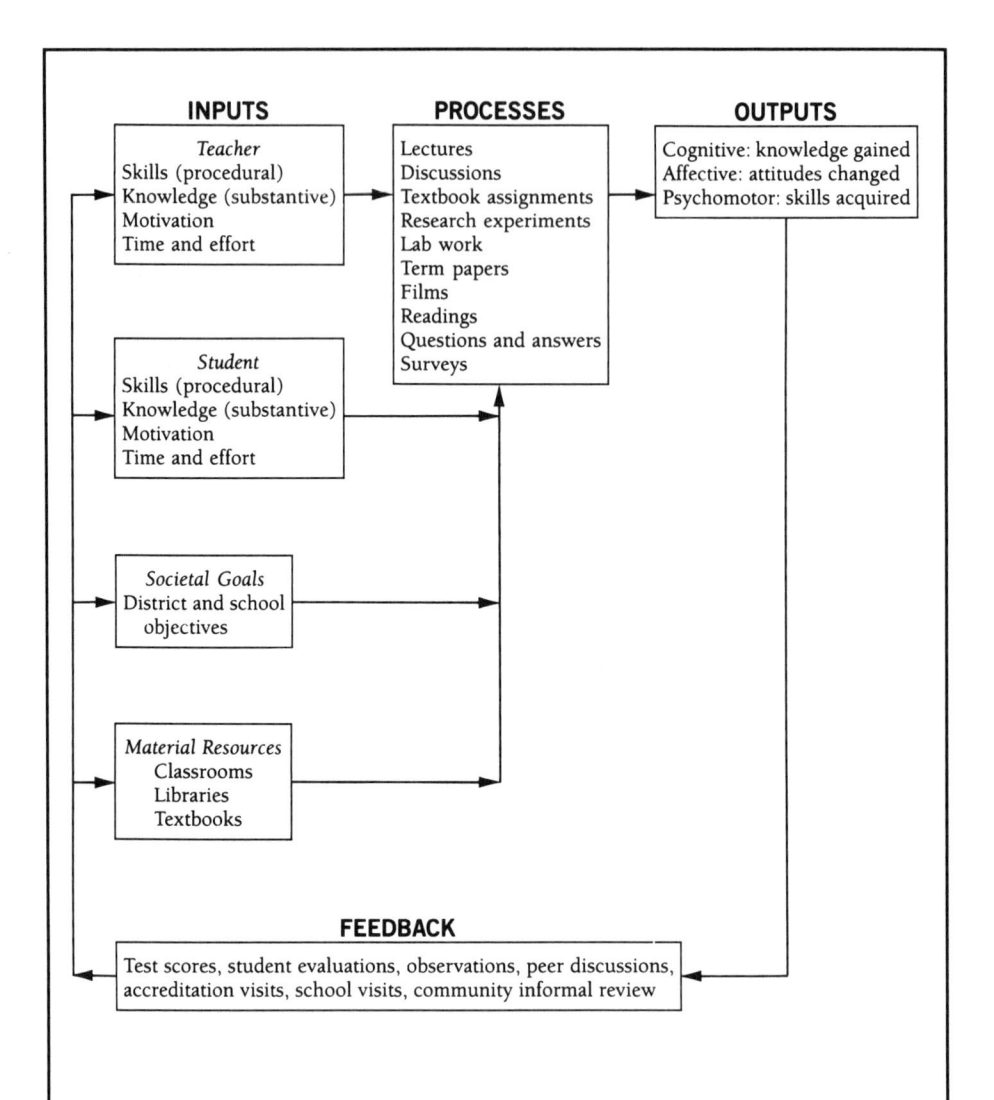

INPUTS	PROCESSES	OUTPUTS
Teacher Skills (procedural) Knowledge (substantive) Motivation Time and effort	Lectures Discussions Textbook assignments Research experiments Lab work Term papers Films Readings Questions and answers Surveys	Cognitive: knowledge gained Affective: attitudes changed Psychomotor: skills acquired
Student Skills (procedural) Knowledge (substantive) Motivation Time and effort		
Societal Goals District and school objectives		
Material Resources Classrooms Libraries Textbooks		

FEEDBACK

Test scores, student evaluations, observations, peer discussions, accreditation visits, school visits, community informal review

Structure of the educational system: a Systems approach (from Leo W. Anglin, Jr., Richard M. Goldman, and Joyce Shanahan Anglin, 1982, p. 7). © 1982 by Harper & Row, Publishers, Inc. Reprinted by permission of Harper & Row, Publishers, Inc.

The educational system consists of inputs, processes, outcomes, and feedback. Inputs represent the starting points and include teacher, student, society, and material resources. The processes include various learning methodologies. Outcomes are classified into three categories: Cognitive (knowledge gained), Affective (attitudes changed), and Psychomotor (skills acquired). The system is continuously monitored through the feedback component. The feedback is used to confirm successful practices and to identify those areas that need to be redesigned, revised, or eliminated from the educational system.

Fig. 2.2

Teaching at the Schoolhouse—What's It Like? 49

Jackson emphasizes four major roles the teacher must assume to be successful in this drama: traffic cop, judge, supply sergeant, and timekeeper. The traffic cop" role involves the teacher's spending a great deal of time both preventing and unraveling physical and psychological traffic jams:

Physical: "Tom, you may go and get a drink when Nancy returns."

Psychological: "Jennifer, since you gave the first answer you will need to wait a few minutes before answering again so that other students can have their turns."

The role of "judge" involves the teacher as an evaluator. The teacher is called upon to place a value on many aspects of school life from on- or off-task behavior to students' attitudes. Anglin, Goldman, and Anglin, in discussing this role of the teacher, include evaluations of clothing, language patterns, assignment results, study behaviors, and many other actions and interactions by and among the students.[7]

Examples: "I'm pleased with the way you completed that assignment, Judy." "Troy, you run out that door again, and you'll be sent to the office."

The teacher uses both verbal and nonverbal communication in his role as "judge."

The teacher as "supply sergeant" plays a very practical role in this age of tight budgets and frequent shortage of needed materials. Teachers often must scrape and scrounge to find materials they believe are needed to fulfill their responsibilities effectively. This is unfortunate, but still a reality in many schools. As a teacher, you will need to act wisely in relation to supplies and equipment uses.

Examples: "Janie, give each student one box of crayons. Children, your crayons must last until Christmas." "Class, this new microscope is a very costly one. Each of you will need to use it with great care."

As "timekeeper" the teacher's role in the schoolhouse drama is most obvious. Whether you teach in a traditional or a nontraditional setting, certain tasks, responsibilities, or operations need to be accomplished within a time limit. Jackson reminds us that "school is a place where things often happen not because students want them to, but because it is *time* for them to occur."[8]

Examples: "Janet, you're late again coming from your physical education class. Miss Jones has told me she allows adequate time. Please see me immediately after this class so we can work this out." "It's nine twenty-five. We'll have to stop now so this group can go to the computer lab. We have a tight schedule in there, so we must move quickly."

Are you still remembering that teachers can make a difference, and asking yourself, "Will I fit into the schoolhouse?"

Anglin and his associates make a helpful analysis of unique aspects of the schoolhouse, listing conditions typically found in classrooms that do *not* occur in other learning environments outside the schoolhouse:

---

7. Leo W. Anglin, Jr., Richard M. Goldman, and Joyce S. Anglin, *Teaching: What It's All About* (New York: Harper, 1982).
8. Jackson, p. 13.

Teachers' Instructional Problems

In 1974 B. R. Bartholomew asked readers of *Today's Education* to react to a series of statements summarizing common problems faced by teachers. The respondents were asked to indicate if they perceived each problem to be negligible, moderate, serious, or critical. Bartholomew summarized the responses in the following way, listed in order of their effect on teachers' work. The first problem would have the most effect on teachers' work and the last problem would have relatively little effect on teachers' work, according to these teachers. Do you think the problems would be the same if a survey were taken today?

Parents apathetic about their children's education*
Too many students indifferent to school*
Physical facilities limiting the kinds of student programs*
The wide range of student achievement
Working with too many students each day
Too many non-instructional duties
The values and attitudes of the current generation
Diagnosing student learning problems
The lack of instructional materials
The quality of instructional materials
Disruption of classes by students
Little help with instruction-related problems from school administrators
The psychological climate of the school*
The mandated curriculum not appropriate for students
Evaluating student achievement
Chronic absence of students from school*
Feeling under pressure too much of the time
The inflexible routine of their situation
The diverse ethnic-socioeconomic backgrounds of students
Student health and nutrition problems that affect learning
Too few opportunities to improve professional skills
The rapid rate of curricular change
Lack of freedom to teach the way they want
Not assigned to teach what they are qualified to teach
Student use of drugs

*Problems that appear to affect secondary teachers more than elementary teachers. Used by permission.

Fig. 2.3

Compulsory nature of classroom attendance
Crowded conditions found in all classrooms (as compared to other environments in society)
Continuous use of praise and punishment
Social conditions that require an imbalance of power between teacher and students[9]

The pros and cons of these aspects need to be fed carefully and thoughtfully into the prospective teacher's philosophic perspective as an aid to improving clinical performance.

Rosenshine's view of the classroom, while limited to young learners (grades 1 to 5) and focusing primarily on reading and mathematics, contains some conclusions concerning classrooms in which students appear to achieve at high levels, and this information needs careful reflection as you feed it into your philosophic perspective. The successful academically-achieving classroom is characterized by the following:

The teacher using direct instruction
The teacher limiting student's choice of activities
The teacher working with large groups or entire class
The teacher focusing discussion on factual-level questions
The students tending to have high self-esteem[10]

In response to criticism that such a classroom sounds like a cold, impersonal place, Rosenshine emphasizes, "Teachers in more formal classrooms today are warm, concerned, flexible, and allow much more freedom of movement. But they are also task oriented and determined that children shall learn."[11] As you consider his findings, remember he is focusing on children in grades 1 to 5, and results are being measured by achievement tests that measure primarily factual information rather than high-level cognitive processes such as problem-solving and creativity. But his results add to our understanding of what teaching is like at the schoolhouse.

In another study, Dunkin and Biddle drew some conclusions with which we will be dealing in other chapters. But one of their statements is helpful here in relation to the teacher's attitude toward the social forces of the schoolhouse: "The truly wise teacher is one who views the classroom social system as an asset rather than a hindrance."[12] This wise teacher, drawing from his or her repertoire of

---

9. Anglin, et al., p. 56. ©1982 by Harper & Row, Publishers, Inc. Reprinted by permission of Harper & Row, Publishers, Inc.
10. B. Rosenshine, "Primary Grades Instruction and Student Achievement Gain" (paper presented at annual meeting of the American Educational Research Association, New York, April 1977).
11. Ibid., p. 22.
12. M. Dunkin and B. Biddle, *The Study of Teaching* (New York: Holt, Rinehart, and Winston, 1974), p. 29. Used by permission.

resources, including the understanding of the social system of the classroom, can use that system as a positive force in the clinical setting to help improve personal performance and, most importantly, student learning.

Remember, in this chapter we are seeking to give you a "feel" for the schoolhouse to help you determine whether you think you will fit into the picture. We have reported on some samplings of schoolhouse life from separate studies by Jackson and Rosenshine, and considered some comments by Anglin and his associates. We turn now briefly to some common, typical, but nonetheless important characteristics that might be termed "everyday facts of teaching at the schoolhouse."

In most cases, you will be expected to teach six hours a day, 180 days per year. However, one recommendation of the National Commission on Excellence in Education is to extend the number of hours per day and the days per year in school.[13]

Teaching loads. At the preschool, kindergarten, and elementary levels you typically would work with the same group of students each day and all year. If you have a self-contained classroom, you will probably have between 25 and 30 students. You may be asked to supervise children during recess periods and at lunch time.

At the middle and secondary school levels, the typical teaching load is five different classes of 30 students each, with one preparation period each day. You would therefore typically be teaching approximately 150 students. You may also be asked to be a sponsor or supervisor for a cocurricular activity that occurs after the school day is over.

Evaluations. Evaluations of some sort—report cards; written comments on students' achievements, behaviors, attitudes, and development; parent conferences—are required in almost all schools. You will need to become adept at accurate and helpful evaluations of your students.

Requirements at various grade levels. Most states require teachers to cover specific subjects at the various grade levels. The local school system may add to the state requirements and even produce a uniform syllabus. Usually, a state publishes a list of approved textbooks, and the local school district selects those to be used in its schools from that approved list.

Elementary schools typically have one or two classes at each grade level, a student enrollment of 150 to 300, seven to fifteen teachers, a principal, secretary, custodian, and cafeteria workers.

There is greater variance in size and other factors in secondary schools. Usually they will have a range of 500 to 2,000 students and from 20 to 70 teachers. The administrative organization for both middle and secondary schools is likely to be more extensive than that of the elementary school, although this obviously

---

13. National Commission on Excellence in Education, "Our Nation Is at Risk," *Chronicle of Higher Education* 26 (4 May 1983):11-16.

varies with the particular situation. It is likely that a teacher has contact with any particular student for no more than one hour per day.

In all schools, typically there will be in-service training and faculty meetings, and those take place at the end of the school day or on special days scheduled in advance for this purpose.

We have been referring thus far primarily to public schools. In the interest of a more comprehensive coverage, we turn now, however briefly, to private and alternative schools, because there are some important differences.

PRIVATE AND PUBLIC SCHOOLS: SOME DIFFERENCES

Private schools, along with alternative or choice schools, are enjoying steady and continuing growth.[14] The Project on Alternatives in Education (PAE)[15] completed a national survey of alternative schools in North America, the most extensive survey ever undertaken of such schools, and, while identifying 2,500 schools, indicated there may well be two to four times that number. Responses from 1,200 of these alternative schools provide a substantial data base for describing their nature and operation.

High morale. One of the most prominent findings is that staff morale is extremely high: 90 percent of the responding staff members displayed real ownership of their programs. They were willing to take on even more professional activity and obligation.

Attendance by students rises in 81 percent of the responding schools, attributed largely to very different teacher-student relationships. Most responding schools identified the quality of these relationships as the feature making them most different from other schools in their district.[16]

Raywid lists a number of factors she believes contribute to the success of alternative schools. Many of those would apply also to private schools.

Smallness. Smallness seems necessary to developing and maintaining many of the positive features of alternative schools.

Choice. Students in 79 percent of the responding schools are there by choice. In 85 percent of the schools, teachers are there by choice.

Extended roles. Since these schools are small, they typically lack support services. There is evidence that significant gains can result from extending areas of individual responsibility within institutions.[17] The PAE survey found evidence that everyone in an alternative school—students as well as staff—has greater amounts

---
14. "Schools of Choice: Their Current Nature and Propects," by Mary Anne Raywid, June 1983, © 1983, *Phi Delta Kappan, Inc.* 64, no. 10:684-88. Used by permission.
15. All survey data came from *The Current Status of Schools of Choice in Public Secondary Education* (Hempstead, N.Y.: Project on Alternatives in Education, Hofstra U., 1982).
16. Raywid, "Schools of Choice."
17. F. Newman, "Reducing Student Alienation in High Schools: Implication of Theory," *Harvard Education Review* 51 (November 1981):553-54.

of responsibility and is allowed more discretion than in conventional schools.[18] There is an emphasis upon interacting with students *pleasantly*, since discipline problems diminish sharply in alternative schools.[19]

Autonomy. Staff members are allowed to design and carry out their own vision of schooling. "Teachers play an important part in hiring staff and allocating funds . . . the greater the school's autonomy, the more prerogatives students enjoy."[20]

Continuing evaluations. Eighty-five percent of the responding schools undergo regular formal evaluation. This probably leads to a constant awareness of problems and a quicker response to take corrective measures.

Insight: Why Parents Send Children to Private Schools

Private school parents are not just fleeing public schools or engaged in white flight. . . . Most seek the ethos or tradition which that school represents. That tradition is usually a way of talking about character. It represents some agreement about which virtues are most worth having. A primary function of private schools is to make visible an otherwise invisible collectivity, to draw together a public that shares similar preferences. The private school is both a symbolic and an actual representation of valued moral and intellectual goods. The fundamental role of leadership in a private school is to bring a person into communication about ways of inculcating and sustaining those values. The leaders of such schools are chosen because they exemplify those values; they are 'the best of us,' persons capable of symbolizing the tradition and of drawing others into it. . . . The quality and character of the teachers are believed to make a great difference. The community stretches through time and measures individuals against perduring standards. Traditions are a way of pointing to those standards and sensing their weight. The parents choose to enroll their children in that community. . . .*

Gerald Grant, "The Character of
Education and the Education of Character,"
Daedalus 110 (Summer 1981): 144-45.

Fig. 2.4

*Reprinted by permission of *Daedalus,* Journal of the American Academy of Arts and Sciences, "The Character of Education and the Education of Character," 110 (Summer 1981), Cambridge, MA.
18. Cited in Raywid.
19. D. Duke and C. Perry, "Can Alternative Schools Succeed Where Benjamin Spock, Spiro Agnew, and B.F. Skinner Have Failed?" *Adolescence* 13 (Fall 1978):375-92.
20. Raywid, p. 686.

Teachers as central. These schools, according to the PAE report, make teachers the central factors for the improvement of their educational programs.

Teaching methods. Over half of the responding schools pointed to this factor as one of their outstanding features. Independent study continues to be most "frequently identified learning arrangement in today's alternatives."

Raywid suggests that "perhaps the single dominant theme expressed by the various studies of effective schooling is that success is linked to what is variously called school culture, climate, or ethos."[21] Researchers who try to isolate the differences between public and private schools are finding that the contrasts are to be found in the general *climate* of the schools.[22]

THE DAYS AT THE SCHOOLHOUSE: TYPICAL SCHEDULES

If you teach at the elementary level, you will need to plan a six-hour schedule daily. If you are in a self-contained classroom, you will be expected to teach all subjects, although many elementary schools have music, math, and art specialists. Your children will need to be encouraged to stay on task, and you will need to be well aware not only of the general developmental characteristics of your students but of as many individual characteristics as possible.

If you teach at a secondary school, *pacing* is perhaps the key concept. Typically, you will teach five sections of the same class, with one preparation period per day. Secondary teachers sometimes have problems maintaining their enthusiasm and their energy as they teach the same material for five hours. Planning becomes a matter of using your resources wisely to work out quality presentations ahead of time so that visual aids and discussions, for example, become constructive tools rather than being used as crutches or substitutes for preparation. It is exceedingly important for you to be consciously aware of your own mental health as you teach day by day, and we shall return to that topic in chapter 19 with some specific suggestions.

THE WAYS OF THE SCHOOLHOUSE: REQUIREMENTS AND REGULATIONS

For any particular school and school system, requirements must be met by the teacher. And certain regulations will govern your overall conduct and procedures.

RECORD KEEPING

You will need some time each day to complete forms and do bookkeeping. These will include such items as attendance, keeping tabs on school property and books, assignment of lockers, playground equipment, collection of lunch money,

---

21. Ibid., p. 687.
22. D. Erickson, "A New Strategy for School Improvement," *Momentum*, December 1982, pp. 4-11.

Insight: The Stability and Similarity of Classrooms

In 1968, Philip Jackson wrote his oft-quoted book *Life in Classrooms*. He points to stability as one characteristic of classroom environments:

> This is not to say, of course, that all classrooms are identical, anymore than all churches are. Clearly there are differences, and sometimes very extreme ones, between the settings. One has only to think of the wooden benches and planked floor of the early American classroom as compared with the plastic chairs and the tile flooring in today's suburban schools. But the resemblance is still there despite the differences, and, more important, during any particular historical period the differences are not that great. Also, whether the student moves from first to sixth grade on floors of vinyl tile or oiled wood, whether he spends his days in front of a blackboard or a green one, is not as important as the fact that the environment in which he spends these six or seven years is highly stable.*

A study of classrooms in grades 1 through 12 in selected Israeli schools found that the processes used in all classrooms did not differ much from one to the other. One example of this similarity is the finding that the following elements crossed elementary, middle, and high school classroom settings:
1. a large percentage of talk by teachers
2. the small number of students who received positive comments from teachers
3. students not much involved in the lesson (students listened, teachers talked).†

Question: Could the stability mean most classrooms are in a "rut"? Is the similarity a positive or negative factor in the teaching-learning process?

---
*Reprinted by permission of the publisher from Jackson, Philip, *Life in Classrooms*. (New York: Teachers College Press, © 1990 by Teachers College, Columbia University. All rights reserved. pp. 4-7.
†Israeli schools study by Goldman, Friedman, and Bogin, "The School System and Its Relationship to Irregular Attendance" (report funded by the Israeli Ministry of Education and the University of Haifa; Haifa, Israel: U. of Haifa, 1971).

Fig. 2.5

signatures of parents for field trips, and requisition forms for needed materials for any special projects.

REPORT CARDS

There is much more to a report card than just marking down a number or a letter. Again, it takes careful planning of ways to evaluate student performances as objectively as you possibly can. Later chapters in this book help you specifically to use objectives, evaluate with quality, and communicate results clearly to students and parents.

If you teach at elementary level, you need to devise plans for evaluating students on several subjects, and in many schools additionally on behaviors, attitudes, and developmental levels. At the secondary level, careful planning helps you work out assignments and do your evaluations on staggered schedule so you do not have to read 150 papers or correct 150 tests on the same day.

RULES

There will be definite rules to follow in most schools. You will be expected to enforce the rules with students as well. These range from dress codes in some schools to smoking regulations in most. The enforcement of rules is not usually the teachers' favorite occupation, but our advice is to enter into it with an attitude of accepting your responsibility and doing it well. Where you feel it may be helpful, talk to others in a constructive manner about changes and suggestions in relation to the rules and regulations.

REPRESENTATIVES OF THE SCHOOL DISTRICT (SCHOOL BOARDS)

Americans believe in democratic governance. This means as citizens we have a voice in selecting leaders and establishing policies. Public school teachers are expected to abide by decisions made by school boards. But within that framework, you will have the opportunity in most school systems to make your voice heard. The difficulty of doing that varies from district to district. In our view, the same belief in democratic governance that allows citizens to select school boards also allows teachers to make their voices heard. As professionals, teachers should seek to make both their approvals and suggestions for improvement known in a responsible manner and through appropriate channels.

RENEWAL OF CONTRACT

Although the merit of tenure is constantly being discussed, most school districts award tenure to teachers after the end of their third year. Usually tenure will mean that the contract is renewed automatically each year thereafter unless there are very substantial reasons for nonrenewal. It is obvious, therefore, that you will be evaluated thoroughly during your first three years in a school system, and especially the first year or two of your teaching career. In our experience, the teacher who welcomes and understands the need for evaluation will be the one who

ACTUAL **PROJECTED**

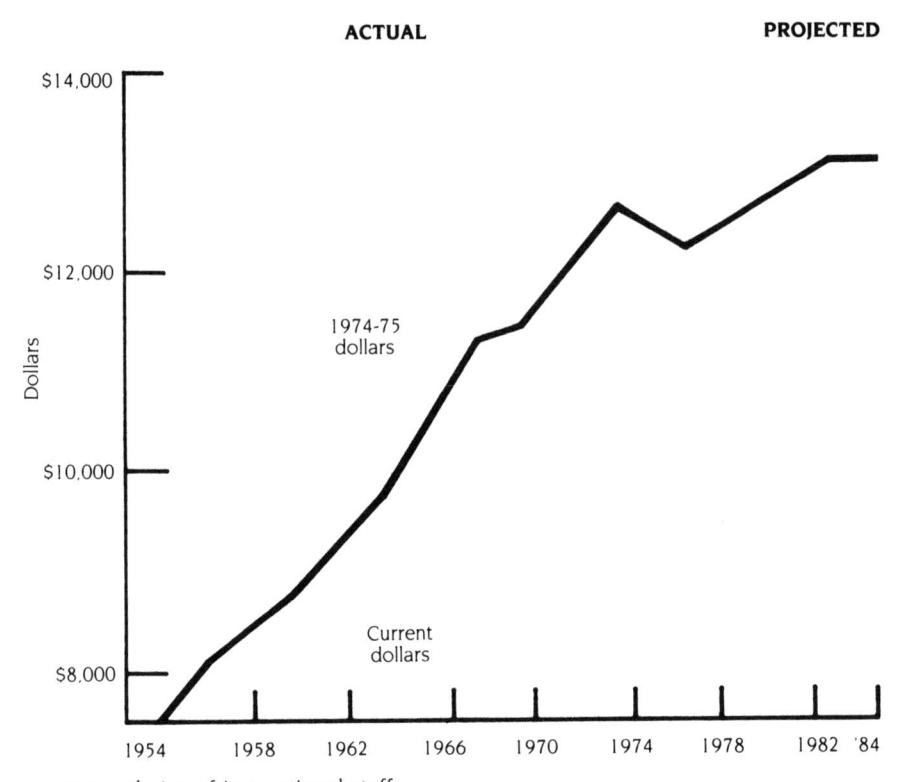

Average salaries of instructional staff.
From Mary A. Golladay, *The Conditions of Education: A Statistical Report on the Condition of Education in the United States* (Washington, D.C.: U.S. Department of Health, Education and Welfare/National Center for Education Statistics, 1976), p. 132.

Fig. 2.6

needs have little fear of the positive outcome of the evaluation. You are hired by the school to help your students learn. You will want to keep tangible evidence of their progress for use in your evaluation and for your own feedback.

REACHING AGREEMENTS WITH OTHER FACULTY MEMBERS

While you really do have a great deal to say about what happens in your classroom, what you do in your classroom also impacts other teachers in theirs. The opposite is likewise true. It is necessary for faculty to get together at certain intervals to discuss procedures, make compromises where there may be conflicts, and generally seek satisfactory solutions to individual and common problems. In my judgment, the wise principal will call an occasional faculty meeting just to informally chat together about topics of the faculty's own choice.

GENERAL RESPONSIBILITIES

No text can capture every detail of the teacher's responsibilities. In the school where you work, there will always be responsibilities of a more general nature—the ones not listed anywhere, nor referred to in any document. They may range from volunteering to help with a reception at the school to offering to help the teacher next door in a moment of special need.

As you continue to size up yourself as to whether you can fit in at the schoolhouse, we turn now to some criticisms of the schools and their processes, and then conclude the chapter by focusing on "you in the schoolhouse" to help you get some usable handles for your decision about teaching.

THE WAVES AT THE SCHOOLHOUSE: CRITICISMS AND A BRIEF CRITIQUE

In this section we will review briefly six major high school reform projects, all expected to be completed by the mid-80s; we will cite the key items in the report "Our Nation Is at Risk," a major document issued by the National Commission on Excellence in Education in early 1983; we will look at some responses to the commission's report; we will examine the Effective Schools Approach to discovering what features mark successful schools, and will relate the Alternative Schools Approach to current criticisms of public schools.

Perhaps it will be helpful to remind you once more our purpose in this chapter is to provide a sampling of criticisms rather than any exhaustive treatment of the issues. Few of us need to be reminded of evidence that secondary schooling has fallen into something less than we would like it to be. Most citizens are aware of the troubling performance of America's public high schools. There are no less than six major high school reform projects in full swing as of this writing.

SIX HIGH SCHOOL REFORM PROJECTS OF THE 80S

An Education of Value. A study of the values underlying secondary schooling is being conducted by the National Academy of Education. Judith B. McLaughlin is executive director of the project.

The Paideia Proposal. Mortimer J. Adler, director of the Institute for Philosophical Research, is the leader of some two dozen intellectuals who propose a grand redesign of curriculum, instruction, and teacher preparation for public schooling.

Project Equality. George H. Hanford, president, has initiated ten years of studies and actions by the College Board intended to redefine and strengthen the academic preparation of college-bound high school graduates.

Redefining General Education in the American High School. Gordon Cawelti, Executive Director of the Association for Supervision and Curriculum Development, has organized a network of seventeen high schools to consult with each other as they individually revise their curricula for general education.

A Study of the American High School. The Carnegie Foundation for the Advancement of Teaching (Ernest L. Boyer, president) will combine its own inquiries with a synthesis of other studies to describe the condition of secondary schooling and to propose solutions for its problems. Paul L. Houts directs the project.

A Study of High Schools. Chairman Theodore R. Sizer, Executive Director Arthur G. Powell, and several colleagues, under the auspices of the National Association of Secondary School Principals and the National Association of Independent Schools, are working on a study that will prescribe secondary schooling to meet America's needs for the rest of this century.[23]

Dennis Gray points out that although it would be impossible to forecast what the reports will say, there are some preliminary indications of what the common themes will be: strong emphasis on academic goals; a core curriculum for most if not all students; much consternation about the education and professional training of teachers; considerable attention to mathematics, science, computers, writing, history, and foreign languages; an assumption that nearly every high school graduate will sooner or later enroll in post-secondary education of some sort; and a general concern for the progression from schooling to life after high school graduation.[24] The concluding remarks of this article are significant: "Schools cannot be reformed by adding to them nor by rearranging what they do. Reform means saying no to claims that rob schools of the time, money, dedication, and energy they need to concentrate on teaching and learning."[25]

OUR NATION IS AT RISK

"Our Nation Is at Risk" is the report of the National Commission on Excellence in Education. Citing the "rising tide of mediocrity," which has undermined education in America over the last two decades, the commission called for tougher requirements for high school graduation, higher salaries for teachers, and new incentives to attract academically gifted students into the teaching profession.[26] The commission's recommendations for upgrading academic standards were strongly endorsed by Education Secretary Terrel H. Bell, who appointed the eighteen-member panel of educators in August 1981.

Although a number of criticisms were quickly leveled at the commission's report, that of Gordon Cawelti of ASCD represents, we believe, a constructive point of view.[27] Cawelti suggests both the problem and solution are grossly over-

---

23. Dennis Gray, "The 1980s: Season for High School Reform," *Educational Leadership* 39, no. 8 (May 1982):564-69.
24. Adapted from Gray, p. 565. Used by permission.
25. Ibid., p. 568. Used by permission.
26. National Commission on Excellence in Education, "Our Nation Is at Risk."
27. Gordon Cawelti, "Cawelti Response to Commission on Excellence Report" (mimeographed, ASCD, June 1983).

simplified. He agrees that many high school graduates are not pressed to reach their academic potential and leave school without having attained even minimal language or math skills. But the report, he says, fails to analyze some of the more subtle facets having to do with student motivation—anxiety, uncertain job outlook, and so on. "The report's chief weakness is that it gives no suggestions whatsoever as to what national priorities must be changed if we are to move to a 200-day school year and pay competent teachers competitive wages."[28] Among further criticisms, Cawelti says the arts and vocational education are missing, and those are needed for curriculum balance.[29]

Insight: Basics for College-Bound Students

In May 1983, following closely on the heels of the report by the National Commission on Excellence in Education, the College Board urged mastery of six basic subjects and six intellectual skills for college-bound students.

The subjects: English
Mathematics
Science
Social Studies
Foreign Language
The Arts

The intellectual skills: Reading
Writing
Speaking and Listening
Mathematical Ability
Reasoning
Studying

The report "Academic Preparation for College: What Students Need to Know and Be Able to Do" was prepared by the College Board as part of the Educational Equality Project, a ten-year effort to develop and implement a national standard for academic achievement in secondary education. The Board is suggesting the report as a guide for secondary schools to use for evaluation and revision of their academic standards and curricula.

Fig. 2.7

28. Ibid., p. 2.
29. Ibid., p. 5.

COLLEGE BOARD BASICS

Unrelated officially to this report, but psychologically well-timed, is the College Board's call for mastery of six basic subjects and six intellectual skills by college-bound students.[30] Because of the College Board's influence, these recommendations are apt to be given heavy consideration, and you will want to study them carefully. (See Insight, fig. 2.7.)

EFFECTIVE SCHOOLS APPROACH

The Effective Schools Approach seeks to uncover important differences among schools by identifying and then investigating those unusual schools that are successful beyond expectations. This approach has developed a five-factor effective schools model: strong administrative leadership; a safe and orderly school climate; an emphasis on basic academic skills; high teacher expectations for all students; and a system for monitoring and assessing pupil performance.[31]

A number of criticisms are being brought in relation to this model and approach. They include the following:

1. No one knows how to create effective schools.
2. The language is fuzzy.
3. Effectiveness is a constricted concept, ignoring many skills, habits, and attitudes beyond the reach of paper-and-pencil tests.
4. Most of the research has been done in elementary schools, and findings have little applicability to the secondary school.[32]

This model is mentioned here because we believe that while it may contain weaknesses as do all models and approaches, it is generating a great deal of debate and discussion that in the end should prove beneficial to our schools.

ALTERNATIVE SCHOOLS APPROACH

"Recent studies indicate that the most effective schools are distinguished, not by elaborate facilities, extensively trained teachers, small classes, or high levels of financial support, but by outstanding social climates."[33]

This is another approach to helping our schools become more effective.

---

30. B. Watkins, "Mastery of Six Basic Subjects and Six Intellectual Skills Urged for College-Bound Students," *Chronicle of Higher Education* 1 (18 May 1983):14-16.
31. R. Edmonds, "Programs of School Improvement: An Overview," *Educational Leadership* 40 (December 1982):4-11. See also J. Ralph and J. Fennessy, "Science or Reform: Some Questions About the Effective Schools Model," *Phi Delta Kappan* 64, no. 10 (June 1983):689-94.
32. "Effective Schools: A Friendly but Cautionary Note," by Larry Cuban, June 1983, © 1983, *Phi Delta Kappan*, Inc. 64, no. 10:695. Used by permission.
33. Erickson, p. 46.

Raywid suggests that there is no reason the sort of choices offered in the private schools cannot be offered within a single public school district. Fred Hechinger reports on the results in one such district in Jefferson County, Colorado. In that district, a student can choose among fundamental schools, open schools, neighborhood schools, and others. Hechinger concludes that when public education offers these kinds of options, it gains in strength and also in public support.[34]

Thus, although the schools are being constantly criticized for what they are doing or not doing, nevertheless in the decade of the 80s many agencies and individuals are concerned and seeking to provide constructive remedies and reforms.

You in the Schoolhouse?

No one can answer this question for you. We urge you, no matter what motivation has brought you to this point of interest in education as a career, to examine carefully and honestly whether you think you fit into the schoolhouse.

To be effective in the schoolhouse requires a belief that teachers can make a difference, an informed philosophic perspective, the skills to perform as a clinician, and a great deal of energy to keep up with the daily schedule. Exceedingly important to your personal mental health is your own assessment of whether you would derive satisfaction from teaching.

Think of yourself as going to the schoolhouse five days a week and becoming involved in the activities there. Would you look forward to it a majority of the time, or would you grate against it? Perhaps, like many students at this point, you are not sure. We urge you to continue exploring the advantages and disadvantages with colleagues, veteran teachers, new teachers, students in the schools, and administrators. As you visit schools and observe educational happenings, the decision you make will become more realistic.

Hindsight

In this chapter we have endeavored to help you look at the schoolhouse through the teacher's glasses. We have emphasized the conviction based on research, observation, and experience that teachers can have a major influence on the way students learn and develop. We have urged you to share in the samplings of schoolhouse behavior in the context of the question: "Will I fit?" At the same time, we cautioned you not to be overwhelmed by the criticisms leveled against the schoolhouse, its personnel and processes.

We have looked at Jackson's four roles of the teacher as traffic cop, judge,

---

34. Fred Hechinger, "About Education: A School System Changes the Mix," *New York Times*, 2 November 1982.

supply sergeant, and timekeeper. We have considered Anglin and associates' unique conditions of the schoolhouse and considered Rosenshine's formal but flexible and warm classrooms. We have reviewed some "typical" schoolhouse situations with reference to what is expected of the teacher at different levels. We sampled some of the differences among private, alternative, and public schools.

Finally, we looked at criticisms of the schoolhouse and some suggested current programs for the improvement of our public schools. We urged you to continue exploring in depth the advantages and disadvantages of teaching to arrive at a realistic answer as to whether teaching is for you.

Incidentally, if you reach a "no" answer, you have not failed. You have progressed a significant step further in your career planning. You can then pursue other possibilities for your future.

CHALKBOARD CHALLENGES

1. Interview some local teachers, one from each level of teaching, if possible. Find out what it is like to be a teacher in today's schoolhouse. Ask questions about such areas as major kinds of discipline problems and how they are handled; frustrations and interruptions; use of equipment; adequate supplies; whether the teachers believe they have genuine influence on the learning and development of their students and what evidences lead them to their beliefs. Make some notes from your interviews in your teacher's notebook.

2. Interview a school board member if possible, or a custodian, or a cafeteria worker to ascertain his point of view on what is happening at the schoolhouse. Make clear you are not looking for or listening to criticism of the administration or other school workers but that you are exploring for basic information to help you make your decision about teaching. Always let the Director of Field Services at your college know if you are going into a school building to interview. Usually, he will have helpful suggestions. And, of course, the first person you talk with in the schoolhouse is the principal to state your reason for being there and ask his or her permission to interview. Be careful also not to disrupt classes or other activities at the school. It is usually best to make an appointment ahead of time for the interview.

3. Make a survey over a month's time of your local newspaper(s). Note what educational issues are receiving the attention of the media. This will help you understand better public perceptions of the schoolhouse. Make a listing of these issues in your notebook.

4. If you have opportunity, why not select as your topic for a class or term paper, "What's Happening at the Schoolhouse?" This will help you to pull together your observations and ideas about this subject.

5. As part of your notebook, develop a simple chart that has two columns: Similarities of Classrooms and Differences in Classrooms. As you visit classrooms,

including those at the college level, sampling as many as you can at different levels, note the similarities and differences you observe in the appropriate column. This can become a valuable piece of work for you over a period of time and will serve you well especially during student teaching time and early teaching years. Make a deliberate effort as a result of your visit and notations to develop your own view of the classroom based on research, observation, and experiences. Another section of your notebook might be entitled "My View of the Classroom."

Want to Know More?

One way to take a look at the schoolhouse is by reading *Life in Classrooms*, by Philip W. Jackson (New York: Holt, Rinehart, and Winston, 1968). This frequently-quoted book is written in such a manner that you pick up the feeling and flavor of the schoolhouse along with the author's insights.

FIRST YEAR TEACHING

For a particular focus on the first year of teaching, the following two books are helpful:

Kevin Ryan, et al., *Biting the Apple: Accounts of First Year Teachers*. (New York: Longman, 1980).

Kevin Ryan, ed., *Don't Smile Until Christmas: Accounts of the First Year of Teaching*. (Chicago: U. of Chicago, 1970).

For a perspective on the contexts of teaching, read the article "Good Teaching in Its Contexts," by Richard L. Turner, *Phi Delta Kappan*, 52, no. 70:155-58.

EFFECTIVE SCHOOLS

Effective Schools Research is the source of much discussion and debate during the 1980s. For three stimulating articles concerning this topic, all contained in the *Phi Delta Kappan* for June 1983 (vol. 64, no. 10), look for these titles:

"Science or Reform: Some Questions About the Effective Schools Model" (Ralph and Fennessey, pp. 689-94).

"Effective Schools: A Friendly but Cautionary Note" (Cuban, pp. 695-96).

"A First Look at Effective Schools Projects in New York City and Milwaukee" (Eubanks and Levine, pp. 697-702).

GENERAL EDUCATION

Redefining general education in our secondary schools is another major issue of the 1980s. The May 1982 issue of *Educational Leadership* (vol. 39, no. 8) devotes three-fourths of its articles to this subject—an excellent compendium, relevant regardless of the level or setting in which you teach or plan to teach.

SCHOOL BOARD

"How Well Does the Public Know Its School Boards?" is the title of a brief, fact-filled report by Boardman and Cassel in the June 1983 issue of *Phi Delta Kappan* (vol. 64, no. 10, p. 740). You may be surprised at the results of this survey.

Another major report is one entitled "A Study of Schooling," which includes a number of articles in the April 1983 *Educational Leadership Journal*. This study looks at improving schooling in the 1980s by John I. Goodlad, who is dean of the Graduate School of Education at UCLA. Then in the same issue are responses and commentaries on Goodlad's report. See especially pages 3-37. The articles involved include a review of Goodlad's new book entitled *A Place Called School*. We consider this virtually "must" reading for the student of education.

Part 2

The Developmental Process

3

Concepts and Theories

CONTENTS

	PAGE
Key Terms	69
That's Debatable!	71
Foresight	72
Difficulties in Defining Development	73
Why We Need Theories	73
Five Assumptions Regarding the Nature of Human Development	74
Continuum of Developmental Theories	77
Early Developmental Theories: Gesell and Watson	81
Current Developmental Theories	84
Implications for the Teaching-Learning Process	98
Hindsight	100
Chalkboard Challenges	101
Want to Know More?	102

KEY TERMS

Accommodation
   The changing of the individual's intellectual structure to fit the new information
Applied behavior analysis
   Application of principles of learning discovered in controlled settings to wider social contexts

Assimilation
> The changing of new information to fit the existing intellectual structure of the individual

Concrete operational stage
> The third stage of cognitive development (Piaget), in which logical thought can be applied to specific situations involving actual objects

Constructionist
> A theoretical approach that sees the child as "constructing" knowledge by coordinating many schemata, as opposed to the idea of the child's simply copying or imitating what he sees in his environment

Continuous development
> A term conceptually opposite of "stage development"; children develop gradually and continuously into adults; the child looked upon as a miniature adult

Critical period
> A limited period during the child's early years in which a certain type of learning occurs because of neurological development

Development
> Orderly, directional change (generally associated with age) characterized by increasing differentiation and complex organization

Enactive representation
> Associated with infancy and very early childhood, in which children represent past experience through their motor acts (Bruner)

Formal operations stage
> The fourth stage of cognitive development (Piaget), in which logical thought can be applied abstractly, with symbols substituting for objects

Iconic representation
> Associated with the preschool and early elementary years, in which children are able to form visual images of stimuli encountered in their environment, to retain these images, and to recall them in the absence of the real object or event (Bruner)

Learning
> (1) A change in behavior due to experience (behaviorist)
> (2) A change in behavioral repertoire due to experience (social learning theory)
> (3) The personal discovery by an individual of his or her relationship to an object, event, process, idea, other persons, God, or self; may or may not be outward behavior that is quantitatively measurable as a result of the inner discovery (author's)

Maturation
> Changes in behavior, genetically determined, biological in nature, which occur independent of experience

Operation
In Piaget's theory, the ability to manipulate concepts internally in increasingly complex ways
Preoperational stage
The second stage of cognitive development (Piaget), in which representation of objects and ideas begins to replace seeing, feeling, touching as a mode of thought
Psychosocial
The concept referring to the individual's establishing basic orientation to himself and his social world throughout the life cycle
Schema
A structurized system of assimilations and accommodations; a behavior pattern (Piaget)
Sensorimotor stage
The first level of cognitive development (Piaget), in which the objects of thought are limited to what can be seen, felt, and heard
Sociobiology
A relatively contemporary and highly controversial science that asserts that man's behavior, like that of all animals, is genetically influenced (not that man necessarily behaves like an ape, but that the same mechanism, heredity encoded in genes, operates on both)
Stage development
Periods of development marked by qualitative changes (changes in kind) at the beginning and the end
Symbolic representation
Associated with the later elementary school years, when the thought of the child becomes more flexible and abstract due to the child's increasingly complex use of language; words may represent ideas and relationships for which there are no concrete referents (Bruner)
Transductive reasoning
The child reasons that one event causes a second event when the two are not related; characteristic of the preoperational stage in Piaget's theory

That's Debatable!

THE PRESENT MOMENT—WHERE ARE WE?

My basic argument in this essay has been that throughout most of the period during which psychology and the practice and philosophy of education have interacted, the interaction has been dominated by developmental and differential psychology. As a dominant source of educational theory, these two branches of psychology have had some peculiar characteristics. Most important, neither has believed very strongly in the power of the educational enterprise—especially direct instruction—to affect seriously the capabilities of children; and neither has offered any substantial help to educators in thinking about how to design environments that would optimize learning. Developmental psychology, adopting a strong child advocacy position, has offered a theory of natural development which was better at suggesting ways of *not* interfering with development than ways of actively promoting it. While the influence of child psychology has surely been a humanizing one on the schools, the movement as a whole has never been very helpful in suggesting how human capacities might be developed to levels beyond those traditionally considered normal or natural. Differential psychology, too, has offered help in describing and classifying children. But in its origins it saw education as capable of *adapting* to children's capabilities—by offering more or demanding less—but not of *creating* capabilities. As long as society was comfortable with schools geared to particular social classes and to high dropout rates or low achievement for large segments of the population, this set of beliefs was perhaps adequate and comfortable.

We are attending now to formerly invisible segments of the population. We are seeking mass levels of competence in literacy, and in mathematics that only a century ago were sought for only a relatively small and elite group. As our aspirations for education increase, we are developing increased concern for the question of how to modify what would be the "normal"—but socially unacceptable—course of development for some children. . . . Only to the extent that education comes to trust more fully in the possibilities for changing human capability and makes deliberate efforts to improve environments for learning will it be able to successfully address the challenge of higher educational standards for larger segments of the population.

Psychology's assumptions will shift in response to the changes in social goals and social assumptions. As a result, psychology's contributions to the science of education are likely to develop in directions that might surprise those whose predictions are shaped by the psychology of the past.[1]

Foresight

The study of human development is a fascinating one, with new findings and insights cropping up almost continuously. These findings may support or challenge the cumulative body of knowledge, but all those interested in how people develop—including teachers—need to keep feeding this kind of information into their repertoire of resources.

It is imperative that the teacher understand the characteristics of the age group he or she teaches. The relationship of behavior to the age of the child raises many difficult issues. This creates difficulties in defining development, and we shall be talking about that in this chapter along with the reasons we need theories of human development. We shall look at five assumptions on which you eventually must "make up your mind" regarding the nature of human development. After

---

1. Excerpted from Lauren B. Resnick, "Social Assumptions as a Context for Science: Some Reflections on Psychology and Education," *Educational Psychologist* 16, no. 1 (Spring 1981):20-21. Copyrighted 1981 by Division 15 of the American Psychological Association; reprinted here with permission.

Concepts and Theories

reviewing briefly early developmental theories, we shall move to the major current concepts and theories and relate their implications to the teaching-learning process.

What we are concerned with is how children grow and change through time. As we discuss these changes, you will begin to see a pattern of development. The behavior of a child is to a large degree a function of his or her age. But remember, there are many important differences in the behavior of children the same age. Different children grow up at different rates and in different ways. Still, there is enough similarity in the development of children to make these patterns a vital part of your knowledge for relating to your students.

We repeat: the study of human development is fascinating. We hope at least some of that fascination will be "catching" as you read this chapter.

DIFFICULTIES IN DEFINING DEVELOPMENT

As a competent teacher, you will need to adapt your ways of teaching to the characteristics of the students in your educational setting. One major part of those characteristics is represented by the developmental levels of the children whom you teach.

But human development is a difficult topic to define (we use "define" in the broadest sense of trying to organize the field). It is difficult because developmental psychology includes so many areas that have been studied intensively; often separate courses are offered on infancy, early childhood, childhood, and adolescence. It is also necessary to analyze many different forms of behavior and to follow through to see how each type of behavior changes as the child matures. Various writers in the field have used different strategies to deal with these problems, and this of course means that there are a good number of approaches to the field of human development. The very large number of approaches in itself can stagger the perception, especially of the relative newcomer to the field.

We therefore write these two chapters—this one and the next—with the intention of calling to your attention certain aspects of human development that particularly concern teachers and to encourage you to relate these aspects to the teaching-learning process. This chapter deals with the concepts and theories of development; the next describes some of the characteristics and sequences of development for various age levels.

WHY WE NEED THEORIES

Theories are important for two reasons: First, theories call attention to the overall sequence, continuity, and interrelatedness of aspects of development. Second, it is important for the teacher-to-be to have been exposed to a number of theories so he will see the importance of developing his own theory of development as a part of his repertoire of resources, which he can then bring to the teaching-learning process. Although that personal theory may be very tentative, nevertheless it is an organizing factor into which the teacher can feed his observation of behaviors at the various developmental levels. In this way the teacher's observations help him deliberately to define and refine his theory, and, conversely, the theory helps him make sense of his observations. The resulting philosophic perspective strengthens the teacher as a clinician in the teaching-learning process. To put it differently, the value of a theory for the teacher is its deliberate organizing effect upon the discrete events and observations of the teacher's clinical practice. The one serves to strengthen the other.

At the same time, the teacher needs to remember that the development of an appropriate theory is a difficult matter. There is a sense in which a theory is never adequate and always needs more data. A theory of development needs to account for as many facets of behavior related to developmental levels as possible. This is a gigantic undertaking, one that needs constant effort, and yet one to which each of us must give careful attention based on the cumulative knowledge of the field and our own careful observations and reflections.

FIVE ASSUMPTIONS REGARDING THE NATURE OF HUMAN DEVELOPMENT

To help us in developing appropriate theories relating human development to the teaching-learning process, there are at least five assumptions or issues with which we must struggle. Our decisions in relation to these assumptions will ultimately help to shape our theories.

INBORN DIFFERENCES AMONG PEOPLE

Although this may seem an obvious kind of issue, it really is quite controversial. For example, on the one hand you have the sociobiologists who insist that behavior must be attributed almost entirely to genetic explanations.[2] The whole field of genetics has spurred increased interest in this topic of inborn differences among people. And it raises many pertinent questions: If an individual's behavior is a result of his genetic inheritance, can you hold him responsible for his behavior? If at the other extreme, an individual's behavior is a result of environmental influences almost exclusively, can you hold that individual responsible for his behavior? Are there differences among various races or as a result of ethnic backgrounds? The child with Downs Syndrome (mongoloidism) has an inborn difference that directly relates to the manner and the environment in which that child can be educated. To what extent are the various learning styles of children due to inborn differences? And the list of questions continues on, each with a significant impact upon both the theory and practice of the philosopher-clinician teacher.

---

2. H.E. Fitzgerald and T.H. Carr, eds., *Annual Editions: Human Development 83-84* (Guilford, Conn.: Dushkin, Sluice Dock, 1983), p. 3.

Concepts and Theories

MALLEABILITY OF HUMAN BEHAVIOR

Malleable means "able to be shaped." The question this assumption asks is, How much can human behavior be influenced by forces outside the individual? When we talk about the shaping of human behavior, we are dealing at least in part with this assumption. Again the theorists are divided sharply on this issue, depending on the amount of influence they attribute to genetic inheritance as being the cause of human behavior. Obviously, if you believe that human behavior is quite malleable, then your approach to the teaching-learning process will be to bring the proper environmental forces to bear upon the individual to achieve appropriate results. If on the other hand you believe that human behavior is not very malleable, a great deal less emphasis will be placed upon the environmental influence in the individual's development, and much more emphasis will be placed upon the maturation factor.

ACTIVE VERSUS PASSIVE ROLES OF HUMANS

This assumption may be illustrated by a simple reference to a billiard ball lying on the pool table. The ball just stays in one position. It does not move until it is tapped by the tip of the cue stick, and then it will roll at the speed with which it is hit and in the direction it has been hit until that force from outside itself is expended. This passive role describes human beings as being largely at the mercy of environmental forces.

On the other hand, if you believe that the human being has an active role, you believe the individual has the ability to change circumstances in his environment by acting upon the forces outside himself. Once again, this is an issue that divides the theorists. The behaviorists see the human being as largely passive, and the cognitive theorists view the human being as one who is able to act upon his or her environment. As with all extreme differences, many theorists fall in between, and are known as interactionists.

INNATE GOODNESS OR EVIL OF HUMANS

Is the human being innately good, evil, or neutral? The broad stream of Christian tradition of course believes the nature of human beings is innately evil. In that stream of thought, it is necessary for the child's development to exercise firm discipline and to help the individual keep his evil nature under control. At the other extreme is the humanists' position, which looks upon the nature of the human being as basically good. The child has within himself or herself the potential to grow into a fully functioning human being. It is then the job of educators and all others who deal with that child to help facilitate the development of that potential in him. Behaviorists would say that the human being is really an organism, and therefore this is a neutral kind of issue, since the organism develops by responding to a greater or lesser degree to the stimuli with which it is presented. Once again the position one takes in relation to this assumption will result in significantly influencing the kind of approach one takes in the teaching-learning process.

RELATIONSHIP OF CHILD TO ADULT BEHAVIOR

Is the child just a miniature adult? Does the child put his world together the same way the adult does, cognitively speaking? Does the child just gradually and continuously grow and develop into an adult, or is there a difference in the quality

---

Insight: Freud's Stages of Development

In contrast with Erik Erikson's "eight ages of man," which extend over the human being's entire lifetime, Sigmund Freud's description of human development concentrates almost solely on the early years of life. Here is a brief summary of those stages described by Freud:

Oral stage—approximately the first year of life, when the mouth region provides the greatest sensual satisfaction. "Incorporativeness" (first six months) and "aggressiveness" (second six months) are derivative behavioral traits.

Anal stage—approximately the second and third years. The site of greatest sensual pleasure shifts to the anal and urethal areas. Derivative traits: "retentiveness" and "expulsiveness."

Phallic stage—approximately the third and fourth years. The site of greatest sensual pleasure is the genital region. Behavioral traits: "intrusiveness" (male) and "receptiveness" (female).

Oedipal stage—approximately the fourth and fifth years of life. At this stage, the child looks upon the parent of the opposite sex as the object or provider of sensual satisfaction, and the same sexed parent becomes a rival in the child's perception. Derivative behavioral traits: "seductiveness" and "competitiveness."

Latency stage—approximately the sixth to eleventh years. Oedipus conflict resolved as child identifies with parent of the opposite sex, thus satisfying sensual needs vicariously. Derivative behavioral trait: "conscience" (the internalization of parental moral and ethical demands).

Puberty stage—approximately the eleventh to fourteenth years. Integration and subordination of oral, anal, and phallic sensuality to a unitary genital sexuality. The object of this genital sexuality is another person of the opposite sex. Derivative traits (along with control and regulation of genital sexuality): "intellectualization" and "estheticism."

Fig. 3.1

Concepts and Theories

(kind) of the child's way of thinking and seeking to make sense out of his world? Stage theorists such as Piaget would say that the child very definitely is *not* a miniature adult but that the child goes through "discontinuous" stages, and those stages are qualitatively different each from the other. The child must be understood on this basis rather than on the basis that the child learns in the same way as an adult, or makes sense out of his experiences the way an adult does. Behaviorists, on the other hand, would claim that the child *is* a miniature adult, and he learns the same way as an adult through stimulus and response, reward and punishment, imitation and modeling. Because the differences between the child and adult are primarily quantitative, the child therefore gradually and continuously develops until he becomes an adult.

Although we have dealt with these assumptions only briefly, we believe that your decisions regarding these assumptions will largely determine your approach to a theory of development. As we move to a discussion of some particular theories, you are urged to keep these five assumptions in the forefront of your thinking. And you are urged to keep some notes in your teacher's notebook concerning your own reflections about them.

CONTINUUM OF DEVELOPMENTAL THEORIES

The multidisciplinary field of human development is concerned with stability and change throughout the life span. There is no single theory at present that gives comprehensive direction to the study of human development.[3] Nevertheless, most developmentalists would agree that age is an important variable in explaining the similarities and differences among children. But there is wide disagreement as to *why* age is so important and the amount of influence either genetics or the environment has upon development.

We have chosen to use a developmental continuum as a means of understanding at least the basic differences in these approaches to human development, and we have chosen theorists we believe represent approaches that hold significant implications for the teaching-learning process. We have adapted this continuum from Lahey and Johnson, and as a means of approaching this continuum let us look first at the unfolding-molding dichotomy summarized in figure 3.2.[4]

UNFOLDING-MOLDING DICHOTOMY

Some have criticized the Unfolding-Molding dichotomy because of its two extreme viewpoints, but it is nevertheless a most helpful kind of device for grasping developmental theories.

Unfolding viewpoint. You will note that the unfolding view sees the child

---

3. Ibid.
4. B.B. Lahey and M.S. Johnson, *Psychology and Instruction* (New York: Scott Foresman, 1978), p. 24. Used by permission.

GALLERY OF GREATS

Sigmund Freud
Personality patterns have their roots in
childhood experiences.

If there is a single name more people know than any other in the fields of psychology and medicine, it is probably Sigmund Freud. Born in Europe in 1856, belonging to a tightly-knit family, he reportedly suffered depression and anxiety during his youth. His main career thrust was to discover the relationship between personality structure and actual behavior. That thrust took him through medical school graduation from the University of Vienna in 1881 to the beginning of World War II in 1939—his last year being spent in England after having been a captive of Hitler.

The "Father of Psychoanalysis," Freud's major contribution was his insight into the causes of behavior. Despite criticism and some of his associates' leaving, he continued to elaborate his theory of sexuality as a determinant of behavior during the early years of life. The psychologist's task was to uncover the psychic material of the past and help the individual understand how it was determining his current behavior. The unconscious was the key to human behavior and motivation.

Perhaps most important among all the contributions of Freud is the realization that we need to recognize and develop control over our destructive human drives. Few would disagree with that, even though there is substantial disagreement about the manner in which such control is to be accomplished.

primarily as a biological organism. In this viewpoint the maturational process is the chief factor in development, and maturation is simply the unfolding of the genes as the child moves along in age. Learning is a function of maturation, and the behavior of children depends on their biological readiness. It is important to note that the

---

Issues Defining the "Unfolding"-"Molding" Viewpoints*

Unfolding Viewpoints	*Molding Viewpoints*
Age depicts the underlying process of biological maturation, as determined by the genes.	*Age* depicts the backdrop against which specific experiences accumulate as a result of the childrens' interaction with their environment.
Norms and *stages* are the benchmarks of the natural process of unfolding.	*Norms* and *stages* are useful only as descriptions of what has occurred in a given environment.
Learning is a function of maturation—what children can learn depends upon their biological readiness.	*Learning:* what children can learn depends upon what they have learned previously.
Teachers and parents play the role of a "gardener," planting the seeds and cultivating, but waiting for the final product to emerge from within the child.	*Teachers and parents* play the role of "potter," starting with a ball of clay and actively shaping the final product by structuring learning experiences.

*From B. B. Lahey and M. S. Johnson, *Psychology and Instruction* (New York: Scott Foresman, 1978), p. 24.

Fig. 3.2

environment has only a minor influence on development, according to the unfolding viewpoint. Lahey and Johnson provide a very helpful picture when they use the gardener as representing the role that teachers and parents play, "planting the seeds and cultivating, but waiting for the final product to emerge from within the child."[5] Differences in children's behavior from those of the typical patterns of development (developmental norms) are the result of the fact that some individuals simply mature (biologically) faster than others.

It is important to note that those known as stage theorists will be found on the unfolding side of the continuum, because the stages are passed through in a fixed sequence under the control of biological mechanisms. A later stage of development cannot be reached until the child has passed through all earlier stages in sequence. Thus, behavior is a function of the maturational process for those who view development from the unfolding viewpoint.

"Experience plays a limited role in determining the rate at which the stages will be completed, in the same way that the sun, water, and nutrients play a role in influencing the growth of a tree. A child growing in a poor environment can be stunted like a tree growing in a poor soil, but experience cannot influence the nature or sequence of the stages anymore than soil can determine what kind of tree will grow from a seed. Acorns always produce oaks, regardless of the soil they are planted in."[6]

Molding viewpoint. If one comes at development from the molding viewpoint, one is saying that changes in behavior do not emerge automatically from within children but result from influences in the environment that act upon children in very predictable ways. Age is seen as important in development only in that with increasing age children increase their range of experiences. What children can learn depends on what they have learned previously. So learning, which is defined as change in behavior due to experience, for the purposes of our discussion at this point, is the principle that guides or controls development. And as Lahey and Johnson point out, "the acquisition of readiness is simply a matter of preparing for more complex behaviors through the learning of prerequisite skills."[7]

Those who stress the environment as the main influence shaping behavior— for example, behaviorists—will be found on the molding side of the dichotomy. Behaviorists believe that behavior is a function of experience. The similarities in the environments of most children are responsible for typical behaviors to appear at certain times and to appear sequentially.

Again, Lahey and Johnson offer a very helpful illustration in referring to teachers and parents playing the role of a potter, "starting with a ball of clay and actively shaping the final product by structuring learning experiences."[8] This dichotomy has enormous implications for the teacher in the teaching-learning process, and we will discuss some of those implications at the end of this chapter.

5. Ibid.
6. Ibid., p. 25.
7. Ibid., p. 26.
8. Ibid., p. 24.

Unfolding-Molding Continuum*

		BLOOM		
WILSON		HAVIGHURST		SKINNER
GESELL PIAGET BRUNER		HUNT	BANDURA	WATSON

Unfolding	Molding

*Adapted from B.B. Lahey & M.S. Johnson, *Psychology & Instruction* (New York: Scott Foresman, 1978).

Fig. 3.3

DEVELOPMENTAL CONTINUUM

With this brief background preparation, we turn now to the developmental continuum itself based on the unfolding-molding dichotomy as shown in figure 3.3.

Note that the unfolding anchor point is at the left end of the continuum and the molding viewpoint is at the right end of the continuum. This illustration provides an image that will help you substantially in understanding the approaches of the main developmental theorists. You will note immediately that Erikson and Maslow are not on this particular continuum, although Erikson certainly would be at about the same place on the continuum as Piaget, since both are stage theorists. However, we have chosen to put Erikson and Maslow on a second continuum, which we call the psychosocial continuum, and that is shown in figure 3.8.

EARLY DEVELOPMENTAL THEORIES: GESELL AND WATSON

It is probably accurate to say that this dichotomy we have been discussing is more characteristic of the early developmental theories, as many of the present theories really would be classified as *interaction* theories. That is, they emphasize that there is an interaction between maturation and experience. One exception to that would be the sociobiologists under Edward O. Wilson, who could be placed at or very near the extreme unfolding end of the continuum. We will return to the sociobiologists shortly.

There are two early developmental theorists about whom we wish to comment briefly, and they represent the pioneering spirit in the field of human

---

Insight: How Accurate Are Early Impressions?

Most teachers form early impressions as to the "good" pupils and the "less than excellent" pupils, academically speaking, in their class. The author has known teachers who almost seem to have formulated a mental normal curve with each pupil perched appropriately thereupon within the first couple of weeks of school! Even kindergarten teachers appear to have caught this "disease" and form early impressions before much instruction has occurred. How accurate are these early impressions?

Harold Stevenson's research group at the University of Michigan's Center for Human Growth and Development conducted a study to find out the answer to our question. The group kept teacher ratings of 217 kindergarten children confidentially on file and later compared them with academic achievement test scores of these children at the end of the second and third grade.

Conclusions:

1. The kindergarten teachers predicted later achievement better than chance or random predictions, but were only moderately accurate overall.
2. Many of the early impressions proved to be inaccurate.
3. Teachers' ratings were more accurate than those of parents.*

An earlier piece of research suggests that the ratings of kindergarten teachers are generally more accurate than batteries of readiness tests, especially in choosing those students who are most in need of special academic instruction.†

Cautions:

1. Early teacher ratings are only moderately accurate.
2. Children change rapidly during elementary school years.
3. Pay no attention to the "rumors" you hear about children: observe them carefully and work diligently with them in your teaching-learning setting to help them develop and learn.

*H. W. Stevenson, T. Parker, A. Wilkenson, A. Hegion, and E. Fish, "Predictive Value of Teachers' Ratings of Young Children," *Journal of Educational Psychology* 68 (1976):507-17.
†W. E. Ferinden, S. Jacobson, and N. J. Linden, "Early Identification of Learning Disabilities," *Journal of Learning Disabilities* 3 (1970):589-93.

Fig. 3.4

Concepts and Theories

development. Their positions are used as opposing anchor points on the continuum, because Arnold Gesell believed strongly that development is a function of biological maturation,[9] whereas John B. Watson formulated a theory of development that placed total emphasis upon learning as the process that shapes the child.[10]

NORMATIVE RESEARCH

In the early 1900s, Gesell began a series of research projects at the Yale Child Development Center that involved the observation of large numbers of children. Gradually, Gesell's studies and observations included children at all age levels up through adolescence. His research was *normative* in nature, which means he wanted to develop descriptive behavior typical of children at various ages. Gesell published three books at the end of an enormous amount of research on many aspects of children's behavior in the 1940s and 1950s, dealing with infancy, childhood, and adolescence.[11] Parents still turn to these books and the detailed descriptions they provide of how a particular aged child should behave, to determine if their child's course of development is normal.

Gesell proposed that the similarities in the behavior of children the same age were due to the unfolding or, as he called it, the "ripening" of the nervous system. Gesell placed very little emphasis on learning: "environmental factors support, inflect, and modify; but they do not generate the progression of development ... the maturational matrix is the primary determinant of child behavior."[12]

WATSON: TOTAL EMPHASIS ON ENVIRONMENT

At the opposite end of the continuum—the molding end—is John B. Watson, who had a very strong conviction that in order for psychology to progress as a science it was necessary to focus on the relationship between observable behavior and the environmental events that affect that behavior. Watson formulated a theory of development that placed total emphasis on learning as the process that shapes the child:

> Give me a dozen healthy infants, well formed, and my own specified world to bring them up in and I will guarantee to take any one at random and train him to become any type of specialist I might select—doctor, lawyer, artist, merchant chief

---

9. Arnold Gesell, "The Ontogenesis of Infant Behavior," in L. Carmichael, ed., *Manual of Child Psychology* (New York: Wiley and Sons, 1954).
10. John B. Watson, *Behaviorism* (Chicago: U. of Chicago, 1925). Original publisher: W.W. Norton & Company, Inc.
11. Arnold Gesell and Frances L. Ilg, *Infant and Child in the Culture of Today* (New York: Harper, 1943). See also Gesell and Ilg, *The Child from Five to Ten* (New York: Harper, 1946); Gesell, Ilg, and Ames, *Youth: The Years from Ten to Sixteen* (New York: Harper, 1956).
12. Gesell, "Ontogenesis," p. 358. Used by permission.

and, yes, even beggar man and thief, regardless of his talents, penchants, tendencies, abilities, vocations, and race of his ancestors.[13]

Watson urged parents to take an objective and firm yet kindly stance toward their children. But he continued to warn them against the unfolding viewpoint:

These two early developmental theorists, almost directly opposite in their approaches to human development, nevertheless set the stage for the many controversies and differences in approach on the human development theoretical scene.

CURRENT DEVELOPMENTAL THEORIES

As we discuss the current developmental theorists, we urge you to keep the continuum in front of you and use it to help you distinguish among the various approaches. We also urge you to think about where you might put yourself on this particular unfolding-molding continuum, however tentative your approach might be. By relating frequently to this continuum you will be helped in developing your philosophy—that is, your professional perspective—toward the teaching-learning process.

We have chosen these particular theories for discussion by using three major criteria: (1) they cover the range of the continuum, and they are representative of the several approaches; (2) a considerable amount of scientific support can be summoned for each of the theories; and (3) the theories have significant implications for the teaching-learning process. Again, remember that we have two continua: one is the unfolding-molding continuum on which most of the theorists we shall be discussing may be found; the second continuum is labeled the "psychosocial continuum" and contains just two of the theorists we are discussing, Abraham Maslow and Erik Erikson. We recognize that usually only Erikson is placed in the psychosocial realm in terms of developmental theory as a major current theorist, but we believe that Abraham Maslow has great value in being placed also on this continuum, at least for learning purposes, and we will of course explain our reasoning when we reach the second continuum.

---

13. Watson, *Behaviorism*, p. 82.

STAGE THEORIES: PIAGET AND BRUNER

When Jean Piaget died in 1980, we lost one of the greatest minds of our time in the area of cognitive development. His theory of cognitive development is a *stage* theory, because he believed that children go through a series of sequential stages in the development of their thinking abilities. Each stage is *qualitatively* different from the others—that is, they are different in kind as characterized by the way children think, the kinds of things they think about, the kinds of errors they make in solving problems, and the way they put their world together and try to make sense out of it.

Piaget further believed that all children, regardless of the culture in which they live or their learning experiences, go through the stages in the same sequence, and a child cannot reach a higher stage of thinking without having gone through the lower stages. Each of the stages is controlled by maturational unfolding, and Piaget's many experiments with children and his observations of their thinking behavior led him to the conclusion that a child can think only in a certain way, characteristic of a particular stage, until maturationally he develops and then is able to think differently according to the next stage.

For Piaget, a child is not a miniature adult, but a child's thinking—the way a child makes sense out of his world—is different in *kind* from the thinking of adults.

We have placed Piaget a little to the right of Gesell and Wilson on the continuum, because although Piaget does believe that children cannot accommodate new learning experiences until they have reached appropriate maturational levels, he believes that the environment is involved in the cognitive development of a child. Piaget is a *constructionist,* a term that means that a child does not merely copy or imitate what he sees outside himself, but rather that the child constructs out of his experiences with the environment that which becomes reality for him. How a child constructs that reality depends upon the maturational stage he has reached.

Let us look at Piaget's four stages and characterize each of them briefly.

Sensorimotor stage (birth to two years). Piaget believed that infants are primarily occupied with processing sensory input and, of course, trying to coordinate motor behavior in response to sensory stimuli. The newborn infant has a set of reflexes that are really automatic behaviors in response to specific stimulation, such as grasping your finger if you place it in the palm of the baby's hand. She will not, however, *intentionally* reach to grasp a toy that might be lying in her crib. But by the time she is one, she will happily bang any object against the side of the crib just to enjoy the sound of the banging. She is at this point beginning to try to make sense of her environment. But it is important to note that her knowledge of the environment at this age comes through motor behavior and physical contact with whatever is in the environment.

By the end of the sensorimotor period, Piaget states that the beginnings of internalized thought appear. The two-year-old, says Piaget, can both think about and systematically search for toys and other objects that are out of her sight.

Basically, the sensorimotor stage is a stage in which the child is getting used to what is in her environment and learning how to coordinate motor behavior in response to all of the sensory stimuli. Incidentally, the ages Piaget assigns to these stages are not necessarily rigid; in fact, they are flexible and must be interpreted as such if you are to understand Piaget properly. But the stages do appear in every child, and every child must go through the previous stage before going on into the successive stages.

Preoperational (two to seven years). During this stage a child's language becomes functional. In the early part of the preoperational stage the language and thought of the child is egocentric; he sees things from his own point of view only. He engages in what is known as *transductive reasoning.* That is, the child cannot handle two variables at the same time in a logical manner, so he will assign cause and effect to two events when there really is no relationship between them. A good example of this is something I said at about the age of five. Having an older brother whose birthday came four days after mine, I kept asking my parents how my brother was older than I when my birthday came before his. This is a typical example of transductive reasoning. The preschool child will likely treat two objects the very same way even though they have just one thing in common. For example, many children will call any four-footed creature a cat or a dog, depending on what label they have assigned to four-footed creatures. During the last half of the preoperational stage, children do begin to grasp logical concepts and become less egocentric in their thinking. Still, their thinking is unsophisticated, and they have difficulty manipulating more than one idea or concept at a time.

Concrete operational stage (seven to eleven years). This is about the time, of course, that children enter elementary school, and some significant changes begin to take place in their thought processes. Piaget points out that their most important change is their newly acquired ability to use mental operations in making sense of their environment. The word *operation* for Piaget means "the ability to manipulate concepts internally." During this stage the child can manipulate two or more objects logically, but the child's thinking is still very closely tied to objects and events that are present or that he or she has previously experienced in a concrete manner. And this is the reason for naming this the "concrete operational stage"—the child can think logically as long as he has something in front of him to which he can concretely relate. This has significant implications for the child in the teaching-learning process, which we shall see when we talk about those implications at the end of this chapter.

The formal operational stage (eleven to fifteen years). The abstract quality of thought is the key feature of this particular stage. Young people are able to think about and consider events that are not immediately present, or even that they have never experienced directly. They can formulate hypotheses, they can problem-solve, they can reverse logic, and they can "imagineer."

All children do not pass through the stages of development at the same speed. Children usually do not acquire all the characteristics of a new stage all at once, but rather one at a time over a period of time.

When the child has to change new information to fit his existing intellectual structure, Piaget calls this *assimilation*. When the child changes his intellectual structure in order to fit the new information, he terms that *accommodation*. As a child deals with the objects and influences of his environment, he constructs a *schema,* which is a way of looking at the world that makes sense to him. It is really, says Piaget, a structurized system of assimilations and accommodations—a behavior pattern.[15]

According to Piaget, human beings inherit two basic tendencies: *organization* (the tendency to systematize and combine processes into coherent systems) and *adaptation* (the tendency to adjust to the environment). Piaget believes that intellectual processes transform experiences into a form that a child can use in dealing with new situations, and that those intellectual processes seek a balance through the process of *equilibration.* Piaget believes that equilibration is self-regulation that children use to help make sense out of their world and that it also serves to bring stability to their ideas of the world.

Children will not move from one stage of development into the next until they are biologically capable of doing so. Yet Piaget recognizes that biological readiness by itself does not guarantee that a child will begin to think in a more sophisticated manner. Piaget emphasizes that cognitive growth is an active process, and that the child does act upon and does seek to adapt to the environment. Therefore, if opportunities for learning are restricted, by which Piaget means if there are not very many situations in which the child has an opportunity to interact with objects or people in the environment, the child's cognitive abilities will not develop as they should. At the same time, Piaget believes strongly that just providing children with stimulating learning experiences will not hasten their cognitive development. For Piaget, learning is under the control of development, rather than development being under the control of learning. There is little doubt that Piaget, after a lifetime of study and writing, has had a major effect on how we think about children.[16]

Jerome Bruner and representation. Jerome Bruner also formulated a stage theory of cognitive development that parallels Piaget's in many ways but is different enough that it requires some mention here. Bruner had a strong commitment both to the discovery of how children acquire and use information and also to the application of that knowledge in ways that would improve the educational process.[17] In 1964 Bruner published an article in which he proposed that we can understand how children think through a process he called *representation.*[18]

---

15. Jean Piaget, *The Origin of Intelligence in Children* (New York: International U., 1952). Also Jean Piaget, *Science of Education and Psychology of the Child* (New York: Grossman, 1970).
16. Piaget, *Origin of Intelligence.* Also Jean Piaget, *The Language and Thought of the Child* (New York: Harcourt, Brace, and World, 1929).
17. Jerome Bruner, *The Process of Education* (Cambridge, Mass.: Harvard U., 1960). Also Jerome Bruner, *The Relevance of Education* (New York: Norton, 1971).
18. Jerome Bruner, "The Course of Cognitive Growth," *American Psychologist* 19 (1964):1-15.

Representation, according to Bruner, refers to the cognitive behaviors that occur when people process and remember information. Those behaviors revolve around coding and storing information in such a manner that they can retrieve it for use at some future time. Bruner suggests that if we did not have that ability to handle information, the complexity of events would simply overwhelm us.

As this theory affects the cognitive development of children, Bruner points out that children use different techniques to represent their environment at different stages in their development. In infancy and early childhood, children use a technique Bruner calls *enactive representation*. Children represent their past experiences through their motor acts.

During the preschool and early elementary years, children use the technique Bruner calls *iconic representation*. Children are able, suggests Bruner, to form visual images of stimuli encountered in their environment, to retain those images, and to recall them in the absence of the real object or event. Although objects exist independent of their actions toward them, nevertheless the perceptual images formed by preschool children are based primarily on physical appearance and are very inflexible.

In the later elementary school years, Bruner says that children begin to use *symbolic representation*. This means that children's thought becomes more abstract and probably more flexible, and it is not tied strictly to concrete images. For Bruner, this results because of the child's increasingly complex use of language. Words may even represent ideas for which there are no concrete referents. Bruner is a *stage* theorist, and he agrees that biological maturation is an important variable in the development of thought, yet he emphasizes that we need to encourage maturity by providing appropriate learning experiences. Bruner would say that readiness is not something to wait for, but something to teach. Bruner appears to place greater emphasis on the role of language in cognitive growth than does Piaget. It is the child's increasing flexibility with language that permits him to solve more complex problems. While Bruner states that the three kinds of representation typically appear in a fixed order, he also stresses that even young children may have all three levels available to them. So there is a bit more flexibility in Bruner's theory in regard to the three levels of representation typically appearing in fixed order than would be the case with Piaget's theory. We will look further at the implications for the teaching-learning process of Bruner's theory when we reach that topic in the chapter.

CRITICAL PERIOD THEORIES: HUNT AND HAVIGHURST

J. McVickers Hunt. Rather than tracing the development of thought throughout childhood, Hunt concentrated on the early childhood period. We have placed Hunt approximately in the center of the continuum because he places emphasis on neural development, and yet he seeks to tie that development to the nature of the child's preschool experiences. Hunt in his hypothesis attempts to integrate what is known about the functioning of the central nervous system with what is known about the development of intellectual skills.[19] He argues that early experience affects neurological development. "If the individual is deprived of important stimulation during early childhood, the central processes within the brain that mediate intelligent behavior will not become firmly established."[20]

Hunt analyzed Piaget's theory extensively and came up with the proposition that we ought to use Piaget's concepts to determine the level of development and then enhance the neurological development of young children by matching the learning experiences with the developmental level.

"In the light of evidence now available, it is not unreasonable to entertain the hypothesis that with the sound scientific educational psychology of early experience, it might become feasible to raise the average level of intelligence as now measured by a substantial degree. In order to be explicit, it is conceivable that this 'substantial degree' might be in the order of thirty points of I.Q."[21]

We label Hunt's theory a "critical period theory" of development because it deals with the idea that if the environment inhibits or prevents appropriate learning during a very limited period of time in the early life of a child, then the resulting faulty learning will be permanent or at least difficult to change. The critical period idea is based on the well-known process of "imprinting" in birds, described by Conrad Lorenz in 1937.

The research of Benjamin Bloom lends considerable support to Hunt's theory.[22] Bloom concluded that for each intellectual or personality characteristic studied there was a period of relatively rapid growth, as well as periods in which little development occurred. He postulated that the environment would have its largest effect on the development of the characteristic during its period of most rapid growth. Bloom came up with some other startling conclusions, one of which was that if a deprived child suffers losses in intellectual development, those losses are quite permanent and very difficult to recover, even if the child is placed in an enriched environment after age four. Conversely, the child who is subjected to an enriched environment in early childhood years is not likely to lose his intellectual advantage, even if the environments to which he is exposed between the ages of four and seventeen are less stimulating. The net result of this and other research appears to be that there are indeed critical periods that occur primarily during early childhood years. The research continues as psychologists and others seek to ferret out the full significance of the critical period theory.

Robert Havighurst. We place Robert Havighurst at approximately the center of our continuum also, because of his proposition that a developmental task is a challenge that arises at a certain time in one's life. For Havighurst, the idea of ages and stages embraces all of life, not just early childhood. The developmental tasks

---

19. J. McVickers Hunt, *Intelligence and Experience* (New York: Ronald, 1961).
20. Lahey and Johnson, p. 45. Used by permission.
21. Hunt, p. 267, Copyright © 1961. Reprinted by permission of John Wiley & Sons, Inc.
22. Benjamin Bloom, *Stability and Change in Human Characteristics* (New York: Wiley and Sons, 1964).

are typically rooted in biological, psychological, and cultural factors. According to Havighurst, failure to accomplish the task that is associated within a level of development will result in the individual's feeling inadequate and will predispose him to failure in later developmental tasks. On the other hand, if one succeeds in developmental tasks at the appropriate time in one's life, this fosters a good self-concept, a strong identity, and realistic expectations—all of which combine to forecast success for that individual in forthcoming tasks.[23] According to Havighurst, through one's life there is one developmental task after another to be accomplished until one finally reaches the task of facing the death of one's spouse and of one's self with acceptance and composure.

An entire book was written by Havighurst outlining the many tasks beginning in infancy and continuing on to maturity.[24] Figure 3.5 lists as an illustration of these tasks the developmental tasks of middle childhood.

In summing up the critical period theorists, the main idea is that, due at least in part to the maturation process, there are certain critical kinds of learning or critical tasks to be done in certain very limited periods in the individual's life. If that learning does not occur, or the tasks are not accomplished within that critical period, then the learning may never occur at all or may be much more difficult, or the individual may be predisposed to failure in later developmental tasks.

Havighurst: Developmental Tasks of Middle Childhood

This example should be regarded as illustrative of tasks Havighurst sets forth at other age stages. These tasks embrace the age stage from about six to twelve years.*

Learning physical skills for games
Building wholesome attitudes toward self
Learning to get along with peers
Learning an appropriate sex role
Learning to read, write and calculate
Developing concepts necessary for everyday living
Developing a scale of values
Achieving personal indepedence
Developing democratic attitudes towards social groups and institutions

*Robert Havighurst, *Developmental Tasks and Education* (New York: David McKay, 1972).

Fig. 3.5

23. Robert Havighurst, *Developmental Tasks and Education* (New York: David McKay, 1972).
24. Ibid.

Insight: Matching Learning and Developmental Levels

The majority of contemporary psychologists fall between the "molding" and "unfolding" ends of the continuum and believe that both learning and the process of development play important roles in intellectual growth. Harvard psychologist Jean Carew and her associates have published observations of young children in natural situations that they feel illustrate this interaction of learning and development. The following excerpts describe two parents informally teaching their young children. In the first example, the parent seems to successfully match the child's developmental level, but the information given by the second parent seems unusual to the young child.

EXCERPT 1: *Good Match with Developmental Level*

"Father is reading to John, age thirty-three months, Ezra Keets' story 'Goggles.' They turn to a picture showing the dog Willy running away with the goggles through a hole in the fence. In the picture the dog's face is half hidden behind the fence. John looks and tells Father: 'Doggie face broken.' Father explains, 'No, it's not broken, it's hiding behind the fence.' John looks puzzled. He asks, 'Hiding?' Father demonstrates. 'See my hand. Now see it hide when I move it behind the book?' John watches intently. Father continues, 'Now, see it come out again. It's not broken. It was hiding.' John imitates Father's actions several times, passing his hand behind the book and watching it reappear."*

EXCERPT 2: *Poor Match with Developmental Level*

"Amy and her mother are putting together a puzzle (on the cover of the box is a picture of the completed puzzle: Raggedy Ann, Teddy Bear, and Doggie having a tea party). Amy tries to fit one of the pieces but is having no success. The piece she holds is a picture of a cookie. Mother tells her, 'See, the cookie is going into Teddy's mouth, not his foot. Look at the picture. That piece doesn't go there.' Mother points to the detail in the picture on the box. Amy looks briefly but immediately resumes her attempt to place the piece incorrectly. Amy announces, 'It doesn't fit. It's too fat.' She takes another piece and tries to place it in the puzzle without referring to the picture, apparently relying on shape correspondence and memory. Mother asks her, 'You don't think the picture helps?' Amy replies, 'No, it's the way it comes out after.'"†

---

*J. V. Carew, I. Chan, and C. Halfar, *Observing Intelligence in Young Children: Eight Case Studies* (Englewood Cliffs, N.J.: Prentice Hall, 1976), pp. 59-60.
†Carew, et al., p. 61.

Fig. 3.6

BEHAVIORISTIC THEORIES: SKINNER AND BANDURA

We have placed Bandura, as a behaviorist, on the molding end of the continuum but to the left of Watson and Skinner, because Bandura does not deny the influence of genetic and biological factors or age on child development as Watson and even Skinner seem to do.

"The number and kinds of responses a child is capable of displaying at any point in his life are determined by his status in the animal kingdom (species characteristics), his biological maturational stage, and his history of interaction with his particular environment from fertilization on."[25]

Because in chapter 5 we discuss in depth the behaviorist approach to learning, we are not going to do so here. Behaviorists have made their greatest contribution, in my judgment and others', in the field of *learning* theory rather than the field of developmental theory. But we do need to note that in contrast to the majority of developmental theorists, behaviorists use a model that affirms behavior is a function of experience. Behaviorists see development as a result of the child's interacting with his or her environment over periods of time, and that interaction causes changes in behavior. The *key* point is that the changes in behavior are not due to any maturational factor nor to the passage of time reflected in age, but rather to the experience or, if you will, the learning of the child from his or her interactions with their environment. Some psychologists place Bandura with Bijou and Baer in the category of "applied behavior analysts."[26] This kind of approach is concerned with application of principles of learning discovered in controlled settings such as laboratories to a wider range of human problems found in broader social settings such as classrooms, prisons, mental hospitals, and the like. "The goal of applied behavior analysis is to develop a comprehensive set of principles based on rigorous research that will not only explain why we behave the way we do, but that will also yield practical and effective techniques for modifying the environment to maximize human development."[27]

Behaviorists cite and emphasize the need to directly encourage or produce development by shaping the child's behavior—that is by gradually rewarding closer and closer approximations of the behavior you want the child to reach eventually. Conversely, behaviorists have been critical of developmental psychology and the unfolding theories of Gesell, Piaget, and Bruner.[28] Behaviorists reject the use of age in combination with concepts as explanations for changes in

---

25. S.W. Bijou and D.M. Baer, *Child Development: A Systematic and Empirical Theory* (New York: Appleton Century Crofts, 1961), p. 15.
26. Lahey and Johnson, *Psychology and Instruction.*
27. Ibid., p. 45.
28. D.M. Baer, "The Control of the Developmental Process: Why Wait?" in Esselroade and H.W. Reese, eds., *Life Span Developmental Psychology* (New York: Academic, 1973). Also S.W. Bijou, "Ages, Pages and the Naturalization of Human Development," *American Psychologist* 23 (1968):419-27.

behavior. Additionally, they would insist that the child learns by the same environmental mechanisms that produce behavior change in the adult organism.[29]

In more recent years, Albert Bandura has produced what has come to be called a "social learning theory" in which "modeling" is a central facet. We will discuss these in detail in chapter 5, but although they would certainly serve to keep him to the left of Watson and Skinner on our continuum, nevertheless Bandura would still be classified as a behaviorist who is seeking explicit ways people learn, and his basic premise still is that behavior is a function of experience rather than of maturation.

What has come to be called "the environmental-behaviorist position" emphasizes learned aspects of behavior, giving little attention to genetic or cognitive explanations. The relationship of the behaviorists' approach to learning and its implications for the teaching-learning process will be explored in chapter 5.

SOCIOBIOLOGY APPROACH: WILSON AND COLLEAGUES

We have placed Edward O. Wilson on the extreme left end of the continuum, for sociobiology argues that the same mechanism—heredity, encoded in genes—operates on both apes and humans, as well as all other animals. Wilson is quoted as saying, "Biology is the key to human nature."[30]

Sociobiologists argue that the universal prevalence of behavioral traits among humans—such as incest taboos, kin groups, law making, and the like can be accounted for only by genetic influence and that, this being the case, the traits must in some way be selected for by evolution.[31]

Although sociobiology is a young science, and being denounced as "sosobiology" and "science with transparent political messages," sociobiology, proponents believe, puts forward an argument that binds human beings and animals together under consistent principles of natural law.[32] This is an approach that makes development of behavior almost exclusively the province of maturational forces, although some adherents claim that genes do not have the last word in the matter. (See Insight, figure 3.7, "Is There a Human Nature?"). The student of human development needs to watch the sociobiology movement carefully, as indeed the other approaches, for evidences of support for its theories. One of the dangers cited in relation to sociobiology is that all too often this kind of theory has been made to serve the ends of racist and other repressive social and political doctrines that essentially assert that some people are genetically inferior.[33]

---

29. D.M. Baer and J.C. Wright, "Developmental Psychology" in M.R. Rozenzweig and L.W. Porter, eds., *Annual Review of Psychology* (Palo Alto, Calif.: Annual Reviews, 1974), p. 1.
30. Fitzgerald and Carr, p. 4.
31. Ibid.
32. Ibid.
33. Ibid.

> ### Insight: Is There a Human Nature?
>
> What can sociobiology tell us about ourselves? When presented with the widely differing attitudes of a Zulu warrior and a Wall Street banker, we may conclude that, in fact, there is no such thing as a "human nature." Sociobiologists, however, believe that the similarities between the two men are profound.
>
> Evidence of a human nature can be found in the long list of behavioral traits common to every culture in recorded history; the list includes incest taboos, male dominance, kin groups, lawmaking, age-grading and many others. Sociobiologists conclude that the universal prevalence of these traits can only be accounted for by genetic influence, and that, this being the case, the traits must in some way be selected for by evolution.
>
> Genes do not have the last word in the matter: human beings are not windup toys made to march in an unalterable cadence. Humans are a combination of genetic and cultural influences—genes prescribe only the capacity to develop certain traits, but culture molds the individual personality and can mitigate the gene's influence. There seems to be no gene favoring the wearing of top hats, for instance, but every human society has developed certain characteristic body adornments.
>
> From Richard Nalley, ed., "Sociobiology: A New View of Human Nature," *Science Digest*, July 1982. Used by permission.

Fig. 3.7

PSYCHOSOCIAL THEORIES: ERIKSON AND MASLOW

I must begin with an apologetic or, if you will, explanation for bringing together on a psychosocial continuum Abraham Maslow and Erik H. Erikson. My reasons are twofold. First, there is a legitimate thread that binds them together, albeit on the opposite ends of a psychosocial continuum; second, by presenting these two major contributors to developmental theory in such a manner, the intention is to clarify the stance of both theorists, especially for the student who is just being introduced to the field. We will look now at the psychosocial continuum as shown in figure 3.8.

First of all, as we are viewing the concept *psychosocial* for our purposes, it represents the individual's seeking to find an orientation for himself or herself in relation to the society in which the individual lives. Out of the conflict or confrontation of the individual with the social forces, there emerges a sense of self.

PSYCHOSOCIAL CONTINUUM-DEVELOPMENT OF SELF IN RELATION TO SOCIAL CONTEXT

MASLOW   ERIKSON

LESS ←———— DEPENDENCE ON SOCIAL CONTEXT ————→ MORE

Fig. 3.8

This is the thread we propose binds Maslow and Erikson together on this psychosocial continuum. Call it the development of self out of conflict with social forces, or call it the "psychosocial development of the ego" with which Erikson's observations and theoretical constructions are primarily concerned, there does appear to be a common thread running along this continuum.

By showing these two major contributors to developmental theory at opposite ends of the continuum, we believe that each of their positions can be made clear, especially to the relatively new student in the field. Let us look first at Erikson's position. He posited that (1) side by side with the stages of psychosexual development described by Freud were psychosocial stages of ego development, in which the individual established new basic orientations to himself and his social world; (2) personality development continued throughout the whole life cycle; and (3) each stage had a positive as well as a negative component.[34]

Erikson identifies eight stages in the human life cycle, in each of which a new dimension of social interaction becomes possible—that is, a new dimension in a person's interaction with *himself* and with his *social environment*.[35]

Compare this with Maslow's self-actualization theme—the actualizing of one's potential, and it appears that although the goals may be stated in different ways, nevertheless they are very similar: the development of a healthy and healed self as a result of a confrontation with the social environment and the individual's interaction with himself.

---

34. David Elkind, "Erik Erikson's Eight Ages of Man," *New York Times Magazine*, 5 April 1970.
35. Ibid.

Gallery of Greats

Erik H. Erikson
Our identity, or self-concept, is crucial to the view we take of other people, work, and life satisfaction. (Courtesy of the Harvard University News Office)

"Identity crisis" is a phrase used by many people who do not realize Erik Erikson is the man who pointed this out as a problem more than two decades ago. Erikson is concerned with the development of the ego, which holds the individual's attitudes and concepts about himself or herself and the world. Born in Frankfurt, Germany, of Danish parents in 1902, Erikson has been able to "Americanize" psychoanalytic theory without rejecting or ignoring Freud's singular contribution.

White hair, mustache, resonant accent, gentle manner—these are some of the descriptions of this theorist, whom we are told is rather shy, uncomfortable in the public's eye, and yet warm and outgoing with friends. He began as an artist doing portraits of children in Vienna, and he worked also as a tutor with a family whose members were friendly with Freud's. Erikson met Freud on informal occasions when the two families went on social outings together. He became interested in psychoanalysis and completed his training with Anna Freud and August Aichhorn. At the same time, he was trained and certified as a Montessori teacher, and thus a combination of his interests in psychoanalysis and education was strongly evidenced. When Erikson treated children, he insisted on visiting their homes and having dinner with their families.

Through much of his life, having held several appointments simultaneously and traveling extensively, Erikson seems to follow his own inner schedule rather than being driven by any outside forces.

Self-actualization is a term introduced by Maslow to identify an unusual degree of mental health.[36] "It refers to bringing into actuality an unusually large amount of one's vast and unique potential for becoming human."[37]

A textbook is not a place to seek to establish a new relationship between two theorists. Obviously, this is more appropriately done in a journal article or a book dedicated to that particular purpose. We do not wish to push this relationship too far, but again affirm that for both of these theorists, although one by the psychoanalytic route (Erikson) building on Freud's foundations but Americanizing them, and the other via what has come to be known as "third force" psychology, at least broadly the goals would appear to be similar; the development of a fully functioning human being.

Maslow will be discussed in more detail in chapter 7 where we analyze the humanistic approach to learning. Erikson's emphasis upon the problems unique to adolescents and adults in our society has helped to balance the previously one-sided emphasis on childhood as the exclusive domain for considering personality development. As Anglin points out,

> so few of the many people today who talk about the "identity crisis" know anything of the man who pointed out its pervasiveness as a problem in contemporary society two decades ago. Erikson has, however, contributed more to social science than his delineation of identity problems in modern man. His descriptions of the stages of the life cycle, for example, have advanced psychoanalytic theory to the point where it can now describe the development of the healthy personality on its own terms and not

---

36. Abraham Maslow, "Further Notes on the Psychology of Being," *Journal of Humanistic Psychology* 4 (1964):45-58. Also Abraham Maslow, *Motivation and Personality* (New York: Harper and Row, 1970).
37. Robert D. Strom and H.W. Bernard, *Educational Psychology* (Monterey, Calif.: Brooks Cole, 1982), p. 27.

Insight: Erikson's Eight Stages of Psychosocial Development

Stage	Developmental Issue
1. Infancy	trust versus mistrust
2. Early childhood	autonomy versus shame and doubt
3. Play age	initiate versus guilt
4. School age	industriousness versus inferiority
5. Adolescence	identity versus role diffusion
6. Young adulthood	intimacy versus isolation
7. Adulthood	generativity versus self-absorption
8. Senescence (mature age)	integrity versus disgust or despair

Fig. 3.9

---

merely the opposite of the sick one.... Erikson emphasizes the inherent strengths of the human personality by showing how individuals can use their neurotic systems and conflicts for creative and constructive social purposes while healing themselves in the process.[38]

The student is urged to look carefully at Insight, figure 3.9, for a summary of Erikson's eight stages of psychosocial development. And there are further reading suggestions for all of these theorists under Want to Know More? at the end of this chapter.

IMPLICATIONS FOR THE TEACHING-LEARNING PROCESS

In chapters 5, 6, 7, and 8 we will deal in detail with the behavioristic, the humanistic, the cognitive, and the Christian approaches to learning. For the student just being introduced to the field of developmental theory, the basic question is whether behavior is a function of experience or a function of the maturational process. If you find yourself leaning to the maturational end of the continuum, then the implications for the teaching-learning process are in the direction of providing many situations in which the child may cognitively act upon objects and relate to people in his or her environment and construct their schemata from that experience, as the maturational unfolding permits them to develop stage by stage. In this case, you will want to concentrate on making opportunities available that will be appropriate in keeping with the child's particular stage of development and the many processes within that stage.

On the other hand, if you lean toward the behavioristic end of the continuum, then the implications for the teaching-learning process go in the

---

38. Elkind.

Concepts and Theories 99

direction of behavioral objectives, providing the proper stimuli in order to get the appropriate responses from your students, and what will probably be a very structured teaching-learning process.

The critical period approach which for Hunt focused on early childhood but for Havighurst went throughout the life cycle, is one that lends itself to the teaching-learning process for lifelong learning. If you are teaching the preschool child, you would want to concentrate on researching carefully the evidence in relation to the critical periods and tie in Havighurst's developmental tasks. If you are teaching elementary age children, middle school, senior high, or adults, both Erikson's eight-stage psychosocial theory and Havighurst's developmental tasks would be appropriate to review carefully.

Our primary concern for you at this point is that you have found a means by which to manipulate the concepts and theories of human development; that you

Stage vs. Continuous Development

Stage development: sequential, qualitative (quantitative within stages)

STAGE 1, STAGE 2, STAGE 3, STAGE 4

PIAGET, BRUNER

Continuous development: gradual, smooth, quantitative

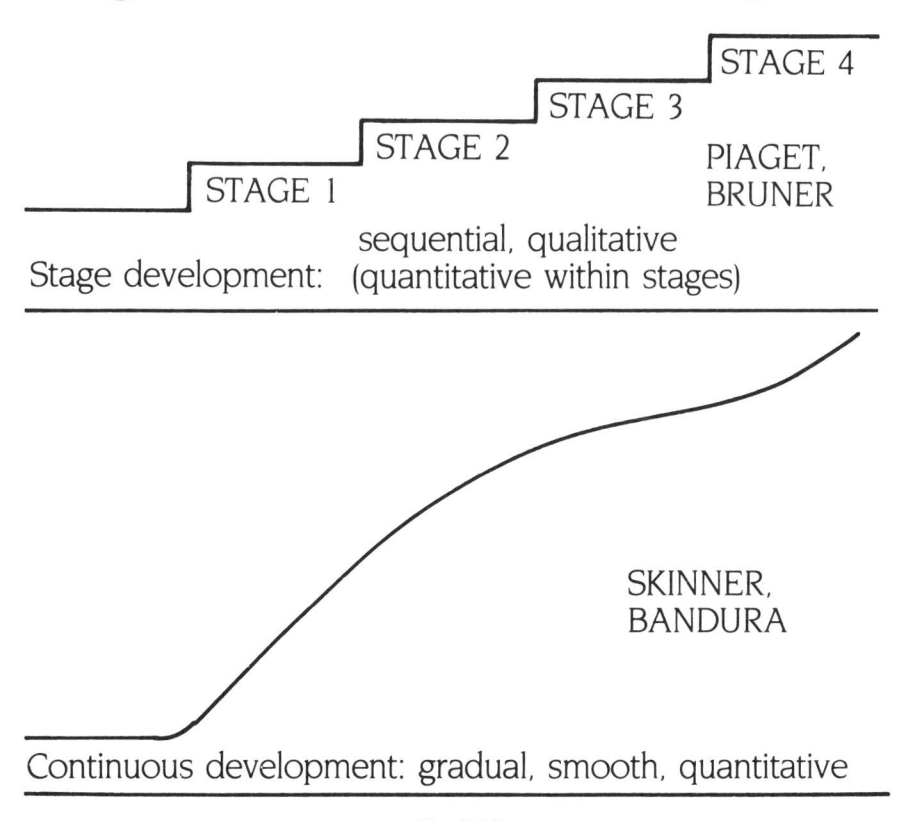

SKINNER, BANDURA

Fig. 3.10

have been able, at least tentatively as you have thought through the assumptions and the theories, to place yourself somewhere on one of the two continua (and they are not mutually exclusive but rather different in kind); and that you consciously and deliberately reflect upon these developmental theories in relation to their implications for you in the midst of the teaching-learning process, for they will enhance greatly your repertoire of resources, enabling you to bring a richer philosophic perspective to your performance as a clinician in the classroom.

Hindsight

We hope that you had your curiosity piqued as you studied this chapter—that you became curious enough to want to read much further about the various aspects of human development. Although there are many difficulties in defining development, we need to continue to construct theories based on the cumulative knowledge of the field, observations, and the experiences. We reviewed five assumptions regarding the nature of human development: inborn differences among people, malleability of human behavior, active versus passive role of humans, innate goodness or evil of humans, relationship of child to adult behavior. Each of these represents an issue about which you will need to make your decision.

We built our discussion of developmental theories around two continua: the

Developmental Pathways

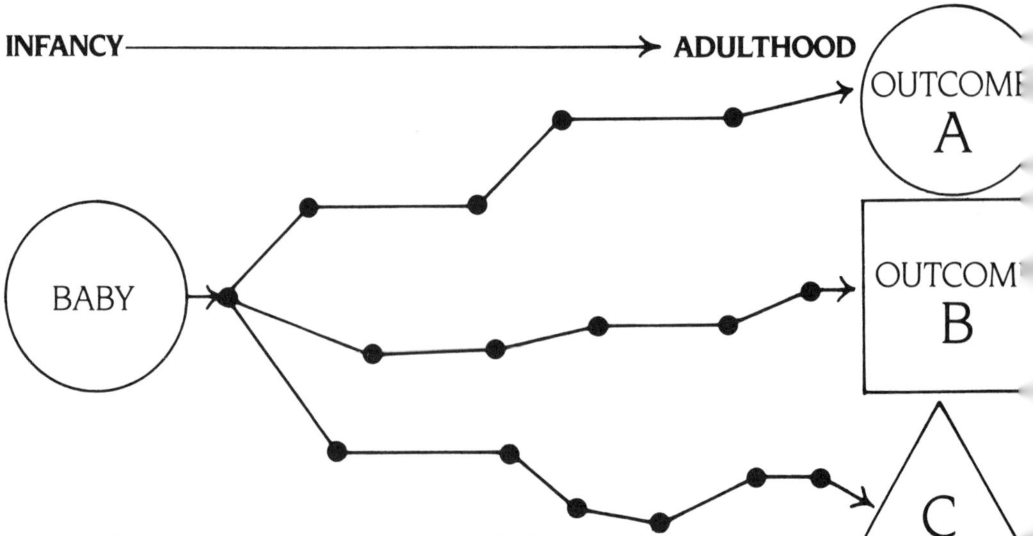

INFANCY ⟶ ADULTHOOD

BABY → OUTCOME A / OUTCOME B / OUTCOME C

The multiple influences upon and from within an individual as he or she develops are represented by the dark dots. Maturational and environmental factors interact to influence outcomes.

Fig. 3.11

Concepts and Theories

first an unfolding-molding continuum and the second a psychosocial continuum. We looked at early developmental theories as represented by Gesell and Watson. We looked at representatives of current developmental theories; stage theories as represented by Piaget and Bruner; critical period theories as represented by Hunt and Havighurst; behavioristic theories as represented by Skinner and Bandura; psychosocial theories as represented by Erikson and Maslow; and the relatively young science of sociobiology as represented by Edward O. Wilson and his colleagues. We briefly indicated some implications of developmental theories for the teaching-learning process. Those implications will be spelled out in rather detailed fashion in chapters 5 to 8 as we discuss four major approaches to learning.

We emphasize the need for the competent teacher to keep abreast of the up-to-date research in the field of human development and to feed that kind of information into his or her repertoire of resources.

CHALKBOARD CHALLENGES

1. It is exceedingly important for the competent teacher to understand at least the basics of developmental theory in order to be able to apply it in an intelligent manner to the teaching-learning process. Therefore, we suggest that perhaps your first order of business in relation to this chapter should be to write in your teacher's notebook a brief summary of each of the theories described in this chapter. We have found that students frequently do not wish to take the time to complete a task of this sort. But we urge you to consider how important this kind of information becomes in the development of your philosophic perspective, which in turn leads to significant improvement in your clinical performance in the teaching-learning process. We suggest that you label a section of your teacher's notebook "Developmental Theories," then simply write the name of each theorist and the corresponding kind of theory (stage, behavioristic, psychosocial, critical period, sociobiology); then, under each of those headings carefully summarize the major points appropriate to that theorist and that theory. However you do it, the major emphasis is on understanding the theory well enough so that you can effectively use it in your teaching.
2. Take a careful look at both the unfolding-molding continuum and the psychosocial continuum presented in this chapter, and remember that they are not necessarily mutually exclusive. They are simply different in *kind*. As you summarize each of the theories, and therefore are thinking carefully about them, deliberately reflect upon where *you* belong on either or both of the continua. Remember that your "perch" is very likely to be a temporary one; nevertheless, try to get positioned somewhere on the continuum, understanding that as you read, reflect, and experience further you are apt to move one way or the other. The major point here is that once you get yourself positioned on the continuum, you will much more probably think carefully about that position and will be likely to have good reasons for moving one way or the other. We have

found through student feedback in our classes that this exercise gives students a sense of direction and provides help for their learning and their practice.
3. Once you have positioned yourself, even though temporarily, on one of the continua, then ask yourself, "What are the implications of my position for my teaching?" To specifically implement this, we suggest that in your notebook you make two columns: the first headed with the word *If* and the second column headed with the word *Then*. Under the "If" column, list your position on either or both of the continua, and in the "Then" column, write some of the specific implications of that position for the level of the teaching-learning process in which you plan to become involved.

Incidently, it is helpful to write the implications for teaching for several school levels just to see how your position, developmentally speaking, flows through to the various age groups. We are going to give you two examples here of how this might work. Let us suppose that in the "If" column you chose Erikson's position on the psychosocial continuum. In the "Then" column you might write something like the following for *preschool and kindergarten level,* "Am I providing plenty of opportunities for younger pupils to develop a sense of autonomy? What else can I do to foster independence?" For the *elementary grade level* to implement Erikson's theory, you might write a question such as, "Am I setting up learning experiences so that my pupils can be successful in the completion of their assignments and therefore acquire feelings of real accomplishment?" At the *secondary grade level,* you might write for Erikson's theory, "Since it is important to help the young people develop a sense of identity, perhaps I need to take more personal interest in students so that they can have a sense of being recognized as individuals. Perhaps I need to say hello to more students personally and learn to talk with each student in my classes, if at all possible, even if the conversation is a brief one." Sometimes even the briefest word from the teacher helps the student to feel like he or she is somebody worthwhile.

Let's go on to another example of the "If"-"Then" columns in your notebook. Let us suppose that on the unfolding-molding continuum you chose Piaget's spot. Then for the preschool through primary grades you might ask questions like the following over in the "Then" column: "How can I arrange learning experiences so that my students only have to deal with one thing at a time, and so they can manipulate lots of objects?" Or at the secondary level, "How can I better teach problem solving skills for this formal operational level?" Use these examples to help get you started.

WANT TO KNOW MORE?

PIAGET

From the many books Piaget has written, we suggest two to introduce you to his thought. Jean Piaget and Barbara Inhelder, *The Psychology of the Child,* trans.

Concepts and Theories

Helen Weaver (New York: Basic Books, 1969). Jean Piaget, *Science of Education and the Psychology of the Child.* (New York: Grossman, 1970).

ERIKSON AND HUNT

To introduce you to Erik Erikson, we suggest *Childhood and Society,* (New York: Norton, 1963).

To introduce you to J. McVickers Hunt, we suggest the book entitled *Intelligence and Experience,* (New York: Ronald, 1961).

BRUNER

If you want to know more about Jerome Bruner, we recommend either or both of the following: J. S. Bruner, *The Process of Education* (Cambridge, Mass.: Harvard U., 1960). J. S. Bruner, *The Relevance of Education* (New York: Norton, 1971).

HAVIGHURST

For an introduction to Robert Havighurst and his theory of developmental tasks, read: *Developmental Tasks and Education* (New York: David McKay, 1972).

Some of the implications of Havighurst's work concerning youth and cultural pluralism, youth and the meaning of work, and youth in social institutions may be found in Robert Havighurst and P. H. Dryer, eds., *National Society for the Study of Education 74th Yearbook,* Part I, *Youth* (Chicago: U. of Chicago, 1975).

MASLOW

For a brief introduction to Abraham Maslow, take a look at "Further Notes on the Psychology of Being," *Journal of Humanistic Psychology* 4 (1964): 45-58. (Further suggestions will be given for reading Maslow's writings at the end of chapter 7, which discusses the humanistic approach to learning.)

SKINNER

A brief introduction to B. F. Skinner might be the book *About Behaviorism.* (New York: Knopf, 1974). (A number of further suggestions will be given for reading in depth about Skinner's work at the close of chapter 5, which discusses the behavioristic approach to behaviorism.)

BANDURA

If you wish to read further about Albert Bandura's social learning theory, we suggest his book *Social Learning Theory,* (Englewood Cliffs, N.J.: Prentice Hall, 1977).

SOCIOBIOLOGY

A helpful introduction to the young science of sociobiology would be the article entitled H. E. Fitzgerald and T. H. Carr, eds., "Sociobiology: A New View of Human Nature" in *Annual Editions Human Development 83-84* (Guilford, Conn.: Dushkin, 1983), pp. 4-9.

FREUD

Calvin S. Hall, *A Primer of Freudian Psychology* (New York: New American Library, 1979), contains an overview of Freud's writings for those who are starting to examine his ideas.

CHILD DEVELOPMENT

If you are interested in tracing the development of the concept of childhood, the following two books are recommended: Phillippe Aires, *Centuries of Childhood* (New York: Vintage, 1962).

This book covers the study of the concept of childhood from the middle ages to the present view and is traced through paintings, diaries, school curricula, and the history of games.

William Kessen, *The Child* (New York: Wiley, 1965). This book contains selected readings from two hundred years of Western writing about children.

4

Characteristics and Sequences

ANN MCFARLAND

CONTENTS

	PAGE
Key Terms	105
That's Debatable!	106
Foresight	106
Characteristics	108
Sequences and Age-Level Characteristics	115
Controversial Issues: Readiness and Acceleration	121
Age-Level Characteristics and Their Significance	124
Hindsight	125
Chalkboard Challenges	126
Want to Know More?	126

KEY TERMS

Physical development
    The simple changes in an individual's size and weight, and the gradual quantitative changes that can be charted for other physical and anatomical features

ANN MCFARLAND, Ph.D., Florida State University, is associate professor of education at Liberty Baptist College, Lynchburg, Virginia.

Cognitive development
All events and processes of the human mind[1]
Cognition
The process by which one comes to know. It involves the mental processes of imagination, memory, perception, and reason. Also concerned with how a person takes random stimuli from the environment and then organizes and processes this material into meaningful information[2]
Peers
Those of equal status with whom we interact on a regular basis
Social
Refers to the child's interaction with other individuals in his environment
Socialization
The process through which the child acquires the attitudes and behaviors considered important and appropriate by the society in which the child lives
Emotional development
Children's feeling and their affective responses
Personality
A person's unique pattern of traits[3]

THAT'S DEBATABLE!

What could an acceptance of acceleration by the public mean to children? Some school systems have already adopted programs for four-year-olds. Would we eventually require schools to provide formal education for children two years and younger? We can not overemphasize the importance of the informal education provided by the home, nor fail to stress that parents are responsible for their children. Is there a possibility that the federal government would sponsor day-care programs for all children? Would home schooling eventually be required to use books and curriculum recommended by the government instead of materials of their choice? The question then becomes, *Who is raising our children?*

FORESIGHT

Are children becoming robots? Are we limiting their ability to think and make decisions to pushing a button? Have we programmed them to make the same decisions as everyone else?

Each child is a unique individual and should be guided to develop socially, emotionally, physically, mentally, and spiritually at his own rate. Emphasis should

---

1. Steven R. Yussen and John W. Santrock, *Child Development* (Albany, NY.: Delmar, 1983), p. 159.
2. Janie D. Osborn and D. Keith Osborn, *Cognition in Early Childhood* (Athens, Ga.: Education Associates, 1983), p. 3. Used by permission.
3. Yussen and Santrock, pp. 355-56.

be on the total development of the child under God.

The responsibility of providing the basic necessities (food, clothing, and shelter) as well as an environment conducive to producing an individual who is an asset to his country, rightly belongs to the parents. But as America has become more mobile and society more complex, many parents have become dependent upon the government, school, and church to support them in or take over their child-rearing tasks.

A child living in today's culture is aware of life on a universal scale. His world consists of more than home, community, and country. He has journeyed into many nations and space by the simple turning of a knob. Many children have had numerous opportunities to travel by car, bus, train, or airplane. Today's child is living in the midst of a culture boom which brings art, music, education, travel, and drama to him in large quantities. Not only is he exposed to viewpoints of people other than his parents through the media, but many children are also placed in child care centers at an early age. The child's development also reflects the behavior of those who bring up and instruct him.

The variety of these experiences gives the child a rich understanding and appreciation of life, a background that affects his basic stores of ideas, skills, and attitudes. He now has a mind full of concepts unknown to him previously, and those concepts need to be developed through many different activities. A child who grows up unable to appreciate and work with people whose appearance, language, or customs are different from his own will be severely handicapped in the world of tomorrow.

As we move into an age of technology and computers, parents and teachers need to focus on the concern that the child shall not become a victim either of overexpectancy or underexpectancy. We stifle his initiative and crush his will if we overestimate him. If we underestimate him, we bore him. All children must be prepared to think clearly for themselves—evaluating new knowledge—not only in science and technology but also in human relationships. Each child has his own timetable of development in all areas. Therefore, we need to know the child's level of development in order to give him the guidance necessary to develop his God-given potential and cope with a changing world in a manner pleasing to the Lord.

As we gain further insight into the characteristics and sequences of development, it is important to remember that all children pass through the same sequence of growth, but not in the same way. Few children grow evenly in all aspects of growth. Growth is an inner force and must be observed on a long-term basis because growth is slow. Parents and teachers need to observe a child's growth carefully; for if the child seems to differ too much from other children his age, we need to find out *why*.[4]

---

4. Ann McFarland, *Stepping Stones: Early Childhood Education Curriculum Guide* (West Liberty, Va.: Region Six Educational Services, 1973), pp. 1-2.

Characteristics

PHYSICAL DEVELOPMENT

To a large extent the factors influencing growth are genetically determined.[5] But certain basic traits and growth sequences are typical of all humans. The general course of development is similar for both sexes, although girls tend to mature more rapidly and earlier than boys. Gesell developed a progressive growth pattern and divided the *Cycle of Development* into seven stages: (1) Stage of the Embryo (0-8 weeks), (2) Stage of the Fetus (8-40 weeks), (3) Infancy (from birth to 2 years), (4) The Pre-school Age (2-5 years), (5) Childhood (5-12 years), (6) Adolescence (12-20 years), (7) Adult Maturity.[6]

Patterns of growth are important; they can be used as clinical instruments to determine whether a child is healthy and developing normally. In addition, we can use growth patterns to make predictions concerning normal transitions from period to period. By observing a child's physical development, we can check his weight in proportion to body type; observe his nutritional state as shown by his weight gains, skin, and muscle tone; check his teeth and find out the stage of his skeletal development and test his coordination. These observations help us know how a child is growing in relation to the average for his age.

Used correctly, this knowledge can assist us in planning a program that will correct the deficiencies and further develop his strengths. A child who lags in physical development may be unable to keep up in activities that demand use of the fine coordination skills of small muscles.[7]

In addition, we must not overlook the importance of experiences in development. Experiences constitute a main ingredient in development. Experiences include: the child's biological environment (nutrition, medical care, drugs, etc.), and the child's social environment (family, peers, media, etc.).[8]

Knowledge of the child's experiences, as well as his physical development, is essential for optimum growth. The importance of physical development to learning cannot be emphasized enough; however, Linskie gives us another important clue in maintaining good physical health. "A certain amount of personal freedom is another requisite for physical well being."[9]

COGNITIVE DEVELOPMENT

Historically children have been viewed as miniature adults. This belief led to the idea that the only difference in the intellect of the young child and the adult was

---

5. Robert M. Gagné, *The Conditions of Learning*, 2d ed. (New York: Holt, Rinehart, and Winston, 1970), p. 2.
6. Arnold Gesell and Frances L. Ilg, *The Child from Five to Ten* (New York: Harper, 1946), p. 10.
7. Gladys G. Jenkins, Helen S. Shacter, and William W. Bauer, *These Are Your Children*, 3d ed. (Glenview, Ill.: Scott Foresman, 1966), pp. 12-16.
8. Yussen and Santrock, p. 10.
9. Rosella Linskie, *The Learning Process: Theory and Practice* (New York: Van Nostrand, 1977), p. 5.

a matter of quantity of learning. Adults possessed more information and were capable of complex thought because they had lived longer and had more experiences.[10]

Jean Piaget, the major cognitive development theorist, has essentially redefined the whole field of cognitive development for us. He was concerned with the broad nature of thinking and was interested in how the child learns, what he can learn, and how he uses what he has learned. The Christian is vitally concerned with bringing these processes within the biblical framework.

Mental growth and capacities can be observed through standardized psychological tests given and interpreted by a trained professional. In the past, academic exercises were pushed both at home and school in order to produce higher scores on standardized tests and IQ tests.[11] However, the work of neuropsychologists in recent years has given credence to the idea that intuitive, creative, synthesizing thought is as valuable as analytical thought.

Some educators now regard the affective component to learning as complementary to the cognitive; believing that feelings, values, and attitudes are important in cognitive learning. The true goal of cognitive development should be to give each child ample opportunity and encouragement to achieve levels reasonable for his age and commensurate with his mind.

This goal can best be met by providing a balanced program that keeps children in contact with their feelings, encourages original ideas and problem solving, fosters the use of language, and provides practice in certain reasoning and thinking skills. Cognitive development must be approached as an essential part of development dependent upon the total development and not as an isolate. God is concerned with the total person.

SOCIAL-EMOTIONAL DEVELOPMENT

In order for a child to be emotionally stable, certain basic emotional needs must be met. He must have the security of knowing he is loved; that he belongs and that he is wanted. In addition, he must have the self-confidence that comes from being able to meet situations adequately. As he tries to cope with the normal problems of growing up, success must at least balance with failure in order for him to feel adequate. Success/failure must be related to God's purposes.

Emotionally healthy children have access to the full range of their feelings and are beginning to learn to deal with these feelings in appropriate ways. They are not excessively withdrawn or aggressive.[12] A child's emotional development is reflected in his behavior. If he appears to be relaxed, happy, free from undue strain and tension, and able to meet situations appropriate to his age, his emotional needs

---

10. Osborn and Osborn, p. 4. Reprinted by permission.
11. Jenkins, et al., p. 15.
12. Joanne Hendrick, *The Whole Child: Early Education for the Eighties,* 3d ed. (St. Louis: Times Mirror/Mosby, 1984), pp. 101-17.

are probably being cared for adequately. Behavior in excess of the normal reaction is the child's way of showing that his growth is being blocked or restricted.[13] (See Insight, fig. 4.1 for Erikson's eight stages of psychosocial development.)[14]

Although environmental factors influence emotional growth, a child's behavior, motivation, and ability to live up to his potential are affected by his self-concept. His attitude toward the demands placed upon him is largely determined by his self-concept.[15] In addition, his self-concept is greatly influenced by the attitudes shown toward him by those with whom he is most intimately connected. An accurate self-concept is significant. The first step in developing self-concept is the recognition that one is a unique individual created by God. It has been suggested each of us has six selves: (1) people we really are, (2) people we think we are, (3) people others think we are, (4) people we think others think we are, (5) people we really want to become, (6) people we think others want us to become.[16] Although self-concepts may or may not be close approximations of reality, they are always in the process of change.

Social development closely parallels emotional growth. It involves the child's feelings and relationships with people among whom he is growing up. The child's first social relationships take place in the home.

It is during the preschool years that a child begins to develop relationships with others as he moves out into the neighborhood. As children grow older the amount of social play increases between them and they make more friends. The group emphasizes to its members that they favor positive friendly behavior and dislike aggression and selfishness.[17]

School-age children spend as much time as possible with their peers. It is from his peers that a child learns first-hand about social structures, in groups and out of groups. Peer group interaction is the context within which the child most easily masters his aggressive impulses. Thus peer interaction serves to support the child's social development. If positive relationships with peers are not developed during childhood, the possibilities of later maladjustment are greater.[18]

Differences in personality, environment, ability, and training affect the ease with which children develop socially. Group acceptance is not the only criterion of social adjustment. Before attempting judgment, we need to know more about the child and his total situation.

As teachers and parents, we can help children form good relationships by reducing frustrations for them when possible, helping them express their feelings in acceptable ways to relevant people, identifying and describing their feelings for

13. Jenkins, et al., p. 17-20.
14. L. Joseph Stone and Joseph Church, *Childhood & Adolescence*, 4th ed. (New York: Random, 1979), p. 39.
15. Jenkins, et al., p. 20.
16. F. Philip Rice, *The Adolescent: Development, Relationships, and Culture*, 3d ed. (Boston: Allyn and Bacon, 1981).
17. Hendrick, pp. 101-17.
18. Charlesworth, pp. 286-87.

them, recognizing the signs of stress, and handling emotional problems on a long- and short-term basis when necessary.

A child whose social development is healthy will be able to relate to other people. It is more significant that he relate to his family and some close friends his own age, than to other large or small groups.[19] As with all other aspects of development, the Christian parent/teacher views social developments within the

---

19. Hendrick, pp. 209-15.

biblical framework, the child growing up in the nurture and admonition of the Lord.

MORAL DEVELOPMENT

People have very definite opinions about acceptable and unacceptable behavior, ethical and unethical conduct, and the manner in which acceptable and ethical behaviors are to be nurtured in children. It is impossible to consider moral development as a separate entity, as it is so intricately related to a child's social-emotional and intellectual status.[20]

It is the social learning theory that has been the primary influence regarding studies of moral behavior. Piaget and Kohlberg stress that moral thinking is primarily determined by the maturation of cognitive capacities and that the social environment provides the raw material on which cognitive processes actively operate. Peer interaction plays a major role in the social stimulation that challenges the child to change his moral orientation. The child is provided with the opportunity to take the role of the other person and to generate rules democratically due to the mutual give and take of peer interaction. This theory is supported by other psychologists' studies of moral reasoning. Christian peers are important.

Most of the research in this area focuses on the development of moral reasoning and the making of moral judgments. According to Piaget and Kohlberg, as an individual becomes less egocentric, his moral judgments become more mature.[21] Thus, most children before age four are probably too egocentric to comprehend rules that others have made. In order for children to feel guilt and behave morally, identification with some adult authority and acceptance of that authority's standards are probably necessary. Fear and anxiety of losing favor with adult authority is responsible for moral development in early childhood. Moral sanctions emanate from within, once the child has developed a sense of guilt.[22]

Initially, Piaget studied the morality of children by observing them at games of marbles and questioning them about the rules they followed. He also used pairs of stories about young children who had done something wrong to find out about a child's moral reasoning. These responses helped Piaget develop a two-stage theory of moral development in childhood. (See Insight, fig. 4.2 for this theory.)[23]

Using procedures based on those of Piaget, Kohlberg presented children with moral dilemmas and found three major levels of moral reasoning (with two subtopics at each level). His research spanned the years from seven to sixteen and

20. Benjamin B. Lahey and Martha S. Johnson, *Psychology and Instruction* (Glenview, Ill.: Scott Foresman, 1978), pp. 60-62.
21. Charlesworth, pp. 291-92.
22. Allison Clarke-Stewart and Joanne B. Koch, *Children: Development Through Adolescence* (New York: Wiley & Sons, 1983), pp. 326-29.
23. Charlesworth, p. 293.

Insight: Piaget's Two-Stage Theory of Moral Development

Age	Stage	Characteristics
4-7	Moral Realism (Preoperational)	Centers on consequencces of act. Rules are unchangeable. Punishment for rule breaking is automatic.
7-10	Transition (Concrete Operational)	Gradually changes to second stage thinking.
11+	Moral Autonomy, Realism, Reciprocity (Formal Operations)	Considers intentions. Realizes rules are arbitrary conventions. Punishment is socially determined, not inevitable.

Fig. 4.2

linked the youngsters' cognitive abilities[24] (Insight, fig. 4.3).[25]

In addition to nourishing the development of morals, we must also nourish a child's capacity to grow spiritually. But that nourishment must meet the needs and capacities of the child at a given age.

At age four the child is becoming assertive, has an active mind, and usually asks many questions. Some of those relate to God and creation of the universe. Gesell's research gives evidence that the "intangible creative force called God is often grasped rather well by the mind of a four-year-old."[26]

The four-year-old is very interested in death but does not understand death's finality. However, the five-year-old brings God within the scope of the everyday world. Age six is usually described as the peak period of a child's interest in a creative power to which he can relate. Prayers are becoming important, and the child thinks of God in terms of creation.

The way a child thinks about God is greatly influenced by his experience with his own father or others in a parental role. The disciplinary action taken after a child has misbehaved will influence his concepts of sin and forgiveness.

Children show a similar pattern of development in their religious concepts regardless of their background. "The growth in understanding right and wrong is a slow process, dependent upon a growing ability to think, to reason, to make comparisons, to foresee consequences."[27] However, a child of three is usually aware that some behavior is considered good and some behavior is considered bad by adults.

---

24. Stone and Church, pp. 448-49.
25. Joseph T. Lawton, *Introduction to Child Development* (Dubuque, Iowa: Wm. C. Brown, 1982), p. 351.
26. Gesell and Ilg, *Child Development*, p. 86. Quoted in Sarah H. Leeper, Ralph L. Witherspoon, and Barbara Day, *Good Schools for Young Children*, 5th ed. (New York: Macmillan, 1984), p. 326.
27. Ibid.

"Moral education is the intervention by the school, direct and indirect, that affects the moral behavior and the capacity of the child to think about right and

---

Insight: Kohlberg's Six Stages of Moral Reasoning

Stage	Moral Concepts
Level 1. Preconventional Morality (Ages 4 to 10 years) Stage 1: Concern with obedience and punishment	Children determine the badness of actions by the degree of punishment that results. Good behavior is associated with avoiding punishment.
Stage 2: Concern with satisfying needs	Good behavior is associated with satisfying one's own desires and needs without considering the needs of others. Although children show some awareness of fairness, it is usually in the sense of what they get out of the exchange. "You can play with my action-man if I can play with your new soccer ball."
Level 2. Conventional Morality (Ages 10 to 13 years) Stage 3: Concern with the "good-boy," "nice-girl" image	Children behave in accordance with rules and standards in order to gain the adults' approval rather than to avoid the physical consequences of bad behavior. There is a growing awareness of the need for rules, and the goodness or badness of behavior is judged in relation to the intention of acts.
Stage 4: Concern with law and order	At this stage children have an unquestioning attitude toward authority and to social rules. All laws are made to be obeyed, and that is the duty of each person without any exceptions being possible.
Level 3. Postconventional Morality (Ages 13 to young adulthood or never) Stage 5: Concern for the rights of the individual	Good behavior is now defined in terms of the rights of the individual according to rules and standards agreed upon by society in general. It is now considered acceptable to change rules or laws if this is necessary for the greatest good, or even to break the rules in certain circumstances—though intention then becomes very important.
Stage 6: Concern for ethical principles	Decisions about one's actions are now based on personal ethical principles derived from universal laws, which are consistent with the general good and with concern for others. Personal moral beliefs and values are steadfastly adhered to even when they are sometimes contradictory to laws established to preserve social order. For example, a man may steal a drug to save the life of his wife because preserving human life is a higher moral obligation than not stealing.

Adapted from L. Kohlberg in D.A. Goslin, ed., *Handbook of Socialization Theory and Research.* Copyright 1969 by Rand McNally. Used by permission.

Fig. 4.3

wrong."[28] The teacher's values concerning ideas, individuals, events, etc. determine her actions, words, and the activities used in the classroom. The values taught should reflect those of the home, the school, organized religion, and various agencies of the community.

In an age where there is constant change in the home, school, and community there is likely to be a confusion of ethical values. We need to be concerned that children develop a conscience. A review of the literature indicates that growth of conscience is influenced greatly by two factors; the presence of affection and a nurturing relationship between the adult and the child, and the use of induction techniques (giving a child a reason he should or should not do something). The use of induction techniques help children grow toward moral maturity. At the same time, we can reinstate the "golden rule—Do unto others as you would have them do unto you." This begins to teach them perspective—thinking of the other person and taking his point of view into consideration.

The development of conscience assists in guiding children in the development of self-control. Individuals who have developed self-control are trustworthy and responsible. They can be depended upon to do the right thing whether they are being observed or not. In addition, the control is internal, which makes it more consistent and more valuable for mental health. An individual who is "inner" controlled makes choices in his own behalf. Therefore, discipline should be more than getting the child to do what we want, it should be the development of self-control, which is necessary for moral and spiritual growth.

For Christian parents and teachers, the desired goal for behavior goes beyond that of self-control or "inner control." The ultimate goal is "Christ-controlled" behavior.

SEQUENCES AND AGE-LEVEL CHARACTERISTICS

At birth, an infant cannot think, use language, run, walk, or even deliberately plan his movements. His process of socialization with others takes the form of a cry or gurgling sounds. Although he is not helplessly passive, he does not have any control over his movements. During the first months of life, babies respond with zeal to circumstances designed to meet their interests and abilities and in fact act selectively upon their environment.

It is during the first six years of life that the most dramatic changes occur in humans. The impact of the informal education provided by the family cannot be overemphasized. However, since very few infants are involved in formal education programs, we will focus on the sequence and age level characteristics of children ages two through sixteen years.[29]

---

28. Ibid., p. 315.
29. Burton L. White, *The First Three Years of Life* (Englewood Cliffs, N.J.: Prentice-Hall, 1974), pp. 15-26.

While all ages are important and indicate growth changes, the most rapid growth occurs during the preschool years and adolescence. As you review the basic characteristics that follow, you need to consider that our expectations of what is considered normal behavior changes with the age of the child. As a teacher, you need to know what to expect of children of the particular age group that makes up your class. Remember that you must also consider individual differences, but a knowledge of the similarities found among children of the same age can assist you in establishing a classroom conducive to learning.

PRESCHOOL: TWO TO SIX YEARS

Physical development. Age 2. Height: 32-33". Weight: 23-30 lbs. Teeth: 16. Runs, walks, and climbs; runs without falling; walks up and down stairs alone, alternating his feet; expands his large muscle activities and interests; attempts to dress and undress himself; can kick a large ball; builds a tower of six cubes; and turns pages of a book singularly.

Ages 3-4. Average 3-year-old: Height, 38"; Weight, 33 lbs.
Average 4-year-old: Height, 39"; Weight, 35 lbs.
Temporary teeth generally complete.
Can go up and down stairs unaided alternating his feet, accelerates and decelerates with ease, negotiates sudden stops, runs, turns and jumps smoothly, rides tricycle (very rapidly at age 4), improved dexterity of hands and fingers, builds tower of 9 to 10 cubes (increasing as matures), and dresses and undresses himself.

Ages 5-6. Average 5-year-old: Height, 41"; Weight 39 lbs.
Average 6-year-old: Height, 44"; Weight, 42-45 lbs.
Teeth: transition to permanent.
Can lace shoes (some can tie shoelaces), physical skills are beginning to be important in influencing status among peers, transition from temporary to permanent teeth begins, can catch and throw a ball, walks, runs, jumps with adult smoothness, is able to draw a recognizable human figure, stands and balances on tiptoe for a short time, skips using alternate feet, and small muscle and eye-hand coordination developing.

Cognitive development. 2-3-year-olds: Can name many objects, beginning to use language as a means of communication, strong interest in investigating the functions and details of household objects; understands and uses abstract words such as "up, down, now, and later"; and the ability to reason, solve problems, and make comparisons is developing.

3-4-year-olds: Little differentiation of fantasy and reality, beginning of categorization (groups of objects which have similar functions or look alike), questions everything and asks many questions, shows more interest in the wider world, and distinguishes "indoor" from "outdoor" voice. Rapid language development; uses numbers, but doesn't understand concept of quantity; can follow instructions if not more than two ideas involved; can make a choice between two

GALLERY OF GREATS

Arnold Gesell
Growth and development occur in an unvarying sequence. (Courtesy of Gesell Institute)

Arnold Gesell was the first to convince psychologists and educators that growth takes place in stages. Although he earned a Ph.D. in psychology under T. Stanley Hall, Gesell went on to study medicine at Yale University. The Yale Clinic for Child Development was organized while he was still a medical student in 1911.

Gesell became convinced that children's behaviors were programmed by evolution. Therefore, if he could carefully observe children, he could discover when these biologically-determined behaviors would unfold. For thirty years, including the period of the establishment of the Institute of Child Development at Yale, Gesell and his cohorts made thousands of observations of children and published books giving detailed descriptions and containing developmental graphs as to the average ages at which many behaviors appeared. During the 1930s and 1940s, parents measured their children's growth and development every six months using such books as The First Five Years of Life and The Child from Five to Ten.

Although many modern psychologists disagree with Gesell's point of view and believe he overgeneralized and oversimplified, many of the methods he developed for observing children are still widely used. His now famous tables of expected ages for behaviors in children have been used as a guide for many pediatric examinations.

alternatives; interested in words—likes to play on words; has very little concept of size and space relationships, and counts, names colors, and recognizes that people can gain meaning from the printed word.

5-6-year-olds: Expresses ideas in artwork and language, memory good for concrete sequences (numbers and letters), can remember more than two ideas; can verbalize similarities and analogies; appreciates humor and unusual situations; plays simple letter and number games; questions change—"Why?" becomes "How?"; can tell left and right on himself but not on others; and eager to explore, investigate, experiment.

Social-emotional. 2-3-year-olds: Says no but submits anyway; shows trust and love; shows strong desires for independence in his actions; enjoys a wider range of relationships and experiences; likes to try out adult activities, does small household chores, runs errands, and strives for mastery over objects.

Ages 3-4: Likes surprises and unusual stimuli, sense of humor is developing; fears the dark, being left alone; egocentric, cooperative, and imaginative; interest in other people is increasing, seeks and needs parental guidance; increasingly independent and outgoing, loving and affectionate; quarrels, argues, competes and bosses about age four; is learning to express empathy; imaginary playmates not uncommon; beginning of strong feeling of family and home, and enjoys new people and experiences.

Ages 5-6: Expresses feelings freely, often in extreme form (joy, jealousy, fear, affection), violent outlets common (5½ to 6½); sense of humor expressed in riddles, nonsense words, and practical jokes; beginning to conform to peers regarding language, dress, etc.; play groups small and of short duration; increasingly realistic, less fanciful; and adult reassurance of competence and basic worth is essential.

Moral development. Ages 2-3: Preconscience age. May feel badly about doing something because he will be punished, but he does not have a real guilt feeling.

Age 4: Personal values that have been subtly shaped since infancy emerge. Takes some responsibility for his own actions. Learns to distinguish between right and wrong. Feels guilty about thoughts and actions he knows are wrong.

Ages 5-6: Evidence of developing conscience; resulting behavior may be rigid and expressed in extremes. Beginning to accept rules, but doesn't understand the principles behind them. Takes some responsibility for his own actions. Is developing a sense of fairness. Feels guilty about thoughts and actions he knows are wrong.

ELEMENTARY SCHOOL: SEVEN TO TWELVE YEARS

Physical development. 7-8 years: Will continually repeat a performance in order to master it. Shows extremes in outdoor play, at times "tearing about" and at other times just "hanging around." Beginning to lose interest in highly structured games. Receptive to learning new techniques in sports. Increase in speed and smoothness in fine motor development. Eye-hand coordination greatly improved.

9-10 years: Works and plays hard. Interested in competitive sports and team sports. Boys are quick to assume an active fighting posture and strike out at each other and wrestle. Physically active. Ten-year-olds hurl words back and forth. Like rough and tumble games (boys). Enjoy bicycles.

11-12 years: Skating, skiing, sledding, swimming, some sailing. Hiking, walking in the woods, nature interests. Bicycling, horseback riding. Running and hiding games. Spectator sports. Seasonal sports: baseball, football, basketball, hockey. Nonathletic girls now losing interest in sports.

Cognitive development. 11-12 years: Many still excited about learning. Thrive on competition. Better able to arrange, classify, and generalize. Most think they have too much homework at twelve. Homework may cause trouble. Strongest feelings are expressed about math, most liked and disliked subject.

Social-emotional. 11-12 years: Moves from being sensitive, proud, competitive, argumentative, and uncooperative with parents at age eleven to being as expansive, outgoing, enthusiastic, and overgregarious at age twelve. Dramatizes and exaggerates his expressions and frequently responds to anger. At age 12 he either loves or hates, no middle ground. Gang is very important. Developing loyalty. Most prefer same sex friendships. Girls tend to have "on again-off again" friendships and long telephone conversations.

Moral development. 7-8 years: Usually blames others for his actions; able to reason, seldom needs punishment. Skepticism about God may appear, and he is unable to accept death as a biological process until age eight. Beginning to feel shame in numerous situations; admits to wrongdoing but gives strong alibis. Highly motivated by money, and chief interest in religion is heaven.

9-10 years: Essentially truthful and honest; accepts blame fairly well and can be appealed to through fairness. Thinks in terms of right and wrong and is aware that adults have different standards of right and wrong. Most 10-year-olds ask searching questions about God, life, and death. Most are ready for a full explanation of death.

11-12 years: Puzzled by right and wrong and is apt to go by feelings and/or common sense. Conscious of choice of peer acceptance and own ethical standards. Concerned with fairness; however, truth is not sacred. At twelve, he becomes a diplomat but does not veer very far from the dictates of his group. Right and wrong choices are a deliberate, weighted process; accepts blame. Now wondering about religion, and his belief in God is more important than attending Sunday school.

JUNIOR HIGH—HIGH SCHOOL: THIRTEEN TO SIXTEEN YEARS

Physical development. Swimming and sailing, skating and skiing, tennis, bicycling, and horseback riding. Walking (girls mostly to a friend's house, movie). Hunting, fishing, sports (boys mostly).

Cognitive development. 13-14 years: May like a subject, regardless of difficulty. Feel they have too much homework, but are conscientious about completing assignments at age thirteen; tendency to need less help at age fourteen. Many enjoy evaluating teachers and subjects. Ease of achievement not always a criterion of interest.

15-16 years: Wide range of attitudes toward school subjects (resentment, to indifference and apathy, to enjoyment of intellectual challenge). All believe there is too much homework, and many don't do it. Great individual variation appears at age sixteen. Most sixteen-year-olds take responsibility of doing homework.

Social-emotional. 13-14 years: Extremely sensitive and vulnerable; easily hurt, irritated, or annoyed. Extremes of behavior apparent at age thirteen. Expansive and outgoing at age fourteen. Becoming more interested in the opposite sex (some dating). Each class has its "group" of popular students. Girls active with friends, telephone very important. Boys still growing.

15-16 years: Exhibits more self-confidence, determined, and self-controlled. Mature enough to be aware of problems; may be unhappy with himself. Becoming analytical about his emotions at age sixteen but generally takes things in stride. Lots of friends. Friendship for girls very important. Some dating. Boys usually go around with a group; one or two close friends. Most prefer friends' company to that of family.[30]

Moral development. 13-14 years: Considers ethics in the sense of how they help you relate to self and others. Extremes of ethical behavior seen at thirteen; accepts conscience as part of self; tries to be truthful. At fourteen, he tends to "stretch" truth occasionally; shows respect and interest in other people and now thinks of relationships of one group with another in terms of ethics. Majority express a belief in God.

15-16 years: Becoming more aware of conventions of rules and of religious codes. Questions of right and wrong often relate to social custom. Most are honest and accept blame. At sixteen, he is surprised to find his ideas are like his parents'. Many unsure about ideas of death and deity. Believing fifteen-year-olds accept God as a spirit and person, while the sixteen-year-old is unable to pinpoint his belief.

---

30. Arnold Gesell, et al., *The First Five Years of Life* (New York: Harper, 1940); Gesell and Ilg, *The Child from Five to Ten;* Arnold Gesell, Frances Ilg, and Louise B. Ames, *Youth: The Years from Ten to Sixteen* (New York: Harper & Row, 1956); Leeper, et al., *Good Schools for Young Children;* McFarland, *Stepping Stones.* Used by permission.

Controversial Issues: Readiness and Acceleration

Readiness and acceleration are difficult to separate, although their approaches concerning development (particularly cognitive development) are totally

---

Insight: Those High School Years

The "search for independence" is the appropriate label for the high school (secondary) years. High school students should be helped to consolidate their ideas about themselves and what they want to do in life. They need to be prepared for adulthood.

Concerns over physical appearance and relationships with persons of the opposite sex are of high priority. Eating and sleeping patterns may be erratic.

On the whole, students are becoming more independent. There is still dependence upon the peer group, but generally much less at age seventeen than at age fourteen.

The search for independence brings a great deal of stress—typically—to the student's relationship with his family. Conflict with authority figures frequently boils to a head, usually because it has not been handled appropriately prior to this time. Often, this conflict revolves around dangerous or antisocial practices: cheating, vandalism, the use of drugs and alcohol. Firmness, consistency, and love for the young person are the essential ingredients for the adult (parent or teacher) in relating to the teenager-becoming-an-adult.

It is difficult for even caring adults to allow the young person more freedom in making decisions, because the outcomes may be in conflict with adult (society's) standards.

The value of teaching children early that they must be submissive to appropriate authority is nowhere more evident than during the high school years. To exercise authority properly, it is essential to have been (and to be) submissive to those in proper authority over you. Without this kind of understanding and experience, there is little chance of resolving conflict with authority during the high school years.

In the Christian perspective, the search for independence is the search to become that person God is calling you to become—physically, mentally, spiritually—and vocationally. The *motive* is service, not self. The *method* is prayerful, reflective thought, not egotistical defiance and, perhaps, violence. The matter is one of stewardship under God, not self-aggrandizement.

Fig. 4.4

different. Readiness is usually considered in terms of reading and school-entrance age, although there is a readiness factor connected with all development.

Readiness is characterized by levels of individual development and by levels of tasks for which an organism is ready at a given time. It is not all or none; rather, it is cumulative and developmental in nature and influenced by numerous factors.[31]

According to Brenner readiness has two aspects: temporary and permanent. Temporary readiness is indicative of readiness for a given task at a given time, and permanent readiness applies to an individual's continuous readiness for school throughout his school life.[32]

The method of determining when a child is ready for formal learning has been debated for years. The majority of school systems in the United States use chronological age as the criterion for school entrance, and age and grade level are synonymous. Research indicates that chronological age should not be the lone indicator of readiness, but that readiness should be based upon physical growth in conjunction with cognitive functioning.[33] Readiness should function as a means to identify an optimal-time for the individual and the school curriculum.[34]

A review of numerous studies indicates that 25 to 33 percent of first-grade pupils are retained each year. Approximately two-thirds of those retainees are boys. Apparently boys have more difficulty adjusting to school.

The differences in achievement between boys and girls are usually explained as developmental or the differences in culturally defined expectations for boys and girls. Research attempts to correlate physical maturation and readiness for school and formal learning have involved the eyes, ears, motor performance, and tooth eruption. Most researchers agree that there is a general transitional period in growth at about the age of seven, and that the readiness necessary for formal learning activities required by the school is usually acquired at age seven or eight.

One of the prime factors that creates an environment of failure for children is the inadequate recognition of the importance of readiness, both in terms of cognitive maturation and cumulative learning.[35] Researchers have found that adverse psychological effects can be caused by ignoring readiness.[36]

In a 1957 study, Brenner discovered that children who were forced into an

---

31. Martha Ann McFarland, "Detention as a Predictor of Readiness, Reading Readiness, and Reading Achievement in Kindergarten, First-Grade and Second-Grade Boys." (Ph.D. diss., Florida State University, 1979), p. 15.
32. A. Brenner, "Nature and Meaning of Readiness for School," *Merrill-Palmer Quarterly* 3, no. 3 (Spring 1957):114-35.
33. McFarland, "Detention," pp. 36-37.
34. E.J. Ogletree, *Understanding Readiness: A Rationale (A Rejoinder to Jensen)*. National Institute of Education. U.S. Department of Health, Education and Welfare, 3, 1973 (ERIC Document Reproduction Service No. ED 076 226).
35. A.R. Jensen, *Understanding Readiness: An Occasional Paper*. Office of Economic Opportunity, U.S. Department of Health, Education and Welfare, 1969 (ERIC Document Reproduction Service No. ED 032 117).
36. Frances Ilg and S.B. Ames, *Is Your Child in the Wrong Grade?* (New York: Harper & Row, 1966), p. 64; Jensen, *Understanding Readiness*; Ogletree, *Understanding Readiness*.

activity before they were able to undertake it were "stultified."[37] In a study conducted by Ogletree, children who had been forced or persuaded to learn academic content prior to their readiness exhibited greater incidents of maladjustment than those who were ready to learn.[38] Wagoner also found training to be more harmful when it is given earlier than the development of the power it is expected to train.[39] Jensen and Goleman support Halleck's theory that "the brain matures by its own preprogrammed laws, and learning and experience cannot change that progression."[40]

Due to the differences in the rate of development in children, we are unable to pinpoint a specific age at which they are ready to begin formal schooling. Research supports the concept that average children can learn before we ordinarily consider them to be ready to do so if they are taught properly. This raises the question, What are the advantages or disadvantages of accelerating learning?

Proponents of acceleration emphasize the results of research done during the late 1950s and early 1960s. This research demonstrated that a child can master rather complex learnings, such as the abilities to read and to master complex mathematical concepts, at a very early age.[41] Research conducted by Becker, Englemann, and Thomas suggests that it is unnecessary to wait until children are completely "ready" for reading instruction, that better learning is produced when instruction is provided earlier.[42]

Much of the research in this area has been conducted almost totally with experimental programs. These programs were generally concerned with the concept of learning as being the acquisition of specific materials. Acquisition of knowledge is widely lauded as superior to the kind of learning that grows out of meaningful experiences and results from the interest and needs of the children.

Contemporary social and cultural conditions have always influenced education. The space age created a need for highly structured areas of knowledge and concern for the quality of education. Thus the best development for each child could become secondary to the aim of having children acquire as much specific knowledge as can be learned in the shortest possible time.[43]

Since research usually focuses on a specific area of development instead of a combination of all areas, additional research is needed in the area of readiness and acceleration. Until research is conclusive, we must make our own judgment concerning acceleration of learning.

We need to question the reason(s) for acceleration. It is believed that only in

37. Brenner, pp. 114-35.
38. Ogletree, *Understanding Readiness*.
39. L.C. Wagoner, *The Development of Learning in Young Children* (New York: McGraw-Hill, 1933), pp. 63-79.
40. R.P. Halleck, "The Bearings of the Laws of Cerebral Development and Modification on Child Study," *National Educational Association Journal of Proceedings and Addresses*, 1897, no. 36:833-43.
41. Leeper, et al., pp. 43-45.
42. Lahey and Johnson, pp. 78-83.
43. Leeper, et al., pp. 43-44.

America would pride be so great that the needs of children are secondary to superior test scores at an earlier age. Is acceleration to compensate for normal development different from using structured teaching to accelerate development beyond the norm?

Current research does not indicate an advantage to teaching children complex skills, nor does it show harm as long as the child is enjoying the learning experience and the possibility of success is high. Therefore, we need to be aware of the child's interest and enthusiasm and be sure he has the necessary entering behaviors for reading, advanced math, etc. If he has those and is also curious and eager to learn, why not capitalize on this?

AGE-LEVEL CHARACTERISTICS AND THEIR SIGNIFICANCE

The significance of age characteristics in children's learning can be witnessed in a majority of classrooms. A typical classroom in the United States is characterized by silence, conformity, docility, and regimentation. Yet, research has indicated that active interactions of the learner with the physical and social environment are the most significant school-related factors which stimulate (or retard) mental growth and development.[44] Learning is not the teacher's pouring knowledge into passive recipients; but rather active, interested, curious, and involved students seeking answers about God, His world, themselves, and others.

Teachers have the responsibility to structure the learning environment to include activities and materials to meet the needs and interests of all children. Lecturing and teacher demonstrations cannot take the place of individual experience with reality. We need to utilize all available scientific knowledge about development and plan curriculm that is consistent with children's level of development.

One of the most powerful forces in shaping the cognitive development of children is the attitude of the teacher toward the nature of intelligence and what constitutes learning. A teacher must be alert, generate positive feelings, provide relevant experiences, encourage autonomy on the part of students, and assist them in synthesizing their experiences.

Students usually achieve what is expected of them. Thus a mutual respect between the teacher and learner must exist for meeting the needs of each student.

Developmental norms present ways of measuring developmental progress. We must not forget that the variability in the rate of development among children is very prevalent and only large deviations from the norm should be considered abnormal.[45] In addition, we need to use the knowledge available to us about development, learning disabilities, and preventive and remedial techniques that

---

44. Linskie, p. 4.
45. Sara W. Lundsteem and Norma Bersteen Tarrow, *Guiding Young Children's Learning* (New York: McGraw-Hill, 1981), pp. 80-85.

build upon strengths to assist us in teaching.

In planning our curriculum, we need to consider the levels of development (all, not just mental), otherwise the learner can only fail. Since we are not the only force assisting the child, there is a need for the teacher to be familiar with the disciplines, traditions, customs, taboos, and attitudes of the community in which she teaches, especially those of the homes of children in her class.[46]

With all of the materials and programs available to us today, the child will still fail if he is expected to achieve at a level beyond which his whole body has developed. The key to learning is the teacher. As a *key,* she must not only be familiar with the characteristics of growth and development but also be able to implement those into the curriculum in order to help each student develop his God-given potential. This is not an easy task, but is one that should be shared with parents and administrators.

HINDSIGHT

In considering the characteristics and sequences of development, we emphasized the major areas of development. They are: physical, cognitive, social-emotional, moral, and spiritual. Experts in the area of growth and development believe all children pass through the same sequence of growth, but not in the same way, and each child has his own timetable of development.

Experiences constitute a main ingredient in development. These experiences include the child's biological environment (nutrition, medical care, drugs); and the child's social environment (family, peers, media). Although children mature at different rates, Piaget suggests that the sequential order of the stages and phases of cognitive development do not vary. Some educators now regard the affective component to learning as complementary to the cognitive; feelings, values, and attitudes are important in cognitive learning. The true goal of cognitive development should be to give each child ample opportunity to achieve levels reasonable for his age and commensurate with his ability. Emotional stability is dependent upon the child's security of knowing he is loved; that he belongs and that he is wanted. In addition, he must have the self-confidence that comes from being able to meet situations adequately. Differences in personality, environment, ability, and training affect the ease with which children develop socially. A child whose social development is healthy will be able to relate to other people. It is more significant that he relate to his family and some close friends his own age rather than to a large or small group.

Peer interaction plays a major role in the social stimulation that challenges the child to change his moral orientation. Fear and anxiety of losing favor with adult authority is responsible for moral development in early childhood. Most of

46. Jenkins, et al., pp. 304-5.

the research in this area focuses on the development of moral reasoning and the making of moral judgments. It is not concerned with the reason the child made the decision.

In order for children to feel guilt and behave morally, identification with some adult authority and acceptance of that authority's standards are probably necessary. Moral sanctions emanate from within once the child has developed a sense of guilt. Therefore, we need to assist the child in developing a Christian conscience in order to instill self-control and Christ-controlled behavior.

Sequence and age-level characteristics providing information of all areas of growth for the two through sixteen years of age were given. These are significant in a teaching-learning situation in order to provide for the need and interest of children. The teacher is the *key* to learning and needs to plan curriculum activities that create enthusiasm and curiosity in the learner as well as success.

Two controversial aspects of development are readiness and acceleration. Maturationists believe schooling should wait until a child is ready. Some even advocate beginning school at a later time. Others indicate that children are able to read and therefore we should accelerate cognitive development. Current research does not indicate an advantage to early learning, nor does it indicate harm as long as the child is enjoying the learning experience and the possibility of success is high.

CHALKBOARD CHALLENGES

1. It is extremely important that the competent teacher be able to observe behavior in children in order to plan for optimal development.

We suggest that you observe a child in a nursery* school or day care center for two hours. Write down everything the child does and says. Do not attempt to evaluate behavior of the children or teacher. After completing the observation, list behavior that indicates the age characteristics and sequence of development the child appears to be in. Record this in your teacher's notebook.

2. Do the same activity with a different age group and compare their levels of development. Record this in your teacher's notebook.

3. Observe the same children again in three months and note the development growth gained. Record in your teacher's notebook.

WANT TO KNOW MORE?

AGES AND STAGES

Arnold Gesell, Frances Ilg, and Louise B. Ames, *Youth* (New York: Harper & Row, 1956).

*You may select other grade levels.

Frances Ilg and Louise B. Ames, *Child Behavior* (New York: Harper & Row, 1955).

Gail Sheehy, *Passages: Predictable Crises of Adult Life* (New York: Bantam, 1976).

Burton L. White, *The First Three Years of Life* (Englewood Cliffs, N.J.: Prentice-Hall, 1975).

COGNITIVE DEVELOPMENT

Janie D. Osborn and D. Keith Osborn, *Cognition in Early Childhood* (Athens, Ga.: Education Associates, 1983).

Rosella Linskie, *The Learning Process: Theory and Practice* (New York: Van Nostrand, 1977).

B. Inhelder and Jean Piaget, *The Growth of Logical Thinking from Childhood to Adolescence* (New York: Basic, 1958).

S. F. Witelson, *Sex and the Single Hemisphere: Specialization of the Right Hemisphere for Spatial Processing* (Science, 1976).

READINESS

Louise B. Ames, C. Gillespie, and J. U. Streff, *Stop School Failure* (New York: Harper & Row, 1972).

B. Carll and N. Richard, *School Readiness: Our Piece of the Puzzle* (Peterborough, N.H.: New Hampshire School Readiness Project, 1965).

Frances Ilg and S. B. Ames, *Is Your Child in the Wrong Grade?* (New York: Harper & Row, 1966).

E. J. Ogletree, "Bioplasmic Forces: A New Concept of Readiness," *Reading Improvement* 10, no. 2 (Fall 1973): 34-36.

Raymond S. Moore and Dorothy A. Moore, *School Can Wait* (Provo, Utah: Brigham Young U., 1979).

Part 3

The Learning Process

5

The Behavioristic Approach

CONTENTS

	PAGE
Key Terms	131
That's Debatable!	133
Foresight	133
Background Influences	134
Realism: The Laws of Nature	134
Positivism: Empirical Verification	134
Materialism: Matter and Motion	135
Ivan Pavlov: Classical Conditioning	135
E. L. Thorndike: Instrumental Conditioning	135
John B. Watson: Environmental Shaping	135
Clark Hull: Quantitative Behaviorism	136
Current Concepts	139
Concepts in the Classroom	149
Criticisms and Critique	152
Hindsight	154
Chalkboard Challenges	154
Want to Know More?	155

KEY TERMS

Behavior modification
    A carefully designed process by which desired behavioral outcomes are

gradually achieved through the appropriate use of positive reinforcers

Chaining
The process whereby the individual hooks together a "chain" of small, individual conditioned behaviors to reach a complex skill

Classical conditioning (respondent conditioning)
A stimulus is presented to bring forth a response, a new stimulus is presented simultaneously with the old one, and then the old one is dropped, allowing the new one to bring forth the original response (Pavlov)

Extinction
A behavior which has been reinforced weakens or disappears when reinforcement is stopped

Loss of reinforcement
A behavior will weaken if its occurrence consistently results in the loss of reinforcers

Modeling
The presentation of desirable behavior to others in the hope they will imitate it

Negative reinforcement
When a behavior consistently terminates or prevents an unpleasant (aversive) consequence, that behavior will increase in strength

Operant (instrumental) conditioning
A behavior (response) is expressed and is strengthened or weakened by positive reinforcement, punishment, negative reinforcement, or loss of reinforcement

Positive reinforcer
Roughly synonymous with "reward." When any behavior is followed by a positive reinforcer, that behavior is strengthened

Programmed learning
The process by which the subject matter is broken up into small steps, so that each student will be reinforced as he or she successfully completes each step

Punishment
Any consequence which weakens a behavior when it consistently follows that behavior

Schedules of reinforcement
Fixed-ratio schedule: reward the behavior regularly, based on occurrence of the behavior (for example, every third time it occurs)
Fixed-interval schedule: reward the behavior regularly, based on the passage of time (for example, every two minutes)

Shaping
Reinforcing behavior by gradual steps into a refined form, by requiring increasingly better approximations of the behavior before providing reinforcement

Stimulus generalization
A reinforcer not only strengthens the original behavior, but by being associated with many behaviors, eventually strengthens any behavior with which it is associated

Stimulus pairing
The function of any stimulus transfers to a previously neutral stimulus, if the two consistently occur together

Token economy
A system using tokens, later to be exchanged for reinforcers, to control misbehavior and encourage learning

Vicarious learning
An individual learns by watching a model perform a specific behavior, noting the results, and then imitates whatever behavior brings pleasant consequences

That's Debatable!

IS MAN FREE TO LEARN?

B. F. Skinner: "The hypothesis that man is not free is essential to the application of scientific method to the study of human behavior. The free inner man who is held responsible for his behavior is only a prescientific substitute for the kinds of causes which are discovered in the course of scientific analysis. All these alternative causes lie outside the individual."[1]

Carl R. Rogers: "I am emboldened to say that personal freedom and responsibility have a crucial significance, that one cannot lead a complete life without such personal freedom and responsibility, and that self understanding and responsible choice make a sharp and measurable difference in the behavior of the individual. Man is subjectively free; his personal choice and responsibility account for the shape of his life; he is in fact the architect of himself. The truly crucial part of his existence is the discovery of his own meaningful commitment to life with all of his being."[2]

Jesus Christ: "Ye shall know the truth, and the truth shall make you free" (John 8:32).

Foresight

Just how do people learn? Has any one approach to learning proved itself

---

1. B.F. Skinner, *Science and Human Behavior* (London: Macmillan, 1953), p. 477. Used by permission.
2. Carl Rogers, *Freedom to Learn* (Columbus, Ohio: Merrill, 1969), quoted in James W. Noll, *Taking Sides: Clashing Views on Controversial Issues,* 2d ed. (Guilford, Conn.: Dushkin, 1983), p. 100. Used by permission.

superior to others? Are there ways in which we ought to design the learning process for maximum results? Why do we remember some items easily and forget others just as easily? Can we do anything to help people remember better and forget less? How can we help students who learn something in one situation, transfer it into other situations later?

In the six chapters of part 3, we will be considering these and similar questions vital to our understanding of the learning process.

There are a number of systematized approaches to learning. To help you compare the four major approaches, we have used the same structured outline in each case: background influences, current concepts, concepts in the classroom, and criticism and critique. We believe this outline will not only aid you in more easily making comparisons, but also will help you in your developing of the philosopher/clinician model, since the background influences are related to the clinical setting.

In this chapter, we deal with the first of the four approaches to learning, behaviorism, which has been a major force in the learning process since the middle of this century.

BACKGROUND INFLUENCES

REALISM: THE LAWS OF NATURE

One of the three major background influences feeding into behavioristic thinking is the position known as philosophical realism. George Knight emphasizes this aspect succinctly:

> With realism, behaviorism focuses on the laws of nature. Mankind from the behaviorist perspective is a part of nature and, as a result, operates according to nature's laws. Reality for the behaviorist is independent of the human arena. The task of the behaviorist is to observe living organisms, including man, in an attempt to discover the laws of behavior. After these laws have been discovered they will provide a foundation for a technology of behavior.[3]

POSITIVISM: EMPIRICAL VERIFICATION

A second major background influence is positivism. Auguste Comte (1798-1857) divided the history of mankind into three eras, and each of those eras was characterized by a particular way of thinking. The last (and highest) level is called the "positive" stage. It is in this stage that men do not attempt to go beyond whatever is observable and measurable. Spirits, gods, essences, and inner principles are rejected as means of explaining events. These, according to the positivists, belong to earlier, less dependable ages. Behaviorists have built on this

---

3. George R. Knight, *Philosophy and Education, An Introduction in Christian Perspective* (Berrien Springs, Mich.: Andrews U., 1980), p. 118. Used by permission.

The Behavioristic Approach

foundation, demanding "scientific" verification, and rejecting any inner feelings and causes because they cannot be measured.

MATERIALISM: MATTER AND MOTION

Materialism is a third major background influence affecting behavioristic thought. The "bottom line" description of materialism is that reality may be explained by the laws of matter and motion. This, of course, means a rejection of any beliefs concerning mind, consciousness, or spirit in man. These are looked upon as leftovers from a prescientific era.

It becomes evident why behaviorism, building on this three-tiered foundation, has had a strong appeal for those interested in scientific methods and "objectivity" in education. We should note here also its substantial appeal for the business community, which is concerned with visible, measurable results, efficiency, accountability, and economy.

IVAN PAVLOV: CLASSICAL CONDITIONING

A number of significant persons also are part of the background influence of behaviorism. Ivan Pavlov (1849-1936), a Russian physiologist, with his study of reflex reactions, was really the pioneer of behaviorist psychology. (See Insight, fig. 5.1, for a description of his classical conditioning with dogs.)

E. L. THORNDIKE: INSTRUMENTAL CONDITIONING

Another influential giant in the development of behaviorism is E. L. Thorndike (1874-1949). Once called the "dean of American educational psychology," Thorndike formulated the theory of connectionism, or S-R (stimulus-response) theory. He proposed that learning could be explained by the formation of bonds between a stimulus and a response. Three laws of learning were postulated: the law of effect, the law of readiness, and the law of exercise. (See Insight, fig. 5.2, for an explanation of these three laws.) Teaching machines, programmed instruction, and applied computer technology all have their roots in the S-R bond theory. And the relationship of modern behaviorism to Thorndike's studies is strongly evident. Thorndike laid the foundation for modern "instrumental conditioning" (an animal first makes a response, then receives a reward; the response is "instrumental" in bringing about its reinforcement; there is feedback from the reward that strengthens the response the animal is learning; the animal is more likely to make that response in the future).

JOHN B. WATSON: ENVIRONMENTAL SHAPING

Most scholars would agree that John B. Watson (1878-1958) has earned the

> **Insight: Classical Conditioning**
>
> Classical conditioning is connected with Pavlov's teaching his dog to salivate at the ringing of a bell. In Pavlov's experiment, the sound of a bell occurred prior to, or simultaneously with, the dog's salivation, which was caused by the presence of food. After this bell was rung for a frequent number of times when the food was presented, the dog then salivated at the ringing of the bell, even when the food was not presented.
>
> In classical conditioning, a neutral stimulus (bell) is presented along with the original stimulus (the smell of the food). In this manner, an organism learns to respond to the neutral stimulus in the same, or similar, way it responds to the old (unconditioned) stimulus. The neutral stimulus (bell) becomes the conditioned stimulus, and the response that follows the ringing of the bell becomes the conditioned response.
>
> It is important to note that in *classical* conditioning, the stimulus is presented in order to get a response. In *operant* conditioning (Skinner) the response (behavior) is made first and then the reinforcement follows.
>
> In the classroom, a good example of classical conditioning would be the development of the fire drill for the students. The ringing of the fire bell in itself really means nothing, unless associated with it are the instructions to the student that when that bell rings, a certain response is to follow, namely taking the proper route to the nearest exit. In effect, the bell is a neutral stimulus, but it is presented with the original stimulus (your instructions as to what the bell means), and then the bell takes on the meaning of your instruction.

Fig. 5.1

title of "father of modern behaviorism." Following in the footsteps of Pavlov, Watson emphasized behavior as a matter of conditioned reflexes and stressed environmental shaping of children's behavior. As we have noted in an earlier chapter, Watson stated bluntly that by controlling the child's environment, he could behaviorally engineer the child into any kind of person he chose.

CLARK HULL: QUANTITATIVE BEHAVIORISM

Clark Hull's (1884-1952) approach has been labeled "deductive" or "quan-

The Behavioristic Approach

titative" behaviorism because his theoretical model was a Newtonian mechanism, and he sought to maintain a consistently objective approach to psychological study. Hull stressed conditioning as the basic learning process, but was deeply concerned with what happened "objectively" in the behaving organism's nervous system between the stimulus and the response. Additionally, he thought of

---

Insight: Thorndike—Three Laws of Learning

Edward L. Thorndike formulated three primary laws of learning: readiness, exercise, and effect.

1. *The Law of Readiness.* This law simply means that an organism will learn more quickly if it is ready to learn. For example, if you are hungry, not having eaten all day long, and someone invites you to go to a hamburger stand, you are going to respond immediately because of your readiness to do so. In your classroom, if you conduct the class in such a manner as to have the children anticipating with excitement the particular item or principle or event about which they are going to learn, they will be much more apt to learn it.

2. *The Law of Exercise.* This law, by its very title, gives itself away. Exercise strengthens the bond between stimulus and response. To put it another way, the more one practices a certain response, the more apt it is to be retained. In your classroom, if your students are learning the multiplication tables, and the stimulus is your giving to them the numbers to be multiplied, such as two times two, or four times four, and then the appropriate answer, the more times this is gone over, the more probable it is your students will retain the results.

3. *The Law of Effect.* A response (behavior) is strengthened if it is followed by pleasure and weakened if followed by displeasure. That is, of course, the forerunner of B. F. Skinner's reinforcement theory. It is the idea of a reward's strengthening any particular behavior.

Critics of Thorndike's laws of learning emphasize that they appear to be quite mechanical, they do not appear to leave room for any sort of cognitive processing on the part of the student, and they do not require that there be any kind of purposiveness in humankind or the animals.

Fig. 5.2

GALLERY OF GREATS

John Broadus Watson
The data of psychology should be the observable response. (Courtesy Culver Pictures)

John B. Watson was born in Greenville, South Carolina, in 1878. He admitted he was lazy in public school, but he received a master's degree from Furman University in 1900. Unable to "comprehend" John Dewey at the University of Chicago, he changed majors and received his Ph.D. in psychology from Chicago in 1903.

Believing firmly that the study of animal responses was the approach for understanding human responses, Watson set up an animal laboratory at John Hopkins University in 1908. In 1913, a new school of thought called "Behaviorism" was begun with the publication of Watson's paper "Psychology as the Behaviorist Views It." He ruled out mentalistic concepts such as mind *and* consciousness *and insisted that psychology must be deterministic, mechanistic, and materialistic.*

In 1920, amidst great notoriety, John Hopkins asked him to leave after his wife divorced him. Later that same year, Watson married Rosalie Rayner, his research associate, and entered the advertising business in New York City.

Watson asserted he could make a child do almost anything if he had control of the child's environment. He died in 1958, having made educational psychology more behavioristic. In particular, he stressed the idea of conditioning in the classroom. This laid the foundation for Skinner and others, who developed "behavior modification" for the teaching-learning process.

reinforcement in terms of need or drive reductions. Learning did not occur with a single S-R event, but rather was stamped in through a process of repeated need or drive reductions. Hull developed an intricate system of definitions, postulates, and theorems to bridge the gap from the simpler conditioning to the more complex forms of learning.[4] We consider Hull to be the "curious, laborious detail man" of behaviorism.

Current Concepts

What are the current concepts as they relate to the learning process? Again, in each of these approaches, a selection must be made from a larger list of possibilities. B. F. Skinner, the father of operant conditioning (contingent reinforcement), and Albert Bandura's social learning theory are representative of the current behavioristic approaches.

CONTINGENT REINFORCEMENT: B. F. SKINNER

Contingency reinforcement, or operative conditioning, was the result of the work of B. F. Skinner, bringing together the contributions of many who preceded him. Skinner, known as "the father of operant conditioning," has developed units of learning called "contingencies of reinforcement." The contingency of reinforcement is a sequence within which a response (behavior) is followed by a reinforcing stimulus. This is also known as "operant conditioning," since the operant (any particular behavior) is conditioned to occur more frequently, less frequently, or not at all—depending upon whether it is reinforced, punished, or ignored. Skinner established several principles of learning built upon contingency reinforcement.

Positive reinforcement. The principle of positive reinforcement states that when any behavior is followed by a reinforcer, that behavior will strengthen.

It is important to understand that while a reinforcer may roughly be thought

---

4. Morris L. Bigge, *Learning Theories for Teachers,* 4th ed. (New York: Harper & Row, 1982), p. 94.

of as a "reward," it is not always a pleasurable consequence. An individual may desire to help young delinquents, for example, and may be reinforced by the opportunity to be a house father or house mother to them. This is not "pleasurable" in the traditional sense, but still acts as a reinforcer.

Negative reinforcement. If a behavior consistently stops something unpleasant (aversive) or prevents it from happening, that behavior will increase in strength.

In our second-grade classroom, our teacher had a cardboard cutout of a coffee pot. On one side was a horribly unpleasant looking face; on the other, a beautiful, smiling face. Each morning our teacher asked whether anyone had drunk coffee. If any student answered yes, the coffee pot face was turned unpleasant face outward. If all answered no, the pleasant face smiled at us all day long! The behavior of not drinking coffee was strengthened because it kept the unpleasant (aversive) face from scowling at us all through the school day.

Loss of reinforcement. This principle of learning states that a behavior will weaken if its occurrence consistently leads to the loss of reinforcers.

A sophomore in high school is hopelessly in love with a lovely young lady. He wants to do everything to please her. He looks forward to her reinforcing comments about how he looks and how he dresses. Suddenly, one day his girl friend makes a comment about the shirt he is wearing—and has worn on a number of previous occasions. She doesn't really care for the color. His reinforcement is suddenly lost, and it is not likely he will wear that shirt again—at least not for as long as he is madly in love with that girl!

Punishment. Any unpleasant consequence following a behavior that consistently weakens that behavior can be called a punishment. It is well to remember that different things are punishing to different individuals, and in different circumstances. A teacher may punish a child by simply saying no in a deliberate manner, but it may also be seen by the child as a way to receive the attention of the teacher, which a child desperately needs and wants. Punishment in that case becomes a reinforcer.

Psychologists and educators disagree as to whether punishment really permanently stops the unwanted behavior and also as to how often and how severe punishment should be. Most would agree, however, that punishment should fit the misbehavior, and that strong physical punishment should be used only as a last resort. But it is important for the child to know that, if necessary, the teacher or principal *will use the strong forms of punishment.*

Strong forms of punishment (such as spanking) should be used only after other procedures have failed, or when the behavior is so dangerous or upsetting it must be quickly eliminated. When a spanking, for example, is administered at school, we recommend that (1) it not be done hastily or in the presence of other children, (2) parents understand fully why it has been done, and (3) it be done always in the presence of another responsible adult (for example, teacher and

The Behavioristic Approach

GALLERY OF GREATS

Burhus Frederick Skinner
"I was a witness to minds being destroyed." (After a visit to his daughter's arithmetic class in elementary school)

The son of a lawyer, B. F. Skinner was born in Susquehanna, Pennsylvania, in 1904, and received his Ph.D. in experimental psychology from Harvard in 1931. Highly influenced by the ideas of John B. Watson, Skinner trained pigeons in such a thorough manner during World War II that they could guide a missile right down the smokestack of a naval destroyer.

While he was chairman of the Psychology Department at Indiana University (1945-48), Skinner developed his famous "air crib," a glass-enclosed, hygienic box for raising small children. His attempt to market this as the "Heir Conditioner" failed. With his inventive mind, Skinner developed such items as a music box to place in a toilet for toilet training of children (it played "Blue Danube" when it got wet!), the Skinner Box to help study animals with precision, and the teaching machine (programmed instruction) to help children learn step-by-step.

The "Father of Operant Conditioning" and the force behind Behavior Modification, now retired from active teaching, Skinner is without question a pioneer in the shaping of behavior. Since moving to Harvard in 1948, he has wielded a monumental influence over a generation of students in experimental psychology.

principal), (4) the child understand clearly what the spanking is for, and (5) the adults involved reestablish good relationships with the child following the punishment. The time lapse between punishment and reestablishment of positive relationships will vary with the age of the child and the particular circumstances that occasioned the punishment. We do not generally recommend spanking a student after he is in high school, but rather using other forms of punishment such as withdrawal of privileges.

Educators need to be aware of the danger of misuse or abuse of punishment techniques. The student who is kept at his work by threat of punishment may learn to dislike school. Punishment often causes the child to be hostile, to dislike the one administering the punishment, to become stubborn, and to cease from engaging in behaviors similar to those for which the child is being punished, even though some of those similar behaviors may be desirable.[5]

Although punishment is necessary in our view, it should be used sparingly and wisely. In the majority of cases, punishment can be replaced with more positive forms of discipline. This usually will prove to be more successful in meeting the goals of the teaching-learning process.

Stimulus pairing. A stimulus is any object or event in the environment. It can reinforce, punish, or be neutral. The function of any stimulus can transfer to any previously neutral stimulus, if they are consistently paired (i.e., if they occur together).

In the classroom the teacher may feel her words of praise ("that's good!") are not as strongly reinforcing as she would like them to be. By handing out a simple token when she says, "That's good" (thus pairing two stimuli) she will strengthen the reinforcement value of her words, especially when the children know the tokens are exchangeable for free time or some other pleasurable consequence.

However, this principle of stimulus pairing may often work against a teacher, if the teacher is not aware of how to use it wisely. For example, students are cheating on tests. The teacher always puts his book down on his desk before he stands up to walk around the room to check on the students' progress. Standing up is a stimulus to the students to stop cheating (when the teacher is coming around to

---

5. Albert Bandura, *Principles of Behavior Modification* (New York: Holt, Rinehart, and Winston, 1969).

The Behavioristic Approach

watch me) and the putting down of the book on the desk by the teacher is a neutral stimulus insofar as cheating is concerned. The students will stop cheating at those moments, and never get caught. Their cheating behavior is stopped temporarily by a previously neutral stimulus (putting the book down on the desk) now associated (paired) with a stimulus (standing up) that has the function of stopping cheating behavior momentarily.

Stimulus repetition. This principle states that a stimulus presented repeatedly or for a long period of time will lose some or all of its stimulus function. This principle is reflected repeatedly in our everyday experience. Suppose there were only one television program on all the time, and that was all you could watch. You would soon grow tired of watching.

But it can be used in powerful ways in the classroom, particularly to help students gradually adjust to a hard task or process. It is used in teaching public speaking. The more the student gets up in front of the group, the more at ease he or she becomes.

Like the other principles of learning, this one can work against you if you do not use it wisely. If you never change the format of your class lectures, they will lose some or all of their ability to gain and keep students' attention.

Schedules of reinforcement. Different kinds of reinforcement schedules affect behavior in differing ways.

A *continuous reinforcement schedule* (rewarding every time the desired behavior occurs) has an effect on performance different from that of an *intermittent reinforcement schedule* (rewarding only certain times the behavior occurs). Different schedules of intermittent reinforcement cause different results.

A *fixed-ratio schedule* (rewarding every second or fourth response, for example) has a different result from a *fixed-interval schedule* (rewarding every two or four minutes).

These kinds of schedules, plus a variety of others, can produce a substantial variety of behavioral results.[6]

Thomas summarizes Skinner's viewpoint by saying:

> From his behaviorist perspective, child development is a process of the growing individual's learning increasingly complex and refined ways of acting as a result of the consequences that have followed the behavior he has attempted. The role of parents and teachers is therefore two-fold: (1) to get children to try desirable acts and (2) to arrange consequences of childrens' acts so that the desirable behavior is reinforced and undesirable behavior is extinguished through nonreinforcement or punishment.[7]

---

6. Ernest Hilgard and G.H. Bower, *Theories of Learning,* 4th ed. (Englewood Cliffs, N.J.: Prentice-Hall, 1975), pp. 216-217.
7. From R. Murray Thomas, *Comparing Theories of Child Development,* p. 390. © 1979 by Wadsworth Publishing Company, Inc. Reprinted with permission.

Educational Psychology

GALLERY OF GREATS

Albert Bandura
A large part of what a person learns
occurs through imitation or modeling.
(Courtesy Albert Bandura)

Albert Bandura is an important contemporary psychologist who has become known as a "social learning theorist." He is concerned with how learning takes place in the midst of the social situation. The individual learns to modify his behavior as a result of watching how others in the group are reacting or responding, and the consequences they incur as a result of their behavior.

Perhaps Bandura's largest contribution involves his efforts to develop an all-inclusive approach to learning. Although still viewed as a behaviorist by many, he nevertheless sees behavior, internal cognitive structures, and the environment as interacting. Persons are not only shaped by their environment, but also choose and shape their environments.

An important aspect of Bandura's approach is his insistence that people can learn new responses by observing the behavior of others. His academic home is Stanford University.

SOCIAL LEARNING THEORY: ALBERT BANDURA

Social learning theory is so-called because it places great emphasis on social variables as determinants of behavior. Rather than depending upon studies of animal learning as previously, or the study of a single person learning, the social learning theorists seek conclusions from the studies of the interaction of two or more persons.

Albert Bandura, a Stanford University psychologist, while certainly a behaviorist, nevertheless differs in at least four important ways from Skinner and the more "traditional" behaviorists (Skinner's position is actually coming to be designated as "radical behaviorism"). As Thomas has pointed out, these four major areas include (1) the way a child acquires a novel (new) behavior, (2) the manner in which one learns from models, (3) the influence of consequences on future actions, and (4) the development of complex behaviors.[8]

New behavior. Rather than agreeing that a child learns new sounds through lucky coincidence of each sound and reward (for example, "dah-dah" followed by smiles and hugs), Bandura believes the child's learning comes from his actively modeling (imitating) what he sees and hears other people say and do.[9] New behaviors are not just lucky hits. Children seek to reproduce what they observe. And the child will learn even when the reinforcement is only vicarious. Five-year-old Sue sees Jane's mother smile when Jane says thank you for some cookies she just received. Even though the reward (smile) happened to Jane (vicarious), Sue learns to say thank you in similar situations in the future.

Can a person learn something he sees or hears if this is not a current need-fulfilling satisfaction, or if there is no reward? To this, the issue of "incidental learning," most behaviorists say no. Bandura and other social learning theorists say yes, at least sometimes. What happens, according to Bandura, is that the individual stores up a repertoire of reactions, and given the appropriate situation will display a particular reaction.

"When exposed to diverse models, observers rarely pattern their behavior exclusively after a single source, nor do they adopt all the attributes even of preferred models. Rather, observers combine aspects of various models into new

---

8. Thomas, p. 409.
9. Bandura, *Principles of Behavior,* pp. 118-20.

amalgams that differ from the individual sources. . . . Different observers adopt different combinations of characteristics."[10]

Learning from models. In the Insight box (fig. 5.3) we have detailed carefully the process of learning from models as Bandura views that process.

We certainly do not completely understand how observational learning takes place. However, some of the learning conditions have been ferreted out. Bandura insists the primary reason a child learns from hearing or seeing a model is that the information he receives from the observation helps the child decide how that behavior might or might not be of benefit to him in future situations. The information received is stored as symbols in the memory, and the child holds these until he may need them at some future point.[11]

The influence of consequences. What is the influence of consequences in relation to future actions? That is, how does the reward (reinforcement) value of what happens now affect the manner in which I may behave in the future?

Skinnerian-type behaviorists believe that the strengthening-of-response-tendencies for reinforcement is *automatic*. It is as though a person says, "it worked well for me this time, so I will do it this way in the future," even though the person does not consciously say that to himself.

Bandura disagrees with this approach. His response (and that of a number of other social learning theorists) if asked how consequences influence subsequent behavior would be: "Although the issue is not yet completely resolved, there is little evidence that reinforcers function as automatic shapers of human conduct. . . . A vast amount of evidence lends validity to the view that reinforcement serves principally as an informative and motivational operation rather than as a mechanical response strengthener."[12]

By "informative," Bandura means that whether the consequences are rewarding or punishing, they "inform" the individual how and when he might want to use this behavior subsequently.

By "motivational role of consequences," Bandura simply means that a child will be more likely to learn the behavior if he likes the result the behavior produces in the model situation.

> In summary, then, Bandura does not believe that consequences reinforce responses automatically and strengthen the response that immediately precedes the consequences. Instead, he sees consequences as *regulators* of future behavior—they regulate by means of giving the individual information about likely future consequences and by motivating her to act in one way rather than another in order to obtain the results she seeks.[13]

10. Albert Bandura, *Social Learning Theory,* © 1977 p. 21, 48. Adapted by permission of Prentice-Hall, Inc., Englewood Cliffs, N.J.
11. Ibid., pp. 22-29.
12. Ibid., p. 21.
13. Thomas, p. 416.

Insight: Learning From Models

The process of learning from models consists of five main functions:

1. The child must attend to the pertinent clues. The child may misdirect her attention at the time the model is observed, and therefore fail to perform the behavior properly later. A teacher can help by directing the child's attention to those parts of the model's performance that are most important.

2. The child must code for memory. That is, a visual image must be stored in the memory for the particular behavior that the child has witnessed. Older children learn more readily from looking at others' performances than do younger children, because of the cumulative effect of the storage in the memory. The development of language, and of schemes for coding the observations, improves the child's ability to profit from watching models.

3. The child must be able to retain in her memory that which she has observed, so that it will be available when needed. Memories do fade or disappear with time. And so memory-aiding techniques such as rehearsal or review or practice, or making an image very vivid for the child, help to maintain the image in the child's memory.

4. The child must reproduce the observed motor activities accurately. The child must not only get the idea of the behaviors to perform but she must also get the muscular *feel* of behavior. According to Bandura, usually the child cannot do this perfectly on the first trial, and thus the child needs a number of trials in which she seeks to approximate the behavior. The older child will probably perform the model activities better, because her muscular development is better advanced than the younger child's.

5. The child must be motivated to carry through all the steps in the process of learning from models. The crucial role of the consequences of the behavior enter the picture at this point. The child must understand that in the future this would be a good way to behave under particular sets of circumstances.

Fig. 5.3

Complex behaviors. How do we acquire complex behaviors? Element by small element, say the Skinnerian behaviorists. Piece by piece, we build up a pattern of

> **Insight: Which Models are Children Likely to Follow?**
>
> Experimental studies show that:
> 1. Children are more likely to model their own behavior after the actions of people they look upon as important, than after people whom they do not look upon as important.
> 2. Children are more likely to adopt behavior patterns from models of their own sex than from models of the opposite sex.
> 3. Models who receive rewards such as fame, high society status, or money are more influential with children than those who do not have these kinds of rewards.
> 4. Models who are punished for their behavior are usually not followed by the children.
> 5. Children follow models who are more similar to themselves in age or social status than those who appear to the child to be quite different from himself or herself.
>
> Through the observation of models, Bandura believes that children can add new options to their repertoire of possible behaviors, and figure out under which circumstances these options should be used.
>
> From A. Bandura and R. H. Walters, *Social Learning and Personality Development* (New York: Holt, Rinehart, and Winston, 1963), pp. 10-11, 50, 84, 94-100. Used by permission.

Fig. 5.4

behavior through the accrual of successive elements.

Bandura differs. Note this significant reply to the Skinnerian behaviorist:

> Patterns of behavior are typically acquired in large segments or in their entirety rather than through a slow, gradual process based on differential reinforcement. Following demonstrations by a model, or following verbal descriptions of desired behavior, the learner generally reproduces more or less the entire response pattern, even though he may perform no overt response, and consequently receive no reinforcement, throughout the demonstration.[14]

14. Albert R. Bandura and R.H. Walters, *Social Learning and Personality Development* (New York: Holt, Rinehart, and Winston, 1963), p. 106. Used by permission.

The Behavioristic Approach

Bandura would agree, however, that once the new (total pattern of) behavior has been learned through observation, its future use by the child will be largely governed by schedules of reinforcement and punishment.

Thomas summarizes Bandura's social learning perspective in relation to child development as a:

> process (1) of the child's gradually expanding his repertoire of answers or possible actions by means of both observing others and trying the actions himself and (2) of the child using information from the observed consequences to guide future decisions about when one response will be more appropriate than another to fulfill needs and attain rewards. Like Skinner, Bandura does not separate development into a series of stages, but he considers the process of cognitive and social growth to be one of gradual accrual of an ever widening array of response possibilities for increasingly differentiated stimulus situations.[15]

CONCEPTS IN THE CLASSROOM

Let us go back for a moment and recall that our model for the teaching-learning process is one of the philosopher/clinician, meaning that the philosophical outlook, based on a vast repertoire of resources, is essential for the teacher to bring to the clinical (classroom) setting if he or she is to be effective. It is for this reason, as well as for others, we seek to describe briefly how the behavioristic approach (and others in succeeding chapters) can be applied to the classroom (clinical) setting of the teaching-learning process. In each case we will view five items: the teacher, the student, the curriculum, the methodology, and the social function of the school. Each of the approaches will then receive a short critical consideration for the purpose of helping the student to clarify the pros and cons of the particular approach involved.

THE TEACHER

In the behavioristic approach the teacher is the *manager of the learning environment*. The teacher's role is to create an effective learning environment. Skinner believes the primary missing ingredient in most classrooms is positive reinforcement. He has criticized traditional education for using aversive (punishing) forms of control such as homework, scolding, withdrawing of privileges, spanking. By studying animals, he contends, scientists can refine the techniques of teaching by applying their findings to human beings. The task of the teacher, Skinner would say, is to arrange the learning environment in such a manner that it provides positive reinforcement for the desired student behaviors. Those undesirable acts, unrewarded, will disappear through extinction over a period of time.

---

15. Thomas, p. 417.

THE STUDENT

The student is a neutral human organism (animal) whose behavior is controlled through contingency reinforcement. He learns the same way other animals learn. The student is not a being related to God. Man is a part of nature. He does not have any special dignity or freedom. As Skinner puts it, "a small part of the universe is contained in each one of us. There is no reason why it should have any special physical status because it lies within this boundary."[16] While man is a complex natural organism, he is still primarily part of the animal kingdom. The teacher, as an expert in contingency reinforcement, controls the student's learning behavior through the use of that expertise, shaping the student as closely as possible to the desired goal.

THE CURRICULUM

In the curriculum, the subjects may vary, but the curriculum is always geared to the science of the society. "Your schools (and their curricula) are viewed as ways of designing a culture. Skinner and other behaviorists claim that environmental conditioning and programming have always been a part of education and schooling. What they are calling for is a more conscious use of the laws of learning to control individuals so that the quality of life and the chances of racial survival will be enhanced."[17]

THE METHODOLOGY

Behavioral engineering is clearly the methodology of the behavioristic approach to the classroom. This is evident whether one is talking about programmed learning/teaching machines, behavioral modification, computer-assisted instruction, individually prescribed or guided education, the self-scheduling system, or modeling techniques. "From the behaviorists' perspective, people are programmed to act in certain ways by their environment. Behavior may be modified by manipulating environmental reinforcers."[18]

We must cite here the important connection that has developed between the behaviorist approach and the business community. Such values as efficiency, economy, precision, and objectivity are central considerations in both behavioristic education and the business community.

Behavioristic techniques have been applied to such business practices as advertising, sales promotion, systems management—with a large measure of

---

16. B.F. Skinner, *About Behaviorism* (New York: Alfred A. Knopf, 1976), p. 24. Used by permission.
17. Knight, p. 121.
18. Ibid.

Insight: Behavior Modification

Ozmon and Craver have summarized the basic procedures for behavior modification in the normative classroom.
1. Specify a desired outcome, what needs to be changed, and how it will be evaluated.
2. Establish a favorable environment by removing unfavorable stimuli which might complicate learning.
3. Choose the proper reinforcers for desired behavioral manifestations.
4. Begin shaping desired behavior by utilizing immediate reinforcers for desired behavior.
5. Once a pattern of desired behaviors has been begun, slacken the number of times reinforcers are given.
6. Evaluate results and reassess for future development.

From Howard Ozmon and Sam Craver, *Philosophical Foundations of Education* (Columbus, Ohio: Merrill, 1976), p. 149. Used by permission.

Fig. 5.5

success. Many in the business community are therefore enthusiastic in joining behavioristic psychologists in calling for *accountability* in education. "If you are accountable, you produce results effectively and efficiently. An ever increasing interest has developed in applying business management techniques, objectives, and many measures based on performance in the teaching-learning context."[19] Your attention is called to the behavior modification process detailed in Insight, figure 5.5.

THE SOCIAL FUNCTION OF THE SCHOOL

Why is the school there, and what is its purpose? The behaviorists answer: students should learn those things deemed important for survival by a given society in a given environment.

Whatever is necessary for your society to survive is the banner flying over the

---

19. Ibid., p. 123.

behavioristic school. As society determines the techniques, attitudes, skills, behaviors necessary for that survival, these should become central as the goals of the school system. To put it another way, the school is there to assure the survival of its society by managing the learning environment so as to produce participants appropriately trained to assure that survival. Schools are there to make your society (culture) what society wants itself to be.

CRITICISMS AND CRITIQUE

REGARDING HUMAN NATURE

The behaviorally-oriented educators view man as a highly evolved and evolving animal at best. This logically implies that the "nature," if any, with which the educator will be working is less than "human." What is the nature of the student? For the behaviorist, a "neutral human animal," whose behavior can be controlled through contingency reinforcement—basically training and manipulation. Critics from the humanistic position are quick to point out that this rules out the "human spirit"—the vast inner potential of a human being that makes the human being what he is. Critics from the Christian standpoint quickly contrast the neutral animal nature with the sin nature of the human being, a cardinal belief of orthodox, evangelical, and fundamental Christians. Both humanists and Christians would point out that to equate training and manipulation (behavioristic) with the total educational process is simplistic. What plays in the Madison Avenue of advertising is not sufficient for either the Metropolis of Humanism or the City of God, when applied to the education of our children.

REGARDING FREEDOM AND DIGNITY

Closely aligned to the human nature controversy is the issue of the freedom and the dignity of the human being. Many critics contend that Skinner and other behaviorists have cut the "human" out of human being. Each critic defines a bit differently what they mean by this kind of criticism. However, it seems fair to say that most critics would agree that the S-R approach leaves man dehumanized and with a metallic ring to his nature. It appears equally fair to say that if Skinner were to formally describe "nature" for the human animal, it would approximate the following:

> Man has inherited the ability to profit from the consequences of behavior. He (she) has an important genetic endowment—an adaptability, a highly sensitive genetic potential for operant conditioning. This is the result of the evolutionary process, and it is the key to the survival of the human animal as a species. (Author's compilation)

If the above is fair to Skinner, then it leaves itself open to a severe criticism

The Behavioristic Approach

concerning the lack of freedom and dignity in the human being. For example, an animal dies; a human being with dignity *has to die*. This kind of example obviously raises the entire question of meaning, life perspective, goals, risk taking, choices—and many other characteristics which can be gathered together to make up what, at least loosely, would be termed by many the "human qualities of living." Animals fight to survive. Human beings, while fighting to survive, nevertheless struggle for much, much more—the worthwhileness of living.

For the humanist, with his emphasis upon *human potential*, the S-R approach appears as a myopic, too-mechanical view of the human being, which leaves him something considerably less than *human*. For the Christian, the S-R approach is not only myopic on the horizontal level, depriving the human being of his dignity, freedom, and deeper struggling; but on the vertical level as well, stripping man of the most essential of his relationships—that of his relationship with God. Such a relationship—and more broadly the biblical view of man—accounts not only for his God-given dignity and freedom, but most importantly for his perverse nature and need for salvation in Jesus Christ.

Skinner would probably respond that the scope of his work is that of describing the reality of how and why people act as they do. They may have inner feelings, for example, and while they come from their own systems, they cannot be measured. Therefore, he is not going to spend time conjecturing on their pros and cons.

Nevertheless, behaviorism does seem open to criticisms of a myopic view of man, the failure to account for his perverse nature, the attempt to account for why pigeons peck (a behavior) and a baby coos with delight (a behavior) on the basis of reinforcement only (is this the only difference between a baby and a pigeon behaviorally?), and the oft-discussed controversy over who controls the controllers if behavior can be controlled by contingency reinforcement.

IMPLICATIONS FOR THE TEACHING-LEARNING PROCESS

The implications for the teaching-learning process are rather obvious. How one views the student—as an animal to be trained and manipulated for society's survival, or as a person created in the image of God—has significant implications for how one approaches the teaching-learning process. Goals, methodology, the curriculum, the role of the teacher, and the nature of the student obviously are affected at the core by such assumptions.

Commenting on *Walden Two,* Skinner's portrayal of the ideal behavioristic society, Stevins summarizes:

> Behavioral engineering rules out the risk and the achievement of freedom, love, self giving, commitment, self discipline, loyalty, memory, creativity, and hope. The significance of politics, the integrity of art, the warmth and support of human

intimacy—all are lost. . . . the most precious part about man is his humanity. *Walden Two* commends its deliberate abandonment.[20]

From the evangelical/fundamentalist Christian point of view, the S-R approach's greatest deficit is its lack of any possibility of the individual relating with God through Jesus Christ, bringing life its fullest meaning and affecting the educational process at its very heart.

HINDSIGHT

We have reviewed the behavioristic approach to the learning process, pointing out the background influences of realism (concern with the laws of nature), positivism (including its primary emphasis on empirical verification), and materialism (concern with the laws of matter and motion). Several key figures were addressed, including Pavlov (classical conditioning), Thorndike (instrumental conditioning), Watson (environmental shaping), and Hull (quantitative behaviorism).

Emphasis was placed on B. F. Skinner's contingency reinforcement, highly influential for the last twenty-five years in psychology and education; and Bandura's social learning theory, which is gaining increasingly wider acceptance, with its modeling and vicarious learning concepts.

The S-R concepts were discussed in relation to the classroom—with the implications for the role of the teacher, the nature of the student, the curriculum, the methodology, and the social function of the school.

We concluded, as we will for each of the approaches to be discussed, with a critique and criticism of the behavioristic approach, with particular concerns for its implications relating to the view of human nature and its undercutting of the significance of human dignity and freedom.

CHALKBOARD CHALLENGES

1. Can all behavior be explained in behavioristic terms? For example, in your ninth-grade classroom, Mike makes the comment, "I don't see why it isn't OK to steal sometimes, if it doesn't hurt anybody." *Stealing* is a *behavior*. Consider how you explain this behavior in behavioristic terms. Wrong reinforcers used? Wrong schedules of reinforcement used? Is it enough to go about correcting the behavior without talking about inner motives? Without relating it to the Christian ethic? Is the survival of a society as a species adequate motivation for not stealing? Also apply this to other behaviors you can think of. Test out the adequacy of behaviorism in explaining and controlling behavior in the classroom setting.

2. One of the frequent criticisms of behaviorism revolves around the issue of

---

20. D.B. Stevens, *B.F. Skinner's Walden Two* (New York: Seabury, 1968), p. 28.

control—if behavior can be controlled through contingency reinforcement, who will control the controllers? That is, who will decide ultimately what behaviors are appropriate? Behaviorists would reply that since survival of the society is paramount, that is the ultimate reference point. How does this translate into the daily routines of the classroom with the behavioristic approach of behavioral engineering? Do you still have the question, Who's the chief engineer? Do other approaches face this same question? You may wish to write a term paper for this or another class on the following or similar topic: "The ultimate standard of behavior in the behavioristic approach."

3. Read *Walden Two,* the description by B. F. Skinner of his ideally managed society. Concentrate on the educational processes of that society. Put yourself in the middle of those processes. In your teacher's notebook, make two columns; head one column with the words "I Like" and the other column with the words "I Don't Like." It may be quite interesting to you how your list turns out as you consider yourself in the middle of the educational processes of *Walden Two.*

4. Should a token economy be used in a "normative" classroom? Again, use your teacher's notebook. Make two columns, with one headed up "Advantages" the other "Disadvantages." You might, for example, begin by listing under the advantages column something like "a clearly detailed way to maintain behavioral control," and over under the disadvantages column "kids learn for tokens, rather than personal growth occurring." See how many of the advantages and disadvantages you can list in these columns with reference to the use of token economy in a normative classroom.

Want to Know More?

B. F. Skinner, *About Behaviorism* (New York: Knopf, 1974). This is an up-to-date, highly readable overview of Skinner's behaviorism.

——————. *Beyond Freedom and Dignity* (New York: Alfred Knopf, 1971). A detailed plan for change that challenges many of Western man's most sacred ideals and personal freedoms.

——————. *Cumulative Record: A Selection of Papers,* 3d ed. (New York: Appleton Century Crofts, 1972). Representative articles from various stages of Skinner's career.

——————. *Science and Human Behavior* (New York: Macmillan, 1953). One of Skinner's earliest books setting forth his point of view.

——————. *Walden Two* (New York: Macmillan, 1948). A setting forth of Skinner's ideal managed community and how it would work.

Francis Schaeffer, *Back to Freedom and Dignity* (Downers Grove, Ill.: InterVarsity, 1972). A reply in Christian terms to B. F. Skinner.

Albert Bandura, *Social Learning Theory* (Englewood Cliffs, New Jersey: Prentice Hall, 1977). The social learning theorist sets forth his point of view.

E. L. Thorndike, *Educational Psychology: Briefer Course* (New York: Teachers College, Columbia U., 1921).

Robert Bolles, *Learning Theory* (New York: Holt, Rinehart, and Winston, 1975). A review of major learning theories.

6

The Cognitive-Discovery Approach

CONTENTS

	PAGE
Key Terms	157
That's Debatable!	158
Foresight	160
Background Influences	160
Gestalt Psychology	160
Current Concepts	163
Jean Piaget: Active learner—processing of stimuli	163
Jerome Bruner: Cognitive structure	165
David Ausubel: Meaningful learning of material	166
Concepts in the Classroom	167
Criticisms and Critique	173
Hindsight	177
Chalkboard Challenges	179
Want to Know More?	181

KEY TERMS

Advance organizer (Ausubel)
    Introductory material, usually general and abstract, providing students ahead of time with some structure to aid them in learning the specific information to follow

Cognition
: The process of thinking and knowing: we receive raw, sensory information and transform, elaborate, store, recover, and use it

Cognitive structure
: The student's grasp of the overall pattern of a field of study, emphasizing relationships within the field

Discovery learning (Bruner)
: The process of confronting children with problems and urging them to seek solutions independently and through group discussions, rather than presenting carefully prearranged and sequenced materials

Field theory (Lewin)
: Stresses that psychological fields are changed in similar fashion as magnetic fields, as positive and negative forces act on human beings

Gestalt psychology
: An approach developed largely by early German psychologists, which concentrates on the significance of perceiving stimulation in patterns and relationships

Insight
: For the cognitive theorists, the perception of new relationships by an individual

Life space (Lewin)
: All the elements within the child's psychological environment that influence the child's behavior at a given moment

Mediator
: A word or idea, produced by the student himself, to tie together two words, ideas, or objects in a way to make sense out of them

Valence (field theory)
: A positive or negative force influencing an individual's behavior

Vector (field theory)
: The direction of a valence influencing an individual's behavior

That's Debatable!

WHICH IS BETTER: THE NEW OR THE OLD MATHEMATICS?

In recent decades, a great deal of controversy has arisen concerning the teaching of mathematics in our nation's schools. The controversy has centered on what has come to be called the "new math" versus the "old math."

At the heart of the new math the basic idea is that children should work from the concrete and familiar toward the abstract and unfamiliar.[1] This basic idea at the core of the new math is congruent with what we have called in this chapter the discovery-learning model.

---

1. H. Ballew, "The New Mathematics as Scapegoat," *The Elementary School Journal* 78 (1977):107-9.

The Cognitive-Discovery Approach

The thrust of the new math came from the fact that in 1957, the Soviet Union orbited the first artificial satellite into space. This frightened many Americans because they believed that the Russians were far ahead of us in technology, particularly space technology, and that we had to engage in some "crash" programs to catch up. So it was that early in 1958, a group of mathematicians meeting at the Massachusetts Institute of Technology developed the first version of what now is called the new math.

In general, the new math really brought some very sophisticated language related particularly to algebra and other higher mathematics down to the elementary school level. Such terms as *set theory, associative properties,* and *commutative properties* of fields and groups were brought into the teaching-learning process. Sets of objects that children already understood (such as a set of blocks, or a set of dishes) were used to relate the familiar concrete world of the children to the world of mathematics.

Arguments against the new math. Parents soon came to be highly critical of the new math with comments such as, "My son or my daughter sure isn't learning to count or compute like I used to." Parents and other critics pointed to the results of the scholastic aptitude tests, where the mathematics scores dropped constantly from the early 1960s right to the present day. Proponents of the back-to-basics movement, like Frank E. Ambruster, opposed the new math.

Arguments for the new math.

> Skills in computation are no longer essential. Calculating machines are available to everyone with prices that are in keeping with their needs. The introduction of the calculating machine has increased rather than lessened the importance of learning arithmetic. The need for extreme skill and speed, however, in obtaining answers has disappeared. The demand is now for the understanding of arithmetic, its logical structure, and its practical application.[3]

The above quotation appeared in *The Arithmetic Teacher* in 1957. Still others (the National Council of Supervisors of Mathematics) want to identify the types of skills required for modern living and then formulate programs that will help children to acquire those needed skills.

Where do you think the cognitive theorists such as Piaget, Bruner, and Ausubel might stand in relation to the old and the new math? Why?

---

3. A. Schott, "New Tools, Methods for Their Use, and a New Curriculum," *The Arithmetic Teacher* (1957):204. Used by permission.

Foresight

Since the 1920s and 30s (John Watson's heyday) many—probably the majority—of American psychologists have endorsed the behavioristic (environmentalists, S-R, associationism) approach to learning and behavior. But a substantial number of American psychologists have pointed to the limitations, inconsistencies, and dangers of the behavioristic approach. Many of these have been attracted to ideas developed and proposed by Europeans—ideas markedly different from those contained in the behavioristic approach.

Europeans have been more inclined to speculate about nonobservable and unmeasurable forms of behavior than Americans. Sigmund Freud, for example, proposed that our behavior is influenced by unobservable and unconscious influences. And Jean Piaget's great driving force was to analyze children's thinking (what goes on *within,* rather than outwardly observable behavior only).

The Gestalt psychology with its emphasis on subjective perceptions of patterns and relationships, Wolfgang Kohler's experiments in insight learning, Kurt Lewin's field theory with its changing psychological forces influencing the individual's perception and behavior, combined with Piaget's emphasis on cognitive operations, Jerome Bruner's cognitive structure and discovery learning, and David Ausubel's meaningful learning of materials, gradually emerged into what is referred to as the *cognitive-discovery* approach. This approach is so-called because it stresses thinking (cognition) and the ways we discover solutions through insights and perceiving of relationships.

In this chapter, we shall look at the background influences, current concepts, and classroom practices of the cognitive-discovery approach, and consider carefully its advantages and disadvantages.

Background Influences

GESTALT PSYCHOLOGY

This view refers to the tendency of people to perceive stimulation in good "form." The German word *gestalt* is usually translated as "form" or "pattern" and emphasizes that many things are learned when we arrange ideas into a total "configuration," or pattern. Gestalt psychology, originating with the early German psychologists, stresses the significance of relationships in learning. Several principles emerge from the Gestalt background influence.

Meaningful configurations are greater than the mere sum of their parts. Biehler contrasts this approach to learning with that of the behaviorists:

> The S-R theorist conceives of learning as the adding together of associations. The separate frames of a program, for example, are combined in sequence to lead to the terminal behavior. The Gestalt view calls attention to the fact that many things are

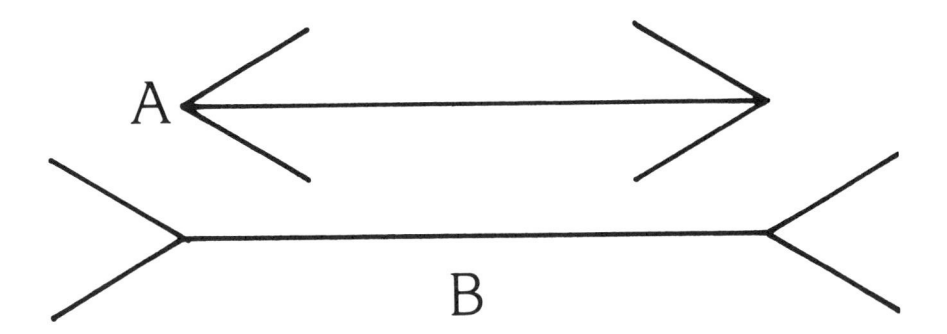

The horizontal lines shown here are the same length. But the arrangement of the diagonal lines causes line B to appear longer than line A.

Fig. 6.1

learned when we arrange ideas into patterns. We do not just *add together impressions;* we grasp how they are related.[4]

Perceptions are influenced by the arrangement of stimuli. The early German psychologists were highly preoccupied with perception—how we interpret the things we observe, sense, or think about. They demonstrated that our perceptions are definitely influenced by the manner in which items are arranged.

For example, in figure 6.1, while the horizontal lines are of exactly identical length, the manner in which the lines are arranged causes line *b* to appear longer than line *a*. Although subjective, organized perception is the basis for learning, our perceptions are influenced by the arrangement of the stimuli.

Learning is by insight, by perceiving relationships. Gestalt psychologist Wolfgang Kohler conducted a now-famous experiment in 1916, which demonstrates this principle.

A chimpanzee named Sultan was confined in a cage containing some short sticks, among other objects. As Sultan manipulated the various objects, he discovered he could use a stick to pull objects to him. Kohler decided one day to put a banana and a long stick outside the cage, and he placed them at such distances

---

4. Robert F. Biehler, *Psychology Applied to Teaching* (Boston: Houghton Mifflin, 1978), pp. 292-93. Used by permission.

as to prevent Sultan from reaching them with his arm. However, the stick was closer than the banana. After Sultan tried to reach the banana with a short stick already in his cage, but failed, he stomped to a corner of his cage. Kohler tells us that as Sultan sat looking at the two sticks and the banana, he suddenly jumped up, ran over and picked up the short stick, raked in the long stick, and then used the long stick to pull the banana to his cage. Kohler suggested that Sultan suddenly perceived the relationships between the two sticks and the banana, and that this is the kind of perception—insight—by which learning takes place. Insight develops from the sudden organization of perceptions.

Learning is a matter of reorganizing the individual's world of experience. This is a principle developed by those who have come to be known as "field" theorists. Primary among these theorists was Kurt Lewin. To help understand Lewin's approach, think of a magnetic field surrounding two bar magnets (fig. 6.2). Physicists have demonstrated (and probably you have observed or done it yourself) the concept of field forces by placing bar magnets on a table, surrounded by iron filings. The filings arrange themselves in precise, differentiated and symmetrical patterns around the magnets. If you change the position of the magnets, the patterns change in the magnetic field. Lewin developed a similar system for depicting how human behavior is influenced by positive and negative forces (valences) and by the direction of those forces (vectors). Past experiences and current interests, indeed all the elements within the child's psychological environment, make up what Lewin calls the "life space" of an individual. Any slight

Magnetic Fields Simulate Psychological Fields

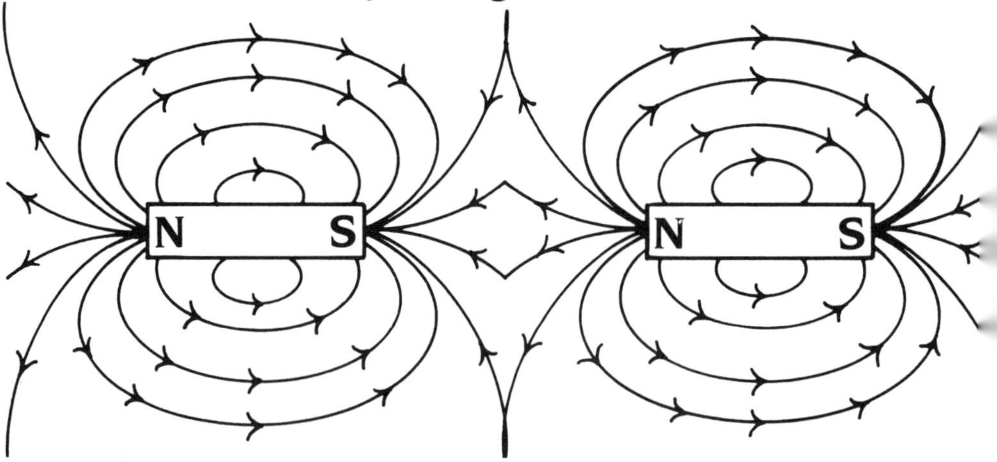

These magnetic fields represent the positive and negative forces operating in the psychological fields of human beings. If the magnets' positions are changed, the magnetic fields would be changed.

Fig. 6.2

The Cognitive-Discovery Approach

alteration in the situation may cause the "field" to change, and the individual to perceive things differently. The individual reorganizes the world of his experiences, perceives the pattern of his field differently.

Think for example of a three-year-old girl whom we shall call Lucy, who accompanies her parents to the beach for the first time. The ocean waves come crashing in, and Lucy is quite frightened of them since this is her first experience at the seashore. Her parents are lying a little distance away on the sand, and Lucy begins playing with a large beach ball. The beach ball goes into the ocean surf about the distance of six inches to a foot, and Lucy begins to cry loudly because she thinks the beach ball is lost. She runs to her father, and her father gets up and comes and retrieves the ball from the ocean water and gives it back to Lucy. The father goes back to lie down, and it is only a matter of seconds before the ball is once again in the surf. Lucy comes crying again to her parents. This time her mother goes and retrieves the beach ball for her. This particular kind of incident is repeated several times, and gradually, with the assurance of her parents, Lucy realizes that the beach ball is not going to be lost in the ocean and that the ocean will not hurt her if she stands on the sand at the very edge and reaches for the ball. So she is able to retrieve the ball herself after a number of experiences of this kind. What has happened is that she has reorganized the world of her experiences into a different kind of pattern of relationships. She now is able to see the ocean surf in a different relationship to the other parts of her experience and to herself, thus enabling her to have learned to get the beach ball from the surf.

The life space concept calls attention to the fact it is not always possible to draw conclusions simply by observing outer behavior, which the behaviorist maintains as his privilege. To understand Lucy's behavior, one would need to understand how she was subjectively changing her perceptions of the ocean, the ball, and herself, reorganizing her "field" in a way which enabled her to get the beach ball on her own.

CURRENT CONCEPTS

We have chosen Jean Piaget, Jerome Bruner, and David Ausubel as current representative theorists for the cognitive-discovery approach.

JEAN PIAGET: ACTIVE LEARNER—PROCESSING OF STIMULI

In chapter 3 we discussed Piaget's theory of cognitive development. You may wish to go back and refresh your memory concerning that theory. In the present context, we are stressing his concept of the student as an active learner-processor of stimuli. Piaget urges us to assume that children have a built-in desire to learn. This is so because children are pretty much forced (Piaget calls it "impelled") to make some kind of sense of their experiences and observations. They have to "put the world together" somehow.

Another important emphasis from Piaget is his conviction that learning is its

Gallery of Greats

Jean Piaget
"What children understand reality to be is never a copy of what was received by their sense impressions; it is always transformed by their own ways of knowing."*

Few would question that Jean Piaget, the world-famous Swiss cognitive theorist, is the most influential psychologist of our generation. We lost a magnificent mind when Piaget died in September of 1980 at the age of eighty-four. It is hard to imagine this man with a white fringe of hair, dark suit and vest, and meerschaum pipe held tight in his

---

*David Elkind, "Piaget," *Human Behavior* 4 (August 1975). Copyright ©1975 by *Human Behavior* Magazine. Reprinted by permission of the publisher.

teeth as a boy of ten, when his article on an albino sparrow gained attention from adult scholars. He earned his doctorate in science from the University of Neuchatel at the age of twenty-one and went on to write more than thirty books in his long, productive career. Piaget's approach to his work was to set up a problem for a year or more and then intensively pursue it. He usually met with his colleagues and graduate students once a week, and from those sessions new insight and ideas emerged to stimulate still further investigation. Elkind tells how Piaget at the end of each year gathered up all the data collected and moved to a secret hideaway in the mountains. There he took long walks, cooked loose omelets, reflected, and wrote material for his books in longhand on square pieces of paper.

own reward. A child who actively processes the stimuli in his or her environment so that it makes sense will not need a reward, because the child's own satisfaction will be all the reward he or she needs.

There is a clear difference here from the behavioristic approach. Instead of asking a child to complete a certain number of tasks or sequences, and then giving him a reward, Piaget maintains that as the child actively processes his interactions with objects, events, and people, he forms his own conceptions (schemes) of how it all fits together, and this is a self-rewarding process. Cognitive theorists believe such conceptions are much more meaningful and permanent than those ideas or sets of ideas acquired by learning (perhaps only memorizing?) material painstakingly arranged by other people. The child should be encouraged, according to Piaget, in his active processing of stimuli, and this will be a self-rewarding experience.

JEROME BRUNER: COGNITIVE STRUCTURE

Jerome Bruner, formerly of Harvard and now of Oxford University, is a leading spokesman for the cognitive-discovery approach. He has been an outspoken critic of the S-R view, and developed an alternative approach to programmed learning known as "discovery" learning, which we will assess later in this chapter.

Bruner stresses the importance of what he calls "cognitive structure." His interest in the cognitive-discovery approach began in 1951 when he studied carefully and wrote an article on perception.[5] This was followed by one on thinking in conjunction with Goodnow and Austin in 1956.[6] Bruner's experience as director of the important Woods Hole Conference on Education in 1959 (called to improve science education in public schools as a result of Sputnik) resulted in the summarizing of the major outcomes of that conference in a book called *The Process of Education* in 1960.[7] Many view this work as a classic statement on education.

5. Jerome S. Bruner, "Personal Dynamics and the Process of Perceiving" in R.R. Blake and G.V. Ramsey, eds., *Perception: An Approach to Personality* (New York: Ronald, 1951), pp. 121-47.
6. J.S. Bruner, J.J. Goodnow, and G.A. Austin, *A Study of Thinking* (New York: Wiley, 1956).
7. Jerome Bruner, *The Process of Education* (New York: Vintage, 1960).

Bruner became interested in the teaching-learning process in general, and his interest resulted in two further books: *Toward a Theory of a Instruction* in 1966 and *The Relevance of Education* in 1971.[8] All of these books are considered highly significant to the cognitive-discovery approach.

In *The Process of Education,* Bruner stresses students should be assisted in grasping the overall structure of a given field of study. (Biehler notes that *structure* is still another way to translate *Gestalt,* and it emphasizes the significance of relationships).[9] Bruner contends that if you help a student grasp the total pattern of a field of study, retention is more probable, the learning of principles which can be used in varying situations in the future will occur, and a good foundation is laid for mastering more difficult information.

According to Bruner, too much learning occurs as step-by-step study of statements or formulas to be reproduced by the student on cue, but which the student is not able to use outside the classroom. Using programmed materials makes students too dependent upon others, and causes students to conceive of learning as something they do to get a reward.

DAVID AUSUBEL: MEANINGFUL LEARNING OF MATERIAL

Ausubel has been concerned with the meaningful learning of verbal material.[10] While viewed primarily as a cognitive psychologist, he advises teachers not to be tied to any one point of view because of the complexity of learning.

Because so much of our formal learning is linguistic (language centered), Ausubel focuses on meaningful verbal instruction and learning. A simple principle is stressed; tell the student how to perform a physical act, and don't let the individual "plunge in and drown." A lot of time can be saved, insists Ausubel, if we understand that the human brain functions in such a way that the student learns by just being told clearly. Otherwise, bad habits or wrong directions may have to be corrected, as in learning to swim, for example.

According to Ausubel, several principles or understandings will facilitate the learning of new materials: advance organizers, progressive differentiation, integrative reconciliation, and consolidation.

Advance organizers are introductory materials providing students ahead of time with some structure for learning more detailed information to follow. Usually, the advance organizers will relate the new material to something the student already knows to help make it meaningful.

---

8. Jerome Bruner, *Toward a Theory of Instruction* (Cambridge: Harvard U., Belknap, 1966). Also Jerome Bruner, *The Relevance of Education* (New York: Norton, 1971).
9. Biehler, p. 294.
10. David Ausubel, *Educational Psychology: A Cognitive View* (New York: Holt, Rinehart, and Winston, 1968). Also David Ausubel, "Enhancing the Acquisition of Knowledge," in National Society for the Study of Education, 79th Yearbook, Part I: *Toward Adolescence: the Middle School Years* (Chicago: U. of Chicago, 1980).

The Cognitive-Discovery Approach

Progressive differentiation consists of moving from general explanations to increasingly detailed accounts of differences and distinctions.

Integrative reconciliation consists of careful, precise indications of ways in which the new material is similar or dissimilar to what the student already knows.

Consolidation is a commonsense matter of insisting on mastery of basic knowledge before going on to new items to be learned.

Overall, Ausubel asserts that meaningful learning is a matter of *subsuming* new information into the currently existing body of knowledge of the individual. The cognitive structure has been established by previous learning, and the new ideas are subsumed into the existing structure. Ausubel advises teachers at all levels to check carefully with their students as to the meaningfulness of their present understanding. Most of all, relate the new material in some relevant manner to the student's present state of understanding, because the learning of meaningful material is much less likely to be interfered with or interrupted than the learning either of nonsense or rote materials.

To summarize current concepts of the cognitive-discovery approach, before proceeding to apply them to the classroom, the basic principles would be: (1) The perceiving of relationships by the learner—*insight*—is the manner in which meaningful learning occurs. (2) The learner is an active processor of the objects, events, and people—the stimuli in his environment; when he works the matter through and makes sense out of it, it is self-rewarding. (3) The provision of cognitive structure for a field of learning substantially aids in retention, application of principles, and the laying of the foundation for learning more difficult information. (4) It is important to find ways of making the subsumption of new ideas into the existing cognitive structure of the student a meaningful process; it is therefore important for the teacher to check frequently with the current understanding of her students in relation to the materials being discussed.

CONCEPTS IN THE CLASSROOM

Biehler summarizes the educational application of the cognitive-discovery view in the following manner:

> Cognitive psychologists assume that behavior is significantly influenced by the way organisms perceive things and that learning occurs when an individual gains insight or becomes aware of a new pattern of relationships. Those who endorse this view urge teachers to arrange learning situations to help students develop new insights. Because every student will have had different previous experiences, it is impossible to predict exactly how any particular individual will develop insight. Consequently, cognitive-discovery psychologists reason that learning situations should be arranged to allow for a variety in the ways students gain understanding.[11]

---

11. Biehler, p. 298. Used by permission.

THE TEACHER

For Piaget, the teacher becomes *the arranger of opportunities* permitting children to interact with their environment. Children learn best when they discover things for themselves. The teacher, therefore, should arrange the teaching-learning process in such a manner as to encourage students to interact with people, places, things, and ideas. The teacher should suggest lines of inquiry, keep the students within the "ball park," encouraging self-discovered learning.

This process would vary depending upon the cognitive stage of the child. For example, if the child is in the "concrete operational" stage (approximately seven to eleven years of age), it is important for the teacher to encourage a great deal of hands-on experience and give the child frequent opportunities to explain how he sees things from his point of view. Exercises need to be used which permit students to explain their answers. If the student gives a wrong answer, he should be asked to explain his reasoning in a nonthreatening way. Group or class discussions can be tied in carefully to a film just shown, or a chapter just read, giving students ample opportunities to make sense out of the material.

For Bruner, the teacher becomes *the presenter of materials* which stimulate problem solving and discovery learning. (Discovery learning is discussed under methodology later in this chapter.) It is important for the teacher to call attention to and take advantage of cognitive structure. In whatever materials the teacher presents, she should stress relationships among the various items or segments. The teacher needs to provide necessary background information through reading, presentation, films, or in other manners. The teacher can structure a discussion by posing a specific question, presenting a controversial issue, or asking students to pick a topic for discussion. It is helpful to ask questions that stimulate students to analyze, evaluate, probe, synthesize, and use logic carefully as they seek solutions.

For Ausubel, the teacher is seen as *an organizer of materials* for meaningful learning. It is important for the teacher to present materials clearly, along with instructions. By using advance organizers, either written or verbal, the instructor helps the students to "get the big picture," making it more likely they will learn further details accurately. If the student can know what the ballpark looks like, and what the rules are, he will be more able to do what is necessary to run the bases or carry the football or whatever may be appropriate to the ballpark "structure."

Ausubel also makes a distinction between reception and discovery learning. In *reception* learning, all of the content to be learned is presented to the learner in final form. In *discovery* learning the individual has to discover what it is to be learned before the material can be incorporated into the student's existing knowledge and structures. We can summarize Ausubel's differences here by pointing out that it is probable that the mastery of many of our traditional school subjects can be obtained through reception learning, for they lend themselves to the presentation of detailed materials in final form. However, many of our day-to-day problems of living, which cannot so easily be detailed in final form ahead of time, probably are solved through discovery learning.

The Cognitive-Discovery Approach

Another important aspect of Ausubel's approach would involve the understanding that both reception and discovery learning can be pursued in either a meaningful or a rote manner. We cannot assume that reception learning is always rote, and that discovery learning is invariably meaningful. Insight, figure 6.3, elaborates on this point and also clarifies further Ausubel's approach to the learning of information.

Insight: Ausubel's Approach to Learning

Many teachers of public speaking and homiletics have given the age-old advice to their students: "tell them what you are going to tell them; then tell them; then tell them what you have told them." In a very real sense, Ausubel's approach to learning follows that advice.

1. Lessons should start with advance organizers to help students see the overall structure of the knowledge to be learned.

2. Point out concepts which are new or which are central to the discussion, and be sure to briefly lay out the learning objectives.

3. Present the material in small, logically organized steps, arranged so that the material is easy to follow.

4. Have frequent communication from your students as they learn, so that you will be able to evaluate whether each step in the sequence is mastered before you move on to another part of the material.

5. Summarize the materials when the lesson is completed, using main points, and tying in the material so that it holds together and makes some sense for the students.

6. Be sure to follow the lesson with review questions, assignments which cause the students to probe, or to engage in activities that will get the material in understandings put into their own words. It is important for the students to be able to apply what they have learned, or to extend it in some way into practical areas that have meaning for them.

This bringing of the materials to the students in a carefully arranged and sequenced fashion is termed by Ausubel "reception learning." His approach does place most of the burden for ensuring learning on the teacher's shoulders. So while his approach is cognitive, rather than behavioristic, nevertheless the teacher becomes more central in the teaching-learning process than is the teacher in either Piaget's or Bruner's conceptions.

Fig. 6.3

For Ausubel, the successful teacher will find ways to help the students subsume (tie in) new ideas into their cognitive structures. To accomplish this, the teacher must strive to relate new ideas in some meaningful way to what the student already knows, and in this process check frequently with the student's understanding of the material at hand or already learned.

THE STUDENT

For all cognitive theorists, the student is viewed as *an active, self-motivated information-processor*. The student is one who *can* reason and *wants* to reason in order to make sense out of his or her situation or set of circumstances. "Help the student investigate and find satisfying answers" is the motto of the cognitive-discovery approach in the teaching-learning process. This is at odds with the behavioristic approach, which sees the student as passive and neutral, whose behavior can be modified by conditioning and modeling. In the cognitive-discovery approach, the student is an inquiring, reasoning person who should be encouraged to solve problems and discover solutions for himself. The student's life space (or psychological field) contains constantly shifting patterns, and this field becomes very much involved in the push and pull of the teaching-learning process.

THE CURRICULUM

The curriculum from the cognitive-discovery point of view, whatever the particular materials, needs to reflect at least three basic characteristics: (1) rather than being carefully prearranged and sequenced (as in programmed learning) it should provide ample opportunities for the student to explore and interact with people, places, ideas, and objects in his or her environment. We should note here that the one exception to this would be Ausubel, with his reception learning, where he believes the material should be presented to the student in final form. (2) Along with providing cognitive structure (i.e., an overall view of the field or segment of study), it should be so arranged to provide the students opportunities for discovery learning, and encouraging the student in problem solving. (3) It should be arranged so as to provide advance organizers to help the student see ahead, and meaningful contact points to help the student relate the new materials to what is already known. Instructions need to be given clearly to prevent the development of bad learning habits or erroneous conclusions. Of course, the child's learning level must be considered as curriculum materials are developed, presented, and used.

THE METHODOLOGY

The methodology of the cognitive-discovery approach is multifaceted, but always geared to the student as a curious, motivated-to-learn, wanting-to-make-sense-out-of-my-situation processor of information and problem solver. Rewards are not necessary since the student finds satisfaction in resolving whatever the

The Cognitive-Discovery Approach

Insight: Four Features of a Theory of Instruction (Bruner)

Jerome Bruner, in his book *Toward a Theory of Instruction*, outlines four features he believes should be included within a theory of instruction.

1. The theory should make clear and precise the conditions that predispose individuals toward learning. Bruner believes that the experiences that contribute to an individual's desire to learn, not only in general but to master particular material, should be stated clearly.

2. Bruner emphasizes that a theory of instruction should describe precisely the ways in which a particular body of knowledge is to be structured so that the students can most readily grasp it and use it. Bruner believes that no matter what the content of the learning, if that material is organized appropriately, it can be presented in a form that is simple enough for any learner to understand.

3. The third feature in a theory of instruction, according to Bruner, should be a detailing of the most effective sequences by which that material may be presented, taking into account the learner, the difficulty of the material, and the logical sequencing of its ideas and content. Bruner's thrust is that the process of instruction should increase the learner's ability to "grasp, transform, and transfer what he is learning."

4. Bruner stresses that a theory of instruction should make very clear the nature and the pacing of the rewards. Bruner stresses that, ideally, educators should move gradually from rewarding extrinsically to helping the student to grasp intrinsic satisfaction. This is, of course, a part of the cognitive view, that the student should become less dependent upon the teacher's rewarding behavior and more dependent upon his own intrinsic satisfaction in seeking to work through to a solution of the learning task itself. Bruner stresses in this regard that the timing of when rewards are given is of great importance. If the student gets rewarded too early, he may not be interested in exploring any further. If he gets rewarded or feedback comes too late, it may not really be relevant or helpful. In effect, Bruner is adding what we might term "sensitive timing" to the already great responsibility of the teacher in the teaching-learning process.

Jerome Bruner, *Toward a Theory of Instruction* (Cambridge: Harvard U., Belknap). Copyright ©1966 by the President and Fellows of Harvard College. Reprinted by permission.

Fig. 6.4

> **Insight: Four Advantages of Discovery Learning (Bruner)**
>
> In an article "The Act of Discovery," in the *Harvard Educational Review*, Bruner sets forth four advantages for discovery learning.
>
> *First*, it greatly helps memory retention, because a student is required to organize information in a meaningful way.
>
> *Second*, discovery learning aids greatly the "intellectual potency" by making available to the students information that they can readily use for their problem solving.
>
> *Third*, it makes the child less dependent upon motivation outside himself, because it concentrates upon the satisfactions that are built in to the discovery process itself.
>
> *Fourth*, discovery learning promotes the acquiring by the child of the skills and procedures needed to engage in discovery learning in the future.
>
> It is readily apparent that this model for learning is almost totally different from a highly structured and finely detailed model offered by behavioristic psychologists such as B. F. Skinner, who believe in and promote the techniques of programmed instruction.
>
> J. S. Bruner, "The Act of Discovery," *Harvard Educational Review* 31 (1961): 21-32.

Fig. 6.5

situation might be. Since the child *wants* to learn, the methodology should take full advantage of that desire, and techniques should encourage the self-discovery kind of learning, in which the child develops his own—rather than ready-made—conceptions.

Bruner's "discovery approach" to learning has become a source of great controversy, but illustrates in a representative fashion the methodology of the discovery concept in the classroom. One of his first efforts was teaching geography to a fifth-grade class. He gave his students blank outline maps and asked them to try to figure out the locations of major cities, railroads, highways, and other items. The students were not permitted to use books or maps or other reference materials. They had to struggle through on their own by asking questions.[12]

Some years later, Bruner developed his MACOS (man: a course of study) materials for teaching elementary school social studies. He describes his course this way:

---

12. Bruner, *The Process of Education*.

The Cognitive-Discovery Approach

> The content of the course is man; his nature as a species, the forces that shaped and continue to shape his humanity. Three questions recur throughout; what is human about human beings? how do they get that way? how can they be made more so?[13]

In discovering answers to these questions, several techniques are needed. (1) *Contrast is emphasized.* (Human beings are contrasted with animals, the prehistoric man is contrasted with modern man, etc.) (2) *Informed guessing is stimulated.* (Asking students to make an "educated guess" as to how, for example, Eskimos know which breathing holes to use in hunting seals under the ice. Students are then shown a film to demonstrate the actual process.) (3) *Participation is encouraged.* (Arranging for students to function in various capacities in relation to the situation being studied, to experience what it might be like.) (4) *Awareness is raised.* (Students are asked to focus consciously and deliberately on how they are seeking to solve the problems.)

These and other techniques are used for purposes of helping to induce discovery by the student of his or her own answers. At the same time, the student hopefully learns how to go about solving problems and working them through to solutions. Bruner summarizes his own approach to the teaching-learning process as follows:

> To instruct someone in a discipline is not a matter of getting him to commit results to mind. Rather, it is to teach him to participate in the process that makes possible the establishment of knowledge. We teach a subject not to produce little living libraries on the subject, but rather to get a student to think mathematically for himself, to consider matters as an historian does, to take part in the process of knowledge getting. Knowledge is a process, not a product.[14]

THE SOCIAL FUNCTION OF THE SCHOOL

From the cognitive-discovery viewpoint, the social function of the school is rather simply stated; learner interest should be stimulated so they can actively process information, and learn how to become problem solvers as they confront the variable circumstances of the real world.

CRITICISMS AND CRITIQUE

REGARDING SELF-MOTIVATION

It is a fair criticism of this approach to observe that not every child is

---
13. Bruner, *Toward a Theory of Instruction,* p. 74. Copyright © 1966 by the President and Fellows of Harvard College. Reprinted by permission. Chapter 4 describes MACOS and how these materials were used to develop a "discovery approach."
14. Ibid.

motivated highly enough to function well in a relatively low-structure situation of discovery-learning. Many children, for a variety of reasons, simply are not motivated to function in this kind of teaching-learning environment. The results may be that not only does this kind of child get left behind academically, but suffers damage to his or her self esteem because "I can't come up with any discoveries on my own." Indeed, it appears very likely that a small handful of children will come up with most of the discoveries in a class, and this sets up an obviously unhealthy situation leading to much student frustration.

REGARDING THE EFFICIENCY OF DISCOVERY LEARNING

Students living in a high-tech society need to know a multitude of things. Critics point out that it is impossible for students to learn through discovery processes even a fraction of what they need to know. Further, critics emphasize it is foolish to ignore most of what has been discovered by many thinkers over a long period of time.

Even the most competent teachers using this method admit that real discovery is rare, is certainly inefficient and time-consuming, and if used *exclusively,* the student probably could not learn enough to be ready to enter college. A very straightforward question appears fair to ask of the cognitive-discovery proponents; what is wrong with a well-informed teacher telling someone else clearly and enthusiastically what she has learned?

REGARDING PARENTAL VIEWS OF THE TEACHER

Another source of criticism is the reaction of parents when it appears the children are not learning as much as they should. With the discovery method, measurable achievements such as parents like to see in their children will tend to be lacking. Where are the arithmetic papers, the spelling words, the artwork, the English themes, and all of the other projects parents expect to see? Although criticism of teachers by parents is going to occur under almost any system, under the discovery approach it becomes excessive. Parents believe their children are getting cheated, are not learning what they should, and criticisms can become highly vocal and disrupting to the teaching-learning process.

REGARDING BEHAVIORISTS' CRITICISM

Representative of the behaviorist's criticism of the cognitive-discovery approach is a rather complete critique set forth by B. F. Skinner in *The Technology of Teaching*.

> [This method] is designed to absolve the teacher from a sense of failure by making instruction unnecessary. The teacher arranges the environment in which discovery is to take place, he suggests lines of inquiry, he keeps the student within bounds. The important thing is that he should tell him nothing.

> **Insight: Language in Cognitive Learning**
>
> Most of the cognitive theorists emphasize the unique abilities of human beings, and stress the conceptual aspects of learning over its behavioristic components. One of the most important unique abilities is that of using language to "mediate" learning. The word *mediate* can be thought of as building bridges between two thoughts, a thought and an object, or any of two or more items to relate them in some kind of meaningful fashion.
>
> While language abilities are present from birth, most cognitive theorists would agree that they do not become efficient tools for learning until around the age of six. Therefore, even cognitive theorists usually do not emphasize the importance of language in studying the learning process in very young children.
>
> However, once language abilities have developed to the point where they can mediate learning (e.g., "watch very carefully to see what happens when I add this extra weight on this side of the scale") cognitive theorists then concentrate heavily on the use of language in the learning process. The efficiency of learning is greatly enhanced by the use of language, according to cognitive theorists. For example, if teaching an animal to go and bring an article back in order to get a reward, many trials and errors are usually necessary over a period of time. In using language as a direct verbal instruction tool with human beings, a teacher can say to the student, "Max, please bring the globe from the back of the room up to the front, so that we can look to see where Key West is actually located." Language, according to the cognitive theorists, helps to make learning easier and more efficient.

Fig. 6.6

The human organism does, of course, learn without being taught. It is a good thing that this is so, and it would no doubt be a good thing if more could be learned in that way. Students are naturally interested in what they learn by themselves because they would not learn if they were not, and for the same reason they are more likely to remember what they learned in that way. There are reinforcing elements of surprise and accomplishment and personal discovery which are welcome alternatives to traditional aversive consequences. But discovery is no solution to the problems of education. A culture is no stronger than its capacity to transmit itself. It must impart an accumulation of skills, of knowledge, and social and ethical practices to its new members. The institution of education is designed to serve this purpose. It is quite impossible for the student to discover for himself any substantial part of the wisdom of his culture, and no philosophy of education really proposes that he should. Great thinkers build upon the past, they do not waste time in rediscovering it. It is dangerous to suggest to the student that it is beneath his dignity to learn what others already know, that there is something ignoble (and even destructive of rational powers) in memorizing facts, codes, formulae or passages from literary works, and to be admired he must think in original ways. It is equally dangerous to forego teaching important facts and principles in order to give the student a chance to discover them for himself. Only a teacher who is unaware of his effects on his students can believe that children actually discover mathematics, that (as one teacher has written) in group discussions they "can and do figure out all the relationships, facts, and procedures that comprise a full program in math."

Still another difficulty arises when it is necessary to teach a whole class. How are a few good students to be prevented from making all the discoveries?[15]

IMPLICATIONS FOR THE TEACHING-LEARNING PROCESS

From a Christian standpoint, it appears fair to make at least the following comments. Since teaching is a calling under God, and parents as well as classroom teachers are charged with bringing up children in the "nurture and admonition of the Lord," this calling must be carried out in a highly responsible fashion and in accordance with biblical values.

Since the child is created in the image of God, the Christian, with prayer and dedicated determination, sets out by the grace of God to help that child develop his God-given potential to the fullest extent. But the child's nature includes sin. So the question becomes, for the Christian, How can I best help the child fulfill his God-given potential and at the same time, deal with his sinful nature?

The sin is dealt with in only one way; the child must be taught that he is a sinner and only by accepting Jesus Christ as Savior can he be saved, reconciled through Christ to the God who created him and loves him.

At the same time, God expects us to develop our potential (talents). Parents and teachers have a major role to play in the process, obviously. The very best in the teaching-learning process, sifted through the standards of the Bible, must be the Christian educator's goal. Several guidelines emerge. (1) Our time, effort, and money within Christian education are matters of stewardship under God. This does not imply necessarily that the teaching-learning process must operate like a highly efficient business—that is, where efficiency is the dominant force. Rather, understanding the nature of the teaching-learning process, we want to operate as efficiently as possible while helping children reach Christian goals, which have been based on the Bible. (2) Our efforts in the teaching-learning process ought to contain the very best from research and practice. There are many areas—especially in the early years of learning—where memorization is highly valuable. There are situations in which discovery-learning techniques may be used effectively. (For example, what do you think you would do in Joseph's place, if you were in

---

15. B.F. Skinner, "Why Teachers Fail," in *The Technology of Teaching* (New York: Appleton Century Crofts, 1968), pp. 109-11. This material first appeared in *Saturday Review,* 16 October 1965. ©1965 Saturday Review magazine. Reprinted by permission.

The Cognitive-Discovery Approach

authority in Egypt, and your brothers, after treating you so badly, came seeking food?) Cognitive structure is very helpful in laying out a certain period of history, or a particular set of philosophic beliefs, or a book of the Bible, or the entire Bible, or other fields or units of study. (3) Our efforts, while involving real pain, joy, and struggle, must always be resolved in light of biblical principles. For example, MACOS has been highly criticized by many Christians because of the personal/social values it teaches which Christians view as unacceptable. We need to understand clearly what a program such as MACOS teaches, and then carefully appraise it in light of biblical values, which must always be the standard and take priority.

The cognitive-discovery approach, while having a number of values that can be incorporated into a Christian approach, nevertheless appears to this writer not to be practical if used *exclusively* in the classroom. However, if used selectively, as a part of the teacher's repertoire of resources, and with a deliberate awareness of biblical principles, it can help to enrich the Christian teaching-learning process enormously. For the Christian especially, it becomes a matter of using God-given cognitive processing capabilities to their maximum effectiveness for the glory of God.

HINDSIGHT

While behaviorists treat learners as passive organisms and concentrate upon how they can be manipulated by the environment, Gestaltists believe that organisms are active processors of the stimuli in their environment. Behavior results primarily from internal motivation rather than external stimulation. Perception—at the heart of learning and understanding—is subjective. Gestaltists insist we do *not* take the isolated bits of information and gradually through successive approximation and reward, impose meaning on them. Rather, the active perception itself includes the meaningful patterns by which we interpret the stimuli. Perception, as demonstrated by the Gestaltists, is both *subjective and organized*. The tendency of people to perceive stimulation in *good form* causes objective input to be distorted. The same stimuli can be perceived by different persons in totally different ways, depending upon the beliefs, values, and perspectives of the perceiver.

Learning through insight is also demonstrated by the Gestaltists. Complex learning can take place through insight—the sudden organization of perceptions into a new, meaningful configuration. This contrasts with the behaviorists' slow, trial-and-error, building of predictable behavior through rewarding correct responses. Learning can occur in one trial, and without the use of reinforcement. Gestalt psychology laid the foundation for the development of the cognitive approach to learning.

The cognitive approach to learning defines learning as the active restructuring of perceptions and concepts, rather than passive responses to external stimuli

Insight: Techniques of Open Education

In his book *Open Education: Promise and Problems,* Vito Perrone discusses in detail the techniques of open education. While there are many variations in the application of this approach, Perrone points out that most open education would feature the following characteristics:

1. *Many activities.* Usually, one will find many activities occurring simultaneously, and children move from one activity to another. The classroom atmosphere is very informal, and students are not only permitted, but encouraged to talk to each other.

2. *Several learning areas.* Usually, an open classroom will be divided into several separate learning areas. Many things can be used to divided these areas, from planters to portable screens or bookcases. Perrone points out that in the elementary school, the more common areas would be those for language arts, reading, science, math, drama, art, and various crafts.

3. *Cooperative planning sessions.* At the very beginning of a school day, students usually are encouraged to go around to the various learning areas and look at the materials and see what may be there for that day. After an hour or thereabouts, the teacher will get the pupils together for a cooperative planning session. During this session the teacher may highlight certain activities or materials that are available in the different learning centers, and the students are encouraged to share with others particular items of interest they may have found that were interesting to them. Each student is then asked to work out a particular personal plan for that day, and the plan usually includes times when the student will meet with the teacher to ask questions, discuss items, get any particular help that may be needed. Sometimes this may be an individual meeting with the student, sometimes in small groups, depending upon the needs in the plan. And then at the end of the day, the students are asked to come together again to share highlights of what they have learned or found particularly of interest during the day.

4. *Individualized planning.* One thing that perhaps is misunderstood about open education is that it probably involves more work on the part of the teacher than does the traditional type of classroom. The teacher concentrates on what each pupil is learning. During the day the teacher will move around from learning area to learning area to observe what the students are doing, to chat with them, and the teacher keeps individual records of the progress of the children. Most teachers I have known in this situation are very careful to write at least some item of

> note in the child's record each day. The teacher will also take great pains to collect log books or other records the children have kept for themselves regarding their activities, and any work that they may have done in relation to those activities, such as reports that they might have prepared.
>
> Although most open education techniques have been developed and used at the elementary school level, the advocate of open education would probably stress that the child in the concrete stage of operations has the need for this direct experience and then interaction with peers in the manner which open education provides. When students get to a stage of formal operations, this kind of experience is not so much needed, since they can sort out and reverse logic and try different approaches to problems, even in a traditional class setting as they listen and participate. However, it may be a good idea to bring into the teaching-learning process at the secondary school level, for example, frequent opportunities for students to engage in individualized kinds of projects. This encourages a change of pace in the classroom activities, and encourages as well greater student initiative.
>
> Adapted from *Open Education: Promise and Problems* by Vito Perrone, Fastback #3. ©1972 Phi Delta Kappa Educational Foundation. Used by permission.

Fig. 6.7

and use of reinforcers. The cognitive theorists emphasize the unique abilities of human beings related to the ability to conceptualize, and stress the importance of the use of language (after the age of six when it has developed sufficiently) to mediate learning. Because people are active information processors, they are continually discovering new concepts, facts, and insights.

In this chapter, we looked at Piaget, Bruner, and Ausubel as representatives of the current cognitive-discovery approach, applied their theories to the classroom, and critiqued them in the light of other approaches and the Christian perspective.

CHALKBOARD CHALLENGES

1. Using Piaget's suggestion that conceptions children develop on their own are idiosyncratic (egocentric), be sure to give your students lots of opportunities to explain how they see things.

2. Take advantage of structure (Bruner, Ausubel). (1) Explain what "structure" means clearly to your students. The idea of the ballpark as an *overall structure* in which many detailed events will occur during a game is one helpful approach,

one to which the majority of your students can relate in a meaningful way.

(2) Stress relationships in the material or ideas you present. Give students handles they can grasp. For example, if you are studying the causes of the Civil War, a brief film or slide presentation of related events in that war could provide the structure needed to stimulate detailed discussion of causes of the war.

(3) Use advance organizers. For the Civil War, a provocative question such as, "Which side, North or South, was really justified in its point of view?" As students begin to share opinions, you have helped them focus in on an increasingly detailed discussion of the causes of the Civil War.

(4) Have students break up into two discussion groups—one taking the point of view of the North, the other of the South. Be sure to provide them clear resources to which they can turn as they work their way through to their conclusions. You may wish to have each member of each group spend five minutes jotting down their ideas (thus helping to provide their own structure) regarding their own point of view before discussing as a group.

(5) After first reactions, probe for further insights if needed. Try to get each member of the group involved in evaluating, analyzing, questioning, and synthesizing.

(6) A concluding event may be a good idea. For example, the concluding event for the Civil War discussion might be a class notebook, in which causes of the Civil War are listed with supporting evidence, as arrived at by the class discussions. This puts a "final touch" on structure, and provides satisfying closure for the work of the students.

3. Make use of the techniques of open education (see Insight, fig. 6.7). If you decide to try this method, be very sure you are thoroughly prepared ahead of time. The open classroom is the logical outgrowth of the discovery approach to learning. In your teacher's notebook, head one column "Advantages of the Open Classroom" and the other "Disadvantages of the Open Classroom." After experimenting, with the blessing of your school principal, with this approach you should have a substantial number of items in both lists based on your firsthand experience.

4. Choose a particular segment or unit of study. Think through carefully how a behaviorist would conduct the teaching-learning process, and then how a cognitive-discovery teacher would conduct the teaching-learning process. Project what you think the results might be in each case. Then, try out the two approaches with two different classes, or with two groups within the same class. Evaluate the results carefully, including achievement scores, attitudes, amount of participation, intensity of participation, and similar factors. Record the results in your teacher's notebook, including suggestions as to which approach you believe is more effective for you, and the strengths and weaknesses of each.

5. If you are a Christian, you may find it helpful to do a careful evaluation of the cognitive-discovery approach, using such Christian perspectives as stewardship of time, energies, talents; the role of the teacher, the sinful nature of human

The Cognitive-Discovery Approach

beings, and other similar Christian principles. This can be a very useful, practical kind of procedure for each of the approaches to the teaching-learning process. You may find that by developing a core list of Christian perspectives, and using that list with reference to each approach, you will clarify substantially the elements of your own approach and why you are using those elements in your approach.

WANT TO KNOW MORE?

GESTALT PSYCHOLOGY?

Read chapter 23 of Edwin G. Boring, *A History of Experimental Psychology*, 2d ed. (Englewood Cliffs, N.J.: Prentice-Hall, 1950).

FIELD THEORY?

A good summary of Lewin's theory appears in chapter 15, "Behavior and Development as a Function of the Total Situation," *Manual of Child Psychology*, ed. Leonard Carmichael, 2d ed.

AUSUBEL

Advance organizers and other aspects are explained in *Educational Psychology: A Cognitive View* (New York: Holt, Rinehart, and Winston, 1968). A broader explanation of Ausubel's ideas can be found in "Enhancing the Acquisition of Knowledge," in National Society for Study of Education, 79th Yearbook, Part I: *Toward Adolescence: The Middle School Years,* (Chicago: U. of Chicago, 1980).

BRUNER

Read his book *Toward a Theory of Instruction* (Cambridge: Harvard U., Belknap, 1966). In particular, chapter 4 relates how MACOS materials were used to develop a discovery approach.

SMALL GROUP DISCUSSION

A good analysis of small group discussion, from the cognitive-discovery point of view, is offered in Herbert A. Thelen's *Classroom Grouping for Teachability* (1967).

OPEN EDUCATION

In Britain—read *Children and Their Primary Schools* (1967)—also called The Plowden Report.

In America—read Alvin Hertzberg and Edward Stone, *Schools Are for*

Children: An American Approach to the Open Classroom (1971). The Center for Teaching and Learning at the University of North Dakota has been the center of the open education movement in the United States. *Open Education: A Promise and Problems* was written by the dean of that center, Vito Perrone.

7

The Humanistic Approach

CONTENTS

	PAGE
Key Terms	183
That's Debatable!	184
Foresight	185
Background Influences	187
Progressivism: Principles Adopted by Humanists	187
Existentialism: Uniqueness of the Individual Child	188
Humanistic Psychologists: Actualizing Potential	189
Romantic Critics: Human Health and Growth in Schools	189
Current Concepts	191
Concepts in the Classroom	195
Criticisms and Critique	199
Hindsight	202
Chalkboard Challenges	203
Want to Know More?	204

KEY TERMS

Affective
    Refers to the way people feel about their perceptions of themselves, other people, and their world

Confluent
    The merging of the affective and cognitive domains in the teaching-learning process

Open schedules
: Schedules not "hemmed in" by tight time requirements, so as to permit students more flexibility in learning

Prosocial behavior
: Refers to "actions that are intended to aid or benefit another person or groups of people without the actor's anticipation of external rewards. Such actions often entail some cost, self sacrifice, or risk on the part of the actor"[1]

Role playing
: The assumption of the role of another person by a student for the purpose of helping the student appreciate the feelings and perspectives of the person whose role has been assumed

Simulation games
: Games in which the students seek to find solutions; in the process they are caused to clarify values, perspectives, and feelings

Self-actualization
: The process of discovering, becoming, and developing one's real self and one's full potential

Third-force psychology
: Associated with Abraham Maslow and emphasizing "the human being in the process of becoming," rather than as reactive (S-R) or reactive-in-depth (Freud)

Values clarification
: The process of looking intensively at one's values so as to become keenly aware of them, thus helping the individual to be able to choose more intelligently

THAT'S DEBATABLE!

ARE THE CRITICS JUSTIFIED?

Presented here is a representative summary of criticisms brought against humanistic education. Are they justified?

1. The humanistic view is not based on empirical data.

2. The achievements of Summerhill's students are unimpressive, and graduates are not atypically creative. (Using Summerhill as an example of humanistic education.)

3. Humanistic teachers tend to look down on other educators who do not share their views. (They are not as genuine, sensitive, etc.)

4. The values clarification process has weaknesses. Students will not

---

1. P. Mussen and Eisenberg-Berg, *The Roots of Caring, Sharing, and Helping* (San Francisco: Freeman, 1977), pp. 3-4.

The Humanistic Approach

automatically choose prosocial values when left to their own value processing. Children in the concrete stage of development are not capable of abstract thought necessary to the formulation of value systems. Secondary students (newly arrived "formal" thinkers) tend to overlook realities.

5. Humanistic educators may function as untrained psychotherapists in psychotherapeutic sessions, and this can be harmful, even dangerous. Teachers have no right, according to some critics, to probe the child's mind and unleash the child's emotions.

6. Humanists who have really tried to teach by building up strong personal emotional ties with each of their students, have not been able to sustain this approach for more than a year or two.[2]

7. Humanists reject up front the one element considered absolutely essential by those who believe in the Judeo-Christian approach: the necessity of a vital personal relationship with God, and the implications of that relationship for the teaching-learning process.

Foresight

How does the student feel about his or her perceptions of self, others, and his world? This represents the key question for the humanistic approach to education.

Humanistic psychologists and educators would agree with the cognitive-discovery theorists on the importance of perception and awareness in the learning process and as determinants of behavior. But the special emphasis of the humanists in education is the impact of the schooling process on the *affective* (emotional level) development of students.

Likewise, humanists emphasize the development of the *human potential* of each person. Some contend that this focus in the learning process helps the overall school performance. Others are not certain, but argue that the development of personal potential is, in itself, a significant objective of schooling, whether or not it helps cognitive performance or mastery of various subjects.

In this chapter, you will discover the major background influences leading to educational humanism, probe carefully the humanistic principles, and focus on how they translate into classroom practices.

We continue to emphasize the philosopher-clinician model; it is highly important to understand the beliefs and principles for each point of view, in order to understand their recommendations for and practices in the clinical setting of the school. You are urged to examine critically and carefully your own outlook as you think about and discuss these approaches to learning. Consciously build up your own "repertoire resources," and consider thoughtfully how you will put them into practice in the classroom.

---
2. See Herbert Kohl, *Thirty-six Children* (New York: New American Library, 1967) and George Dennison, *The Lives of Children* (New York: Random House, 1969).

GALLERY OF GREATS

Jean Jacques Rousseau
"Everything is good as it comes from the hands of the Maker—but degenerates once it gets into the hands of man."

Jean Jacques Rousseau (1712-1778), the Swiss-French moral philosopher, was born in Geneva. His mother died at his birth. Rousseau was abandoned by his father when he was ten and tried his hand at a multitude of activities including music, poetry, drama, engraving, and the priesthood. He was converted from Protestantism to Catholicism, and then back to Protestantism. Although badly treated by many people, Rousseau was in many ways his own worst enemy. He died of apoplexy (brain hemorrhage) in France, July 2, 1778.

Among the most famous of his works, Emile stands out with reference to

The Humanistic Approach

education. Rousseau stressed the child's need for self-expression and urged mothers to spend time with their children, surround them with affection, breast-feed them instead of handing them over to a wet nurse, and allow them to grow to health outdoors rather than "civilized pallor at home." A child's religious education should begin late, after the child is already familiar with the wonders of the universe. Emile's deistic doctrine caused the Roman Catholic church to order him arrested. "Man is good by nature, and must discover that nature, and follow it." Rousseau's philosophy was a forerunner of the educational humanism of today, with its thrust of actualizing one's potential.

BACKGROUND INFLUENCES

Four major influences have fed into what has come to be called "educational humanism": progressivism, existentialism, humanistic psychologists, and Romantic critics.[3]

PROGRESSIVISM: PRINCIPLES ADOPTED BY HUMANISTS

As an educational theory, the progressive influence needs to be seen as a reaction against traditional education, which had emphasized formal methods, disciplined minds, and literary classics in the teaching-learning process.[4] To understand progressivism and therefore humanism (since humanism adopted or absorbed most of the progessive ideas) it is important to examine briefly three significant intellectual forces that fed progressive education: John Dewey, Sigmund Freud, and Jean Jacques Rousseau.

John Dewey: no absolutes. Dewey's pragmatic position gave no place to such concepts as *Absolute Truth*. Man lives in a constantly changing world of experience, and what works today may not be sufficient for tomorrow. Therefore, truth is relative. And the same principle holds for values—there are no absolute principles on which we can lean. The individual acts upon his environment, undergoes the consequences of that action, and from this "transaction" develops truth, values, and reality. Dewey's pragmatism removed the absolutes from philosophy and education.

Sigmund Freud: no repression. The psychoanalytical theory of Freud targeted the repression of painful or unauthorized feelings or thoughts as the major source of mental illness. The opposite of repression is self-expression for children, and a more open learning environment in which students can express themselves (their instinctive impulses in Freudian terms). This is seen as "creative self-expression." Repression was wrong.

Jean Jacques Rousseau: no adult interference. Rousseau's Emile (1762) gave the

---

3. George Knight, *Philosophy and Education: An Introduction in Christian Perspective* (Berrien Springs, Mich.: Andrews U., 1980), p. 98. Adaptations used by permission.
4. Ibid., p. 91.

clear message that adult interference with children's goals or what they learned was a major cause of children's problems. The child with his needs and interests should be placed at the center of the learning process, and interference from adults should be minimal.

These intellectual influences were developed into progressive educational theory by a group of educators which included Carleton Washburne, William H. Kilpatrick, Harold Rugg, George S. Counts, Boyd H. Bode, and John L. Childs.

> Through their influence and energy, progressive education became the dominant theory in American education from the 1920s to the 1950s. By the middle of the 1950s, when progressive education lost its organizational existence, it had changed the face of American education. Perhaps part of the reason for its organizational demise was the fact that many of its ideas and programs had been adopted to some extent by the public school establishment, and the progressives had therefore less to "holler" about. On the other hand, it should be recognized that progressive theory in its completeness never did become the major practice in the vast majority of school systems—what was adopted were bits and pieces of progressivism that were amalgamated with other educational methods in an eclectic fashion.[5]

The progressivists condemned the authoritarian teacher, reliance on textbooks, memorization of factual data, the isolation of education from reality within the school walls, and the use of fear or physical punishment as a form of discipline.[6]

Many of the progressive principles found their way into the educational humanism of the late 1960s and early 1970s, and continue to this very day. These principles include: (1) the child is the central focal point of the school; (2) the child is an active learner and will learn if adult authorities do not insist on imposing their wills upon the child; (3) there can be no authoritative teaching of a particular, "essential" body of knowledge, so the teacher becomes a guide and fellow traveler with the students; (4) the school should reflect the realities of the larger society, rather than being a preparation for "reality to come" after graduation; (5) the teaching-learning process should teach problem solving, rather than particular bodies of subject matter; and (6) cooperation rather than competition, and a democratic atmosphere, should characterize the school (student government, free discussion of ideas, and faculty and students planning together for learning).

Again, it is significant to note that organized progressivism came to an end in the 1950s but the humanists adopted most of the progressive principles. Progressive education is a most important contribution to educational humanism.

EXISTENTIALISM: UNIQUENESS OF THE INDIVIDUAL CHILD

Existentialism added a second kind of impetus to the development of educational humanism. Existentialism begins with a statement, "I exist," and

---

5. Ibid., p. 92.
6. Allan C. Ornstein, *An Introduction to Foundations of Education* (Chicago: Rand McNally, 1977), p. 204.

generally describes the individual as having been thrust into existence without any vote. Therefore, the individual must struggle on his own to find meaning for life. As a result, the uniqueness of the individual student and the need to search for personal meaning in that individual's existence have been intensified in the humanistic approach.

HUMANISTIC PSYCHOLOGISTS: ACTUALIZING POTENTIAL

A third background factor contributing to educational humanism has been the third-force psychology. Whereas Abraham Maslow, Carl Rogers, and Arthur Combs develop their approaches with their own variations, they agree on the need for facilitating the self-actualization of the student. The student has "human potential," and it is of highest priority that he or she discover what that potential is and develop it to become a fully functioning human being.

Maslow believed that too much of psychological study had focused on animals and mentally ill people. He chose to focus on those whom he believed were mentally extremely healthy (self-actualized) and developed principles and practices based on them. He emphasized the possibilities of growth for the individual, rather than their control by environmental forces, or by unconscious repressions. For Carl Rogers's approach to learning, please see Insight, figure 7.1. Combs summarizes his perspectives on humanistic learning as follows:

> To understand humans ... it is necessary to understand the behaver's perceptual world, how things seem from his point of view. This calls for a different understanding of what the "facts" are that we need in order to deal with human behavior; it is not the external facts that are important in understanding behavior, but the meaning of the facts to the behaver.[7]

These humanistic psychologists emphasize the importance of understanding the individual's perceptions, needs, and emotions, not just to help them achieve in school, but far more importantly, to help them fulfill their basic human potential.

ROMANTIC CRITICS: HUMAN HEALTH AND GROWTH IN SCHOOLS

The fourth background influence helping to fuel educational humanism has been a group of writers who have come to be called the "romantic critics." Knight describes them superbly:

> These writers arose in the social turbulence of the 1960s in a storm of protest over the repressive, mindless, and inhuman conditions of modern schools. They argued that schools had become intellectually deadening and psychologically destructive because they were preoccupied with order and punishment, rather than human health and growth. . . . the literature produced by the romantic critics was

---

7. Arthur Combs, R. Blume, and H. Wass, *The Professional Education of Teachers*, 2d ed. (Boston: Allyn and Bacon, 1974), p. 15. Used by permission.

> **Insight: Carl Rogers—Humanistic Learning Principles**
>
> As one of the best known and most widely read enthusiasts for humanistic education, it is important to understand how Rogers views the teaching-learning process.
>   1. Human beings have a natural potentiality for learning.
>   2. Significant learning takes place when the subject matter is perceived by the student as having relevance for his or her own purposes.
>   3. Learning then involves a change in self-organization—in the perception of one's self.
>   4. Those learnings that are threatening to the self are more easily perceived and assimilated when the external threats are at a minimum.
>   5. When threat to the self is low, experience can be perceived in differentiated fashion, and learning can proceed.
>   6. Much significant learning is acquired through doing.
>   7. Learning is facilitated when the student participates responsibly in the learning process.
>   8. Self-initiated learning that involves the whole person of the learner—feelings as well as intellect—is the most lasting and pervasive.
>   9. Independence, creativity, and self-reliance are all facilitated when self-criticism and self-evaluation are basic, and evaluation by others is of secondary importance.
>   10. The most socially useful learning in the modern world is the learning of the process of learning, a continuing openness to experience, an incorporation into one's self of the process of change.
>
> Adapted from: Carl Rogers, *Freedom to Learn* (Columbus, Ohio: Merrill, 1969).

Fig. 7.1

eloquent, poignant, and popular. As such, it made a large impact on the reading public and developed a grass roots sympathy for experimentation in humanistic education.[8]

Representative of the kind of literature published by these critics are: *How Children Fail* by John Holt; *Thirty-six Children,* by Herbert Kohl; *Death at an Early Age,* by Jonathan Kozol; *The Lives of Children,* by George Dennison.[9]

---

8. Knight, p. 98.
9. John Holt, *How Children Fail* (New York: Pitman, 1964); Jonathan Kozol, *Death at an Early Age* (Boston: Houghton Mifflin, 1967).

The Humanistic Approach 191

As noted by Knight, the major thrust of these writings was to influence popular opinion toward the humanistic approach to education—a most significant accomplishment.

CURRENT CONCEPTS

You will remember that many of the progressivists' principles were either adopted or absorbed by the educational humanists from the mid 1950s on. Here, then, we will highlight current concepts that have been fed by progressivism and the other background influences.

CREATE LEARNING SITUATIONS IN WHICH CHILDREN WILL BE
FREE FROM FEAR OF FAILURE, COMPETITION, AND SEVERE DISCIPLINE

Humanists feel that in most schools the fear of failure is too much a part of the school climate; that competition which becomes intense really hinders good learning rather than promoting it, for most children; that severe discipline is not needed if children are seen as naturally good, curious, and eager to learn.

Holt incorporated this view of human nature and how it affects the learning environment in his book *Freedom and Beyond:*

> ... that children are by nature smart, energetic, curious, eager to learn, and good at learning; and that they do not need to be bribed and bullied to learn; that they learn best when they are happy, active, involved, and interested in what they are doing; and that they learn least, or not at all, when they are bored, threatened, humiliated, and frightened.[10]

CREATE TEACHING-LEARNING RELATIONSHIPS CHARACTERIZED BY MUTUAL TRUST

Humanists criticize the traditional schools for typically operating as though the teacher and the students were enemies. They feel such an atmosphere is destructive of individual growth and creativity. Energy spent in the adversary relationship needs to be channeled toward positive growth based on trust between the teacher and the students.

Many humanists believe that schools must be concerned about teaching prosocial behavior. If you look back at the key terms, you will refresh in your thinking the definition of prosocial behavior by Mussen and Eisenberg-Berg.[11] Essential to their definition is the encouragement of students to become more considerate and helpful toward others, without looking for rewards, and making self-sacrifices, if needed, to benefit others. Just how to teach children these kinds of behavior has not been determined by hard empirical evidence, but many believe

---

10. John Holt, *Freedom and Beyond* (New York: Dell, Laurel, 1972), p. 10. Used by permission of author.
11. Mussen and Eisenberg-Berg.

that relationships in the teaching-learning process permeated by feelings of trust and security form the atmosphere in which prosocial behavior can best be learned.

CENTER ON SELF-ACTUALIZATION RATHER THAN
MASTERY OF INFORMATION AND SUBJECT MATTER

A climate of openness, with emphasis on the use of the student's imagination, fantasy, an awareness of his or her own feelings, should be encouraged.

Simpson and Gray, in their book *Humanistic Education: An Interpretation*, present a review of curricula that can be used to help self-actualization (through bringing affect into the curriculum).[12] It is not our purpose to review all of these here, but rather mention one for the elementary level and one for the secondary level as examples.

"The magic circle," recommended for elementary level (based on the human development program developed by Harold Bessel and Uvaldo Palomares) encourages students to increase *awareness* of themselves by discussing with other students such things as: something I like about you, something I like about myself, and similar themes. Good and Brophy describe clearly the intended effects of this particular exercise:

> [It] allows students to hear positive comments about themselves from other students. They also have a chance to experience the feeling of someone's saying something nice about them, and a chance to verbalize that feeling. Through such activities students can progressively consider the events that keep them from doing as they wish, and look at their behavior as it affects other people.[13]

For the secondary level, an activity known as Trumpet March: Diagram and Details (developed by the Center for Humanistic Education at the University of Massachusetts) gives students the opportunity to gain information and evaluate it in relationship to themselves and others. Figure 7.2 gives a brief excerpt of the steps and questions found in the Trumpet March.[14]

THE TEACHING-LEARNING PROCESS SHOULD BE CONFLUENT:
THE COGNITIVE AND AFFECTIVE SHOULD MERGE

Brown was one of the first to use the term "confluent education" in 1971, and has recommended a number of activities for engaging in confluent education in the areas of English and social studies.[15] Many humanists believe, however, that

---

12. E. Simpson and M. Gray, *Humanistic Education: An Interpretation* (Cambridge, Mass.: Ballenger, 1976).
13. Thomas Good and Jere E. Brophy, *Educational Psychology: A Realistic Approach*, 2d ed. (New York: Holt, Rinehart, and Winston, 1980), pp. 294-95. Used by permission.
14. Simpson and Gray, pp. 89-91.
15. G. Brown, *Human Teaching for Human Learning* (New York: Viking, 1971).

> **Excerpts of Steps and Questions Contained in Trumpet March**
>
> Step One: Experience Confrontations
> > I interact with a situation that generates data; and
>
> Step Two: Inventory Responses
> > How did I respond? What was unique? What common?
> > > a. What did you just do? Describe your behavior.
> > > b. What were you aware of?
>
> Step Three: Recognize Patterns
> > What is typical of me?
> > > a. Did you do anything that surprised you?
>
> Step Four: Own Patterns
> > What function does this pattern serve for me?
> > > a. How does it serve you?
> > > b. How does your pattern make you feel good?
>
> Step Five: Consider Consequences
> > What does happen or could happen in my life because of this pattern?
>
> Step Six: Allow Alternatives
> > Will I allow myself any additional patterns of response?
> > > a. What are the first steps you could take to change?
>
> Step Seven: Choose
>
> From Thomas L. Good and Jere E. Brophy, *Educational Psychology: A Realistic Approach*, 2d ed. (New York: Holt, Rinehart, and Winston, 1980), p. 296, as excerpted from Simpson and Gray, 1976, pp. 89-91. Used by permission.

Fig. 7.2

confluent education must go beyond the feelings or reactions about subject matter. Although a proponent of Christian education, I have found it helpful to have students explore from time to time how they feel about the course, the way it is taught, what makes them want to come to class, and what makes them not want to come to class.

But beyond this, when students interview someone in the community or the college, or reflect on an experience unrelated to the subject matter per se, they frequently are surprised at how well they have done, or the particular direction of their experience, and they "almost grow in front of their own eyes," as one student expressed it on one occasion. (From the Christian viewpoint, this kind of growth experience and increase in self-awareness is made possible by the wisdom of the God who created us, and is always encouraged to be seen and used in that perspective.)

> **Insight: Becoming More Human**
>
> Humanists' interest in self-perceptions is not geared only to improving achievement in the classroom. Humanists emphasize the significance of understanding the student's point of view in order to help that student fulfill his or her basic potential. Good and Brophy cite the following quotation as one which captures some of the spirit of becoming more human:
>
>> If I had my life to live over, I would try to make more mistakes next time. I would relax, I would limber up, I would be crazier than I have been on this trip. I know very few things I'd take seriously anymore. I'd certainly be less hygienic. I would take more chances, I would take more trips, I would scale more mountains, I would swim more rivers, and I would watch more sunsets. I would eat more ice cream and fewer beans. I would have more actual troubles and fewer imaginary ones. You see . . . I was one of those people who lived prophylactically and sensibly, and sanely, hour after hour, and day after day. Oh, I've had my moments and if I had it to do all over again, I'd have many more of them. In fact I'd try not to have anything else, just moments, one after another instead of living so many years ahead of my day. I've been one of those people who never went anywhere without a thermometer, a hot water bottle, a gargle, a raincoat, and a parachute. If I had it to do all over again, I'd travel lighter, much lighter than I have. I would start barefoot earlier in the Spring and I'd stay that way later in the Fall. And I would ride more merry-go-rounds, and catch more gold rings, and greet more people, and pick more flowers, and dance more often. If I had it to do all over again—but you see, I don't.
>
> From Thomas L. Good and Jere E. Brophy, *Educational Psychology: A Realistic Approach*, 2d ed. (New York: Holt, Rinehart, and Winston, 1980), p. 285. Used by permission.

Fig. 7.3

EMPHASIS PLACED UPON SELF-EXPRESSION AND VALUES CLARIFICATION

Simon, Howe, and Kirschenbaum and numerous others have insisted that a part of the teaching-learning process must be the clarification of values by the student.[16] For example, one suggestion by Simon, Howe, and Kirschenbaum for helping students feel positive about themselves (Strategy 11) is that students move

16. S. Simon, L. Howe, and H. Kirschenbaum, *Values Clarification: A Handbook of Practical Strategies for Teachers and Students* (New York: Hart, 1972).

quickly around the room telling what they are proud of. In another suggestion (Strategy 62) they provide words and music so this can be done in the form of a song. Other exercises from various authors include situations in which value choices must be made, in order to help the student become aware of his valuing processes. In many of these, the teacher is asked to refrain from interjecting her values into the process. This has some possible serious disadvantages (see Criticisms and Critique, further along in this chapter).

The effort, however, is intended to encourage students to become people who are aware of their valuing processes and who will therefore, it is hoped, not make choices or decisions in a mechanical or unfeeling manner.

Concepts in the Classroom

THE TEACHER: FACILITATOR OF A WARM, NON-THREATENING LEARNING ENVIRONMENT CENTERED ON THE INTERESTS OF THE CHILD

There are at least two key elements involved here: the teacher is not to be an authority in the traditional sense of being a dispenser of certain essential information, but on the other hand, the teacher obviously possesses greater knowledge and has more life experience than her students.

The term *facilitator* combines these two key elements: the teacher who knows more and has had more experience than her students uses these advantages, not to pound facts into her pupils in an authoritarian manner, but rather to facilitate (make easier) their learning how to learn for themselves, so they can become self-sufficient adults in a constantly changing environment.

THE STUDENT: BASICALLY GOOD, CURIOUS, EAGER TO BECOME ACTIVELY INVOLVED IN THE TEACHING-LEARNING PROCESS

An essential question for any teacher (it appears to me at least) is to ask one's self constantly, Who are the students? What is their nature? For the humanists the answer is they are basically curious and eager to learn. All kinds of implications emanate from this answer. Some possible ones are: (1) If students are basically good, very little discipline is needed. (2) If I want students to learn how to learn for themselves, a flexible open classroom is best. (3) If a student is by nature curious and eager to learn, the motivation is already there. What I need to do is provide a variety of materials/experiences to facilitate the student's enriching of himself.

Our point here is only that from the clear answer to the questions above, will come much of the teacher's methodology in the teaching-learning process. It is also *crucial* in the maintenance of the teacher's own mental health to be very clear about the answer to these and similar questions, as we shall consider in a later chapter.

THE CURRICULUM: A VARIETY OF LEARNING MATERIALS,
USUALLY SET UP IN ACTIVITY CENTERS

Students can use, manipulate, or read materials as needed. This translates into what has come to be called the open classroom. But the open classroom ranges all the way from almost total "laissez-faire" (do as you please) to a rather carefully

---

Insight: The Humanistic Teacher

Who is the humanistic teacher? The responses to that question are apt to be as wide and varied as the number and diversity of individuals responding. But Patterson summarizes his answer to the question in terms of three significant dimensions which he believes are incorporated in one way or another by most of the writers who are seeking to define the humanistic teacher. These three dimensions are as follows:

1. *Humanistic teachers are genuine.* "He doesn't feel one thing and say another. He does not project blame for his feelings and reactions on to the students. He accepts responsibility for his own behavior."

2. *Humanistic teachers have respect for the child as a person.* "There is an acceptance of imperfections, mistakes, and errors, changes in mood and motivation, as aspects of being human. There is a confidence in the basic goodness of each individual, in the capacity of the individual to grow and to develop, to actualize his potentials in an appropriate environment."

3. *Humanistic teachers have empathic understanding.* This is understanding that goes beyond the ordinary types of information that a teacher might receive by looking at a student's record, or just through informally observing the students in the everyday teaching-learning process. Empathic understanding means that the teacher attempts to put himself in his student's place, and seeks to understand how the student might be perceiving and feeling his world at that moment.

Patterson and others point out that these are the ideals of humanistic teachers, and that constant encouragement is needed for teachers to develop these kinds of characteristics.

From C. H. Patterson, *Humanistic Education*, ©1973, pp. 103-4, 107. Adapted by permission of Prentice-Hall, Inc., Englewood Cliffs, N.J.

Fig. 7.4

The Humanistic Approach

structured daily/weekly program for students as they use the learning centers. In many respects, it is more energy consuming for the teacher in this kind of operation, where there are many individualized concerns to manage in relation to student progress, time for sharing individually, and similar details.

THE METHODOLOGY: FACILITATE COMMUNICATION AND PARTICIPATION; WORKING WITH INDIVIDUALS AND SMALL GROUPS

It is difficult to discuss in detail, in a limited space, the many outworkings of humanistic methodology. Insight, figure 7.4, will be helpful in summarizing the approach of the humanistic teacher. It is fair to state that any methodology that encourages the child to participate, communicate, and evaluate for himself, which helps the child to become a fully functioning human being, which facilitates the development of his human potential in a growth-oriented direction—is a methodology of which a humanist would approve.

THE SOCIAL FUNCTION OF THE SCHOOL: EDUCATION FOR DEMOCRACY

The aim is to facilitate the self-actualization of the individual so he or she becomes able to deal with the variable circumstances as a fully functioning human being. As illustrations of the diversity in which humanistic schools function, we shall look briefly at four "instructional formats" which have had rather widespread influence as alternatives to the more traditional approaches to the teaching-learning process.

Summerhill: A. S. Neill. In 1921, A. S. Neill, an English school teacher who had experienced difficulty in the public school system, established his own school and called it Summerhill. In 1960 he wrote a book by the same title describing his experiences over the forty years of the schools' existence.[17] For Neill, the child is "innately wise, and if left to himself without any adult interference, will develop as far as he is capable of developing."[18] If you show a child how to do something, you have robbed that child of the joy of discovering, and made him feel inferior, because he must depend on help from someone else.

Students were not forced to attend the lessons by the teacher at Summerhill but could be barred from future sessions by those who attended regularly if they so voted. Afternoons were free for everybody, faculty and students alike. Every Saturday night a grievance meeting was held, and everyone voted as to whether a particular complaint was justified or not. If it was justified, the individual involved might have to pay a fine or lose a privilege, in addition to refraining from the action. General school policies were determined at these meetings by faculty and students discussing together. Summerhill was a full-time boarding school, and thus in a

---

17. A.S. Neill, *Summerhill* (New York: Hart, 1960).
18. Ibid., p. 4.

sense a successful experiment; nevertheless, even most humanists would agree its policies and techniques would not be usable in an American public school.

The open classroom: Herbert Kohl.[19] The open classroom seeks to provide a schooling experience that does away with the inflexibility of the traditional classroom. It is decentralized, divided with clusters of desks in learning areas. A variety of learning materials available for students to read and use are provided. There is no rigid schedule. Teachers spend their time with individuals and small groups rather than with whole classes. The goal is to develop a learning community where students and teachers work and learn together.

Kohl describes the open curriculum as he sees it:

> The role of the teacher is not to control his pupils but rather to enable them to make choices and pursue what interests them. In an open classroom a pupil functions according to his sense of himself rather than what he is expected to be. It is not that the teacher should expect the same of all his pupils. On the contrary, the teacher must learn to perceive differences, but these should emerge from what actually happens in the classroom during the school year, and not from preconceptions.[20]

Schools without failure: William Glasser. This humanistic approach was proposed in 1975 by William Glasser, a psychologist, based on what he sees as ways to avoid two kinds of human failure: "failure in love and failure to achieve self worth."[21] Traditional schools have not provided the atmosphere in which these two needs can be met. The school must provide a warm, nonthreatening environment in which the need for love and self-worth can be met.

The free school movement: Jonathan Kozol. In 1972 a fourth humanistic proposal was made by Kozol, who felt deeply that the traditional school could not provide the appropriate conditions for learning because of the pressures upon it to be a baby-sitter and an indoctrinator.[22] The free school movement can therefore be seen as a revolt against the traditional public schools; a revolt by unhappy parents and teachers who did not want their children in an authoritarian system. Each of these schools is quite different, and most have not lasted very long. The idea, however, is to develop "free children"—by which is meant, children who will be nondependent, who will stand on their own with courage, and who will be able to deal adequately with a rapidly changing, complex society.

These four examples illustrate the variable proposals by humanistic educators to humanize schooling. Knight makes a point worth noting: most of these efforts have been aimed at the elementary level.[23]

---

19. Reprinted with permission from The New York Review of Books. Copyright © 1969 Herbert Kohl.
20. Ibid., p. 20.
21. William Glasser, *Schools Without Failure* (New York: Harper & Row, Perennial Library, 1975), p. 14.
22. Jonathan Kozol, *Free Schools* (Boston: Houghton Mifflin, 1972), p. 14.
23. Knight, p. 102.

CRITICISMS AND CRITIQUE

REGARDING VALUES CLARIFICATION

From a behaviorist's standpoint, values are considered as too nebulous to deal with, unless translated into specific behavioral responses, which can be measured. The ultimate value for the behaviorists would be the *survival* of the society, rather than individual values.

The cognitive-discovery theorist agrees with the importance of developing values, but even more important is the development of the child's cognitive, problem-solving abilities. It is obvious the cognitive-discovery and the humanistic approaches contain many areas of overlap.

The Christian theorist, committed to the Judeo-Christian ethic, insists on the values clarification process "going somewhere"—that genuine discussion among students is excellent, but that the role of the parent and teacher is to raise the child in "the nurture and admonition of the Lord." Therefore, if in a values clarification discussion a child decided it was OK to steal, the Christian teacher would find it necessary to interject his or her instruction to help the child think through that stealing violates one of the Ten Commandments and the New Testament teachings of Christ. It is important and fair to note that the Christian teacher does not do this as an evasion of the hard reality but to confront the hard reality with a Christian solution and seek to determine how it can work in that situation. Christians need to develop a solid educational approach to *Christian values clarification,* based on the Word of God, directed by the Holy Spirit, and applied to the hard realities of the world in which we live.

REGARDING THE JUSTIFICATION OF CLAIMS

While individualized education has proved useful in a number of ways for helping students master subject matter, the data for more favorable *affective* responses as a result of individualization are, at best, contradictory. The evidence is even less for prosocial gains.

Admittedly, individualization is difficult to define. Even so, the affective gains in individualized programs are not all that impressive, and do not appear to be better than the affective gains of students in "regular" classrooms.

Wright's study is representative in the comparisons of open and traditional classrooms.[24] He compared fifth-grade pupils from open and traditional classrooms on several items (socioeconomic status, ability, past achievement) and also their cognitive and affective outcomes. Results: students' affective outcomes, after two years in the school program, were the same in open and traditional classrooms; the students in the traditional classrooms, however, were superior on cognitive measures.

---

24. R.S. Wright, "The Affective and Cognitive Consequences of an Open Education Elementary School," *American Education Research Journal* 12 (1975):449-78.

> **Insight: Cognitive Versus Affective Goals**
>
> Research points to the fact that affective gains and cognitive gains do not necessarily happen at the same time. It is probably a healthy approach for a teacher to realize that she cannot be all things to all people, for there are simply just too many teaching tasks and concerns to keep up with.
>
> A large study of the relationship between affective and achievement growth in elementary and secondary schools conducted by Ligon and associates suggests that there is no clear relationship between affect and achievement.
>
>> Raising a child's self concept or improving his attitude towards school does not insure an increase in his achievement level. Compensatory education programs which claim that activities designed to improve a child's self-concept or attitude towards school will in turn improve the child's achievement, may be well advised either to address improvement in achievement more directly, or to set up affective objectives separate from achievement objectives.
>
> From G. Ligon, J. Hester, N. Baenen, and P. Matuszek, "A Study of the Relationship Between Affective and Achievement Measures" (paper presented at the annual meeting of the American Education Research Association, New York, April 1977).

Fig. 7.5

As Good and Brophy point out, students enrolled in open education programs do not consistently report more favorable affective responses than students in self-contained classrooms.[25]

Additionally, students in open classrooms usually score higher on anxiety scales—in other words, show a higher level of anxiety.

REGARDING THE NATURE OF THE STUDENT

The humanistic approach assumes the student is basically good, curious, eager to learn. The behaviorist disagrees, insisting that motivation to learn is an extrinsic matter, coming from environmental impact through contingency reinforcement.

The cognitive-discovery theorist agrees essentially with the humanist, but again insists that the *cognitive* development is of the *highest* importance. This point must be made, however. There is no guarantee that if the cognitive development

---

25. Good and Brophy, p. 293.

The Humanistic Approach

occurs, the affective development occurs as well, or vice versa. In fact, this is highly doubtful. Which, then, we must ask, is the most essential feature of the student's nature: the cognitive or the affective? At this point a real difference would arise between the cognitive-discovery theorists and the humanistic theorists.

The Christian finds himself in total disagreement with the humanistic view of human nature. "All have sinned, and come short of the glory of God" (Romans 3:23). The human being is created by God, in His image. Therefore he or she has potential. But that potential means nothing ultimately, if the individual is not redeemed through Jesus Christ. And discipline is required in order to help the child mature as a Christian.

REGARDING THE POSSIBILITY OF MISGUIDED THERAPY

A final note of caution must be made. In the small group or individual learning sessions, because of the intimate and personal sharing involved, sometimes intentionally and sometimes unintentionally, the sessions are in danger of becoming therapy sessions within the teaching-learning process. Troubled students begin to share their deepest needs, and empathetic teachers respond with every desire to help as fully as possible. It is a situation that can quickly turn into a misguided therapy session, with the teacher wanting to help, but untrained as a therapist. The teacher who chooses to use the humanistic approach would be well advised to explore and become aware ahead of time of the dangers involved in the situation, so as to prevent the teaching-learning process from turning into a misguided therapy process.

IMPLICATIONS FOR THE TEACHING-LEARNING PROCESS

Carl Rogers summarizes his point of view relative to what should occur in the classroom under the humanistic approach:

> The [learner must] be in contact with, be faced by, a real problem . . . instead of organizing lesson plans and lectures, the teacher concentrates on providing all kinds of relevant raw material for use by the students, together with clearly indicated channels by which the student can avail himself of these resources . . . [the teacher] does not set lesson tasks. He does not assign readings. He does not lecture or expound (unless the students ask him to). He does not evaluate and criticize unless the student wishes his judgment on a product. He does not give examinations. He does not set grades.[26]

Rogers's ideas emerged from seminar sessions where people eagerly pay to attend. What works for him in that setting might not work amidst the everyday

---

26. Carl Rogers, "Learning to Be Free," in Carl Rogers and Barry Stevens, eds., *Person to Person: The Problem Being Human* (Lafayette, Calif.: Real People Press, 1967).

routines of a public or private school classroom, where the teacher is under regulations and is with the students at least some part of every day for 180 days per year.

Arthur Combs has been more closely tied to everyday education practices through working with teachers and students, and makes some suggestions especially in regard to the characteristics of humanistic teachers, and how to put humanistic assumptions into practice in the classroom.[27] He emphasizes the need to feel adequate.

A volume highly regarded by humanistic enthusiasts is the *Humanistic Education Sourcebook,* compiled in 1975.[28] It contains a series of fifty-six articles, and provides ideas for teachers who desire to put humanistic education into practice in the classroom.

Perhaps one of the books containing the most specific implications for the humanistic classroom is the one by Howe and Howe, entitled: *Personalizing Education: Values Clarification and Beyond.*[29] A sampling of their chapter titles reveals a representative list of humanistic implications for the teaching-learning process:

Chapter 4: Developing a Climate of Acceptance, Trust, and Open Communication

Chapter 8: Helping Students Choose Their Values Freely, from Alternatives, After Weighing the Consequences

Chapter 12: Adapting Curriculum to Serve Student Interests, Needs, Concerns, Goals, and Values

Chapter 15: Goal Sheets and Learning Contracts: Facilitating Student Self-directed Learning

Chapter 16: Developing and Managing a Choice Centered Classroom

HINDSIGHT

Educational humanism developed from the amalgamation of four sources: progressivism, existentialism, the humanistic psychologists, and the romantic critics.

Both humanistic and cognitive psychologists agree there is danger of excessive regimentation and control, if the behavioristic approach is carried to the extreme. Humanists emphasize that emotions, feelings, self-fulfillment, and

---

27. A.W. Combs, *The Professional Education of Teachers* (Boston: Allyn & Bacon, 1974); A.W. Combs, "Humanistic Goals of Education," in Donald A. Read and Sidney B. Simon, eds., *Humanistic Education Sourcebook* (Englewood Cliffs, N.J.: Prentice-Hall, 1975), pp. 91-200; A.W. Combs, "The Personal Approach to Good Teaching" in Read and Simon, eds., *Humanistic Education Sourcebook,* pp. 249-61.
28. Read and Simon, eds., *Humanistic Education Sourcebook.*
29. Leland W. Howe and Mary Martha Howe, *Personalizing Education: Values Clarification and Beyond* (New York: Hart, 1975), pp. 5-6.

interpersonal trust need to be stressed along with cognitive development. Some humanistic educators argue teachers should merge thinking, feeling, and action, while other emphasize the techniques of values clarification.

The central principle of humanistic education is: let students have opportunities to make their own choices and decisions. Since each person has human *potential,* facilitate the development of that individual's potential into a fully functioning human being.

The critics of humanism have attacked this point of view from many angles, including such items as: their presentation of vague, unjustified propositions; the making of overly elaborate claims; and psychotherapy conducted by teachers untrained as psychotherapists.

Chalkboard Challenges

1. Children should be helped to understand the needs and interests of others who differ from them in SES (socioeconomic status), age, and other significant ways. For example, encourage children to talk with grandparents and report on how they feel about items selected for their report. Have an elderly person who is a community or church leader come in to the class to share with the children. At the secondary level, more specific interviews with elderly people can be assigned, and reports made. Or, an elderly leader may be glad to come to class and hold a "press conference," with students acting as reporters.

2. Think back over teachers you have had in your school years. Pick two or three who in your estimation were most "humanistic." Would you label them "good teachers"? If so, why? If not, why not? Were they successful also in teaching basic subject matter material? You may wish to record some of your thoughts on these matters in your teacher's notebook.

3. Aesthetic education is very important to many humanistic teachers. Their interest is not necessarily in improving the performance abilities of students, but in helping them become more aware and appreciative of the beauties in art, nature, music, architecture, and other areas. For example, show your students pictures of different kinds of architecture, or types of art, or let them listen to different types of music. When they say, "I like it," or, "I don't like it," ask them to share why with the class, or a small group within the class. From this kind of experience, a unit on the humanities could develop to help students define and refine their tastes. Even better, if possible, take your class on trips to museums, tours of homes representing various architecture, etc., and then have them share as suggested above.

4. Do you agree it is important to help children develop prosocial behavior? How would you go about encouraging your students to become more considerate, helping, and self-sacrificing toward others? One specific example might help to give you food for thought on this issue. Research suggests that prejudices toward specific individuals can be improved by student group work demanding shared

participation. Read *The Jigsaw Classroom,* by Aronson, et al., 1978, for techniques and curriculum topics you could use in the classroom for this purpose.[30] Then record other ideas in your teacher's notebook as to other techniques you might use to aid in facilitating prosocial behavior. What dangers, if any, do you see in using this kind of technique in the classroom?

WANT TO KNOW MORE?

CONTROL

If you want to know more about early discussion of the issue of control in the teaching-learning process read Carl R. Rogers and B. F. Skinner, "Some Issues Concerning the Control of Human Behavior," *Science* 124 (1956): pp. 1057-66.

AFFECTIVE TOPICS AND ISSUES

Read E. Simpson and M. Gray, *Humanistic Education: An Interpretation* (Cambridge, Mass.: Ballinger, 1976).

VALUES CLARIFICATION

Read S. Simon, L. Howe, and H. Kirschenbaum, *Values Clarification: A Handbook of Practical Strategies for Teachers and Students* (New York: Hart, 1972).

HUMANISTIC TECHNIQUES

Read Donald A. Read and Sidney B. Simon, eds. *Humanistic Education Sourcebook* (Englewood Cliffs, N.J.: Prentice-Hall, 1975).

---

30. E. Aronson, H. Blaney, C. Stephan, J. Sikes, and M. Snapp, *The Jigsaw Classroom* (Beverly Hills, Calif.: Sage, 1978).

8

The Christian Approach

CONTENTS

	PAGE
Key Terms	205
That's Debatable!	206
Foresight	206
Background Influences	207
Current Concepts	213
Concepts in the Classroom	218
Criticisms and Critique	221
Hindsight	223
Chalkboard Challenges	224
Want to Know More?	225

KEY TERMS

Consensus
    General agreement, even though there may be disagreement on some specifics

Enlightenment
    A movement which began in the seventeenth century in Europe and grew to vitally affect American outlook on life in the past sixty years; it celebrates the self-sufficiency and reason of man and looks with disdain on traditional views, especially those relating to God

Secular humanism
    An approach to life that makes man the measure of all things and rules out God as unnecessary

Ultimate reality
    That which is the very essence of all that is; that on which we stake our lives as eternally dependable

That's Debatable!
Can the Humanist Reality Enhance the Human Potential?

Humanists, of course, will answer in the affirmative. They believe that getting rid of the supernatural entanglement leaves the human being free to develop his or her potential.

This is highly debatable. Christians insist on pressing the logic here. If the ultimate reality is not the God of the Bible, then matter plus energy, shaped by chance *is;* that makes man nothing more than a temporal creature of the natural order and therefore not deserving of any special attribution of dignity, worth, or respect. The only human potential, it appears then, is the potential a higher-level animal can claim—a higher-level animal that is the result of an accident in the natural order of things. The humanists are in a trap of their own making. And no matter how many attributes they seek to infuse into this human animal by issuing manifestos, the ultimate reality of matter-and-energy-shaped-by-chance (MESC approach) gives them no logical reason to live except to survive. To survive for a brief split second of time, and disappear forever. Survive for what? For the sake of survival of the race? Why? And how does survival for a brief split second of time enhance the human potential? The very potential the humanist seeks to enhance is not even there to begin with under the view of reality the humanist espouses.

Foresight

The explosive growth of Christian schools represents both a phenomenon to be celebrated and a real danger. It is, of course, a matter of joy and satisfaction for Christians to see so many Christian schools being established.

But it represents a great danger as well. How many of these schools are carefully planned and well developed, so as to bring glory to God? How many are barely planned and poorly developed and become masterpieces of shoddiness?

The Christian approach to education is today a peak on the educational landscape. It does indeed represent an approach at odds with that of the secular humanism of our public school systems. Christians increasingly are becoming aware of the absolute incompatability of these two ultimate realities on which the Christian and the secular humanism approaches to learning, respectively, are founded. The battle is joined, and educators need to be keenly aware of the issues involved.

The Christian Approach

This chapter explores the background influences, issues, and implications of the Christian approach to the teaching-learning process.

BACKGROUND INFLUENCES

CHRISTIAN CONSENSUS

The scope and space of this book do not permit a detailed coverage of the long history of Christian education. It is a fascinating study, and for that purpose we recommend a recent book by Kenneth O. Gangel and Warren S. Benson, which provides an excellent look at the history and philosophy of Christian education.[1]

Rather, we have chosen to consolidate multifaceted background influences into what Francis Schaeffer has called a "Christian consensus," which existed in our nation until about sixty years ago. Dr. Schaeffer describes it with superb accuracy:

> The term, Christian consensus, needs clarification. In using [this term] I do not mean to say that everyone at the time of the Reformation in northern Europe was truly a Christian; nor, when [this term] is used in reference to our own country, that everyone in our country was a genuine Christian. Rather this refers to the fact that the Christian worldview, and Biblical knowledge in particular, were widely disseminated throughout the culture and were a decisive influence in giving shape to the culture. In other words, at the time of the Reformation and in our country up until the last forty to sixty years, the large majority of people believed in basic Christian truths such as: the existence of God; that Jesus was God's Son; that there is an afterlife; that morality is concerned with what truly is right and wrong (as opposed to relative morality): that God is righteous and will punish those who do wrong; that there truly is evil in the world as a result of the fall; and that the Bible truly is God's Word.[2]

Dr. Schaeffer goes on to point out that in the Reformation countries and in America up until the last sixty years or so, most of our people believed these things, even though their belief often was not in the sense that they really personally trusted Jesus Christ as their Savior.

> Going back to the founding of the United States, this consensus was crucial. This does not mean that it was a golden age, nor that the founders were personally Christian, nor that those who were Christians were always consistent in their political thinking. But the concept of a Creator and a Christian consensus . . . was crucial in their work.[3]

After pointing out that this broad dissemination of biblical knowledge can

---

1. Kenneth O. Gangel and Warren S. Benson, *Christian Education: Its History and Philosophy* (Chicago: Moody, 1983).
2. From *The Great Evangelical Disaster*, by Francis A. Schaeffer, copyright © 1984, pp. 183-84. Used by permission of Good News Publishers/Crossway Books, Westchester, Illinois 60153.
3. Ibid.

Gallery of Greats

Francis A. Schaeffer
"The world must have the proper answers to their honest questions, but at the same time, there must be a oneness in love between all true Christians. This is our final apologetic."*

Francis Schaeffer wrote his final book, The Great Evangelical Disaster, *in 1984 while he lay dying of cancer. He left behind an enormous legacy for modern man to ponder.*

Widely recognized as one of the most influential Christian thinkers of our time,

---

*From The Great Evangelical Disaster (Westchester, Ill.: Good News, Crossway, 1984), p. 165.

Dr. Schaeffer, with his wife, Edith, founded L'Abri Fellowship, an international Christian study center, including extensions in Switzerland, England, France, Sweden, the Netherlands, and the United States.

*More than three million copies of his twenty-three books are in print, translated into twenty-five languages. Three books—*How Should We Then Live? Whatever Happened to the Human Race? *and* The Great Evangelical Disaster—*have been produced as major films and film series.*

A frequent lecturer at leading universities in the United States and abroad, Dr. Schaeffer's unchanging theme—expressed in careful, yet pungent, manner—is the uncompromising truth of biblical Christianity and its urgent relevance to all of life, including the teaching-learning process.

appropriately be termed a "Christian consensus," Dr. Schaeffer says:

> It may be correctly stated that this consensus had a decisive influence in shaping the culture of the Reformation and the extensions of these cultures in North America.... We must be careful, however, not to overstate the case and imply that the United States ever was a "Christian nation" in a truly Biblical sense of what it means to be a Christian, or that the United States could ever properly be called God's chosen nation.
>
> Moreover, we must acknowledge that there is no golden age in the past to which we can return, and that as a nation we have always been far from perfect. As I have mentioned in the past we have had blind spots and serious shortcomings.... But having made all of these qualifications, we must nevertheless acknowledge that in so far as the northern European countries of the Reformation and extensions of these countries such as the United States do in fact represent a Christian consensus, this consensus has profoundly shaped these cultures, bringing forth many wonderful blessings across the whole spectrum of life. Moreover, the opposite is also true: in so far as our culture has departed from a Christian consensus, as it has so rapidly over the last forty to sixty years, this has had a devastating effect upon human life and culture, bringing with it a sweeping breakdown in morality and in many other ways as well.[4]

THE TEACHING-LEARNING PROCESS IN AMERICA

Within this consensus, the teaching-learning process developed in America. For example, Thomas describes the good child of Puritanism as: "One who keeps himself engaged in profitable tasks and does not idle away his time, obeys his superiors, does not lie or swear or steal, studies hard in school, forgives his enemies, speaks well of others and treats them with kindness, reads the Bible and prays regularly, attends Church, abides by the Ten Commandments, loves Christ, and accepts Christ as his Redeemer from sin."[5]

Veltkamp points out that "the thrust of education was basically religious in its

---

4. Ibid.
5. From R. Murray Thomas, *Comparing Theories of Child Development*, p. 59. © 1979 by Wadsworth Publishing Company, Inc. Reprinted with permission.

concern for sin and one's duties towards God and man, as evidenced especially in the New England Primer and in the charter of Harvard college, which includes 'training in knowledge and godliness' as one of its goals."[6]

After the colonial period, education was highly influenced by the European "age of enlightenment," and stressed equality of all men under the law, the dependability of nature, the innate goodness of man, and the superiority of natural rights over birth, status, or any kind of special privilege.

A significant figure in America during the nineteenth century was Horace Mann, who "believed that religion had nothing to contribute to education for a happy life," and promoted the idea of a free public school, suggesting that "democracy be substituted for Christianity as the bright ideal for mankind."[7]

Horace Mann is a symbol of the changes that began to occur in American Society during the nineteenth century, for it was about this time that the ideas of the enlightenment began to wield a significant influence upon Christianity in America.

So there can be little doubt as to what the enlightenment ideas were, it is fair to describe it as an intellectual movement that celebrated the self-sufficiency of human reason, and carried a severe skepticism about any traditional authority of the past. (See Insight, fig. 8.1, for a more detailed description.)

A NEW CONSENSUS

We turn to Francis Schaeffer once again for a constructive passage about the new consensus, which has developed over the last sixty years as a result of the enlightenment influences in America.

> ... a consensus that stands in total antithesis to Christian truth at every point—including the denial of the supernatural; belief in the all-sufficiency of human reason; the rejection of the fall; denial of the deity of Christ and His resurrection; belief in the perfectibility of man; and the destruction of the Bible. And with this has come a nearly total moral breakdown. There is no way to make a synthesis of these ideas and Christian truth. They stand in total antithesis.[8]

Dr. Schaeffer points out that, along with this change, "those holding the liberal ideas of the enlightenment and the destructive methods of Biblical criticism came into power and control in the denominations. By 1930 liberalism had swept through most of the denominations, and the battle was all but lost."[9]

The latter point is a most critical one, since for the most part, the rapid

---

6. James J. Veltkamp, "A History of Philosophic Patterns of Thought," in Paul A. Kienel, ed., *The Philosophy of Christian School Education,* 2d ed. (Whittier, Calif.: ACSI, 1978), p. 164. Used by permission.
7. Ibid., p. 165.
8. Schaeffer, *The Great Evangelical Disaster,* pp. 35-36.
9. Ibid., p. 34.

> **Insight: The Enlightenment: What Was It?**
>
> The Enlightenment combines opposition to all supernatural religion and belief in the all-sufficiency of human reason, with an ardent desire to promote the happiness of men in this life. Most of its representatives rejected the Christian dogma and were hostile to Catholicism as well as Protestant orthodoxy, which they regarded as powers of spiritual darkness depriving humanity of the use of its rational faculties. Their fundamental belief in the goodness of human nature, which blinded them to the fact of sin, produced an easy optimism and absolute faith in human society once the principles of enlightened reason had been recognized. The spirit of the Enlightenment penetrated deeply into German Protestantism in the nineteenth century, where it disintegrated faith in the authority of the Bible and encouraged biblical criticism on the one hand and an emotional pietism on the other.
>
> From F. L. Cross, ed., *The Oxford Dictionary of the Christian Church* (London: Oxford U., 1958), pp 104-5. Used by permission.

Fig. 8.1

growth of the Christian day school movement (estimated at 20,000 schools or more, and new ones beginning at the rate of three or four per day) has its roots in the new fundamentalist/evangelical churches which have rejected that denominational liberalism.

Schaeffer once more on a new consensus: "I have described this new consensus as secular humanism. The enlightenment worldview and the worldview of secular humanism really are essentially the same, with the same intellectual heritage."[10]

Before turning to current concepts of the Christian approach, we need to reaffirm clearly the background influences and how they have operated to bring about the current confrontation between the secular humanism consensus and the Christian consensus.

1. It is not difficult to understand the totally different thrusts of the two influences: the one celebrating the total insufficiency of man without God; the other celebrating the total self-sufficiency of man without God. The one places basic faith in the revelation of God through His inspired, inerrant, infallible Word—the Bible; the other places basic faith in man's power to reason, value, and

---

10. Ibid., p. 36.

choose on his own, without any need of God and the Bible.

2. The educational implications arising from the confrontation are life and death matters: teachers, curricula, educational philosophies, objectives—the kind of person we wish to produce—all are drastically affected by these two exclusively different world views. Value orientations are totally at odds.

3. For the current situation to be appropriately appraised, it is important for fundamentalists, evangelicals, and secular humanists as well, to understand the exclusive nature of these two world views. It is apparent we are not talking about minor differences in beliefs or differences among denominations, or about people who are just trying to be "hard-headed." The struggle is between two mutually exclusive views of ultimate reality, which affect *inevitably* not only spiritual matters, but the whole spectrum of life—including education, government, law, culture, ethics, and aesthetics.

We turn now to further elaboration of these two world views, and for our purposes in this text, how their current concepts translate into the operation of the teaching-learning process.

Insight: Humanist Manifesto II: Key Points

1. Traditional theism, especially faith in a prayer-hearing God, assumed to love and care for persons, to hear and understand their prayers, and to be able to do something about them, is an unproved and outmoded faith.

2. Salvationism, based on mere affirmation, still appears as harmful, diverting people with false hopes of heaven hereafter. Reasonable minds look to other means for survival.

3. No deity will save us, we must save ourselves.

4. Promises of immortal salvation or fear of eternal damnation are harmful.

5. The human species is an emergence from natural evolutionary forces. The total personality is a function of the biological organism transacting in a social and cultural context.

6. There is no credible evidence that life survives the death of the body.

7. Moral values derive their source from human experience. Human life has meaning because we create and develop our future.

8. Reason and intelligence are the most effective instruments that humankind possesses. The controlled use of scientific methods must be extended further in the solution of human problems.

9. We believe in maximum individual autonomy consonant with social responsibility.

10. The right to birth control, abortion, and divorce should be recognized. The many varieties of sexual exploration should not in themselves be considered evil. Moral education for children and adults is an important way of developing awareness and sexual maturity.

11. The individual must experience a full range of civil liberties in all societies. This includes a recognition of an individual's right to die with dignity, euthanasia, and the right to suicide.

12. All persons should have a voice in developing the values and goals that determine their lives.

13. The state should encourage maximum freedom for different moral, political, religious, and social values in society.

14. We leave the door open to alternative economic systems if they can increase economic well-being for all individuals and groups.

15. We believe in the right to universal education. We believe in equal rights for both women and men to fulfill their unique careers of potentialities as they see fit.

16. We look to development of a system of world law and of world order based upon transnational federal government.

17. The world community must renounce the resort to violence and force as a method of solving international disputes.

18. The world community must engage in cooperative planning concerning the use of rapidly depleting resources.

19. World poverty must cease. Therefore, extreme disproportions in wealth, income, and economic growth should be reduced on a worldwide basis.

20. The world must be open to diverse, political, ideological, and moral viewpoints and evolve a worldwide system of television and radio for information and education.

21. At the present juncture of history, commitment to all humankind is the highest commitment of which we are capable; it transcends the narrow allegiences of church, state, party, class, or race in moving toward a wider vision of human potentiality.

From *Humanist Manifesto II* (New York: Prometheus, 1973). Used by permission.

Fig. 8.2

CURRENT CONCEPTS

THE CHRISTIAN WORLD VIEW AND THE
HUMANIST WORLD VIEW ARE MUTUALLY EXCLUSIVE

A comparison of the two Insight boxes (figs. 8.2 and 8.3), summarizing the key points of the *Humanist Manifestos* and *A Christian Manifesto*, serve to make this point abundantly evident.

Insight: A Christian Manifesto: Key Points

1. Little by little, as a result of the influence of the Enlightenment in our nation, morality and freedom started to crumble.
2. Something fundamental has changed. Law and government no longer provide a foundation of justice and morality but have become the means of licensing moral perversions of all kinds.
3. Education has become the enemy of religious truth and values.
4. The media have provided the means for propagating the change.
5. We have failed to understand the problem—to see that the whole foundation for society has shifted radically from its original Judeo-Christian basis to a humanistic basis.
6. We need a massive movement in government, law and all of life—to reestablish the Judeo-Christian foundation and turn the tide of moral decadence and loss of freedoms.
7. Christians must change the course of history by returning to biblical truth and by allowing Christ to be Lord in all of life. This will involve a head-on confrontation with the false view that material and energy, shaped by chance, is the final reality.
8. When the state directly defies the absolute law of God, its authority becomes illegitimate. In this case, the Christian is bound to resist the state by whatever means necessary—through direct legal and political action and possibly through massive demonstrations of civil disobedience.

From Francis A. Schaeffer, *A Christian Manifesto* (Westchester, Ill.: Good News, Crossway, 1981).

Fig. 8.3

In *A Christian Manifesto,* Schaeffer points out the problems we face today have

come about due to a shift in worldview—that is, through a fundamental change in the overall way people think and view the world and life as a whole. This shift has been *away from* a worldview that was at least vaguely Christian in peoples' memory (even if they were not individually Christian) *toward* something completely different—

The Christian Approach

toward a worldview based upon the idea that the final reality is impersonal matter or energy shaped into its present form by impersonal chance.[11]

So the battle is not just over religious truths, as seen by Dr. Schaeffer and Christians who take a position similar to his. It is over the ultimate nature of *reality*. Is it matter plus energy shaped by impersonal chance? Or is it the God of the Bible?

If we agree to the former, logically we live in a universe that has no meaning or purpose, no foundation whatever for law and morality, no concept of what it really means to be human. And this kind of ultimate reality (humanistic) furnishes no basis for any value to be placed upon human life.

For many Christians, this is perhaps the greatest irony in this situation: that the humanistic world view, with its attempt to place high emphasis on *human potential*, in effect destroys it because the ultimate basis of their reality furnishes no grounds for the value of human life!

CHRISTIANS SEE THE VIEW OF SCRIPTURE AS THE "WATERSHED" ISSUE

If the Bible is viewed as the inspired, infallible, inerrant Word of God, then it is to be taken quite literally, as the standard of authority for faith and practice.

If the Bible is viewed as anything less, such as good guide or a great piece of literature, then it is not binding or trustworthy as the authoritative standard for faith and practice. Fundamentalist/evangelical Christianity is committed to the inerrancy and authority of the Scriptures, both the Old and the New Testaments. Therefore the Christian views all of life, including the teaching-learning process, quite differently from the secularist.

Explains Warren Young, "Today secularism is the integration of life around the spirit of a specific age rather than around God. It is living as if the *material* order were supreme and as if God did not exist."[12]

Schaeffer explains "the term, humanism, means man beginning from himself, with no knowledge except what he himself can discover and no standards outside of himself. In this view man is the measure of all things, as the Enlightenment expressed it."[13]

Thus, putting these two terms together, the phrase "secular humanism" refers to an approach to all of life, including education, which sees no need for God, no knowledge except what man himself can dredge up, no standard beyond man by which to measure anything, which leaves man to begin, struggle all the way, and end with himself. (See That's Debatable! in this chapter.)

---

11. From *A Christian Manifesto* by Francis A. Schaeffer, in *The Complete Works of Francis Schaeffer*, vol. 5. Copyright © 1984, p. 423. Used by permission of Good News Publishers, Crossway Books, Westchester, Illinois 60153.
12. Warren Young, "Secularism," in Everett F. Harrison, ed., *Baker's Dictionary of Theology* (Grand Rapids: Baker, 1960), p. 477. Used by permission.
13. Francis A. Schaeffer, *A Christian Manifesto* (Westchester, Ill.: Good News, Crossway, 1981), p. 24.

> **Insight: Fundamentals of the Faith**
>
> In resisting the influences of Darwinism, higher criticism, and secularism, early Fundamentalist leaders identified five basic fundamentals. They were considered the essential points of Christianity. The Fundamentalist leaders argued that anything less than these fundamentals was not another form of Christianity but was not Christian at all. The fundamentals were first articulated and defended at the Niagara Bible Conference at the end of the nineteenth century. They were further solidified with the publication of *The Fundamentals* in 1909.
>
> These five basic fundamentals included: (1) The inspiration and infallibility of Scripture; (2) the deity of Christ (including His virgin birth); (3) the substitutionary atonement of Christ's death; (4) the literal resurrection of Christ from the dead; (5) the literal return of Christ in the Second Advent.
>
> Although some have expanded this list to include such issues as: a literal heaven and hell, soul winning, a personal Satan, and a local church, nevertheless the doctrinal character of fundamentalism still centers around the five fundamentals listed.
>
> From Ed Dobson, "Fundamentalism—Its Roots," *Fundamentalist Journal*, September 1982, p. 26. Excerpt from *Fundamentalist Phenomenon*, edited by Jerry Falwell with Edward Dobson and Edward Hindson. Copyright © 1981 by Jerry Falwell. Reprinted by permission of Doubleday & Company, Inc.

Fig. 8.4

The term *Christian* as used in this volume refers to that individual who believes the Bible to be the inerrant, infallible, inspired Word of God; who accepts the Bible as authoritative for all of life; who has accepted Jesus Christ as his Savior, understanding this is the *only* way to salvation; who believes that Jesus Christ is Lord of *all* of life; who believes the fundamentals of the Christian faith (see Insight, fig. 8.4), and who espouses the Christian world view, "beginning with the central reality, the objective existence of the personal—infinite God—[believing that] Christianity is not just a series of truths, but Truth—about all of reality. . . . and then, in some poor way living upon that Truth—[so as to] bring forth not only certain personal results,"[14] but also government, legal, and educational results; in fact, results in every ramification of life.

Some will criticize this description as too detailed or too limited. But our

14. Ibid., p. 20.

concentration in this chapter is upon the Christian approach to education, and the burgeoning numbers of Christian schools, which are becoming such a large factor in the educational scene, are being planted and operated by Christians who would place themselves, we believe, generally within the description above. Therefore we believe it is a most pertinent kind of description and extremely relevant for our purposes in this chapter.

CHRISTIAN EDUCATION: A RIGHT AND A RESPONSIBILITY

For Christians, it is not only a right, but a responsibility for parents to educate their children in a teaching-learning process where the Christian world view prevails. Several corollaries follow from this concept:

(1) Public schools are generally viewed by Christians, and with a great deal of validity, as operating under the secular humanism philosophy. Let us hastily comment that not all Christians agree on this point, that there are many who espouse the Christian world view (teachers and students) in our public schools and that public schools vary sometimes substantially from place to place. However, it appears the evidence is there to justify generally the predominance of the secular humanism philosophy in our public school systems.[15] Most Christian parents simply do not want their children educated in that kind of atmosphere.

(2) There is no insistence on the part of the Christian that everybody be *forced* to go to a Christian school. These parents want the right to try to convince others, in the plurality of our society, just as they want others to have their right to try to set forth their point of view. Genuine plurality and the exercise of responsible freedom means that public, private, and Christian schools should be *equally available* to parents and their children. Each has the opportunity to seek to persuade others by reasonable means of its virtues. None should seek to *force* its point of view on others.

(3) The child *belongs to the parent,* not to the state. Christian schools are extensions of the home and the church. The Christian parent desires the schools to reflect and teach the same Christian values that are encouraged and taught at home. The child is made in the image of God, and the responsibility of the parent is to do everything possible to rear their child in such a manner that the child will genuinely *receive Christ as Savior* and *grow to Christian maturity.*

(4) Increasingly, large numbers of Christians are becoming aware of these differences and are ready to battle for their convictions concerning child rearing and the teaching-learning process, wherever and whatever the battle may take.

Franky Schaeffer puts it bluntly: "It is well to remind ourselves as Christians that we have a higher calling than being 'open-minded' or even of being 'good Americans' or 'pluralistic.' Our calling is to *acknowledge Christ* before men. If we think acknowledging Christ before men is without cost, . . . we have fooled

---

15. Jerry Falwell, "Education," in *Listen America* (New York: Doubleday, Bantam, 1981), pp. 177-94.

ourselves. Obviously, to acknowledge Christ must cost us something in our daily lives, right where we are."[16]

Franky Schaeffer then goes on to point out that the point being made here is not just theoretical. If a staff member at a secular or so-called Christian college is acknowledging Christ in his discipline, he will not get on very well with those of the secular philosophy that have already thrown out all the absolutes. And although Franky Schaeffer is somewhat discouraged with the number of people who call themselves by the name of Christian who are compromising with the secular philosophy, nevertheless increasing numbers of Christians are indeed making their voices heard and declaring their willingness to carry the battle as far as it has to be carried in order not to compromise their convictions about the Christian view of ultimate reality.

We turn now to look at how Christians translate those convictions into the teaching-learning process.

CONCEPTS IN THE CLASSROOM

THE TEACHER

The teacher, from the Christian position, is an academically well-prepared Christian, who believes teaching is a calling of God, communicates the subject matter of his or her literary specialty in the context of the Christian world view, and is committed to the redemptive and restorative purposes of Christian education under the leadership of the Holy Spirit. By *redemptive* is meant the redemption of man from his sin, and by *restorative* is meant the restoring, after redemption, of the image of God in man. Another way to state this would be to say that man is created in the image of God, and once he is redeemed from his sin, then the task of Christian education is to encourage in every way the individual to develop the mind of Christ as fully as possible while here upon the earth. (See Insight, fig. 8.5, for a further description of the kind of teacher the Christian education process wishes to produce.)

THE STUDENT

The student is a sinner whose greatest need is to know Jesus Christ as Savior and Lord. He was created in the image of God and therefore has infinite potential. The Christian world view sees the human as a *total* person who needs to engage in an educational process resulting in balanced development for the spiritual, social, mental, and physical aspects of the individual.

---

16. From "How to Become a Jellyfish," in *Bad News for Modern Man* by Franky Schaeffer, copyright © 1984, pp. 78-79. Used by permission of Good News Publishers, Crossway Books, Westchester, Illinois 60153.

THE CURRICULUM

The curriculum is described by the Christian as Bible-centered spiritual and moral instruction integrated with quality academics in a balanced curricular offering, since God is the ultimate Reality, the Creator of everything, and therefore truth in all fields stems from Him. The Bible provides the *unifying focus* for all knowledge. Honesty, respect for authority, the work ethic, reverence for God and life, and religious liberty for all are emphasized.

THE METHODOLOGY

For the Christian school, a wide variety of methods are used based on the following guidelines:

(1) From externally imposed control to a Christ-controlled life is the goal in Christian education and discipline.

(2) Educate the student to think for himself, rather than to merely respond to environmental cues. In this process, the Bible is used as the standard, and the student is instructed to depend upon the guidance of the Holy Spirit to develop his thinking as he deals with the various bits of information and ideas and experiences in which he becomes involved.

(3) The aim is for the student consciously to choose to respond to the love of God as revealed in the Bible and in Jesus Christ.

(4) Though widely variable, methods should be in harmony with the Old and New Testaments. For an excellent list of methods used in the New Testament, the student is referred to a book edited by Paul Kienel, entitled *The Philosophy of Christian School Education,* pp. 104-110. The list is much too long to include in the present chapter, but I highly recommend this list for the student's review of methodology which goes back to the Scriptures, yet is very relevant in today's teaching-learning process.

(5) Careful attention is given to the individual needs and learning styles of students. In Christian education, this is done not out of the progressivist background, but out of the background that God has created each individual with dignity and worth and with individuality.

(6) Methods are used to help students develop mentally, spiritually, physically, and socially toward Christian maturity.

THE SOCIAL FUNCTION OF THE SCHOOL

Conservative. This function of the school involves the transmitting of the unchanging truths of Christianity to children in cooperation with the home and the church. It is looked upon as a conservative social function, since it is a matter of transmitting those things which are to be conserved from the great body of Christian truth.

Insight: The Kind of Teacher We Desire to Produce

C —*Christ centered*
He has accepted Jesus Christ as his personal Savior, and the living Lord rules his life. He is anxious to share his testimony and has learned how to do it appropriately and effectively.

H —*Historically knowledgeable*
Since history is God's story, he not only knows the basic story of civilization, but understands that God is working out His purpose in the lives of men and nations. He pursues his role as a teacher in light of that perspective.

A —*Affectively wholesome*
The emotional aspects of his personality are controlled by the Holy Spirit. He possesses self-esteem, not in his own merits, but as the result of being a sinner saved by grace. This gives him dignity and worth in the sight of God. He knows how to love himself as a yielded servant of God.

M—*Morally upright*
He possesses moral integrity and maturity based on the Word of God "hidden in his heart." His values are those set forth in the Word. He can be trusted—he has developed Christian character.

P —*Physically able*
He understands his body to be the temple of the Holy Spirit. He strives to keep it fit and able by following good rules of health, including proper food and exercise. He may be physically handicapped, but is still able to perform his duties acceptably.

I —*Intellectually mature*
He is conversant with the liberal arts. His cognitive abilities are mature. He exercises good judgment, listens and evaluates with excellence, is a good problem-solver, able to grasp concepts well, and sees the parts in terms of the total pattern of events. He is committed without mental reservation to Jesus Christ.

O —*Oriented to his profession*
He is knowledgeable concerning the teaching profession, issues, history, and philosophy of education. He understands professional ethics, and is particularly oriented to the Christian school movement. He views his profession as a calling under God, and engages in his teachings as unto the Lord. He is able to translate this knowledge into actual teaching of students.

> N—*Notable in his relationships*
> The Spirit is evident in his behavior. The fruits of the Spirit can be seen in his life. He knows how to relate to others in meaningful and Christlike manner. He is prompt in appointments, responsible in duties, loving in his conduct, serious in his leadership. He knows how to love his neighbor, because he loves God.
> S —*Spiritually discerning*
> He reads the Word of God regularly and treasures it. He is theologically sound. He is concerned to win others to the Lord and help them grow in His grace and knowledge. He reflects spiritual discernment in his thinking, his conversation, his conduct, and his prayer life, all of which are bound together by the working of the Holy Spirit in his life.

Fig. 8.5

Revolutionary. The revolutionary function involves the conversion of men and women from their old way of life to the Christian way, and through these changed lives an impact is made upon the society for the Christian world view. The idea here is that the social function of the school is a *spiritually revolutionary* function. The Christian is not referring to violence of any kind at this point. However, Christians are being called upon and urged strongly to become involved in the civic and political processes of their communities, their states, their nations. They are being urged to register, to vote, to become aware of the issues and the candidates, to run for political office themselves, in order that the Christian world view through the influence of their personalities, may make a significant impact upon society.

It is important to note here that the Christian is not referring to the church as a formal institution interfering with the political processes but to the individual Christian as a responsible citizen making his or her influence felt in the civic and political life of society.

CRITICISMS AND CRITIQUE

REGARDING HUMAN NATURE

One of the criticisms brought frequently against the Christian approach points out that either the Christian view (all have sinned) is not justifiable or that there is no such thing as a "human nature."

While the heart of the Christian's answer is his belief in the inerrancy of

Scripture, and that he has scriptural authority clearly for this view, one can look further at everyday evidence regarding the nature of men and women through observation of their behaviors. The front page of any daily newspaper makes it evident that the behavior of human beings is filled with destructiveness, greed, deception, theft, lust.

One finds newscasts abounding with stories of frauds, rapes, murders—even in small towns and rural areas, which make rather evident the contention that the nature of man is not "basically good." Admittedly, newscasts many times dwell on news that is negative, because that is what makes the news what it is. But survey after survey of criminal activity and negative human behavior would support the contention that human nature is filled with evil motivations and behaviors.

Thus, the Christian responds not only that he has scriptural support for his contention that all have sinned, and not only with observations of negative human behavior, but even further with a reverse criticism to the critics: that other approaches to the teaching-learning process *fail to account* for what is exceedingly evident to the Christian—the perverse nature of human beings, and their need for salvation in Christ.

There are those who would bring the question then to something akin to the following: Is there more good behavior or more bad behavior among members of the human race? The Christian would not deny that there are many noble things that one human does for another human being, but nevertheless still would point to the way society is structured, based on the nature of man—namely, policemen are necessary, military organization is necessary, locks on doors are necessary, bankers want security before they will loan money, prisons are filled to overflowing, and security men are needed at almost every plant or educational institution of any kind in our society. There is only one answer to all of these situations, and that is that the individual human being has something in his nature which certainly cannot be called "good and trustworthy." And to the Christian, what others refer to as negative factors in human behavior is clearly defined as "sin" in the Scriptures. The Christian contends that since this is a characteristic of the nature of man, any approach which does not take that into consideration is not an adequate approach to the teaching-learning process.

REGARDING THE QUALITY OF CHRISTIAN EDUCATION

Critics frequently point to the poor equipment, poorly trained teachers, inadequacy of curricular materials, and other weaknesses in the quality of Christian schools.

There is no question some of this criticism is justified. If the Christian ideal, for example, is a teacher academically well-prepared in her literary speciality, combined with a heart committed to Christ, then to have a poorly trained teacher is a violation, at least in part, of that Christian ideal. If Christ is Lord of *all* of life, that certainly *includes the teaching-learning process.* To engage in it with less than reasonably adequate buildings, personnel, curricula, or equipment is rejecting a part of life (even temporarily) as being under the Lordship of Christ. To be sure, the best of everything does not insure *Christian* education, but to use this as an excuse for inadequate conditions is to dishonor the Master Teacher whom Christians desire to serve.

Increasingly, churches are being advised to plan carefully in relation to Christian schools, to implement only what can be done well, while constantly seeking ways to reach more people with *quality* Christian education, centered in the Bible as its unifying focus.

Quality teachers, *quality* administrators are being trained; *quality* materials are being written and/or improved; *quality* equipment is being produced; *quality* buildings are being designed and built. All because of the conviction on the part of Christians that everything should be "done as unto the Lord." And this means a striving for excellence in all things, including the teaching-learning process, according to the Christian point of view.

I have heard well-meaning people say, "A really good teacher can teach almost anywhere." Yes, but how much *more* effective could that same teacher be with improved quality in his or her situation! Ugly buildings do not reflect a God of things that are lovely. Poorly planned learning experiences fly in the face of the scriptural injunction to let all things be done decently and in order.

Deliberate shoddiness anywhere in the teaching-learning process deserves criticism, and the Christian school is no exception.

IMPLICATIONS FOR THE TEACHING-LEARNING PROCESS

From the Christian standpoint, the teaching-learning process in the clinical setting of the school is an extension of the same process at home. Parents turn their children over to experts in fields where they, the parents, cannot be experts. They want their children to have excellent academic training in an atmosphere where the Christian world view prevails. Parents share in this process in appropriate ways, at the same time keeping in touch with the nature and quality of the teaching-learning process in which their children are involved.

Hindsight

There was a "Christian consensus" in our nation until about sixty years ago, when the Enlightenment consensus (finally labeled secular humanism) began to take over. The Christian consensus is totally at odds with the secular humanism consensus, because of the exclusive nature of the ultimate realities they espouse: the God of the Bible versus matter-plus-energy-shaped-by-chance (MESC). As the Christian world view translates into the classroom, most Christian parents want the very best in academic education for their children, conducted in a setting in which the Christian world view prevails. They see the teaching-learning process in the school setting as the extension of the process at home. The goal is to lead children to a genuine acceptance of Christ as Savior, followed by a life-long development toward Christian maturity.

CHALKBOARD CHALLENGES

1. Interview a teacher or administrator at a Christian school to find out how he views his job. Does he really view it as a calling? How does he think of his students? How does this affect his teaching methods? What are his joys and what are some of his really tough spots? *Note:* always work through your director of field activities or similar person in the education department to coordinate any visits to schools for interviews. The public relations aspect is most important; never enter a school without calling ahead and making arrangements to talk with the individual you want to see, after clearing with your field director at the college.

2. In your teacher's notebook make two columns. In one column, list the main points of *Humanist Manifesto II*. In the other, list the points (correlated as to issues) from *A Christian Manifesto* by Francis Schaeffer. You may wish to keep these for future reference, or discuss the implications of each with friends or in a class session. What do they mean for your own calling as a teacher?

3. Observe in your own school or visit another school. Note the quality of the building, rooms, equipment, curriculum materials, personnel. If you were chief administrator of that school, what would you change, and why? What would you not change, and why? The purpose of this challenge is to help you clarify in your own thinking what *quality* means and how to work this out in practical ways in the situation. You may find it useful to make a priority list of items you would improve as money became available. (Again, be sure you have made all your clearances with the appropriate persons ahead of time.)

4. Think carefully about the Insight box (figure 8.5), The Kind of Teacher we Want to Produce. In the Christian context, what would you add or take away? Why? What are the areas (using the listing as a kind of checklist for yourself) where you believe you are fairly competent or ready? In what areas do you need to improve? You may wish to make some comments to yourself in your teacher's notebook as to how you will specifically go about improving in those areas where you feel improvement is needed.

5. Perhaps your class, a group within your class, or you yourself would like to accept a challenge of designing a Christian school, including building, equipment, curriculum, personnel, budget. It probably is better to limit yourself to a K-6 school, or a middle school, or a secondary school; or perhaps just to one classroom at the level where you think you want to teach. When you have completed your project, take it to a Christian school expert (administrator, teacher, etc.) and ask that individual to critique it for you. You might be surprised! And you will have engaged in a valuable learning experience that will provide many lessons for future years.

WANT TO KNOW MORE?

Francis Schaeffer, *A Christian Manifesto* (Westchester, Ill.: Good News, Crossway, 1981). This book is literally a call for Christians to change the course of history by returning to biblical truth and by allowing Christ to be Lord in all of life. This will involve a head-on confrontation, according to Schaeffer, with the secular humanism view of reality.

Franky Schaeffer, *Bad News for Modern Man: An Agenda for Christian Activism* (Westchester, Ill.: Good News, Crossway, 1984). The message of this book is that unless Christians mend their ways and once again become the true people of God preaching and living out and acting upon the faith once delivered to the saints— they risk compromising the gospel beyond the point of recovery.

Kenneth O. Gangel and Warren S. Benson, *Christian Education: Its History and Philosophy* (Chicago: Moody, 1983). A historical flow of philosophical thought from a Christian point of view, with emphasis on the Christian education aspects and their implication for us not only today, but into the future.

Francis A. Schaeffer, *The Great Evangelical Disaster* (Westchester, Ill.: Good News, Crossway, 1984). In this book, Dr. Schaeffer exposes the rise of compromise and accommodation on the part of those who profess to be Christians, and the tragic consequences of this for our society.

Paul Kienel, ed., *Philosophy of Christian School Education,* 2d ed. (Whittier, Calif.: ACSI, 1978). A compilation of excellent articles providing a philosophy of Christian school education for those who are concerned with the rapid growth of Christian schools.

Frank Gabelein, *The Pattern of God's Truth* (Chicago: Moody, 1968). This book has become a must for beginning students in Christian education.

Jerry Falwell, *Listen America* (New York: Bantam, 1980). An outstanding Christian leader presents his point of view on crucial issues for our American society.

9

Varieties, Conditions, and Designs

CONTENTS

	PAGE
Key Terms	226
That's Debatable!	227
Foresight	228
What Is to Be Learned?	228
Mastery Approach to Learning	229
Varieties of Learning: Robert Gagné's Analysis	244
Systematic Instructional Design: Robert Glaser	249
Implications for the Teaching-Learning Process	250
Hindsight	250
Chalkboard Challenges	251
Want to Know More?	253

KEY TERMS

Affective domain
    Includes objectives for developing appreciation, interests, attitudes, values

"Beta" hypothesis
    Practice the wrong response, then relearn the right response

Cognitive domain
    Includes objectives for recalling knowledge and developing intellectual skills

Instructional objectives
    Statement which describes the goals you expect the student to reach when you complete instruction

Psychomotor domain
    Includes objectives for developing manipulative and motor skills
Mastery learning
    Progress from one learning unit to another should be based upon fully learning each successive task
NAEP
    National Assessment of Educational Progress, set up in 1964 by the Educational Commission of the States to provide information about the knowledge, understanding, skills, and attitudes American children acquire in our public schools
Task analysis
    The arranging of skill components in order
Taxonomy
    A comprehensive scheme for classifying learning objectives

THAT'S DEBATABLE!
The Cons and Pros of Mastery Learning

THE CONS

It is too costly in terms of money, time, and effort.
Determining the mastery criterion is a highly subjective exercise.
It slows the progress of brighter students because they have to wait until the slower students have passed the criterion test.
It causes students to be lazy, because there is no penalty for failure.
It won't work with lower achieving students.
It still keeps the possibility of failure in the picture.
Teachers emphasize lower levels of objectives because they are easier to write.
Mastery is not really mastery because you are just testing students over on exactly the same material.

THE PROS

Benefits have to be compared with the costs, and that's a value judgment for those involved.
Almost any educational decision is made on a subjective basis, after considering the experience and judgment practices of others.
Research has not shown that brighter students learn less in mastery approaches than in nonmastery ones.
If the criteria are set high enough the bright students will have to work to pass the requirements.
Those students who are least likely to stick with mastery learning would probably be least likely to stick with any system since they attribute their failure to

how difficult the task is, or to luck, rather than to their own ability or how much effort they put into it.

No matter what the system, students will compare themselves with others in one way or another, and competition and failure are a part of daily living. They cannot be eliminated.

Although it is easy to focus on the lower level objectives, the teacher who makes a decision to use the mastery approach must be willing to work at the most complex objectives as well as the easier ones.

In mastery learning students are not retested using the same tests as the original ones. An alternative form of a test is used to cover the same knowledge and skills but with different test items.

Foresight

In the preceding four chapters, you were introduced to four different approaches to the learning process: behavioristic, cognitive-discovery, humanistic, and Christian. The teacher needs to develop a clear philosophic approach to the teaching-learning process, but without compromising basic convictions. He should be able to synthesize carefully and thoughtfully (rather than muddling through in hit-and-miss fashion) aspects of other approaches into his or her own view, thus enriching and strengthening his or her own distinctive approach and influence as a teacher.

As we begin to move in this chapter gradually from the more philosophical to the more clinical aspects of the teaching-learning process, we believe it is extremely important to understand how to "synthesize without compromise." For example, I make no secret of my wholehearted and whole-minded commitment to the Christian approach. However, without compromising my convictions regarding that approach, with its God-centered ultimate reality, I can appreciate and use effectively social learning theory, cognitive structuring, and I have deep interest in the wholesome affective development of each student, for I am concerned with the development of the total person toward Christian maturity. This process of "reflective commitment" allows me to remain open for full and serious consideration of new ideas. I filter them through my philosophic position, but I am careful in my use or nonuse of them not to violate the integrity of that position.

We look in this chapter at the variety, conditions, and designs of learning, including the concept of mastery learning, the advantages and limitations of instructional objectives, and a discussion of the National Assessment of Educational Progress (NAEP).

What Is to Be Learned?

There has been conflict for centuries concerning what is to be learned and *how* it is to be learned. A story attributed to Thales, a Greek philosopher (625 B.C.), goes like this:

On one occasion he was transporting several large sacks of salt by donkeys to a neighboring town. While crossing a shallow river, one of the donkeys slipped and fell. Naturally, some of the salt dissolved in the water, resulting in a lighter load. When the same donkey came to the second water crossing, it purposely fell in an effort to further lighten its load. At the next seaboard town, Thales purchased a large quantity of sponges and loaded them on the donkey's back. At the next water crossing, the donkey again went into its stumbling act, needless to say, for the last time.

Another of the Greek philosophers writes a very up-to-date sounding piece:

At present, opinion is divided about the subjects of education. People do not take the same view about what should be learned by the young, either with a view to human excellence or a view to the best possible life; nor is it clear whether education should be directed mainly to the intellect or to moral character . . . whether the proper studies to be pursued are those that are useful in life, or those which make for excellence, or those that advance the bounds of knowledge . . . men do not all honor the same distinctive human excellence and so naturally they differ about the proper training for it.

(Attributed to Aristotle)

Regardless of one's view of what is to be learned, we want to help as many students as possible to master the curriculum.

Mastery Approach to Learning

Mastery learning is not really new as an idea. In 1922, Carleton Washburne devised the Winnetka plan,[1] and Henry C. Morrison developed a similar approach in 1926 at the University of Chicago laboratory school.[2] Common to both plans were the defining of mastery learning using objectives, well organized learning units made available to the students, the use of tests to ascertain whether students had met objectives at the end of the instructional unit, and, for students who needed it, remedial instruction.[3]

This approach was forgotten during the 1940s and 1950s, and it was John B. Carroll, in 1968, who supplied the motivation for its reemergence. His basic idea was simple: that teachers allow more time and provide more instruction for students who learn more slowly and with greater difficulty than their classmates.[4] (See Insight, fig. 9.1, for the teacher's function in mastery learning according to Carroll.)

Benjamin Bloom in 1968 was impressed by the Carroll model, and used it as a basis of his statement to promote mastery learning: "Most students (perhaps over

---

1. C.W. Washburne, "Educational Measurements as a Key to Individualizing Instruction and Promotions," *Journal of Educational Research* 5 (1922):195-206.
2. H.C. Morrison, *The Practice of Teaching in the Secondary School* (Chicago: U. of Chicago, 1926).
3. R.F. Biehler and J. Snowman, *Psychology Applied to Teaching*, 4th ed. (Boston: Houghton Mifflin, 1982), p. 486. Used by permission.
4. J.B. Carroll, "A Model of School Learning," *Teachers College Record* 64 (1963):723-33.

> **Insight: Mastery Approach—The Teacher's Responsibility**
>
> Carroll makes the point that "teaching ought to be viewed as a process concerned with the management of learning." He suggests the following as functions of the teacher in the mastery approach.
> Specify what is to be learned.
> Motivate pupils to learn it.
> Provide instructional materials [to foster learning].
> [Present] materials at a rate appropriate for different pupils.
> Monitor students' progress.
> Diagnose difficulties and provide remediation.
> Give praise and encouragement for good performance.
> Give review and practice.
> Maintain a high rate of learning over a period of time.
>
> From John B. Carroll, "Problems of Measurement Related to the Concept of Learning for Mastery," *Educational Horizons,* 48, no. 3 (1970), pp. 71-80.

Fig. 9.1

90 percent) can master what we have to teach them, and it is the task of instruction to find the means which will enable our students to master the subject under consideration. Our basic task is to determine what we mean by mastery of the subject and to search for the methods and materials which will enable the largest proportion of our students to obtain such mastery."[5]

PREPARING INSTRUCTIONAL OBJECTIVES:
ROBERT F. MAGER AND NORMAN C. GRONLUND

Two things that stimulated the wide use of mastery learning were the formulation of instructional objectives and the development of a comprehensive description of the hierarchial nature of learning (taxonomy of instructional objectives).

Robert F. Mager describes an instructional objective as "an *intent* communicated by a statement describing a proposed change in the learner—a statement of what the learner is to be like when he has successfully completed a learning experience. It is a description of a pattern of behavior (performance) we want the learner to be able to demonstrate."[6]

---

5. Benjamin S. Bloom, *Learning for Mastery.* Reprinted by permission of the Center for the Study of Evaluation, University of California, Los Angeles. *Evaluation Comment,* 1968, *1* (2), 5.
6. From *Preparing Instructional Objectives* by Robert F. Mager. Copyright 1984 by David S. Lake Publishers, Belmont. Reprinted by permission of David S. Lake Publishers, Belmont, California.

Instructional objectives are simply statements that describe the goals you want the student to attain when instruction on a particular sequence is completed. While objectives may be general or quite specific, they can be most helpful to you as a teacher in helping to clarify your ideas about a particular unit of instruction. It is easy to get sidetracked—"run the rabbit trails"—while teaching. Writing out objectives will help both you and your students to concentrate on the most useful learning experiences in relation to each goal. While testing is discussed in a later chapter, we can mention here that if achievement tests are based on objectives (and you have stayed faithfully with the objectives during your instruction) they are more likely to be fair and valid measures of your students' learning. Still another advantage is that objectives make clear to the students exactly what is expected and provide the opportunity, at least, for students to make more efficient use of their time.

How do you write good instructional objectives? In Mager's book *Preparing Instructional Objectives* (a pioneer book in the field) he emphasizes three essential steps:[7]

(1) Specify the terminal behavior expected of the student. The emphasis should be on observable performance, on what students must be *doing* when they indicate they have achieved the objective. Mager cautions teachers to avoid general terms such as "understand" or "appreciate," since they do not precisely communicate the behavior expected of the student. He suggests that terms like "give examples of," "point to," or "separate into categories" describe terminal behaviors that you can more readily observe.

(2) Specify the conditions under which the terminal behavior is expected to occur. For example, in the following statement the terminal behavior is clearly specified, but the conditions are not: "The student will put a list of words in alphabetical order." This could be greatly improved by adding more details, as follows: "Given a list of words, each beginning with different letters of the alphabet, the students will put these words in alphabetical order." Or another example, "The student will be able to show that he can multiply numbers," could be vastly improved as follows: "Without the use of a calculator or any other instrument, the student will write down on his paper the multiplication process for any two, three-digit numbers." The purpose for adding these details is to make very clear what you are expecting, and to prevent the student from misinterpreting a particular objective or from confusing one objective with other similar objectives.

(3) Specify the level of performance acceptable for mastery of the objective. To put this in simple language, we are simply answering a question, "How well does the student have to perform so that we may decide that he or she has met this objective?" Acceptable levels of performance may be stated in various ways.

For example, if a student has been given a list of problems to solve, after specifying the other details of the objective, then we might say the student must

7. Ibid.

solve 80 percent of the problems correctly. Or, in another kind of situation, emphasizing time limits on getting the work done adequately, if the student has been given a paragraph to write concerning, let us say, his favorite athlete in the Olympics, after specifying the other details of the objective, we may add, "The student will complete this assignment in ten minutes." Or, in still another kind of situation, we may be concerned with precision or accuracy, and so if the student, for example, were typing the paragraph in the previous example, after giving a time limit we could add the words "with no more than two errors."

In *Stating Behavioral Objectives for Classroom Instruction,* Norman E. Gronlund points out that Mager's objectives are most appropriate for teaching skills and specific items of information, since each objective is an end in itself. Gronlund is concerned with objectives for more advanced types of instruction, and he suggests writing a general objective first, and then clarifying it by noting samples of the type of performance that indicates the student understands that general objective. To put it another way, Gronlund is interested in *sampling type objectives,* because he believes they put greater emphasis on more general principles. To master principles, in Gronlund's opinion, is more likely to lead to learning that involves a higher level of understanding as compared to simple recall.

Gronlund recommends the following procedure for preparing objectives.

(1) State the general instructional objectives as *expected learning outcomes.*

(2) Place under each general instructional objective a list of specific learning outcomes that describes the *terminal behavior* students are to demonstrate when they have achieved the objective.

    a. Begin each specific learning outcome with a verb that specifies definite, *observable behavior.*

    b. List a sufficient number of specific learning outcomes under each objective.

    c. Be certain that the behavior in each specific learning outcome is relevant to the objective it describes.

(3) When defining the general instructional objectives in terms of specific learning outcomes, revise and refine the original list of objectives as needed.

(4) Be careful not to omit complex objectives (for example, critical thinking, appreciation) simply because they are difficult to define in specific behavioral terms.

(5) Consult reference materials for help in identifying the specific types of behavior that are most appropriate for defining the complex objectives.[8]

When students first look at instructional objectives, as in the above listing, they sometimes become discouraged because they fail to see how this can translate into a specific classroom situation. Here is a brief example from Gronlund of how you might follow his suggestions:

---

8. Norman E. Gronlund, *Stating Behavioral Objectives for Classroom Instruction* (New York: Macmillan, 1972), p. 17.

Understands scientific principles
Describes the principles in his own words
Identifies examples of the principle
States tenable hypotheses based on the principle
Distinguishes between two given principles
Explains the relationship between two given principles.[9]

Rather than becoming discouraged, we encourage the student to look very carefully at instructional objectives and how they can translate effectively into the teaching-learning process.

It becomes obvious it will be easier for you to write some kinds of objectives more readily than others. For example, it is easier to write objectives when simple recall is the behavior desired. It is more difficult when we are writing objectives for higher level cognitive processes, such as critical thinking, or perhaps most difficult of all when we are dealing with affective areas, such as values or attitudes. But objectives can be written, and effectively so, for all levels of learning. Bloom's *Taxonomy* helps us to comprehend how this may be done. A taxonomy is simply a comprehensive scheme for classifying learning objectives.

TAXONOMY OF EDUCATIONAL
OBJECTIVES: BENJAMIN S. BLOOM

Bloom and his associates developed a system for categorizing objectives into three domains: cognitive, affective, and psychomotor. Within each domain, objectives can be arranged in a hierarchy of categories from simple to complex. We look briefly now at each of these domains.

Taxonomy of educational objectives: Handbook I; Cognitive Domain.[10] This book presents a comprehensive classification of all the cognitive objectives schools might want to use. There are six hierarchically-ordered levels of instructional outcomes: Knowledge, Comprehension, Application, Analysis, Synthesis, Evaluation. The hierarchy description means that understanding depends upon the mastery of each level of information, relationships, etc. before proceeding to the next level. It is a scheme built on a step-by-step process. Insight, figure 9.2, gives a brief outline of the taxonomy for cognitive objectives.

The effectiveness of cognitive objectives has been evaluated by several researchers (E. G. Faw and Waller, 1976;[11] Hartley and Davies, 1976;[12] and Melton,

9. Norman E. Gronlund, *Measurement and Evaluation in Teaching,* 4th ed. (New York: Macmillan, 1981), p. 46. Used by permission.
10. Benjamin S. Bloom, et al. *Taxonomy of Educational Objectives: Handbook I: Cognitive Domain* (New York: McKay), 1956. Used by permission.
11. H.W. Faw and T.G. Waller, "Mathemagenic Behaviors and Efficiency in Learning From Pro's Materials," *Review of Educational Research* 46 (1976):391-720.
12. J. Hartley and I.K. Davies, "Pre-Instructional Strategies: The Role of Pretests, Behavioral Objectives, Overviews, and Advanced Organizers," *Review of Educational Research,* 46 (1976):239-66.

> **Insight: Bloom's Taxonomy of Educational Objectives: The Cognitive Domain**
>
> | CATEGORIES OF OBJECTIVES | EXPLANATION |
> |---|---|
> | Knowledge | Recalling or recognizing facts, concepts, rules |
> | Comprehension | Understanding facts and concepts by summarizing, interpreting, translating, etc. |
> | Application | Using facts and concepts to solve new problems |
> | Analysis | Identifying component parts of a whole and their interrelationships |
> | Synthesis | Integrating components into a new whole |
> | Evaluation | Judging or comparing ideas, procedures, products, etc. |
>
> From Benjamin S. Bloom et al, *Taxonomy of Educational Objectives:* Handbook I, Cognitive Domain (New York: Longmans Green, 1956). Used by permission.

Fig. 9.2

1978[13]). Biehler and Snowman report the major conclusions of these researchers as follows:[14]

(1) Objectives work best when students are aware of them, treat them as directions to learn specific sections of material, and feel they will aid learning.

(2) Students of average ability profit more from being given objectives than do students of higher or lower ability.

(3) Objectives may be less effective with students who are submissive, internally motivated, and conscientious.

(4) Objectives work best when they are clearly written and the learning task is neither too difficult nor too easy. Consequently, providing objectives for application, analysis, and synthesis tasks tends to be more useful than providing objectives for knowledge or evaluation tasks.

(5) There should not be so many objectives specified that the probability of achieving any given objective is decreased.

(6) Intentional learning—correctly answering questions directly related to objectives—is enhanced, but at the expense of incidental (or unintended) learning.

(7) Learners given objectives tend to spend more time studying material relevant to the objectives.

Taxonomy of educational objectives: Handbook II: Affective Domain.[15] In addition to the concern about cognitive objectives, many teachers and students are

---

13. R.F. Melton, "Resolution of Conflicting Claims Concerning the Effect of Behavioral Objectives on Student Learning," *Review of Educational Research,* 48 (1978):291-302.
14. Biehler and Snowman, p. 321.
15. D.B. Krathwholl, B.S. Bloom, and B.B. Masia, *Taxonomy of Educational Objectives Handbook II: Affective Domain* (New York: McKay, 1964). Used by permission.

Gallery of Greats

Benjamin Bloom
One of the major difficulties in education has to do with the definition of goals.

One of the best known scholars in the field of educational psychology is Benjamin Bloom. Born in 1913, he completed a master's degree at Penn State and his Ph.D. at the University of Chicago in 1942, where he has remained for the duration of his professional career.

Bloom became known for his insistence on precise thinking about education, and from this precision developed the taxonomies for both the cognitive and affective domains—listing educational objectives and relating each objective to specific classroom procedures. This classification of objectives has become a standard.

Turning next to the nature-nurture controversy with reference to intelligence,

Bloom published another "classic," Stability and Change in Human Characteristics. *His work emphasizes the critical importance of early experience and early learning factors in the process of intellectual growth.*

A more recent book, All Our Children Learning, *stresses the need for each child to be given the opportunity and encouragement to succeed in the learning process through a mastery approach. Dr. Bloom has contributed a lifetime of significant scholarship to the field of educational psychology.*

Insight: Bloom's Taxonomy of Educational Objectives: Affective Domain

CATEGORIES OF OBJECTIVES	EXPLANATION
Receiving (attending)	To produce in the student the willingness to receive or attend to certain stimuli
Responding	A commitment of the student to do something with or about the stimulus
Valuing	A belief or attitude is expressed about the value of something
Organization	Organizing two or more values into an internalized system
Characterization by a value or value complex	A way of life is built around the value system

From David B. Krathwohl, Benjamin S. Bloom, and Bertram B. Masia, *Taxonomy of Educational Objectives: Handbook II: Affective Domain* (New York: McKay, 1964). Used by permission.

Fig. 9.3

interested also in affective objectives. *Handbook II* was prepared to help teachers describe and attempt to reach objectives which have to do with appreciation, interest, attitude, and values. The third Insight box (fig. 9.3) gives a brief outline of the taxonomy for the affective domain.

Although there has been considerably less research on the validity of the affective domain as compared to the cognitive domain, in a very real sense the humanistic approach to education may be looked at as describing the advantages and disadvantages of emphasis on affective objectives.

As Biehler and Snowman point out, this kind of education (geared to the affective domain) is much less popular in the 1980s than it was in the 1970s.

> Many schools that emphasized humanistic education in the 1960s and 1970s now stress mastery of subject matter. It seems likely that the reduced popularity of humanistic teaching in this decade is traceable, at least in part, to cultural trends (for example, a move from liberal toward conservative political thinking); a high rate of

unemployment, which causes students to want to acquire skills that will make them attractive to employers. Perhaps the main reason for the return to "basics" though, is the well publicized discovery that many contemporary high school graduates are not well educated in basic academic skills.[16]

It is important, even though we are expected and need to concentrate on basic cognitive kinds of objectives and basic academic skills, in terms of the development of the total person to give substantial attention to the development of the affective domain.

Taxonomy of educational objectives: Psychomotor domain. No matter what grade level or what subject you teach, you are bound at some point to want to help your students acquire certain kinds of physical skills. If you are teaching in the primary grades, you will want your students to learn how to print clearly. In junior and senior high school there are many psychomotor skills that are of major importance: typing, driving a car, playing a musical instrument, operating certain kinds of tools in the shop, etc. Therefore, the taxonomy of education for the psychomotor domain will be of great value to you for developing either a unit or a course that emphasizes psychomotor abilities. See figure 9.4 for this taxonomy, which was developed by Elizabeth Jane Simpson in 1966.[17]

Two comments I have found helpful in my experience may also be helpful to you as you develop your approach to the teaching-learning process. One relates to task analysis, the other to the "beta" hypothesis. Task analysis is simply the orderly arrangement of the components necessary to a particular skill. To do this, you must isolate the components of a particular skill, next arrange the components in the most efficient order, and then train the student to follow the chain of links exactly. A note of caution is in order, because this technique may work fine for teaching someone to install a particular part in a car, but it often does not function very well with more complex tasks. What happens is that if students are required to concentrate too much on each of the separate steps or components of the skill, then they may not be able to put these steps together in a very natural smooth way. There is an old story of a centipede that walked along in fine order until he was taught the techniques of task analysis. That is, he was taught to think about which leg moved precisely before and after the other of his many legs. He concentrated so much on that task analysis, that he became totally paralyzed and fell over motionless on the ground, unable to walk. This kind of situation can happen to students as they are learning a psychomotor skill. It is well to be aware of this. There are no easy guidelines as to when and when not to use a task analysis as you go about your teaching.

The "beta" hypothesis is a fascinating technique. It is common sense to say that emphasizing the right way to perform a skill is usually the most helpful kind of

---

16. Biehler and Snowman, p. 333.
17. E.J. Simpson, *The Classification of Educational Objectives: Psychomotor Domain* (Urbana, Ill.: U. of Illinois, 1966).

> **Insight: Bloom's Taxonomy of Educational Objectives: Psychomotor Domain**
>
> | CATEGORIES OF OBJECTIVES | EXPLANATION |
> | --- | --- |
> | Perception | Becoming aware of objects and their qualities through one or more of the senses |
> | Set | The readiness to perform a particular action |
> | Guided response | Performing under the guidance of a model |
> | Mechanism | The ability to perform a task consistently with some degree of confidence and proficiency |
> | Complex overt response | The ability to perform a task with a high degree of confidence and proficiency |
> | Adaptation | Performing new but related tasks based on previously learned motor skills |
> | Origination | From understanding, abilities, skills developed in the psychomotor area, the student creates new performances |
>
> Adapted from Elizabeth Jane Simpson, "The Classification of Educational Objectives: Psychomotor Domain," *The Instructor,* August/September 1971. Copyright © 1971 by The Instructor Publications, Inc. Used by permission.

Fig. 9.4

guidance. But if a student has an unusually stubborn problem in trying to learn a particular skill, it may be helpful to deliberately exaggerate the mistake. This is the technique referred to as the "beta" hypothesis, and it was first described by Knight Dunlap in 1949.[18] Exasperated by a quirk in his typing technique that caused him to type *hte* for *the,* Dunlap deliberately banged out several dozen *htes* and discovered he was then in a position to relearn the correct movements. His explanation was that he had fixated the wrong response to the point that it had become an automatic reaction. By deliberately concentrating on the error, he had been able to bring it under his own control, and then he could relearn the right response. This is a most helpful technique to use when you get in a situation in the classroom where a student "just can't seem to help himself in doing the wrong thing." Have him do the wrong thing and enjoy it and exaggerate it. Then, have him go back and relearn the right way to do it. It works amazingly well in many situations.

NATIONAL ASSESSMENT OF EDUCATIONAL PROGRESS

It will be helpful to you, whether you teach in a public or a private school, to be very much aware of the National Assessment Program and its objectives. This program developed because many individuals were convinced that education was

---

18. Knight Dunlap, *Habits: Their Making and Unmaking* (New York: Live Right, 1949).

not all that it should be, but they had no way of really organizing their impressions into an effective program. In other words, there was no trustworthy way to ascertain what students were learning—or not really learning—in American schools. It was for this reason that in 1964 the Education Commission of the States was formed for the purpose of initiating what came to be called the National Assessment of Educational Progress.

The purpose of the National Assessment Program was direct: to provide information about the knowledge, understanding, skills, and attitudes that American children acquire in the public schools. In order to achieve this purpose, the decision was made to test thousands of individuals periodically at four age levels—nine, thirteen, seventeen, and twenty-six through thirty-five—in ten different learning areas: art, career and occupational development, citizenship, literature, mathematics, music, reading, science, social studies, and writing. Various groups of educators, teachers, scholars, and lay people drew up educational goals and objectives for each of the ten areas. Examinations were then prepared to evaluate how well those objectives were being achieved. And then a rotating schedule for administering the test was developed, and the examinations were given to representative samples of the student population involved.

The results are reported in terms of geographic region, size of community, type of community, age, sex, race, and socioeducational background. General trends are noted, and information is given on specific questions.

Overall, the National Assessment reports must lead us to only one conclusion: the public schools are not meeting many objectives in an effective manner. Here is one sample of a report from *Update on Education: A Digest of the National Assessment of Progress,* in 1975:

> The general level of writing skills shown nationally was not very high. At age nine, few individuals have mastered the basics of written English; by age seventeen about half the individuals had some mastery of basics but they rarely attempted anything beyond the simplest construction or use anything beyond a rather limited vocabulary. At no age did many individuals show much of a flare for writing . . . Americans seem to have difficulty writing in business situations of even the simplest nature. Only at age seventeen did even slightly more than half manage to fill in correctly a simple information form asking for name, address, birthdate, and current date . . . the vast majority of young Americans can read fairly simple material, but many cannot; many young Americans are handicapped by deficient reading skills. They cannot follow simple directions, and they find it difficult to draw inferences or conclusions based on what they do understand when they read.[19]

Subsequent NAEP reports have shown few improvements in the performance levels since the 1975 summary. On the basis of these data, it seems fair to say

---

19. National Assessment of Educational Progress, *Update on Education: a Digest of the National Assessment of Educational Progress* (Denver: NAEP, 1975), pp. 5-8.

that there is great need for improvement in American education.

Biehler and Snowman make a salient point in regard to the NAEP report:

> Until recently educators often argued it was impossible to determine how effective the schools actually were. That is no longer the case. National Assessment not only supplies information about educational deficiencies, it provides teachers with general and specific information about educational deficiencies, it provides teachers with general and specific leads they might follow in helping students overcome such weaknesses. These specific leads are supplied in the form of lists of objectives and information regarding how well these objectives are being met.[20]

Although the National Assessment objectives and reports are based on public school education, those who are in private schools can profit greatly from the use of these objectives, adapting them to their own particular school setting. The lists of objectives under each of the ten learning areas indicate what kinds of objectives experienced educators believe should be stressed by teachers of those subjects, and also reflect the basis of the information supplied in the National Assessment reports. If you would like more complete information about any of the lists, including all of the subobjectives for different grade levels, you can obtain booklets from the National Assessment organization at the address listed under Want to Know More? at the end of this chapter. The Insight box (fig. 9.5) shows a sampling of objectives taken from NAEP booklets for the spring of 1981. We have chosen the mathematics, reading, and literature objectives for our sampling. And you will note that while we have just illustrated sub-objectives under one section of the general objectives, in the actual report each major objective has sub-objectives listed under it. The student should be aware that these objectives are occasionally revised, and so the very latest ones at the time of this book's publication may vary somewhat.

In many states, a statewide report in the form of assessment of the performance abilities of students is also done, and the results are published comparing each of the school districts in a particular state.

CRITIQUE OF THE MASTERY APPROACH

A review by James Block and Robert Burns in 1976 of over two dozen studies on mastery learning produced the following conclusions. Sixty-one percent of the time, mastery-taught students scored significantly higher than nonmastery-taught students. For retention levels, mastery-taught students scored significantly higher 63 percent of the time. The one aspect of the mastery approach that appeared to produce the strongest effects was the requirement that a criterion test be passed before the student goes on to further instruction. Reflecting affective outcomes, mastery taught students were more interested in the subject matter being learned,

20. Biehler and Snowman, p. 352. Used by permission.

Varieties, Conditions, and Designs

Insight: NAEP Objectives: A Sampling

Mathematics Objectives

I. Mathematic knowledge
II. Mathematical skill
    A. How well can students perform computations, including computations with whole numbers, integers, fractions, decimals, percents, ratios, and proportions?
    B. How well can students make measurements?
    C. How well can students read graphs and tables?
    D. How well can students perform geometric manipulations like constructions and spatial visualizations?
    E. How well can students perform algebraic manipulations?
    F. How well can students estimate the answers to computations and measurements?
III. Mathematical understanding
IV. Mathematical application

Reading and Literature Objectives

I. Values reading and literature
II. Comprehends written works
III. Responds to written works in interpretative and evaluative ways
    A. Extends understanding of written works through interpretation
        1. Demonstrates an awareness of the emotional impact of written works
        2. Applies personal experiences to written works
        3. Applies knowledge of other works or fields of study
        4. Analyzes written works
IV. Applies study skills in reading

From NAEP booklets supplied by the National Assessment of Educational Progress in spring 1981.

Fig. 9.5

and yet showed greater improvement in self-concept, self-confidence, and attitudes toward the teaching-learning process.[21]

At this point, the author must caution the student to go back and remember the bandwagon effect. For these results seems to indicate that the mastery approach is the ideal approach to the teaching-learning process. There is no question that the mastery learning approach has made positive contributions to the improvement of the teaching-learning process. The research findings indicate that students taught under the mastery approach two-thirds of the time learn more than students taught under nonmastery conditions. On the other hand, there are a number of limitations and cautions you need to be aware of in relation to the effectiveness of the mastery

---

21. James H. Block and R.B. Burns, "Mastery Learning," in L.S. Shulman, ed., *Review of Research in Education*, vol. 4 (Itasca, Ill.: Peacock, 1976).

learning approach. Listed below are eight common objections to the mastery learning approach.

(1) The amount of materials required and the time required is very costly in terms of money, time, and effort.[22] Even though this objection may be true, a decision concerning any kind of learning should never be based only on the cost involved. Of course this is a value judgment that has to be made by the people involved in the particular school system where the teaching-learning processes take place.

(2) The mastery learning approach involves a high degree of subjectivity, as the standards for achievement are determined.[23] The subjectivity involved in the teaching-learning process of any kind is reflected in our philosopher/clinician model. The professional judgment of the teacher and others concerned with the teaching-learning process must be involved. This objection does not appear to me to be one that carries much weight, since it could be applied to almost any approach to instruction. The important thing is to look at the experiences and the judgments of others along with the data appropriate to the situation and then seek to make a good professional judgment in relation to the particular item involved.

(3) The progress of brighter students is slowed, because the moving on to a new topic cannot proceed until the slower students have passed the criterion test.[24] It has not actually been shown that brighter students learn less in the mastery approach than in nonmastery approaches. However, it is possible to individualize learning in the mastery approach. It would appear this would be one way to overcome this objection.

(4) Since there is no penalty for failure, this may cause great numbers of students to prepare as little as possible for an examination.[25] They may pass without putting forth very much effort, but if they fail, all that happens is that they find out what they have to learn in order to pass the retest. It appears to me, at least, that this is one of the more weighty objections to the mastery learning approach, but it can be helped somewhat at least by setting the criteria sufficiently high (but still within a realistic realm) for the passing of the objectives.

(5) The students who do not have the willingness to persevere are going to be penalized by the mastery approach to learning.[26] Again, it appears this is one of the more weighty objections to this approach. And we are really concerned here with the problem of motivation, in which we know that those students who are less likely to persevere attribute their successes and failures to how difficult the task is or to plain luck, rather than to their own lack of ability or lesser degree of effort.

---

22. D.J. Mueller, "The Mastery Model and Some Alternative Models of Classroom Instruction and Evaluation: An Analysis," *Educational Technology* 13, no. 5 (1973):5-10.
23. Ibid.
24. J.K. Smith, "Perspectives on Mastery Learning and Mastery Testing," (ERIC/TM Report 63, Princeton, N.J.: ERIC Clearing House on Tests, Measurement, and Evaluation, 1977).
25. W.F. Cox, Jr., and T.G. Dunn, "Mastery Learning: A Psychological Trap?" *Educational Psychologist*, 14 (1979):24-29.
26. Ibid.

(6) Competition or failure is not eliminated by the mastery learning approach.[27] The matter of competition or failure on the part of students is, needless to say, a highly controversial issue. Those who tend toward the humanistic approach, with its emphasis on the affective domain, would be more highly concerned about this kind of consequence than those who placed their emphasis on other areas of the teaching-learning process. Competition and failure are very much a part of daily living, and it does not appear a realistic goal to try to eliminate them totally from the teaching-learning process. If a student is in the teaching-learning process where the mastery approach is used, he may compare himself in terms of whether it takes a longer or shorter time to reach a particular standard than the other students around him.[28] In other approaches, students may compare themselves, and in fact do, in terms of grades or test scores. Not to be overlooked is the fact some have argued there are beneficial effects to failure.[29] It is possible that some students may be motivated by the desire to avoid failure, just as others are motivated by the desire to succeed. Also, the experience of failure (and we do not say this lightly) can be a constructive kind of contribution to the instructional process. For it says to the students who fail, You need more concentration, more time, more effort, and perhaps you need to learn how to study and to develop more effective learning strategies, in order to achieve a particular goal.

In dealing with the failure syndrome, educators certainly need to be sensitive to the devastating effects it can have in the lives of certain students. We must work to counteract those devastating effects. However, for many students, the experience of failure can be a very constructive contribution in the teaching-learning process.

(7) It is difficult to write the more complex cognitive and affective objectives; therefore, the focus may be on the easier, lower level objectives.[30] There is no question that this is one of the real abuses of the mastery learning approach, but it is not the fault of the approach itself. If a teacher decides to use the mastery learning approach, part of that decision must be the willingness to work hard at the task of writing clear objectives at the more difficult levels and in the more difficult areas.

(8) When students are retested on the same material, this does not prove that they have mastered the material.[31] This does not appear to be a very weighty objection, since most of the advocates of mastery learning emphasize that while the retest should in fact cover the same facts and skills as the original test, nevertheless this should be done with a different form of the test, including different tasks or test items.

From my own experiences, readings, and observations, the following appears to be true: Just as with any other approach to learning, some students will get you to the point of infuriation, if you let them, by the lengths to which they will go in

27. Ibid.
28. Mueller, 1973.
29. R.E. Ebel, "The Failure of Schools Without Failure," *Phi Delta Kappan* 61 (1980):386-88.
30. Cos and Dunn, 1979.
31. Ibid.

trying to beat the system. I have found that "A" students will do well under most any system of learning and are the ones who will get into the best colleges and get the best jobs. They simply have learned how to cope with and successfully overcome any kind of a system in the teaching-learning process. We will deal with that kind of student, and the ways in which his energies and brightness should be channeled, in another chapter of this book which includes a discussion of gifted and talented students.

I believe that the individual whom we label the "average" or "C" student is the one that really might be helped most by the mastery approach to learning. This student probably has not felt able to compete for high grades with the "A" students, but under a mastery scheme, he is likely to try harder and perhaps improve his learning, his attitudes, and his self-concept. Students who find it very difficult to learn usually feel even more inadequate when the mastery approach to learning is used. The logic of this is not hard to follow: when the opportunities are plentiful, and every encouragement has been given, and the student who has difficulty learning still fails, he has no one then to blame—not even the system—but himself.

We want all of our children to learn as much as they can, and we want them to improve not only in their cognitive domain, but in their affective and psychomotor domains as well. As teachers, we need to be concerned with the development of the total student. If you decide to use the mastery approach to learning, be realistic about it, and about the students whom it will help, and those whom it is not likely to help. Don't expect utopian results, don't look upon mastery learning as a bandwagon to jump on and automatically succeed in the teaching-learning process. Be sensitive to how you can best use it and the students with whom you can most effectively use this approach. This is another one of those critical areas in which you as a teacher-philosopher must use good judgment influenced by information and feedback from the actual clinical process in order to arrive at an appropriate decision.

VARIETIES OF LEARNING: ROBERT GAGNÉ'S ANALYSIS

We turn now to a brief discussion of the varieties of learning. It is important for you to be aware of these different kinds of learning, for a child who is learning the alphabet is engaged in a different kind of learning from the child who is trying to find the answer to a mathematical problem. And each of those kinds of learning is different from a child who is engaged in discussing the rights and responsibilities of human beings.

Robert Gagné is an educational psychologist who has developed a very helpful way of analyzing the different types of learning. In his book *The Conditions of Learning* and another entitled *Principles of Instructional Design* Gagné distinguishes five different types of learning and makes suggestions as to how instruction can be designed appropriate to each type.[32] Most educational psychologists believe that Gagné's analysis is sound and practical.

VERBAL INFORMATION

This is simply the student's learning labels and facts. If a student takes a blank map of the United States and fills in the name of each state, for example, the student is engaging in labeling. When students are able to use labels in the formation of a sentence, expressing a relationship between two or more objects or events, they have learned a fact. For example, "Georgia is located just north of Florida." Or, "Hurricanes travel much more slowly than tornados, and can be easily tracked," or, "Ten computers in one lab plus ten in another equal a total of twenty computers available." Any of these statements are considered verbal information in the form of facts.

It is important to note that the learning of relationships between objects, events, or ideas is essential to the learning of verbal information. A distinction here is made by psychologists between meaningful learning and rote learning. They define meaningful learning as learning that relates the new bit of information to what students already know. This is in contrast to rote learning, in which students simply memorize verbatim the information. To go back to our illustration of a blank map of the United States, the student needs to associate the name of the state with its shape, its location, its capital, and other features about that state. As the student learns each new bit of information, he or she needs to associate the idea in some way with what she already knows about that particular state; then the learning will be more meaningful.

One further item needs to be noted about verbal learning. Although many people criticize rote learning, the knowledge of a number of facts is necessary for further learning and for getting along in everyday situations. So again, the prospective teacher is cautioned not to jump on the bandwagon of "rote learning should be avoided at all costs," for it simply cannot be avoided at all costs. A certain amount of rote learning is necessary in order to form the foundation for further meaningful learning. Again, the best judgment of the philosopher/clinician is needed to make good decisions about the learning of verbal information.

INTELLECTUAL SKILLS

One kind of distinction between verbal information and intellectual skills is one of learning *that* versus learning *how*. Lahey and Johnson describe the difference this way: "the student who knows *that* immunology is the branch of medicine

---

32. Robert M. Gagné, *The Conditions of Learning*, 2d ed. (New York: Holt, Rinehart, and Winston, 1970). Also Robert M. Gagné, and L.J. Briggs, *Principles of Instructional Design* (New York: Holt, Rinehart, and Winston, 1974).

concerned with protection from disease has learned a fact. The student who knows *how* to look up the meaning of 'immunology' in a dictionary has learned an intellectual skill. Intellectual skills make it possible for the student to think in terms of classes of objects and events, rather than working with a confusing blizzard of individual facts or instances."[33]

Some examples of the kinds of intellectual skills students learn in the classroom would be counting, diagramming sentences, reading, learning to tell time, sketching a picture, or programming a computer. When you are teaching intellectual skills, you will need to be aware that your students need to *understand* concepts and to *follow* rules.

Forming concepts. To learn a concept means to learn how to put ideas or things into groups on the basis of certain characteristics they share, even though individual items in that group may differ in noncritical ways.

Let us take as an example the learning of the concept *square.* What is critical to a square? Answer: four straight sides of equal length joined at right angles. Students must be able to positively identify squares, and also to learn what is not a square. Squares can be huge or tiny, green or black, but the size or color are not critical ideas for the definition of the square. The student must be able to distinguish a square from a triangle or a circle or other figures. Concept learning, then, involves demonstrating the meaning of objects, events, and symbols, and goes beyond just simply stating verbal information.

Combining concepts into rules. After students have learned the basic concepts in a given area, they need then to learn how to combine those concepts into rules and further to use the rules to solve problems. Rules are simply statements that inform the learner how he or she is to perform. For example, if we use the rule for finding the area of a rectangle, it would be "width times height." This informs the student how to find the area of a rectangle. Another favorite of mine is "i before e except after c"—a rule that informs the student how to deal with a certain kind of spelling pattern.

When we are teaching rules to students we need to present the student with a verbal statement of the rule, then give examples of the rule, and then ask the student to practice application of the rule in a number of differing situations.

COGNITIVE STRATEGIES

For Gagné, cognitive strategies are the skills we use in organizing our thought processes: learning to listen, asking questions, criticizing, formulating hypotheses, and similar types of mental operations. This is a type of learning that permits students not only to solve problems but to come up with solutions to problems that they have never encountered previously. Others have referred to this

---

33. Benjamin B. Lahey and Martha S. Johnson, *Psychology and Instruction* (New York: Scott Foresman, 1978), p. 92. Used by permission.

as learning to learn or productive thinking, but Gagné calls this kind of learning *cognitive strategies*.

ATTITUDES

Gagné defines an attitude as "an internal state which affects an individual's choice of action toward some object, person, or event."[34] It is not hard to see that attitude learning falls into a different kind of category, simply because we go about learning attitudes differently from the way we go about learning information, skills, or strategies. Two of the most important conditions in the learning of attitudes are (1) how successful students are in that particular activity with which the attitude is involved and (2) the models the child is exposed to.

Perhaps one of the outstanding examples, and one of the most serious examples, of attitude learning occurs for a child who has great difficulty in learning to read. That child develops a negative attitude toward reading, simply because of the miserable experience the child is having. Teachers need to become aware of this kind of situation very early in the child's development, and seek to have the child experience success in learning to read, or in whatever area might be troubling the child. Relating this to our previous comments about failure in the classroom, if the failure experiences are handled correctly by the teacher, many times they can be turned around and made into constructive contributions for the progress of the child. For example, if a child is having a hard time learning to read, the teacher not only will want to help him improve the reading by the application of every technique appropriate to the situation, but at the same time help the child to understand that everybody fails in one thing or another; the thing to do when one fails is not to become discouraged or give up but simply to get up and try again. This kind of attitude on the part of the teacher, along with skillful application of the strategies for helping the child to improve his reading, will have the probability of bringing about the development of a better attitude toward reading.

In relation to learning by modeling, we certainly do learn attitudes indirectly by observing the behavior of people who are important to us, as was just indicated in relation to the teacher in the reading situation. Parents, teachers, peers, and other important people in the child's eye wield great influence by behaving in the sorts of ways that reflect the attitudes they want the children to develop. In any classroom, these attitudes certainly would include fairness, kindness, respect for each human being, and very importantly in the teaching-learning process, the development of a love for learning, so that students will think of the school as an exciting place to come, rather than one that is a drudgery.

MOTOR SKILLS

Gagné's fifth category of learning involves motor skills, defined as those

---

34. Gagné and Briggs, p. 62. Used by permission.

activities which require a precise sequence of bodily movements. It is not hard at all to think of examples of motor skill learning, from skipping, riding a tricycle in the preschool and early elementary grades to swimming, playing a musical instrument, typing, driving a car, and many, many others which require that we learn how to coordinate our muscular movements.

Demonstration, practice, and feedback are necessary components of efficient motor skill learning.[35] It is almost impossible to learn a complex motor skill until we have watched someone else demonstrating how to do it, then have an opportunity to try it out ourselves, and then have someone knowledgeable tell us how well we did and where we need to improve.

Motor learning usually takes place more gradually than other kinds of learning, and practice can certainly improve the motor skill over a period of time. Motor skills, once we have learned them, are not easily forgotten. For example, if you have learned to swim as a child, but perhaps have not had the opportunity to swim for a good number of years, and suddenly you have the opportunity, you will discover that you have not forgotten how to swim. The same is true for the kind of skill it takes to balance and ride a bicycle again, even though you may be a little shaky at first.

So if we seek to summarize Gagné's five categories of learning, and remember that the goal of education is to teach children to think independently, to solve problems on their own (and most educators would agree at least on these goals, although they would then relate them perhaps in different ways to their particular philosophical approach), we can say that most problem solving certainly requires the recall of certain verbal information and the use of certain intellectual or motor skills. Attitudes are obviously essential, for a problem will not be solved by an individual if he does not have an interest in solving it, if he does not see a reason to solve it, and therefore want to go about spending the time and effort it takes to find the solution.

Of course cognitive strategies are absolutely essential. They involve the manner in which the individual comes to the problem, and what she brings with her to attempt to find the solution. Perhaps you share with me the experience of knowing great numbers of people who might be able to recall facts almost perfectly, or who have the motor skills to solve problems, and who have the intellectual skills necessary, but who simply cannot get their thinking organized to make sense out of problems—even everyday problems—and so they become very ineffective in their daily living and problem solving. One of the most important parts of cognitive strategy is to learn how to organize one's thinking, to make the very best use of the verbal information and the other skills that one has developed. Knowing how to approach and find solutions to problems that one has never faced before is a very critical kind of thing to learn in a world that is changing so rapidly from day to day. There is a tremendous satisfaction for an individual once he has resolved a problem

---

35. Lahey and Johnson, p. 96.

that previously was very new to him, has learned something new about the world in which he lives, and has developed a more positive attitude in relation to the area the problem involved.

SYSTEMATIC INSTRUCTIONAL DESIGN: ROBERT GLASER

When we talk about systematic instructional design, we are talking about a concern for integrating every part of learning into the total teaching-learning process. The teaching-learning process is made up of a number of distinct and yet interrelated parts or components. For the most effective results in the teaching-learning process, all of those components must work together. While there are many models for systematic instruction we have chosen one which we believe to be representative and comprehensive—Robert Glaser's model, which contains four phases.[36]

The first phase of Glaser's model is the specification of instructional goals. This simply means that you identify the goals you want the student to reach, and write the objectives needed to reach those goals.

In phase two, the aim is to assess entering behaviors. For example, for a course in educational psychology, if I am assessing entering behaviors, I can do it in several ways. I can use a teacher-constructed test to see how much the students know about educational psychology at the point they come into the class. Or I can use a standardized test, or a questionnaire that has to do with attitudes or interests, or I could use observational checklists, or if it is a small group, and the time is available, I can assess entering behaviors by conversation with each of the students. Or I can combine any one or more of these with the other sources to endeavor to form a fairly solid idea of what the student knows about educational psychology. Now this means that I do not simply teach the course the same way every time, but I try to adjust it in terms of where I start and how rapidly I may move through these various segments, depending on these entering behaviors.

And this leads us to phase three of Glaser's model, which is to implement instructional procedures. That is, on the basis of entering behaviors in relation to the instructional goals, I then engage in the teaching-learning process.

And finally in phase four, I assess terminal behaviors following all of the course instruction. Glaser has referred to this fourth phase as the "quality control" component of teaching. We need some measure of the student's progress in relation to the goals that were specified in phase one. Evaluation and assessment are subjects of other chapters in this text, but we simply point out here that achievement tests based on instructional objectives can be very effective in measuring not only how far the student has progressed, but also in helping to identify weaknesses in the total instructional process as it has been carried out. This four-phased model can be used for an entire course as has just been illustrated,

---

36. *Education* (New York: Wiley and Sons, Copyright © 1962). Reprinted by permission of John Wiley & Sons, Inc.

or for any particular unit or segment of a course that is being taught. We need always to feed back the evaluation results into the total instructional system in an effort to make that system more effective as a part of the teaching-learning process.

IMPLICATIONS FOR THE TEACHING-LEARNING PROCESS

The overall implications from looking at objectives, taxonomies, and varieties and designs for the teaching-learning process is that having a better understanding of the kinds of learning, and then adapting one's objectives to the kinds of learning, as well as to the three domains involved, should vastly improve the effectiveness of that process.

To consider seriously whether one is going to use the mastery learning approach, for example, is hopefully to compare that approach with other kinds of approaches to the teaching-learning process and thereby to help the teacher make a deliberate and thoughtful decision as to that approach. A great many educators would probably agree that one of the greatest "sins" in relation to the teaching-learning process is that so many times, in spite of all the books and articles and conferences, we end up just bumbling our way through in a hit-or-miss fashion. We hope this is not true but fear that it is. Therefore, regardless of one's approach to the teaching-learning process, objectives, written clearly and realistically, can be most helpful in organizing and clarifying not only what the teacher is going to do in that instructional process, but also what the students are expected to do.

The concept of designing instruction, as in Glaser's model, is one that can help to bring the many components of the instructional process together into some kind of integrated whole. This concept of designing instruction applies not only to a particular class, or a unit of instruction in that class, but to the entire spectrum of the teaching-learning process over the years in a particular school system. What kinds of things are our children learning? What are the places that need to be improved in the K-12 teaching-learning process? Are we leaving out some of the components, or are we putting in components that may not be as necessary as others may be? Again, these questions can be asked of any school system, public or private, large or small, and should result, if taken seriously, in a much better design of the teaching-learning process for that system.

A final comment involves the advantage of including administrators, teachers, and students in the use of objectives and in the design of instruction, and certainly the involvement of parents, since after all, the children do belong to them, and not to the state or the school system. With such involvement of the professionals and the parents, as well as the students, a continual appraisal of the teaching-learning process can be made, and the quality of education in that process should be substantially improved.

HINDSIGHT

Whatever our approach to education, all of us would agree we want to help as

Varieties, Conditions, and Designs

many students as possible to master the curriculum. One way that has proved quite effective in moving toward that goal is the mastery approach to learning. A part of the mastery approach is to prepare and write clear and relevant instructional objectives. These objectives can be written for the cognitive, affective, and psychomotor domains. The more complex the learning process, the more difficult the writing of objectives, but it can be done. The teacher who decides to use this approach should certainly commit himself or herself to the writing of objectives for the three domains and from the simple to the more complicated levels of learning. A number of objections have been raised concerning the mastery approach, and those have been discussed in this chapter.

We have presented Robert Gagné's five varieties of learning, with some suggestions as how each can be used in the teaching-learning process. Finally, we presented the concept of systematic instructional design, as represented by Robert Glaser's four-phased model.

CHALKBOARD CHALLENGES

1. Talk with your students about objectives and their importance. One excellent way to get into this subject is to ask students, Which subject do you like best? How and why did you come to like this subject best? What subject do you like the least? What made you come to the conclusion that this is your least favorite subject? As students answer these questions, as a teacher listens really carefully to discern each element of their likes and dislikes in relation to a subject, gradually lead the conversation, either from things involved in making a subject their favorite, or things involved in making a subject their least favorite, around to the part that objectives could have played, or did play, in relation to their favorite or least-liked subject.

For example, a common answer might be, "I hate math." When you ask the student to discuss why he dislikes math, you will find probably somewhere in that discussion that the student did not understand a particular mathematical operation, and from that point became more and more lost, and then finally grew to dislike the subject. How would objectives have helped? How would mastery learning have helped? Could this approach have made a difference in the student's coming to like mathematics, rather than to hate it?

Write in your teacher's notebook your ideas about relating this kind of conversation to the use of objectives in your class. And of course, a very constructive result of this kind of conversation is that students see the need for objectives and, with proper leadership in the class discussion, can come to see and appreciate the objectives in the particular subject you teach, or in several subjects you teach if you are in the elementary area.

2. Write and get a copy or copies of pamphlets from the National Assessment Program in order to get familiar with these and know how to use them to help at the grade level in which you expect to teach, and then give some thought, if you are in a private school rather than a public one, as to how these objectives and assessments

can be put to use in your particular school setting. Again, you want to look especially at the objectives that are written for the grade level in which you are interested and write in your teacher's notebook some of your ideas applying these in your own teaching-learning situation. These can be of great help to you as well in your student teaching process.

3. Think about ways you can make the teaching-learning process more fascinating and exciting for your students, no matter what kind of learning you may be talking about. One of the ways this can be done is borrowed from what our school band or our school dramatic players usually do, and that is to have a dress rehearsal or, as the athletic teams, have a scrimmage before the season actually starts. Why not apply this idea of dress rehearsal or scrimmage to other areas of the teaching-learning process? For example, if you are teaching a high school business class, try to arrange to have your classroom look as much as possible like an office. Have the students operate in a "scrimmage" session frequently, to see if they achieve the kinds of things they will be called upon to achieve when they get out into the "real world of business." If you are teaching a Home Economics class, it is a natural for you to have your "Home Ec" class prepare a dinner or at least refreshments for guests whom they invite to come. This gives a note of realism to the teaching-learning, and you will find your students more highly motivated and working harder to achieve the objectives that have been prepared for that particular segment of learning. If you are teaching in junior high school (or middle school as it is often called) and you have objectives you want to achieve concerning sentence structure and grammar, let them scrimmage by pretending that they are an organization that owns a major athletic team. There are certain letters they have to write, and there are reports that have to be made, and those have to be done with good sentence structure and using good grammar, and this becomes a most effective way to have those students engage in a "scrimmage session." You may want to jot down in your teacher's notebook some ideas revolving around these situations, and situations that apply particularly to your subject area or your level of teaching.

4. In relation to systematic instructional design, use Glaser's four-phased model, (this particular exercise would be good for junior high school, secondary, or college level) in reference to the training of an astronaut for a space trip. Do not let it become too complicated, as students may get discouraged. But have them think through some of the basic things the astronauts would need to know, and then use the four-phased instructional model of Glaser to design a program for training those astronauts, including evaluation and feedback once they have returned to earth. Put down in your teacher's notebook the many kinds of objectives, including some from each of the three domains, that can become involved in such a project as this. Each of the five varieties of learning, as suggested by Gagné, become involved. And again, you have set up in effect a "scrimmage" session with the students to test their abilities in a live situation.

Want to Know More?

SYSTEMATIC DESIGN

W. Dick and L. Carey, *The Systematic Design of Instruction* (Glenview, Ill.: Scott Foresman, 1978). A helpful book to read to help you understand the importance of having a systematic design for instruction.

NATIONAL ASSESSMENT REPORTS

For a complete list of National Assessment objectives and reports, write to National Assessment of Educational Progress, 1860 Lincoln Street, 300 Lincoln Tower, Denver, CO 80295.

EDUCATIONAL OBJECTIVES

As a good introduction to educational objectives, read Robert Mager, *Preparing Instructional Objectives,* 2d ed. (Palo Alto, Calif.: Fereon, 1975).

For a better understanding of the taxonomy of educational objectives, and to help you gain insight into how objectives and evaluations can be brought together in the teaching-learning process, examine Benjamin S. Bloom et al., eds., *Taxonomy of Educational Objectives, Handbook I: Cognitive Domain* (New York: McKay, 1956).

MASTERY LEARNING

For a review of mastery learning, read J. H. Block and R. B. Burns, "Mastery Learning," in L. S. Shulman, ed., *Review of Research in Education,* vol. 4 (Itasca, Ill.: Peacock, 1976).

GAGNÉ

Two books by Gagné may be very helpful to you. R. M. Gagné, *The Conditions of Learning* (New York: Holt, Rinehart, and Winston, 1970), and R. M. Gagné and L. J. Briggs, *Principles of Instructional Design* (New York: Holt, Rinehart, and Winston, 1974).

10
Remembering, Forgetting, and Transferring

CONTENTS

	PAGE
Key Terms	254
That's Debatable!	255
Foresight	255
Framework for Information Processing	256
Factors Improving Memory Capability	264
Factors That May Cause Forgetting	267
The Transfer of Learning	268
Implications for the Teaching-Learning Process	270
Hindsight	271
Chalkboard Challenges	272
Want to Know More?	273

KEY TERMS

Chunking
    A technique for holding separate items of information in short term memory by grouping them

Distributed practice
    Short concentration periods spaced out over time

Information processing theory
    Study of the ways sensory input is transformed, stored, recovered, and used

Interference theory
   The theory that previous, future, or coactive current learning may interfere with each other and may cause confusion or forgetting
Long-term memory (LTM)
   Permanent storehouse of information with unlimited capacity
Massed practice
   Intensified concentration upon learning material in a short period of time
Metamemory
   Knowledge of how your memory works
Mnemonic devices
   Special mental "hooks" for helping recall
Sensory register (SR)
   Information held briefly for decision on processing
Serial position effect
   Tendency to remember more easily items at the beginning and ending of a list
Short-term memory (STM)
   Ordinarily thought of as "working memory"
Transfer
   What is learned in one situation carries influence in other situations

That's Debatable!
Is Modular Learning Better?

Students constantly complain about having three tests, a paper, and a lab all on the same day. If questioned at length, they almost always state they have "let one or two of the subjects go" in order to concentrate (cram!) for the others: a prime example of what I term "coactive interference." It is difficult to see how this can produce the thoughtful, meaningful learning we say we espouse.

Would it not be better to have students concentrate on one subject at a time for a prescribed period of weeks? Would retention be better? Transfer? Understanding of relationship between ideas, concepts, principles?

Is modular learning better beginning in junior high? What do you think? What other alternatives can you come up with which enhance learning, memory, and transfer in relation to the overall design of the teaching-learning process?

Foresight

Regardless of one's approach to learning, all of us want our children not only to learn but to remember what they learn and to be able to transfer what they learn in one situation to many other situations.[1]

---

1. Benjamin B. Lahey and Martha S. Johnson, *Psychology and Instruction* (New York: Scott Foresman, 1978), p. 89.

Learning, remembering, forgetting, and transferring are closely related processes.

>When an individual learns a skill, strategy, attitude, or a bit of information, something is presumably stored in the person's memory. At a later time the individual may retrieve from memory storage what he or she has learned. If the previous learning can be recalled, retention has occurred. If previous learning cannot be recalled, forgetting has occurred. Finally, if learning in one situation has some influence, either positive or negative, on learning in another situation, transfer has occurred.[2]

This chapter is about how human memory works and how we might improve it, and how information we learn can more effectively be transferred in an appropriate manner to other situations. The study of how input from outside or from within ourselves is encoded, processed, stored, retrieved, and used is known as Information Processing Theory. Knowledge of how your memory works (metamemory) can improve your remembering, decrease your forgetting, and thus make available more information for you to transfer to more situations. And that is highly important, especially in an information society such as ours.

FRAMEWORK FOR INFORMATION PROCESSING

Those who have studied information processing have identified essentially *three memory structures* and *five control processes*. Memory structures are used to help us understand more clearly how our memory operates. They are: (1) the sensory register (SR—not to be confused with S-R for stimulus-response), (2) short-term memory (STM), and (3) long-term memory (LTM). Each of these "storage structures" varies as to how much information it can hold and for how long.

The *control processes* are (1) recognition, (2) attention, (3) rehearsal, (4) encoding, (5) retrieval. They are called control processes because they control the flow of information between the memory structures and also the way that information is encoded. You, the student, decide when and how to use them. They are under your direct, conscious control.

That fact is highly significant in talking about using them in the learning process, as we shall see shortly. As we discuss each of these memory structures and control processes, it may help you to glance occasionally at the Insight, figure 10.1, to help you keep in mind the overall framework for information processing.

THE SENSORY REGISTER

The sensory register is so called because information we receive is thought to be "registered" (encoded) in the same form we perceive it. The SR holds information just long enough (three seconds) for us to decide what we want to do

---

2. Lahey and Johnson, p. 102. Used by permission.

Insight: Framework for Information Processing

I. SENSORY REGISTER (SR) 3 seconds, 12 items
   Recognition
   Attention/Distraction
II. SHORT-TERM MEMORY (STM) 20 seconds, 7 items
   Maintenance (rote) rehearsal
   Elaborative rehearsal
III. LONG-TERM MEMORY (LTM) unlimited capacity?
   Episodic Memory
   Semantic Memory
   Elaborative Encoding
IV. METAMEMORY
   Knowledge of How Your Memory Works

Fig. 10.1

with it. After three seconds, if we do not pay any attention or recognize the information, it will decay badly and totally disappear from our system. Interestingly, the SR can hold about twelve pieces of information at one time. Twelve items for three seconds! Long enough for a typing student to remember a word to get it typed. If you read a page of a textbook without paying real attention, you will probably waste your time. You might say, "I read it," but it will have disappeared from your information processing system, because you did not pay adequate attention/or did not want to recognize the information.

This is so because the two controlling processes that determine what you do with information in your SR were not put to work. They are *recognition* and *attention*.

Recognition. Follow closely to understand how recognition works. It depends on two sources of information; partly from the stimulus itself (called bottom-up processing), and partly on information from long-term memory (called top-down processing). For example, as I watch the wild rabbits feeding and playing in our yard, I am drawing on the stimulus itself (rabbit) by noticing the physical features that make this animal a rabbit rather than something else; but I am also drawing on LTM ideas associating the rabbit with fond memories of hunting trips, beagle hounds, good times with fellow hunters, and southern fried rabbit. The context in which perception takes place tends to cause us to *recognize* certain kinds of information. The best way to make recognition effective is to make use of all available sources of information.[3]

Attention. If you stop to think about it, you become aware the environment

---

3. R.L. Klatzky, *Human Memory: Structures and Processes,* 2d ed. (San Francisco: Freeman, 1980), p. 64.

usually throws more information our way than we can handle at one time. Again, follow the logic closely. From all the influences impinging on us at one moment, only a fraction of them are noticed and recorded in the SR. And out of the already selected information recorded in the SR, most of us only process about one-third. We continually *pay attention* to one item to the exclusion of something else. It is a kind of "selective focusing," and that is why it is called *attention*.

Attention also operates as a kind of general monitoring system to detect changes in our environment. As I am writing these words, it happens to be quite late at night and the house is quiet. If suddenly our dog begins to bark, or the rescue squad goes down the highway with its ambulance sirens screaming, I notice. In technical language, the values of the stimuli in the environment change, and *distraction* occurs.[4] In college, I had a roommate who could not study unless the radio was playing. On the other hand, I could not concentrate when it was playing. There are great individual differences in distractibility. Again, LTM information plays a major role. "Perceivers pick up only what they have schemata for and willy-nilly ignore the rest."[5] In simpler terms, we choose what we will pay attention to by anticipating the information it will provide. You may find yourself daydreaming in a class simply because you do not expect to hear anything of interest or value in the teacher's lecture.

Two other points of significance are worth noting about the attention controlling process. First, LTM contains all of our store of knowledge—and we use that body of knowledge to evaluate whether new information is worthwhile. Therefore children, who have a lesser store of knowledge than adults, have a harder time distinguishing worthwhile stimuli from nonworthwhile stimuli. So they are more apt to be distracted from the task at hand. Their attention span is shorter.

Second, although bizarre stimuli may catch our attention, there is little evidence that such stimuli *improve recall* for adults or children.[6]

THE SHORT-TERM MEMORY

After you have attended to and recognize information as worthwhile, you transfer it to STM. By short-term is meant about twenty seconds. A familiar illustration of this revolves around a telephone call that you are about to make. If you are distracted for about twenty seconds, you probably will forget that number. STM is often called the "working memory," since it holds the information we are aware of at a given moment. The capacity of STM? Seven unrelated items of

4. A.L. Glass, K.J. Holyoak, and J.L. Santa, *Cognition* © 1979, McGraw-Hill. Used by permission.
5. U. Neisser, *Cognition and Studies* (San Francisco: Freeman, 1976), p. 79.
6. D.W. Kee and S.Y. Nakayama, "Children's Noun Pair Retention: Assessment of Pictorial Elaboration and Bizarreness Effects" (paper presented at the biannual meeting of The Society for Research in Child Development, New Orleans, 1977); J. Snowman, "Bizarre Versus Non-Bizarre Elaborative Prompts in Children's Noun Pair Learning" (paper presented at the annual meeting of the American Educational Research Association, San Francisco, 1979); K.A. Wollen, A. Weber, and D.H. Lowry, "Bizarreness Versus Interaction of Mental Images as Determinants of Learning" *Cognitive Psychology* 3 (1972):518-823.

information (sometimes called "chunks").

In the absence of further processing, one big disadvantage of STM is how quickly information can be lost. Through a process called *rehearsal*, this disadvantage can be helped.

There are two kinds of rehearsal: *maintenance rehearsal* to maintain information in the STM for immediate use, as in the telephone illustration above. This has no effect upon LTM.

Elaborative rehearsal helps the transfer of information to LTM along with maintenance in the STM. In elaborate rehearsal, the individual links up related information from LTM with material being learned. A perfect illustration of this occurred recently in relation to the paging number of our son who is a medical student. Obviously, he spends a great deal of time in a hospital, and in order to reach him while on duty in case of an emergency he gave us his paging number. I wanted to memorize it—a four digit figure. Then I realized that it was the same number my father had on his badge for forty years while working in a steel mill. This is elaborative rehearsal—more often called *mediation*—in which information from LTM is linked up with new information to enhance the learning of it. It is the rule, rather than the exception. But you have control. If the information is for future use, use elaborative rehearsal. If it is just for the moment, use maintenance rehearsal.

Biehler and Snowman make an important point concerning the relationship of age to the ability to use rehearsal.

> Kindergarten pupils rarely engage in spontaneous rehearsal. By the age of seven, however, simple rehearsal strategies are typically used. When presented with a list of items, the average seven-year-old rehearses each word, by itself, several times. From the age of ten, rehearsal becomes more like that of an adult. Several items may be grouped together and rehearsed as a set.[7]

THE LONG-TERM MEMORY (LTM)

The third memory structure is LTM. Most cognitive psychologists believe (on the basis of neurological, experimental, and clinical evidence) that the storage capacity of LTM is unlimited, and contains a permanent record of everything an individual has learned.[8] There is some doubt on the latter point, however.[9]

Neurological evidence. This evidence comes from the work of a Canadian neurosurgeon, Wilder Penfield, 1969, who operated on over one thousand patients with epileptic seizures.[10] In his efforts to determine the source of the seizures,

---

7. Robert F. Biehler and Jack Snowman, *Psychology Applied to Teaching*, 4th ed. (Boston: Houghton Mifflin, 1982), p. 202. Used by permission.
8. Biehler and Snowman, p. 203.
9. E.F. Loftus and G.R. Loftus, "On the Performance of Stored Information in the Brain," *American Psychologist* 35, no. 5 (1980):409-20.
10. W. Penfield, "Consciousness, Memory, and Man's Conditioned Reflexes," in K. Pribram, ed., *On the Biology of Learning* (New York: Harcourt, Brace and World, 1969).

Penfield stimulated electrically various parts of the surface of the brain. As he carried out this procedure, many of his patients reported they had vivid images of events they had not thought of for a long time out of their past. In today's language, it would be like running a neurological video tape on the screen.

Experimental evidence. An example of experimental evidence involves how well people can recognize pictures they have seen some time before. For example, thirty-six hours after viewing better than twenty-five hundred pictures, the average number of identifications made by a group of college students was about twenty-two hundred and fifty, which amounts to about 90 percent.[11]

Clinical evidence. As we read case histories of individuals which have been written by psychologists and psychiatrists, we run on to great numbers of individuals who have been able to recall events that apparently they had forgotten, through hypnosis and other techniques.[12]

The nature of LTM. LTM plays an exceedingly important role throughout the information processing system. When you think of the LTM as your permanent record area, then you know that interests, skills, attitudes, values, and knowledge—all of these which you have experienced are residing there, and they influence what you perceive, and how you interpret what you perceive, and whether you process information for short-term memory or for long-term memory. Retrieval from LTM has been likened to that of retrieval from a well-run library. It is extremely rapid and precise, and therefore information in the LTM needs to be organized. And it is important to understand the nature of LTM.

One excellent way of understanding the nature of LTM is to consider the kinds of information that are stored there. Endel Tolving has helped us a great deal in this area by making a distinction between *episodic* and *semantic* memories.[13] According to Tolving, *episodic* memories have a personal reference and take the form of "I did this particular thing, in a particular place, at a particular time." Obviously then, episodic memories are recognized by date, place, and time, and therefore accurate recall of this kind of information depends on being given or being able to spontaneously generate the appropriate context within which that particular memory is held. If you think about your own experiences in this regard, you will soon agree that you, like the rest of us, many times do not pay very good attention to precisely when and where certain events have taken place, and so if we are asked to recall that information for that particular event, it may be inaccurate.

On the other hand, Tolving tells us that *semantic* memories, as he terms them, "represent objects—general and specific, living and dead, past and present, simple and complex—concepts, relations, quantities, events, facts, propositions, de-

11. L. Standing, J. Conezio, and R.N. Haber, "Perception and Memory for Pictures: Single Trail Learning of Twenty-five Hundred Visual Stimuli," *Psychonomic Science* 19 (1970):73-74.
12. M.H. Erdelyi and B. Goldberg, "Let's Now Sweep Repression Under the Rug: Towards a Cognitive Psychology of Repression," in J. Kihlstrom and F. Evans, eds., *Functional Disorders of Memory* (Hillsdale, N.J.: Lawrence Erlbaum, 1979).
13. E. Tolving, "Episodic and Semantic Memory," in E. Tolving and W. Donaldson, eds., *Organization of Memory* (New York: Academic, 1972).

tached from autobiographical reference."[14] But what this means is that information in our semantic memory can be used to make inferences, generalizations, and to apply formulas and rules. Tolving points out that recall from semantic memory probably will be more accurate than recall from episodic memory, because the information "is usually encoded as part of, or assimilated into, a rich multidimensional structure of concepts and their relations, and such imbeddedness protects the stored information from interference by other inputs."[15] An oversimplified illustration of this, but one that may help to make the point, is that the semantic memory is like a piece of glassware that we surround with a great deal of packing material in order to keep it from being broken. Therefore, it arrives at its destination in one piece.

It is important to note that there is a very significant relationship between semantic and episodic memories. *Any of the information which is in your semantic memory was originally part of your episodic memory.* As you experience many and varied things in many and varied environments, concepts, rules, facts, and so on, are developed and become a part of your semantic memory.

Again, Biehler and Snowman make an important point in relation to the use of these memories and how information is presented in the classroom. They point out that if you present information in class very quickly, and with very little illustration, that kind of information is very probably going to go into episodic memory. This means that the retrieval of that information will be quite difficult in the absence of specific contextual cues. If you want information to be integrated into semantic memory, you need to provide the kind of learning environment that emphasizes mastery, good organization, and carefully-thought-through encoding strategies.[16]

Encoding and retrieval. It remains for us to make clear, or as clear as we have evidence to substantiate, how information becomes encoded in LTM to begin with; and once the information is there in LTM, how we can gain access to it. The answer to those questions is the process known as *elaborative encoding*. This encoding improves the organization and meaningfulness of the information being learned. Therefore, the information we store in our LTM is stored so that retrieval is quite easy when it becomes necessary.

Imagine the new library for a school that has just been built, and imagine that one-half of the books in that library are shelved according to the Library of Congress system or the Dewey Decimal system: that is—a system that is organized and meaningful, once it is understood. The other half of the books are shelved at random without any kind of system. The obvious question is, which of the books would be easier to find? The point is that for information to be stored in LTM, the very process required to store it there—*elaborative encoding*—ensures that it is encoded in an organized and meaningful way, rather than randomly.

---

14. Ibid., p. 389. Used by permission.
15. Ibid., p. 391.
16. Biehler and Snowman, p. 205.

262   Educational Psychology

Elaborative encoding may be accomplished either through visual modality or through verbal modality. Just a little bit later in this chapter we will discuss how various factors affect memory and forgetting, and you will want to remember the influence of these two modalities on long-term memory in relation to the discussion of those factors.

THE METAMEMORY

Metamemory simply refers to your knowledge of how your memory works. For example, if you know that information which is fascinating to you is going to be remembered better than that which is boring to you; or that older children recall more than younger children; and that usually the longer you wait after learning something before you try to recall it, the less you are apt to remember about it, you are talking about metamemory. The point here is that having a knowledge of how your memory works really can help you to use your memory processes much more effectively.

Robert Kail has organized metamemory research into several categories, and has come up with the following conclusions, which he emphasizes are *tentative*:[17]

**Insight: The Measurement of Retention:
The Three Rs**

In his famous study, Ebbinghaus used the method of relearning to measure retention. After learning a list of nonsense syllables, he waited a period of time and then relearned the list. In order to determine the percentage of the material retained or "saved" from one learning session to the next, he used the following formula:

$$\frac{\text{time for original learning} - \text{time for relearning}}{\text{time for original learning}} \times 100$$

For example, if the original learning required 10 minutes and the relearning required only 2 minutes, the formula would read:

$$\frac{10-2}{10} \times 100 = 80 \text{ percent retention}$$

Psychologists still use the method of relearning in studies of memory. But they also use two other methods in memory research

---

17. Robert Kail, *The Development of Memory in Children* (San Francisco: Freemen, 1979).

today, methods more familiar to the classroom teacher. Recall involves measuring the extent to which one can reproduce what has been previously learned and is the method used in essay and completion tests. Recognition, on the other hand, requires only that the individual be able to identify what he or she has learned. Multiple-choice and matching tests are good examples of the recognition method.

In general, recognition is the most sensitive measure of retention and recall is the least sensitive. In other words, students might be unable to recite or write what they learned, but still be able to indicate some retention by picking out correct choices from a number of alternatives. Of course, recognition tests are not always "easier" than tests of recall. Sometimes the alternatives in a multiple-choice test are worded so poorly or are so similar that it is difficult for the student to identify the correct response.

It is impossible to say which method for measuring retention is better. Certainly recall, recognition, and relearning all have their place in education. Recall comes closest to guaranteeing that the student has learned the material. However, we simply do not expect students to be able to recall everything they have learned. We are often satisfied if students are able to recognize facts and relationships or if they are able to relearn material more efficiently at a later time.

From Benjamin B. Lahey and Martha S. Johnson, *Psychology and Instruction* (New York: Scott Foresman, 1978), p. 104. Used by permission.

Fig. 10.2

(1) Although most children of school age understand that we need to make an attempt to store information in memory, that awareness does not always translate into an effective memory strategy. (2) Most children understand that memory improves with age and that they cannot remember all types of information equally well. (3) Kindergarten children generally believe they can hold more information in STM than they actually can. (4) By third grade, most children can predict their memory performance relative to their classmates with some degree of accuracy. (5) Most children know that information that is more familiar to them will be easier to recall than that which is less familiar to them. (6) By first grade, most children will tell you that recognition is easier than recall, and they can explain why. (7) Paraphrased recall is less demanding than verbatim recall, and by fifth grade virtually all children understand this difference. (8) The older a child is, the more likely that child is to recognize that a learning task will be remembered better if you organize it well. (9) First-graders typically don't know what they don't know. Third

graders, by contrast, know to some degree what they don't know.

Factors Improving Memory Capability

Many factors contribute to the improvement of memory. We look now at some of the more prominent ones.

OVERLEARNING

Overlearning simply means learning beyond essential mastery of the information. The salute to the flag, repeated each day in the classroom, is an excellent example of overlearning. By going over and over and over a piece of information, far beyond the essential learning of it, one is much more apt to remember it.

MNEMONICS

There are many kinds of mnemonics, and they are simply special mental "hooks" for helping us to recall information. For example, a *rhyme* such as "thirty days has September, April, June, and November" would be an example of this kind of mnemonic device.

Another kind of mnemonic is what is called an *acronym*. For example, in order to learn the spaces on a music staff, the letters F-A-C-E become a helpful device.

An *acrostic* is a third kind of mnemonic, in which you make up a sentence so constructed that each word begins with each of the items to be learned. An example of this would be an acrostic to help learn the lines on a music staff: *Every-Good-Boy-Does-Fine.*

Many of you have used the mnemonic known as the *pegword*. This is used most often in helping to learn a list of items. The idea here is simply to hook up the list of items with the memory pegs and the pegs you have already learned in association with a word that rhymes with them. For example, let us assume the first peg is called one-fun, and you want to use that peg to help learn the first item on your list. Let's imagine the first item on your list is animal cracker. Then you might imagine that one kind of fun (one-fun) is to eat animal crackers, and so on.

Reputedly, the oldest known mnemonic is called the *loci,* and many people like this method. The word *loci* means "places," and so places are used as memory pegs: many times stores on a particular street or the rooms in a particular house are used as memory pegs. Usually, a minimum of ten such places are needed in order to make this system work. Although there are some rather detailed rules for this method, let us suppose that we are using ten rooms with which you are very familiar. You get an image of these rooms in your mind and number them from one to ten, with each room being quite distinctive from the others. In each room a particular kind of furniture or piece of furniture should be located. Thus you have

Vocabulary Items and Keywords Used in Teaching a Foreign Language		
Spanish	Keyword	Translation
Charco	[charcoal]	Puddle
Arena	[rain]	Sand
Gusano	[goose]	Worm
Lagartija	[log]	Lizard
Rodilla	[road]	Knee
Prado	[prod]	Meadow
Cebolla	[boy]	Onion
Nabo	[knob]	Turnip
Payaso	[pie]	Clown
Trigo	[tree]	Wheat
Postre	[post]	Dessert
Chispa	[cheese]	Spark
Butaca	[boot]	Armchair
Cardo	[card]	Thistle
Carpa	[carp]	Tent

(From Raugh & Atkinson, 1975).

Fig. 10.3

in your memory ten very distinct rooms, each with a number and each with a distinctive piece of furniture. Then, for the list of items you want to remember, you mentally walk through each of these rooms and place an image of the item you want to remember underneath or on a particular piece of furniture. Then when you want to recall, you simply retrace your steps back through each of the rooms, retrieve each image from where it was originally placed, and then decode each image into either a written or a spoken word.

Although the loci method is probably the oldest, the newest is probably that known as *keyword*. This method first appeared in a study by psychologists Raugh and Atkinson in 1975 (see fig. 10.3), and it was used in relation to the improvement of retention of a foreign language vocabulary.[18] Imagine a 3-column list of words: first in Spanish, the word to be learned; and then the middle column has the key word, which is an English word that *sounds* like the Spanish word; the third column has the actual meaning of the Spanish word. For example, if I am trying to learn the Spanish word *charco* (which means "puddle"), I look at the *key* word in English which is *charcoal,* and I may then form a mental image of a *charcoal puddle* to help me remember the Spanish word *charco*. When mental imagery is used, you should not be bothered by how ridiculous it might seem to you or to someone else, as long as it works. Incidentally, Raugh and Atkinson found that subjects who used

---

18. M.R. Raugh and R.C. Atkinson, "A Mnemonic Method for Learning a Second Language Vocabulary" *Journal of Educational Psychology* 67 (1975):1-16.

the key words in mental imagery retained 88 percent of the words they had studied. In contrast, subjects who had simply learned the associations between the English and Spanish words in a rote manner retained only 28 percent of the words.

Why do these mnemonic devices work? The definition of mnemonic device which we have given really provides the answer: the devices provide mental "hooks" which make it much easier to encode and retrieve information. Items that are otherwise unrelated are organized, and some kind of meaning is brought to the items to help you remember them. It should be noted as well that mnemonic devices can be great motivators in getting students to learn information which otherwise might be quite boring or quite tedious.

CLUSTERING

Clustering simply means that material is reorganized into more meaningful subgroups and then the subgroups can be learned as "clusters." Gordon Bower and his colleagues conducted a study which showed the effectiveness of clustering as a memory aid.[19] In this study the students who memorized a list of words clustered into logical groupings recalled two to three times as many words as those who just memorized them as separate words in random order.

MASSED VERSUS DISTRIBUTED PRACTICE

Massed practice simply means that there is intense concentration on a subject matter crowded into a short period of time. Contrasted with this is the idea of distributed practice, in which practice sessions are shorter and separated by rest intervals. If you have crammed for an examination, you have engaged in massed practice. Cramming may help you to pass that immediate exam, but retention is exceedingly poor, so that overall this kind of cramming is not a really effective way to learn. As a general conclusion, massed practice is less effective than distributed practice.[20]

THE SERIAL POSITION EFFECT

If you have a list of words to remember, the words that come first or last are the ones you are more likely to remember. This is called the serial position effect.[21] This principle can be used to great advantage simply by arranging those items that you have the most trouble remembering as the items which are first and last on a list. Or, if you do not want to rearrange the list, then you might use the device of overlearning for those items that are in the middle of the list.

19. G.H. Bower, M.C. Clark, D. Lesgold, and D. Winzenz, "Hierarchical Retrieval Schemes in Recall of Categorized Work Lists," *Journal of Verbal Learning and Verbal Behavior* 8 (1969):323-43.
20. B.J. Otherwood, *Experimental Psychology: An Introduction* (New York: Appleton Century Crofts, 1949).
21. Ibid.

Factors That May Cause Forgetting

We need to say at the outset that there is no single, easy explanation as to why we forget material. We are quite surprised many times to discover that we have forgotten information we understood quite well just a brief time previously. And the same surprise occurs when we discover we are able to remember little, trivial kinds of items from many years ago. We discuss now three theories of forgetting, which at least will contribute somewhat to our understanding of this complex process.

THE DISUSE THEORY

The easiest way to express the *disuse theory* is: "what you don't use, you lose." If you do not make use of information you once learned over a period of time, you are apt to forget it. The presumption in this theory is that probably some kind of physiological memory trace is formed in the brain when learning occurs, and if that trace is not made use of from time to time, it fades away.

Very frankly, there is not very much experimental evidence for this theory. Most of the illustrations for this theory come out of our personal experiences. If, for example, you do not use algebra for a good number of years after having learned it, you become "rusty" and are not sure what to do in a given situation where the algebraic operation is required. Many psychologists and educators are apt to take the position that although disuse may be involved, there is much more to forgetting than disuse alone.

THE REORGANIZATION THEORY

Here is a theory proposed by Frederic Bartlett back in 1932. The *reorganization theory* refers to a kind of forgetting that happens when you remember part of what you have learned, but you forget many of the details. According to Bartlett, the memory trace does not just fade over a period of time; it becomes distorted, and that makes us forget the details of past events and fill in the gaps with whatever makes sense to us at the present time. Inaccurate memories result because the information we originally learned has been actually reorganized over a period of time.[22] For example, let us assume you were present at an event that took place one year ago. That event was videotaped so that every detail was preserved. It is now one year later, and you are asked to recount the details of that event. You present a very good account, which makes sense to you, which holds together and has continuity. However, when compared to the actual videotape of that event, you discover that you actually had forgotten some of the details, and had replaced them with other details which filled in the gaps and helped the story to make sense as you told it now. This is very difficult for most people to accept, unless they experiment with it and read about what others have done in this regard.

22. F.C. Bartlett, *Remembering* (London: Cambridge U., 1932).

INTERFERENCE THEORY

The *interference theory* stresses that either previous, future, or coactive current learning may interfere with each other and cause forgetting.

Interference can be *retroactive,* which means that later learning moves back and interferes with the retention of earlier learning. Or, interference can be *proactive,* meaning that earlier learning moves forward and interferes with later learning. Interference is the greatest when the information to be learned is similar to the material with which it conflicts, either previous or yet to be learned.

The author contends that the greatest kind of interference in most of our school systems is *coactive.* That is, with students taking four or five subjects and having to make preparations for them each day, the pressures, content of the subject area, material to be prepared, exams to be taken, papers to be written, etc. really create great psychological interference, preventing the student from learning meaningfully and thoroughly. In my judgment, a much better way to learn is through modular sequencing, in which the student concentrates on only one subject for a certain period of time (for example, four weeks) and then having finished with that subject, goes on to concentrate in another one for a prescribed period of time. We would recommend this kind of learning beginning with the middle school years. An excellent question for research would be the following: Does modular learning increase the retention, and provide a more meaningful interrelationship both among subject areas within a given course, and between courses?

THE TRANSFER OF LEARNING

We reaffirm that we not only want our children to learn, and remember what they learn, but we want them to be able to *transfer* what they learn from one situation appropriately to other situations.

Negative transfer occurs when what the student learns in one situation has a damaging or destructive effect on what is learned in other situations. Teachers need to be very much aware of the kinds of situations in which negative transfer can occur and try to avoid them.

Positive transfer occurs when we help our students to learn in one situation so that that learning will be able to help the student in many other situations with which he must deal. Are there ways in which transfer can be increased and enhanced? In *The Conditions of Learning* Gagné makes a distinction between vertical and lateral transfer.[23] In *vertical transfer* what a student learns in one situation helps the student to master either more advanced or more complicated skills in other situations. They would apply, for example, in mathematical skills, where the simpler skills of adding, subtracting, multiplying, and dividing are needed to compute the standard deviation. We need to be sure students have

---

23. Robert Gagné, *The Conditions of Learning,* 2d ed. (New York: Holt, Rinehart, and Winston, 1970).

learned the prerequisite skills needed for the higher or more complex levels of learning to which they proceed.

Quite helpful also in this regard is to show students how what they are learning currently really will be useful and helpful to them later, and this can be pointed out in specific ways that will increase the likelihood of transfer, and especially vertical transfer. When students really do not *understand* what they have learned, and they do not see any reason for having to learn it, they are not very likely to apply the learning from that situation into any other situation, other than perhaps in a negative kind of way.

In *lateral transfer,* as the phrase implies, students apply what they have learned in one situation to other situations that are very similar in what is required of them. For example, here is a student who has learned how to work on the engine of a car in a vocational program, and he goes out to get a job in a garage as a mechanic. The skills he learned in the vocational school in this particular instance are very similar to those which he will need out on the job as a mechanic. Therefore, we hope that lateral transfer will occur. There are areas in which students need to learn the kinds of skills they can recall and use in everyday situations, from balancing their checkbooks to voting in an election.

Positive transfer, whether vertical or lateral, is much more apt to occur if the learning situation can be made similar to the everyday situation into which the student will go to use the particular skills or knowledge he is acquiring. On-the-job training is excellent, as are field trips to have the students exposed to everyday working situations, and similar kinds of activities.

It is also very helpful if the kind of situation in which the student is learning can be changed somewhat, with a rather full explanation by the teacher, so that the context is somewhat different. For example, let us suppose a student is studying in a particular course about the importance of voting, knowing the candidates, understanding the issues involved, and how to relate them to the larger picture of

---

Insight: The Transfer Picture

POSITIVE TRANSFER:	learning in one situation helpful in other situations
NEGATIVE TRANSFER:	learning in one situation has a damaging effect in other situations
VERTICAL TRANSFER:	learning in one situation allows mastery of more complex skills in other situations
LATERAL TRANSFER:	learning in one situation applied to other situations of similar complexity

Fig. 10.4

life in our nation and internationally. It would be helpful for the student to have the opportunity to actually work in a real election as a volunteer in some capacity. But if that is not possible, then within the classroom itself a number of differing sets of circumstances could be set up, so that, for example, the student could act as one who is passing out literature for a candidate, or as a judge at the polls, or perhaps even as a candidate.

The basic thrust of transfer, because it is what we are striving for in the teaching-learning process, is to help the student look upon what he or she is learning now as related to what he or she will be doing later, "out there in the real world." The more experiences the student can have under good guidance, or the more simulations which can be entered into and talked about in the classroom, with good oversight by the instructor, the better the transfer process is apt to be. We want our students to be able to transfer what they learn from their current situation to as many other situations as may be appropriate.

IMPLICATIONS FOR THE TEACHING-LEARNING PROCESS

Teachers should try to help students minimize forgetting and maximize positive transfer. We are convinced that every teacher ought to learn thoroughly information processing theory. We say this recognizing that someone approaching the learning process from the behaviorist standpoint is not primarily interested in mental processes. While the cognitive psychologists are the ones primarily interested in this kind of theory, we feel certain the humanists share that interest as well, for values are learned, attitudes are learned, affective areas of the student's life are tied in intricately with the cognitive aspects. The educator who espouses the Christian approach will see these processes as God-given processes that are to be used to help the whole person grow toward Christian maturity.

Since information processing is under the direct and conscious control of the individual, individual responsibility is certainly one of the prime concerns that need to be taught. As children develop and learn, they need to be taught the importance of using the controlling processes of the system in order to remember better, and therefore to have much more information available to transfer to new situations. Because we are living in that kind of society now—that is, where no one can really predict the kinds of situations that may arise, and because our technology is changing the situations with which we have to cope, we need individuals who can have the greatest possible amount of information to transfer to the greatest possible number of situations in an appropriate manner. Whether from the pulpit or the school lecturn, whether through parents at home, whether from the counselor's seat, or the facilitator of the small group, understanding the information processing system is of significant concern for everyone involved in the teaching-learning process. The alert teacher who really wants to do a superb job will want to take advantage of every possible bit of knowledge that can be made available through this process.

I presume that many people who come from the Christian approach will be reading this book. It is for that reason we point out that from the preacher in his message on Sunday morning and Sunday evening and at other times in the services of the church, to the Sunday school teacher, to the youth leader, to the children's chairman—all through the activities of the church—the teaching-learning process really is the process in which we are all engaged, for better or for worse. As a matter of stewardship under God, Christians believe it is their responsibility to use every opportunity in an effective manner to be sure that *what* they preach and teach and counsel has the *highest probability* of being transferred appropriately to the many daily situations in which people find themselves.

HINDSIGHT

Learning is important, but we also want our students to be able to remember what they have learned and to be able to transfer what they learned from one situation to as many situations as possible in an appropriate manner.

We want our teachers, and through our teachers our students in our schools, to become knowledgeable of the information processing theory, with its three memory structures and five control processes. To understand and use these structures and these processes we believe will make every teacher a better teacher, and outcomes will be improved. We need to understand how to use the factors that improve memory capabilities, and how to minimize the factors that cause forgetting. In particular, we need to become keenly aware of the interference theories of forgetting. Of particular concern is the concept of coactive interference to which we have called attention in this chapter. Many changes could be made in our school systems which would improve the thoroughness of our learning, and at the same time would remove the excessive psychological pressure on students when they have to carry five or six subjects at the same time. We would like to challenge some of the brightest and best minds who are interested to research whether modular learning really does improve retention and transfer and relatedness among subject areas and ideas, as compared with the more traditional four-and-five-subjects-at-the-same-time method.

Every teacher, pastor, parent, counselor, and youth or children's leader ought to be vitally interested in working to produce positive transfer in the students for whom they are responsible. For our society is one, with its rapidly changing technology and circumstances, that needs people with the greatest amount of information and the greatest ability to transfer that information to many and varied sets of circumstances.

The behaviorists may not look upon information processing theory with as much enthusiasm as those of other approaches, and that is understandable. The cognitive theorists are the ones who are highly interested in this approach, and the humanists also share a deep concern for cognitive development, and therefore, presumably, for how information processing theory operates. For the Christian, it is a matter of using God-given processes and structures to help the individual develop in the most effective manner toward Christian maturity.

CHALKBOARD CHALLENGES

1. Think back over your own school career. Was there any course or section of that course that helped you to improve your memory? Since the whole purpose of the teaching-learning process is to help students learn, remember well, and be able to transfer what they have learned to other situations, do you find the answer to your previous question surprising? Would you agree with Cermak that it is time our school systems let all of our students in on these memorization techniques? "Courses on how to improve one's memory should be reintroduced into our curriculums and taught as actual academic courses."[24]

2. The research seems to indicate rather overwhelmingly that most children and adults are not efficient learners.[25] Think about it once again in your own experience: students' attempts at encoding rarely go beyond rote rehearsal such as rereading a textbook chapter, or outlining or underlining or highlighting. Why do you think this is so? Is it because students are not taught how to make the most of their memory capability? You may want to record some of your thoughts on these particular kinds of questions in your teacher's notebook to think about from time to time, and perhaps to add future comments in relation to this highly significant matter.

3. Which mnemonic devices do you think you can use for yourself as a student, and then as a teacher in the future? This is not as easy a question as you might think. Think about your teaching style and learning style, what you feel comfortable with, and which of these mnemonic devices you would best be able to use. Try out some of them with a group of friends, and in turn let them try out some if they so desire. By this kind of practice and testing, you will soon find that there are certain ones you can best use in your learning and in your teaching.

4. One of the keys for improving long-term memory is to make the information meaningful to the student. This is done by creating a relationship between what the student already knows and the new information. This interrelationship between the two sets of information needs to go beyond the surface kind of rote memorization, and techniques that may help us remember bits of information but do not do much to help with interrelationships among ideas, concepts, and principles. Can you think of some ways in which you, when you become a teacher, can help your students probe more deeply and create better relationships among ideas? Think about this and write down your ideas in your teacher's notebook. You will probably discover there are many of these ideas you can begin using immediately yourself as a student to deepen the meaning of your

---

24. Reprinted from *Improving Your Memory* by Laird S. Cermak, p. 133, by permission of W.W. Norton & Company, Inc. Copyright © 1975 by W.W. Norton & Company, Inc.
25. L. Annis and D. Annis, "A Normative Study of Students' Preferred Study Techniques" (paper presented at the annual meeting of the American Educational Research Association, San Francisco, April, 1979. Also R.A. Bjork, "Information Processing Analysis of College Teaching," *Educational Psychologist* 14 (1979):15-23.

learning and, therefore, improve your long-term memory and give you more information to bring to more situations.

5. Take a subject that is one of your favorites, and develop one fifty-minute class session concerning that subject at the level at which you hope to teach. If you are planning to teach at elementary level, of course you will need to break the fifty minutes down into much shorter periods and perhaps cover different subject areas. Consciously, carefully, and thoughtfully build into this one-class session the information processing theory, and indicate how you would deal with the various components of that theory, including the three memory structures and the five control processes. You may find this one of the most helpful exercises you have ever done, in terms of providing information for yourself which will be highly transferable to future classroom situations. Therefore, you will want to write in your teacher's notebook, perhaps the entire procedure for that class, or at least those aspects which pertain to the information processing theory.

6. On the basis of our assumption that many people of Christian persuasion will be reading this book, how does the Christian approach to learning utilize the information processing theory? May we suggest that you think about tying in the ultimate reality of God, the total development of the individual, the matter of stewardship under God, and similar ideas. Again, make good use of your teacher's notebook to record any ideas you feel are important for you to keep in this manner. Incidentally, the teacher's notebook idea in itself is one thing needed for promoting a deeper kind of "interrelationship thinking" among ideas, concepts, and principles!

WANT TO KNOW MORE?

LEARNING STRATEGY

If you want to know more about helping students develop a comprehensive learning strategy system (which includes two major components: concentration management and networking), then you will want to read the following research: Donald Dansereau, "The Development of a Learning Strategies Curriculum," in H. F. O'Neal, ed., *Learning Strategies* (New York: Academic, 1978); D. F. Dansereau, K. W. Collins, B. A. McDonald, J. C. Garland, G. Diekhoff, and S. H. Evans, "Development and Evaluation of a Learning Strategy Training Program," *Journal of Educational Psychology* 71, no. 1 (1979):64-73; and C. F. Holley, D. F. Dansereau, B. A. McDonald, J. C. Garland, and K. W. Collins, "Evaluation of a Hierarchical Mapping Technique as an Aid to Prose Processing," *Contemporary Educational Psychologist* 4 (1979):227-37.

A technique called *mapping,* very similar to networking, and the use of it for a group of eighth-graders is reported in B. B. Armbruster and T. H. Anderson, *The Effect of Mapping on the Free Recall of Expository Text,* Tech. Report #160 (Champaign, Ill.: Center for the Study of Reading, 1980).

MEMORY DEVELOPMENT

Read Robert Kail, *The Development of Memory in Children* (San Francisco: Freeman, 1979). Chapter 4 deals with the nature of recognition memory beginning with infants and going through children at ten years; chapter 1 contains an excellent outline of how encoding strategies develop from early childhood to adulthood.

INFORMATION PROCESSING

One of the books that covers very well the structures and processes of information processing theory is Roberta Klatzky, *Human Memory: Structures and Processes,* 2d ed. (San Francisco: Freeman, 1980).

For a very readable account of how information processing theory relates to classroom teaching and learning, read Frank Smith, *Comprehension and Learning* (New York: Holt, Rinehart, and Winston, 1975).

METAMEMORY

As we indicated, metamemory is a very new area, and there is not much available to read beyond individual research articles. Chapter 3 of Robert Kail's book *The Development of Memory in Children,* already mentioned, probably provides the best coverage available at this time.

Part 4
The Teaching-Learning Process

11
Management—Classroom Control

CONTENTS

	PAGE
Key Terms	277
That's Debatable!	278
Foresight	278
The Scope and Function of Classroom Management	279
Discipline and Control	279
A Continuum of Approaches to Classroom Discipline	281
Developing Responsible Classroom Managers	282
Preventive Management Medicine	285
Classroom Management and the Teaching-Learning Process	294
Hindsight	296
Chalkboard Challenges	296
Want to Know More?	298

KEY TERMS

Appropriate behavior
   Behavior that is productive and contributes to the teaching-learning process
Classroom management
   "Encompasses the provisions and procedures necessary to establish and maintain an environment in which instruction and learning can occur."[1] It includes management of time, space, materials, and guest personnel

---

1. Daniel L. Duke, "Editor Preface," in *Classroom Management*, ed. Daniel L. Duke, Seventy-eighth Yearbook of the National Society for the Study of Education, Part 2 (Chicago: University of Chicago Press, 1979), p. xii. Used by permission.

Corrective classroom management
The appropriate handling of inappropriate behavior in such a manner as to bring minimal disruption to the teaching-learning process and the providing of steps to help prevent such behavior in the future
Discipline
As a noun—One aspect of classroom management, defined as the set of appropriate behaviors permitted in the classroom
As a verb—Taking action to correct a student's inappropriate behavior with the goal of restoring the student as one who has appropriate behavior
Inappropriate behavior
Behavior that is disruptive, irrelevant, or unproductive in relation to the goals of the teaching-learning process
Preventive classroom management
The organization of the classroom environment to maximize student learning and minimize inappropriate behavior

That's Debatable!
Discipline or Permissiveness

In response to those who would counsel permissiveness, Dr. James Dobson counsels discipline.

> It is a great mistake to require nothing of children—to place no demands on their behavior. Whether a high school girl wears slacks or dress is not of earth-shaking importance, although it is significant that she be required to adhere to a few reasonable rules. If one examines the secret behind a championship football team, a magnificent orchestra, or a successful business, the principal ingredient is invariably *discipline*. How inaccurate is the belief that self-control is maximized in an environment which places no obligations on its children. How foolish is the assumption that self-discipline is a product of self-indulgence. How unfortunate has been the systematic undermining of educational rules, engineered by a minority of parents. Despite the will of the majority, the anti-disciplinarians have had their way. The rules governing student conduct have been cut down, and in their place have come a myriad of restrictions on educators. School prayers are illegal even if addressed to an unidentified God. The Bible can be read only as uninspired literature. Allegiance to the flag of our country cannot be required. Educators find it very difficult to punish or expel a student. Teachers are so conscious of parent militancy that they often withdraw from the defiant challenges of their students. As a result, academic discipline lies at the point of death in a nation's schools.[2]

Foresight

A relatively inexperienced elementary teacher asked an older, more experi-

---
2. From *Dare to Discipline* by James Dobson, p. 87. Published by Tyndale House Publishers, Inc., © 1970. Used by permission.

enced colleague to come into her room and observe her students' involvement. During the observation, it became readily apparent that, during small group activities, as many as seven or eight students would be out of the room (in the restroom, they said) at any one time.

As the two teachers discussed the situation, the younger teacher said, "Yes, I had noticed that. But the students really do need to go to the restroom, and I thought it unreasonable to not let anyone go." The teacher then decided to try a strategy that was suggested by the observer. She took two pieces of cardboard, labeled one "boys" and the other "girls," and hung them up in the back of the room. She then told the children, "Only one person can leave the room at a time. When you go out, simply turn the card over so that the blank side is showing; when you come back, return the card to its original position. If the blank side is showing and you want to go to the restroom, you must wait until the other student returns."

When the observer returned several days later for another observation, she reported a dramatic change. Children had quickly adapted to the new routine and were no longer leaving the room en masse. The result was higher student involvement.[3]

The story provides a striking example of how a change in a classroom management strategy worked wonders! That is what this chapter is about: the strategies and processes involved in developing well-organized classrooms. Such a classroom is essential to maximize student involvement in the teaching-learning process.

THE SCOPE AND FUNCTION OF CLASSROOM MANAGEMENT

As pointed out in our key terms, classroom management encompasses all the elements necessary to establish and maintain the kind of surroundings conducive to an effective teaching-learning process. As I heard one teacher put it, "It includes the whole ball of wax to keep something academically worthwhile happening and the students involved in productive learning!"

DISCIPLINE AND CONTROL

Discipline is often mistakenly thought of as classroom management. But it represents a narrower reality and so cannot be used as a synonym for classroom management. However, it is highly important to understand what discipline involves and how, as one aspect of classroom management, it relates to the larger picture in a vital manner.

Virtually every year since 1969, discipline has ranked as the number one concern of parents in relation to schools, as reflected by the annual Gallup polls. And beginning teachers as well worry greatly over their ability to "maintain discipline in the classroom." Administrators also listed discipline as their main

---

3. David A. Squires, William G. Huitt, and John K. Segars, *Effective Schools and Classrooms: A Research-Based Perspective* (Alexandria, Va.: ASCD, 1983), pp. 18-19.

concern and felt more time should be devoted to dealing with it as a key issue.[4] At least in a general way, parents, teachers, and students do understand that "if discipline is not maintained, the amount of appropriate learning taking place will be very little."

Discipline is the kind of concern which suffers in its discussion and application from both extremes. On the one hand, traditionally (and still currently) it is perceived as a totally negative kind of thing, where the parent or teacher stands in authoritative fashion holding a bullwhip and constant threats of punishment over the students' heads. At the other extreme, substantial numbers of psychologists and educators appear to be saying, "Don't be too hard on the child. Don't punish him—it's not his fault." Added to these extremes, not surprisingly, is the failure to agree on what discipline (as a set of behaviors) we deem appropriate in a classroom. Both parents and teachers have different views of discipline, and in the confusion, the discipline problem gets worse decade after decade. Now let us attempt to put into a paragraph or two an approach to discipline that will be helpful. Discipline may be operationally defined as a set of behaviors considered appropriate in a particular teaching-learning setting. Discipline is but one aspect—although a highly significant aspect—of classroom management. Discipline *does* have to do with *control,* however we seek to bring it about—externally or internally: control in the sense of placing reasonable limits on the set of behaviors in which a child may engage in the particular educational clinical setting.

How can we most effectively (both from the enhancement of the teaching-learning process and the development of the student) exercise control in order to maintain discipline appropriate to the educational setting? Or, to put it another way, *discipline* itself is not so much the issue of disagreement, but rather *the manner in which we exercise control to maintain discipline.*

SELF-DISCIPLINE

Wayson and Pinnell make an excellent point when they remind us that *"self-discipline* is the most essential goal of a curriculum that aims to help citizens attain and preserve freedom. Because we do not see that discipline is the heart of a curriculum, we fail to use methods that will stand some chance of teaching the discipline necessary for people in free societies."[5] While we find ourselves in disagreement with the methods they propose, nevertheless their thrust in the direction of helping the student achieve self-discipline—as part of the teaching-learning process over a period of time, helping the student move from externally

---

4. Daniel L. Duke, "How Administrators View the Crisis in School Discipline," *Phi Delta Kappan* 59 (1978):325-30.
5. William W. Wayson and Gay Su Pinnell, "Creating a Living Curriculum for Teaching Self-Discipline," in Daniel L. Duke, ed., *Helping Teachers Manage Classrooms* (Alexandria, Va.: ASCD, 1982), p. 117.

imposed controls to internal controls, in relation to reasonable limits on behavior—is a thrust in the appropriate direction.

Their definition of discipline also is helpful, "Discipline is the ability and the will to do what needs doing for as long as it needs doing and to learn from the results."[6]

A final point here in relation to the development of self-discipline is in the individual. While the behavior of all of us is a result of the interaction of many influences, if we talk about self-discipline, we are assuming self-accountability (the responsibility of each person for his own behavior). On this point, there is a great deal of controversy. But we need to beware of the trap: if genetics are at fault, or on the other hand environment is at fault, then we can make either or both of them into scapegoats, and the individual is attributed no accountability whatever for his or her behavior. In such a setting, the idea of "self-discipline" loses all its meaning. If students, or any other group of human beings, decide they are *not* personally accountable for their behavior, a very dangerous situation has developed for which there are no controls except whimsical violence.

Discipline is a crucial issue in the teaching-learning process. It is certainly not the whole of classroom management, but it cannot be bypassed or treated lightly, either from the standpoint of the well-managed classroom or the development of the student.

A Continuum of Approaches to Classroom Discipline

After pointing out the weaknesses of simplistic approaches to discipline, Vernon Jones emphasizes that "student behavior and school discipline are best viewed as environmental management issues. Any attempt to assist teachers in creating more productive learning environments must focus on a wide range of factors influencing individual and group behavior in school settings, methods for diagnosing school and classroom factors that may be eliciting the problem, and the options available for influencing student behavior."[7]

Jones continues, "Prior to learning specific management skills, teachers should have an overview of the various management methods that have been popularized during the past decade. This overview helps teachers clarify the issues surrounding classroom management and often significantly reduces confusion created by the highly theoretical or narrow approaches they have previously encountered."[8]

Insight, figure 11.1 reflects Jones's continuum of approaches to classroom discipline.

---

6. Ibid.
7. Vernon Jones, "Training Teachers to Be Effective Classroom Managers," in Daniel L. Duke, ed., *Helping Teachers Manage Classrooms*, p. 54.
8. Ibid.

> **Insight: A Continuum of Approaches to Classroom Discipline**
>
> | Instruction/ Organization | Interactive/ Interpersonal | Problem-Solving | Behavioristic | Behaviorism/ Punishment |
> |---|---|---|---|---|
> | Madeline Hunter | Carl Rogers | William Glasser | Bill Walker | Lee Carter |
> | Carl Wullen | Tom Gordon | Frank Maple | Wesley Becker | James Dobson |
> | Jahanna Lemiech | William Purkey | Tom Gordon | Daniel O'Leary | |
> | Carolyn Evertson | Richard Schmuck | | | |
> | Jere Brophy | Curwin and Fuhrman | | | |
>
> From Vernon Jones, "Training Teachers to Be Effective Classroom Managers," in Daniel L. Duke, ed., *Helping Teachers Manage Classrooms* (Alexandria, Va.: ASCD, 1982), p. 54. Reprinted with permission of the Association for Supervision and Curriculum Development. Copyright © 1982 by the Association for Supervision and Curriculum Development. All rights reserved.

Fig. 11.1

Consistent with our philosopher-clinician model, it is important to reflect upon the knowledge of the various approaches to classroom management. Most teachers who seriously engage in this process usually discover that one single approach will not answer all their problems, and yet the information gained can greatly enhance their own understanding; again, a case of "synthesizing without compromising" the integrity of one's position.

Developing Responsible Classroom Managers

Evertson and Emmer define effective management as consisting "of those teacher behaviors that produce high levels of student involvement in classroom activities and minimize student behaviors that interfere with the teacher's or other students' work and efficient use of instructional time."[9]

They then pose a critically important question: Is there any significant relationship between good classroom management and increased student achievement academically? Research is cited, including their own, which provides an answer of, "Yes, a moderate relationship."

It appears, then, that good classroom management is one enabling factor contributing to student achievement gained through an effective teaching-learning process.[10]

---

9. Carolyn M. Evertson and Edmund T. Emmer, "Preventive Classroom Management," in Daniel L. Duke, ed., *Helping Teachers Manage Classrooms*, p. 6.
10. P. Jackson, *Life in Classrooms* (New York: Holt, Rinehart, and Winston, 1968); B. Bloom, *Human Characteristics in School Learning* (New York: McGraw-Hill, 1976); J. Brophy, "Teacher Behavior and Its Effects," *Journal of Educational Psychology* 71 (1979):733-50. T.L. Good, "Teacher Effectiveness in the Elementary School: What We Know About It Now," *Journal of Teacher Education* 30 (1979):32-64; D. Medley, *Teacher Competence and Teacher Effectiveness: A Review of Process-Product Research* (Washington D.C.: American Association of Colleges for Teacher Education, 1977).

TWO STUDIES: THIRD GRADE AND JUNIOR HIGH, AND RESULTS

Evertson and Emmer conducted what we consider two outstanding studies regarding the strategies and processes for well-managed classrooms.[11] They are outstanding not only because of excellent design, but also because, importantly, one is at the elementary level, and the other is at the junior high level, thus providing a look at two rather different teaching-learning situations.

The focus for the first study, conducted in twenty-seven self-contained third-grade classrooms, was to determine how teachers organize and manage their classes beginning with the first day of school. Results are shown in the second Insight box (fig. 11.2).

A second study at the junior high level was conducted in seventh- and eighth-grade math and English classes. As a result, major differences between good and poor management behaviors were found, and were very similar to the results for the elementary school studied. These results are condensed in the third Insight box (fig. 11.3).

Together these studies point the way to some basic strategies for effective

---

Insight: Results of a Third-Grade Study on Classroom Management

(1) Better managers demonstrated an ability to analyze the tasks of the first few weeks of school in precise detail.

(2) Better managers incorporated the teaching of rules and procedures as a very important part of instruction during the first few weeks.

(3) Better organized teachers were able to see through the eyes of the students in planning the classroom and in introducing the students to new routines during the year.

(4) The more successful teachers monitored students closely during the first few weeks and dealt with problems immediately.

From Carolyn M. Evertson and Edmund T. Emmer, "Preventive Classroom Management" in Daniel L. Duke, ed., *Helping Teachers Manage Classrooms* (Alexandria, Va.: ASCD, 1982), p. 8. Reprinted with permission of the Association for Supervision and Curriculum Development. Copyright © 1982 by the Association for Supervision and Curriculum Development. All rights reserved.

Fig. 11.2

11. Evertson and Emmer, "Preventive Classroom Management," in Duke, *Helping Teachers Manage Classrooms*. (Research reported in this chapter was supported in part by the National Institute of Education, Contract No. OB-NIE-G-80-0116, P2, the Classroom Organization and Effective Teaching Project, Research and Development Center for Teacher Education, the University of Texas at Austin. The opinions expressed do not necessarily reflect the position or policy of the National Institute of Education and no official endorsement by that office should be inferred.)

> **Insight: Results of a Junior High Study on Classroom Management**
>
> (1) Even though all of the teachers had rules and procedures, the more effective managers had more complete systems and were more successful in teaching and installing rules and procedures.
> (2) The more effective teachers were rated as being more consistent in managing behavior.
> (3) More effective managers kept better track of student progress and completion of assignments.
> (4) Effective managers were more successful in presenting information clearly, in giving directions, and in stating objectives.
> (5) More effective managers wasted less time in their activities and had more on-task time.
>
> From Carolyn M. Evertson and Edmund T. Emmer, "Preventive Classroom Management," in Daniel L. Duke, ed., *Helping Teachers Manage Classrooms* (Alexandria, Va.: ASCD, 1982), p. 9. Reprinted with permission of the Association for Supervision and Curriculum Development. Copyright © 1982 by the Association for Supervision and Curriculum Development. All rights reserved.

Fig. 11.3

classroom management. The differences between the third grade and the junior high management function were more a matter of accommodation to age and classroom grouping, than real differences in *kind*.

Other effective classroom strategies to complement the above-listed ones include: (1) structuring the physical environment to prevent distraction;[12] (2) planning smooth transitions between activities;[13] (3) pacing activities so that students become neither confused or bored;[14] and (4) avoiding negative affect when controlling students' behavior.[15]

THE HOW OF HANDLING CLASSROOM MANAGEMENT

I posed a scenario to our older son who is fairly well along in medical studies

---

12. D.C. Berliner, "Impediments to the Study of Teacher Effectiveness," *Journal of Teacher Education* 27 (1976):5-13.
13. M. Arlin, "Teacher Transitions Can Disrupt Time Flow in Classrooms," *American Educational Research Journal* 16 (1979):42-56.
14. C. Fisher, N. Filby, R. Marliave, L. Cohen, M. Dishaw, J. Moore, and D. Berliner, *Teaching Behaviors, Academic Learning Time and Student Achievement: Final report of Phase III-B, Beginning Teacher Evaluation Study* (San Francisco: Far West Laboratory, 1978). Also J.S. Kounin and P.H. Doyle, "Degree of Continuity of a Lesson's Signal System and the Task Involvement of Children," *Journal of Educational Psychology* 67, no. 2 (1975):159-64.
15. R. Soar and R. Soar, *Setting Variables, Classroom Interaction, and Multiple Outcomes* (Final report for National Institute of Education, Project No. 6-0432, Gainesville: U. of Florida, 1978).

for his M.D. degree. "Suppose that when you went to your office in the morning, thirty children, each with a different problem, were there in your waiting room. They couldn't leave until three P.M., except for a brief lunch, and you had to treat them all at one time. How would you handle it?"

His reply: "I'd treat them one at a time, of course, in the order in which they arrived and signed in. The only exception would be an extreme emergency which warranted prompt attention to a child." Then he added, "I hope I'd have more intelligence than to have that many appointments scheduled all at the same time. Part of my preventive medicine would be to think about the situation ahead of time, and try to schedule reasonably."

I didn't have the courage to tell him I was thinking of the teaching-learning process in the classroom, where this very kind of situation happens to teachers on a five-day-a-week basis! "Treat them one at a time!" "Schedule them one at a time!" How nice—but realistically, we do not have that choice. Admittedly, there are some other differences between the two situations, but the "How shall I handle it?" remains.

Lortie hits the bullseye in describing the task of the teacher: "The teacher . . . is expected to elicit work from students. Students in all subjects and activities must engage in directed activities which are believed to produce learning. Their behavior, in short, should be purposeful, normatively controlled, and steady; concerns with discipline and control, in fact, largely revolve around the need to get work done by immature, changeful, and divergent persons who are confined in a small space."[16]

We have already discussed some suggestions from Evertson, Emmer, and their associates coming out of some excellent practical research. We look now at some other ways to develop an effective classroom management system.

PREVENTIVE MANAGEMENT MEDICINE

Our son's comment about preventive medicine, especially his comment concerning thinking about it ahead of time, caught fire in my mind. How can we handle classroom management by thinking about it ahead of time, planning, and preparing for it? We have long been convinced that the first few days of the school year are of exceeding importance in establishing the management system one is going to use. And perhaps, toughest of all, how can the systems be maintained throughout the school year?

A disclaimer statement must be made here. We have no easy answers; neither do we claim these suggestions will work for everyone, for there is a sense in which effective classroom management has to develop a certain "fit" between the teacher and the particular clinical setting. What we do say is that we, and others, have found the following suggestions helpful, and offer them for your serious consideration for possible inclusion in your "repertoire resources."

16. D. Lortie, *School Teacher: A Sociological Study* (Chicago: U. of Chicago, 1975), p. 151.

AHEAD OF TIME (BEFORE THE SCHOOL YEAR BEGINS)

What are your students going to be doing? What kinds of behavior are you going to expect from them? Form a set of rules? Yes—but communicating a clear-cut set of expectations is far more difficult, because the expectations must be geared to various activities—from seatwork, all-the-class-at-once, small groups, to different-in-kind activities within each of the groupings.

Let us look at just one example to model the preparation of expected behaviors. Suppose, as you sit with a small group in your class, asking questions about something they have just read (fourth-grade level), one student consistently answers all the questions, shutting out the other students. By your preventive management planning, you could designate the expected behavior in this situation, such as, "No one answers twice until everyone has had a turn." A little thing? Maybe. But the cumulation of these "little things" can disrupt severely your teaching-learning process.

It is amazing how many areas there are in which a teacher needs a clear set of expectations to communicate clearly to her students. The tables in figures 11.1 and 11.2 list expectations and procedures for the elementary level and the middle school (junior high classrooms.) We are grateful to Carolyn Evertson, Edmund Emmer, and their associates for the use of these tables from the Research and Development Center for Teacher Education at the University of Texas. We recommend these expectations for your careful study.

Expectations and Procedures for the Elementary School Classroom

Area of Behavior	A Common Expectation or Procedure
A. Student use of classroom space and facilities	
1. Desks or tables and student storage space	Students are usually expected to keep these clean and neat. Some teachers set aside a particular period of time each week for students to clean out desks. Alternatively, straightening out materials could be a good end-of-day routine.
2. Learning centers/stations	Appropriate behavior at the center, access to the center, care of materials, and procedures for coming and going should be considered.
3. Shared materials, bookshelves, drawers, and cabinets	Access and use should be spelled out.
4. Teacher's desk and storage areas	Frequently these are off limits to students, except when the teacher's permission is given.
5. Drinking fountain, sink, pencil sharpener, and restroom	Decide when and how these can be used. Most teachers prefer not to have lines waiting at any of these locations.
B. Procedures concerning other areas of the school	
1. Out-of-class restrooms, drinking fountains, office, library, resource rooms	Appropriate student behavior needs to be identified. Procedures for students coming to and going from these areas should be decided upon.

Management—Classroom Control

2. Coming and going from the classroom	Students need to learn how to line up properly and how to pass through the halls correctly. Consider such things as the condition of the room before lining up, and whether talking is allowed.
3. Playground	Expectations need to be identified for coming from and going to the playground, safety and maintenance rules, and how to get students' attention for lining up or listening. Some teachers use a coach's whistle.
4. Lunchroom	Expectations for table manners, behavior, and noise level should be identified.
C. Procedures during whole class activities	
1. Student participation in class discussions	Many teachers require students to raise their hands to be called on before speaking during whole-class activities.
2. Student involvement and attention	Students are expected to listen to the person who is talking.
3. Assignments	Many teachers record assignments on a chalkboard or elsewhere, or have students copy the assignments in notebooks.
4. Talk among students during seatwork	Some teachers require silence; others allow quiet talk (very soft whispering). Also, teachers sometimes use a cue or signal to let students know when the noise level is unacceptable. For example, a bell rung once means no more talking. Also needed are procedures for students working together, if this is to be allowed, and some procedure to enable students to contact the teacher if they need help. Typical procedures involve students raising hands when help is needed or, if the teacher is involved with other students or in group work, the use of classroom monitors.
5. Passing out books, supplies	Supplies that are frequently used can be passed out by a monitor. Students need to know what to do while they wait for their materials.
6. Students turning in work	Teachers frequently have a set of shelves or an area where students turn in assignments when they are finished. Alternatively, a special folder for each student may be kept.
7. Handing back assignments to students	Prompt return of corrected papers is desirable. Many teachers establish a set time of the day to do this. Students need to know what to do with the material when they receive it (place it in a notebook or folder, or take it home).
8. Make-up work	Procedures are needed for helping students who have been absent as well as for communicating assignments that must be made up.
9. Out of seat policies	Students need to know when it is acceptable to be out of seat and when permission is needed.
10. What to do when seatwork is finished	Some teachers use extra credit assignments, enrichment activities, free reading, etc.
D. Procedures during reading groups or other small-group work	
1. Student movement into and out of group	These transitions should be brief, quiet, and nondisruptive to other students. Many teachers use a bell to signal movement from seatwork to small group. This works when there is a preset order that students know.
2. Bringing materials to the group	Students need to know what they are to bring with them to the group. One way to communicate this is to include a list of the materials along with posted assignments.
3. Expected behavior of students in the group	Just as in whole-group activities, students need clear expectations about what behaviors are appropriate in small-group work.
4. Expected behavior of students not in the small group	Students out of the group also need clear expectations about desirable behavior. Important areas include noise level, student talk, access to the teacher, and what to do when the seatwork

	assignment or other activites are completed. Effective managers avoid problems by giving very clear instructions for activities of students out-of-group. Checking briefly between groups also helps prevent problems from continuing as well as allowing monitoring. Student helpers may also be identified.
E. Other procedures that must be decided upon	
1. Beginning the school day	Establishing a consistent routine, such as the Pledge of Allegiance, date, birthdays, an overview of the morning's activities, or passing back graded papers helps start the day while still giving time for late arrivals and for administrative matters to be accomplished.
2. Administrative matters	Such details as attendance reporting, collecting lunch money, and other record-keeping must be done while students are in the room. Teachers can set aside a specific time of the day for performing these tasks during which the students are expected to engage in some activity. For example, 10 minutes of quiet reading fills the time constructively while allowing the teacher to handle administrative tasks with little interruption.
3. End of school day	Routines can be planned for concluding each day. Straightening desks, gathering materials, singing a song, or reviewing activities and things learned during the day provide some structure for this major transition time.
4. Student conduct during interruptions and delays	Interruptions are inevitable and sometimes frequent. Students can be taught to continue working if interrupted, or to sit patiently and quietly otherwise.
5. Fire drills and other precautionary measures	School procedures need to be identified and carefully taught to the children.
6. Housekeeping and student helpers	Most children love to help, and the teacher need only identify specific tasks. They are also a good way to help some children learn responsibility. Some possibilities: feeding classroom pets, watering plants, erasing chalkboards, acting as line leader, messenger, etc. A procedure for choosing and rotating responsibilities among students needs to be established.

Note: This table is adapted from the manual *Organizing and Managing the Elementary School Classroom*, by Carolyn M. Evertson, Edmund T. Emmer, Barbara S. Clements, Julie P. Sanford, Murray E. Worsham, and Ellen L. Williams (Austin, Tex.: U. of Texas, Austin, Research and Development Center for Teacher Education, August 1980). Reprinted by permission.

Fig. 11.4

Expectations and Procedures for Junior High School/Middle School Classrooms

Area of Behavior	A Common Expectation or Procedure
A. Procedures for beginning class	
1. Administrative matters	The teacher needs procedures to handle reporting absences and tardiness. Students need to know what behaviors are expected of them while the teacher is completing administrative procedures. Some teachers begin the period with a brief warm-up activity such as a few problems or a brief assignment. Others expect the students to sit quietly and wait for the teacher to complete the routine.
2. Student behavior before and at the beginning of the period	Procedures should be established for what students are expected to do when the tardy bell rings (be in seats, stop talking), behavior during PA announcements (no talking, no interruptions of the teacher), what materials are expected to be brought to class each day, and how materials to be used during the period will be distributed.

Management—Classroom Control

B. Procedures during whole-class instructional activities

1. Student talk — Many teachers require that students raise their hands in order to receive Permission to speak. Sometimes teachers allow chorus responses (everybody answers at once) without hand raising, but the teacher then needs to identify and use some signal to students which lets them know when such responding is appropriate.

2. Use of the room by students — Students should know when it is appropriate to use the pencil sharpener, to obtain materials from shelves or bookcases, and if, and when, it is appropriate to leave their seats to seek help from the teacher or other students. Unclear expectations in this area result in some students spending time wandering about the room.

3. Leaving the room — Some procedure needs to be established for allowing students to use the restroom, go to the libarary or school office, etc. Usually the school will have some specified system. We have noted that teachers who are free with hall passes frequently have large numbers of requests to leave the room.

4. Signals for attention — Frequently teachers use a verbal signal or a cue such as moving to a specific area of the room, ringing a bell, or turning on an overhead projector to signal to students. Such a signal, if used consistently, can be an effective device for making a transition between activities or for obtaining student attention.

5. Student behavior during seatwork — Expectations need to be established for what kind of talk, if any, may occur during seatwork, how students can get help, when out-of-seat behavior is or is not permitted, access to materials, and what to do if seatwork assignments are completed early.

6. Procedures for laboratory work or individual projects — A system for distributing materials when these are used is essential. Also, safety routines or rules are vital. Expectations regarding appropriate behavior should be established for students working individually or in groups, and when extensive movement around the room or coming and going is required. Finally, routines for cleaning up are suggested.

C. Expectations regarding responsibility for work

1. Policy regarding the form of work — Procedures can be established for how students are to place headings on paper, for the use of pen or pencil, and for neatness.

2. Policy regarding completion of assignments — The teacher will have to decide on whether incomplete or late work is acceptable, and under what conditions, and whether a penalty will be imposed. In addition, some procedure for informing students of due dates for assignments should be established, along with procedures for make-up work for students who were absent.

3. Communicating assignments to students — An effective procedure for communicating assignments is to keep a list of each period's work assignments during a 2- or 3-week period of time. Posting this list allows students who were absent to easily identify necessary make-up work. Another useful procedure is to record the assignment for the day on an overhead projector transparency or on the front chalkboard, and require students to copy the assignment onto a piece of paper or into a notebook. Students who do not complete assignments in class will then have a record of what is expected when they return to the assignment at home or during a study period.

4. Checking procedures — Work that is to be checked by students in class can save the teacher time and provide quick feedback to students. Procedures should be established for exchanging papers, how errors are to be noted, and how papers are to be returned and passed to the teacher.

5. Grading policy	Students should know what components will be included in determining report card grades and the weight, or percent, of each component.
D. Other procedures	
1. Student use of teacher desk or storage areas	Generally these are kept off limits to students, except when the teacher gives special permission.
2. Fire and disaster drills	Students should be informed early in the year about what they are to do during such emergencies. Typically, the school will have a master plan and will conduct a schoolwide drill.
3. Procedures for ending the class	Expectations regarding straightening up the room, returning to seats, noise level, and a signal for dismissal may be established. When cleanup requires more than a few seconds, teachers usually set aside the necessary time at the end of the period to complete the task before the bell rings.
4. Interruptions	Students need to know what is expected during interruptions (continue working or sit quietly).

Note: This table is adapted from Tables 2 and 3 in the manual *Organizing and Managing the Junior High Classroom* by Edmund T. Emmer, Carolyn M. Evertson, Barbara S. Clements, Julie P. Sanford, and Murrey E. Worsham (Austin, Tex.: U. of Texas, Austin, Research and Development Center for Teacher Education, August 1981).

Fig. 11.5

The remaining items for completion *ahead of time* include: *Formulating a set of rules based on your expectations.* Some teachers find they need just a very few rules, others make out a rather detailed list of rules. It is really a matter of what you feel comfortable with as you engage in the teaching-learning process in your particular setting. *Decide and write down what happens when students follow the rules, and when they don't. Plan ways to provide special incentives*—from free reading time to a certificate of award, from a word of praise to providing individual contracts for students under certain special circumstances.

To summarize your ahead-of-time planning: (1) write down your expectations of students, (2) develop rules based on those expectations, (3) lay out consequences of appropriate or inappropriate behavior, (4) plan special incentives.

WHEN THE SCHOOL YEAR STARTS

This is an exceedingly important time for the teacher to establish the basis of an effective classroom management system. Every teacher knows the excitement of the first few days of school: students in a different setting, with a different teacher (you!), different learning materials, different classmates (at least in part). Generally (and there are exceptions), students are more receptive to new ways of doing things as the new school year starts.

In addition, many students feel highly anxious at the beginning of a new school year. You can help allay some of their anxieties by communicating clearly your expectations and thus producing a more structured atmosphere to help these students feel more secure.

It is always easier if students do not have to unlearn inappropriate behaviors.

So take advantage from the first moment to teach appropriate behavior, before undesirable behavior has an opportunity to get established.

Research suggests seven principles which good classroom managers use at the beginning of the year.[17]

(1) Take some time during the first day or class meeting to discuss your rules. During the first several weeks, point out examples of appropriate behaviors in relation to the rules.

(2) Make the teaching of rules/procedures a part of your regular teaching routine. State rules, demonstrate them, and in elementary grades it is a good idea to let the students have the opportunity to practice them.

(3) Don't try to teach every rule the first day! Teach them as they are needed, and be sure they are understood and used correctly.

(4) Promote a high rate of success during the first few days of school by involving children in easy tasks. Early success helps to provide a positive outlook and makes task engagement easier.

(5) For the first few days, give the same assignment to the whole class, and use only simple procedures. This gives both you and the students opportunity to adjust.

(6) Include in your lesson plans provision for teaching rules and procedures where appropriate. Allow time, for example, to be sure students know, in detail, what to do. When the students do seatwork for the first time in your class, they need to know what paper and other materials to use, what heading you want on the paper, and so on.

(7) Do not assume students know how to do something after just one practice attempt. The more complex the procedure, the more it should be reviewed. Once students can read, rules can be posted at the appropriate spot (for example at each learning center).

The overall bottom line for the start of a new school year is: keep it simple, do it right, promote success, and teach your rules and procedures as a part of your regular teaching-learning process, thus establishing appropriate behavior from the outset.

DURING THE SCHOOL YEAR

We have discussed the need to plan ahead of time in order to get off to a good start at the beginning of the year. We turn now to the question of how to maintain good classroom management *during the school year*.

Exciting maintenance. The key phrase here, in my experience, has been "exciting maintenance." By "exciting" is *not* meant that the teacher goes to class every morning ready to put on a three-ring circus to keep the students entertained. This soon becomes a losing battle, and the teacher will exhaust herself.

---

17. Evertson and Emmer, pp. 23-24.

What *is* meant by "exciting" is that the teacher does not allow herself to become bored or boring as the maintenance of this classroom management system is carried out. The effective classroom manager will do her maintenance in an *interesting* manner, "keeping the edge on" with occasional special incentives and surprises.

How do you spell *relief* from the doldrums in the middle of the school year? I-N-C-E-N-T-I-V-E, S-U-R-P-R-I-S-E, T-H-E U-N-E-X-P-E-C-T-E-D.

"I've declared this to be National Sweetheart Week. At the end of the week, since it's Valentine's Week, I'm going to give a heart-shaped box of candy to the student who accumulates the biggest number of points. You'll be declared the Miss Academic Sweetheart or Mr. Valentine of our class." (Make sure that these points emphasize credit for a lot of appropriate behavior). However, we do not recommend the use of a point system based on a prize for more than a week, lest it become cumbersome and lose its appeal. Also, you may just wish to make a proclamation of "Academic Sweetheart" or "Mr. Valentine" without the box of candy. With children, always clear with parents first about candy or other edibles.

"This week you have a choice. You can either work the regular math assignments and take the test on Friday. Or, you can work the special math puzzler problem I'll give you, and if you get it right by Friday, you will not have to take the test. Either way, you'll be working on the math procedures you need to learn this week." This not only encourages completion of the task, but adds the "edge" of a choice.

What about the maintenance of your classroom management system? There are two main functions during the year which subsume a great many smaller, but important, functions.

Two Main Functions.

(1) Monitoring Appropriate Behavior

Keeping an eye on student behavior is usually called *monitoring*. This involves watching students' behavior in the classroom and also keeping up with student progress in the academic areas. The objective always is to find any difficulties while they are small, prevent them from growing to class-disrupting proportions, and resolve them in such a way that the student is encouraged to grow.

If a student is failing an assignment early, best to catch it early through the monitoring process, and correct the inappropriate behavior before it becomes a habit.

The teacher, in order to monitor student behavior, should virtually always be in a position where she can scan the entire class and its activities.

If a particular time of the day appears to encourage disruptive behavior, and this happens frequently, the teacher needs to look carefully at the circumstances occurring at that time of day to discover the causes of inappropriate behavior and take steps to remedy them.

(2) Managing Inappropriate Behavior

Stop inappropriate behavior as quickly as possible—this is always the rule. This establishes the credibility of the rules, and the teacher makes clear through her action she is going to use the system, and use it consistently. Effective classroom managers do not overreact or become emotional about inappropriate behavior. Research indicates good managers use the following procedures for dealing with inappropriate behavior.[18]

(a) Simply ask a student to cease the inappropriate behavior and stay with the student until the behavior is appropriately performed.

(b) Keep eye contact with the student until the appropriate behavior returns.

(c) If necessary, remind the student of the appropriate procedure.

(d) Ask the student to state the appropriate procedure behavior. Help the student understand it clearly.

(e) Impose the consequences for violation of the procedure. (Usually, to do the procedure over correctly). If the student understands the procedure but is not performing it appropriately (for attention-getting or other reasons), use a mild penalty as per your rules, which have previously been clearly communicated.

(f) If off-tasks, inappropriate behavior seems to be widespread in the class, inject variety, change, "excitement" as previously noted.

Serious disruptive behavior. Occasionally, in spite of the teacher's best efforts at classroom management, serious disruptive behavior may occur. When it does, three procedures are usually appropriate:

(1) Talk with the student out of the presence of the class (in the hall, for example).

(2) If the school has a procedure for dealing with this kind of inappropriate behavior, invoke it.

(3) Follow up with all appropriate personnel, from principal to parents, to *explain* and *prevent* such behavior in the future.

THE EFFECTIVE CLASSROOM MANAGER: A PROFILE

Evertson and Emmer provide us with a profile of an effective classroom manager, as a result of the extensive research in which they and their associates engaged.

> The effective classroom manager has a clear set of expectations about appropriate and inappropriate behavior at the beginning of the year and communicates to students in a variety of ways. The better manager establishes routines and procedures to guide student behavior in a variety of classroom activities and takes considerable care in teaching the system to the students. Departures from expected behavior are generally dealt with promptly so the students receive feedback, and the consequences are clear and consistent. The teacher monitors student behavior carefully and, thus, is aware of small problems before they become big ones. Better managers are also better communicators and are able to explain, give directions, and communicate information correctly.[19]

18. Ibid., p. 27.
19. Ibid., p. 24.

CLASSROOM MANAGEMENT AND THE TEACHING-LEARNING PROCESS

Throughout this chapter, we have sought to tie a comprehensive view of classroom management to the teaching-learning process. Two significant areas need yet to be mentioned.

THE LIVING CURRICULUM

The "Living Curriculum" resolves from organizational factors combining to quietly, pervasively, and rather consistently "teach everyone in the school 'how we do it around here.' They comprise a powerful instruction in the school."[20]

Research makes it rather evident that eight such factors "have a strong relationship to the quality of discipline, as they combine to create the Living Curriculum."[21]

These factors include: (1) patterns of communication, problem solving, and decision making, (2) patterns of authority and status, (3) procedures for developing and implementing rules, (4) student belongingness, (5) relationship with parents and community forces, (6) processes for dealing with personal problems, (7) curriculum and instructional practices, (8) the physical environment.

Although we do not have the space to include a detailed discussion of these eight factors, the reader who wishes to do so will find an excellent discussion by Wayson and Pinnell in their chapter "Creating a Living Curriculum for Teaching Self-Discipline" in *Helping Teachers Manage Classrooms*, an ASCD publication.[22] It is a significant presentation worthy of serious reflection.

THE UNIQUE CHRISTIAN CONTRIBUTION

The Christian approach has a most helpful kind of contribution to make to our understanding of discipline in relation to classroom management and the teaching-learning process.

A Christian emphasizes that discipline is a positive word coming from the same root as "disciple."

Concerned with training and nurturing, it is the firm foundation for the

---

20. Wayson and Pinnell, p. 118.
21. William M. Wayson, et al., "A Handbook for Developing Schools with Good Discipline" (report of the Phi Delta Kappa Commission on School Discipline, Bloomington, Ind., 1982). Also G.S. Pinnell, et al., *Directory of Schools Reported to Have Exemplary Discipline* (Bloomington, Ind.: Phi Delta Kappa International, 1982); United States Department of Health, Education and Welfare, "Violent Schools-Safe Schools," 1978; J.M. First and M.H. Mizell, eds., *Everybody's Business: A Book About School Discipline* (Columbia, S.C.: Southeastern Public Educational Program, 1980); Susan C. Kaeser, *Orderly Schools That Serve All Children: A Review of Successful Schools in Ohio* (Cleveland: Citizen's Council for Ohio Schools, 1979).
22. Wayson and Pinnell, "Creating a Living Curriculum," pp. 118-39.

teaching process. Almost all we do in relation to the student includes a phase of discipline. With the young child discipline is generally external—a direction and control by parents and teachers. As the child matures, our goal is to encourage and train for more and more self-control in the life of the child. This will obviously necessitate less and less external control from parents and teachers. The process of disciplining is a positive challenge in responsibility. There will always be a negative part of discipline, of course—punishment. However, we cannot let the need for punishment overshadow the positive side of discipline—and nurturing of children, the disciplining of students. We must find a balance between positive discipleship and the effective punishment.[23]

Insight: Techniques to Improve Discipline

1. Use simple analogy-parable.
2. Use humor to win the class. (Don't ridicule.)
3. Have fun with your class.
4. Remove the cause for poor behavior, if possible.
5. When something happens, discuss *why* with the child.
6. Stop the problem at its inception.
7. Avoid tattling.
8. Don't let the child get the upper hand.
9. Concentrate upon improvement.
10. Show the child how to do better.
11. Speak to the individual rather than the entire class. Give specific directions.
12. Relate the punishment to the offense.
13. Use a positive approach rather than a negative one. "I think James is almost ready" is preferred to "I don't see one person who is ready."
14. Recognize a ripple effect of discipline. Clarity and reasonable firmness produce the best results.
15. Wise and infrequent use of punishment. Use punishment when it is necessary.

From James W. Braley, "The Christian Philosophy Applied to Methods of Instruction" in Paul A. Kienel, ed., *The Philosophy of Christian School Education*, 2d ed. (Whittier, Calif.: ACSI, 1978), p. 121. Used by permission.

Fig. 11.6

23. James W. Braley, "The Christian Philosophy Applied to Methods of Instruction," in Paul A. Kienel, ed., *The Philosophy of Christian School Education* (Whittier, Calif.: Association of Christian Schools International, 1978), pp. 119-20. Used by permission.

These qualities are further practicalized by Braley, whose words we just quoted, when he gives us a suggested list of Techniques to Improve Discipline (fig. 11.6) and Approaches to Avoid In Discipline (fig. 11.7).

Finally, Braley caps his discussion of discipline with the reminder that after punishment is administered, it is highly important to reestablish a positive relationship with the child.

"This is often a time when the spirit of the child is softest. By reassuring the child of your interest and affection, you can often provide a time of positive reaction to the discipline. It will not always work, but it is worth the effort."[24]

HINDSIGHT

With this chapter we began part 4 of the book, *The Teaching-Learning Process*. We are getting to the heart of the "clinician" portion of our philosopher-clinician model.

Discipline is an exceedingly important aspect of a comprehensive view of classroom management. We have used research and practical experience to relate essential factors and features of effective classroom management for the teaching-learning process. We have espoused the point of view that we are managing for reasonable control of student behavior, and our goal is to help the student to the point where his or her control will grow to be self-control, rather than externally manipulated control. We presented, again from the best of the research, a profile of the effective classroom manager.

Finally we touched on the highly significant areas of "Living Curriculum" and the unique Christian contribution in reference to discipline, classroom management, and the teaching-learning process.

CHALKBOARD CHALLENGES

1. Think back over your own earlier experiences with classroom control in your school. Analyze those experiences. Which techniques *really* worked? Which ones did you feel were unfair? Why?

2. As a result of your analysis in number 1, make a list of procedures/techniques you believe are worthy of using in relation to classroom management. Make the list a part of your teacher's notebook. It's a list you will use often!

3. In your teacher's notebook, set up a page for each of the major educational approaches in relation to classroom management. For example, on the behavioristic page write "Behavioristic Approach to CRM" at the top, and then list those procedures/techniques you perceive the behaviorist as using to establish and maintain a system of CRM. Do the same for the cognitive-discovery approach, the

---

24. Braley, "The Christian Philosophy," p. 122.

> **Insight: Approaches to Avoid in Discipline**
>
> 1. Don't make consistent use of rigid, regimented control. This does not mean that we are not firm and that there are not rules to guide the individual in the class.
> 2. Don't permit yourself to become preoccupied with a student's limitations.
> 3. Don't punish a child when you are angry.
> 4. Don't lose your composure—appear calm.
> 5. Don't expose the class or the individual to frequent, prolonged displays of emotion.
> 6. Don't punish the entire group for just one (or a smaller group).
> 7. Don't shame a student before all the other members of the class.
> 8. Don't talk down to students.
> 9. Don't use sarcasm or ridicule.
> 10. Don't use punishment for retribution. (Don't try to get even with the child.)
> 11. Don't make idle threats.
> 12. Don't depend on loud methods of discipline.
>
> From James W. Braley, "The Christian Philosophy Applied to Methods of Instruction," in Paul A. Kienel, ed., *The Philosophy of Christian School Education,* 2d ed. (Whittier, Calif.: ACSI, 1978), pp. 121-22. Used by permission.

Fig. 11.7

humanistic approach, and the Christian approach. Reflect carefully as you write. Then go back over the four lists and check those items with which you basically agree. How do they fit with the philosophic integrity of your approach to the teaching-learning process?

You can use this exercise profitably as you reflect, analyze, and gain further experience in the teaching-learning process from the teacher's point of view. Constantly work toward a position that has philosophic integrity rather than one which is based on a hit-or-miss nature. "Synthesize without compromise!"

4. There is a real and basic difference between the Christian approach to discipline and the other basic approaches, based on the nature of the child as sinful, rather than good or neutral. Test out the logic of these approaches as to practices and results, personally and socially. You may want to record some of your thoughts in your teacher's notebook.

WANT TO KNOW MORE?

CLASSROOM MANAGEMENT RESEARCH

Two excellent books from the Association for Supervision and Curriculum Development are considered "must" reading for students who want to really be up to date on the research with relation to classroom management. The first of these is Daniel L. Duke, ed., *Helping Teachers Manage Classrooms* (Alexandria, Va.: ASCD, 1982). The second is David A. Squires, William C. Huitt, and John K. Segars, *Effective Schools and Classrooms: A Research Based Perspective* (Alexandria, Va.: ASCD, 1983).

CHRISTIAN PERSPECTIVE

Two excellent books from the Christian point of view will be most helpful to the student interested in that perspective. The first is Paul A. Kienel, ed., *Philosophy of Christian School Education,* 2d ed. (Whittier, Calif.: ASCI, 1978). The second is James Dobson, *Dare to Discipline* (New York: Bantam, 1970).

GENERAL CLASSROOM MANAGEMENT

From the Research and Development Center for Teacher Education University of Texas at Austin come two manuals based on thorough research: Carolyn M. Evertson, et al., *Organizing and Managing the Elementary School Classroom,* August 1980, and Edmund T. Emmer, et al., *Organizing and Managing the Junior High Classroom,* August 1981.

12
Management—Classroom Climate

CONTENTS

	PAGE
Key Terms	299
That's Debatable!	300
Foresight	300
Organizing the Classroom	301
The Terrible Ten and Their Transformation	302
Classroom Climate and the Teaching-Learning Process	319
Hindsight	319
Chalkboard Challenges	320
Want to Know More?	321

KEY TERMS

Ability grouping
  The practice of organizing classroom groups to put together students of a particular age/grade who have similar standings on measures of achievement and capability

Authoritarian approach
  An approach to the teaching-learning process in which the teacher maintains virtually total control without participation in decision-making by the students

Authoritative approach
  An approach to the teaching-learning process characterized by a teacher who

is knowledgeable in her subject/literary areas and, while everyone in the classroom knows the teacher is in charge, nevertheless students have ample opportunities to participate in decision making

Classroom climate
The psychological context of the classroom; metaphorically, the classroom's atmosphere for human development and learning

Cohesiveness
Describes closely-knit social groups which satisfy the needs of their members

Democratic approach
An approach to the teaching-learning process characterized by moderate teacher control, with emphasis on student participation in most of the decision-making

Laissez-faire approach
An approach to the teaching-learning process in which the teacher exercises minimal controls over the students or classroom activities

Learning style
A consistent pattern of behavior with a particular range of individual differences

Morale
The affective tone of the classroom or school as a result of students' perceptions of major operational characteristics and their relationship to them

THAT'S DEBATABLE!
Questions for You to Consider

1. Do you favor or oppose the grouping of students by ability? Why?
2. To what extent should teachers become involved in the personal problems of the students?
3. Should the schools compensate for emotional gaps left by destructive home influences?
4. If a child came to your class crying, and saying, "When I left home, my mother was drunk," what would you say or do as a teacher?
5. How much difference do you think the physical arrangements of a classroom make (seating patterns, etc.)?
6. How does the belief that God is a God of beauty translate into the aesthetics of the classroom?

FORESIGHT

How important to you is the atmosphere of your school? Even more so, of your classroom? Are two prominent authors right when they say that "one of the most important potential objectives of schools is . . . the creation of pleasant environments for young people?"[1] These same authors then raise an issue that is blatantly obvious yet for the most part ignored by researchers and practitioners alike: "whatever the preparatory and socializing function of schools, the student still must live seven hours a day for up to thirteen years in them. Is it unreasonable to expect schools to be as comfortable and accommodating as possible?"[2]

We believe a highly significant but sorely neglected area, in terms of research and application, is that of school and classroom climates. It just may be one of the most important keys we have to unlock productive behavior, excellent achievement, and student development.

It is essential to the development of a better teaching-learning process that we look carefully at the relevance of school and classroom climate to student achievement and growth. Likewise, we need to ferret out, as best we can, what components contribute to the school and classroom climate.

That is precisely what we will attempt to do in this chapter, with the aim of helping you to become extremely sensitive to this area and with the encouragement to consider seriously the suggestions made for improving classroom climate. Additionally, we hope that great numbers of you will become leaders in helping to improve the climate of schools and classrooms in which you teach.

Organizing the Classroom

You are talking with your best friend. You are on the bus riding home, and the two of you are discussing what happened in school that day. In the course of the conversation, you find yourself saying, "I hate Mrs. Jones's class." Your friend replies, "Me, too! But I just love art class, don't you?" In that brief part of your conversation, you and your friend have targeted the whole issue of classroom climate in relation to the teaching-learning process.

If you think about the reasons you hate a particular class, and on the other hand, the reasons you love another class, you begin to get at some of the underlying factors that contribute to classroom climate. We have defined classroom climate in this text as "the psychological context of the classroom"—the weather condition, if you will, of the classroom. And that climate is developed by the manner in which the classroom is structured, physically and psychologically, along with the interactions of the students and the teacher on a day-to-day basis. The teaching-learning process always takes place in some kind of context, and to help us understand better the behavior of the individual in the context, we do need to look carefully at the factors involved and how students and teachers may be perceiving them. It must be noted here as well that the total organization of the school also has a tremendous influence on the climate of the individual classrooms.

---

1. Daniel L. Duke and William Seidman, "Are Public Schools Organized to Minimize Behavior Problems?" in Daniel L. Duke, ed., *Helping Teachers Manage Classrooms* (Alexandria, Va.: ASCD, 1982), p. 159.
2. Ibid., pp. 159-60.

The Terrible Ten and Their Transformation

We have chosen to organize the many and variable factors involved in the development of classroom climate under the heading of Terrible Ten, with full understanding that they could be listed under The Infamous Forties, or divided into any other number that one might wish. We recognize others may group these factors differently, but our main concern here is that you understand the high significance of climate as it influences the teaching-learning process, and that you incorporate these factors and others that you may develop from your reading and experiences into your repertoire of resources and from there into your clinical practice of teaching.

FEAR

Here, we restrict ourselves to elements in the physical environment of the school or classroom which may create fear in the hearts and minds of students. One of the major factors in developing a good school climate is to provide an orderly and safe environment.[3] Perhaps we need to make a clear distinction here that we are not referring in this first of the "terrible ten" to a lack of concern for academic achievement or for how students may feel about themselves and their schooling related to the part of the school system to which they belong, but rather we are talking quite literally about physical safety within and around the school.

James Dobson reports that a teacher friend of his recently told him he was looking for a new line of work, and that he was leaving the teaching profession because he is "fearful for his safety, despite the fact that he is a six-foot-five-inch, two hundred twenty pound athlete." Dobson goes on to report concerning this friend's school:

> The students at his school have displayed more and more boldness in their physical confrontation with teachers. For example, a few weeks ago a student put a shotgun against the stomach of a faculty member and demanded the keys to his car. The teacher recognized the boy and thought he was joking; he pushed the gun aside. Again the student pointed his weapon at the teacher and threatened to shoot him if the keys were not delivered. The teacher refused to take the adolescent seriously, and went on his way. He was told later by investigating officers he was lucky to be alive. So many teenagers are using drugs now that their rationality cannot be presupposed. The epidemic of drug addiction has resulted in numerous panic stricken young people who are driven to reduce their inner torment. Everyone near them must share their peril.[4]

Because many parents and would-be teachers are not aware of some of the events taking place in our schools in relation to literal physical safety of students

---

3. David C. Berliner, "The Half Full Glass: A Review of Research on Teaching," in *Using What We Know About Teaching* (Alexandria, Va.: ACSD, 1984), p. 67.
4. James Dobson, *Dare to Discipline* (Wheaton, Ill.: Tyndale, 1970), p. 86-87. Used by permission.

> **Insight: Violence in the Schools**
>
> Communities are beginning to insist that schools be made safe for students to attend. The Safe School Study cites research indicating that teenagers are more likely to be victimized in school than elsewhere. Surveys of students indicate that during a typical month, eleven out of every one thousand have something stolen from them, 1.3 percent were attacked at school and .05 percent were victims of extortion. One out of every five students said they feared being hurt or bothered at school.
>
> Victimization also may be related to school grade-level organization. A comparison of six K-8 schools and eight K-6 schools in a midwestern city finds that students have a significantly better chance of being robbed in the former group. The presence of older students—particularly males—in the K-8 schools apparently caused sixth-graders to be subjected to more victimization than their counterparts in K-6 schools.
>
> It is likely that most victimization occurs outside of class—before school, between classes, in cafeterias, after school, on buses, at special events. Many schools—especially urban secondary schools—currently employ door monitors to register all visitors, uniformed security guards, paraprofessionals serving as campus supervisors, bus supervisors and student patrols.
>
> From "Are Public Schools Organized to Minimize Behavior Problems?" in Daniel L. Duke, ed., *Helping Teachers Manage Classrooms* (Alexandria, Va.: ASCD, 1982). Reprinted with permission of the Association for Supervision and Curriculum Development. Copyright © 1982 by the Association for Supervision and Curriculum Development. All rights reserved.

Fig. 12.1

and teachers and administrators, let us share with you a brief run-down of some representative incidents. As we do so, we do not mean to imply that in every school in America these things are taking place, but only that in many schools of America, there is a real threat to the physical safety of those who are in the school.

A UPI story from Washington in the spring of 1976 stated that assault, mugging, vandalism, and gang warfare were rampant in America's schools. The writer called for a nationwide crime control effort. The situation in our schools was described as "a virtual reign of schoolhouse terror."

One well-known public figure reports that recently while he was in New York, he visited a school where the principal and school teachers literally stay behind locked doors while school is in progress, and armed security guards keep peace in the school. When school is out, and the young people are gone, the metal doors are locked so that the custodian can clean the building. And he concludes that a large number of the public schools in our nation are hazardous places in which to be.

The May 21, 1979, *U.S. News and World Report* states:

> A wave of violence in many of the nation's schools is again playing havoc with American education. Now it is the communities noted for good schools and quality education that are being scandalized by physical assaults and threats against teachers and students. Handguns, ice picks, explosives, and other weapons are turning up increasingly in schools in wealthy suburbs of Los Angeles, Denver, Washington, D.C. and New York, as well as scores of smaller cities across the nation.
>
> "Violence in our schools, reflects violence in our society," says Bennie Kelley, president of the National Association of School Security Directors. "As criminal activity increases in suburbs and smaller cities, it follows that this trend will show up in suburban and rural schools. That is exactly what is happening."[5]

The same issue of *U.S. News and World Report* also contains accounts of brutal violence in schools, as, for example, in Austin, Texas, while thirty of his classmates watched, a thirteen-year-old boy shot and killed his English teacher.

In addition, there is a frightening problem of vandalism in schools. It is not confined to poor urban areas. In December 1978, in a wealthy Virginia neighborhood near Washington, D.C., three young people were charged with arson in a fire that destroyed a high school with damages of 4.5 million dollars. They were the sons of people who were very prominent in the community. More than 25 percent of all schools are subject to vandalism in a given month. The annual cost of school crime is estimated to be around five hundred million dollars.[6]

Certainly fear for one's safety while being in a classroom is a destructive influence on good classroom climate. As much of the research shows, many of those who perpetrate these acts in school and threaten the welfare and safety of others in the school, are people on drugs, alcohol, and those who have dropped out of school and may have a grudge against the school. Many parents are refusing to send their children to schools where the safety of their children is obviously in jeopardy. The local school system must provide a safe and orderly environment before learning can take place, and certainly if one is going to seek to develop a good classroom climate.

ANXIETY

When I think about anxiety in relation to the child and school, the image usually comes to mind of a bug with a thousand antennae, each one of which is

---

5. Excerpted from *U.S. News & World Report* issue of May 21, 1979. Copyright, 1979, U.S. News & World Report, Inc. Used by permission.
6. As reported in Jerry Falwell, *Listen America* (New York: Bantam, 1980), pp. 187-89.

highly sensitive to one thing or another in the bug's environment. There are so many influences in the child's environment—and this differs with each child quite widely—that can create anxiety in the child, it is hard to formulate a list. In relation to the classroom, there is classroom anxiety per se, in which the thought of going to school and being in the classroom makes the child highly anxious. Many students have high anxiety when it comes to test-taking or examinations. The student who is scheduled to make a presentation before a large group, and who is frightened of large groups, is certainly likely to develop a high anxiety level. Many conditions in the home lives of students serve to create a continuing feeling of anxiety, or a certain kind of event on a particular day can send the child to school highly anxious. It may make some children anxious to sit near the teacher, or on the other hand to sit far away from the teacher in the classroom. A child who needs a high degree of predictability in his or her environment may become anxious in a classroom situation that is not rather heavily structured.

Because it is so difficult to make a particular list of anxieties, we have chosen to communicate the flavor and feeling of this particular aspect of the psychological climate of the classroom by the use of several items included in a recent article in a local paper. The reporter picked up in excellent fashion the kinds of things that create levels of anxiety in children with which the school must deal in today's society. Pointing out that teachers find themselves striving for psychological well-being, as well as academic achievement, the reporter points out that about half the children now in first grade will have lived in single-parent homes by the time they graduate from high school. Nearly one of five families is headed by a woman who is divorced, separated, widowed, or has never married, and two-thirds work.[7]

That same report states that high school is home for many students. And most teachers and administrators will agree that they handle many responsibilities traditionally taken care of by the home. And the reporter continues by pointing to the fact that schools and teachers have expanded their role in this regard to include hugging students and helping them decide what is important to them.

Here are some examples of the kinds of situations with which particular local school teachers and administrators have been confronted:

One principal said, "if you get up in the morning and mother is crying and you come to school, and you worry all day long, learning can be almost impossible."

"A mother may be drunk in the morning as her children leave for school. Students come to school with painful medical or dental problems for which the family cannot afford treatment." Students from one-parent homes often cannot concentrate or organize their work and they fear failure, lack self-confidence, and manifest a high degree of anxiety.

One guidance counselor summed up the many kinds of situations with which they deal by saying, "We don't want school personnel to be prying into students' lives, but they are just so upset and there is so much anxiety." And a final

---

7. Ernest L. Boyer, *The High School* (Washington, D.C.: Carnegie Foundation, 1983).

statement in this article makes another important point: no matter how many counseling and assistance programs the schools employ, educators agree they can never replace parents. Instead, they see themselves as working toward the same thing that parents seek—a good education for the child.

To deal with high levels of anxiety in children in great need of security is certainly one of the severe factors in relation to the climate of the classroom. For the manner in which that child is treated in the teaching-learning process can help to allay at least some of this anxiety, or it may increase the amount of anxiety, which can lead to extremely severe problems for the child.

DISCOURAGEMENT

In the context of the classroom climate, we refer here to the student who is discouraged because he really believes that there is no chance of his achieving success within the school system. The reasons for this discouragement may be varied, but it is this student who sees successful achievement as a matter of luck, or knowing the right people, or getting a break, rather than the result of persistent hard work. This is the student who is apt to say something like, "No matter what I do, I won't make it anyway." This is the "I have no chance" syndrome.

As this particular factor ties into the teaching-learning process, it can be greatly affected by the teacher who does not believe that her students can achieve through persistent hard work. The student picks this up quickly, and it simply adds to his discouragement. This student needs to have some honest success experiences in order to help him see that good work will bring him success.

REJECTION

This fourth of the Terrible Ten factors having to do with classroom climate is the one that relates to the much discussed topic of peer influence.

In the same newspaper article just referred to, the reporter writes about a ten-week program for all sixth-graders in the school system through a program known as SODA—short for Students Organized for Developing Attitudes. In 1983 certain high school juniors and seniors participated in concentrated training sessions to prepare them to go into Lynchburg's (Virginia) middle schools as SODA partners.

Each high school student worked with a small group of sixth-graders, helping them to recognize and solve problems effectively. An important aim of this program was to try to teach students to *resist* peer pressure in terms of wrong influences and behavior.

There is no question that, inside and outside the classroom, one of the most powerful social influences on children's behavior is the peer group. It is in late childhood or early adolescence (the peer group influence peaks at about age fourteen) that the peers of the child are usually the strongest forces influencing his or her behavior. There is a real sense in which peers become models for the behavior of other young people. As Lahey and Johnson point out, "peer groups also enforce their norms and standards for conduct through reaction to each individual's behavior. The member of a peer group who shows up in a 'slick' (or whatever the current term happens to be) outfit will be greeted with positive reactions, but the 'square' who dresses like his grandfather may not be well received."[8]

It is obvious that the strong influence of the peer group can be helpful, especially if the influences of the group are consistent with the goals of the school. But peer groups may not always be beneficial for children. They can frustrate members, and they can create severe conflicts by putting pressure on members to engage in behaviors that their families and teachers oppose. And then there is the student who simply has a hard time trying to fit into any group, and really needs some special attention from the teacher, but most of all, from the parents. If the teacher can get in touch with the parents in order to be helpful in this situation, a good teacher-parent relationship can be worked out for the benefit of the student.

The need for each child to feel accepted is the goal, and the wise teacher will very quickly note from observation in her classroom those children who are the leaders of the peer group, those who are the followers, and those who are left out. By working with these influences, and channeling them into the overall structure of the teaching-learning process, the effective teacher will greatly enhance the positive climate of the classroom.

STALEMATE

Here we are talking about something that is difficult to define precisely. But it refers to the morale of the total class, the sense of satisfaction that is there in the classroom as the students work together. Is there a sense that it is worthwhile? Or is there a sense that this outfit never does anything right?

Because this is so often hard to define and to deal with, probably the majority of the time it is not dealt with. But it can be a devastating influence in the climate of the classroom. If students begin to feel that "this is not a good group to be with," there is a very high probability that the achievement levels of most of the students in that teaching-learning process will be lowered. The aim for the teacher is, of course, to develop the genuine response on the part of the class members, "This is the class that I really look forward to."

NO CONSENSUS (ACADEMIC)

The word *consensus* means basic agreement or a sense of agreement on a particular matter. In this particular factor, we are talking about consensus in relation to an emphasis on academics. Some of the questions that can be asked in relation to this particular factor are pointed out by the authors of a book entitled

---

8. Benjamin B. Lahey and Martha S. Johnson, *Psychology and Instruction* (New York: Scott Foresman, 1978), p. 220. Used by permission.

Effective Schools and Classrooms: A Research Based Perspective.[9]
From the student's standpoint, do students master the academic work? Do students bring books and pencils to class? Do students perceive congruence among the faculty in enforcing school rules strictly and in controlling classroom behavior?

The authors of this book point out that students who bring books and pencils to class usually succeed. And such actions by the students serve to reinforce the school's academic emphasis. For example, if students frequently use the school library, this probably is an indicator that those students and teachers look with a high value on the resources of their library. And the question concerning students' perceiving congruence among the faculty in enforcing school rules implies that when this is so, the academic emphasis of the school is enhanced.

Some further questions from the teacher's standpoint also emphasize whether or not there is a consensus concerning academic emphasis: is time spent efficiently and directly on teaching academic skills? Do lessons start on time and continue without interruptions? Do teachers regularly give and mark homework? Do teachers plan lessons in advance? Do teachers expect students to succeed? Obviously, positive answers to these questions indicate that there is a consensus with regard to an emphasis on academic achievement. This is a great "plus factor" in the climate of the classroom.

THE MECHANICAL TEACHER

The mechanical teacher is rather easy to spot by anyone who has been in education for any length of time at all. It is obvious that this teacher is not "with it" in terms of arranging her classroom to accommodate several different approaches to the teaching-learning process; by the way she looks and talks in the classroom, which is indeed a mechanical operation; by the lack of interest shown on the part of her students day after day in her classes.

Under the topic of "how *not* to become a mechanical teacher" we will discuss two major items: four approaches to the teaching-learning process, and the relationship of physical settings to the teaching-learning process.

Four approaches to the classroom. Research has usually distinguished three approaches to the classroom: authoritarian, laissez-faire, and democratic. We believe there is a fourth, authoritative, and therefore we add that to our brief discussion here.

1. Authoritarian. The three styles of leadership were distinguished in a frequently cited study by social psychologists Lewin, Lippitt, and White.[10] In that

---

9. David Squires, William G. Huitt, and John K. Segars, *Effective Schools and Classrooms: A Research Based Perspective* (Arlington, Va.: ASCD, 1980), p. 67.
10. K. Lewin, R. Lippitt, and R.K. White, "Patterns of Aggressive Behavior in Experimentally Created Social Climates," *Journal of Social Psychology* 10 (1939):271-99. Also G. Barker, J.S. Kounin, and J.K. Wright, eds., *Child Behavior and Development* (New York: McGraw-Hill, 1943).

study, the authoritarian leader was one who strongly directed the activities of the members of his group, with very little opportunity for participation in any decision-making. The authoritarian leaders produced a great deal of anger and aggression among the boys, but they did accomplish a great deal in their work activities. However, the boys did not enjoy the authoritarian led group, and they disliked the authoritarian leader.

2. The laissez-faire leader. In the study, the laissez-faire group floundered a great deal and moved in different directions. They really did not enjoy their activities either and were constantly getting into minor squabbles.

3. The democratic leader. In this particular study, the democratic group seemed to fare the best overall. They got along with each other, apparently enjoyed the group more than the others, and still accomplished a great deal.

There have been studies of these three styles of leadership conducted since the original study, and conducted in classroom settings. In a review of this research, Anderson concluded that there was not much difference in the *quality of learning* in the authoritarian and democratic classrooms, but the *morale* was higher under democratic leaders.[11]

4. Authoritative. We believe there is a fourth style of leadership that has much to commend it. By authoritative is meant that the teacher is well-grounded in her subject/literary areas, and there is no question that she is the leader of the classroom. However, in many appropriate places, students are invited and encouraged to participate in decision-making. We believe that under this style of leadership, the class morale can become the highest, for students want someone to give a sense of leadership and direction to their teaching-learning process, and, at the same time, to feel that they have a reasonable part in appropriate decision-making processes. Admittedly, a great deal of research has not been done on this particular style of leadership, and it needs to be done for the sake of comparing styles of leadership in relation to student achievement and the classroom climate.

Physical settings and classroom climate. What we are discussing under this particular section are the ways in which the utilization of physical space in the classroom influences student behavior. The implication is rather clear that the teacher who is "with it" will be alert to this critical factor in the teaching-learning process in relation to classroom climate.

There is no question that school and classroom size influence behavior. However, there is really not much that the individual teacher can do about those factors, except within particular settings where the teacher may break a large class down into smaller subgroups within the same classroom, using different instructional paces in order to maintain the interest of the group—the latter being a good idea in most any size classroom.

Two important findings regarding pacing need to be mentioned briefly here.

---

11. G.J. Anderson, "Social Climate on Individual Learning," *American Educational Research Journal* 2 (1970):135-52.

One comes from a study on student ability and classroom pace, which was conducted by Lundgren,[12] and the second study was by Arlin and Westbury.[13] Lundgren found that teachers gear the pace of instruction to the lower aptitude students, which he calls the "steering group"—not the very lowest students, but those who were close to the bottom of the class. In their study, Arlin and Westbury sought to determine how teacher and student pacing influenced faster students. Their conclusions suggest that less able students put restrictions on how fast more capable students can move through any particular school curriculum. Good and Brophy conclude that probably the most able students are the ones hurt by teacher pacing. They recommend that teachers who want to create opportunities for individual activity on limited time and budgets probably should direct their initial efforts to buying or developing self-study materials for high-achievement students. The logic is that this would allow teachers more time with the lower ability students who apparently need more active teaching and more teacher contact.[14]

A number of studies have been done relating to the manner in which the arrangement of seating in the classroom influences student achievement and classroom climate. Where do students sit if you allow them to choose their own places? They are likely to sit by friends, or in what we might call "habitual places." Seats are not chosen randomly, and this means that for the teacher in that classroom setting, there will probably be some problems built into the seating arrangement. Furthermore, dependent students usually sit in front of the room, and hostile and alienated students sit in the back of the room.

Students who are friends or who like to be with one another are apt to do more talking as they sit together in a classroom than would "nonfriends." Obviously, if you have a number of students who really do not like school, who are tuning out the teacher anyway, and who sit relatively far away from the teacher, the teacher must be prepared to move frequently to that part of the room, especially when presenting information to the class.[15]

An interesting result was found by Adams and Biddle, who studied several first, sixth, and eleventh-grade classrooms. They report that about 64 percent of student participation in classroom discussions was by the students who sat either in the front row or in the strip running up the center of the classroom. They labeled this area the "action zone."[16] Good and Brophy found more even patterns of student participation in those situations where high and low achievement students were mixed together in their seating arrangements.[17]

One of the reasons, but not the only one, that students who sit in the back of

12. V. Lundgren, *Frame Factors and the Teaching Process* (Stockholm: Almqvist and Wiksell, 1972).
13. M. Arlin and I. Westberry, "The Leveling Effect of Teaching Pacing on Science Content Mastery," *Journal of Research into Science Teaching* 13 (1976):213-19.
14. Thomas L. Good and Jere E. Brophy, *Educational Psychology, A Realistic Approach*, 2d ed. (New York: Holt, Rinehart, and Winston, 1980), p. 414.
15. Ibid., p. 416.
16. Adams and Biddle (1970), cited in Good and Brophy, p. 416.
17. Ibid., p. 416-17.

the room do not participate, could be that teachers spend about 70 percent of their entire class time at the front of the class.[18]

The conclusion to this matter appears to be that although no one seating arrangement is going to be ideal for any teacher in all settings, if low-ability students are sitting toward the back of the room, and the teacher does not move around the room, particularly near those students in the back rows, then the low-achievement students are unlikely to make very much progress, and their sense of satisfaction about the class climate is almost certain to decrease. There seems to be some evidence that it would be better to have low- and high-ability students mixed together in the classroom. With this kind of arrangement, the low-ability students who are seated near the front appear to do better, even though high-ability students do well almost anywhere in the classroom.

One further comment is in order. The majority of classrooms now are probably equipped with individual movable desks, and yet one particular seating arrangement seems to be used by some teachers. There is, of course, such a thing as changing too frequently. But it does seem that if the teacher can have in mind two or three patterns for the classroom, depending upon what she wants to do on a given day or at a given time, to shift the desk or table and chairs around into these patterns does provide some variability, and will improve classroom climate. In figure 12.2 several possible classroom seating arrangements are presented with suggestions under each. In figure 12.3 the recommended first-grade classroom is shown, taken from Good and Brophy, and adapted from Wang (1973). We recommend that you study these diagrams so that you might have some idea of what can be done with classroom seating. It definitely has a strong effect on the classroom climate and student achievement.

BOREDOM

How many of us have conducted class with a bored student, usually sitting near the back of the class, and wondered what we could do to stir his interest? Then we hear teachers say, "You are always going to have some bored students, so don't worry about it, go ahead and teach the ones that are really interested." We must admit that that has an appealing ring to it in the midst of the teaching-learning process with all of its responsibilities. But in our better moments we reject that kind of hypothesis.

Some of the more recent research concerning learning styles and teaching styles can be of help in combating this particular monster which seeks to destroy the classroom climate and ruin student achievement. While ability deals with *what* to learn, style is concerned with *how* to learn. Claudia E. Cornett reminds us of this in her book *What You Should Know About Teaching and Learning Styles.*[19] Cornett

18. Ibid., p. 419.
19. *What You Should Know About Teaching and Learning Styles,* by Claudia E. Cornett, Fastback #191. © 1983 Phi Delta Kappa Educational Foundation. Used by permission.

Several classroom seating arrangements

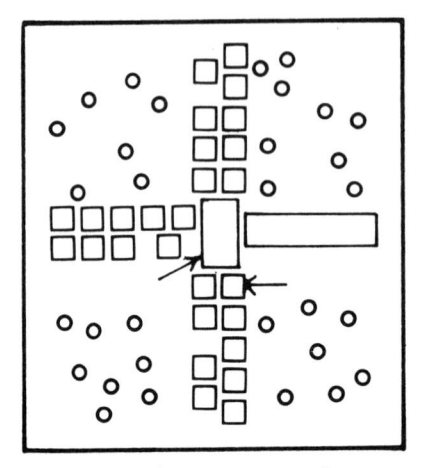

This "cross plan" creates more floor space. The open areas can be used when exploring a variety of different activities.

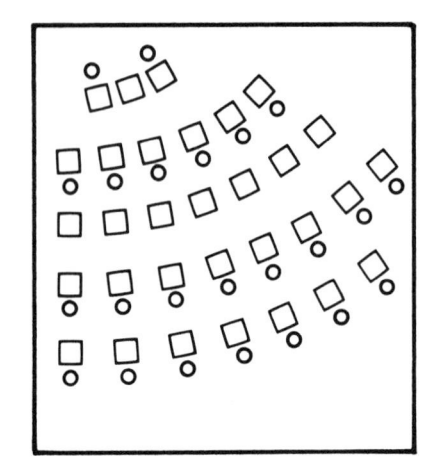

The class directs its attention to one or two people in front of the group. This arrangement can be used to prepare for a lesson or to summarize and evaluate a recently completed activity.

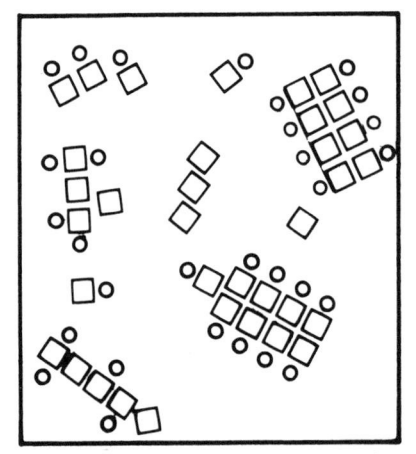

This arrangement allows pupils to work in small group activities and move freely from one work area to another.

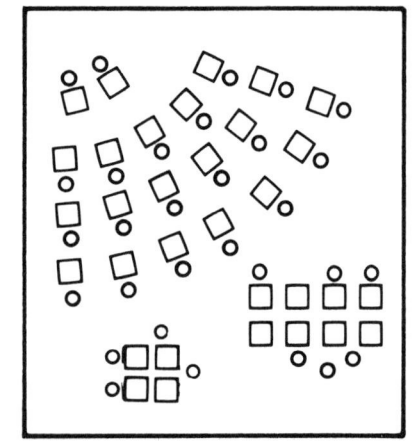

This plan provides for a large group activity while two smaller groups work on projects elsewhere in the room. To minimize distractions, children in the large group face away from the work areas.

Adapted from Reys, R., and Post, T., *The Mathematics Laboratory: Theory to Practice*. Boston: Prindle, Weber, and Schmidt, 1973. Used by permission of Robert E. Reys.

Fig. 12.2

A recommended first-grade classroom

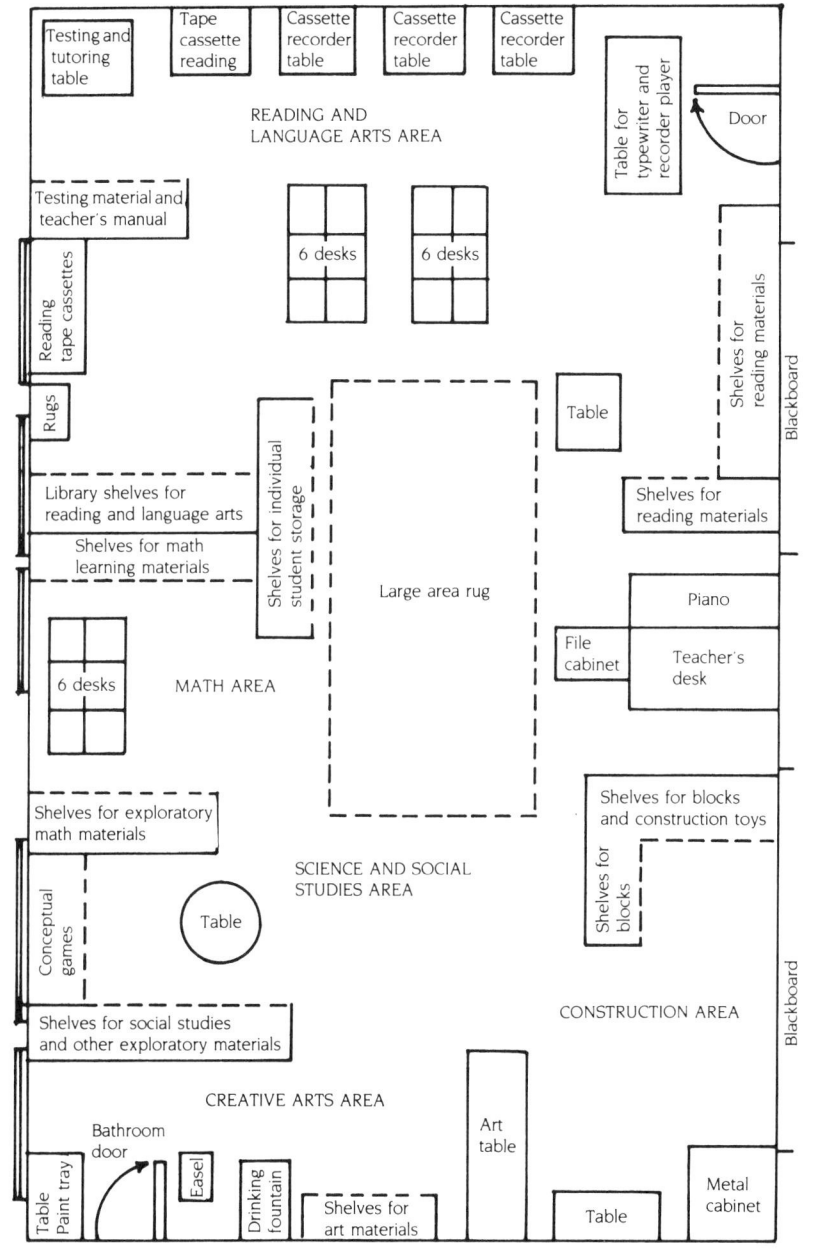

Adapted from Margaret C. Wang (1973). In Good, T. L. and Brophy, J. E., *Educational Psychology: A Realistic Approach*, 2d. ed. (New York: Holt, Rinehart, and Winston, 1980). Reprinted by permission.

Fig. 12.3

then goes on to remind us, "one of the contributions of learning style research is to help educators realize that all people possess ways to learn despite their ability levels. . . . We all possess latent learning styles that are not used until the situation demands that."[20]

The implication of Cornett's statements is that the student who is bored has a learning style just like any other student. But the predominant style being used in the classroom is not reaching that student. Now to be sure, the student has the responsibility to be responsive, and not just to sit there daring the teacher to teach him something. At the same time the teacher, by deliberately changing her teaching style, will be much more likely to get that bored individual involved in the teaching-learning process actively, and therefore bring to that individual a greater sense of satisfaction in relation to his school experience. It is in this way that learning styles affect the classroom climate. Dr. Cornett's book also contains an excellent bibliography on teaching styles and learning styles which will be helpful for you as you pursue this particular topic further.

PIGEONHOLED

What this means to the student is that he or she feels stuck, because either formally or informally the student has been labeled as to ability and perceives the teacher viewing that ability at a certain level. As a result of ability grouping, the student is really saying, "I'm stuck!" If the student happens to be in the top-level ability group, others may perceive him as "stuck *up*." If the student happens to be in the lowest ability group, or even one of the lower ones, other students are apt to perceive the student as "stuck *down*." And the probability is further that, because of the way other students perceive either one of these students, these students may in fact come to perceive themselves in that light. Classroom climate is not helped by and large by ability grouping.

We must make clear that we are talking here about permanent arrangements in groups for a particular class for an entire year. We are *not* referring to temporary groupings on a day-by-day or even a week-by-week basis, based on criteria other than measures of achievement and capability.

The rationale for ability grouping suggests that the members of homogeneous groups will form friendships more easily because they are similar in interests and ability: "that the less able members will not suffer loss in self-esteem because of an inability to compete with the brighter students in ungrouped classes; and that teachers will find it easier to teach children whose level of learning is similar."[21] While these arguments sound plausible and compelling, they turn into poor prophecies indeed.

A large-scale study in 1966 provides a good evaluation of grouping. The

---

20. Ibid.
21. Lahey and Johnson, p. 228. Used by permission.

researchers reached the following conclusions: achievement was lower in most basic school subjects when the students were in homogeneous ability groups than when they were ungrouped. Ability grouping failed to lead to higher self-esteem, and self-esteem actually dropped over the two-year period of the study in the children that had been placed in the lower ability groups. Interest and attitudes toward school were unaffected by grouping.[22]

In a later study, in 1980, Webb shows how the middle-ability child suffers a

---

Insight: Evidence of Attention to Physical Environment

In schools where staffs pay attention to the physical environment and organization:

1. Personal contributions by students and staff are evident in the surroundings; for example, homemade curtains or student art is used in decorations.
2. The school is decorated and inviting on the first day when students enter.
3. Visitors see evidence the students are producing: for example, student work is carefully displayed in hallways, libraries, cafeterias, and classrooms.
4. Students are involved in projects to improve the school environment: for example, beautification projects and planting days are high points of the school year.
5. Bulletin boards are used to communicate information about the school or the whole community: for example, attendance charts may be publicly displayed.
6. Littering is minimal, even at the end of the day.
7. One sees little evidence of vandalism and graffiti.
8. Repairs are made immediately so that the physical facility is in good shape.
9. Parents are advocates for getting help to improve the school facility.

From William W. Wayson and Gay Su Pinnell, "Creating a Living Curriculum for Teaching Self-Discipline," Daniel L. Duke, ed., *Helping Teachers Manage Classrooms* (Alexandria, Va.: ASCD, 1982). Reprinted with permission of the Association for Supervision and Curriculum Development. Copyright © 1982 by the Association for Supervision and Curriculum Development. All rights reserved.

Fig. 12.4

22. M.L. Goldberg, A.H. Passow, and J. Justman, *The Effects of Ability Grouping* (New York: Teachers College, 1966).

loss in achievement, while the low-ability child shows some gains in achievement when that child is in a mixed ability group, over what would be expected if they were in uniform ability groups.[23]

Insight: Ways to Encourage Your Child to Like School

Centuries ago, when public schools were scarce, many a child learned to read and cipher at his mother's side, using a slate and the Bible.

Though parents are less involved in the educational arena today, efforts to return part of their teaching role to them are hardly novel. The parents' interest and support in school activities can make the difference between a child who struggles through his classes and one who shines. Following is a list of suggestions for parents that can help them help their children to like school.

1. Read to your children and listen to them read aloud.
2. Talk to them and listen to what they have to say.
3. Provide them with books and craft materials.
4. Make television work for you by carefully selecting programs and discussing them with the children during or after they have watched them.
5. Teach your children to examine things, such as flowers.
6. Encourage them to listen to horns, whistles, and other sounds (doing this helps children when they must identify letter shapes and sounds as they learn to read).
7. Take very small children to places such as the fire station, giving them a wealth of experiences and memories to refer to as they grow.
8. Encourage children to join family discussions of current events, and be sure to take an interest in events in the child's life as well.
9. Stay in touch with your schools, making sure your children are performing well. Try to work with teachers to resolve any difficulties.
10. Since parents are the primary teachers of their kids, a child only benefits by the involvement of the parents.

From Sharon Sick, "Parents Still Play Key Role in Education," *The News and Daily Advance* (Lynchburg, Virginia), 16 October 1983. Used by permission.

Fig. 12.5

---

23. N.M. Webb, "A Process—Outcome Analysis of Learning in Group and Individual Settings," *Educational Psychologist* 15 (1980):69-83.

The conclusion of this particular matter would appear to be that it is not a good idea to put students into an ability grouping situation for long periods of time. And when we do put them into groups even for a day, or a week, we need to be very careful about the basis on which we select even those groups, for implications may arise from their groups and their performances which will stay with a student all the rest of his school life and even beyond. Obviously, if that is a negative kind of implication, this will greatly lessen their satisfaction with the school, and therefore has a severe effect on the climate of the classroom.

The author would like to emphasize at this point that for junior high level and above, it would seem that random selection to the temporary work groups for a day or a week is in most cases the preferred route to go. Such a method takes the possible onus off the shoulders of any particular student. The author has certainly found it a highly workable and satisfactory method at the college level.

APATHY (SCHOOL)

Again, let us make clear what this particular monster of destruction to classroom climate is all about. We are talking here about the total school's concern as visibly reflected to the students, which the students may perceive as favorable or unfavorable to their welfare and their achievement. The author is convinced that without the administration of the school's setting the tone and the pattern for a good school climate, the classroom climate will be very difficult indeed to establish on the positive side.

A beautiful illustration of the reflection of an administration of the school really caring for the welfare of the students, and therefore producing a healthy school and classroom climate, is shared by Wayson and Pennel in their article "Creating a Living Curriculum for Teaching Self-Discipline."

> Even an old building can be made to look inviting. At A. B. Hart Junior High School in Cleveland, the cafeteria was a big problem. It was an old facility with dark unfinished floors and not much light. Students and staff made red-checked curtains for the windows; the biology department raised plants and hung them all around the room; the art students covered one large wall with a mural depicting the history of the school; a group of students made table and wall decorations. On special occasions the Home Economics department put out tablecloths and centerpieces for some one thousand students who ate in five shifts. The cooperative effort brought people closer together and made them feel successful. Another dramatic example comes from Franklin school in Newark, New Jersey. Staff, students, and parents were so bothered by the condition of the building that they bought paint and redecorated the entire building. Now a school that was covered with graffiti has none.[24]

24. William W. Wayson and Gay Su Pinnell, "Creating a Living Curriculum for Teaching Self-Discipline," in Daniel L. Duke, ed., *Helping Teachers Manage Classrooms* (Alexandria, Va.: ASCD, 1982), p. 135. Reprinted with permission of the Association for Supervision and Curriculum Development. Copyright © 1982 by the Association for Supervision and Curriculum Development. All rights reserved.

> **Insight: Teaching Strategies—Learning Styles**
>
> Following are suggestions for teaching strategies that recognize the varieties of learning styles:
> 1. Use questions of all types to stimulate various levels of thinking.
> 2. Provide a general overview of material to be learned, so that students' past experiences will be associated with the new ideas.
> 3. Allow sufficient time for information to be processed and then integrated using both the right and the left brain hemispheres.
> 4. Expect that at least one new thing will be learned by each student. Go around the room at the end of the period or the school day and have each student tell something he or she has learned. Once this routine has become established, students soon begin actively to seek a "new learning" during lessons, because they know they are expected to share something.
> 5. Set clear purposes before any listening, viewing, or reading experience.
> 6. Warm up before the lesson development by using brainstorming, word associations, fantasy journeys, etc.
> 7. Use spaced practice to facilitate remembering and skill development and have the practice include both verbal and image rehearsal depending upon the nature of the task.
> 8. Use multisensory means for both processing and retrieving information. Write directions on the board as well as give them orally. Have students write down instructions as well as read them.
> 9. Use a variety of review and reflection strategies to bring closure to learning.
> 10. Use descriptive feedback rather than simply praising. Instead of "good job" say "each problem you worked so far is correct."
>
> From Claudia E. Cornett, *What You Should Know About Teaching and Learning Styles*, Fastback no. 191 (Bloomington, Ind.: Phi Delta Kappa Educational Foundation, 1983). Used by permission.

Fig. 12.6

As Wayson and Pennel point out, supervisors and administrators have a tendency to feel that they can do nothing about the physical environment of the school or that it has nothing to do with their jobs. But Wayson and Pennel emphasize that superintendents, supervisors, and specialists can help promote a good school climate by encouraging all staff members to use their planning skills to create a pleasant learning environment, and by encouraging the visible signs that tell students they are welcome and belong in the school.[25]

CLASSROOM CLIMATE AND THE TEACHING-LEARNING PROCESS

It is obvious that the classroom climate—that is, the sense of satisfaction with which the students perceive the operational factors of the classroom—has a tremendously significant influence on the teaching-learning process. In the taming of the Terrible Ten monsters, which are destructive of the classroom climate, there is no easy, one-shot kind of answer. Most educators desire to improve the climate both of the school and of their classrooms. Substantial numbers of teachers have good ideas and put them into effect in their classrooms to improve climate, and thereby enhance student achievement. But there are many teachers who either are not aware of the need to influence classroom climate or perhaps, like many students, have come to feel, "What's the use?" In many situations with which I am familiar the latter conclusion is understandable, but never defensible. The teacher is a professional and as such must be aware of the factors involved in bringing about student achievement, of which the classroom climate is a highly important one. There are many teachers who want to change the climate of their classrooms, but do not know *how* to go about doing it. Therefore, administrators and supervisors need to provide specific help to teachers in making changes in their classrooms. Above all else, the school authorities—whatever their titles—must set the standard and show their genuine interest and support on a daily basis in order to bring about the results in the teaching-learning process that are desirable.

Once again, to look at classroom climate as the outgrowth of a particular philosophical approach to the teaching-learning process may be most helpful. In my judgment, one of the greatest weaknesses in the educational enterprise has been the tendency to look at particular events or temporary movements within the educational process without relating those specific things to a broader philosophic viewpoint. For the viewpoint can bring a great deal of wisdom to the particular movement, and in turn, feedback from the particular movement can enrich the philosophic approach. And of course, this textbook has stressed from the beginning the necessity of the philosopher/clinician approach, in which these two aspects need continuously to be joined. It is probably the case that each of the philosophic approaches we have discussed in this book would consider classroom climate important for different reasons. In the Chalkboard Challenges of this chapter, we will have you think about some of those differences.

HINDSIGHT

In this chapter, we have stressed the importance of the atmosphere of the classroom and the school. If students feel frightened, insecure, or rejected, they

---

25. Ibid., p. 136.

will find it hard to concentrate on learning. If there is little likelihood of success, they are not apt to be very interested in the teaching-learning process.

We have talked about the destructive influences on classroom climate in the form of the Terrible Ten and made some suggestions, based on research and experience, as to how to tame and transform the Terrible Ten. It is important for you to understand that the Terrible Ten is not intended just as a gimmick, but to help you remember the seriousness of the feelings and perceptions that plague many students. They do affect the student's learning and achievement, and certainly the sense of satisfaction the student experiences in relation to the teaching-learning process.

Chalkboard Challenges

1. We mentioned near the end of the discussion that the different philosophic approaches to the teaching-learning process would look upon the matter of classroom climate as important for differing reasons. Think about the four approaches: behavioristic, cognitive-discovery, humanistic, and the Christian approach—how do you think each would view the importance of classroom climate?

Just to get you started thinking, if we contrast the behavioristic approach which has as its major social function for the school the survival of society as a whole, with the Christian social function of the school as the proclamation of the gospel of Christ in order to transform lives and based on the supernatural reality of the God of the Bible, two very different reasons for enhancing classroom climate would become rather apparent. It would be important to the behaviorists for as many students as possible to achieve at a high level for the survival of society. The behaviorists would use what they term various types of "classroom reward structures" to bring about the involvement of as many students as possible, rather than just a few. The Christian approach would be interested in the individual's achieving a real sense of satisfaction in relation to how he or she perceives the teaching-learning process, based on the fact that each individual is made in the image of God and is precious in His sight. Therefore, the Christian would want the student to achieve as highly as possible for the glory of God.

As you think through the various approaches in relation to this particular question, you may find yourself greatly strengthened in the philosophic approach you espouse.

2. Study carefully the classroom diagrams in this chapter, and then design a classroom of your own for the grade level at which you expect to teach, building in at least two or three possible changes or arrangements, depending upon what you wanted to do on a particular day or in a particular week. Add this design and your reasons for it to your teacher's notebook for future reference.

3. Look over the list of the Terrible Ten again and see if you would add to or subtract from the list. We suggest you make your own list of the destructive

influences to classroom morale. In this very process you will become even more sensitive to the importance of these factors in the teaching-learning process.

4. From the Terrible Ten list, or using one of your own from your list, analyze what really brings about the child's finding himself or herself in that particular circumstance. What kinds of action could you take as a teacher to help tame the particular monster you have chosen? Jot down some practical things you could do in your own classroom to transform the monster into a constructive influence for student learning.

WANT TO KNOW MORE?

PHYSICAL SETTING

For an excellent review of the physical setting in relation to the psychological context of classroom climate read chapter 19, "The Physical Setting: Building a Psychological Context for Learning," in Thomas L. Good and Jere E. Brophy, *Educational Psychology: A Realistic Approach,* 2d ed. (New York: Holt, Rinehart, and Winston, 1980).

TEACHING AND LEARNING STYLES

For a very helpful brief review of teaching styles and learning styles, read Claudia E. Cornett, *What You Should Know About Teaching and Learning Styles* Fastback no. 191, (Bloomington, Ind.: Phi Delta Kappa Educational Foundation, 1983).

GROUPING

For an informative look at the issue of grouping students, read Robert Calfee and Roger Brown, "Grouping Students for Instruction," in Daniel L. Duke, ed., *Classroom Management, The 78th Yearbook of the National Society for the Study of Education,* Part II (Chicago: U. of Chicago, 1979).

SCHOOL SAFETY

As a teacher or one about to become a teacher, you will especially want to be familiar with *Violent Schools—Safe Schools,* National Institute of Education: The Safe School Study Report to the Congress, vol. I (Washington, D.C.: National Institute of Education, 1978).

A thorough study of a number of aspects in many classrooms is the basis for *Fifteen Thousand Hours* by Michael Rutter, Barbara Maughan, Peter Mortimore, and Janet Ouster (Cambridge, Mass.: Harvard U., 1979).

13

Classroom Methodology

ANN MCFARLAND

CONTENTS

	PAGE
Key Terms	322
That's Debatable!	323
Foresight	323
Methods: The Use of Procedures to Attain Educational Goals	324
Methods of the Past: Will They Still Work?	324
Methods and Techniques of the Present: Description and Evaluation	325
Methods and Basic Skill Instruction	333
Methods and Content Instruction	341
Study-Skills for Lifetime Independent Learning	345
Appropriate Uses of Methodology in the Teaching-Learning Process	346
Hindsight	346
Chalkboard Challenges	346
Want to Know More?	347

KEY TERMS

Inquiry method
  The process of using one's own intellect to gain knowledge by discovering concepts and organizing them into a structure that is personally meaningful
Unit
  A plan that organizes ideas and knowledge into a meaningful structure for teaching purposes

Individualized instruction
　A system that designs and programs specific learning tasks so individual learners can progress through the program at their own level of readiness and own learning rate
Realia
　Objects and activities used to relate classroom teaching to the real life
Preschool education
　Education that takes place prior to formal academic instruction
Basal reader
　A set of graded reading books that provide a developmental sequence of skills and a controlled vocabulary

THAT'S DEBATABLE!

Process or content? Which is of greater importance in the learning procedure? How do we evaluate learning when using the discovery process? Many teachers feel more comfortable lecturing students and grading written assignments. This indicates to them that the student has learned. But other educators believe the students learn and retain more by discovering information for themselves, particularly in the science area. Perhaps the question we really need to ask is: How can we teach the children ultimately to be responsible for their own learning as they grow in the nurture and admonition of the Lord?

FORESIGHT

In a world that is continually in a process of change, the goals, methods, and curricula of education are also being evaluated and updated to help students cope with change. The major goal of all levels of education should be to assist the child in developing his God-given potential into useful abilities. The underlying goal should be developing one's ability to think. The importance of this is emphasized by Grant, who quotes Fraber and Shearron: "To be free, a man must be capable of basing his choices and actions on understandings that he himself achieves and on values he examines himself."[1] Christians believe that freedom is under the leadership of the Holy Spirit.

Additional goals are set for different age and grade levels. Although these vary according to the philosophy and the type of program, at no time should the purpose of education be degraded to the level of only preparing the child for the next level of learning. We must accept the child as he is, and assist him in living out the kindergarten, first-grade, seventh-grade year to his fullest.

In order to assist you in understanding curriculum and methods used in the classroom, we will look at different types of instruction used currently and in the

---

1. Carl A. Grant, *Bringing Teaching to Life: An Introduction to Education* (Boston: Allyn & Bacon, 1982), p. 91.

past. While studying this chapter, keep in mind the age level you hope to teach and consider methods of instruction available for use in the classroom.

METHODS: THE USE OF PROCEDURES TO ATTAIN EDUCATIONAL GOALS

What is your responsibility in the pupil's process of learning? Can you be held accountable for a pupil's learning or lack of learning? Does the granting of a degree indicate success? How do you assist and guide learning?

If we truly want to be an attribute to students in their quest for knowledge, then we must be aware of the different methods and techniques used in attaining goals. As you gain more knowledge in methods and procedures, you may have a tendency to favor a particular method or procedure. However, as you gain experience in teaching, you will employ and combine many methods and techniques in your attempt to meet the different learning styles and needs of students. It is the teacher's responsibility to present the appropriate knowledge necessary for the student to acquire the skills, knowledge, attitudes, appreciation, and standards of behavior that will serve as a foundation upon which he can build further knowledge. Most school systems depend upon the classroom teacher to determine the methods and procedures to be used in assisting students in achieving the educational goals necessary for success.

METHODS OF THE PAST: WILL THEY STILL WORK?

Much of early education was accomplished in informal settings in the family, church, and neighborhood. The typical methods used were recitation, memorization, and drill.

Early schools also depended upon recitation, memorization, and lecture. The catechetical method was also employed during colonial times. What are the characteristics of these methods, and are they still useful today?

LECTURE METHOD

The lecture method is basically used to convey knowledge. The learners are usually passive, and the teacher has the responsibility of taking the school district's goals and materials and making daily lesson plans for the students. The primary purpose of the lecture is for the teacher to convey whatever material is prerequisite for moving to the next grade level.

This method is still in use today both in universities and elementary schools. The lecture is usually augmented with a variety of mediated teaching methods (such as films, textbooks, videos). The lecture can also be seen periodically in the open classroom when the teacher feels the need to convey information to the whole class.[2]

---

2. Leo W. Anglin, Jr., Richard M. Goldman, and Joyce G. Anglin, *Teaching: What It's All About* (New York: Harper & Row, 1982), pp. 99-115.

RECITATION

Recitation originally required students to enumerate relevant details in front of the class. The teacher would ask the students questions and they would have to recite answers by memory in detail. Today, the most common form consists of the teacher's assigning of homework and devoting most of the next class time answering questions. This method has been modified by reading and teacher-led discussions with specific answers required during class.

MEMORIZATION

Memorization requires pupils to commit to memory specific information deemed important by the teacher. The student will need this information in order to score high on an oral or written examination. Memorization is also used in learning the alphabet and mathematical concepts deemed as important prerequisite skills for reading and advanced math. Memorization's greatest value is in a student's being able to recall information necessary to the acquisition of new materials.[3]

The catechetical method requires children to repeat memorized responses to questions. This method is sometimes used in the reading of poetry or choral readings; however, it is used most often in Christian schools in the teaching of biblical doctrines.

DRILL

Drill is a physical or mental exercise aimed at perfecting a skill. Children usually respond favorably to drill when they understand the value to them. Be alert to specific weaknesses or disabilities and give them opportunities for special drills. Drills can be very competitive, and it helps children commit to memory skills necessary for advancement. This method is still used; however, it usually involves team competition.

These methods are still useful today, although they are generally integrated with other methods of teaching. The methods used for instruction are usually dependent upon the philosophy of the school, the teacher, physical setting, and the subject being taught.

METHODS AND TECHNIQUES OF THE PRESENT:
DESCRIPTION AND EVALUATION

Most school systems and teachers employ a variety of teaching methods and techniques. This is due not only to better teacher preparation, increase in materials, visual aids, and improved facilities, but also an increase of knowledge in development and learning styles.

---

3. Lester D. Crow and Alice Crow, *The Student Teacher in the Elementary School* (New York: McKay, 1965), pp. 198-200.

GALLERY OF GREATS

John Dewey
We learn what we do and we do what we learn. (Courtesy The Granger Collection)

"The Father of Progressive Education," ahead of his time, astute intellect, extremely shy, weather-beaten—these are just a few of the characterizations of John Dewey. Born in Vermont in 1859 of a grocer-tobacconist father and a devout Calvinist mother, he later renounced his belief in any supernatural being and became a pragmatic humanist. In 1889, after several teaching posts, he became chairman of the Department of Philosophy, Psychology, and Pedagogy at the University of Chicago and eventually director of the School of Education.

A poor administrator, Dewey made his wife principal of the University

Elementary School and had to pay for his poor judgment with his resignation. But he had built a good reputation and was asked to join Columbia University as a professor of philosophy, where he spent his remaining years. It has been said that people either "pucker up or duck" when they hear Dewey's name. Whichever one does, one must acknowledge that he has had a profound effect on both the theoretical and pragmatic aspects of American education. Maxine Green says about Dewey:

> Most agree his influence was exerted in the broadening of the curriculum, the correlating of subjects, the development of a less rigid notion of discipline, and the relating of school studies to their application to life.*

And Harold A. Larrabee remarks:

> His appearance was farmer-like, weather beaten . . . he remained seated throughout the hour and seldom seemed to be looking directly at his audience. . . . His facial expression was solemn, though it lighted up at times with something like a chuckle . . . one rarely left the classroom without the conviction that something intellectually and practically important had been said.*

Some of the most noted methods include problem solving, project method, unit plan, socialized recitation, individualized instruction, learning center, and the use of audiovisual aids.

PROBLEM-SOLVING OR INQUIRY METHOD

Bruner defines the inquiry method as the process of using one's own intellect to gain knowledge by discovering concepts and organizing them into a structure that is personally meaningful.

There are five steps in the process of problem-solving. They are:

(1) Identification of the problem. (2) Hypothesizing as to possible solutions to the problem. (3) Exploration—search for evidence to support tentative solutions. (4) Analyze the data, evaluate the data, note any bias, similarities, differences, and so on. (5) Formulate a conclusion—acceptance, rejection, or modification of the hypothesis.

Problem-solving is not to be considered a method but a mode of approach that is characteristic of various teaching methods.[4] Not only must the problem have interest and appeal to children, it must also be suited to their ability to profit from participation in the activity. Intelligent guidance in setting up experiences, in which the children recognize the value to themselves in dealing with them, is

---

*Both quotations above from William W. Brickman and Stanley Lehrer, eds., *John Dewey: Master Educator*, 2d ed. (New York: Society for the Advancement of Education, 1961), pp. 82, 97. Used by permission.

4. Johanna K. Lemlech, *Curriculum and Instructional Methods for the Elementary School* (New York: Macmillan, 1984), pp. 291-304. Used by permission.

required by the teacher. This approach also gives the students practice in applying the scientific method of arriving at solutions to the many problem situations they are likely to encounter throughout life. Proponents of this method consider that knowledge gained as a means of helping in the solution of a problem is learned more effectively than if it were acquired as unrelated facts to be memorized.[5]

PROJECT METHOD—GROUP STUDY

The project or group study method gives students an opportunity to work together on a common project, problem, or topic of interest. Students of various social and academic abilities have an opportunity to gain respect for each other as they use their creative abilities in a team effort.[6] The project must be within the capacities of the students, and adequate materials and equipment must be provided for the successful completion of the project. The project must be evaluated and presented to the class in order to involve the whole class.[7] Group work requires encouragement from the teacher and must be closely supervised to assure that the work is shared equally by group members. Project completion is dependent upon a team spirit in order to be successful.[8]

UNIT PLAN

"A unit is a plan that organizes ideas and knowledge into a meaningful structure for teaching purposes."[9] Basic concepts are selected within a subject area or across subject areas to achieve specific objectives. Not only does a unit plan imply a problem-centered curriculum, but it also places an emphasis on the process in which the learner engages other than the content to be covered. This method changes the goal from accumulating information to developing understandings as a result of experiences.[10] The unit content facilitates communication and should provide integrated experiences to satisfy students' needs and develop understandings, values, and skills. A teaching unit is made for a specific group of students and should be evaluated and restructured before using with a different group of students.[11]

SOCIALIZED RECITATION OR GROUP DISCUSSION

Socialized recitation or group discussion may involve the entire class or small groups. The purpose of group discussion is to encourage reflective thinking for

5. Crow and Crow, pp. 214-18.
6. Grant, p. 199.
7. Crow and Crow, pp. 90-91.
8. Grant, p. 199.
9. Lemlech, p. 305.
10. Daisy M. Jones, *Curriculum Targets in the Elementary School* (Englewood Cliffs, N.J.: Prentice-Hall, 1977), pp. 162-63.
11. Lemlech, pp. 305-22.

everyone participating in the discussion. One of the disadvantages could be that one or two students could monopolize the discussion. The teacher must be sure that the pupil-selected topic is relevant to the purpose of the lesson and that they do not digress from the topic.

INDIVIDUALIZED INSTRUCTION

Individualized instruction "is a system that individualizes instruction by designing and programming specific learning tasks so individual learners can progress through the program at their own level of readiness and own learning rate."[12] The system is over seventy years old and came into existence because of some educators' philosophy that each child is unique and has his own instructional needs. Individualized instruction is characterized by the following components: (1) "A unit for achievement with specific objectives; (2) learning activities in a prewritten learning guide; (3) evaluation of student achievement; (4) teacher involvement; (5) student responsibilities."[13]

Some of the better known programs of individualized instruction include: Individually Prescribed Instruction (IPI), Accordance With Needs (PLAN), Individually Guided Education (IGE), Accelerated Christian Education (ACE), and Alpha-Omega. These programs have been developed by curriculum experts and offer a variety of prepackaged instructional activities which accommodate a wide range of learner differences. The evaluation procedure requires charting the progress of each student as he moves through the curriculum. This, in addition to the amount of time the teachers need to prepare the individual materials, creates a need for a classroom assistant.[14]

LEARNING CENTERS

Learning centers are designed to motivate, reinforce, and support students' learning needs. Their major purpose is to increase self-motivation, self-direction, and to personalize instruction.[15] A teacher can design a center to meet special needs or the needs of all the pupils. The center should have multilevel activities to accomplish the objectives and an accumulation of multimodality materials in order to meet different learning styles. To insure success with learning centers, the teacher must refine techniques of recording children's work and monitoring their progress. You must know who has used the center, who needs to use the center, and

---

12. Gerald L. Gutlek, *Education and Schooling in America*, © 1983, p. 182. Reprinted by permission of Allyn and Bacon.
13. Charles R. Kniker and Natalie A. Naylor, *Teaching Today and Tomorrow* (Columbus, Ohio: Merrill, 1981), p. 305.
14. John O. Bolvin, "Individually Prescribed Instruction," in Maurie Hillson and Ronald Hyman, *Change and Innovation in Elementary and Secondary Organization*, 2d ed. (New York: Holt, Rinehart, and Winston, 1971), pp. 241-45.
15. *Learning Centers: Children on Their Own* (Washington, D.C.: Association of Childhood Education International, 1969), pp. 52-54.

whether the students are accomplishing the goal. The age of the pupils, materials and space available, and the curriculum goals will determine the centers you need.[16] While learning centers are used as a major method in the open classroom, they are often used in a traditional classroom to reinforce skills. Learning centers require a teacher with imagination and a genuine desire for personalized learning. Possible problems are: leaving them open too long, too little explanation of procedures, and a lack of knowledge by the teacher of the amount of work involved with learning centers.

COMPUTERS

Computers have been used by the schools since 1960; however, usage increased when the first commercially feasible computer became available in 1975. By the spring of 1980, students had access to 96,000 microcomputers and 24,000 computer terminals.

Most school systems have used the computer for various managerial and organizational functions such as scheduling students' courses and keeping attendance and grade records.[17] However, with the cost decline, computers are being used for instruction in the classroom.

Computer-based instruction has two major functions: computer-assisted instruction (CIA) and computer-managed instruction (CMI). Because of their data storage capacity, patience, and branching capability, microcomputers lend themselves to individual instructions. They can be used to supplement content area lessons which require drill and practice sessions by providing students with immediate feedback. Problem-solving skills can be developed by simulations where they are required to solve complex problems and the consequence of their decisions is known immediately. The graphic display capabilities help students who lean toward pictorial learning. When using the computer as a word processor, writing skills can be improved. Students are able to concentrate on intellectual content other than mechanical recording of thoughts on paper as the computer can add, delete, or modify expressions more easily.[18] In addition, computers can be used for tutorials, information retrieval, performing routine library research tasks, and connecting school study to the real world.

Teachers receive assistance from the CMI in planning and monitoring student learning experiences; storing and retrieving individual plans; programming tests, assessing exams; computing grades and filing the results. It helps them in keeping records, scheduling, and motivating students.

In spite of the enthusiasm of the results of the use of the computer in the

16. Sara W. Lundsteen and Norma Tarrow, *Guiding Young Children's Learning* (New York: McGraw-Hill, 1981), pp. 428-30.
17. Kniker, pp. 275-76.
18. Kevin Ryan and James M. Cooper, *Those Who Can, Teach* (Boston: Houghton Mifflin, 1984), pp. 428-33.

classroom, there are several major concerns about computers. These include: (1) an overemphasis on problems and ideas that lend themselves to quantification may detract from other forms of thinking; (2) may be addictive and alienating; (3) electronics can be hypnotic and isolating, taking away from or eliminating human experiences and relations; and (4) a fear of computers replacing humans in the work world.

What is the future of computers in education? Will they replace teachers, or will they become another fad?

There will probably be no radical changes in schooling during the next five to ten years, although there will be an expansion in the use of microcomputers in education. (A microcomputer is a small computer built around a microprocessor, which is a tiny electronic chip engraved on a silicon chip, which is smaller than a postage stamp.)[19] Any major investments in computers will be impeded by budget cuts and federal fiscal policies. In addition, there is a lack of high-quality software, and at the present the computer has few if any advantages over a well-programmed text. Another problem that must be overcome is that of teachers' fears. These include: fear of the unknown, fear of obsolescence or replacement, and a fear of math anxiety. However, we must remember that a major goal of education is to prepare students for the world of work. The computer will challenge us to produce students with a greater knowledge of science and technology and with thinking skills to make the best use of constantly developing information techniques.[20]

MEDIA

The tools of the professional teacher are educational media. In the past textbooks have been the major source of assistance for teachers. But the special projects of the 1960s and 1970s spurred the commercial market into implementing changes suggested by the disciplinarians and professional educators. Educational media includes printed, audiovisual, and real materials (realia).

The media available continue to increase and are too numerous to list. We will be discussing some of the major media used in classrooms.

Printed materials. These include maps, globes, graphic materials, atlases, newspapers, encyclopedias, pictures, and comics.[21] The advantage of printed materials is their abundance, and a lot of them can be obtained at little or no cost. It is important that the teacher select pictures that are related to the topic or lesson being discussed and to see to it that the students are aware of the relationships. Teachers must also acknowledge that pictures are subject to cultural, group, and individual interpretation and that an individual's past experiences will affect his

---

19. Ibid., p. 429.
20. Glen Hass, *Curriculum Planning: A New Approach*, 4th ed. (Boston: Allyn & Bacon, 1983), pp. 99-101. Also Ryan, pp. 428-33.
21. John A. Johansen, Harold W. Collins, and James A. Johnson, *American Education: An Introduction to Teaching*, 4th ed. (Dubuque, Iowa: Wm. C. Brown, 1982), pp. 309-331.

understanding of the picture. Pictures have value in gaining students' interest; however, you must remove them once they have served their purpose.

Transparencies. These require the use of an overhead projector and are a good alternative for the chalkboard. They provide a relatively inexpensive method of presenting a visually stimulating lesson and help with classroom managment. You can make a transparency by using a felt-tip marker or a grease or ceramic pencil. If you wish, you can reproduce typed or pencil-drawn materials by using a small thermal copy machine. These can be "dressed up" by superimposing additional transparencies on the original to represent complex ideas. This is also a method that can invite student participation.

Slides. Students can also make slides. They are particularly effective in helping students understand a concept more clearly if the printed word is accompanied (with step-by-step illustrations).

Audiovisuals. These are particularly effective in helping children understand concepts. The use of two senses (eyes and ears) often attracts and holds attention better than other media forms. The audiovisuals utilized in the class are film, filmstrips, television, video tapes, etc.[22] Teacher planning and preparation are crucial to using audiovisual aids successfully.

Films. Commercially prepared films can often be obtained from universities, State Department of Education, libraries, etc. with no charge. They can also be purchased or rented from commercial outlets. Films can be used to aid comprehension and provide vicarious experiences. The teacher can stop the film and reshow scenes to encourage students to predict what may happen next or to focus attention on an important idea. Another aspect of films is classroom production. This encourages creative expression, fosters active involvement and cooperation, and gives students a sense of accomplishment.

Videotape recorder (VTR). The VTR has a number of uses. The equipment includes a microphone, video camera, and a videotape playback unit. The machine is mobile, easy to operate, and can be used to evaluate performance and interaction of the teacher and pupils. VTR is of particular value in the performing arts, and students could use the equipment to make a TV show.[23]

Television. The value of television in education has been debated for years. It is important to remember that equipment must be used correctly and that the teacher must plan and prepare the class for the program. Television, both commercial and educational, can focus on events as they happen. It is of particular value in learning about and observing the legislative and political processes that govern our lives. Teachers must teach children to watch TV critically and discuss the implications of the program with them as soon as possible.[24]

Audio materials. AV materials can serve as an alternate learning resource for

22. Grant, p. 247.
23. Johansen, et al., pp. 309-31.
24. Crow and Crow, pp. 281-82.

students whose preferred learning modality is through verbal instruction. Audio materials include records, cassette tapes, and radio. Tapes have various uses but are of particular value in developing correct oral language patterns which serve as the foundation for learning the grammar and written form of language. Tapes are easy to store, compact, easily repaired, can be reused and are widely available. They are also one of the best means of evaluation.[25]

A word of caution—when using audio aids—you must prepare the materials and the students in order to achieve success.

Realia. Realia refers to the objects and activities used to relate classroom teaching to the real life. This includes such things as animals, pets, plants, insects, models of real things such as skeletons and machinery, simulation devices such as driver trainers and communication kits, as well as computers and other electronic devices.[26] Realia provides opportunities for students to have direct experiences with objects and specimens. It also provides an opportunity for field trips to museums, farms, zoos, and historical places to observe objects they might otherwise have no experience with. If you are not aware of the value of realia it is very easy to take many things for granted. In our modern society many children have not been acquainted with rural life, farm animals, and possibly may not have seen grass. As a classroom teacher, you need to provide as many real-life experiences as possible in guiding childrens' education.

METHODS AND BASIC SKILL INSTRUCTION

We have looked at different methods and media used in presenting instruction and now need to focus on the basic skills necessary for learning. "The overall goal of the preschool is to provide a child with an environment that will promote his optimum development at a period when growth is rapid and the child is vulnerable to deprivation of appropriate opportunities, new knowledge, and new relationships."[27] It is the preschool that gives the child his beginning in formal education. Historically elementary education has sought to provide children with the fundamental skills and basic knowledge necessary to function as members of society. Thus, elementary educators prepare children to use language by teaching reading, writing, and comprehension. In addition, special attention has been given in developing basic mathematic skills. It is the elementary school that builds the foundation of science, math, social studies, art, music, reading, writing, language, and physical education. Therefore a continuing goal is to cultivate fundamental skills and processes.[28] The junior high and high school basically teach educational content, although some high schools are teaching basic skills.

25. Grant, p. 247.
26. Johansen, et al., pp. 309-31.
27. Katherine Read and June Patterson, *The Nursery School and Kindergarten*, 7th ed. (New York: Holt, Rinehart, and Winston, 1980), p. 58.
28. Gutlek, pp. 177-80.

PRESCHOOL EDUCATION

Preschool education refers to the education that takes place prior to formal academic instruction. Although programs may vary due to differences in philosophy, methods, and curriculum, they all reflect the principles of a democracy. Citizens of a democracy, while being aware of diversity, also acknowledge a unifying factor and realize that the majority of citizens possess certain characteristics. The majority of preschools endorse a program that enhances the development of the following characteristics: (1) autonomy, (2) ability to think, (3) ability to make decisions, (4) self-confidence, and (5) ability to relate and work with others.[29]

In addition to preparing children to become competent members of a democratic society, a good preschool recognizes the importance of working cooperatively with parents. The goals focus on all of the children's needs and provide programs which offer a balance between self-directed and teacher-directed activities, quiet and active periods, and include periods of rest, nourishment, and evaluation.[30] Regardless of the age involved, a quality preschool program has the following goals: "(1) To provide children with a foundation for learning. . . . (2) To build a strong sense of self in young children. . . . (3) To help children develop physically. . . . (4) To help children learn to relate effectively with others. . . ."[31] A good preschool program is built on the foundation of sound human relationships involving many people working directly with the children, or working for their benefit.

Methods used in the preschool are dependent upon the philosophy of the school and the community. Although some preschools are highly structured and cater to cognitive development, the majority believe that curricula for young children must be centered in their play activities.

Immediately you begin to question what the young child is learning. Most individuals have not considered the value of play in a child's life. Our culture has basically considered play as something reserved for after work, unproductive and unrelated to intellectual pursuits. If our curriculum limits the time a child spends in play, it also limits the child's opportunity to learn. Piaget indicates that it is through play that a child practices and consolidates all he knows. This leads the child to question his concepts of reality, rethink them, and revise them to fit reality.[32] "What Can a Child Learn From Play?" adapted from JDC Guide for Day Care Centers[33] answers the question as follows:

When he builds with blocks: He learns to use his imagination to create

---

29. Carol Seefeldt, *A Curriculum for Preschool,* 2d ed. (Columbus, Ohio: Merrill, 1980), pp. 5-13.
30. Joanne Hendrick, *The Whole Child: Early Education for the Eighties,* 3d ed. (St. Louis: Time/Mirror/Mosby, 1984), pp. 254-55.
31. Seefeldt, pp. 11-13.
32. Jean Piaget, *Play, Dreams and Imagination in Childhood* (New York: Norton, 1962), pp. 87-104.
33. Adapted from *JDC Guide for Day Care Centers* (Geneva, Switzerland: Joint Distribution Committee).

something from his own thinking. He has the satisfaction of being able to make something. He learns about sizes and shapes, weights and balances, height and depth, smoothness and roughness. He is exercising his body. He may be learning to play with others.

When he paints: He learns about colors and how he can use them. He learns to use his imagination and tranfers his ideas to paper. He gets emotional satisfaction from being able to express himself. He learns how to use small muscle coordination to handle a brush.

When he plays in the doll corner: He learns what the roles of mothers and fathers and children are. He understands what it feels like to play at being somebody other than himself. He learns how to use his imagination. He learns to cooperate with other children.

When he makes a gift out of paper and paste: He learns about doing things for others. He learns how to use materials like scissors and paste. He learns how to use his imagination to make the kind of present he has in mind. He learns about shapes, sizes, color.

When he climbs on the climbing ladder: He learns how to use his body effectively. He experiences joy in achieving a skill. He has the fun and relaxation to be found in bodily movement. He learns the limitations of his body. He learns safety and caution. He learns to take turns and to share a piece of equipment. He learns to use his imagination and finds new ways of using the ladder.

All-around growth and development are enhanced by well-balanced play experiences. These include: (1) active physical play; (2) manipulative, constructive, creative, and scientific play; (3) imitative and dramatic play; and (4) social play. Play is the avenue chosen by children to express their feelings, try out their ideas and abilities, and get acquainted with the world. As experiences broaden and abilities develop, play changes.[34]

The atmosphere in many preschool centers is similar to a home setting where learning is informal, unstructured, and unpressured. The interaction between adults and children is spontaneous, which lends itself to rich language experiences. During play children often talk to themselves or others. Playing with others provides opportunities for children to communicate their ideas, gain cooperation, and respond to other ideas. Teachers can also help develop language by: (1) listening carefully to the children; (2) providing a meaningful base of experience to talk about; (3) developing conversation; (4) using questions to generate language; (5) extending their replies to children's questions; (6) providing consistent practice in auditory training; and (7) seeking professional help for those who need it.[35] Language development is considered to be closely connected with cognitive development; therefore, we need to encourage the use of spontaneous language.

It is of utmost importance that the right equipment, materials, and

---

34. Grace Langdon, "Play-Learning Interests of Children," *Instructor,* December 1969, pp. 40-41.
35. Hendrick, pp. 373-99.

supervision be supplied in order to develop total growth in the child. Play equipment is learning equipment and should be able to withstand hard wear. Play as a learning theory demands careful planning and supervision on the part of the teacher. She must assist children in their development by being either an observer or participant depending on the desire of the children. Preschool centers with play as a means of learning also have periods of formal instruction and give children a foundation for formal learning experiences. Often children learn more readily during play periods than during times of formal instruction. "There is now clear evidence to support the theory that the play of the child is, indeed, his work—a very necessary type of work."[36]

READING INSTRUCTION

Reading instruction probably receives more attention from the public than any other subject. It is believed that an individual who can read with understanding holds the key to all the stored knowledge of civilization. There are many varied reasons for reading, but the ability to read contributes to both societal and individual goals. Reading stimulates the individual to create, critique, and develop intellectually, as well as contributing to thinking ability. It is one of the most important aspects of life since economic competency is directly related to one's ability to read. The importance of reading in the early grades is crucial because of the difficulty nonreaders have in attaining their grade levels or ability levels. It is also the underachievers who tend to have more emotional and social problems, which are compounded as the child advances in school.[37]

MAJOR APPROACHES TO READING

A variety of methods have been used in teaching Americans to read, and apparently all have worked. Evidently all systems have worked for some, though not for all. Two major approaches are basically reflected in beginning reading programs: instruction based on skill and instruction based on experience. Phonics—word and letter patterns—for strong decoding skills are emphasized in programs featuring skills. The language-experience approach uses the child's natural language as the beginning reading content and emphasizes content and meaning.[38] Descriptions of the most commonly used approaches to reading will be discussed.

Language-experience approach. This approach to reading instruction is based on the idea that children will learn to read more quickly if confronted with words

---

36. Seefeldt, p. 98. Used by permission.
37. Dorothy Rubin, *Teaching Elementary Language Arts,* 2d ed. (New York: Holt, Rinehart, and Winston, 1980), pp. 117-18.
38. Sydney L. Schwartz and Helen F. Robinson, *Designing Curriculum for Early Childhood* (Boston: Allyn & Bacon, 1982), pp. 252-54.

they say and think. Students are highly motivated since they are reading about their own experiences. The emphasis of this method is on speaking to express a thought, followed by the encoding of that thought in writing. There are several problems with this method. Of major concern is that skills and vocabulary are not necessarily developed sequentially. In addition, the teacher must determine if the student is decoding or has memorized the content. The integration of all the language arts skills is the advantage of this method.[39]

Kinesthetic approach. This approach teaches reading by using the students' own stories. It differs from the language experience approach in that the student uses a dictionary box when writing a story. If a student asks for assistance with a word during the writing period, the teacher writes the word on a slip of paper. The pupil then traces the word with his index finger, turns the paper over and writes the word from memory. If successful, the word is utilized in the story and then filed in his dictionary box for future use. If the child cannot spell the word correctly, he retraces it until successful. This method is very similar to the language-experience approach and has the same problems.

Individualized approach. This also is a highly motivating approach to reading. The students are given an opportunity to select what they want to read from a wide variety of materials. The assumption is that students will select materials on their own reading level. The teacher meets with each student individually to check comprehension and skill needs. After identifying common learning needs, the teacher organizes small groups for skill instruction. Students select their own reading materials and are not required to read a specific number of books. The approach can be implemented several different ways. Record-keeping is probably the most important aspect of the method.[40]

Basal reader approach. This is the approach used by most teachers. This approach utilizes a set of graded reading books and supplementary materials designed to teach the important skills of reading. Because basal texts provide a developmental sequence of skills and have a controlled vocabulary, reading is learned in small steps.[41] This approach is most used by teachers for the following reasons: (1) a variety of text series are available; (2) a logical, sequential development of vocabulary and skills are provided; (3) teacher manuals provide assistance in organizing the reading program; and (4) the manual gives assistance in motivating reading and in evaluating skill mastery. The main criticism of the basal text is the stiltedness of the writing and the tendency of being written for a "typical" student. However, a creative teacher can add supplementary materials and enrich the reading program.

Phonics approach. This is another popular approach and involves teaching letter sounds for all twenty-six letters of the alphabet, seventy phonograms,

---

39. Rubin, pp. 120-21.
40. Lemlech, pp. 126-27.
41. Edna P. DeHaven, *Teaching and Learning the Language Arts* (Boston: Little, Brown, 1979), pp. 381-84.

thirteen phonic rules, and twenty-six spelling rules. There is an advantage to teaching children to use phonetic clues as a tool for learning to read words, but the importance of sight words cannot be overlooked. Students often complain of the large amount of time spent in drill and comprehension skills, which are usually weak. In addition, they often lack expression in their reading and appear to be uninterested in reading.[42] This method is usually more successful when used as a supplement to another approach.

Most classroom teachers combine two or more approaches in teaching reading. All methods have been successful with some, but not with everyone. The importance of reading to future success deems it necessary that the classroom teacher determine the method that will assure success for each student.

THE LANGUAGE ARTS

The language arts are the heart of the elementary school curriculum. The major skills include speaking, listening, reading, and writing. Reading and listening are considered to be receptive skills, while speaking and writing are viewed as expressive skills. "Language is both the foundation on which a program is built and the source of supply for continuing growth."[43] The skills among the four areas are very similar and make learning in one area complementary to that of another. In fact many of the skills involving language and thought are used in all language arts activities. Our capacity for knowledge and thinking is controlled by the mind, which allows us to organize and share knowledge through the language system. Teaching and learning activities in the language arts are those that focus on developing knowledge and understanding language and those that focus on developing skills in using language. Although all of the areas are interrelated, we will examine speech, listening, and writing.

Speech. Oral communication is important and necessary for success in life. Children learn language by listening, observing, imitating, and experimenting. By the time a child enters school, he has acquired a sizable vocabulary. Teachers need to help children communicate effectively for the following reasons: (1) increasing verbal environment; (2) bombardment of knowledge; (3) need to improve human relationships; (4) help link the past to the present; and (5) to enhance their chance for success in academics and real-life pursuits. Vocabulary development and communication skills are more easily developed in the elementary grades because (1) the classroom facilitates a warm relationship between the teacher and child; (2) interaction can be facilitated by the seating arrangement; and (3) oral skills can be developed in all subject areas throughout the day.[44] Children must be able to

42. Lemlech, p. 128.
43. DeHaven, p. 13.
44. Lemlech, pp. 97-107.

express ideas clearly, interestingly, and pleasantly in order to be competent in using oral language.

Good language programs can only grow out of stimulating experiences that are meaningful to children. Conversation, perceiving and following instructions, formulating questions and inquiries, seeking information, expressing ideas, sharing information, group discussion, listening to stories, books, poems, creative dramatics, dramatic play, and development of vocabulary must be programmed into the curricula to assist children in their effort to communicate effectively. A teacher needs to be aware of the oral skills of each student and assist him in achieving competency in oral communication.[45] It is through many different activities that children discover the relationships of language choice and language function and become flexible and competent in using language appropriately. Children should be helped to use language, other than having it just presented as a subject.

Listening. Listening is probably the most neglected of the language arts skills, although more failure in academic and social growth can be traced to the inability to listen than any other aspect of the language arts. Listening or nonlistening is difficult to detect. We must not take it for granted that a person can listen because he can hear. Hearing depends on the proper functioning of the ears, nervous system, and the brain, whereas listening extends hearing to reaction, identification, and thought. A teacher needs to be aware of and plan for the three types of listening: (1) informational, (2) appreciative, and (3) critical.

A child's background of experiences; his social, emotional, physical, and cognitive development; and the context of the listening material determines how well he listens. Children's listening abilities can be improved through instruction. Therefore, teachers must be aware of their responsibilities that are conducive to attentive listening. To teach listening, the teacher needs to be (1) a good model, (2) a good planner, and (3) be able to evaluate oral directions.[46] Listening can be incorporated into every subject area. It is the teacher's responsibility to develop the skills of listening by providing opportunities for listening and emphasizing the importance listening plays in achieving success.

Writing. Writing is probably the most difficult of the language arts components to teach. The mechanics of handwriting are dependent upon good eye-hand coordination and the development of small muscles in the hand and wrist. Continued practice in writing causes children to become bored and discouraged. In addition, the grading of handwriting can be very painful. Although we need to teach children the mechanics of good writing, it is important to be sure they have developed the maturational level necessary for being able to accomplish the skill.

---

45. DeHaven, pp. 118-24.
46. Paul C. Burns and Betty L. Broman, *The Language Arts in Childhood Education,* 4th ed. (Chicago: Rand McNally, 1979), pp. 97-109.

Good handwriting requires patience, close supervision, encouragement, and lots of assistance from the teacher. Writing papers, stories, essays, and so on is dependent upon the student's ability to understand the relationship of words to thoughts. To be effective it requires a knowledge of writing mechanics such as punctuation, capitalization, spelling, and sentence structure.

How does a teacher teach writing? "The purposes of the writing program include: (1) The development of functional writing to communicate skills; (2) the development of creative writing to express thoughts and (3) skill development in the mechanics of writing."[47]

Student activities such as letter writing, creative writing, informational writing, record keeping, note taking, outlining, research, and proofreading will help accomplish the above goals. In addition, we need to emphasize the relationship between speaking and writing, and work on vocabulary development since the student is dependent upon his speaking vocabulary for written expression.

All of the language arts components are important and interrelated. The development of one area is dependent upon another. Therefore, we should make an extra effort to integrate all of the language arts components into our daily plans.

MATHEMATICS

Mathematics is another of the major areas in the elementary curriculum. It is both a skill and content subject. A solid mathematics program is characterized by three factors: (1) how children learn mathematical concepts; (2) the logical structuring of mathematical ideas; and (3) the functional application of mathematics' content to the world of the child. The mathematical skills children acquire in early childhood lay the foundation for later knowledge. The program should focus on independence of thought and logical reasoning other than the production of correct answers. There should be an emphasis on real-world problems with learning experiences progressing from concrete to abstract. An appreciation and understanding of mathematical concepts, structure, and terminology should be a major goal of the elementary math program.[48] Mathematical ideas are contingent upon discovering and creating patterns and classifying and comparing physical objects. Children must have experience with real things before they can be expected to conceptualize abstract symbols and operations of mathematics. As they learn, children must be involved in trial-and-error processing. There is a memorization factor involved in mathematics. Most educators agree that memorization is usual in learning the names of numbers and in the multiplication operations. Children must be able to build within themselves relationships

---

47. Lemlech, p. 109.
48. Ibid., pp. 178-98. Also Sue Clark Wortham, *Organizing Instruction in Early Childhood* (Boston: Allyn & Bacon, 1984), pp. 87-89.

between meaning and labels for shapes, functional operations, and thought processes in the mental juxtaposing of ideas.[49]

Lemlech reports the seven major content strands of mathematics to be: (1) arithmetic numbers and operations; (2) geometry; (3) measurement; (4) calculators/computers; (5) probability and statistics; (6) relations and functions; and (7) logical thinking. The application for these is problem solving. Calculators and computers are most commonly used in the upper grades after students have achieved the basic computation skills.[50] Mathematics is an essential skill for general kinds of enjoyment, self-protection, and effective functioning in society.[51]

The problems concerned with mathematics are similar to those of reading—the choice of a formal textbook, programmed instruction, or a combination of several series. In addition, teachers must decide whether to emphasize facts and skills or precise vocabulary, insight into the system and how it works, and appreciation of the discipline.

Both the traditional math and modern math have limits and merits. See Insight (fig. 13.1) for comparison and contrast of traditional and modern math. Many teachers use a combination of the methods. Regardless of the system you use, success is dependent on your understanding and skill as a teacher. As a teacher, you must take an active role in encouraging the child to use mathematical concepts and thinking that will foster skill and knowledge in every area of math.[52]

METHODS AND CONTENT INSTRUCTION

Most content instruction begins after third grade. Prior to third grade, emphasis is on developing the skills necessary for learning. Content instruction includes the science and social studies areas of the elementary curriculum. However, math is both a skills and content subject. Although content is important, it is more effective when taught in a meaningful way.

SELECTION AND ORGANIZATION OF CONTENT

The problem of what to teach and how subject matter determines curriculum is determined either by school districts, schools, teachers, or cooperatively. However, the nature of the subject matter is an influential factor in determining the relationship of content to curriculum. It determines whether or not it is to be taught and where it will be placed in the scheme of things.

Piaget's stages for cognitive development as well as Gesell's developmental assessment of readiness can be used to guide teachers in the selection of content

---

49. Edythe Margolin, *Teaching Young Children at School and Home* (New York: Macmillan, 1982), pp. 285-86.
50. Lemlech, pp. 180-81.
51. Margolin, pp. 285-86.
52. Wortham, pp. 87-89.

Insight: Traditional Versus Modern Math Comparison and Contrast

AREA	TRADITIONAL MATH	MODERN MATH
Aims	Skill in computation Mastery of facts Knowledge of subject matter Mental discipline	Insight into the structure of the discipline Precise terminology for naming the concepts Reasoning
Content	Number names Number sequence Computation Notation and numeration Fundamental processes	Vocabulary and sets Theory and logic Principles of association, distribution, and commutation Generalizations
Approaches	Present the facts Memorize the processes Drill for perfection & skill Use processes to solve problems	Meet the situation Experiment with possibilities Discover the patterns and the principles Practice for needed skills
Procedures	Explain the processes Provide repetitive drill Test and retest Memorize rules and formulae Use deductive reasoning Move from definition to theorem	Set the stage Lead the children to experiment Question for insight and understanding Help them draw conclusions Encourage more than one way Use inductive reasoning Move from theorem to definition
Outcomes	Mastery of skills Rote learning Routine application	Insight into the structure of the discipline Appreciation for the orderliness of number relations Independence in approaching new concepts

Advantages	Quick
	Accurate
	Easily tested for mastery
	Objective measurement
	Parents think they understand it
		Leads to:
		  permanent learnings
		  interest for the learner
		  challenge for the teacher
		  independence for future learnings
		  appreciation for the discipline of mathematics

Limitations	Learner becomes dependent on rules and code Subject becomes dull and boring to creative child	Takes longer to arrive at mastery of the process Permits trial and error and inaccuracies while insights are being established Real objectives are not easily measured by objective tests Less emphasis on computation

Pupil lacks insight which leads to independence Provides drill on computation better done by tables of the computer	Parents do not understand

From Daisy M. Jones, *Curriculum Targets in the Elementary School*, © 1977, p. 217. Adapted by permission of Prentice-Hall, Inc., Englewood Cliffs, N.J.

Fig. 13.1

(see chapter 4). Some areas of knowledge require more instruction, maturity, and experience to learn than others. Learnings that require logical and sequential organizations, with each step based on the one that has gone before, implies that sequence and placement of content is influence by the nature of the subject matter. As knowledge continues to *explode* around us, the issue becomes what to teach, when to include it, and whether or not to incorporate this new knowledge into the curriculum.

Information that is organized and includes related experiences is considered to be more meaningful than miscellaneous facts and isolated activities. A teacher who wants to produce learners who can perform on tests and produce scores will use methods that drill for skills and feed for facts. Will this learning last beyond the end of the term? Remember, they accomplished their goal—a high score. A curriculum designed to produce learners who can meet situations, set goals, make decisions, and become self-propelled organizes facts and coordinates learnings to develop understandings and insights.

Your goals will influence the organization of the curriculum. In the past, curriculum has been influenced by religion, nationalism, industrialization, culture, and technology. The points of emphasis have varied and tend to fluctuate with the viewpoint of curriculum specialists and teachers. The question to ask is, "Which is of more value: knowledge, skills and attitudes accumulated, or the processes through which the learner goes in learning how to learn?"[53]

MAKING CONTENT LEARNING MEANINGFUL

All learning requires planning and structure on the part of the teacher. Information that is organized and includes related experiences is considered to be more meaningful than miscellaneous facts and unrelated activities. It is the lack of planning and disorganization on the part of the teacher which creates confusion, lack of achievement, lack of interest and disciplinary problems.

53. Jones, p. 12.

Most educators consider rote learning to be difficult and easily forgotten, whereas meaningful learning is easy and well-retained. Research has supported the theory that meaningful learning is superior to that of rote memory. It is the responsibility of the teacher to present content in a manner that is meaningful to students.

Of particular importance to content instruction is the understanding by the students that important information is to be presented. This requires that the information be presented clearly, logically, and in a simple, precise vocabulary. Most of all it must be understandable. Previews and reviews to lectures and reading assignments are helpful in teaching content. The students are made aware of what they are going to learn or what they should have learned. Content can be presented by balancing product and process. You may use lecture, reading, or research, but you must make learning meaningful to the student. He needs to be able to take the information and apply it to his situation in life in order to maintain learning. Research has indicated that using previews, reviews, and a summary of content are effective in learning content.

TECHNIQUES FOR TEACHING CONCEPTS

The teaching of new concepts to students is probably one of the most important and challenging goals of teaching. The works of educational psychologists have produced guidelines for the teaching of concepts, thus making it easier for teachers. These include: (1) giving a definition of the concept; (2) providing several different examples of the concept; (3) indicating which features of the examples are critical features and which are not; (4) provide examples that may appear to be members of the concept, but are not; (5) give the students a mixture of positive and negative instances of the concept, with an explanation in order to test their knowledge of the concept, and then test them on additional positive and negative instances; (6) begin with simple instances of the concept and move gradually to the more complex ones if possible; and (7) remember that while most students will appear to have grasped the concept, there will be some who will require additional individual work before they grasp it. Several references in this book have cited Piaget's theory that students learn best when they discover for themselves. However, recent research indicates that expository teaching of concepts is more effective than the discovery method.[54] This does not imply that students are not to be involved actively in learning. The many media resources can be extended and useful in teaching concepts.

METHODOLOGY AND REAL WORLD SKILLS

Real-world skills are the skills that are necessary to succeed in life. This is

---

54. Ibid.

very difficult to decide due to the incredible advancements being made in technology. Skills such as cooking, sewing, check-writing, auto-mechanics, as well as other vocational skills, may not be relevant to today's young students. Should those be replaced with skills in using the computer and other electronic devices, or will there always be a need for some basic skills? Although schools have taught students the process of completing applications and check-writing skills, not all have extended this knowledge. The following occurred recently:

A colleague's twelve-year-old son mowed my lawn. After completing the job, I gave him a check for $10. Since the bank was located nearby, I suggested that he endorse the check, and that he could cash it on the way home. He immediately asked what "endorse" meant and then turned the check over and signed it horizontally rather than vertically.

This child was familiar with banks, checking accounts, and the process of writing checks, but this was his first experience with the endorsing requirement.

It is very difficult to determine the exact skills needed for the "real world" because of the fast pace of technology. However, we need to be alert to what students currently need in order to succeed. In addition, we must be alert to technical advancements and the role they play in determining the skills needed for success.

Study-Skills for Lifetime Independent Learning

It is the desire of all good teachers to instill in their students the desire to continue learning throughout life. This becomes more important in a complex society, where changes in all aspects of culture are continually undergoing change.

What are the characteristics of a lifelong learner? Crowley describes lifelong learners as:

1. Highly skilled at locating information
2. Highly effective in applying knowledge they already possess in a variety of situations
3. Accustomed to setting their own objectives
4. Efficient in evaluating their own learning
5. More highly motivated to continue learning than is usually the case
6. Possessing self-concepts favorable to continual learning[55]

In order to accomplish this, we must teach students to be independent learners by teaching them effective study skills. The following tips will assist you in increasing study skills: (1) choose an appropriate place to study, (2) *study*—don't pretend, (3) organize and reduce study material, (4) test yourself or use study partners, (5) self-record and self-reinforce, (6) use spaced study periods, (7) use

---

55. A.J. Crowley, "Lifelong Learning," in Henry Ehlers, *Crucial Issues in Education*, 7th ed. (New York: Holt, Rinehart, and Winston, 1981), p. 184.

mnemonic devices, and (8) continue study after learning content.[56] As a teacher, you need to encourage and reinforce students in their quest for better study skills. Many students who enroll in a basic study skills course in college are made aware of the process involved in effective study for the first time. As teachers, we have an obligation to teach effective study skills, observe those skills, and evaluate them in order to help students achieve success and developed their God-given potentials into abilities.

APPROPRIATE USES OF METHODOLOGY IN THE TEACHING-LEARNING PROCESS

Once a teacher has decided upon the objectives, she must then determine the method to use in order to achieve them. The teacher must give specific attention at this stage of planning to assure that the methodology is appropriate to the attainment of the objective. She must also take into consideration the learning styles and the age-level characteristics of the students in determining the method of instruction to be used. In addition, she must be flexible in her planning and teaching, as well as being comfortable with the content, materials, and methodology used in guiding students toward success.

HINDSIGHT

This chapter has reviewed methods used to attain goals in education. Some of the current methods used include (1) problem-solving, (2) project method, (3) unit plan, (4) socialized recitation, (5) individualized instruction, (6) learning centers, (7) computers, and (8) audiovisual aids. We then considered different methods used in achieving basic skills. A good school accepts the child as he is and presents a program that will assist the child in living his fourth year, tenth year, etc. to his fullest. Most experts stress the importance of play in young children's learning. A brief summary of several approaches to reading was presented, including the advantages and disadvantages of each. Approaches and techniques used in math and language arts were also presented. The selection and organization of content instruction was previewed, emphasizing particular information regarding teacher responsibility. The chapter concluded with a description of a lifelong learner and the importance of appropriate methodology in attaining goals as the student moves toward Christian maturity.

CHALKBOARD CHALLENGES

1. Since you were given a brief view of a good preschool program, we suggest you visit a federally funded preschool program and a private preschool program and identify seven specific learning experiences using play as the method of

---

56. Benjamin B. Lahey and Martha S. Johnson, *Psychology and Instruction* (Glenview, Ill.: Scott Foresman, 1978), pp. 304-8.

attaining the objective. Write a description of those activities.

2. The importance of different methods of presentation was presented to you. In order to increase your experiences with methods, observe in an elementary classroom and list the different methods and approaches used in teaching math and reading. This should be recorded in your teacher's notebook.

3. Compare different materials and basal texts used in the teaching of reading (for example, ACE, McGinn, or Alpha Omega). How are they alike and/or different? We suggest you record this in your teacher's notebook.

WANT TO KNOW MORE?

PRESCHOOLS

For more detailed information on preschools read: James L. Hymes, *Teaching the Child Under Six* (Columbus, Ohio: Merrill, 1968).

CURRICULUM

If you desire more information on curriculum, visit your school's curriculum library or a County School Board office. Also examine the following curriculum:

Abeka Publications, a ministry of Pensacola Christian College.
Box 18,000
Pensacola, FL 32523.

Accelerated Christian Education,
P.O. Box 1438.
Lewisville, TX 75068.

Alpha-Omega
2316 West Huntington
Tempe, AZ 85281.

Bob Jones University Press,
Greenville, SC 29614

Most major educational publishers have series of math, reading, science, and language arts.

14

Student Motivation

CONTENTS

	PAGE
Key Terms	348
That's Debatable!	350
Foresight	350
Motivation and Student Movement Behavior	351
Theoretical Approaches to Motivation	353
Cognitive Approaches	356
Developing a Theoretical Framework of Motivation	361
Classroom Approaches to Motivation	363
Hindsight	369
Chalkboard Challenges	369
Want to Know More?	370

KEY TERMS

Achievement motivation
   A term that refers to individuals for whom success and its visible concomitants are especially important
Actualization
   Stresses the positive nature of behavior and views motivation from the

standpoint that we strive to control our environment
Attribution
Explanations of motivative behavior that suggest our inferences about others and ourselves are formed by attributing motives, as we eliminate alternative explanations
Cognitive theories
Concerned primarily that we understand the processes we use when we interpret information about the motivation of our behavior
Dissonance
Better known as "cognitive dissonance," a theory holding that only when cognitions are dissonant (out of harmony) is motivation activated to resolve the dissonance
Drive reduction
The drive to fulfill biological needs motivates or causes behavior
Extrinsic motivation
Emphasizes the external goals toward which the activity is directed
Hedonism
Motivated by pleasure and pain
Homeostasis
An optimal level exists for various states of the body; and when the body deviates too far from that level, motivational circuits are triggered by the receptors monitoring these states, and behaviors that will bring the body back to its optimal level are begun
Incentive
The goals toward which we strive can in themselves be motivating
Incongruity
Motivation exists whenever an incongruity occurs between past experience and new information
Instinct
Genetic programming in the form of instinctive behaviors may become activated when our physical needs reach certain levels
Intrinsic motivation
The value or pleasure associated with an activity as opposed to the goal toward which the activity is directed
Motivation
A concept used to describe the forces acting on or within a person to explain the initiation, direction, intensity, and persistence of behavior
Meaningfulness
People pursue those objects, events, and experiences that are emotionally important for them
Social motivation
Our interaction with other people, which both generates and directs behavior

THAT'S DEBATABLE!
Origins or Pawns?

Are we primarily motivated from within ourselves or from forces outside ourselves? At any given moment, on any given day, this is a good question to begin a discussion that can quickly become spirited. In thinking about this question, deCharms came to the conclusion that people may be categorized as "origins" or "pawns." An origin is one who believes that his own behavior is controlled by his own choices. A pawn, on the other hand, is one who perceives his behavior as being controlled by outside forces over which he has no control. deCharms believed that the primary motive in humans is to "be effective in producing changes in their environment."[1] In other words, we strive for *personal causation* (i.e., to be people who cause things to happen in our environment).

It is not hard to see that origins would have strong feelings of personal causation, and that much of their behavior results from those feelings of control over their environment. In contrast, pawns feel powerless, and their behavior as well results from their perception of having no control over their environment.

Are you an origin or a pawn? Or is there some of both in you?

FORESIGHT

Recently the author was talking with a group of students about a possible meeting time. After a number of suggestions were made, someone suggested 5:30 without designating whether he meant in the morning or in the late afternoon. One of the students said, "There is no way you're going to get me up at 5:30 in the morning for a meeting!" whereupon I, testing a theory of motivation, said, "What if you really knew that you would get a million dollars if you came to a meeting at five thirty in the morning?" The same student replied, "I would set three alarm clocks, tell my roommates to wake me up, get there early, be sure I knew where I was to meet and with whom I was supposed to meet, and nothing would stop me from being there."

This student's comments illustrate perfectly what motivation is all about. We define motivation as forces acting on or within a person to initiate, direct, intensify, and cause behavior to persist. Interestingly, the student's comments contained each of those aspects of motivation.

In this chapter, we will be talking about motivation—a fascinating subject indeed! All of us in our more serious moments ask questions such as, "What made me act that way?" "I wonder why she did that?" "Look at that human fly climbing up that forty-story building! I wonder why anybody would want to put themselves at that risk, just to get arrested at the top." "It seems like he never sleeps. I wonder

---

1. R. deCharms, *Personal Causation: Thee Internal Affective Determinants of Behavior* (New York: Academic, 1968), p. 269. Used by permission.

what drives him so?" All of these questions or comments relate to the heart of motivation. What causes us to do the things we do, say the things we say, to say them with the intensity or lack of intensity with which we say or do them, and why do we stick doggedly to a task or to a conviction on one occasion, and on another occasion really not fight very hard for it?

In the teaching-learning process, it goes without saying that the teacher must understand and be able to apply the concept of motivation. For the teacher's job is to cause learning and facilitate the development of the students who are in his or her classes. We think you will find this chapter not only interesting, but exceedingly helpful in a practical way as well.

MOTIVATION AND STUDENT MOVEMENT BEHAVIOR

As we carefully consider motivation in the classroom, let us recap the essential teacher behaviors which the extensive research on effective schools and classrooms has evidenced to be so: "Teachers who plan, manage, and instruct in ways that facilitate student involvement, coverage, and success are likely to be considered more effective."[2] If you analyze carefully that brief statement, you will see that what the teacher is really called upon to do is to engage in certain kinds of behaviors, which in turn involve the students in such a way that students move from where they are to a new and more knowledgeable position in relation to the particular subject matter or behavior involved. This is the kind of effect we refer to when we talk about *student movement behavior*. We believe it is helpful to look at motivation, not only in terms of very specific research that has been done—and we shall review that research briefly in this chapter—but also with a general kind of overview. In the classroom itself, in the midst of the teaching-learning process, the teacher may not always be able to remember all of the details of a particular theory. But if the teacher can have a mental image of the student's moving from one position, one conviction, or one point of view to another informed by additional knowledge, understanding, and experience, then the teacher has in mind the overview of motivation that is associated with our meaning of *student movement behavior*.

It is certainly the case that many and varied influences from without and from within will motivate the many different kinds of students with whom we deal. But our goal always is to help them move from one spot to another (in the sense just described) without violating their integrity as individuals.

In relation to this kind of overview of motivation as *student movement behavior*, it is helpful to keep in mind a question: "Is it worth doing?" Whatever it is, desirable or undesirable in terms of the teacher's point of view, or the principal's point of view, or the parents' point of view, the student (or any other human being

---

2. David A. Squires, William G. Huitt, and John K. Segars, *Effective Schools and Classrooms: A Research-Based Perspective* (Alexandria, Va.: ASCD, 1983), p. 10.

for that matter) is not going to move in that direction unless he or she believes that the move is worth it. In our previous illustration, the student who was going to arrive at the meeting at 5:30 in the morning felt that it was worth it if he were going to receive a large sum of money. Otherwise, it would not be worth doing.

Putting these two ideas together—the overview of motivation as *student movement behavior* and the question of *making it worth doing*—the teacher may approach the teaching-learning process with two very valuable tools. Keep in mind constantly that you want to help your students move in a desirable direction according to the objectives of your school and of your course and in terms of their own development and learning. In order to get them to make such movement, the motivation must be some thing, idea, value, or person which makes that movement worthwhile.

Insight: From Jerusalem to Jericho

Seminary students at Princeton University were asked to participate in a study on religious education and vocation. The subjects began the experiment in one room but were then asked to go to another building next door to finish the experiment by giving a short talk on either religious vocations or the parable of the Good Samaritan. Three conditions were run. In the first condition, subjects were told that they were late for the second part of the experiment and should hurry across the alley to the second building. A second group was told that they had just time enough to make it to the other building, and a third group was told that they had plenty of time to get to the building for the second part of the experiment.

Subjects were directed to the building next door. Getting there required crossing an alley that ran between the buildings. In this alley a confederate of the experimenter was slumped against the wall. He was instructed to cough twice and groan as subjects passed him.

The behavior of interest was whether students in training for the ministry would stop to aid the victim and whether the type of talk they were about to give (i.e., religious vocation or the parable of the Good Samaritan) and the degree of hurry (i.e., late, on time, or early) would influence the probability of their giving aid.

Results of the experiment are quite fascinating. The type of talk the seminarian was about to give (and thus was presumably thinking about on his way across the alley) had no effect on helping behavior. Subjects asked to talk on the parable of the Good Samaritan were no more likely to stop than those asked to talk on religious vocations. Thus thinking about helping others did not appear to increase the likelihood of lending aid to a victim. By contrast, the time constraints put on the subjects had a large effect on helping behavior. Subjects who thought they were late and were thus in a hurry were not very helpful; only 10 percent stopped to offer the victim aid. Of the subjects in the "on time" condition, 45 percent stopped to offer aid, while 63 percent in the "early" condition stopped. Clearly the situational factor of time can be crucial in determining helping behavior. Again we see the importance of situational factors in motivating behavior in social situations.

J. M. Darley and C. D. Batson, "From Jerusalem to Jericho: A Study of Situational and Dispositional Variables in Helping Behavior," in M. P. Golden, ed., *The Research Experience* (Itasca, Ill.: Peacock, 1976). Adapted from Herbert L. Petri, *Motivation: Theory and Research*, p. 276. © 1981 by Wadsworth, Inc. Reprinted by permission.

Fig. 14.1

THEORETICAL APPROACHES TO MOTIVATION

As we consider each of these approaches briefly because of the limitations of this particular chapter, keep in mind, both in relation to yourself and in thinking about others, which or what part of any of these approaches really rings true. Each approach is quite different in some respects, others are similar in a number of respects, and indeed very close one to the other. But we include these here because we feel that each one represents an approach that is worth consideration, and which research has shown has a contribution to make as we reflect upon this important matter of motivation.

S-R APPROACH: DRIVE REDUCTION

The S-R approach, of course, is the basic behavioristic approach, and an analysis of this approach suggests that behavior is initiated by the occurrence of an external or internal stimulus, and that the direction of the behavior is then determined by what are called S-R bonds, or habits.

The close relationship between learning and reinforcement is referred to by McCandless.

Good and Brophy describe this kind of motivation as follows:

> The human infant is born with certain biological drives. The S-R point of view begins with the assumption that the drive to fulfill biological needs *motivates* or causes behavior. Through the pursuit or fulfillment of biological drives (e.g., satisfying hunger needs), secondary drives (the closeness of social stimulation) are learned. Progressively, children learn secondary drives (dependence, aggressiveness) that in turn cause behavior.... Once formed, secondary drives or goals function and cause behavior. If secondary drives continue to be reinforced, behavior associated with them continues to be repeated. Hence, the general theme of a stimulus/response theory is that reinforced behavior is *repeated*, while unreinforced or punished behavior tends to *disappear*.[4]

This is called a *drive reduction theory* because it says that learning occurs when a drive is reduced or satisfied. And the S-R theorist would say that the event that reduces the drive is called the reward. However, what may be looked upon as a reward is open to controversy, and therefore it may be the most accurate conclusion to state the situation as Good and Brophy do: "Behaviorists place more emphasis on external rewards and a deliberate and systematic arrangement of reinforcement contingencies, whereas cognitive theorists place more emphasis on internal rewards and related cognitive processes."[5]

NEEDS APPROACH: TENSION REDUCTION

Actually, explaining human motivation with the concept of need was one of the earliest explanations of motivation. In this concept, human behavior is explained in terms of the attempt to fulfill the needs of the human being.

The name of Henry A. Murray is associated with the development of the concept of need. According to Murray, a need is a *tension* that leads the individual to take action in a direction of a particular goal.[6] And what Murray called the "goal state" is an event capable of releasing the tension the individual feels. Murray listed some twenty needs or social motives as a result of his extensive research.

Another part of Murray's theory is this: A need usually is triggered by what Murray calls a "press." A press is an external influence upon the individual's behavior. Murray believed that these two forces, the need and the press, combine to

---

4. Thomas L. Good and Jere E. Brophy, *Educational Psychology: A Realistic Approach*, 2d ed. (New York: Holt, Rinehart, and Winston, 1980), p. 211.
5. Ibid., p. 212.
6. Henry A. Murray, ed. *Explorations in Personality* (Oxford: University Press, 1938).

form what he called a "theme," by which he meant a pattern of behavior. An example of this would be the job assigned to a student of raising the flag outside the school each day. The child feels a need within himself to do this because it makes him feel responsible, and the press in this situation would be the expectation of not only the principal of the school, but of the teachers and other students, that he would carry out this duty daily. Further, Murray would say that once a need is created, it tends to perpetuate itself.

As you think about Murray's approach, ask yourself whether our needs really do cause us to act in certain ways. Ask yourself if you view all of your behavior as purposeful, an attempt to satisfy a need or accomplish a goal. When you become a teacher, you will want to be alert to the needs that your students are seeking to fulfill, and once identified, build those needs into your motivational plans for your students.

Abraham H. Maslow set forth what he termed "a hierarchy of needs" arranged in order of their strength, and suggested that our fundamental needs tend to be satisfied first. Another way to say this, and to understand Maslow's theory, is to say that the appearance of higher needs usually depends upon our first satisfying the lower needs. As Maslow arranges these needs from the lowest to the highest, the result is as follows:

1. Physiological needs (sleep, thirst, etc.)
2. Safety needs (freedom from anxiety and psychological threats)
3. Love needs (acceptance from parents, teachers, peers)
4. Esteem needs (confidence in one's ability)
5. Need for self-actualization (creative self-expression, attempts to satisfy one's curiosity, etc.)[7]

Maslow emphasizes that if an individual is going to seek actively what he or she is or must be, he or she must first resolve the lower needs. In some ways, it resembles the climbing of a ladder with the lower needs being the lower rungs of the ladder, as long as this illustration is not carried too far. And Maslow pointed out as well there are exceptions in the manner in which these needs may be fulfilled hierarchically. You may give up sleep, for example, in order to study for an exam you need to pass in order to graduate.

One of the attractive parts of Maslow's view, whether one agrees with it totally or not, is that he recognizes the influence of the forces that can bring heavy influence upon an individual from one's environment. However, Maslow is hopeful and optimistic that the individual will respond in thoughtful and productive ways to these external forces, rather than simply responding thoughtlessly or unproductively.

Good and Brophy point out that a diligent student who gives up sleep or

---

7. Abraham H. Maslow, *Toward a Psychology of Being*, 2d ed. (New York: Van Nostrand, 1968).

misses a meal in order to do well on an exam may indeed be prompted by forces other than his or her own need for esteem. And they cite a beautiful letter to illustrate this to a student named Jim, at Difficult University. They term this "a warm and informative letter" from Jim's father.

> Dear Son:
> The receipt of your midterm grades has made it necessary that I write. Your mother and I assure you of our continuing love and affection, for we know you are trying. However, we feel you are trying more to test our patience than you are trying to apply yourself to school demands. Rest assured that the money source which supplies your physiological needs (fraternity house bill, warm clothes, money for food, and so forth) will be terminated at the end of the semester if your grades are not significantly improved.
>
> Love as always,
> Your Father[8]

In applying Maslow's needs approach to the classroom (in addition to trying to be reasonably sure that a student's needs are becoming involved in the teaching-learning process, for this is essential to motivation), the overall value, it appears to the author, of Maslow's approach is that teachers may be prevented from moving too rapidly in their efforts to motivate students. In the author's experience, teachers being the kind of people they are—that is, interested in students achieving at their highest possible levels—may make efforts at motivating students through the higher rungs of the ladder before the lower rungs (needs) have been climbed. It is as though the teacher may be trying to get the student to jump to the third or fourth rung, when the student is not even certain he can get a foot up on the bottom rung. This can discourage students; this can cause their motivation to decrease in relation to the tasks of the teaching-learning process. It is interesting to note as well that Maslow's approach to motivation would tie in rather well with the mastery approach to learning, which as you remember called for one task to be mastered, before the next (and a little more difficult) is attacked.

COGNITIVE APPROACHES

Before we look at several specific cognitive approaches to motivation, we need to generally define the kind of approach this is. This approach really emphasizes that the important thing about the behavior of a human being is the manner in which the person thinks about what is happening to him or her. How the individual perceives what is happening to him is more important than the objective reality.

Weiner conducted a study that demonstrates rather conclusively that cognitive perceptions do definitely influence behavior.[9] In that study and as a result

---

8. Good and Brophy, p. 217.
9. B. Weiner, "The Role of Success and Failure in the Learning of Easy and Complex Tasks," *Journal of Personality and Social Psychology* 3 (1966):339-44.

of it, he notes that students with *high anxiety* levels (those who are afraid of failure, for example) do better on experimental tasks if they first experience some success. If they do not do very well on the first task given to them, how they do on their second task deteriorates in quality. For *low-anxiety* students, if a student fails on a task, this appears to help improve a subsequent performance, and if this low-anxiety student has a high degree of success on the first task, it may cause that student not to do as well on subsequent tasks. The point here is that how the individual *perceives* success or failure on a task will have great influence, according to the cognitive approach to motivation, on how well or how poorly that individual will do on subsequent tasks.

Motivational theory has progressed from Maslow's and Murray's *particular* schemes, to emphasis more recently on the individual's perception of events that occur, and as well, on what is known as *intrinsic* motivation.

An excellent segment from Edward J. Murray helps to build the bridge from some earlier theories of motivation to more recent ones.

> In the past, the field of motivation and emotion was dominated by two theories—the classical Freudian and the classical behaviorist. In the Freudian image a man was that of a creature driven by inherited, unconscious sexual and destructive instincts constantly seeking release in a frustrating social environment. The behaviorist view was that of a creature quietly metabolizing in the shade, occasionally goaded into action by the hot sun and the lure of a cold glass of beer. Man is not simply warding off noxious stimuli and seeking the peace of death or Nirvana. He actively interacts with the environment. He is curious, playful, and creative. He conceives great ideas, seeks meaning, and envisions new social goals.[10]

Another way to think of this development of motivational theory is to remember that Freud's theory saw the human being as dominated by unconscious forces which were the result of the individual's having repressed those things he felt he did not want to face or think about. The behaviorist (a la Watson, for example) saw the human being as virtually a billiard ball on the pool table, which just lay there motionless until poked by a cue stick (a force from outside oneself); in this manner the individual's behavior was shaped. Man was a reactive being-in-depth (Freud) or simply a reactive being (behaviorist), and at the mercy of the forces of his environment. The newer view of motivation (by no means noncontroversial) is that man is a being-in-the-process-of-becoming, has purpose, intentions, and acts upon his environment in order to bring about change. We now look briefly at several versions of the cognitive approach to motivation.

INCONGRUITY: J. MCVICKERS HUNT

Hunt's argument is that if activity is intrinsic in its motivation in human beings, then it is not necessary to see behavior as a matter of either avoiding pain or

10. Quoted in Good and Brophy, p. 220.

reducing the tension of needs. And he concluded from a number of animal and human studies he did that when you observe play in young children or in young animals, for that matter, you usually find them in a very satisfied kind of position, which seems to be the condition necessary for them to play.[11]

And then in 1964, Hunt suggested that what he termed "incongruity" may well serve as the basis of motivation. Hunt refers, in seeking to make clear his idea of incongruity, to the temperature at which a thermostat is set in a room, and suggests that the temperature furnishes a standard against which the actual temperature of the room is being tested on a continual basis. Obviously, if the actual room temperature falls below that for which the thermostat is set, an incongruity occurs which starts the furnace operating. Hunt is arguing that a human being may well operate on this same kind of principle. In other words, an incongruity, which he defines as "a discrepancy between what is now and what is perceived or presented," will initiate action on the part of the human being. Each individual, says Hunt, has a particular level of incongruity which is best for him, and it varies then, obviously, from individual to individual.[12]

The application to the classroom is readily apparent. The teacher needs to learn how to present a new challenge, whether it is in the form of new materials, a higher level of difficulty within the materials, or a new kind of idea for operating in the classroom, in order that a certain amount of incongruity will develop in the student's perception of the situation. This, according to Hunt's theory, then should cause the students to do something to reduce that incongruity, and we would hope that "something" would be to study and learn more in order to be able to deal with the new material, or the new level of difficulty, or the new procedure.

The difficulty here is also readily apparent: The optimum amount of incongruity for each student is different. At the same time, the teacher in many situations must deal with the entire class at one time, so that what might be at one optimum level for one student, may be too much or too little for another student. We're back to the pediatrician dealing with thirty patients all at the same time. Here again, the wise teacher will get to know her students, and bring the best measure of professional judgment possible to the particulars of her classroom situation.

DISSONANCE: LEON FESTINGER

You will remember we have talked about this particular concept earlier in this textbook, but we return to it here just briefly to discuss it in the context of motivation. If you have in your thinking two inconsistent opinions, beliefs, or attitudes, dissonance or disharmony will occur. Festinger assumed that cognitive

---
11. J.M. Hunt, *Intelligence and Experience* (New York: Ronald, 1961).
12. J.M. Hunt, "Intrinsic Motivation and Its Role in Psychological Development," in D. Levine, ed., *Nebraska Symposium on Motivation*, vol. 13 (Lincoln: U. of Nebraska, 1965).

dissonance occurs when information or behavior occurs contrary to one's beliefs about oneself. Dissonance is usually looked upon as an unpleasant kind of state, and therefore the individual is motivated to reduce that unpleasantness.[13] If we can say this in another way, it may be helpful: The assumption of this theory is that we attempt as human beings to maintain *consistency* of our beliefs, attitudes, and opinions with our outward behavior.[14] As long as consistency is maintained, no motivation is triggered. An example comes readily to mind: If an individual is considerably overweight, and vacation time is coming up, and that individual wants to reduce and get in shape for the summer vacation, but at the same time loves to eat fattening foods, dissonance has occurred. It may be resolved by the individual's deciding that he will change the nature of his intake of food, or he may seek to rationalize his overweight in any one of several ways. Either way, dissonance has created motivation to either do something about the situation or to rationalize it in order to reduce the unpleasantness.

ACHIEVEMENT: DAVID MCCLELLAND, J. W. ATKINSON

According to David McClelland, achievement motivation refers to individuals for whom success and its visible concomitants are especially important.[15] If children are evaluated as having high achievement motivation, they usually are strongly rewarded by a lot of praise for their good performances, good grades, special awards they receive, etc. It is also an interesting note that the research suggests that students who have high achievement motivation usually have parents who have a very high opinion of the students, who expect success from them at a very early age, and of course reward them with strong emotional praise for their success.[16]

Atkinson has made his contribution to this field in a number of ways, one of which is the idea that human beings are continually motivated. Therefore, we don't need to be concerned with the *activation* of behavior, but with the variables that cause an individual to move from one type of activity to another. To put it another way, our behavior flows in a constant stream, and that stream may be changed in its course from time to time as the situation changes. Further, if we ask what are the major sources that cause the stream of behavior to change, this theory would point to the cognitive processes (conscious thoughts). As we consciously and deliberately think about conditions, situations, ideas, etc., this thinking serves to change

13. L. Festinger, *A Theory of Cognitive Dissonance* (Stanford, Calif.: Stanford U., 1957).
14. R.T. Abelson, E. Aronson, W.J. McGuire, T.M. Newcomb, M.J. Rosenberg, and P.H. Tannenbaum, *Theories of Cognitive Consistency: A Source Book* (Chicago: Rand-McNally, 1968).
15. Benjamin B. Lahey, and Martha S. Johnson, *Psychology and Instruction* (Glenview, Ill.: Scott Foresman, 1978), p. 142.
16. D.C. McClelland, *The Achieving Society* (Princeton: Van Nostrand, 1961).

the flow of the stream of behavior to a new kind of behavior or to dam up behaviors that have been ongoing.[17]

In terms of the application of this particular approach with students, again it becomes a matter of the exceedingly important professional judgment of the teacher, based on information and experience brought together in a definite philosophic approach to the clinical setting. Obviously, the teacher who can observe children well will be able to spot without too much difficulty those who are achievement-oriented. Again, this will not be true in an equal sense for every student in your class. But if you observe carefully, identify those children who are achievement-oriented (many times either the firstborn or an only child, according to research),[18] the teacher will be able to build this particular motivational factor into the teaching-learning process for this kind of individual.

ATTRIBUTION: B. WEINER

The attribution theory primarily concerns those factors assumed by people to cause the behavior of human beings. So, people "attribute" the behavior of others to particular factors—either to personality characteristics (dispositions) or to circumstances of the social situation of the persons involved.

The attribution theory rests on three basic assumptions:

1. It assumes that people do attempt to determine the causes of both their own behavior and that of others.

2. The assignment of causes to behavior is not done randomly; rules exist that can explain how people come to the conclusion they do about the causes of behavior.

3. Causes attributed to particular behaviors will influence subsequent emotional and nonemotional behaviors.[19]

> Attribution theories suggest that we are motivated to try to understand the environment in which we are immersed. This environment includes people with whom we interact and situations in which those interactions occur. Then our brains, having obtained sufficient information, cognitively process it according to relatively standard rules (most of them unknown) and make decisions (i.e. attributions) concerning how one event is related to another.[20]

Attribution theory has been applied most directly to achievement motivation

---

17. B. Birch, J.W. Atkinson, and K. Bongort, "Cognitive Control of Action," in B. Weiner, ed., *Cognitive Views of Human Motivation* (New York: Academic, 1974).
18. R.L. Adams and B.N. Phillips, "Motivational and Achievement Differences Among Children of Various Ordinal Birth Positions," *Child Development* 43 (1972):155-64.
19. E.E. Jones, D.E. Kanouse, H.H. Kelley, R.E. Nisbett, S. Valins, and B. Weiner, eds., *Attribution: Perceiving the Causes of Behavior* (Morristown, N.J.: General Learning, 1972).
20. From Herbert L. Petri, *Motivation: Theory and Research.* © 1981 by Wadsworth, Inc., p. 278. Reprinted by permission.

by Bernard Weiner and his associates.[21] Weiner argued that when we engage in achievement-related behavior, we will ascribe our success or failure at the task as a result of ability, effort, task difficulty, and/or luck. Past successes or failures will have a great influence as to what we attribute our successes or failures currently. Our judgments about our abilities are made, not in a vacuum, but in relation to how other people perform around about us.

MEANINGFULNESS: ERIC KLINGER

Klinger's basic idea is the importance of meaningfulness for people's lives. Meaningfulness is provided by incentives toward which people work. According to Klinger, people will be motivated to pursue those things that are emotionally significant to them. Klinger's view is summed up by concluding that people work (i.e., behave) in order to get those incentives that are prizes.[22]

If is of significance in Klinger's approach that he demonstrates these incentives that provide meaningfulness to people are not events or objects or experiences that are out of the ordinary. He points out that family, children, and personal relationships seem to be the most common sources of meaning for most people.[23]

Developing a Theoretical Framework of Motivation

After reading and reflecting upon the various approaches to motivation (and there are still others we have not discussed in the text) the student begins to feel there is some element of truth in each of the approaches. But at the same time, students frequently become discouraged in terms of a total frame of reference for motivation. That is, they have difficulty trying to formulate in their own minds a model which could include the many and varied elements represented in the various approaches. We are going to discuss classroom approaches to motivation in the coming section. At this point, it is important for you to try to get in mind an overall framework or theoretical model which can include the numerous, and frequently unpredictable, components of motivation.

We have found that sometimes a simple, almost ridiculous-sounding

---

21. I.H. Frieze, "Casual Attributions and Information Seeking to Explain Success and Failure," *Journal of Research in Personality* 10 (1976):293-305, B. Weiner, *Theories of Motivation: From Mechanism to Cognition* (Chicago: Markham, 1972); B. Weiner, I. Frieze, A. Kukla, L. Reed, S. Rest, and R.M. Rosenbaum, "Perceiving the Causes of Success and Failure," in E.E. Jones, et al., eds., *Attribution: Perceiving the Causes of Behavior;* B. Weiner and A. Kukla, "An Attributional Analysis of Achievement Motivation," *Journal of Personality and Social Psychology* 15 (1970):1-20; B. Weiner, D. Russell, and D. Lerman, "Affective Consequences of Casual Ascriptions," in J.H. Harvey, et al., eds., *New Directions in Attribution Research*, vol. 2, (Hillsdale, N.J.: Erlbaum, 1978).
22. E. Klinger, "Consequences of Commitment to and Disengagement from Incentives," *Psychological Review*, 82 (1975):1-25.
23. E. Klinger, *Meaning and Void: Inner Experience and the Incentives in People's Lives* (Minneapolis: U. of Minnesota, 1977).

> **Insight: External and Internal Controls**
>
> Rotter argued that individuals can be placed along a continuum of internality-externality in regard to how they perceive behavior as being reinforced. *Internal individuals* perceive rewards and punishment as resulting from their own behavior; that is, they believe themselves to be in control of their own behavior. *External individuals* perceive the rewards or punishments they receive as being outside of their control. For external individuals, both good and bad events are attributed to luck, fate, powerful others, or conditions over which they have no power.
>
> Rotter developed a twenty-nine-item, forced-choice test that assessed a person's internality-externality. The questionnaire has been widely used, and the locus-of-control research (over 600 published reports) emphasizes the importance of one's perception of who controls the reinforcement that one receives. Internals perceive that they control their own reinforcements, while externals see others as in control of the reinforcements they receive. The importance of the origin of reinforcement has also been noted by researchers and theorists who have examined the concept of intrinsic vs. extrinsic motivation.
>
> J. B. Rotter, "Generalized Expectancies for Internal vs. External Control of Reinforcement," *Psychological Monographs* 80 (1966):1-28. Also J. B. Rotter, "Some Problems and Misconceptions Related to the Construct of Internal vs. External Control of Reinforcement," *Journal of Consulting and Clinical Psychology* 73 (1975):36-67. Cited in Herbert L. Petri, *Motivation: Theory and Research*, p. 316. © 1981 by Wadsworth, Inc. Used by permission.

Fig. 14.2

scheme, can be used as a means of establishing such a framework. We suggest such a framework now, using a line from an old English rhyme: "FE + FI + FO = FUM. The Field of Engagement plus Forces Inside plus Forces Outside equal Factors Underlying Motivation.

The *Field of Engagement* refers to the context in which the behavior is taking place. For the teacher, ordinarily, this will be the teaching-learning process. Probably most of the time this will be the physical location of the classroom or classrooms in which the teacher engages in the teaching-learning process. Motivation leading to behavior does not occur in a vacuum.

The *Forces Inside* refer to factors within the individual which feed into the process of motivation. These factors include one's beliefs, one's perceptions, one's values, plus the physical drives and previously learned ways of behaving.

Student Motivation

The *Forces Outside* include what other theorists have termed "the environmental press." We are referring here to all of the forces of the environment which impinge upon the individual from outside himself. These may be encouraging forces or they may be discouraging forces, depending upon how the individual perceives them in the context of the behavior.

Now in order to establish our theoretical framework so that we may think together about applying it within the teaching-learning process, let's go back for a moment and summarize: We defined motivation as those forces acting on or within a person to explain the initiation, the direction, the intensity, and the persistence of behavior. We have stressed that the results of motivation will cause the student to move in one direction or the other, from one event, idea, or conviction, or location to another. And the student is not going to move in any direction unless he or she feels that it is worthwhile to do so. The intensity and the persistence of the behavior will depend on how deeply worthwhile the student believes the course of action is. Now tie this into our FE-FI-FO-FUM model, to give yourself a mnemonic device you can keep in your thinking as you move into the center of the teaching-learning process, with the goal of motivating your students to move toward the goals you have set.

CLASSROOM APPROACHES TO MOTIVATION

As you move into the classroom, then, remember that the teaching-learning process going on within the classroom (or elsewhere on the school property) represents the *Field of Engagement,* and it is in that context that you need to be able to motivate your students.

To the extent possible (and this is difficult in many situations where there are great numbers of students to whom you must relate, particularly at the middle school and secondary school levels where a teacher may have five groups of thirty or forty students every day), seek to understand as best you can the beliefs, the perceptions, the values, the drives, and the previously learned behaviors of your students. Years of experience have taught us that the teacher simply does not have the time to do this particular job very well in the teaching-learning process in most of our current school situations. Therefore, it may be possible for the teacher only to engage in seeking to understand the *Forces Inside* part of this model when there are some difficulties with a particular student. This is unfortunate, but realistically sometimes the way things work out. Again, we emphasize that to the extent possible—and it's much more possible for the teacher who has a self-contained classroom with the same students day after day—get to understand the *Forces Inside* operating within your students. This does not mean that you become a therapist—we have also cautioned against that earlier in this text—but simply on a day-to-day basis try to discover what those forces are that play such a vital role in the motivational processes of your students.

The *Forces Outside* are going to vary greatly. In terms of the teaching-learning process in your classroom, however, there are many things you can do to improve the quality of the environmental press upon your students. Make your classroom as pleasant as possible in appearance. Have the students in your class become involved in improving the physical setting for their daily hours within that setting. All the way from attractive posters and pictures and learning centers, to an object of interest if you are only in that classroom for one hour per day, can help to improve the environmental press. Again, the arrangement of the classroom as a part of good classroom management will affect greatly the quality of the environment.

We recommend that you give this model careful consideration, and if it is one that is helpful to you, you might want to recite this as you head for your classroom each day: "FE-FI-FO-FUM." It will serve as a reminder of a framework of motivation you can use in many practical ways in your classroom. We believe the FE-FI-FO-FUM approach is at least much better than the HO-HUM approach, since the latter will leave both you and your students bored beyond endurance.

CLASSROOM DEFINITION: STUDENT ENGAGEMENT IN APPROPRIATE WORK

How do you measure in the teaching-learning process whether your students are motivated in the direction of the goals you want them to move? How do you know if you are coming anywhere near getting the job done which you want to do as a dedicated teacher? The operational definition of motivation in the classroom we suggest is your students engaged in the appropriate work. This means that they are engaged in doing what you have planned for them to do, at the time you have planned for them to do it, and all as a part of reaching the instructional goals or objectives that have been established.

The following is shared by the author as an illustration of students engaged in appropriate work.

Not long ago I walked through a school that impressed me as one of the finest I had seen in many years. As I approached the front of the building, there were students, a small group of them, some sitting, some standing on the steps, but they appeared to belong there and were waiting for a van to pick them up to go on an authorized trip. They greeted me pleasantly, which immediately gave me a mindset about the school, of course. As I walked inside, the halls were mostly clear; a few students were walking in various directions, but again, to the best of my knowledge and observation, with definite purposes in mind. The atmosphere appeared orderly but relaxed.

As I made my way to the principal's office to let him know I was in the school (we had a previous appointment), I passed a number of classrooms in the K through 6 part of the school building. Without disturbing the classes, I looked in a classroom window just long enough to note the almost perfect textbook picture of a classroom, at least from my point of view. This happened to be a fourth-grade classroom into which I was looking, and I noticed that the floor was tiled on one-half of the classroom and the other was carpeted. I found out later that each of these classrooms had its own restroom, so the students did not have to go down the hallway to the restroom. The restrooms were located on the tiled end of the floor, with a washbasin outside the restroom, so that students could wash their hands at almost any time that they needed to, with the teacher's permission, and could do it on the tiled part of the floor rather than the carpeted portion. At the carpeted end of the room, a couple of small groups of students were seated on the floor busily engaged in projects which apparently were the appropriate ones for them to be engaged in at that moment. On the tile end of the floor two or three groups of students around appropriate-sized tables were working on a large map, in one situation, and in another, engaged in artwork of some type, and the whole picture of the classroom made me think of the model about which we have just been talking. Here was an operational picture of motivation in the classroom, as a result of excellent classroom management and at least what has to be inferred as a teacher who understood how to get her students involved enthusiastically in the teaching-learning process. Student engagement in appropriate work is one of the best ways for you or anyone else to evaluate whether you are succeeding in motivating your students.

TEACHER STRATEGIES: BASIC RESPONSIBILITIES

Getting the student started on the appropriate seat work. We want to make clear that when we say "seat work," we don't want you to be limited to students sitting stiffly at their desks or in their chairs, and unable to move around the room. It might be better to leave out the word "seat," but it is such a familiar phrase in the teaching-learning process that we have decided to include it. But we do refer to "seat work" as any kind of appropriate activity in the teaching-learning process which is in accord with the teacher's plans and goals and objectives for that particular time.

It is reasonable to predict that students who are performing reasonably well in school will also be doing their assigned seat work reasonably well. They will listen carefully to conversations in the classroom involving the teacher and other students. They will raise their hands to ask questions rather than speaking out, if that is the procedure the teacher requires. When they are involved in group projects, they will be the ones to concentrate on the tasks that have been assigned. A great number of studies have demonstrated a relationship between such behaviors and academic achievement.[24]

Getting the students started on the appropriate seat work is highly important, of course, to the individual student, as well as to the teacher and the general morale of the classroom. We have several suggestions. First, be sure that your objectives are clearly communicated to your students. Be sure that you and your students are

---

24. Good and Brophy, p. 237.

focusing your attention on the same desired outcomes. Many students will work very hard to prepare for a test or an exam and still do poorly, not primarily because of test anxiety, but because the teacher had not made clear the goals for that test or exam, and the student studied the wrong material. As a result, in the student's mind, a relationship between his or her efforts and good outcome simply does not exist, and so the motivation of that student is undermined.

The second suggestion is to be sure you capture the student's attention at the very outset. Without the student's attention, no learning is going to take place, no matter how much teaching you do. Whatever topic you choose, find a way to capture the student's interest at the outset. One teacher made the effort to create student interest in a particular task in the following manner, and this may be a helpful suggestion for you.[25]

> To get students' interest in India, a teacher first held a class discussion, asking each student to tell whatever came first to his mind when he thought of India. Then each student wrote a "pretend" letter to a high school student in India, asking questions about what he most wanted to know. The letters helped the teacher discover the preconceptions (and some misconceptions) the students had and to evaluate their existing interest.

The third suggestion is to allow the students to have some choices wherever this may be possible. This helps to create interest in the task at hand. For example, in the illustration just used, students could have been given choices as to whether they would like to study the geography of India, the agriculture of India, the characteristics of the people of India, and so forth. Then each student or group of students could focus in on the particular aspect they chose, and later feed back the results of their investigations to the whole class. Again, we are aware that unfortunately, because of time restrictions, limited resources, or other reasons, it is often impossible or undesirable to provide opportunities for choice. But used *selectively,* giving the students the opportunity for choice is a good way to help them get started on the appropriate seat work.

Keeping the student engaged in the appropriate seat work. The first suggestion here is that once the seat work assignments have been made, do not go back to your desk and begin to get engaged in paper work yourself, or do not get absorbed with one student for a lengthy period of time. This is the time, once the seat work has been assigned, to monitor carefully each of the students by walking around among them to be sure they are actually doing the work, and doing it in an appropriate manner.

A second suggestion is to say to the students (and the time element would vary here according to the grade level) "You are to have this task done in fifteen minutes. This will be plenty of time if you get right to the work and work steadily

---

25. H. Klausmeier and R. Ripple, *Learning and Human Abilities,* 3d ed. (New York: Harper & Row, 1971).

on it. At the end of fifteen minutes, I am going to check each of your papers to see if you have completed this particular task." This certainly helps to keep the students engaged in the appropriate seat work. One of the worst things a teacher can do, in our judgment, is to assign a task either as seat work or as homework, for that matter, and then not bother to check it. This causes a student to think, *Since the teacher never checks the seat work, or my homework, why should I bother to do it at all?* Again, motivation has been undermined. Always check the work of your students, let them know ahead of time you are going to check it, give them feedback, and follow through on your promises to them.

A third suggestion toward keeping the student engaged in the appropriate seat work is what we have come to call *knowledge of results*. This has been found to be a key aspect of maintaining student interest and performance.[26] If students do not know they are on the right track, they are not very willing to put in more effort going in the wrong direction, or going in an uncertain direction. Also, if the student has developed assumptions or habits that are in error, the longer they are practiced the more difficult they are to change. The earlier the feedback can be provided to the student, the better.

Another suggestion is to make certain that students can work without interruption once the seat work has been assigned. Have you ever had a teacher who assigns you a task and then, when you are a minute or two into it, interrupts and says, "Oh, there's something else I forgot to tell you"? This kind of classroom operation has been labeled a *stop-and-go* situation, and it virtually guarantees that students are going to wait for a while before they bother to become engaged in seat work, and that once engaged, they are going to be on edge because of the expectation of another interruption by the teacher. If a student needs help in the middle of seat work, the wise teacher will have regular routines established, which the students will become used to, such as the student's simply raising a hand or coming to the teacher's desk for help.

Keeping the student interest high throughout the year. Previously in the text, we have talked about "excitement maintenance" in classroom management. Many of us get weary doing the same thing day after day all day long. It is amazing how much a little change of pace will help in the routine of the day. Let the students have fun helping to create a new learning center, or celebrate a special day in a special way in your class, with lots of student involvement according to their interests and their abilities. Occasionally, instead of the usual kind of seat work, the same objectives can be reached by employing the use of the game. We are not talking here about games day in and day out, but the use of an appropriate game to cover appropriate objectives as a "break" in the usual routine for the purposes of exciting and motivating your students. It will certainly help to keep them moving in the direction of your objectives.

26. P. Waller, and J. Gaa, "Motivation in the Classroom," in R. Coop and K. White, eds., *Psychological Concepts in the Classroom* (New York: Harper and Row, 1974).

Helping the student build self-evaluation and regulation. Teachers frequently do not give students enough credit for being able to regulate themselves in terms of the work they are doing in the teaching-learning process. Now obviously, some students have very limited capacity for self-direction or self-regulation (this would certainly be true of very young children), and there are students at all levels and ages who really don't have much interest in planning and evaluating their own academic performance. We must be realistic about this matter, as about all others. But if we can help the student through feedback about his or her academic performance by providing information that will help the student set realistic goals, we will be helping that student immeasurably.

If we give the students some training and give them a specific item or area to observe, many students will be able to become better critics of their own work. If a student is writing a paragraph, for example, the student himself can check to see if that paragraph has a topic sentence, and this can gradually be built into a series of paragraphs where the student checks to see that each of those paragraphs has a topic sentence. And we are helping the students to be self-regulative when we help them in this way. Again, we must be realistic and say that there are many students who either cannot do or are not interested in this kind of self-evaluation and regulation.

One expert has argued that an ultimate teaching goal is to help students realize that education is their chief responsibility, and that the student who understands this goal will be satisfied only with careful work, and thus will become very proficient in evaluating self-performance.[27] We believe that for this to occur, the teacher has to work consistently and persistently with students to help them toward self-evaluation and regulation.

MOTIVATION AND THE TEACHING-LEARNING PROCESS

The teaching-learning process by its very nature involves motivation—the initiation, direction, intensity, and persistence of behavior. The teacher who takes this for granted is apt to run into serious difficulties in the classroom. There is no excuse for a classroom filled with boredom. A good reminder at this point for all of us as teachers is the old saying, "You can lead a horse to water, but you cannot make him drink." When the students come into your classroom for you to engage them in the teaching-learning process, the "horses are at the water." Can you make them drink? The answer is almost certainly, "No," if you are not willing to spend time learning and putting into practice good motivational techniques. You will see student movement toward the water, and the drinking of the water, only when through your practice of good motivational techniques you make them thirsty.

---

27. C. Jencks, "Program Evaluation by Critical Application of a School District's Educational Mode," in R. Weisgerber, ed., *Perspectives in Individualized Learning* (Itasca, Ill.: Peacock, 1971).

Student Motivation

Hindsight

Motivation is a concept used to describe the forces acting on or within a person to explain the initiation, direction, intensity, and persistence of behavior. We have suggested the FE-FI-FO-FUM model for the teacher as a framework for thinking about motivation. There are many components to motivation, some of them from within, some of them from outside the individual, and always these forces are coming together in a field of engagement, a context in which the motivation occurs. The goal is always that of student movement toward the objectives established for the teaching-learning process in a particular setting. This student movement will only occur if the individual believes it is a worthwhile movement to make.

We have discussed various approaches to motivation including the S-R approach, the needs approach, the incongruity, dissonance, and achievement motivation approaches. Additionally, we talked about the place of attribution and meaningfulness in the process of motivation.

The operational definition of motivation within the teaching-learning process is the students' being engaged in appropriate work. We suggested some strategies for getting the students started on appropriate seat work, keeping the students engaged in the appropriate seat work, and keeping the students' interest high throughout the year. Additionally, we made some suggestions for ways the teacher can help students to self-evaluation and regulation in relation to their progress in the teaching-learning process.

Chalkboard Challenges

1. Think of yourself as already being a teacher in a classroom, or, if you are already a teacher, think of your current situation. When you evaluate yourself as a teacher as to whether you are successful or not, do you include student motivation in your evaluation? Some teachers are satisfied if the students just learn the material. Would this be an adequate definition for you in terms of teacher success? Or would you add such things as the enthusiasm of the students about the teaching-learning process as it is conducted in your class, and also the motivation for them to "keep on learning how to learn"? What difference do you think it will make in your students' lives?

2. In relation to motivation, one of the most profitable exercises imaginable, in our opinion, is to think back over your teachers from the beginning of your formal schooling experience until now, and select the ones you feel were the best teachers. Then, analyze what techniques of motivation they used—both generally for the classroom, and whether they used any particular techniques that helped to motivate you. From this review of your teachers and their motivating techniques, we suggest you make a list of techniques you believe you can use in the teaching-

learning process, and keep these in your teacher's notebook.

3. Since many of you reading this textbook presumably are Christian in your approach to the teaching-learning process, what difference does the Christian perspective make in thinking about the motivational process? Can you find scriptural examples of motivation? How would they apply to the modern teaching-learning process? Think about this both in terms of a philosophy of approach (the God of the Bible vs. matter + energy directed by chance) and in terms of particular techniques. Again, we suggest that you make comments in regard to these questions in your teacher's notebook, for they will become a valuable reference for you, and you may wish to add to them or detract from them as you grow in your teaching career.

4. We have stressed in this chapter the essential importance of the teacher's having a theoretical model of motivation with which to think about this whole process as he or she goes into the clinical setting. We have suggested the FE-FI-FO-FUM model, both because we believe it is broad enough to contain the various components of motivation, and because it is easy to remember. Analyze this model, critique it, and try to come up with a better one. We really hope you can, for all of us are seeking the very best model possible to help motivate our students toward the objectives that are established in the teaching-learning process. Here again, you may wish to place your comments upon this model, or your own model, in your teacher's notebook for frequent reference.

WANT TO KNOW MORE?

DISSONANCE

For a good overview of this important topic, see R. A. Wicklund and J. W. Brehn, *Perspectives on Cognitive Dissonance* (Hillsdale, N.J.: Erlbaum, 1976). Also, see E. L. Deci, *Intrinsic Motivation* (New York: Plenum; 1975).

PERSONAL CAUSATION

For a discussion of personal causation as a component of motivation, see R. deCharms, *Personal Causation: The Internal Affective Determinants of Behavior* (New York: Academic, 1968).

ACHIEVEMENT MOTIVATION

For more on achievement motivation as applied to our society, you may wish to read D. C. McClelland, *The Achieving Society* (New York: Van Nostrand, 1961).

MOTIVATION (FIELD)

For a good review of the field of motivation, read Herbert L. Petri, *Motivation: Theory and Research* (Belmont, Calif.: Wadsworth, 1981).

From any of these books suggested here, or from those listed under the reference notes for this chapter, you may wish to investigate any one or more of the many approaches to motivation as they have been described in the chapter. We encourage you to do so as an important segment of your professional growth as a teacher.

15

Student Multipotentiality

CONTENTS

	PAGE
Key Terms	372
That's Debatable!	373
Foresight	374
Multipotentiality: Aptitudes and Abilities	374
Differences in Intelligence	377
IQ Tests	379
The Heredity-Environment Controversy: Jensen	382
Differences in Socioeconomic Status (SES)	386
Sex Differences Among Students	390
Creativity in the Classroom	393
Translating Multipotentiality into Performance	393
Hindsight	395
Chalkboard Challenges	395
Want to Know More?	396

KEY TERMS

Ability
    A trained aptitude
Aptitude
    Ability before it is trained

Creativity
   Unusual and useful solutions to problems, or the production of something novel and enjoyable (art, music, etc.)
Intelligence
   The ability of an individual to be aware of and select from his or her environment those certain necessary elements, which when put together in orderly fashion, enable the individual to achieve a desirable goal
Multipotentiality
   The highly variable capabilities—physical, mental, and spiritual—which are the result of either genetic inheritance or learning in the individual
Socioeconomic Status (SES)
   A complex of attributes (occupation, education, income, housing, neighborhood, etc.) used to try to define what people are like

THAT'S DEBATABLE!

Psychologists who emphasize the role of heredity in producing individual differences in intelligence have valued the classic "research" reports of the late Cyril Burt. Burt, who died at the age of eighty-nine in 1971, enjoyed a reputation as an eminent psychologist. He was the first psychologist to be knighted in Great Britain. Shortly before his death, the American Psychological Association awarded Burt its prestigious Thorndike Prize.

Much of Burt's reputation rested upon his claim that he had conducted surveys of separated identical twins that showed differences in intelligence are chiefly genetic in origin. It was Burt's "work" that led many authorities to the conclusion that 80 percent of the differences in IQ scores found within a population have an hereditary foundation. His ideas strongly influenced British educational practice during the 1930s and 1940s. That nation's 1944 Education Act establishing the three-tier school system (grammar, technical, and secondary modern) was largely a response to Burt's view that intelligence is primarily the product of heredity. Based upon their performance on the IQ tests administered at the age of eleven, children were assigned to one of the three educational levels, with profound consequences for their subsequent vocational opportunities (Wade, 1976).

Leon J. Kamin (1974, 1977) was the first to charge that Burt's identical twin studies contained serious methodological errors, a mass of contradictions, unreported sample sizes, and the straightforward and fraudulent inventing of data to fit his conclusions. Other researchers have since reached similar conclusions (Gillie, 1977; McAskie, 1978; Dorfman, 1978). Subsequent investigations by the London Sunday *Times* suggest that two of Burt's collaborators who are named as authors of research papers (Miss Margaret Howard and Miss J. Conway) may never have existed and that Burt himself wrote the papers in their names (Gillie, 1977).

Even strong proponents of heredity like Jensen have concluded that Burt's data and statistical procedures are "useless for hypothesis testing" (1974:24). In brief, Burt's twin findings are simply too good to be true; they follow precisely theoretical anticipations that would be statistically improbable in real life. It should be stressed, however, that Jensen still maintains that Burt's conclusions are correct. "The one important conclusion that we may draw with complete confidence is that, even if all of Burt's findings were thrown out entirely, the picture regarding the heritability of IQ would not be materially changed" (1977:492).[1]

FORESIGHT

A story prominent some three decades ago is still most appropriate for introducing this chapter on the multipotentiality of individuals. A man was visiting New York City for the first time, and for the first time saw a New York City telephone directory. The visitor, being a novelist, thumbed reflectively through the thousands upon thousands of names in the huge directory, and then made this comment: "There are surely lots of different characters here, but not very much of a plot."

The New York City directory is representative of the population of human beings here upon the earth. We are alike in an amazing number of ways, but there are vast differences among individuals. What accounts for those differences? Genetic inheritance? Environmental forces? Are some people just naturally more intelligent than others? Is there a difference in intellectual functioning between boys and girls? What is creativity, and where does it come from? How is it related to intelligence? Why do certain students reflect a slight gain as measured by their IQ scores through their school years, and others begin to drop off once they get past the first three or four grades? How can we translate this multipotentiality into performance as a result of the teaching-learning process?

These are the questions—the fascinating and difficult questions—with which we deal in this chapter.

MULTIPOTENTIALITY: APTITUDES AND ABILITIES

We need to make clear at the outset that in this chapter we are referring primarily to those individuals who are not handicapped. We look upon the handicapped as "very special people" who also have many potentialities, but who sometimes run into difficulty in finding ways to express those potentialities. And we will discuss those "very special people," who so often amaze us with their sensitivities and their abilities, in chapter 16.

Multipotentiality is a construct referring to the highly variable capabilities—

---

1. James W. Vander Zanden, *Educational Psychology in Theory and Practice* (New York: Random House, 1980), p. 35. Used by permission.

physical, mental, and spiritual—which are the result of either genetic inheritance or learning in any particular individual. There seems to be very little question that individuals differ in intelligence, in aptitudes, in creativity; and the question is constantly raised and argued from many points of view as to the extent to which socioeconomic status (SES) is the result of this multipotentiality.

One of the ways in which people differ is in aptitude. We define an aptitude as an ability before it is trained. Conversely, we define ability as a trained aptitude. Although it is difficult, if not impossible, to determine the limits of multipotentiality for any individual, nevertheless it is obvious from commonsense observation and experience that no matter how much training or practice certain individuals receive, they will not improve beyond a certain level of skill or performance. For example, we have known students who have put in every ounce of energy and time they had to become good enough in their skills and performance to make the first team in a particular sport, but did not succeed. In fact, we have known a number of such young people who have worked much harder and practiced much longer than those who did make the team. Leaving out subjective factors on the part of those who choose the team members, it is obvious that aptitude is what makes the difference. When an aptitude is trained, it becomes an ability.

We can use the word *ability* in relation to an aptitude to mean that point at which the aptitude has been trained enough that the individual reaches a level of skill, corresponding to that aptitude, which is minimally competent. Usually we are talking about a group of aptitudes rather than a single one. Thus, if you have the aptitude needed to learn how to punt a football so that it goes a reasonable distance, but you never get out and train and practice kicking the football, the aptitude will never translate into an ability. However, when you get out and practice so you can kick the football a reasonable distance, then that aptitude becomes an ability.

Further practice will help you to refine the kicking of the football, so that your ability in this particular activity increases in the level of competence. You practice long enough so you can kick the football further and higher, and eventually place it somewhere near where you want it to come down out of bounds near the goal line.

On the other hand, if you do not have the group of aptitudes necessary to kick a football—and as one who played football and has sought to train others through the years, we can assure you there are those that do *not* have this group of aptitudes—then no amount of practice is going to develop you to a level of even minimal competency in this particular skill.

We have taken quite a bit of time and space to discuss the aptitude-into-ability concept, because we believe it makes a point that is not only valid, but also provides understanding as we deal with the potentials that individuals bring to any given situation. The point is that the teacher needs to be alert to the aptitudes that a student may or may not possess. Granted, this is not an easy task, and no teacher can do it to perfection. But the little boy who simply has no aptitude to kick a football may nevertheless possess an artistic set of aptitudes that will enable him,

Gallery of Greats

William B. James
Psychology is a science—teaching is an art; and sciences never generate arts directly out of themselves. An intermediary inventive mind must make the application, by use of its originality. (Courtesy Brown Brothers)

For one who showed little evidence of academic brilliance as a child to become known in his later years as a prophet of American pragmatism, with several outstanding volumes to his credit, was no small accomplishment. For one who was indecisive about his career choices—in a letter written to a friend he had mentioned natural history, medicine, printing, and beggary!—to have graduated in chemistry and physiology, received an M.D. from Harvard Medical School (1869), opened the first psychology lab in America (1879), taught physiology and anatomy at Harvard (1871-97), and made tremendous contributions to the quality of classroom education—was indeed quite a pilgrimage.

James was born in New York City in 1842 and died in New Hampshire in 1910. Turning to philosophy and religion after having written an outstanding two-volume text, Principles of Psychology, between 1879 and 1890, James became a pragmatist with unquenchable thirst for improving the quality of education. His Talks with Teachers *reflects his desire to relate psychology to education, emphasizing that the quality of education rests with the performance of the classroom teacher.*

with good training and practice, to be able to paint beautifully and make his productive contribution to society in that particular fashion. In the teaching-learning process, we need to be very much aware of which aptitudes students possess or do not possess, and then find ways to help translate those aptitudes into abilities.

Differences in Intelligence

Much of the school-related activity in which we engage has to do with the three R's and the various areas such as the sciences, literature, and history. Since some students perform better than others at many of these tasks, the assumption has frequently been made that students differ in their capabilities. We are talking here primarily about mental capacities, or what we more commonly call "intelligence."

CONCEPTS OF INTELLIGENCE

You, like most people, probably have a general idea of what you mean when you say someone is an intelligent person, but if you try to set it down in precise words in a definition, you might have some difficulty. Intelligence is defined in many different ways. We define it in this text as the ability of an individual to be aware of and to select from his or her environment certain necessary elements, and to put them together in orderly fashion to achieve a desirable goal. Some psychologists and educators define intelligence as the ability to think abstractly; or the capacity to profit from experience; or the capacity to adapt to new situations. There are some who would say intelligence is that which we measure by an intelligence test.

There is a common problem we all share in trying to define intelligence: It is an *inferred* capacity based on observation of behavior.

Charles Spearman, in 1927, formulated an early theory of intelligence which stressed the general aspects of intelligence.[2] Spearman was an English psychologist, and he proposed that intelligence is basically a *general* intellectual capacity

---

2. C. Spearman, *The Abilities of Man* (New York: Macmillan, 1927).

and that tests can be constructed to provide for a single pooled score across many items.[3] Spearman believed that all tests of intelligence have two components—the "g factor" and the "s factor." The "g factor" is that portion of variance that all tests of intelligence have in common. The portion that is unique or specific to each test is the "s factor."[4]

It was Spearman's contention that all the tests are at least to some extent measuring "g." And with that logic, he looked upon the "g factor" as a basic intellectual power that runs all through an individual's mental activity. At the same time, Spearman recognized that an individual's performance across various tasks certainly is not perfectly consistent. Therefore, Spearman identified many specific factors (s_1, s_2, s_3, etc.) to identify those particular types of activities. This approach is known as the *two-factor* theory of intelligence.

Other theorists have proposed that intelligence is made up of a number of distinct abilities or traits. One example of this approach can be found in the work of L. L. Thurstone.[5] Thurstone identified seven primary mental abilities: verbal comprehension, word fluency, numeric ability, space visualization, associative memory, perceptual speed, and reasoning. If you were to ask him about an individual's ability, he would respond by showing you a profile representing that individual's scores in these primary mental ability areas.

J. P. Guilford in his milestone text, *The Structure of the Intellect,* proposed that intelligence is made up of 120 separate factors.[6] He claims that research has empirically demonstrated that at least 82 of the 120 factors actually exist.

There is still a further distinction made by some psychologists, primarily Raymond B. Cattell.[7] Cattell distinguishes two kinds of intelligence: fluid intelligence and crystallized intelligence. *Fluid intelligence* refers to a quality of general brightness or abstract mental efficiency, which Cattell emphasizes is independent of either schooling or cultural influences. *Crystallized intelligence* is related to the knowledge and skills that are acquired through the cultural experience and the teaching-learning process. Cattell points out that fluid intelligence can be measured by nonverbal tests involving such things as figure classifications, figural analogies, and number and letter series tests. On the other hand, if one wants to measure crystallized intelligence, one would use tests of general information, such as vocabulary or word analogies.

---

3. E.B. Brody and N. Brody, *Intelligence: Nature, Determinants, and Consequences* (New York: Academic, 1976). Cited in James W. Vander Zanden, *Educational Psychology in Theory and Practice* (New York: Random House, 1980), p. 26.
4. Ibid.
5. L.L. Thurstone, *Primary Mental Abilities* (Chicago: U. of Chicago, 1938). Also L.L. Thurstone, *Multiple Factor Analysis: A Development and Expansion of "The Vectors of the Mind"* (Chicago: U. of Chicago, 1947).
6. J.P. Guilford, *The Nature of Human Intelligence* (New York: McGraw-Hill, 1967).
7. Raymond B. Cattell, "The Measurement of Adult Intelligence" *Psychological Bulletin* 40 (1943):153-93. Also R.B. Cattell, *Abilities: Their Structure, Growth, and Action* (Boston: Houghton Mifflin, 1971).

You need also to recognize here that, while Piaget did not view intelligence in any kind of fixed terms, and therefore apparently had very little interest in a static kind of assessment of individual differences, nevertheless he had a view of intelligence that would be defined as dynamic interplay between the individual child and his or her environment.

IQ Tests

If we think of intelligence as a kind of mental capacity, it is obvious we need to develop some way to measure that capacity. This is usually done by administering an intelligence test to an individual in a test setting which involves the individual's engaging in various verbal and performance tasks. We need to emphasize that intelligence tests do not directly measure an individual's mental capacity. Rather the items on the test represent a diverse sampling of behaviors. The logic is that through these samplings, a result can be obtained which will enable us to infer from the behaviors of the individual on the test an *estimate* of that individual's mental capacity or ability. Those results of the individual's performance on an intelligence test are usually reported as a number, and referred to as the IQ (intelligence quotient). An IQ number simply represents the individual's performance on the items of the test in relation to the *average performance* of individuals of his or her same age.

There are a number of *group-administered* intelligence tests, which means that the test is administered to many individuals at one time. Additionally, the group test is usually administered by a classroom teacher, who follows the exact instructions in the manual that comes with the test. The cognitive abilities test, multilevel addition, is a good example of a group-administered intelligence test.[8] Many psychologists question the validity of group-administered tests, but nevertheless they are used quite widely in many school systems.

Different from the group intelligence tests are those which are administered individually, and by one who is a trained psychologist or counselor qualified to engage in this task. Two such tests are best known: the Stanford-Binet Intelligence Scale[9] and the Wechsler Intelligence Scales.[10]

THE STANFORD-BINET INTELLIGENCE SCALE

For educational purposes, this test is used primarily at the younger ranges (2 to 6), and testing generally takes about an hour. An important characteristic of the Stanford-Binet is that it is an *age-level scale,* which means that test items are

---

8. Thorndike and Hagen, *Cognitive Abilities Test,* Multilevel ed. (Boston: Houghton Mifflin, 1971).
9. L.M. Terman and M.A. Merrill, *Standford-Binet Intelligence Scale: Manual for the Third Revision Form,* form L-M (Boston: Houghton Mifflin, 1973).
10. D. Wechsler, *The Wechsler-Bellvue Intelligence Scale,* 1944. Also D. Wechsler, *Manual for the Wechsler Intelligence Scale for Children—Revised.* (New York: The Psychological Corporation, 1974).

> **Insight: Test Item Samples from the Stanford-Binet Intelligence Scale**
>
> *Age Level*   *Sample Items*
> Two years   Given some blocks and a model, build a 4-block tower.
> Three years   Given paper and pencil, copy a circle.
> Five years   Given pairs of pictures, tell whether the pictures are alike.
> Seven years   Given a sequence of five digits presented orally, listen and repeat them.
> Ten years   Given abstract words, define them.

Fig. 15.1

grouped according to age levels, with the items becoming more and more difficult at each succeeding level. The Insight box (fig. 15.1) reflects samples of test items at various age levels on the Stanford-Binet. The Stanford-Binet test enjoys great popularity among many educators and psychologists, and is made use of frequently as a basis for predicting the future academic success of students. One of the test's limiting features is that it gives only one IQ score. It is very difficult to determine a child's relative strengths and weaknesses from one verbal ability score.

It is important for the teacher to know that the mean (average) score is 100, with a range of "normal" intelligence being from 84 to 116.

THE WECHSLER SCALES

In the late 1930s, David Wechsler, a psychologist at Bellevue Hospital in New York City, decided that there were a number of shortcomings in the Stanford-Binet and set about to develop his own intelligence scale. The first scale he developed was the Wechsler-Bellevue Intelligence Scale in 1944 that was designed primarily for adults. The present version of that test is called the Wechsler Adult Intelligence Scale (WAIS). This is used for testing adults ages sixteen years and over.

Wechsler then developed the Wechsler Intelligence Scale for Children (WISC—now called the WISC-R since it was revised in 1974), for testing children six to sixteen. Then one further test, the Wechsler Preschool and Primary Scale of Intelligence (WPPSI), was developed for children ages four to six-and-a-half. All the tests developed by Wechsler contain separate verbal and nonverbal components. There are six verbal subtests and five performance subtests as indicated in the Insight box (fig. 15.2). The items on the Wechsler test are not organized into age levels, as the Stanford-Binet items are. Instead, the items are graded in order of increasing difficulty within each of the subtests. And one of the advantages of the Wechsler Scales is that the final IQ score is made up of separate verbal and nonverbal performance scales, and you can look at each of these subareas apart from the total IQ score. This is most helpful for the trained psychologist or counselor who understands the meaning of the scores and can apply them to a particular child's situation. The mean score is 100, and the range of "normal" intelligence is 85 to 115.

THE USES AND ABUSES OF INTELLIGENCE TESTS

1. Although intelligence tests are reasonably good predictors of academic success, nevertheless an IQ test score *alone* for a single individual may result in a relatively large error in prediction. Since an intelligence test is really nothing more than a sample of behavior taken at a particular moment in time, it tells us how the child is functioning at that moment—it cannot tell us whether the child will continue to function the same way in the future.

2. An individual's IQ is not absolutely fixed or unchanging. It can fluctuate from time to time, even under the most ideal test conditions. Many things can artificially lower an IQ score: illness, fatigue, fear, boredom.

3. An IQ test score *alone* should never be used in diagnosing a child as mentally retarded, or in making any major decisions about the child's future education. In these kinds of situations, it is mandatory on the part of the professional to use the IQ test in conjunction with other tests and with other information, including the child's family background, health, school history, and observations from other teachers. Since the child belongs to the parents, and not to the school system, the ideal way to proceed is for the school system to be a partner of the parents in informing them of the data they have, in discussing with the parents possible avenues of decision, so that the parents can make an intelligent decision concerning their child.

Insight: Wechsler Verbal and Performance Subtests

Verbal Tests
1. Information
2. Comprehension
3. Arithmetic
4. Similarities
5. Vocabulary
6. Digit Span
   (alternate)

Performance Tests
7. Picture Completion
8. Picture Arrangement
9. Block Design
10. Object Assembly
11. Coding or Mazes
    (alternate)

Fig. 15.2

4. Teachers should be aware that IQ scores are less dependable for some of their students:

(1) Those who come from minority group culture or racial background
(2) Those who find school-related tasks relatively unmotivating
(3) Those who are weak in reading skills or have other difficulties with verbal materials, and
(4) Those who have problems in emotional adjustments[11]

5. Using the terms *underachiever* and *overachiever* is highly controversial. "What these terms really mean is that there is a disparity or gap between a child's IQ score and school achievement, with the IQ score serving as a benchmark for assessing school achievement."[12]

Ziegler and Trickett make this observation regarding these labels:

> If a middle class child does not do very well in school, both the school and the family appear more comfortable if we call the child an *underachiever*. If an economically disadvantaged child does poorly in school, we are tempted to call him or her *stupid*, using the school performance itself as the ultimate gauge of a child's intellectual level. This situation becomes even more ridiculous when we use the nonsensical label of *overachiever*. . . . We cannot be very tolerant of a label that essentially asserts that *some individuals achieve more than they are capable of achieving*.[13]

Some psychologists find these terms helpful, however, although they use them cautiously. These psychologists would point out that if you have a gap between a child's IQ score and his or her school achievement, particularly in the situation of underachievement, the teacher should be alerted to a potential problem. Something, either in the school or in the child's environment, is interfering with the child's reasonable expression of his or her potential.

THE HEREDITY-ENVIRONMENT CONTROVERSY: JENSEN

Psychologists disagree on what intelligence is, how to measure it or infer it, and how many factors of intelligence there are. And they disagree also concerning the relative part that heredity and environment have in producing individual differences in intelligence.

One of the problems is that psychologists disagree to begin with on which is

---

11. N.E. Gronlund, *Measurement and Evaluation in Teaching*, 3d ed. (New York: Macmillan, 1976). Cited in Vander Zanden, p. 30. Used by permission.
12. Vander Zanden, p. 31.
13. E. Zigler and P.K. Trickett, "IQ, Social Competence, and Evaluation of Early Childhood Intervention Programs," *American Psychologist* 33 (1978):789-98.

the right question to ask regarding this particular issue. The first question asked was the "which" question—"Which is more important in the determination of intelligence, heredity or environment?" This question is no longer looked upon as a profitable way to ask the question about this issue, since the either-or nature of the question raises a hopeless division between the two factors. As Vander Zanden points out: "Carried to its logical conclusion, biologically inborn behavior would be defined as behavior that appears in the absence of environment and learned behavior would be that which does not require an organism. The question would be comparable to asking whether oxygen or hydrogen is more important to water. Obviously, without either oxygen or hydrogen, there could be no water."[14]

The "how much" question came next—"How much of the total variation in intelligence within a particular population can be attributed to genetic factors and how much to environmental factors?" Enter Arthur R. Jensen, an educational psychologist at the University of California at Berkeley, who has vigorously championed this particular phrasing of the heredity-environment question.

Jensen points out that as the genetic or biological kinship relationship between two individuals increases (gets closer) the correlation between their IQ scores also increases. The Insight box (fig. 15.3) indicates correlation data between relatives. To understand the data in that Insight box, remember that the nearer the correlation coefficient is to +1.00, the closer is the overall correspondence of the IQ score of one relative to the IQ score of the other relative.

Based on these kinds of data (the studies are known as family resemblance studies), Jensen came to the conclusion that about 80 percent of the variations in IQ

Insight: Median correlation coefficients for intelligence scores showing degree of similarity between performance of individuals of varying degrees of kinship.

Category	Median Coefficient
Foster parent-child	.20
Parent-child	.50
Siblings reared together	.49
Fraternal twins	.55
Identical twins reared apart	.75
Identical twins reared together	.87

From L. Erienmeyer-Kimling and L. F. Jarvik, "Genetics and Intelligence: A Review," Science 142 (13 December 1964): 1477-79, passage. Copyright 1964 by the AAAS. Used by permission.

Fig. 15.3

14. Vander Zanden, p. 21.

scores in the general population is due to genetic differences and 20 percent is due to environmental differences. Many psychologists and educators disagree with Jensen in his claim that the differences in intelligence are mostly a function of heredity. Also many of those who disagree want to ask the question in yet another way. "How do heredity and environment *interact* to affect performance on intelligence tests?"

These psychologists, who would be located over on the environmental end of the continuum, insist that mental abilities are *learned*. And they would hold that one's intelligence is increased or decreased depending upon how rich or how impoverished an environment the individual has been exposed to. One of these psychologists, Leon J. Kamin, states: "There exists no data which lead a prudent man to accept the hypothesis that IQ test scores are in any degree heritable."[15] It is interesting that Kamin was the first to call into question the study by the late Cyril Burt, an English psychologist whose research was looked upon as virtually "classic." Burt's results leaned heavily in the direction of heredity as the main factor in producing individual differences in intelligence. That's Debatable! at the beginning of this chapter contains fascinating and disturbing reading.

The environmental-leaning psychologists of course present data to show that when cultural conditions improve over a period of time so does the overall intelligence test performance of the population. One of the studies they cite frequently is the one which reflects the improvement in the test scores of American soldiers between World War I and World War II.[16]

Some educators are adamant about their insistence that teaching *requires* an individual to take the environmental position.

> The psychologist and the geneticist may wish to speculate about how to improve the gene pool—the educator cannot and should not. The educator must be an environmentalist . . . It is through the environment that he must fashion the educational process. Learning takes place within the child; the educator tries to influence this learning by providing the appropriate environment. If heredity imposes limits—so be it. The educator must work with what is left, whether it be 20% of the variance or 50%.[17]

Arthur Jensen makes this reply to the claims of the environmentalists:

> I do believe that educational policy decisions should be based on evidence and the results of continuing research—and not just the evidence which is comfortable to some particular ideological position, but *all* relevant evidence. I submit that the research on the inheritance of mental abilities is relevant to understanding educational problems and formulating educational policies. For one thing, it means that we

---

15. L.J. Kamin, *The Science and Politics of IQ* (Potomac, Md.: Erlbaum, 1974), p. 1. Used by permission.
16. R.D. Tuddenham, "Soldier Intelligence in World Wars I and II," *American Psychologist*, 3:54-56.
17. B.S. Bloom, "Letter to the Editor", *Harvard Educational Review*, 39:2, pp. 419-421, Copyright © 1969 by the President and Fellows of Harvard College. All rights reserved. Used by permission.

take individual differences more seriously than regarding them as superficial, easily-changed manifestations of environmental differences.[18]

It must be obvious to all but the most casual observer that these issues are extremely controversial, and certainly remain unresolved.

RACE AND IQ SCORES

In a discussion as emotionally-laden as one concerning race and IQ, as well as the following topic of socioeconomic status and differences involved among human beings in that regard, it is wise for every citizen to be aware of the pros and cons in the background of this discussion. And it is mandatory for parents and teachers to be keenly aware of the factors involved, so as to keep the emotional pitch at the lowest level possible and the reasonable factors well in view.

This issue of IQ scores and racial differences exploded anew in 1969 when Arthur Jensen published a paper in the *Harvard Educational Review*.[19] This is a highly prestigious journal, and later issues carried rebuttals by prominent psychologists, and then Jensen's response back to them. News magazines and newspapers also gave great publicity to this issue, and the fire was burning. Jensen found that, on the most widely used intelligence tests, there is an average 15-point difference in the IQ performance between blacks and whites.[20] And Jensen attributes this difference to genetics.

> All the major facts would seem to be comprehended quite well by the hypothesis that something between ½ and ¾ of the average difference between American Negroes and whites is attributable to genetic factors, and the remainder to environmental factors and their interaction with genetic differences.[21]

Many psychologists challenged Jensen's conclusion. They pointed out that the intelligence test scores of blacks who were recruits during World War I, originally interpreted as being inferior to native-born whites, nevertheless turned out to look quite differently during the 1920s when psychologists took a second look at those scores. Then it was found that blacks from the south, where educational handicaps were more severe, scored lower than northern blacks. Blacks from Pennsylvania, New York, Illinois, and Ohio averaged higher scores than whites from Mississippi, Arkansas, Kentucky, and Georgia. One can presume from these results that the educationally and economically superior environmental

---

18. A.R. Jensen, "Reducing the Heredity-Environment Uncertainty: A Reply", *Harvard Educational Review*, 39, pp. 449-83, Copyright © 1969 by the President and Fellows of Harvard College. All rights reserved. Used by permission.
19. A.R. Jensen, "How Much Can We Boost IQ and Scholastic Achievement?" *Harvard Educational Review*, 39:1-123.
20. A.R. Jensen, "Race, Intelligence and Genetics: The Differences Are Real," *Psychology Today* 7 (December 1973):80-86. Also A.R. Jensen, *Educability and Group Differences* (New York: Harper & Row, 1973).
21. A.R. Jensen, *Genetics and Education* (New York: Harper & Row, 1973), p. 358.

opportunities in which the northern blacks were living accounted for their better test scores. A number of distinctions of this kind are presented by those who challenged Jensen's conclusions.[22] Sandra Scarr and Richard A. Weinberg found that a substantial part of the IQ gap between blacks and whites is closed among black children who are adopted as infants by white, middle-class foster parents.[23]

Jensen's critics also say that most IQ tests contain a good deal of material which is termed *culturally loaded*. This means, say the critics, that children of different groups may not really understand the question in the same way. Often black and Spanish-speaking children are afraid of the test-taking process and have a mental set that they are going to do poorly. They may simply not respond as the test is set up to have them respond if they are to score well. Some research has shown that children who may not do very well on intelligence tests still are good problem-solvers in their own environments. These are children who have learned and profited from their experiences in ways that would not be reflected in their IQ test scores.[24]

Again, we emphasize that the issue of intelligence scores and their comparison among races is a highly emotional issue. It is closely linked with the larger nature-nurture controversy. The role of the professional educator (and we would hope of all citizens) is to keep reason in control over the emotional fanning of fires that promote hostility among members of different races. The professional educator should become aware of the research pros and cons, and then proceed to work with each child regardless of racial or ethnic background to help that child grow from wherever he or she is to become more knowledgeable and understanding of themselves and the world in which they live.

Vander Zanden's quote from Cicero at the beginning of his discussion of IQ and race speaks volumes, and needs no further comment in terms of the lessons that history can teach us in this regard. (Even though the author is of British/Scottish descent, we include this quote!)

> Do not obtain your slaves from the Britons, for the Britons are so stupid and so dull that they are not fit to be slaves.[25]

DIFFERENCES IN SOCIOECONOMIC STATUS (SES)

Socioeconomic Status refers to a complex of attributes (occupation, education, income level, housing, desirability of neighborhood, etc.) which are used to

---

22. O. Klineberg, *Negro Intelligence and Selective Migration* (New York: Columbia U., 1935). Also E.S. Lee, "Negro Intelligence and Selective Migration: A Philadelphia Test of the Klineberg Hypothesis," *American Sociological Review* 16 (1951):227-33.
23. S. Scarr and R.A. Weinberg, "IQ Test Performance of Black Children Adopted by White Families," *American Psychologist* 31 (1976): 726-39. Also S. Scarr and R.A. Weinberg, "When Black Children Grow Up in White Homes," *Psychology Today* 9 (December 1975):80-82.
24. E.Y. Babad and M. Budoff, "Sensitivity and Validity of Learning-Potential Measurement in Three Levels of Ability," *Journal of Educational Psychology* 66 (1974):439-47.
25. Vander Zanden, p. 34.

try to define what people are like. "Social class" is a very closely related concept, but it includes other people's perceptions of you and your family.[26]

SES is closely associated with race, ethnicity, and various religious, political, and social customs, in the sense that they tend to correlate. The explanation of the correlation is not always an easy one, but researchers are beginning to ferret out the conclusion that the educational level of the parents is probably one of the most basic characteristics in relation to student achievement. That is, once the educational level of the parents is statistically controlled in an experiment, all or most of the other variables carry very little power for predicting such things as student achievement.[27] And of course to the teacher, the level of the education of parents is especially significant for the reason that it is linked to the interests of the parents in education and certainly determines in some substantial measure the attitude of the parents toward education.[28]

> Parents who are well-educated themselves generally value education and expect and desire their children to become well-educated. They usually show interest in their children's progress and in meeting and collaborating with teachers, and they typically volunteer, participate in PTA and fund-raising activities, and help supervise field trips.[29]

If we look at those who would be classified as low SES parents (that is, those who are not educated very highly) we find a quite different set of attitudes. Many of these parents either quit or were expelled before graduating from high school, and the vast majority of the remainder ended their learning experience at the time of high school graduation. We should not conclude from this that these parents do not know the value of education or that they do not want their children to be educated, for that would be erroneous. However, very few of these parents have a great deal of understanding about how schools operate, nor are they knowledgeable about how to deal with schools and the teaching-learning process.[30] If you ask these parents how they feel when they need to talk to a teacher or the principal, many of them would express fear or anxiety. We must remember that many of these parents had very hard times themselves as students, and so they have mixed emotions when they think about the teaching-learning process and about teachers

---

26. W. Warner, M. Meeker, and K. Eells, *Social Class In America* (Chicago: Science Research Association, 1949). Also R. Hess, "Class and Ethnic Influences Upon Socialization," in P. Mussen, ed., *Carmichael's Manuel of Child Psychology*, 3d ed., vol. 2 (New York: Wiley, 1970).
27. R. Hess, in Mussen. Also H. Stevenson, T. Parker, A. Wilkenson, B. Bonnevaux, and M. Gonzalez, "Schooling, Environment, and Cognitive Development: A Cross-Cultural Study," *Monographs of the Society for Research in Child Development* 43, no. 3 (1978), serial #175.
28. V. Shipman, J. McKee, and B. Bridgeman, with M. Boroson, P. Butler-Nalin, J. Gant, and M. Mikovsky, "Stability and Change in Family Status, Situational, and Process Variables and Their Relationships to Children's Cognitive Performance," report PR-75-28 (Princeton, N.J.: Educational Testing Service, 1976).
29. Thomas L. Good and Jere E. Brophy, *Educational Psychology: A Realistic Approach*, 2d ed. (New York: Holt, Rinehart, and Winston, 1980), p. 485. Used by permission.
30. Hess, pp. 485-86.

and principals. They respect teachers and principals because they tend to look upon them as people with expertise and authority, but they also experience at least some discomfort and, at worst, open hostility toward school personnel. Another factor enters in here which prevents these lower SES parents from having very much contact with school personnel: their schedules, which are usually less flexible if they are working.

However, when all of the above has been said, we have found the vast majority of these parents in our experience to value education highly in terms of their children. It is exceedingly important, in our judgment, for teachers and principals to let these parents know, even if they cannot visit the school very often, that as teachers and school officials, we value their children highly and we *really* want what is best for their children as well. This kind of relationship with low SES parents, as opposed to one that sets us up as high authority figures threatening to expel their child from school, is much to be preferred.

THE DISADVANTAGED: WHO ARE THEY?

Perhaps one of the greatest misperceptions in our land is that of who makes up the group known as "the disadvantaged." It is important to get the facts straight on this matter, because *disadvantaged* is a label that carries with it many negative viewpoints and attitudes, and that includes those of people involved in the teaching-learning process. For example, we know substantial numbers of people who, when they consider someone "disadvantaged," virtually write them off as lost causes, and the whole matter of teacher expectations begins to come into the picture very strongly.

In 1983, in a report released just as this chapter is being written, the Census Bureau stated that the national poverty rate was 15.2 percent. A family of four was classified as poor if it had cash income of less than $10,178.00 in 1983. The poverty rate for children under the age of six was 25 percent for 1983, according to the Census Bureau's report. This means that one child out of every four under the age of six was living in poverty circumstances in 1983.

If we look at poverty *rates,* we see a noticeable difference for black, white, and Hispanic people under the age of eighteen. In that age group, the poverty rate was approximately 17 percent for white, 46 percent for blacks, and 38 percent for Hispanics.

We need to be very sure that we understand these figures, which can easily become confusing. In terms of race and urban versus rural status, the majority of disadvantaged families are white, and a large proportion are rural. Much more attention has been focused on urban blacks, and this causes many people to think that terms like "disadvantaged" refer primarily to that group. But as Good and Brophy point out: "It is true that a greater percentage of blacks than whites are disadvantaged, but it also is true that this percentage is a minority. About 80% of the disadvantaged are white."[31]

---

31. Good and Brophy, p. 487.

CAN EDUCATION OVERCOME SES DIFFERENCES?

For a substantial period of time, many educators believed that educational enrichment was the answer in terms of overcoming SES differences. These efforts were largely influenced by Hunt and Bloom, who placed a great deal of emphasis upon very young children's having the right kind of experiences.[32] For this reason, Hunt and Bloom have been called the "critical period theorists," as noted earlier in this book. A minority of people take this position today.[33] Most psychological and educational experts have given up the hope that SES differences can be overcome quickly or easily. As much as it brings pain to many people, Project Headstart, Project Follow-Through, and other programs aimed at the disadvantaged "no longer are seriously expected to eliminate SES differences in IQ or even educational attainment."[34]

Is there a difference between people who are disadvantaged and those who are classified as "middle class people"? Do their values and attitudes contrast each with the other? Again, from our experience and from the research of others, the conclusion that appears to be most accurate is that the major difference between the disadvantaged parents and the middle class parents is that the disadvantaged parents simply do not have the resources and information to make it possible for them to succeed in getting what they want for themselves and their children.[35]

THE QUALITY OF THE CHILD'S COGNITIVE ENVIRONMENT

Usually, when we think of the disadvantaged or low SES home, we tend to think in terms of the lack of financial resources in that home. And while that is certainly one of the factors, nevertheless it does not seem to be the key to the difficulties which low SES children have in the teaching-learning process. Several researchers have pointed out that what does seem to be at the heart of the success or failure of the child in the teaching-learning process is the quality of what has come to be called the "cognitive environment" of the home.[36] What this research is really saying, if we put it into simple language is, "the cognitive development of boys and

---

32. J. McVickers Hunt, *Intelligence and Experience* (New York: Ronald, 1961). Also Benjamin Bloom, *Stability and Change in Human Characteristics* (New York: Wiley, 1964).
33. B. White, *The First Three Years of Life* (Englewood Cliffs, N.J.: Prentice-Hall, 1975).
34. Good and Brophy, p. 487.
35. Hess, 1970. Cited in Good and Brophy, p. 487.
36. Ibid. See also Shipman, et al., 1976; C. Deutsch, "Social Class and Child Development," in B. Caldwell and H. Ricciuti, eds., *Review of Child Development Research*, vol. 3 (Chicago: U. of Chicago Press, 1973); K. Marjoribanks, "Environment, Social Class, and Mental Abilities," *Journal of Educational Psychology* 63 (1972):103-9; F. Trotman, "Race, IQ, and the Middle Class," *Journal of Educational Psychology* 69 (1977):266-73; R. Wolf, "The Measurement of Environments," in A. Anastasi, ed., *Testing Problems in Perspective*, rev. ed. (Washington, D.C.: Council on Education, 1966); T. Moore, "Language and Intelligence: A Longitudinal Study of the First Eight Years, II: Environmental Correlates of Mental Growth," *Human Development* 11 (1969):1-24; N. Freeberg and D. Payne, "Parental Influence on Cognitive Development in Early Childhood: A Review," *Child Development* 38 (1967):65-87; R. Bradley, B. Caldwell, and R. Elardo, "Home Environment, Social Status, and Mental Test Performance," *Journal of Educational Psychology* 69 (1977):697-701.

girls depends much more on rich interaction with their parents than it does on richness in terms of material possessions."

A superb description of how parents provide a rich, cognitive environment for their children is given by Good and Brophy.

> They label objects and events, explain causal relationships, discuss future activities in advance, and accompany discipline with instructions containing information as well as demands. They also answer the children's questions, encourage their exploratory efforts, and, in general, provide them with a rich context of *meaning* within which to understand and assimilate each new experience. More generally, they model intellectual activity and verbal communication in everyday activities: reading newspapers and books, for both information and pleasure; watching educational as well as purely entertaining television programs, and discussing their content; stimulating mealtime conversations about daily life events; participating in social and political organizations; and visiting zoos, museums, and other educational settings.[37]

For those who are Christian parents, this same description can be used, with the addition of spiritual emphasis throughout these events. The point is, that beginning very early in the child's life, as parents we need to provide a rich cognitive environment, including (and for the Christian, emphasizing) the *spiritual meanings* throughout these relationships and events.

The truly disadvantaged child does not get very much of this kind of interaction with his parents. Frequently, the parents may not even be aware that they need to provide such an environment in the home, or the parents may not really know how to provide that environment.

Where does this leave the teacher who is responsible for this child in the teaching-learning process, while the child is under her care during school hours? It means that quite often many other resources will have to be found, in addition to the resources of the school. It does not mean that the kind of instruction these children receive should differ from those that other students receive. There are some indications that this kind of child does best with teachers whom he perceives as warm and personal, but who at the same time let the child know that they expect him to perform up to his capacities, and not in any way making a "special case" out of this child.[38]

Sex Differences Among Students

In most schools (there are exceptions) there are both male and female students. It is therefore important for the teacher to understand what differences

---

37. Good and Brophy, p. 487. Used by permission.
38. J. Brophy and C. Evertson, *Learning From Teaching: A Developmental Perspective* (Boston: Allyn and Bacon, 1976); J. Kleinfeld, "Effective Teachers of Indian and Eskimo Students," *School Review* 83 (1975):301-44; N. St. John, "Thirty-six Teachers: Their Characteristics and Outcomes for Black and White Pupils," *American Educational Research Journal* 8 (1971):635-48.

may exist in relation to the performance of the male and female student in the teaching-learning process.

SOCIETAL EXPECTATIONS AND SELF-EXPECTATIONS

It is not hard to find expressions of beliefs concerning male and female characteristics and achievement. For example, females are usually looked upon as more social than males; males are supposed to be more aggressive than females; females supposedly lack achievement motivation; females are good in verbal abilities, and males are supposed to be good in mathematics; and males are supposed to be more competitive than females. Frankly, it is not always an easy job to separate the myths from the facts, and even then, as Lahey and Johnson point out, we still have the task of trying to decide whether sex differences are due to genetic factors or learning and cultural expectations.[39] And depending upon which of these beliefs listed above (plus many additional ones which could be listed) turn out to be true, then we have the question, "Should males and females be taught differently?"

INTELLECTUAL FUNCTIONING: MACCOBY AND JACKLIN

Maccoby and Jacklin in 1966 and 1974, respectively, reviewed the literature on sex differences in intellectual functioning.[40] Their conclusion was that there are *not* consistent sex differences. This means there is really no reason to believe that male and female students cannot succeed equally well in the various school subjects or in their subsequent career pursuits.

However, the study did show that boys and girls do achieve in somewhat different ways. For example, Maccoby and Jacklin found that four sex differences are fairly well established. (1) After the age of eleven, females consistently score higher than males on tests of verbal ability. (2) From adolescence onward, males consistently score higher than females on tests of visual, spatial ability. (3) After the age of twelve, males are superior to females in mathematical ability. (4) At all ages, males are more aggressive than females, both physically and verbally. Maccoby and Jacklin cite evidence that aggression and visual spatial ability may have strong genetic components. For other characteristics, such as verbal and mathematic ability, learning and cultural expectations may play a much larger role. But "in either case, environmental experiences influence whether an innate predisposition will be expressed. Females who are encouraged to practice visual-spatial skills, for example, may indeed perform better than males who have not been encouraged to practice such skills."[41]

---

39. Benjamin B. Lahey and Martha S. Johnson, *Psychology and Instruction* (Glenview, Ill.: Scott Foresman, 1978), p. 158.
40. E. Maccoby and C. Jacklin, *The Psychology of Sex Differences* (Stanford, Calif.: Stanford U., 1974).
41. Lahey and Johnson, p. 159. Used by permission.

To complete this brief picture of sexual differences in intellectual functioning, we need to point out that studies have shown subsequently that there is no evidence of male superiority in mathematics achievement when affective variables and exposure to math courses were controlled.[42] Overall, the studies tend to show that the differences in intellectual functioning are not so much matters of genetic inheritance, as they are of societal expectations and practices.

THE TEACHER'S RELATIONSHIP WITH BOYS AND GIRLS

The teacher, whether male or female, needs to understand that the boys and girls who come into his or her class are going to vary widely in terms of their styles of behavior, preferences for work activities, attitudes toward various areas of the curriculum, levels of activity and competitiveness, and so on.

It is important for teachers to understand they are models for the children with whom they engage in the teaching-learning process. Not only the more obvious attitudes and behaviors of the teachers, but also their relationships with the students and with each other and with other school personnel help to make up what has been called "The Hidden Curriculum." This term refers to what is *really being learned* by the students, even though it may not appear in the objectives or the goals for the class. It is learned as students sense and perceive what is really taking place in the school. Therefore, teachers need to be keenly aware of their responsibilities in terms of how their relationships to boys and girls contribute to this hidden curriculum.

There is evidence from a number of studies to show that teachers tend to overestimate achievement potential and intelligence of girls and underestimate the achievement potential and intelligence of boys, and have higher expectations for girls than for boys of equal ability. Also, the same studies indicate that teachers possess more negative attitudes toward boys, particularly regarding how well motivated they are for school and the expectations of the teacher that boys are going to be classroom management problems.[43] It is also easy for the teacher to develop a very strong difference in perception of boys who are high-achieving in the classroom and those who are low-achieving in the classroom, coming to look upon the low-achieving boys as "trouble" and "lazy." The low-achievement boys are more likely to receive criticism from teachers, and that only makes the boys more likely to experience school difficulty. Teachers need to be very sensitive to their perceptions of behavior of boys in the classroom.

In relation to girls, teachers can help to broaden their horizons and perspectives by pointing out to them that there are many fields open to them which they may not imagine. Also, the teacher—male or female—needs to be very

---

42. E. Fennema and J. Sherman, "Sex-related Differences in Mathematical Achievement, Spatial Visualization and Affective Factors," *American Educational Research Journal* 14 (1977):51-72. Also F. Christoplos and J. Borden, "Sexism in Elementary School Mathematics," *Elementary School Journal* 78 (1978):275-77.
43. J. Brophy and T. Good, *Teacher-Student Relationships: Causes and Consequences* (New York: Holt, Rinehart, and Winston, 1974).

sensitive to those occasions on which it would be more appropriate for a boy to talk to a male teacher or for a girl to talk to a female teacher, and help to make it easy for this to happen by arranging for such an opportunity.

The Christian teacher's relationship with boys and girls is a matter of seeing each one as made in the image of God, precious in His sight, and therefore to be dealt with with great care and respect in every aspect of the teaching-learning process.

CREATIVITY IN THE CLASSROOM

Creativity is, of course, of great interest to educators, or it should be. However, it is very difficult to define or to measure. It does have association with IQ, but IQ tests cannot measure it directly. And valid and reliable tests of creativity have yet to be developed, in spite of the work of people such as Guilford, Torrance, and Getzels and Jackson.[44]

We do know that some of the components of creative thinking are divergent production, fluency, flexibility, and originality.

As teachers try to encourage creativity in the teaching-learning process, the first step would be to show the students—that is, let them know definitely—that you value creative thinking, and also provide opportunities within the teaching-learning process for experiences in which students can use their creative talents. You may want to use in your classroom an activity such as brainstorming, where students just come up with all the ideas they can think of concerning a particular issue or subject area or project; you may have your students deliberately search for a novel and useful solution to a particular kind of problem. Encourage the students to bring creative things from home that they might have made there, and take time to look at them and comment about them with the students.

Perhaps one further note in this brief discussion of creativity will be helpful. Although experts do not agree on a definition for creativity, it certainly appears logical that such a definition as Lahey and Johnson have proposed would be minimal: "Creativity is defined as *unusual and useful* solutions to problems or the production of something new and enjoyable, such as works of art."[45] Their definition places emphasis upon creative acts being *both* novel and beneficial.

TRANSLATING MULTIPOTENTIALITY INTO PERFORMANCE

Every educator surely has some notion of the multipotentiality of the individual, else they would not be involved in the teaching-learning process. For without a potential, there is nothing with which to work in order to train or educate

---

44. E.T. Torrance, *Rewarding Creative Behavior in Classroom Activity*. (Englewood Cliffs, N.J.: Prentice-Hall, 1965); J. Guilford, *The Nature of Human Intelligence* (New York: McGraw-Hill, 1967); J. Getzels and P. Jackson, *Creativity and Intelligence: Explorations with Gifted Students* (New York: Wiley, 1962).
45. Lahey and Johnson, p. 100. Used by permission.

it into performance. But there are frankly sharp differences among the various approaches to the teaching-learning process as to the methodology by which that potential should be transformed into ability, and the ultimate goals for which that ability should be used. The behaviorist is really not highly concerned with the nature of human potential, but places his emphasis on using external stimuli to produce the responses desirable, and thereby shapes the behavior of the human animal with the ultimate goal of the survival of our society.

The cognitive theorist emphasizes particularly that part of the human potential which has to do with cognitive processing of information, with the goal of helping the individual learn how to solve problems, in order to be able to meet the varying circumstances of a rapidly changing society.

The humanist is also deeply concerned with the human potential, and places emphasis upon actualizing that potential, especially the affective processes relating to values, attitudes, interests—with the ultimate goal of the human being becoming a fully-functioning person.

The Christian views the multipotentiality of the human being as a gift from the hands of the God of creation. Although made in His image, nevertheless the image has been marred by the fact of sin. Therefore, the multipotentiality, even though developed into ability, has no eternal significance until the individual is redeemed by the grace of God in Christ Jesus. Once this transformation has taken place, all of life becomes a matter of stewardship under God, and as the multipotentiality is translated into ability, the individual then does everything "as unto the Lord."

The ultimate goal for the Christian is not the survival of our society, although his patriotism and love for his nation are among his most precious values; neither is the ultimate goal the development of the individual into a fully functioning human being, even though he is deeply concerned with both the cognitive and affective areas becoming well-developed; the ultimate goal is to live to please the Lord in every aspect of one's living, understanding as the Christian does, that God is the One with whom he shall dwell for all eternity.

God is indeed the Ultimate Reality, but the spires of our churches pointing to the skies do not imply that the Christian is interested *only* in the life to come, to the exclusion of life upon the earth. For ever since sin came into the world, the process of human development and learning has been the permissive will of God. Only Adam and Eve were created as adults. Even Jesus Christ entered into the process of development and learning. What happens to people in this process of human development and learning is of utmost importance to our Lord, and therefore it is important to the Christian. When people are starving, suffering, or seeking help, the Christian should be ready to respond and be prepared with the knowledge, skills, and understanding to respond to meet that need in the name of Christ.

And just at this point, the multipotentiality of the human being transformed by the grace of God and translated into ability comes to its fullest flower here upon the earth. The Christian is to occupy "until Jesus comes," and this occupation in an increasingly technological society requires the best of training and education to translate the many-potentialed human being into a knowledgeable and skilled workman for the Lord. And this is the ultimate challenge for the Christian teacher—to see in the teaching-learning process this very opportunity—to become an authoritative, compassionate leader to be used by the Holy Spirit in the fulfillment of this process.

Hindsight

In this chapter we have talked about the multipotentiality of human beings—the many and varied ways in which students differ. These include intelligence, socioeconomic status, creativity, and sex differences in intellectual behavior, and we have made some suggestions as to how these differences might be dealt with by the teacher in the teaching-learning process. We pointed out that while every educator has some notion of the multipotentiality of the human being, there are sharp differences both as to the method to be used and the ultimate goal to be reached as multipotentiality is developed into ability.

Chalkboard Challenges

1. Think back a moment over all the things you wanted to be and do in your life so far. These probably range from being a fireman or a nurse, through a whole variety of occupations and professions. Presumably you have decided on becoming a teacher, and we commend you for that, for we look upon that as one of the noblest of the professions. But consider for a moment all of the other things you could do if you really wanted to. You may want to make a list of these in your teacher's notebook, to remind you of your multipotentiality—the many aptitudes you have which, if you receive training or education, could be developed into abilities.

2. Think about the part heredity and environment play, respectively, in the matter of individual development, and especially with regard to human intelligence. Rather than trying to arrive at an answer as to which of these two forces plays the greater role, think about how the two of them interact in your life and in the lives of others, and then jot down in your teacher's notebook what your conclusions imply for your own responsibility as a teacher.

3. After reading and thinking about the definitions of intelligence that various psychologists and educators have presented, develop carefully and deliberately your own definition of intelligence. Again, we suggest you write this in your teacher's notebook for frequent reference. You may wish to change it somewhat as you progress through your career.

4. Describe the way in which you think, on the basis of research and experience, intelligence tests can legitimately be used. Put down an example for each of the ways you think such a test might be helpful.

Want to Know More?

BURT'S STUDY

If you really want to know more about the study Burt made, which at one time was considered a classic, and more recently has been called into question, we suggest you read the article entitled "The Genetic Determination of Difference in Intelligence: A Study of Monozygotic Twins Reared Together and Apart," *British Journal of Psychology* (1966):137-53.

Because this study and the questions about it are central to the topic we discussed in this chapter, we suggest that you look at the following references:

N. Wade, "IQ and Heredity: Suspicion of Fraud Beclouds Classic Experiment," *Science* 194 (1976):916-19.

L. J. Kamin, *The Science and Politics of IQ* (Potomac, Md.: Erlbaum, 1974).

L. J. Kamin, "Burt's IQ Data," *Science* 195:246-48.

O. Gillie, "Did Sir Cyril Burt Fake His Research on Heritability of Intelligence? Part I," *Phi Delta Kappan* 56 (1977):469-71.

M. McAskie, "Carelessness or Fraud in Sir Cyril Burt's Kinship Data?" *American Psychologist* 33 (1978):496-98.

D. D. Dortman, "The Cyril Burt Question: New Findings," *Science* 201 (1978):1177-86.

A. R. Jensen, "Kinship Correlations Reported by Sir Cyril Burt," *Behavior Genetics* 4 (1974):1-28.

A. R. Jensen, "Did Sir Cyril Burt Fake His Research on Heritability of Intelligence? Part II," *Phi Delta Kappan* 56 (1977):471, 492.

EFFECT OF EXPERIENCE

Another classic study that still stands firm is that of H. M. Skeels and H. B. Dye, "A Study of the Effect of Differential Stimulation on Mentally Retarded Children," *Program of the American Association of Mental Deficiency* 44 (1939):114-36. This study shows the important influence of experience on intellectual development.

CREATIVITY

If you want to know more about creativity, we recommend a book by E. P. Torrance, *Rewarding Creative Behavior in Classroom Creativity* (Englewood Cliffs, N.J.: Prentice-Hall, 1965).

SEX DIFFERENCES

One of the most comprehensive sources of information on sex differences in intellectual abilities is Eleanor Maccoby and Carol Jacklin, *The Psychology of Sex Differences* (Stanford, Calif.: Stanford U., 1974).

GENETICS

It is presently thought by genetic experts that what is termed "a reaction range" of about 25 points is to be expected for IQ scores. This means that, given a particular set of genes, the difference in IQs ultimately between individuals who grow up in a relatively nonstimulating environment versus those growing up in a highly stimulating environment would be as much as 25 points. If you are interested in reading more about this, you can do so in the article by S. Scarr-Salapatek, "Genetics and the Development of Intelligence," in F. Horowitz, ed., *Review of Research in Child Development*, vol. 4 (Chicago: U. of Chicago, 1975).

16

Mainstreaming Students—Exceptionality

CONTENTS

	PAGE
Key Terms	398
That's Debatable!	399
Foresight	400
Exceptional Students: Who Are They?	401
Exceptional Students: What Do I Do with Them?	403
Meeting the Needs of Exceptional Students	404
Public Law 94-142 and Its Critical Importance	408
Exceptional Students and the Christian School	410
Hindsight	416
Chalkboard Challenges	417
Want to Know More?	417

KEY TERMS

Exceptional children
  Children whose behavior deviates from the norm in ways that are maladaptive to the child or society

Individualized Education Program (IEP)
  Under Public Law 94-142, which took effect in 1977, an IEP must be developed for each exceptional child in the school system

Mainstreaming
  The practice of bringing exceptional children into the regular classroom for

as much time as possible, rather than keeping them in self-contained classrooms. Usually, this means that for certain times during the day, the exceptional child will make use of a special *resource room*

In this chapter we believe it will be more beneficial to define the remainder of the key terms within the context of the chapter itself, since the key terms represent the various kinds of exceptionality and the chapter is structured around those terms. Our intent is to make the learning of these exceptionalities, their characteristics, and how to relate to them in the classroom, easier.

THAT'S DEBATABLE!
Is Mainstreaming the Best Idea?

In this chapter, we briefly call attention to the manner in which exceptional students have been treated in the teaching-learning process. We point to the initial treatment of "putting them all in a room together and making them behave," followed by the concern that each one be diagnosed carefully and then sent off outside the school to a special treatment center, and then finally to the inclusion of the exceptional student in the classroom under the Mainstreaming Act of 1975, which took effect in 1977.

The purpose in the latter two of the three phases has been to do what is best for the student. As one educator put it, "We want to help the exceptional student stand out as little as possible as being different in some awful way from all the other students." To put it another way, we want the exceptional student to feel comfortable in the classroom, and the manner in which that is done predominantly is to mainstream the exceptional student.

However, very recently increasing numbers of educators—although still a minority—have been wondering whether mainstreaming is really the best way of engaging the exceptional student in the teaching-learning process. Is he or she really experiencing social development as a result of the mainstreaming process? Or does the exceptional student really feel so uncomfortable in the regular classroom, and so "different" when he or she leaves to go to the resource room or to the therapist's office, that it really does not provide the best setting for the teaching-learning process?

Those concerned with whether mainstreaming is the answer are concerned, not because they want to get rid of the problems out of the classroom, but because they want to be sure that the underlying purpose of exceptional education is being fulfilled—namely, that the student is really profiting as much as he or she can from the teaching-learning process. Does the mainstreaming method restrict the social development of the exceptional student? Could he or she, by feeling more comfortable in a special classroom with highly trained individuals, profit more from that educational setting?

The research is not at all clear in all areas of this question, and it is debatable!

Foresight

A number of years ago, prior to the passage of Public Law 94-142 (Education for All Handicapped Children Act), we had included as part of our responsibilities consulting with several public school systems. In one school system there was a large high school, which for the most part did a fair job of engaging in the teaching-learning process. But when we conversed with the principal of that particular high school and asked him about their program for exceptional students, we were appalled. For in this otherwise above-average high school, the response to our inquiry was that "all of the slow learners or problem children are in one room down in the basement of the school." When we went down to observe this situation, we found precisely what we had expected: namely, all kinds of exceptional students and those who were not truly exceptional, but "troublemakers," as they were labeled, were lumped together in one dingy, dark, unattractive room. Further, the young man who was teaching them (and there was only one teacher for about thirty-five of these students) although doing his best, had only two years of college, and no special training whatever for dealing with exceptionality of any kind.

In answer to our question about why there was not a fully qualified teacher the administrator commented, "There is no sense in paying a big salary for a fully qualified teacher for these kids. All they need is somebody to keep them in the room, and keep them from getting into trouble, and keep them entertained through the school day."

Aside from the fact that we made a few substantial recommendations regarding this situation, the situation does serve to remind us of what happened in many, probably the majority of schools, for many decades. In our minds, we believed in our national policy of free public education for all. This means that the public schools are available to any student who wishes to enroll. But there have been great numbers of students who have been excluded from that policy, sometimes intentionally—sometimes unintentionally. As Flowers and Bolmeier note, among the reasons for exclusion of students have been such things as mental and physical deficiencies, poor health, pregnancy, flagrant or willful misbehavior, and unconventional dress or disturbing personal appearance.[1]

Along with the "dump them all in one room and keep them quiet" philosophy, there developed another approach of diagnosing the students with special tests and placing them in particular settings that would deal with their special needs. The settings were outside of the regular classroom. This sounded like the proper thing to do with children who had special needs, but research began to question the effectiveness of special classes for these students outside of the regular school setting, and court decisions began to stress the rights of all children to appropriate educational treatment within the regular school setting. So gradually the approach developed to put the children with special needs in the regular classroom setting, at least for the majority of the time, and provide special help for

---

1. A. Flowers and E. Bolmeier, *Law and Pupil Control* (Cincinnati: Anderson, 1964).

Mainstreaming Students—Exceptionality

them where needed.[2] Public Law 94-142 was passed in 1975 and took effect in 1977, and this had an earthshaking impact on the manner in which the exceptional student was to be engaged in the teaching-learning process.

This means that you as a teacher can expect to have exceptional students in your classroom. You need to be prepared to relate with them and to help them achieve the objectives established for them. In this chapter we explain the requirements of Public Law 94-142, the various types of exceptionalities you may see reflected in students in your classroom, make suggestions as to how to deal with them within the teaching-learning process, and then conclude with a special section on exceptional students within Christian schools.

EXCEPTIONAL STUDENTS: WHO ARE THEY?

Depending upon which book you are reading, exceptionality may or may not include those who are gifted and talented. In our view, the gifted-talented student (GT) is an exceptional student, at the opposite end of the IQ scale from the student who is severely or profoundly mentally retarded.

Exceptional students may be handicapped by various physical, sensory, or emotional disabilities—or they may be gifted. As a rule of thumb, the estimate is approximately one-third of the students in any given class will need some kind of modification of their educational programs at some time during their years in school. It is estimated that about 10 percent of the students will need a major modification or special intervention in order to meet their particular special needs. These students may display a great variety of learning problems and definite need for many kinds of special services.

Following are the categories of exceptionality which ordinarily you will need to be aware of and able to relate to in the classroom.

SPEECH IMPAIRED

Speech-impaired students are persons who have disorders of vocal production. These disorders are of such nature that they distract attention away from what the individual is trying to say. The greatest number of students with this disorder have articulation problems involving omissions, substitutions, or distortions of speech sounds.[3]

VISUAL IMPAIRMENT

Visually impaired students either have a limited field of vision or they have defects of visual acuity. Unless this individual also has other handicaps, he can do

---

2. J. Chaffin, "Will the Real Mainstreaming Program Please Stand Up! (Or . . . Should Dunn Have Done It?)" *Focus on Exceptional Children* 6 (1974):1-18.
3. Sharon R. Berry, "Exceptional Students in Christian Schools" (monograph), Norfolk Christian Schools, Norfolk, Virginia, 1979, p. 10. Used by permission.

very well in regular classroom programs. The teacher and the school need to be aware of the Commission for the Visually Handicapped, which offers a wide range of helpful services for this kind of special student. The services include such things as talking books, recording equipment, instruction in Braille, low vision aides, and training on an itinerant basis.

HEARING IMPAIRED

Hearing-impaired students have defects in hearing which limit their ability to take in and process information from their surroundings, which has to do with understanding and production of language. It is not hard to see that this can then affect students' performance across the board in almost every academic subject. Barry points out that typically, the students will function three or more years academically delayed, although exhibiting normal intelligence.[4] This makes programming for hearing impaired students within the regular teaching-learning process quite difficult.

PHYSICAL HANDICAPS

These students are sometimes called orthopedically handicapped, and the first thing to become aware of is whether there are other disabilities in addition to the physical disability. If not, then there need be only modifications in terms of the physical environment.

EMOTIONALLY DISTURBED

These students are sometimes categorized under the label of behavioral disorder. However, the ability to make modifications in your teaching-learning process for emotionally disturbed students obviously depends on how severe the disturbance is. The definition of emotional disturbance includes two factors: (1) reduced functional abilities in academic pursuits, and (2) poor interpersonal relationships. Usually progress of these students academically will be very slight until the conflict with which they are battling is resolved.

LEARNING DISABILITIES

These students are by definition those who have normal intelligence, but are experiencing difficulties in their academic pursuits because of a wide range of perceptual disorders which reflect themselves in dysfunctions in language and mathematics. We wish to stress that these students are usually normal to above normal in intelligence, but have "perceptual short circuits."

4. Ibid, p. 11.

MENTAL RETARDATION

By definition these students are below-average in their intellectual functioning (IQ). We must caution, however, against the use of the IQ test alone as the basis for assigning a student into a program for the mentally retarded. As in every other kind of exceptionality, every resource ought to be brought to bear on the situation that can possibly have some relevance to making an intelligent decision. The various categories for mental retardation are usually designated by two or more standard deviations from the norm on intelligence tests.

Many special education experts recommend that mentally retarded students can best be considered in two major groups: those who can benefit from instruction and being a part of the regular classroom, and those who cannot. Those we call slow learners and the educable mentally retarded students are usually placed in the first group. Trainable to severely mentally retarded students are usually placed in the second group.

THE GIFTED

As we have indicated previously, giftedness is at the opposite end of the continuum of intelligence from mental retardation. Gifted students are defined as those who score two or more standard deviations above the norm on a test of intelligence. Usually this will mean from 130 to 160 on the IQ scale. Dr. Sharon R. Berry describes these students as having "special talents (musical, artistic, etc.), brightness and genius." These students generally possess high levels of academic achievement, interest in a variety of enriched or advanced subjects, skill in creative problem solving, and mental alertness.[5]

EXCEPTIONAL STUDENTS: WHAT DO I DO WITH THEM?

We certainly understand that unless the teacher-to-be has had some experience either within his or her own family or as a teacher's aide in a classroom with exceptional students, this can be a frustrating, even frightening kind of prospect. But we assure you it need not be, even though it is exceedingly important that you understand exceptionality and how to relate to these students in the teaching-learning process. Therefore, we are providing in this chapter four kinds of suggestions, which we think will be of help to you:

    1. The general suggestions made under each type of exceptionality
    2. The quite specific suggestions made under the heading of "Modifications for Special Education Students in the Regular Classroom"

5. Ibid., p. 16.

3. By suggesting exceedingly pertinent material for you to read under Want to Know More?

4. For those of you teaching in Christian schools or planning to teach in Christian schools, some very special suggestions, with deep gratitude to Sharon R. Berry for her very special help in providing these valuable suggestions for the special circumstances for Christian schools.

MEETING THE NEEDS OF EXCEPTIONAL STUDENTS

SPEECH IMPAIRED

In most schools, either a full or part-time speech therapist will be a member of the staff and will provide individual therapy sessions for the students. In the case of the Christian school, as Dr. Berry points out, a therapist would need to be secured from a local university, a clinic, the public schools, or someone who is a private therapist, and the extra costs would have to be arranged for these services.[6]

VISUALLY IMPAIRED

As suggested previously, great use should be made of the Commission for the Visually Handicapped and their wide range of ancillary services. In relation to the Christian schools, these students can be served in the regular programs in cooperation with resources from the community. As a teacher, you will need to make arrangements for these students to have class intervention by those who may be helping them.

HEARING IMPAIRED

It is a good idea here to have a special resource classroom for deaf and hard-of-hearing students, particularly if you have a half dozen or more students and you can find a teacher who is appropriately qualified. Again, volunteers can give great help. In our college, for example, when a hearing-impaired person is in the class, a volunteer who knows sign language comes along and sits in the front of the class where the hearing-impaired student is able to see him clearly, and the volunteer interprets what is being said during the class time. People have asked, "Isn't that disturbing for the rest of the class?" And the honest answer is, "No, after the first class session or two." The reason is that students quickly adjust to and accept this kind of special help for those who have special needs.

If hearing-impaired students do have a special resource classroom, then the idea would be to integrate them into the regular classrooms and activities wherever they have similar needs to students in those classes: lunchtime, physical education, and, in Christian schools, chapel services.

6. Ibid., p. 9.

If a student is only moderately hard of hearing, the participation in the regular classroom becomes a matter of careful seating to be sure the student is near to the source of the sound.

PHYSICALLY HANDICAPPED

The student may require crutches, a wheelchair, or any one of several other possible pieces of equipment to aid him in getting around and overcoming his physical handicap. The buildings must be planned and made accommodating in terms of ramps and toileting facilities especially. Two additional considerations are emphasized by Berry[7]: usually physically handicapped students will be enrolled in programs of physical and occupational therapy, as well as medical follow-up, and while the parents usually assume responsibility for obtaining these services, there is always need for careful coordination with the school personnel to assure the carry-over of special techniques or services. And second, the homebound student needs to be taken into full consideration. Some systems have homebound teachers, others use special telephone systems to allow the student to participate in the teaching-learning process.

Our suggestion is that, if at all possible, the school have a homebound teacher. The opportunities for Christian compassion and service are almost limitless. Here again is the opportunity for a volunteer. Perhaps a retired qualified schoolteacher would be delighted to perform this service at little or no cost to the school.

EMOTIONALLY DISTURBED

With this special needs student, there are the possibilities for assignment in the regular classroom while simultaneously being treated through psychotherapy, or again the use of a resource classroom where the teaching-learning process is structured to meet each student's needs. Quite often, if a special classroom is used, the emotionally disturbed, severe learning disabilities student, and those who are classified as slow learners can be combined.

The emotionally disturbed student can be a student of almost any range of intelligence, but the student who is going to be in your classroom is probably going to be within the normal range or above; although we need to be aware always that, for example, a mentally retarded student can also become emotionally disturbed. As a part of our school consultation responsibilities we became part of a situation where the son of a well-known citizen in a certain town was "streaking" during the evening hours through the middle of the town. The intelligence level of this student was in the bright range, and his parents were both fine, concerned Christian people. Without their realizing it, however, they had become so involved

---

7. Ibid., p. 10.

in other activities that the boy felt neglected, and so chose this method of getting their attention. Fortunately, over a very short period of time, this particular behavioral disturbance was resolved. The point is that the academic progress of the emotionally disturbed student is going to be very slight until the conflict which is causing the behavioral disturbance is resolved. Therefore, the school needs to work very closely with the psychotherapist or school psychologist in conjunction with the teaching-learning process and how it is geared for this particular student.

LEARNING DISABLED

Again, let us remind you these students have normal to above normal intelligence, but are suffering from what we term "perceptual short-circuiting." Another way to describe them is to say that they have "deficit" areas, and need help in those areas, even though they do possess normal or above normal intelligence.

In dealing with these students, the goal should always be to get them to the place where they can function comfortably in the regular classroom. This student will be in your classroom most of the time, and as a result of his individually prescribed program, will be undergoing intensive treatment focusing in on the deficit areas mentioned above. Usually, about ten students are needed along with a therapist who is qualified, before a program for the learning disabled can be established. These students make great use of resource rooms in which their special areas of deficit are dealt with. Depending upon how severe these deficit areas are, the ratio can run from ten to one (students to teacher) to a maximum of sixteen to one for less severe situations. Berry again suggests that in the situation where the Christian school is not able to provide these services—perhaps because the school is young or does not have enough students yet—the parents should be advised by the Christian school to seek resources from their local public education agency.[8]

MENTALLY RETARDED

What the teacher and the school are facing in this situation is a very complex problem indeed: how to provide the kind of instruction that will be helpful for students who cannot function at the level of their age and grade placement. Those who are severely or profoundly mentally retarded in most cases will not be in your classroom. You will be seeing slow learning and educable mentally retarded students, and the research indicates that it is better to keep these students either in or as closely related to the regular classroom as possible, since if they are put into separate classes full-time, the students have lower achievement rates.

Here again, because of the great variability in terms of the academic areas in which mentally retarded students can function, common sense has to be injected in the situation in order to make the decision as to those subjects in which they can

8. Ibid., p. 14.

participate in the regular classroom. For those subjects where they are not able to participate, the resource room is used. And, here again, let us emphasize that the resource room is a place where a great variety of students with learning problems can be served. It is a room that requires highly individualized instruction and a relatively low teacher-student ratio. The teacher in the resource room is making every effort to get the student to the place where he or she can return to the regular classroom, but this is obviously not always possible for some students. In dealing with the mentally retarded students, the program should certainly stress self-help and those skills that the student needs just for daily maintenance and living. Berry recommends "when a population of students can be identified, the best service option is a self-contained classroom for each 8 to 12 students who are within four years chronological and functional age of one another ... Since this level of retardation (trainable and severely mentally retarded) occurs in only one to three percent of the general population, it is unlikely that a group of students would be identified for service in a small Christian school. More often parents must seek public or private school special placement unless the Christian school is large and/ or serves as a regional service center."[9]

GIFTED AND TALENTED

The usual approach to helping these students has been to either offer enrichment programs in addition to their programs in the regular grades or to accelerate the students, advancing them to higher grades.

The optimal program has been an arrangement which allows the students to remain in age-appropriate regular classrooms with opportunities to participate in activities and programs that expand and enrich the regular classroom program. These can be one-day special programs each week, one period each day, Saturday programs, independent studies, or university classes, directed pursuits of personal interests, etc. Adjustments should be made in the regular class to allow students to use time productively after meeting the objectives of the regular curriculum, through projects, participation in special program materials, or attendance in advanced classes.[10]

One of the more promising programs for gifted students is the one known as mentor-assisted enrichment projects (MAEP).[11] In a Phi Delta Kappa Educational Foundation booklet describing this program, Gray lists six major benefits of this program and of using preservice teachers as the mentors for gifted students.

First, MAEP provides an inexpensive means of enabling G/T students to pursue an indepth investigation of a real problem or topic of personal interest to them.

---

9. Ibid., p. 16.
10. Ibid., pp. 16-17.
11. William A. Gray, *Challenging the Gifted and Talented Through Mentor-Assisted Enrichment Projects* (Bloomington, Ind.: Phi Delta Kappa, 1983).

Second, MAEP expands students' cultural awareness and experiential background through field trips arranged by their mentors.

Third, MAEP helps students develop their oral language facility as they prepare, rehearse, and conduct interviews with various people in the work force and community.

Fourth, MAEP fosters students' social and emotional development by enabling them to gain confidence from interviewing strangers during field trips, from giving a class presentation, and from learning how to work together cooperatively.

Fifth, MAEP provides real-life opportunities for students to develop and use high-level thinking skills and to internalize values and attitudes from their experiences throughout the enrichment program.

Sixth, MAEP enables pre-service teachers who serve as mentors to develop such basic training competencies as: doing long-range planning, learning how to ask high-level questions, providing direct instruction when necessary, providing for discovery learning when appropriate, arranging for hands-on enrichment experiences, planning field trips, preparing students to conduct interviews, assisting students in using multi-media materials, and rehearsing students in making interesting and informative presentations.

Additionally, we would recommend for those who are particularly interested in mainstreaming in the secondary schools a booklet sponsored by the Phi Delta Kappa Educational Foundation entitled *Mainstreaming in the Secondary School: The Role of the Regular Teacher*.[12] Another booklet for those interested in the high school student places emphasis on the marginal student at the secondary level and is most helpful in suggesting effective programs for that student. It is entitled *Effective Programs for the Marginal High School Student*, and Gary Wehlege is the author.[13]

Another aspect of the education of the handicapped which is of vital interest to all those involved in the teaching-learning process, is the matter of legal issues. For a very brief booklet, written in understandable language for the teacher and quite current (1983), we recommend Donald G. Turner's *Legal Issues in Education of the Handicapped*.[14]

PUBLIC LAW 94-142 AND ITS CRITICAL IMPORTANCE

In 1975, this law known as the *Education for All Handicapped Children Act*, was passed by the Congress, and it became effective in 1977. It has also been called

---

12. Cynthia L. Warger, Loviah E. Aldinger, and Kathy A. Okun, *Mainstreaming in the Secondary School: The Role of the Regular Teacher* (Bloomington, Ind.: Phi Delta Kappan Educational Foundation, 1983).
13. Gary G. Wehlege, *Effective Programs for the Marginal High School Student* (Bloomington, Ind.: Phi Delta Kappa Educational Foundation, 1983).
14. Donald G. Turner, *Legal Issues in Education of the Handicapped* (Bloomington, Ind.: Phi Delta Kappa Educational Foundation, 1983).

the *Mainstreaming Act,* because it seeks to bring as many exceptional children as possible into the regular "mainstream" of the regular classroom. It mandates that free and appropriate public education in the least restrictive environment will be provided for all children and young people ages 3 through 21. There is no question that this is a landmark act in the history of education, particularly in the history of how exceptionality will be dealt with in the teaching-learning process.

However, it does present many challenges to the regular classroom teacher and to the school system. At the very heart of this act is the referral and placement process built around the development of an Individualized Educational Program

---

Insight: Requirements of Public Law 94-142

1. This law mandates free, appropriate public education.

2. That education must be provided in the least restrictive environment.

3. That education must be provided for all handicapped children and young people, ages three through twenty-one.

4. Development of an Individualized Educational Program is mandated as the result of a referral and placement process.

5. That program must be carefully evaluated for the individual student at least every three years.

Fig. 16.1

Insight: Instances of Exceptionality in Public Schools

Out of students in the public schools, the following represent the numbers which represent the number of students with a particular exceptionality to be found:

Speech disorders	3 in 100
Mentally retarded	1.5-2 in 100
Severely profoundly retarded	1 in 3,000
Hearing impaired	1 in 1,000
Visually handicapped	1 in 2,000
Gifted and talented	1.5-2 in 100
Learning disabled	3 in 100
Physically handicapped	1 in 100
Emotionally disturbed	1-2 in 100

Fig. 16.2

> **Insight: Referral and Placement Process for the Exceptional Student**
>
> The referral and placement process has six distinct steps as follows:
> 1. Receive referral from some source.
> 2. Carry out a five-phase evaluation for appropriate diagnosis.
> 3. Determine what the student is eligible for, and explain that clearly to the parents.
> 4. Develop the Individualized Educational Program for the student.
> 5. Monitor and evaluate the student's progress carefully and specifically.
> 6. Completely re-evaluate the child's eligibility and progress every three years.

Fig. 16.3

(IEP) which is mandated to be developed for each exceptional child, and to be developed without any charge or cost to the parents or the child. In the development of the IEP, two people from the school system and at least one parent must agree on the services the child needs. And related services must be designated and provided such as music, speech therapy, physical therapy, and psychological help.

The referral and placement process contains six steps, and these are shown in figure 16.3. The requirements of Public Law 94-142 are indicated in figure 16.1, and a typical Individualized Education Program for a student is indicated in figure 16.4. We urge the student to look at each of these carefully, because of the exceeding importance of the mandates of this public law.

If we look at the instances of exceptionality in the public schools, we find the results as they are listed in figure 16.2. The expectancy rate—that is, what percentage of the total student population may be classified as exceptional, therefore needing some degree of modification in their instructional programs—for the public school is about 20 percent.

EXCEPTIONAL STUDENTS AND THE CHRISTIAN SCHOOL

Sharon R. Berry conducted a study, in connection with the Association of Christian Schools International (ACSI), of Christian schools with enrollments of over 200 and representing a student population of 130,000. Out of 332 responses from these schools and representing special services for 5,000 exceptional students, the following figures are indicative both of the expectancy rate for

Christian schools (6.8 percent) as well as the high interest of many Christian schools in providing programs for exceptional students.

Sixty percent of the Christian schools surveyed either were going to start, or were going to develop further, special education programs according to their responses. The cost per child per year in a Christian school for these special services is estimated to be about $5,000 over and above the cost of regular schooling. Of the Christian schools surveyed, the students in the various exceptional categories were as follows: 110 were listed as slow learners or problem learners and could probably be categorized as having learning disabilities. There were 42 gifted and talented students. There were 21 educable mentally retarded students. There were 24 emotionally disturbed students. There were 8 visually impaired students. There were 57 students with speech handicaps. There were 21 students with physical handicaps. There were 15 hearing impaired students.[15]

A Philosophy of Exceptionality Education in Christian Schools

While virtually all educators believe that we must make educational opportunities available to all students, the Christian has even more reason to support this point of view, because of his foundations of belief in the God of creation. Dr. Berry treats this subject in a superb way in her monograph *Exceptional Students in Christian Schools*.[16] Using three main assertions, she views carefully the pros and cons of Christian education in relation to exceptionality. Her three assertions are: (1) exceptional students are part of God's creation; (2) exceptional students are members of the Body of Christ; (3) exceptional students are part of God's eternal purpose. Dr. Berry backs up her assertions with biblical foundations. We view the reading of this monograph as *must* reading for the student who is planning to teach in a Christian school, or for the administrator who is planning to be a superintendent or principal of a Christian school, or the teacher or administrator who already is actively pursuing a profession with Christian school education.

Modifications for Special Education Students in a Regular Classroom

The special education department of Lynchburg Christian Academy, Lynchburg, Virginia, under the direction of Dr. Berry, developed a list of modifications with the title identical to our heading, and have given us their permission to include this helpful and practical list of suggestions in this text. We believe you will find these significantly helpful as you prepare to relate to the exceptional student in the teaching-learning process.[17]

---

15. Sharon R. Berry, *Presentation in Graduate Seminar* (Lynchburg, Va.: Liberty Baptist College, Summer 1984).
16. Sharon R. Berry, "Exceptional Students in Christian Schools," pp. 1-8.
17. "Modifications for Special Education Students in the Regular Classrooms," Special Education Department, Lynchburg Christian Academy, Lynchburg, Virginia, 1983. Used by permission.

Short-Term Objectives	Special Education and Related Services	Person Responsible	Beginning and Ending Dates	Review Date
(1) Design a reading program building on Frank's areas of interest.				
A. Develop sightword vocabulary builders using the newspaper and sports books.	EMR Teacher support from remedial reading teacher; supplemental materials	EMR Teacher	March 7 June 1	May 1
OBJECTIVE: improve Frank's sight word vocabulary by 25%				
B. Using math word problems designed to incorporate new vocabulary words, Frank will improve in his ability to deal with math word problems.	EMR teacher; supplemental materials	Math teacher	March 7 June 1	May 1
C. An independent reading list based on occupational opportunities will be developed. Frank will read and discuss such materials.				
D. Frank will be encouraged to report on independent reading to his teacher—later to his peers.	EMR teacher	EMR teacher	March 15 June 1	May 15
(2) Frank will remain in the regular math class.				
A. Teacher will design sequential math materials building on Frank's strengths. OBJECTIVE: Frank will experience academic success.	Math teacher/ Math supervisor	Math teacher	March 7 June 1	May 15
B. Shop teacher will design math problems in that content area. Frank will be allowed to experience finishing a project from the conceptual stage through completion.		Shop teacher	March 7 June 1	May 15

C. Frank will be enrolled in an intramural or P.E. program.	P.E.	P.E. instructor	May 15
(3) Frank will spend two hours per week for three weeks with the vocational counselor discussing his readings in job opportunities.	EMR teacher	Vocational counselor	March 7 June 1 March 30 June 1
(4) Frank will assume increasing amounts of responsibility for his own learning as evidenced by his willingness to complete required projects and seek help from teachers.	EMR teacher	All of Frank's teachers	March 7 May 15 April 20

PLACEMENT DECISIONS

Frank will remain in EMR class for reading and language arts. He will attend a regular math class, shop class, and be enrolled in a P.E. class.

PERCENT OF TIME IN REGULAR CLASSROOM
50%

FOR THE COMMITTEE, RECOMMENDATIONS FOR SPECIFIC PROCEDURES/TECHNIQUES, MATERIALS, INFORMATION ABOUT LEARNING STYLE, ETC.

Frank's basic strength lies in the fact that he recognizes his weakness in reading and that he wants to stay in school. It is extremely important that he be allowed to experience success in an academic setting.

CRITERIA FOR EVALUATION OF ANNUAL GOALS

(1) Reading and math will be evaluated on the basis of teacher test and standardized test.

(2) Social behavior will be based on staff observations and Frank's observations as well as suspensions.

(3) Relations with teachers and peers (most likely dependent upon academic success) will be based on observations.

Committee Members Present
_____
_____
_____

Dates of Meetings
_____
_____

From Thomas L. Good and Jere E. Brophy, *Educational Psychology: A Realistic Approach*, 2d ed. (New York: Holt, Rinehart, and Winston, 1980), pp. 145-47. Used by permission.

Fig. 16.4

A Typical Individualized Educational Program

Child's Name   *Frank West*   Date Returned to Committee *March 2*
School   *Crescent Point High School*

SUMMARY OF PRESENT LEVELS OF PERFORMANCE

Frank wants to stay in school. He recognizes that his reading ability is low and he wants to learn to read. Teacher observations and test scores indicate that he has a basic understanding of the concepts and operations of fundamental mathematics. He has the ability to follow through on assignments which interest him. He experiences the most difficulty when he is asked to do school work which he doesn't understand or is presently incapable of doing. He is extremely unhappy in the self-contained classroom and does not associate with his classmates. He looked forward to being placed in a "regular" classroom but he has trouble controlling his anger when he can't do the required work. He does independent reading (e.g., newspapers and sports books). Teachers and school personnel often view his behavior as inappropriate for school. This has resulted in numerous suspensions.

PRIORITIZED LONG-TERM GOALS

(1) Frank will improve in his reading ability.
(2) Frank will experience success in the regular classroom.
(3) Frank will be given the opportunity to explore a range of career alternatives.
(4) Frank will develop positive relationships with peers and teachers.
(5) Frank will become more of a participant and less of a spectator in areas of interest.

The following modifications were drawn up by the Special Education Department. Our purpose is not to mandate ideas but rather to suggest to you, the classroom teacher, possible ideas that may benefit you and the special education student. Some suggestions will not be applicable to your teacher/student situation as each special student has different needs. The suggestions are based on different characteristics of an exceptional child.

Some of those characteristics are:
1. Poor reading skills
2. Easily distracted
3. Low self-esteem
4. Lack of self-motivation

Mainstreaming Students—Exceptionality

   5. Hyperactivity
   6. Impulsivity
   7. Disorder of memory and thinking
   8. Low tolerance for frustration
   9. Poor ability for abstract reasoning
   10. Poor ability for organizing thoughts
   11. Poor short and long term memory
   12. Slow in finishing work
   13. Poor ability to organize work
   14. Overly gullible and easily led by peers
A. *Classroom Modifications*
   1. Let child sit in front of classroom.
   2. During lectures maintain eye contact with child, calling his name often.
   3. Allow for delays in answering oral questions.
   4. Lecture from student's desk enabling the student to copy your notes.
   5. Allow student to tape class lecture.
   6. Tape reading sections for science, history, etc. where intent is knowledge of content.
   7. Allow student to tape reading assignment and to practice reading along with the tape.
   8. If your book is marked with additional information, allow student to also mark his/her book in same manner.
   9. If student is willing to supply carbon paper and extra notebook paper, allow him/her to have a note taker. The note taker should be chosen by the teacher and the special ed. student will still take down his own notes and is responsible to blend both sets into his personal notes each evening.
   10. Provide copies of your lecture notes.
   11. Use several avenues of providing information to utilize the student's strengths in either auditory or visual channels.
B. *Grading Modifications*
   1. When grading, provide both a content grade and a form grade. The form grade should be incorporated into language and spelling or reduce the overall grade slightly.
   2. Consider not penalizing on grades for nonacademic issues related to their handicaps. (For example, points off for incorrect grading of another child's spelling test when poor auditory memory prevents him from grading correctly.)
   3. In spelling, grade written work but consider giving ½ credit if word can be spelled orally.
   4. Provide opportunities for dropping the lowest grade, for extra credit, projects, special reports, etc.
   5. Give encouragement for every item attempted whether right or wrong.
C. *Homework and Assignment Modifications*
   1. Try to reduce length of assignments (not the content but the drill), if not absolutely needed.
   2. Prioritize problems and questions so that the most important can be done.
   3. Provide choices of assignments (projects versus written work) when possible.

4. For long term assignments, provide a lot of structure with check points. Provide a model for your expected performance.
   5. Have students keep a daily assignment notebook. Double check with the student to make sure he understands the assignment and has all the necessary books and materials.
   6. Use a buddy system to double check assignments.
   7. Give advance notice of homework assignments, preferably Friday for the following week.
   8. Have parents initial homework.
   9. Allow parents to judge a reasonable length of time spent on an assignment and write you a note when a child could not finish in a given time.
D. *Test Modifications*
   1. Allow oral tests or dictated answers when your focus is knowledge of content.
   2. Break down into smaller units allowing student to take one section at a time.
   3. Provide information on tests to the special teachers as soon as possible so that students can be tutored or modifications made.
   4. Allow special education teacher to make a study guide from the test.
   5. Allow special education teacher to re-structure test, if necessary.
   6. In memory tasks on a test, decide if it must be total recall or if recognition is acceptable and inform the student and special teacher.
   7. Provide additional time to take tests or eliminate non-essential items.
   8. Assist students in taking tests in the classroom by calling attention to blanks, allowing student to write only answers instead of full sentences or by having student answer orally to you.
   9. Use aides or student teachers to help give tests individually.
   10. Allow student to take mid-term exams with special education teacher to provide a quiet atmosphere with less pressure.
E. *Misc. Modifications*
   1. Visit child's therapy session.
   2. Provide concrete expression of emotional support.
   3. Use aides, student teachers, and volunteers to provide special help.

Hindsight

For many years, exceptional students were handled in the teaching-learning process on the basis of "put them all in a room and get somebody to keep them under control for the day." Then developed an interest in diagnosing the children and providing programs in special settings outside the regular classroom for these students. Most recently, and particularly through the Public Law 94-142, the direction of the educational process for exceptional students has been to mainstream them, that is, to include them as much as possible in the regular teaching-learning process in the classroom.

In this chapter we have discussed the various kinds of exceptionality you are apt to see reflected in students in your classroom, given you practical suggestions

Mainstreaming Students—Exceptionality

as to how to relate to these students, explained Public Law 94-142 and what it means when you apply it in the teaching-learning process. And, finally, we have included a special section on the exceptional student in the Christian school setting.

CHALKBOARD CHALLENGES

1. Imagine yourself to be the school psychologist, and think through carefully how you would distinguish between a student who is mentally retarded and one who is learning disabled. You may want to write your logic step by step in your teacher's notebook. Be detailed and specific.

2. Review each of the categories of exceptionality to be sure you know how to describe each. And then how to relate to each in the setting of the teaching-learning process. Again, write these items in your teacher's notebook for future reference.

3. Does the Christian approach make any difference at all in the manner in which we view exceptional students and the manner in which we relate to them? In what way?

4. Read over very carefully the Individual Education Program in the fourth Insight box (Fig. 16.4) to become thoroughly familiar with the kind of items that are included. You will be called upon as a teacher to engage in this kind of development of the IEP for individual students as you work with at least one other person from the school and one parent. This will bring you a greater degree of confidence as you learn how to develop these individualized programs for students.

WANT TO KNOW MORE?

Sharon R. Berry, "Exceptional Students in Christian Schools" (monograph) Norfolk Christian Schools, Norfolk, Virginia, 1979. We consider this mandatory reading for every student who is planning to teach in a Christian school. It is excellent reading for a teacher or teacher-to-be in any setting of the teaching-learning process.

Phi Delta Kappa Educational Foundation in Bloomington, Indiana, produces small, excellently researched, simple-to-read booklets it calls "Fastbacks." There are four of these we recommend for your reading:

Cynthia L. Warger, Loviah E. Aldinger, and Kathy A. Okun, *Mainstreaming in the Secondary School: The Role of the Regular Teacher,* 1983.

William A. Gray, *Challenging the Gifted and Talented Through Mentor-Assisted Enrichment Projects,* 1983.

Gary G. Wehlege, *Effective Programs for the Marginal High School Student,* 1983.

Donald G. Turner, *Legal Issues in Education of the Handicapped,* 1983.

17

Measurement—Student Performance

MAURICE STONE

CONTENTS

	PAGE
Key Terms	418
That's Debatable!	419
Foresight	421
How to Select and/or Write a Test	421
How to Interpret Test Results	441
Hindsight	444
Chalkboard Challenges	445
Want to Know More?	446

KEY TERMS

Achievement test
 Designed to assess the degree to which a student has achieved the objectives of a learning experience, that is, knowledge of the content presented in a course

Aptitude test
 A measurement device used to estimate the amount of a specific ability,

MAURICE STONE, Ed.D., Temple University, is professor of education at Liberty Baptist College, Lynchburg, Virginia.

potential, or capacity possessed by an individual in a specific area; for example, artistic aptitude

Central tendency
Any of several statistics indicating the typical performance of students; for example, the mean, the median, and the mode

Criterion-referenced test
A measurement that relates a test performance to specific levels of expected competence

Educational objective
A more or less precise statement of a desired behavior change

Norm-referenced test
A measurement that relates a student's performance to group-established norms

Reliability
That quality of a test which indicates its ability to consistently give the same results; does it *consistently* measure whatever it measures?

Standard scores
Scores based on the relationship between the mean and the standard deviation, for example, T scores, z scores

Standardized test
A published, formal, ready-made test for teacher use

Teacher-made test
An informal test which is not published, although generally typed and duplicated

Validity
The degree to which a measurement procedure truthfully represents that which it is intended to measure; does it *really* measure what it is supposed to?

Variability
Any of several statistics, for example, the range and standard deviation, which indicate the spread of students' scores

See also the glossaries compiled by Green, 1974, and Lyman, 1978.[1]

THAT'S DEBATABLE!
The Testing Trap

What's all the fuss about anyway? If you've been following the news, you know that there has been a definite change in attitude about standardized tests in America. There has always been a trickle of criticism directed at overstated claims regarding the accuracy of these tests, but lately that trickle seems to be turning into a raging torrent of skeptical words. Why are these tests under sustained attack? Don't they help us

---

1. John A. Green, *Teacher-made Tests,* 2d ed. (New York: Harper & Row, 1975), pp. 199-205; Howard B. Lyman, *Test Scores and What They Mean,* 3d ed. (Englewood Cliffs, N.J.: Prentice-Hall, 1978), pp. 170-81.

achieve the goal of using a fair, scientific, and objective method of selection whenever there are more people who want a job or admission to a particular school than there are openings for that job or school? Why are so many people so upset about this type of testing? If there are some problems with the tests, how can you protect yourself and your children? Do we really need to reform tests, and if so, how should we do it? . . .

These are not just academic questions. Standardized tests play a significant part in your life, in the lives of your children, from the day you start school until your last try for a new job or promotion. Standardized tests have become a modern obsession. The scores you receive on these tests at various stages of your life will be used by officials such as teachers, admissions officers, and employers to make decisions about your prospects and your life. Equally important, these test scores influence the way many people think of themselves. The impact can be especially severe for impressionable children. If they are told by supposedly scientific tests, that despite their satisfactory work in school, they are really "slow" or below normal in intelligence, some of them sadly will take that message to heart. Whenever children or adults are convinced that they will fail, they are well on the way to making that prophecy a reality.

Low test scores can stigmatize fully competent boys and girls, women and men. This happens because we as a nation have come to believe in the accuracy and impartiality of standardized tests beyond all reasonable bounds. There is a kind of wishful thinking at work here; we see the supposed power these tests have to predict our lives and the lives of our friends and family. So we reason backward. If tests are this accurate in predicting our destinies, it must be because they are perfect for that purpose, and so this kind of reliance must be fully justified. This assumption about the predictive powers of standardized tests is made by many people who sincerely want a fair chance for everyone in our country. . . . Many of the justifications for the standardized tests that glut our schools, universities, and offices are far less scientific and unchallengeable than many would assume. While these tests can serve a valuable and constructive purpose when used properly, it is vital that we understand and respect their limits as well as their virtues. Otherwise, the way lies open to labeling children and adults, ethnic groups and whole races with false and harmful numbers.

You cannot avoid this threat of test abuse just by leaving the problem in the hands of the experts and hoping that they will come up with a solution. The decision of where, when, and how to use standardized tests reflects our values and priorities as a people. It is a decision that we all must participate in for we will all surely feel its consequences. And it is a decision that we all are *capable* of participating in, for the basic ideas behind the theory of standardized testing are just that: basic. When you strip away the jargon and some of the statistical embellishments, what remains are some fundamentals which are easily understood and dealt with. We are not talking about nuclear physics or quantum mechanics here. If you can add, subtract, multiply, and divide, with or without the help of calculators, you will be able to follow everything said [on this issue] and reach your own conclusions. If you decide to avoid this subject because of the "mystique" of numbers or an excessive deference to professional testers, you will be making a mistake. And you or your children may end up paying a price for that mistake someday. Your ability to handle standardized tests is becoming at least as important a survival skill as balancing a checkbook, filing tax returns, and making change at the grocery store.[2]

FORESIGHT

This chapter attempts to answer two questions. The first question is, "How to select and/or write a test?" Two aspects are covered under this question. First, standardized, ready-made tests; and second, nonstandardized, teacher-made tests. The second question is, "How to interpret test results?" Included under this question are five aspects: (1) measures of central tendency, including the mean, the median, and the mode; (2) the measures of variability, including the range and standard deviation; (3) validity including content, concurrent, predictive, and construct validity; (4) reliability, including retest and split-half reliability; and (5) various scores, including z scores, T scores, stanines, percentiles, and grade equivalency scores.

It should be obvious by now that teaching is an activity for professionals. Not only must the teacher become more expert at determining goals and objectives, selecting learning experiences and establishing classroom climates consistent with those objectives, presenting these experiences in some organized fashion, and guiding and motivating individuals through this organization of experience; she must also develop essential skills in the area of measurement and evaluation. She must learn how to determine, from among other purposes, the extent to which initially stated objectives have been achieved, given the motivational techniques employed through the organization of these experiences.

These measurements have traditionally been classified as either standardized, ready-made tests or teacher-made tests and scales. Both types have much in common, but with some obvious differences. In this chapter these similarities will be highlighted along with the distinctions. The discussion of characteristics of a good measuring instrument includes an interpretation of test results in terms of validity, reliability, variability, and central tendency.

HOW TO SELECT AND/OR WRITE A TEST

STANDARDIZED, READY-MADE TESTS

Standardized, ready-made tests exist in almost every conceivable variable of personal development that is of interest to professional teachers: (1) the cognitive variables, (2) the affective aspects, (3) the psychomotor components, and (4) the interactive dimensions. These four developmental variables would subsume tests of achievement in nearly every subject of the curriculum, as well as special aptitudes, vocational interests, personality, and intelligence.

---

2. Andrew J. Stenio, Jr., excerpt from *The Testing Trap,* pp. xv-xviii. Copyright © 1981 Andrew J. Stenio, Jr. Reprinted with the permission of Rawson Wade Publishers.

These four developmental gradients could be referred to with terms like thinking, feeling, acting, and interacting. They could also be referred to as the rational, emotional, physical, and social aspects of development. The various tests that are on the market within the cognitive domain tend to measure aspects such as information, knowledge, understanding, conceptualizational skills. Tests, inventories, and scales that exist within the affective domain measure aspects of development such as attitudes, opinions, interests, values, preferences, and personal orientations. Tests that exist within the psychomotor, or performance, domain measure aspects such as visual perception and retention, auditory perception and discrimination, muscular coordination, and speech production. Scales within the social domain tend to be interested in evaluating group participation, favorable relationships with one's peers, even ecological or environmental adjustment.

Lest there be some misunderstanding, it should be noted that none of these domains exists in isolation; all of them are interrelated. There is, for example, a cognitive aspect of the affective domain; there is a cognitive aspect of the psychomotor domain; and there is a strong cognitive aspect of the social domain. There is likewise a social aspect of the cognitive area, and of the affective area, and of the active, or performance, area. The crucial point to remember is that none of these domains exists in isolation.

In a contemporary curriculum words such as diagnosis, prognosis, creativity, skills, potential, aptitude, maturation, and exceptionality would apply equally well to each of these four areas. This would also be true of such concepts as norms and profiles, reliability and validity, objectivity and subjectivity, evaluation and assessment, verbal and nonverbal testing, basic learnings and life skills, even competencies and intelligence. Consideration of intelligence, for example, as a function of the cognitive domain only is at best naive. Concluding this point, professional evaluators have spent much time on the *what,* or *thinking,* variables of development. More progress is needed into the *so what,* or feeling, aspects, the *now what,* or acting, components, and the *with what* (or whom) interacting dimensions.

A few years ago several teachers were asked, "What types of test information would you prefer?" Figure 17.1 is a summarization of their responses to that question. Seven obvious conclusions could be drawn from this summary. First, a noteworthy finding was the very high preference for reading comprehension test information and emotional well-being and social adjustment test information. On the other hand, teachers showed a very low preference for vocational aptitude ratings such as clerical, musical, mechanical, artistic, or manual aptitudes. In the general communications area, one should note that reading and listening comprehension, as well as general vocabulary and spelling test information was desired above reading speed and verbal fluency data. Third, in the interests and attitudes area, teachers showed a preference for emotional, social, and school adjustment information above vocational and educational plans. Fourth, in the mental and physical aptitudes and abilities categories, teachers would choose

Teachers' Preferences for Test Information—MEASUREMENT AREAS (41)

Ratings Summary	General Communications	English & Literature	Mathematics, Sciences	Natural Sciences	Social Sciences	Aptitudes & Abilities — Mental	Aptitudes & Abilities — Physical	Interests & Attitudes
5.0	Reading Comprehension[C]							Emotional Well-being
4.5	Listening Comprehension[C] General Vocabulary							Social Adjustment
4.0			Computation[C] Concepts[C]			Study Habits & Skills Creativity		
3.5	Spelling		Story Problems				Non-verbal	School Subjects
3.0		English Usage[C]		Comp.[C]	Comp.[C]	Verbal Reasoning[C] Everyday Problem-solving[C]		
2.5	Reading Speed	English Comp.	Charts, Graphs[F]	Application Vocabulary	Application		Spatial[V]	General
2.0	Verbal Fluency	Library Research			Vocabulary		Manual[V]	
1.5		Essay Writing English Rules[F] Literature Facts		Facts[F]	Facts[F]	Artistic[V]		Vocational[V]
1.0						Musical[V]	Mechanical[V]	Educational Plans
0.5							Clerical[V]	

$Q_{3.5+}$ Very high (Reading, Listening, Vocabulary, especially Emotional and Social).
Q_3/Q_1 Top quarter (most "attractive" to teachers) vs. bottom quarter ("unattractive") tests.

C/F Teacher-preference tendency ("comprehension" tests over "factual" tests).
V   Low vocational aptitude ratings (Clerical, Musical . . . Spatial).

"Very Desirable" — 5.0–4.0
"Desirable" — 3.5–2.5
"Nice" — 2.0
"Not very Attractive" — 1.5–0.5

Adapted from R. H. Baurenfeind, "School Testing Programs," in Stone and Shertzer, eds., *Guidance Monograph, Series III: Testing.* (Boston: HMCO, 1968). Copyright 1968 by Houghton Mifflin Company.—Guidance Monograph Series, Series III, Testing "School Testing Programs" by Robert H. Baurenfeind. Used by permission.

Fig. 17.1

study habits and skills, creativity, and verbal reasoning abilities over the more specialized aptitudes in such areas as spatial ability, plus manual, artistic, mechanical, musical, and clerical abilities. Fifth, in the social and natural science areas, including mathematics, one should note that the teachers showed a preference for comprehension and application test information over the more specific vocabulary and factual type of information.

One might assume that teachers have developed some confidence in their abilities to secure test information in some of these areas that don't receive a high preference—in areas such as vocabulary and factual information. Still another finding from the area of English and literature related to the desire of teachers for tests in English usage and composition over English rules and literature facts. Finally, mention should be made of the overall teacher-preference tendency for tests to measure comprehension, over those tests designed to measure specific vocabulary or factual recall of information.

A next logical question is, "Where will a teacher locate standardized tests to meet her instructional needs?" The Insight box (fig. 17.2) contains a list of twenty-five publishers and distributors of such tests. Attention is called to the more-or-less arbitrary ranking of these sources according to the potential reference to these companies in a comprehensive and contemporary school testing program as partially outlined above. Approximately one-third of these publishing houses supply standardized, cognitive achievement survey test batteries as shown in figure 17.3. A special feature of figure 17.3 is the specific reference to the academic ranges measured by each achievement battery. Standardization of any one of these achievement tests is a complicated, involved, and time-consuming process. It is extremely difficult for a classroom teacher, preoccupied with determining goals and objectives, selecting learning experiences and climates, organizing and presenting materials, guiding and motivating the students, and all the other details of pedagogy, to be an expert and conscientious tester as well. Consequently, she must often seek assistance from those who devote their professional lives to developing tests ready-made for teachers. A ready-made test will generally provide helpful information, but ultimately a test's worth can be decided only by using it in one's immediate context, and then determining how well it assessed those cognitive, affective, active, or interactive objectives of individual students.

How is a standardized or ready-made test prepared? Traditionally the preparation of a standardized test would follow three stages. Stage one would be the stage of specifications and construction; stage two would be the stage of administration and finalization; and stage three would be the stage of publication and distribution.

Stage one of a standardized test construction procedure would include at least five steps. The first step deals with the determination and selection of the objectives the test is to measure. Usually those objectives are determined on the basis of a national survey of relevant courses and curricular guides. It should be pointed out that these objectives would probably fall within those four areas that

Insight: Publishers and Distributors of Standardized Tests*							
	Ranking						
	1	2	3	4	5	6	10
Addison-Wesley Publishing			X̲				
American College Testing		X					
American Council on Education	X̲						
American Guidance Service				X			
Bureau of Educational Research	X						
CTB/McGraw-Hill Publishing				X̲			
Consulting Psychologists Press						X	
Educational and Industrial Testing				X			
Educational Testing Service				X̲			
Harvard University Press	X						
Institute for Personality and Ability Testing					X		
Jastak Associates	X						
NCS Interpretive Scoring		X					
Psychological Corporation							X̲
Psychological Research Center	X						
Psychological Test Specialties		X					
Research Psychologists Press		X					
Riverside Publishing					X̲		
Scholastic Testing Service		X̲					
Science Research Associates						X̲	
Scott, Foresman, and Co.				X̲			
Sheridan Psychological Services		X					
C.H. Stoelting Company		X					
U.S. Employment Service		X					
Western Psychological Services		X					

*Arbitrarily ranked according to potential usage/reference in a comprehensive and contemporary school program.
(Underlined X's indicate a publisher of one or more standardized achievement test batteries, i.e., surveys of general academic development.)

Fig. 17.2

have been discussed above; that is, the cognitive, affective, psychomotor, and social domains.

Step 2 deals with the establishment of a table of specifications as seen in the Insight box (fig. 17.4). The table of specifications might include choosing the type of questions most likely to measure the various aspects of the terminal behaviors; it might deal with the particular types of objectives that are being measured. For example, in figure 17.4 you could note that knowledge objectives exceed comprehension objectives by 70 percent to 30 percent respectively, and that in terms of question type, analogous-type questions exceed multiple-choice type questions by a similar distance of 70 percent to 30 percent.

At step 3 numerous items are written; numerous questions are constructed to fit the table's specifications. Considerable care is taken to insure that a comprehensive coverage of a subject is insured and that ambiguity is avoided in the writing of the items. This reduction of ambiguity requires the efforts of a team of experts—

Popular Standardized Cognitive Achievement Survey Test Batteries: Surveys of General Academic Development

Battery (recent editions)	Publisher	Academic Range				
		Primary	Middle	Inter-mediate	Senior High	College
California Achievement Tests	McGraw-Hill	X	X	X	X	
Comprehensive Tests of Basic Skills	McGraw-Hill	X	X	X	X	
CAP Achievement Series	Scott, Foresman	X	X	X	X	
Iowa Tests of Basic Skills	Riverside	X	X	X		
Iowa Tests of Educational Development	SRA			X	X	
Metropolitan Achievement Test	Psychological Corp.	X	X	X		
SRA Achievement Series	SRA	X	X	X		
STS Educational Development Series	Scholastic Testing Service			X	X	
Sequential Tests of Educational Progress	Addison-Wesley		X	X	X	
Stanford Achievement Test	Psychological Corp.	X	X	X		
Stanford Test of Academic Skills	Psychological Corp.				X	X
Tests of Achievement and Proficiency	Riverside			X	X	
Tests of General Educational Development	ACE		X	X	X	X

Fig. 17.3

Insight: Two-Way Table of Specifications (For: Anastasi, *Psychological Testing*, 5th ed., ch. 1 Quiz)

Chapter Content	Pages	Objectives (%)			Question type (%)	
		Knowledge	Comprehension	Total	M-C	Analogy
1. uses of psychological tests	3-5	5	10	15	10	5
2. early interest in classification	5-6	5	5	10	5	5
3. first experimental psychologists	6-7	5		5		5
4. contributions of Francis Galton	7-8					5
5. Cattell and early "mental tests"	8-10	5		5		5
6. Binet and rise of intelligence tests	10-11	15		15		15
7. group testing	11-12	5		5		5
8. aptitude testing	12-15	5	10	15		15
9. standardized achievement test	15-16	5		5		5
10. assessment of personality	17-18	10	5	15	5	10
11. sources of information about tests	19-21	10		10	10	
TOTAL		70%	30%	100%	30%	70%

Fig. 17.4

professional test specialists, both in the area of the writing of test items and in the particular subject matter or measurement area that is to be tested.

At step 4 preliminary or experimental forms of the test or tests are assembled. In step 5 specific detailed directions or instructions for standardized administration in various locations are prepared. Several crucial questions have already been answered early on in this stage. Two basic questions have to deal with the *how* and the *what* of this particular test that is being designed. *How* questions have to do with method. Method questions typically subsume items such as: Will it be a maximal or a typical performance test? Will it be an individual or a group test? Will it basically emphasize survey or diagnostic qualities? Will it be a measurement of the product or the process involved? Will it be basically a quantitative or a qualitative estimation? Will it be objective or subjective in nature? Will it be basically a language test or a nonlanguage test?

What questions deal with purpose or scope. What will be the purpose of the test? Will it be used to measure mental ability, such as intelligence, or some other forms of aptitude or achievement, or will it be a test to measure interest, attitudes, or even personality? Other questions dealing with the method of testing sometimes revolve around whether or not it will be a speed or a power test and whether or not it will be an emphasis upon common skills as opposed to basic skills. More recently we are seeing an emphasis upon the distinction drawn between criterion-referenced and norm-referenced evaluations. It should be apparent that most classroom tests that are designed by teachers are given to the students at this point and then scored, but the standardized test is subjected to several more operations before it is put to use. The nature of these procedures is indicated by the term "standardized."

Stage two, administration and finalization, also contains five steps. At step 1 several preliminary experimental, or trial, forms of the test may be administered to reasonably representative samples or groups of students or individuals comparable to those with whom the test is designed to be used: that is, if the test is designed to measure mathematics computation skills in a middle schooler, the test is administered to middle schoolers with a wide range of abilities. The general purpose of this administration is to permit item analyses data to be obtained for later purposes. Several forms of the test are constructed and given until the initially stated requirements of the test are met. The flaws in the initial design of the test become visible both during the administration and the scoring of the test and in the statistical analysis of the responses to various items, both in terms of reliability and validity. That process of testing is repeated until a sizeable pool of acceptable items is available.

At step 2, on the basis of these accumulated data, the table of specifications and various item analyses techniques items are either retained or selected for inclusion in the final forms of the test. The test items and the directions are reanalyzed for flaws, and the final form is then put into shape. It should be noted that items that appear to be most valid in terms of how well they discriminate between students who scored high on the test and those who scored low are typically put into the final test.

At step 3, final forms of the test are administered to a different and proportionate sample of students or individuals reflecting regional or urban, rural, and social class differences in order to gather data on which to base the national norms. This test is given under carefully controlled conditions to this representative sample of thousands of students to obtain comparative samples of behavior under different situations and different environments.

At step 4, norm tables are prepared on the basis of the scores from this administration or procedure. This construction of norm tables is what allows the classroom teacher to compare a particular pupil or group of students to students all over the country.

At step 5 a manual is written. The manual will contain answers to such questions as: how the test was constructed, what kinds of items are included, which content areas were surveyed, what groups produced the particular norms, and so on. With some manipulation of statistics, one or more of three basic types of norms are computed, for example, percentile ranks, age and grade equivalents, and standard scores. The manual may also provide substantial claims on the reliability and validity of the test and detailed directions for selecting, administering, scoring, interpreting, reporting the results, and a variety of other bits of information.

Stage three, the stage of publication and distribution, also contains five steps, but these technical marketing concepts will not be covered in this chapter.

It should be highlighted that teacher-made tests may approximate over a period of time some, if not many, of these steps as well; that is, they may be objective, they may have a table of specifications drawn up, the items would be written in terms of that table of specifications, there would be initial forms of the test constructed, these initial forms would be revised over a period of time, and local norms would be established. If differences do exist, they tend to be in the size and number of the groups tested, the higher levels of statistical rigor applied to the data, the availability of a manual, which includes sophisticated data regarding reliabilities and validities. That is, an achievement test, published by one of the concerns that specialize in such measuring instruments, is devised in essentially the same way as a classroom test, up to a point.

The standardization of the testing conditions. A crucial point to keep in mind about administering ready-made tests is the need to follow the suggested procedure. If the instructions supplied for giving a test are not followed exactly, the scores of some students may be distorted by variables that were not present when the test was standardized. Students must be provided the opportunity to respond to commercially prepared tests in the standard manner recommended by the test publisher.

A standardized test generally provides precise directions about the manner in which the test is to be administered. Theoretically, the directions are the same each time the test is given. Such directions usually designate a constant length of time to be allowed for the test, plus the directions to be given to those being examined; they also sometimes describe the exact conditions that should be controlled to ensure comparable performance. Usually included in the directions is information on: the types of pencils and scratch paper recommended, controlled seating and spacing arrangements, specific preparation of the students for taking the test, distributing and collecting the testing materials, the answering of relevant questions from the pupils, and enforcing the prescribed time schedule. For example, maintaining the precise time limits helps to ensure that all individuals taking the test have equal opportunity to perform the tasks in that test. It should also be noted that there are some unprepared teachers that are apt to feel that they should give some students a little extra help, which, of course, often destroys the value of the test, for the

---

**Insight: Administering Standardized Tests
(A "Tale of Two Teachers/Principals")**

One teacher taught in a school with an easygoing, pleasantly addlepated principal; the other, under a very efficient, well-organized principal. A notice was sent to each school announcing that achievement tests were to be administered on a given day. The relaxed principal took a quick glance at the memo, put it on top of the pile on his desk, and forgot about it. The other principal obtained copies of the test booklet and called a special teachers' meeting devoted to familiarizing everyone with the nature of the test and its administration.

When the tests were delivered to the schools on the specified day, the casual principal took them around to his teachers, said, "You're supposed to give these tests," and wandered off. The efficient principal had the booklets distributed to the classrooms, where both students and teachers were poised and prepared. It happened that this particular test featured an answer sheet which was a bit unorthodox. All the teachers who were forced to give the test on the spur of the moment did not catch this, and even those who did discover it were unable to alert their pupils to it very effectively. The teachers in the other school had warned the students ahead of time and quickly demonstrated the way to record answers before the students got to work. Needless to say, the scores earned by students in the two schools varied considerably.

From Robert F. Biehler, *Psychology Applied to Teaching* (Boston: Houghton Mifflin, 1971), pp. 414-15. Used by permission.

Fig. 17.5

teacher cannot, therefore, compare the performance of individuals if some of them have been given the directions as stated, while others have received a little assistance, however kindly intended, on the side. The test directions usually encourage the testee to do his very best, that is, to exhibit maximal performance; or to say merely what he thinks or feels—an example of typical performance. Since ready-made tests scores often play a major role in the academic futures of the pupils, it is important to enhance the validity and the reliability of these tests by providing the most standardized testing situations possible. (In this regard, please see "That's Debatable!" and the Insight box, fig. 17.5, for an interesting comparison.)

Evaluating and selecting a standardized test. The most popular and available source of information on standardized tests are the Buros *Mental Measurements Yearbooks* (MMYs). The table in figure 17.6 contains a percentage listing of approximately one thousand standardized, ready-made tests that are available to the schools. It is apparent from this table that 25 percent of the one thousand, or 250 tests, are classified as natural science measures. Of these 250 tests, 60 percent, or 150, are mathematical in nature and 40 percent, or 100, are classifiable as life science tests. Furthermore, humanities represents one-fifth of the one thousand studies, with 25 percent of these measuring English and composition skills. Approximately 75 tests are listed in the area of reading. Around 100 tests would be classified as multiple aptitude or some related miscellaneous category. Over 200 tests are available in specific vocational areas as well.

With this wide assortment of tests available, how does the teacher or school

Rounded Percentages of Mentions of Standardized Tests in the Most Recent *MMYs* Listed Below in Various Broad Fields (Approximately 1000 Titles Included)

Broad Field	Percent	Sub-fields	Percent
Natural Sciences	25		
		Math Sciences	60
		Life Sciences	40
Humanities	20		
		Foreign Languages	50
		English & Composition	25
Communications	15		
		Reading	50
		Vocabulary	15
Social Sciences	10		
		History	20
		Social Studies	20
Specific Vocations	20		
Multi-aptitude Batteries and Miscellaneous Categories	10		

Fig. 17.6

select the "right" test? Given a well-defined context, including the teachers available, the purpose of evaluation, and budget limitations, answers to the following questions relevant to that context can generally be answered in the MMY or some other source to be noted later, for example:

When was the test published?
How much time is required to administer the test?
For which group, or groups, was the test designed?
Is the content appropriate for your objectives?
Are the directions adequate?
How much effort is required to score it?
Must the examiner be specially trained to administer the test?
What are the qualities of the standardization sample?
What types of scores are generated by the results of the test?
Are equivalent forms of the test available to allow for pre- and post-testing in an instructional situation?
How appropriate are the types of reliability to the particular test?
What were the specific procedures followed in assessing the validity of the test?
Is empirical evidence provided indicating exactly what the test does measure?

In addition to the *Mental Measurements Yearbooks,* numerous other indexes are available, including the *Education Index,* the *Current Index to Journals in Education,* the *Educational Resources Information Center,* even *Psychological Abstracts.* All of these indexes and abstracts will have information on tests and other scales listed under headings such as: Attitudes, Behavior, Intelligence, Interests, Personality, Reading, Social Acceptance, and so on. In addition to these particular headings, there are other headings such as: Educational Measurements, Evaluation, Questionnaire, Psychological Tests, Self-Appraisal, Sociometry, and Testing Programs.

Numerous journals also contain helpful information on the usage of standardized tests in various situations and studies. The *Psychological Bulletin, Psychological Monographs, Psychological Reports, Psychological Review,* as well as the journals of *Applied Psychology, Consulting Psychology, Educational Psychology, Educational Measurement, Clinical Psychology, School Psychology,* and *Educational Research* contain a wealth of information on testing. In addition to these, there is also *American Psychologist, Educational and Psychological Measurement Journal, Child Development, Perceptual and Motor Skills,* and numerous other journals available to the teacher looking for information on testing.

Standardized tests for the busy team of educators. The table in figure 17.7 presents a list of some more-or-less standardized tests for which the author of this chapter has developed an affinity over the past twenty-five years as a teacher, educa-

Standardized Tests/Techniques (Restricted to two per classification)

Intelligence (individual)	Ammons Quick Test of Intelligence
	Slosson Intelligence Test
Intelligence (group)	California Tests of Mental Maturity
	Otis-Lennon Mental Ability Test
Multiple Aptitude	Differential Aptitude Tests
	SRA Primary Mental Abilities
Creativity	Mednick Remote Associates Test
	Torrance Tests of Creativity
Reasoning	Watson-Glaser Critical Thinking Appraisal
	Wilkens Syllogistic Reasoning Test
General Achievement	Metropolitan Achievement Test
	Stanford Achievement Test
Minimum Competency	McGraw-Hill Basic Skills System
	Jastak Wide Range Achievement Tests
Separate Subjects	Evaluation and Adjustment Series
	Sequential Tests of Educational Progress
Phonics	Botel Phonics Mastery Test
	California Phonics Survey
Word Recognition	Daniels/Edwards Word Recognition Lists
	Slosson Oral Reading Test
Vocabulary	EDL Word Clues Test
	WBED Vocabulary Development Series
Spelling	Stone Spelling Checks
	Temple University Spelling Inventory
Reading (individual)	Botel Reading Inventory
	TU Informal Reading Inventory
Reading (group)	Delaware County Silent Reading Test
	Gates-MacGinitie Reading Test
Visual Survey	Kerns Visual Screening Report
	Keystone Visual Survey Test
Auditory	Gates Auditory Perception Test
	Monroe Auditory Word Discrimination Test
Visual-motor	Harris Tests of Lateral Dominance
	Purdue Perceptual-motor Survey
Multiple Modality	Detroit Tests of Learning Aptitude
	Illinois Test of Psycholinguistic Abilities
Social Adjustment	Mother-child Relationship Evaluation
	TU Social Adjustment Inventory
Behavioral Development	Bonaker-Yingling Trait List
	Jaffe Diagnostic Interview Evaluation

Self-report Personality	Eysenck Personality Inventory
	Taylor Biographical Inventory
Personal Values	AVL Study of Values
	Shostrom Personal Orientation Inventory
Occupational Interests	Hackman-Gaither Vocational Interest Inventory
	Minnesota Teacher Attitude Inventory
Study Habits and Skills	Brown-Holtzman Survey of Study Habits & Attitudes
	Spitzer Study Skills Test
Incomplete Sentences	Rotter Incomplete Sentences Blank(s)
	TU Sentence Completion Test
Drawing "Pictures"	Bender Visual-Motor Gestalt Test
	Buck House-Tree-Person Technique

Fig. 17.7

tional consultant to numerous government projects, director of remedial clinics, and college counselor and professor. Note that there has been a restriction of two tests per major classification. A third selection test policy would have allowed the Guilford Series under the Creativity classification, The Stanford Diagnostic Reading Test under Reading, and so on. Some of these tools are becoming a little dated, others require strict scoring to maintain decent reliabilities, but most tend to be easy to administer and provide a heavy load of valuable qualitative and diagnostic data. No attempt is made to suggest that those listed are one whit better than any other that could have been listed, for example, the exclusion of the popular Weschler and Binet Scales, the Kuder, and the Strong Campbell Inventories. Some of these tests have been discussed in an earlier chapter.

TEACHER-MADE EVALUATION TOOLS OR TESTS

Whether in the realm of ready-made or teacher-made tests, one must start with the purposes and aims of one's educational system or program. Every legitimate instructional objective has two parents: the educational goals of the institution and the instructional needs of the child.

Within the opportunities offered by a broad and balanced academic program, any person desiring to be educated—regardless of age, sex, economic status, geographic background, or racial heritage—will be personally dedicated to continuing his development as guided by the following responsibilities and imperative needs: The student will learn (1) consumption responsibilities, (2) recreation responsibilities, (3) occupation responsibilities, (4) symbolization responsibilities, and (5) socialization responsibilities. These five cardinal area or personal and institutional aims of education could just as easily and respectively be called the development of adequate parentalship, sportsmanship, workmanship, scholarship, and citizenship. These five essential areas of education are treated in a separate insert in this section and each is identified with a letter, C-R-O-S-S respectively, which stand for: consumption, recreation, occupation, symbolization, and socialization. These five areas of educational responsibility are not necessarily listed in any priority. They are, however, a cross to be worn or borne by every educator.

Within each of these five cardinal areas are four domains: a cognitive domain, an affective domain, a behavioral domain, and a social domain. The cognitive domain deals with thinking duties, the affective domain subsumes feeling duties, the behavioral domain includes acting duties, and the social domain encapsulates the interacting duties. For too long education has been hung up at the cognitive area in the *what* dimension. It is now time to march on with confidence into the *so what*, the *now what*, and the *with what* or *whom* areas of education. For the sake of brevity only two broad goals per major category have been listed.

Personal and Institutional Aims of Education
Five Cardinal Areas

Within the opportunities offered by a broad and balanced academic program, any person desiring to be educated—regardless of age, sex, economic status, geographic background, or racial heritage—will be personally dedicated to continuing his/her development as guided by the following responsibilities and imperative needs:

C CONSUMPTION RESPONSIBILITIES (Parentalship)
  A. Cognitive/Thinking Duties (what?)
   1. To consider the family unit as a scripturally established, basic institution within which he learns to become socially and economically literate
   2. To understand the values received by the household consumer and the economic consequences of his actions as an informed and efficient buyer
  B. Affective/Feeling Duties (so what?)
   1. To value and conserve the scriptural ideals for the family as these benefit the optimal development of individuals
   2. To develop sound, judgmental standards for guiding his personal and domestic expenditures
  C. Behavioral/Acting Duties (now what?)
   1. To become more personally skilled at establishing and maintaining the conditions conducive to successful family life
   2. To become more capable of planning the economic aspects of his family and personal life by purchasing and using goods and services intelligently
  D. Social/Interacting Duties (with what?)
   1. To maintain a family relationship, based upon well understood scriptural principles, within the democratic cooperation of its members
   2. To take when necessary the appropriate leadership responsibilities to provide the protective measures which would safeguard the economic interests of his home and family

R RECREATION RESPONSIBILITIES (Sportsmanship)
  A. Cognitive/Thinking Duties (what?)
    1. To demonstrate sufficient mental resources for the development of a suitable range of creative and personal interests
    2. To increasingly understand the basic scientific facts concerning the nature of the divinely created world, including man and his potential for either healthy or unhealthy mental and physical growth
  B. Affective/Feeling Duties (so what?)
    1. To find ongoing personal satisfactions in the beauty expressed through literature, art, music, drama, nature, and other creative expressions
    2. To exercise his opportunities for the pursuit of happiness through the attainment and preservation of mental and physical health
  C. Behavioral/Acting Duties (now what?)
    1. To give responsible direction to his own life as he wisely budgets the worthy uses of his own leisure time as a skilled participant and spectator in many individualized and group sports and other esthetic and recreational pastimes
    2. To assure himself and, eventually, his dependents of optimal growth to adult status by protecting and maintaining his own mental and physical health
  D. Social/Interacting Duties (with what?)
    1. To maintain a balance between activities that yield personal satisfactions with those that are socially useful
    2. To work and play with others in a cooperative manner which will improve the general health of his wider community

O OCCUPATIONAL RESPONSIBILITIES (Workmanship)
  A. Cognitive/Thinking Duties (what?)
    1. To exhibit a mental and spiritual orientation for a life of educated, vocational production, given the essential and suitable personal abilities
    2. To progressively understand the skills and knowledge requirements plus other occupational information regarding the opportunities for various jobs
  B. Affective/Feeling Duties (so what?)
    1. To willingly assume the attitudes that assist the worker to be an intelligent and productive participant in economic life
    2. To personally feel the satisfaction that comes from the self-discipline required to establish good work habits
  C. Behavioral/Acting Duties (now what?)
    1. To acquire the skills which will improve his own vocational competency and efficiency by allowing him to make the necessary adjustments to be successful in his chosen vocation
    2. To develop salable skills within reasonable opportunities for personal growth which comes from engagement in absorbing personal goals
  D. Social/Interacting Duties (with what?)
    1. To engage in supervised and exploratory vocational experiences at all steps of vocational awareness and selection
    2. To appreciate the social value and usefulness of his chosen occupation as he lives and works cooperatively with others

S SYMBOLIZATION RESPONSIBILITIES (Scholarship)
  A. Cognitive/Thinking Duties (what?)
     1. To cultivate his God-given abilities, within his command of the fundamental academic processes, to observe critically, think rationally, and communicate clearly
     2. To demonstrate his understanding of the physical world through the acquisition of the verbal and numerical symbols of his mother tongue
  B. Affective/Feeling Duties (so what?)
     1. To experience satisfactions from his intellectual curiosity and academic achievements
     2. To express an insatiable appetite for learning through the solution of verbal and mathematical problems
  C. Behavioral/Acting Duties (now what?)
     1. To be increasingly skilled in the basic decoding skills of listening and reading
     2. To become more efficient in the basic encoding skills of speaking and writing
  D. Social/Interacting Duties (with what?)
     1. To demonstrate his ability to think and evaluate for the constructive benefits to others as well as himself
     2. To become more adequately prepared for intelligent and self-directed lifelong learning

S SOCIALIZATION RESPONSIBILITIES (Citizenship)
  A. Cognitive/Thinking Duties (what?)
     1. To grow in his insight into the ethical values and scriptural principles which should undergird the civic rights and duties of a citizen in a democratic society
     2. To understand basic social structures, processes, pressures, and legal responsibilities with the necessary cognitive defenses against propaganda
  B. Affective/Feeling Duties (so what?)
     1. To respect and observe the law and be legally sensitive to the disparities of human circumstances within the context of his appreciation of a variety of human values from different persons
     2. To appreciate our democratic heritage by enjoying the rich, sincere, and varied social life and by showing tolerance for honest differences of opinion
  C. Behavioral/Acting Duties (now what?)
     1. To maintain successfully, by individually observing the amenities of social behavior, certain definite civic, social, and community relationships
     2. To be personally diligent, socially competent, and progressively more mature in his performance of his obligations, as a member of his community, to correct unsatisfactory social conditions
  D. Social/Interacting Duties (with what?)
     1. To cooperate in social relations with his peers and as a member of a state, national, and world community which would measure all progress by its contributions to the general welfare
     2. To act with an unswerving loyalty to democratic ideals and be prepared to assume full responsibilities of American citizenship

A few keys in each domain should be noted; for example, in the thinking domain: words such as understanding, information, knowledge, rationality, and insight; in the feeling domain, words such as valuation, judgment, satisfaction, willingness, respect, and sensitivity; in the acting domain: words such as skillfulness, utilization, direction, competency, and adjustment; and in the interacting domain: words such as relationship, leadership, cooperation, engagement, community, and loyalty.

These educational goals must now be translated into instructional objectives and specific learning outcomes. The test items written by the teacher, or teachers, are dependent upon the preciseness of those objectives. Unfortunately, in many schools, these necessary connections between institutional aims, educational goals, and course objectives are difficult to detect. The negative fallout, in terms of both staff and student confusion, is almost unavoidable in these situations. Summer workshops and other forms of inservice and collective dialogues should be directed at either establishing or revising this communication between goals and objectives.

Once the connections have been made, the teacher can begin to select or devise techniques of evaluation. References listed at the end of this chapter contain excellent details on the planning, preparation, reproduction, administration, scoring, and analyzing of various forms of teacher-made tests. The numerous

An Example of an Anecdotal Record Form

Date: __9/24/84__ Pupil: __Laurie D.__
Time: __12:20 p.m.__ Grade: __9__

OBJECTIVE DESCRIPTION OF INCIDENT (the pupil's actions):
While scoring the math homework papers collected in the Period I Math section, I noticed that Laurie seemed to be getting the correct answers to several problems, but her work, i.e., the procedures shown for deriving those answers, did not seem to support her answers. Eight of ten answers to the problems appear to have been erased prior to the writing of her final answers.

SUBJECTIVE EVALUATION OF INCIDENT (your reaction to them):
I suspect that the homework assignment was too difficult for Laurie. She has probably "borrowed" answers from a friend prior to turning in her paper.

SUGGESTED REMEDIATION/COURSE OF ACTION (your interpretation of the cause of the action is implied):
An attempt will be made to insure that future homework assignments can be done independently by each student, expecially Laurie D.

Observer: __R. Tschetter (teacher)__

Fig. 17.8

advantages and limitations of each form are also supplied. Traditional classifications include both essay and objective test items, such as multiple choice, matching, and true-false.

Because the tools and techniques of observation are frequently overlooked by teachers, these will be emphasized here. Observation tools include anecdotal records, checklists, rating scales, participation charts, and sociometric devices. Despite the obvious difficulties encountered with validity and reliability, the teacher who overlooks the advantages of these forms of *direct* observational data will be, in our opinion, disregarding "acres of diamonds."

Anecdotal records (here the word *anecdotal* means "to not give out," that is, information kept within the confines of the significant instructional staff) can be kept on children who need special observation in any area or domain of development. A school system should have standard record forms which include spaces for the data, time of day, pupil's name, and observer's signature. Care should be taken to distinguish objective description from subjective evaluations. Some forms also include suggested courses of action as seen in figure 17.8. Forms should be written out daily and kept as long as useful, for example, for staffing purposes or parent conferences.

The professional educator will also use *checklists* to secure information helpful to each child. Some checklists are used as a basis for referring a child for special help, as the *Bonaker-Yingling Trait List* in figure 17.9. This trait list is used to refer children who may need more assistance in their perceptual development (items 1-15), their emotional growth (items 16-28), or for greater intellectual stimulation (items 29-30). Typically the higher the saturation of checks made by the teacher, the higher the priority for immediate attention by ancillary staff personnel.

Bonaker-Yingling Trait List
(Teacher Referral of Pupil Needs)

Student's Name _____ Parents _____
School _____ County _____ Address _____
Grade _____ Date of Birth _____ 19_____ Teacher _____

TO: The Classroom Teacher

This form is used to identify a pupil who has some kind of a problem which interferes with adaptation to the school program; the pupil who is not making the desired progress and needs special attention to locate the problem.

The classroom teacher is the one person who is most likely to be aware of the unmet needs and problems of the students. These students may have emotional, social, physical, or mental problems. Gifted students who are not being challenged sufficiently by the regular school program should also be reported.

You are the key person to make the report. No progress is possible until the individual pupil is identified. You are not expected to be a diagnostician, or to pinpoint the exact nature of the problem. Please use this form to identify each pupil you consider to be in need of attention.

Please give a description of this pupil's problem(s) based on your observations:

_____
_____

In your opinion what services or programs, not currently available, would benefit this pupil? _____
_____

TRAITS

(Check (✔) all applicable to this pupil)

_____1. Has severe word recognition difficulties.
_____2. Does not learn by reading but can only learn by listening.
_____3. Loses place easily while reading.
_____4. Does not express self well orally. Has great difficulty in writing and spelling.
_____5. Writes laboriously, cramped fingers, uneven pressure.
_____6. Speaks indistinctly, slurs, mumbles.
_____7. Does not grasp concepts of numbers, space, time, directionality.
_____8. Makes oral and written reversals. Has difficulty with left to right progression.
_____9. Cannot concentrate. Has short memory span. Does not hear fast. Can hear but fails to understand.
_____10. Does not voluntarily work up to potential.
_____11. Day dreams excessively. Does not participate.
_____12. Is very verbal. Makes excuses. Tries to cover up failures.
_____13. Has no inner motivation, no curiosity.
_____14. Is eager, enthusiastic. Well informed but cannot read.
_____15. Is physically awkward. Lacks basic coordination. Drops things frequently.
_____16. Is extremely hyperactive. Has little self-control, impulsive.
_____17. Has good and bad days, behavior varies.
_____18. Does not respond to teacher's voice or to other sounds outside his range of vision.
_____19. Has difficulty in focusing. Eyes wander, jerky.
_____20. Feels inadequate. Is often depressed. Lacks confidence.
_____21. Does not relate well to other children.
_____22. Appears upset. Is often disturbed about family problems.
_____23. Has temper tantrums when not given his own way.
_____24. Withdraws from class mentally, physically, socially.
_____25. Is extremely aggressive.
_____26. Is frequently tired. Lacks energy or strength.

____27. Is unhappy, scowls, surly, obstinate.
____28. Is overly sensitive. Feels unwanted. Cries easily.
____29. Is unchallenged by present program level.
____30. Is active, curious. Works ahead of assignments.

E.S.E.A. (Elementary Secondary Education Act), Title 1 funded research project.
Fig. 17.9

Other checklists might be used to note early indicators of talents or gifts as in figure 17.10. The potential range of interest is almost infinite, but teachers can gather direct observations for subsequent occupational-vocational counseling purposes. Note that a checklist simply indicates the presence or absence of a behavior.

Space does not permit a lengthy discussion of any of these observational techniques. Only one kind of *rating scale* is shown in figure 17.11. This Chen Course Evaluation Form is an example of a numerical-descriptive rating scale. In addition to the numerals one to five, abbreviated and consistent descriptors are also supplied for each rating level. Note, for example, that items 1, 2, and 4 could be subsumed as in a cognitive category; items 3 and 6 in an affective dimension; items 5 and 8 in a behavioral domain; and item 7 in a social classification. There is a danger illustrated in this rating scale known as reponse-set, that is, the students can easily and generously mark all of the ones, or severely mark all of the fives.

Participation charts, sociometric devices, autobiographical sketches, case studies, and other observational techniques will be discussed at a later time.

Checklists

Our example examines a complex trait we might designate as an interest, talent, or gift in music:

	Yes	No
1. Comments on the music played on the radio or television.	___	___
2. Talks about musical topics, in general.	___	___
3. Creates special friendships with teachers of music.	___	___
4. Learns to play a musical instrument.	___	___
5. Reads biographies about musicians.	___	___
6. Volunteers to play her instrument for the enjoyment of others.	___	___
7. Joins a local, school or community, musical group.	___	___
8. Spends hard-earned money purchasing printed music.	___	___
9. Selects and customizes assignment in other context areas to coincide with music (e.g., in history class, she writes on the topic of the history of violin making).	___	___
10. Attends a summer camp for musicians.	___	___

Fig. 17.10

Measurement—Student Performance 441

Chen Course Evaluation Form

Course and number _____ Section _____
Major _____ Classification _____
Q.P.A. _____ No. of Psychology Courses taken _____
Social Security Number _____
Rate the course on each of the following items by drawing a circle around the number that best indicates its position in comparison with other courses you have taken. The course: _____

	Outstanding	Superior	Competent	Only Fair	Less Value Than Other Courses
1) Has interpreted ideas and theory clearly	1	2	3	4	5
2) Has increased my skills in thinking	1	2	3	4	5
3) Has broadened my interest in teaching	1	2	3	4	5
4) Has given me new viewpoints	1	2	3	4	5
5) Has shown ability to relate and communicate	1	2	3	4	5
6) Has fulfilled my personal and vocational needs	1	2	3	4	5
7) Has provided opportunity for interaction	1	2	3	4	5
8) Has motivated me to do my best work	1	2	3	4	5

Dr. S. Andrew Chen. Doctoral research at University of Pittsburgh, 1970.

Fig. 17.11

How to Interpret Test Results

CENTRAL TENDENCY

Figure 17.12 contains the scores of twenty-five students on a hypothetical science quiz. The maximum raw score was ten, and the lowest raw score was four. Figure 17.13 presents a tally of these separate scores, that is, how many scores appear at each of the possibilities from four to ten. Note that the most common score is seven, that is, seven students received this score. Seven is, therefore, the *mode* of this distribution of scores. Seven is also the score which divides the number of scores into two equal groups; therefore, it could also be called the *median*. If we were to add all the scores, we would obtain a total of 175. This total divided by the number of scores, that is, 25, equals the *mean*, that is, 7. Because this group of scores is symmetrical, or evenly distributed on each side of the mid-point, these three measures of central tendency are identical.

Student Scores on a Ten-item Science Quiz

Student	Score	Student	Score
A	6	N	9
B	9	O	10
C	5	P	7
D	8	Q	5
E	7	R	8
F	6	S	7
G	8	T	6
H	4	U	8
I	7	V	7
J	6	W	7
K	8	X	9
L	5	Y	6
M	7	Z	(absent)

Fig. 17.12

Science Quiz Score Frequencies

Score	Tallies	Frequency (f)	Cf
10	I	1	25
9	III	3	24
8	IIII	5	21
7	IIII II	7	16
6	IIII	5	9
5	III	3	4
4	I	1	1
3		0	0
		N = 25	

Fig. 17.13

VARIABILITY

Two common measures of variability are used. The first is the *range*. The range is simply the highest score minus the lowest score plus one. In the science quiz, the scores received ranged from ten to four. Seven different scores were received: ten, nine, eight, seven, six, five, and four. This is equal to the range, that is, ten minus four plus one equals seven.

The standard deviation (SD) is a little more complicated than the range, but

Method of Computing Standard Deviation
(for Science Quiz)

Magnitude of scores	Number of scores of magnitude	Total value of all scores of each magnitude	Total value of the scores of each magnitude squared	
10	1	10	$(10^2 \times 1)$	100
9	3	27	$(9^2 \times 3)$	243
8	5	40	$(8^2 \times 5)$	320
7	7	49	$(7^2 \times 7)$	343
6	5	30	$(6^2 \times 5)$	180
5	3	15	$(5^2 \times 3)$	75
4	1	4	$(4^2 \times 1)$	16
	N = 25	175 (total of all scores)		1277 (total of each score squared)

$$\frac{\sqrt{1277 - 25 \times 7^2}}{(n-1)} = \frac{\sqrt{1277 - 1225}}{24} = \frac{\sqrt{52}}{24} = \sqrt{2.16} = 1.47 = SD$$

Fig. 17.14

since the SD is used in so many other calculations, it assumes some more significance. Calculation of the SD is shown in figure 17.14.

VALIDITY

Of the many types of validity, the following four will be discussed.

1. *Content validity* indicates the specific content of a test is appropriate for the way the test is used. There is an attempt to answer the question: How well does the test sample in the area being measured?

2. *Concurrent validity* is the measure of the accuracy of a test to measure its relationship to contemporary criteria. There is an attempt to answer the question: How well does this test correlate with other current and relevant evidences of classroom achievement?

3. *Predictive validity* answers the question: How well does this test anticipate future performance of the student?

4. *Construct validity* attempts to answer the question: How well does this test correlate with a psychological basis underlying both the test and a theoretical position?

Different types of tests require different types of validity. A good achievement test would be expected to have high content validity, and an occupational interest survey might be expected to have high "predictivability."

RELIABILITY

Of the many types of reliability, only two will be mentioned here: (1) *Test-retest reliability* indicates the degree of stability between two sets of test scores obtained from one group of students, for example, in a pretest-posttest situation with the same test in an equivalent form. (2) *Split-half reliability* deals with the extent of relationship between two parts of the same test, for example, the odd-numbered items related to the even-numbered items. Some tests, for example some speed tests, are not amenable to the latter type of reliability.

VARIOUS SCORES

Many current tests make extensive use of various forms of scores. The following four types will be discussed:

(1) *z scores* are computed by finding the difference between the individual's raw score and the mean of the base group and dividing this difference by the standard deviation of that group. For example, student 0 in our science quiz above, with a raw score of 10, would have a z score of approximately 2.0, more exactly, plus 2.04.

(2) *T scores* have an arbitrary mean of 50, and a standard deviation of 10. A T score of 70 equals a z score of plus 2.0, and a T score of 35 equals a z score of minus 1.5

(3) Stanines have a mean of 5, a standard deviation of 2.3, and an arbitrary range of 1-9 ("stanine" is a contraction of two words, "standard" and "nine"). Twenty percent of the scores fall with the fifth stanine, while only 4 percent fall in each of the first and ninth stanines.

(4) *Percentile scores* indicate the percentage of persons in the sample who fall at or below a given raw score secured by a single individual. A P_{50} score means that the individual has scored as well as, or better than, 50 percent of the standardization sample.

Each score has it limitations and its advantages, but all are being used in our schools today.

HINDSIGHT

In retrospect, we want to emphasize the necessity for carefully establishing one's specific objectives prior to either selecting a ready-made test or constructing one's own teacher-made tools. These objectives, which are fathered by the purposes and aims of one's institution, as well as the specific needs of a child or group of students, lend the necessary direction to a teacher's choices of tests, items, formats, and so on.

Ready-made tests offer the advantages of the rigorous standardization procedure, plus a set of norms to which one's classroom can generally be referenced or compared. Teacher-constructed tests could supply local norms as well as test data that compare quickly to various local criteria of achievement, even some forms of mastery in all four domains of achievement—the rational, attitudinal, behavioral, and social components of a complete education. With proper selections and interpretations of tests, the C-R-O-S-S should be bearable by any teacher.

Chalkboard Challenges

1. In a sense this chapter is a summarization of a vast number of ideas. Many areas could not be treated because of limitations of space. As a challenge to you, the student, select one area that you consider to be inadequately summarized and volunteer to present an oral report to the class in that particular area. For example, you might select some tests that all fall within a similar area or content area, or some concepts that could be stated more clearly.

2. To facilitate your own comprehension of some of the more difficult concepts, you might involve yourself in the charting of some related ideas, for example, the various types of validity or reliability, many of which were not even stated here. You might at this point construct an overhead transparency and color it well, illustrate it well, and plan to share it, either orally or in some written fashion, with your classmates or the professor, or both.

3. The area of tests and measurements is replete with pressing controversial issues: for example, measurement in the affective domain, minimum competency testing, the value of diagnosis in teaching, the fairness of tests to both sexes, the fairness of tests to various ethnic groups, testing individuals with special handicaps or needs, the role of objectives in educational evaluation, the relative value of norm versus criterion referenced tests, the use of tests in selection decisions, and numerous other pressing issues. The student could identify with one of these pressing controversial issues. Spend some time in the library, locate some articles that relate to that particular issue, and share a condensation, even a potential solution, or a step in the direction of a solution, to some of these pressing issues.

4. Begin your own test file. Locate the addresses of some of the publishers; secure their ideas on the tests that they publish, especially those tests related to your particular speciality. For example, if you plan to be a mathematics teacher, begin to locate those tests that relate to your particular area. If you plan to be a teacher of English, begin to locate those tests that relate to that particular area as well, and begin to develop your own personalized file that will be of valuable use to you in a few short semesters.

5. Practice actual calculations. Identify with some college professor who is giving tests, and ask to use his or her test data. Calculate percentiles, T scores, z scores, and other types of calculations that may be of help to that professor. Report your information back to this class.

6. Try your hand at constructing your own test. Look at the various types of tests that were mentioned in this chapter. Establish your own objectives. Try to write an objective test. Try to write also an essay or subjective test. Report to the class the particular challenges or problems that you faced in this area.

7. Create a thirty-minute multimedia presentation on testing and measurement that would be intended for a group of teachers of the sort that you might someday be working with. Include the various ideas that have been discussed in this particular chapter or an assortment of those ideas as you consider them relevant to that particular group of teachers.

Want to Know More?

OBJECTIVES

From the many books on the writing of objectives, we suggest three that have helped many students:

William J. Kryspin and John F. Feldhusen, *Writing Behavioral Objectives: A Guide to Planning Instruction* (Minneapolis: Burgess, 1974).

Paul D. Plowman, *Behavioral Objectives: Teacher Success Through Student Performance* (Chicago: Science Research Associates, 1971).

W. James Popham, *The Uses of Instructional Objectives: A Personal Perspective* (Belmont, Calif.: Fearon, 1973).

STATISTICAL MEASURES

For the conscientious student who is looking for more help on statistical measures and test scores we recommend the following three books:

Frank F. Gorow, *Statistical Measures: A Programmed Text* (San Francisco: Chandler, 1962).

Howard B. Lyman, *Test Scores and What They Mean*, 3d ed. (Englewood Cliffs, N.J.: Prentice Hall, 1978).

G. Milton Smith, *A Simplified Guide to Statistics for Psychology and Education*, 3d ed. (New York: Holt, Rinehart, and Winston, 1962).

TEST CONSTRUCTION

If you would like more help on the constructing of classroom tests, these three books would be of help:

Frank F. Gorow, *Better Classroom Testing* (San Francisco: Chandler, 1966).

John A. Green, *Teacher-Made Tests*, 2d ed. (New York: Harper & Row, 1975).

Lillian C. Howitt, *Practical Classroom Testing* (Englewood Cliffs, N.J.: Teachers Practical Press, 1961).

CONTROVERSIAL ISSUES

For the student interested in some of those chalkboard challenges related to the issues in tests and measurements, these three books would be recommended:

Collins Lacey and Denis Lawton, eds., *Issues in Evaluation and Accountability* (London: Metheun, 1981).

Gallery of Greats

Edward L. Thorndike
Exercise: "Practice makes perfect."
Effect: Rewards strengthen a behavior.
Punishment weakens a behavior.
(Courtesy The Granger Collection, New York)

A personality driven by his sense of perfection, with little regard for those who had come before him, Thorndike based his theories on scientific data, observation, and took great pride in his work. He began life in 1874 in Williamsburg, Massachusetts, and by 1922 had become director of the University Division of Psychology in the Institute of Educational Research at Columbia University. His two most famous "laws" were the laws of exercise and effect, even though both had some flaws in them.

Exercise alone, without feedback, does not necessarily improve performance.

And there are situations in which rewards do not strengthen behavior, nor punishment suppress it. Nevertheless, Thorndike extended Pavlov's work from the laboratory to more natural settings, involving learning through trial and error, and became a forerunner of Skinnerian behaviorism. Thorndike is known also for his attack upon the "mental discipline" approach to education, which affirmed that by studying science and the classics, one could train the mind. His work has contributed greatly to modern reinforcement theory, which is reflected in the many forms of programmed learning to be found in schools today.

Lawrence Lipetz, ed., *The Test Score Decline: Meaning and Issues* (Englewood Cliffs, N.J.: Educational Technology Publications, 1977).

Andrew J. Strenio, Jr., *The Testing Trap* (New York: Rawson, Wade, 1981).

MEASUREMENT AND EVALUATION

The student who is looking for a well-rounded look at the whole area of measurement and evaluation in teaching couldn't go far wrong with these three following recommendations:

Norman E. Gronlund, *Measurement and Evaluation in Testing*, 3d ed. (New York: Macmillan, 1976).

Tom Kubiszyn and Gary Borich, *Educational Testing and Measurement: Classroom Application and Practice* (Glenview, Ill.: Scott Foresman, 1984).

William A. Mehrens and Irvin J. Lehmann, *Measurement and Evaluation in Education and Psychology*, 3d ed. (New York: Holt, Rinehart, and Winston, 1984).

For the student who has developed an intense fascination for the field of measurement and evaluation we would recommend these three books:

Scarvia B. Anderson, Samuel Ball, and Richard T. Murphy, et al., *Encyclopedia of Educational Evaluation* (San Francisco: Jossey-Bass, 1975).

Paul L. Dressel, *Handbook of Academic Evaluation* (San Francisco: Jossey-Bass, 1976).

W. James Popham, ed., *Evaluation and Education: Current Applications* (Berkeley, Calif.: McCutchan, 1974).

TESTING SPECIALTY

If the student plans to go on into graduate school and specialize more in either administration or some higher levels of education, these following three books are highly recommended.

Anne Anastasi, *Psychological Testing*, 5th ed. (New York: Macmillan, 1982).

Paul McReynolds, ed., *Advances in Psychological Assessment*, vol. 1 (Palo Alto, Calif.: Science and Behavior Books, 1968).

Richard M. Wolf, *Evaluation in Education: Foundations of Competency Assessment and Program Review*, 2d ed. (New York: Praeger, 1984).

18
Measurement—Student Feedback

MAURICE STONE

CONTENTS

	PAGE
Key Terms	449
That's Debatable!	451
Foresight	451
How to Report Test Results	451
Uses and Abuses of Tests	459
Other Means of Evaluation	462
Hindsight	463
Chalkboard Challenges	463
Want to Know More?	463

KEY TERMS

Academic
   Generally a designation of the cognitive aspects of instruction, specifically the formalized school subjects such as the sciences, humanities, etc.

Acceleration
   Developmental progress more rapid than the average in any of several possible areas such as mental, physical, social

Basic skills
   The minimally required skills in reading, writing, and arithmetic essential to further academic development

Chronological age
: A person's "calendar age"; the length of time one has lived; abbreviated "CA"

Curriculum
: All the academic subjects plus other planned or incidental experiences through which the institutional goals and objectives are to be accomplished

Evaluation
: An interpretation of test results which includes comparative-judgmental terms, such as bigger, faster, better

Exceptional children
: Children who deviate from norms in ways that suggest the need for specialized instructional programs

Feedback
: Initial, medial, or final information on learning given to teachers, students, and parents to facilitate maximal developmental progress

Formative evaluation
: Evaluation during instruction to provide corrective feedback for the benefit of both the students and the teacher

Grade equivalents
: The grade levels which correspond to the mean scores on standardized tests of a normative sample of children at each grade level

Grades
: The symbols, or marks, (A, B, C, etc.) given by a teacher to indicate the extent of a student's accomplishment in a particular assignment or course of instruction

Halo effect
: A factor influencing, either positively or negatively, evaluations of products or processes from students known in other ways

Interaction
: Mutual influence between the participants in a defined group

Mastery learning
: Progress from one learning unit to another should be based upon fully learning each successive task

Participation chart
: A record of both the quantity and quality of each individual's contributions to a group exchange of ideas

Remedial teaching
: Specialized instruction aimed at correcting specific learning dysfunctions

Sociometry
: Procedures for describing, measuring, and interpreting group interaction structures

Summative evaluation
: Evaluation at the end of an instructional sequence used to provide a final estimate of student achievement

That's Debatable!

What is important, I think, is the process that has carried me to the point where I can say with conviction, "grades, as used in 97 percent of our schools, are *the key factor* in the perpetuation of a schooling process which has failed to accomplish its own expectations." I need not cite the unhappy facts of illiteracy, conflict, and teacher despair that characterize our schools. Parents, students, and teacher are trapped in a system in which the real, but hidden agenda is control, not learning, and where the ultimate weapon of control is the grade.

Those who support traditional grading will argue that the fact rests with the teachers (always convenient scapegoats), rather than with the grading system itself. This argument, wrongly, I think, idealizes the teacher as a being with no faults, no weaknesses, no personal opinions—a fantasy of perfection. But grading forces every teacher, no matter what her/his beliefs, to adopt an evaluation system the essence of which is to hamper, to devalue, and to destroy individual self-worth. No matter what good intentions a teacher caught in this system may harbor, or how she/he may play down the negative aspects of grades; no matter how the class may be involved in decisions about grading standards, or what humane strategies may be used to counteract the atmosphere, one bitter reality remains: at semester's end, the verdict comes, camouflaged as an A, B, C, D, or F.

Let there be no misunderstanding. I believe that grading is morally wrong, practically ineffecive, and a major deterrent to learning. I believe that no teacher should be forced to grade, and no student be graded. These are basic rights. I do not say that evaluation is unimportant to the learning process. It is important. I do not suggest we sweep away grades with one immediate stroke. I do say that every teacher, student, and parent should strive to eradicate the grading game as quickly as practicable. With that key out of the lock, we can open the door to more successful teaching and more beneficial learning.[1]

Foresight

In the former chapter, the selection, construction, and interpretation of tests was discussed. This chapter treats the subsequent questions of reporting the results of those tests to both the student and his parents. We are also reminded of the numerous uses and potential abuses in various testing and reporting practices. A brief summary statement is added at the end dealing with some of the many other means of facilitating maximal student achievement of the desired instructional objectives.

How to Report Test Results

Both the student and the parents are entitled to receive feedback from the tests administered to them. School personnel, including the guidance and

---

1. James A. Bellanca, *Grading* (Washington, D.C.: National Education Association, 1977), pp. 7-8. Used by permission.

counseling staff, the instructional team, and the administrative and ancillary personnel, share a common responsibility, that of communicating measurement and evaluation contents to various publics, or groups. In this next section we delineate not only "what is said" but "to whom." Interested groups include: the parents of minors, one's colleagues, and the student himself. Methods, or media, include: report cards, conferences, personal letters, and ongoing daily feedback to the individual student.

ASSIGNING GRADES/MARKS

Teachers who assign marks continue to consider them an unfortunate chore; the older the student becomes the more they distrust them; and measurement experts find great discomfort in their souls upon contact with them—yet they continue to impose a mysterious and charming effect on many educators. In spite of the wisest counsel, they remain as one of the most popular means of transmitting achievement data for students. And, in spite of their questionable philosophical origins, they continue to thrive in the strangest places.

The research literature on grades continues to overflow with pervasive and persistent problems. These challenges posed by the assignment of grades need much more attention from many more teachers and others than they typically receive. If one places confidence in the research, grades continue to be a poor indication of actual achievement, they are often assigned with an insufficient data base, there is an extensive oversimplification of a very complex performance implied when a simple letter seems to say it all about a student.

On top of this problem, the problem of oversimplification, is the relative absence of objectivity in determining them. The assignment of grades is replete with judgment and measurement errors. The students can easily manipulate the teacher by feigning interest in the content being taught, by sitting at the front of the class, by asking questions, by visiting the teacher in off class hours, etc. The halo effect runs rampant. Personality conflicts between the teacher and an individual student can awaken a negative halo. The journals are filled with articles on the influence of cultural bias in the assignment of grades. Male/female contaminants are also a significant factor. Male teachers tend to favor female students over male students, especially the more attractive female students. Female teachers conversely tend to favor male students over female students. And in spite of all these persistent problems, they continue to impart that sense of finality that they rarely deserve.

What, then, are the functional purposes of grades? What principles does a teacher follow while assigning marks? A few points should be underlined at this point: (1) There should be a consensus within a school system on the specifics of a grading policy. If that consensus is absent, numerous harmful vibrations can develop. This grading policy agreed upon with the school staff should be flexible enough to account for shifts in student body characteristics or class size or different levels of course work. (2) Each student should be kept aware of the progress of his grade during the course. This tends to provide an additional motivational factor. (3) The grading policy of each course, of each class, should be fully explained to the students at the beginning of each semester. It should be fully comprehended by each student, as well as by the parents of younger children. The weightings given to various activities relative to the course objectives should also be made obvious to the students. (4) The marks received by a student should constitute the most accurate reflection of his achievement of the instructional objectives set for a particular course. Some teachers use initial diagnostic tests, followed by formative and summative test data in these calculations. The more accurate the grading system, the greater the help to the student and his parents in the making of educational plans. (5) Grades should *not* be used for disciplinary purposes. This policy tends not to work. In summary, the assignment of a mark or a grade should *only* be done in reference to the function that mark is designed to serve.

How does a teacher choose a standard for her grading policies? Some criterion is needed before a grade can be given. The research literature provides no direct theoretical basis for any of several methods. The choice of a method tends to be solely a matter of school policy. We shall look at three popular grading methods: (1) The individual or variable standard method, sometimes referred to as ability grading, is an attempt to award grades based upon the ability of each individual student. (2) The fixed standard for all students method generally employs a criterion set by the teacher prior to the offering of her class. This is the most frequently used method in this country. The grade assigned is indicative of a level of mastery with respect to the established or set criteria. Unfortunately, standards do vary between teachers, and classes do vary from year to year. (3) The group or norm-referenced standard method is a relative approach. The student's achievement is compared to the achievement of a group, for example, his class or former classes taught by that instructor. If the grades approximate a normal curve, those students above the average tend to recive A's or B's. Those below the average tend to receive D's or F's.

REPORT CARDS

A school's report card policy should answer the following three questions: (1) To whom? (2) For what purpose? (3) To what degree of detail? Given an answer to these three questions a report card should (a) accurately reflect the educational philosophy of the school system, (b) be understandable by both the student and his parents, (c) be moving in the direction of computerization of data transmitted, (d) be supplemented with conferences with the parents and the student, and (e) be consistent with legal restrictions, for example, the Family Educational Right to Privacy Act and the Buckley-Pell amendment to the General Education Provision Act.

PARENT-TEACHER CONFERENCES

The parent-teacher conference is an important addition to any other written communication with the parents, especially for younger children. If the conferences are regularly scheduled, what topics could a teacher discuss with the parents? Typical comments relate to the following: (1) the child's progress and his classroom work, (2) his interests and attitudes, (3) his work habits at school, (4) his relationships with other children in the classroom, on the playground, and in other groups plus his relationships with teachers and other staff members. In addition to these four, teachers typically will comment on possible problems, either learning problems, emotional, behavioral or health, or social problems. The reader should note the cognitive, affective, behavioral, and social dimensions of both the progress and problem dimensions in the previous listings.

It should not be assumed that conferences automatically produce positive results. Various problems can occur, and they typically occur in at least two areas. One is in the area of training and the other is in the area of timing. First, in terms of training, teachers, as a rule, are generally not well prepared for conferences. They need to develop a system for handling their data; they often relate information to a parent that ends up being used against the child. Parents need some very careful training in how to avoid that kind of sharing of information. Second, in terms of training, the parents or the teacher often becomes defensive, even argumentative, especially if the parents are very bright, or if the teacher has failed to anticipate the questions that the parents might raise in that conference.

In terms of timing, most teachers feel as though there is an excessive amount of time required in the preparation and conducting of parent-teacher conferences, and this consumption of time keeps them from other pressing and essential responsibilities. It is important, however, that if parent-teacher conferences are scheduled, they should be scheduled during the school day, remembering that a teacher has many other responsibilities. And many parents at the upper elementary or lower secondary levels may not be willing to take the time necessary to schedule a parent-teacher conference, especially if the child has half a dozen teachers. And it should be remembered that some parents will not show up at all. It is important in these situations to be very careful to schedule those conferences when the parents are available. Typically it is the parents who need to see the teacher who fail to show up. Another aspect of timing has to do with the frequency of the conferences. In most school situations, the first conference is scheduled very early in the year before the teacher really gets to know the child, and the second conference is scheduled so late in the year it really is too late to do anything about any particular problem the child might be having, especially with that teacher.

It should be obvious by now that a good parent-teacher conference typically requires some adequate training and preparation on the part of the teacher. Several points will be suggested. These points could also be employed in telephone contacts, even in some forms of written comment to the parents. The following points are divided into four areas; the communication process, the offering of help,

> **Insight: Some Observations on Parent-Teacher Conferences**
>
> Teachers at the elementary level generally must report student progress, in whole or in part, through parent conferences. In some schools this means "interpreting" a standard report card to the parents; in others, simply giving an oral analysis of strengths and weaknesses. Parents often dislike the latter kind of report unless the teacher shows them something specific to back up her remarks. One parent, for example, said that she and her husband got the same answer to all their queries about their son's progress: "He's doing just fine." He was doing "fine" even in reading, although he was two grade levels below the level he should have been. The parents suspected that the teacher didn't *know* their son's status.
>
> In your school teacher-parent conferences, keep in mind that unless you have kept systematic records of student performance, your only recourse will be to keep smiling "and perspiring" and repeating, "he's doing just fine." Picture an interview with aggressive parents who have ambitions for their son far exceeding your estimate of his ability. Whether an actual report card is used or not, life will be much simpler if you can support your judgments with evidence. Such evidence will also permit you to do a better job of teaching.
>
> From Robert F. Biehler, *Psychology Applied to Teaching* (Boston: Houghton Mifflin, 1971), p. 401. Used by permission.

Fig. 18.1

establishment of atmosphere, and general professionalism.

Communication. Be a good and willing listener. Let the parents talk. Don't try to out-talk them. Don't lecture. Don't interrupt when they are talking. Use this occasion to learn the environmental pressures on the child and the gripes of the parents. Accept the parents' feeling and attitudes. This does not mean that you approve or disapprove of them, you merely accept the fact that those feelings and attitudes are there.

Second, remain alert throughout the conference. Try to develop real interaction. In order to gain helpful information about the child ask leading questions, rather than those which could be answered with a yes or a no. It is better to ask, "How does Johnny feel about school?" rather than, "Does Johnny like school?"

Third, be honest. Be truthful. Be sincere. Low test scores should be honestly but tactfully explained.

Fourth, keep your terminology simple. Explain unusual words. Put your stress upon understanding. Use understandable language, the language of the parent—that is, talk parent talk, not "pedagese." Don't say "peer group"; say "children of the same age." Don't drop a word curtain between you and the parent.

Offering help. Be constructive in all suggestions to the parents. By all means avoid open or implied criticism of the parent. The more mature teachers typically have discovered that most parents are honestly attempting their very best efforts in behalf of their children. Second, be careful about advice but suggest several possible remedies for a problem and allow the parent to choose which he will try. This is not only good conferencing, it is good salesmanship. Third, help the parents find their own solutions to the problem. Participate minimally, however, in the planning. Encourage the parents to suggest their own remedies for any problem that has appeared. If the problem is too complex for the school, be ready to suggest other sources of help. Last, avoid direct comparison of the child with other children. Encourage the parents not to compare one child with another, especially a brother or sister. Your objective is to help those parents to achieve a better understanding of their child as a unique and valuable individual.

Conference atmosphere. First, establish a friendly, comfortable, informal atmosphere free from interruptions. Try to establish immediate rapport with those parents. Second, be positive throughout, especially at the beginning and the end of the conference. Try to end the conference by enumerating the strong points of their child. Third, by all means, invite those parents to visit and participate in the school functions on a regular basis. Let them know that the doors of the school are open to the parents. It is especially important to plan later visits for parents who have been critical of the school program.

Professionalism. Observe professional ethics at all times. Don't ask embarrassing questions. Don't belittle another teacher or administrator. Some parents will try to tempt you into unethical conduct. No matter how you feel about the teacher the child had last year, don't join in when the parents criticize him. Keep them to the subject, which is: How can we help your child right now? Second, respect the parents' and the children's information as confidential. Don't forget the Buckley amendment. Don't ever betray their confidence in you. Remember what you can and cannot say. It is a good idea to find out beforehand what information you are not supposed to give to parents. In some school districts, for example, you do not reveal the child's IQ. Third, base your judgment on all available facts and on actual situations. As a general rule, it is a good idea for the teacher to avoid the expression of judgments or opinions unless asked for by the parents. Fourth, it is a good idea to take notes during the conference, but let the parents know what notes you have taken by reviewing them with the parents at the end of the conference. A quick summarization will relieve the minds of some parents as to what has been written. Remember that in a parent-teacher conference situation, the parents become your partners in evaluation. It is often highly desirable for the teacher to present information and let the parent make some value judgments based upon this information. The teacher in summarizing the notes and the aspects of the conference can concur with the parental judgments or add independent evaluations.

PERSONAL LETTERS

To provide for greater flexibility in reporting pupil progress to parents, some teachers have turned to using *all* letters of the alphabet to evaluate the students' work. These informal letters of evaluation are periodically sent to the parents, kept on file in the school, and eventually sent to college admissions officers and prospective employers. Frequently teachers are provided with a form to guide them in their written evaluations. Such a form might have spaces for the teacher to discuss unique strengths, weaknesses, or learning needs and suggest recommended plans for improvement. In addition, it might have a more detailed breakdown of various aspects of a subject, for example, reading, writing, discussion skills, and so forth. This tends to make clear each student's progress in every area of development of concern to the school program. Now this approach to reporting information to parents has its advantages and its disadvantages. There are four significant advantages: (1) These evaluations are much more helpful to the student than letter or number grades. They serve an obvious educational value by clarifying and elaborating specific points in other objective records. (2) Written evaluations are often much more meaningful to both the parent and college admissions officers. Physical, social, and emotional development, along with subject matter achievement can be reported. (3) They encourage the teacher to think more about each pupil as an individual, rather than as a set of numbers in her gradebook. (4) Note that the school with an ongoing written evaluation and parent response system tends to encourage continuous attention to each student's needs, better school-community relationships and parental responses, which in turn help the teacher to write more meaningful evaluations.

As the sole method of reporting progress, written evaluations in the form of personal letters to the parents have their limitations: (1) They allow teachers to be even more subjective than usual in evaluating students. Teachers might unconsciously minimize the strengths and focus on the weaknesses of students they dislike. This subjectivity is often misunderstood by the parents. (2) Unfortunately, not all teachers know how to write meaningful, helpful, individualized evaluations. Some teachers will tend to rely upon such vague terms as "excellent," "fair," "poor," "needs improvement," "a good worker," and so forth. Their evaluations will be no more meaningful than letter grades. Bad writing damages the reputation of all teachers. Although not an inherent disadvantage of the method, most letters tend to become very monotonous, stereotyped, and therefore not too informative. (3) If the letters are adequately constructed and thought-filled it becomes a very time-consuming method of evaluation for the teachers. (4) Written evaluations create extra work for the school's records office, as well as reducing the systematic and organized quality of those records. The traditional continuity of more objective reporting systems is often destroyed in this process. (Note the example of a reasonably good letter in Insight, fig. 18.2.)

IN-CLASS FEEDBACK TO STUDENTS:
TESTS AS LEARNING EXPERIENCES

It may first be useful to consider the function of feedback in the evaluational process. (See Insight, fig. 18.3, for further comments on feedback.) How does feedback aid learning? A logical, two-fold answer is that it probably focuses the learner's attention on certain important aspects of the learning task, or it may raise the learner's level of interest.

Uses and Abuses of Tests

USES

Tests have three major uses: instructional, administrative, and guidance. Tests are put to an instructional use when they are used to adapt students to courses, or courses to students. They are put to an administrative use when decisions have to be made about curriculum, placement of students, or the adding or dropping of courses. Tests are put to a guidance use when they are used to help students make choices as to future vocational or occupational plans.

It is also possible to look at tests in terms of their ability to benefit either the student, the teacher, or the administrator.

We shall look at the potential uses of tests in seven different areas.

1. To *facilitate student progress,* that is, to help the student make progress in achieving learning outcomes considered by society, the teacher, and himself to be of value. This is the most important purpose of any evaluation and to help the student overcome incorrect responses or inappropriate methods and to learn what is correct or acceptable.

2. To *assess student achievement,* that is, to get reliable information on how well the student is learning so as to ensure improvement or reasonable progress. Or to ascertain what he knows at the start or has learned at the end of an instructional sequence.

> **Insight: Feedback**
>
> The term "feedback" is one that psychologists have borrowed from the field of electronics. It refers to a process whereby data are "fed back" into a system (either a human organism or a group can be considered a "system") in order to modify and correct its behavior. A thermostat serves this type of function for a central-heating system. When the temperature falls below a certain level, this information is fed into the system, which then turns on the furnace. To transfer this concept to the learning process, we can say that if data regarding a learner's performance on a task can be fed back to him, he is in a position to guide and direct his efforts more effectively and efficiently. This principle is also used in those teaching machines in which learners find out immediately whether their answers are right or wrong. A considerable number of research studies show that learners tend to function more successfully if they receive reports as to their success or lack of it. . . . Students who received teachers' comments on their quiz papers showed more improvement on the next quiz than did students whose papers were only graded. . . . Students retained or (remembered) material covered in quizzes best when they received feedback in terms of the instructor's discussing the correct answers with them. This method was more effective than having students look up the answers in the book or having them check their replies against a list of answers written on the chalkboard. All three of these methods were, of course, better than no feedback at all.
>
> From Henry Clay Lindgren, *Educational Psychology in the Classroom,* 3d ed. (New York: Wiley and Sons, 1967), pp. 432-33. Used by permission.

Fig. 18.3

3. To *understand the individual student,* for example, to ascertain and understand the affective characteristics and kinds and levels of abilities essential to, or in relation to, achieving the instructional objectives; or to secure information about each student's cognitive, psychomotor, and affective abilities to decide whether the child is making the progress of which he is capable.

4. To *facilitate self-understanding,* that is, to help the students in a relatively short time to understand themselves as individuals and as members of a group; to set realistic goals and evaluate their progress toward those goals; to make decisions about what is important in life and what they can attain with regard to the kinds of abilities and characteristics they possess and to help the students to identify their own strengths and weaknesses by allowing the students to share in all phases of

gathering, interpreting, and using information for self-understanding and improvement, withholding information, however, that might have a detrimental effect.

5. To *evaluate the instructional programs*, a form of curriculum development; namely, to determine whether the teaching methods are effective and whether the teacher's objectives are realistic; or to analyze the teaching-learning situation as a help in deciding the causes of good or poor learning performance in terms of realistic objectives, effective teaching methods, the difficulty level of a test, or student characteristics.

6. To *assist in the administrative and curriculum judgments*. For example, to select students and materials for classes of superior, retarded, or average learners, or to select students for retaining, promoting, accelerating, or recommending for college.

Uses of Test Information: Tests as Learning Experiences

The success of any testing program, whether standardized or teacher made, is dependent upon the realization by all concerned that testing, when properly used, is an effective facet of the learning process. Achievement testing is one valuable source of feedback information to both the instructor and the student regarding the effectiveness of their respective efforts. Test results should have a positive effect upon the student's learning process, classroom activities, and curriculum planning. Teachers who merely construct and administer tests for the purpose of recording marks in the grade book are failing to realize the full potential of the measurement process. An effective test should serve the instructor, student, and the school in which it is used.

Historically, examinations have been administered as achievement tests following instruction, or as *post*-tests. Examinations may also be administered prior to instruction as *pre*-tests, usually as diagnostic instruments. Regardless of when tests are administered, they should be used as an integral part of the learning program, not an appendage thereto. Test results should be returned to the students and the individual items reviewed. . . . In the final analysis, the measure of an effective test is the degree of feedback realized from using the instrument.

Karl C. Garrison and Robert A. Magoon, "Measurement and Evaluation in the Classroom," *Educational Psychology: An Integration of Psychology and Educational Practices* (Columbus, Ohio: Merrill, 1972), p. 548.

Fig. 18.4

7. To *contribute to the knowledge of abilities and instruction in general,* that is, to help make precise and accurate judgments in a behavioral science about the complex human abilities and interactions in the teaching-learning process or processes, or to carry out the kind of research with children of school age to make these processes more exact and less of a trial-and-error situation.

ABUSES

We shall merely list fourteen common abuses of tests.

(1) When the teacher tries to make the test the object of instruction, that is, she teaches for the test

(2) When she assumes that all students will respond equally to the testing situation, for example, in terms of emotional tension

(3) When she concludes that tests provide the *only* valid clue to student progress

(4) When she believes that standardized tests measure only recall of facts

(5) When she insists that achievement and intelligence are distinct

(6) When she holds to the belief that achievement test norms are standards

(7) When she assumes the standardized tests are pefectly reliable

(8) When she overemphasizes the prediction functions of tests

(9) When there is the assumption that two tests with similar titles must therefore be measuring similar things

(10) When she assumes that two tests with dissimilar titles must therefore be measuring dissimilar things

(11) When she ignores the standard error of measurement

(12) When she tries to convert the scores from ability tests to I.Q. scores

(13) When she allows her school system to continue to use measurements of student interests that are based upon forced-choice "ipsative" instruments

(14) When there is an allowance for the intermixing of national norms from different tests

This list, it seems, could go on almost indefinitely. The potential abuses of tests are quite numerous.

Other Means of Evaluation

Other means of evaluation might include projects, field trips, small group analysis, one-on-one interviews, class discussions, or term papers. Most of these other means tend to be rather subjective. However, many constitute important objectives of most courses. Most teachers include some evaluation of these other means in their grading policies. Although many are highly subjective, the research indicates that reliability, at least, increases with usage.

Hindsight

The conflict over grading techniques continues. The introduction of supplemental methods of communicating student progress to parents and others is encouraging. Teachers will need to be educated in the nuances of these less traditional reporting techniques, however. With increased awareness within the teaching profession of the various testing procedures may come decreased abuse of these tests. Other means of evaluation commonly employed by the classroom teacher should be continued with the essential refinement provided by some of the references cited.

Chalkboard Challenges

1. The student might attempt a listing of the advantages and disadvantages of one of the techniques treated in this chapter.

2. The student could try to establish a grading policy for a future teaching situation. Explore the recent literature in depth. Prepare a brief oral report for peer consumption, specifically those colleagues who might have a reason to be interested in your findings.

3. Explore the controversy raging over letter grades. Interview classmates who are willing to share their experiences pro and con on this issue. Present a summation to your classmates.

4. Select an alternative to the traditional five-point letter grading system and defend its merits before an appropriate college committee, for example, a committee on academic standards and admissions.

5. Interview some parents who have recently been involved in some actual parent-teacher conferences. Collate, organize, and condense your findings in a written report. Suggest improvements in the training of teachers for these conferences.

6. Visit a local school to observe a school psychologist administering some tests.

7. Team up with a teacher and help her work out any "wrinkles" in her grading policy. Report back to the class.

Want to Know More?

Please refer to the section at the end of chapter 17. The references suggested are basically identical.

Part 5

The Teacher in the Teaching-Learning Process

19

Personal and Professional Development

CONTENTS

	PAGE
Key Terms	467
That's Debatable!	468
Foresight	468
The Personal Development of the Teacher	469
The Professional Development of the Teacher	476
Hindsight	484
Chalkboard Challenges	485
Want to Know More?	486

KEY TERMS

Teacher burnout
    A condition that results from working too hard for too long or enduring too much stress over a short period of time. Symptoms vary from fatigue to depression to quick anger

Teacher competency
    The ability of a teacher to responsibly perform his or her duties appropriately

Teacher morale
    The extent to which teachers experience a sense of general well-being and satisfaction in their job situation

THAT'S DEBATABLE!
Can I Survive My First Week As A Teacher?

May Richstone, in an article entitled "First Week Survival Kit" in *Instructor* magazine, gives these survival hints:
1. Hang onto your sense of proportion.
2. Try for understanding.
3. Never say fail.
4. Speak privately of private matters.
5. Write encouraging notes.
6. Remove the child briefly, if necessary.
7. Save your breath—no long barrages of words.
8. Criticize the act, not the child.
9. Preparation and pace preclude many problems.
10. Invest in a timer.
11. Vary the activities.
12. Stroll to the trouble spot in advance.
13. Make a home visit.
14. Enjoy the children, and they will respond and try to please you.[1]

(Note: Not all hints are included.)

FORESIGHT

The school's most important influence is the teacher. There is no question that the teacher sets the tone of the classroom and establishes the nature of the teaching-learning process in his or her classroom. The teacher provides the direction for the behavior of the students. The personality of the teacher is very important, and we do not mean that every teacher has to be a star. What we do mean is that the teacher needs to have a good understanding of himself or herself, and of why he or she is there in the classroom, and of the nature of his or her relationships with students, the administration, the parents, and the community. A teacher needs to be able to communicate with other people authoritatively (not in an authoritarian manner), reasonably, and appropriately for the situation in which he or she is involved.

The personal and the professional roles of the teacher overlap, but it is helpful, we believe, to look at each of these areas, once we have acknowledged their overlapping influences.

Teachers can suffer burnout, maladjustment, and even mental illness just as can anyone else, but the incidence of these illnesses are no higher among teachers than for comparable professionals.

---

1. May Richstone, "First Week Survival Kit for the Brand-New Teacher," *Instructor* 80 (August/September 1971). Adapted from *Instructor*, August/September 1971. Copyright © 1971 by The Instructor Publications, Inc. Used by permission.

Personal and Professional Development

In this chapter we talk about these maladjustments, how many of them may be prevented, and the necessity for the teacher to learn how to maintain good mental health. We also provide what we have termed the teachers' evaluation clinic, which is a brief look at the various relationships in which the teacher will be engaged from day to day and week to week. Finally, we discuss the role of the competent teacher in a pluralistic society.

THE PERSONAL DEVELOPMENT OF THE TEACHER

SIGNIFICANCE OF SELF-UNDERSTANDING

It is just as important for teachers to understand their own behavior as it is for them to understand the behavior of the students with whom they relate in the teaching-learning process. Lindgren suggests that as a reasonable hypothesis, our insight into and understanding of our students are approximately proportional to the insight and understanding we have regarding ourselves, our behavior, and the effect we have on others.[2]

One of the things that all of us tend to do is to pretend that all the defense mechanisms we read about are always a part of someone else's behavior. Then we discover some of these same quirks in ourselves. Now there is a real difference here: In the first instance, we understand what defense mechanisms are and we see them readily in the lives of other people, and this affects the manner in which we relate to our students and our colleagues. The second level occurs when we are able to see these things operating in ourselves, and therefore we are much more apt to effectively work with our students and our colleagues, simply because we are working on a level of *understanding,* rather than a mere level of information. Because we have developed some self-understanding, we carry a greater feeling of understanding and respect for others.

It is a helpful thing for teachers to understand that the same kinds of pressures that affect the lives of students, also affect the lives of teachers. There are the expectations of the culture, the stresses of community, the necessity of balancing one's personal desires and standards with those of the larger community. There are times when teachers experience their "good days," there are times when teachers experience "bad days." Students, principals, parents, school board members—all these have their good days and bad days as well.

As teachers, we need to try to be aware of how other people perceive us. And it is not necessary to assume a certain set of personality characteristics in order to be an effective teacher. Teachers who are effective with one level of students may not be as effective with students at different levels in their mental and emotional development. All of us have seen the contrasts in teacher personalities, and while certainly there are discernible differences between those who are "good" teachers

---

2. Henry Clay Lindgren, *Educational Psychology in the Classroom,* 6th ed. (Oxford: University Press, 1980).

and those who are "bad" teachers, nevertheless all teachers do not have to be "clones" of one particular model. For example, an outgoing teacher can work with a certain group of people who respond to her outgoingness. In the next room there is another teacher who dresses well, is well-trained for her job, but is quiet and perhaps even perceived as being somewhat shy by others. A smaller number of students may relate to this second teacher, but because she is understanding and caring, there are students who find in this quiet teacher someone with whom they can talk. The second group of students would not receive the help they need, were it not for the second teacher.

In 1977 a study was made of college instructors who had received distinguished teaching awards.[3] The purpose of this study was to determine, if possible, what these instructors were like and what really led to their receiving or being worthy of receiving the distinguished teaching awards. The largest number of common attributes (twenty-three) focused on teaching style and technique. But there were other descriptions of these teachers which are significant: enthusiastic, stimulating, expecting much, willing to listen, innovative. The teachers were further described as being willing to explain the relevance of material, prepared and organized, showed concern about their pupils' progress, graded fairly, and were helpful advisors. In terms of personal qualities, these distinguished teachers were seen as vigorous and enthusiastic, friendly, sincere, and respectful of students as persons. In addition, they were seen as identifying with young people. We'll return to this study when we talk about the professional development of the teacher.

The better you as a teacher or a teacher-to-be can understand yourself and how others perceive you, the better you'll be able to understand and relate to those with whom you work.

INCIDENCE OF TEACHER MALADJUSTMENT

Typically, beginning teachers are filled with hope and great expectations about the profession of teaching and their part in it. But it has been noted by a substantial number of observers and researchers that those enthusiastic feelings deteriorate over a period of time to a disappointing and sometimes very alarming degree, and such disappointment may lead to teacher maladjustment, burnout, and psychosomatic illnesses.

These same things occur in the other professions as well. It is at least encouraging to note that the incidence of maladjustment, burnout, and mental illness is no greater among teachers than it is, proportionately, among lawyers, doctors, nurses, business managers, or day laborers.[4]

---

3. Charles A. Goldsmid, J.E. Grueber, and E.K. Wilson, "Perceived Attributes of Superior Teachers (PAST): An Inquiry into The Giving of Teacher Awards," *American Educational Research Journal* 14 (1977):423-40.
4. Christena Maslach, "Burned Out," *Human Behavior* 5, no. 9 (1976):16-22. Also Daniel Yankelovich, *Family Health in an Era of Stress* (Minneapolis: General Mills, 1979).

Any professional group needs to be concerned about the health of its members. There are very close ties between an individual's work and his or her health. This has been researched and highlighted from the coal miners with black lung disease to nurses in operating rooms who have a high incidence of spontaneous miscarriages due to their exposure to anesthetic gasses.[5]

In the mid-seventies a poll was conducted by the *Instructor,* a teacher magazine with nearly 300,000 subscribers. The American School Health Assocation cooperated in this study, and in the September 1976 issue of the magazine, a questionnaire was included to which 9,000 teachers responded. The results: these teachers had missed an average of 4.5 days at work during the previous school year because of illness. Twenty-seven percent indicated they had chronic health problems. Seven percent said they had had psychiatric treatment, and forty percent indicated they were currently taking prescription drugs. Seventy-eight percent of the teachers rated their health as good to excellent.

SYMPTOMS OF TEACHER MALADJUSTMENT

A National Education Association survey found that one-third of teachers were dissatisfied with their jobs. An even greater proportion—forty percent—would not choose teaching again if they had another chance. It is no secret that hundreds of teachers leave the profession each year and seek a livelihood in other professions or occupations. And, of course, some do suffer breakdowns in mental health or develop mental illness.[6]

This kind of disillusionment has most recently been termed "burnout." This has also been called battle fatigue and combat neurosis, among other labels. Teacher burnout is a condition that results from a teacher's working too hard for too long or enduring unusually intense stress or pressure over a short period of time.[7] The symptoms of burnout vary among individuals, but some of the common warning signs are constant fatigue, frequent headaches, digestive problems, insomnia, very frequently feelings of futility or depression, and a quickness of temper and anger. Some have reported cardiovascular disorders, breathing problems, and ulcers. And then there are others in whom burnout takes the form of boredom or loneliness. There is no question these kinds of problems can interfere with professional competence, and as you see an individual who used to be moderate in temperament becoming cross, shouting, sometimes not able to plan his work, suffering feelings of guilt—all of those may be signs of burnout. (Please note we are not attempting here to give a medical or psychological diagnosis by a

---

5. W.J. Blot, L.A. Brinton, J.F. Fraumeni, Jr., and B.J. Stone, "Cancer Mortality in U.S. Counties with Petroleum Industries," *Science* 198 (1977):51-53. Also G. Bronson, "Long Exposure to Waste Anesthetic Gas Is Peril to Workers, U.S. Safety Unit Says," *Wall Street Journal,* 1 March 1977, p. 10.
6. L. Landsmann, "Is Teaching Hazardous to Your Health?" *Today's Education* 67 (1978):49-50.
7. Donna Sommons, "Burn-out: The Dangers of Overworking," *Family Weekly,* 9 March 1980, p. 15.

textbook but simply are describing typical symptoms reported by many who have been diagnosed as having burnout.)

Those with whom we have had contact who suffer from burnout tend to be perfectionists, want to do everything exceptionally well, and therefore appear to be very vulnerable to the kinds of pressures that operate in the teaching-learning process. Some of these people may be "going great guns" on Monday, and the next day have totally broken down in terms of mental health. Others develop the symptoms gradually over a period of time. Again, we want to stress that these are not intended to be diagnoses, but rather personal observations in which we have been involved. Any person with serious burnout symptoms should consult a professional for help.

The first Insight box (fig. 19.1) is worthy of your careful consideration, for it presents characteristics of maladjusted teachers in relation to student needs. It is important especially because it describes maladjusted teacher behaviors, with which each of us needs to be familiar.

CAUSES OF TEACHER MALADJUSTMENT

Some of the factors that tend to bring about burnout are, of course, found in all the professions. Two significant ones include overload and the general press of numerous forces in people which cause the individual to behave "according to rules" rather than taking time to deal genuinely with each problem as a human being.[8]

In a study at Michigan State University's Institute for Research on Teaching, Michael Vavrus surveyed 275 prospective and in-service teachers on the basis of "alienation."[9] In this study, alienation was defined as the "withdrawal of self-investment from a job." The results indicated that prospective teachers were significantly less alienated than in-service teachers, and that the more teaching experience a person had, the more alienated and less involved the teacher was likely to be. In this particular survey, much of the dissatisfaction reported by the teachers had to do with being left out of decision-making at schools. So one of the causes of teacher maladjustment may indeed be frustration because they are not permitted to be as involved as they would like to be in making decisions in which they are vitally interested and which vitally affect the teaching-learning process.

In the poll cited previously undertaken by *Instructor*, eighty-four percent of the teachers responding said that health hazards existed in teaching. *Stress* was identified as the most common problem. And they reported the causes of stress or tension as being large class sizes, the lack of teaching materials, an increase in severe discipline problems, increased pressures from the public on teachers, and

---

8. Maslach, pp. 16-22.
9. Michael Vavrus, *The Relationship of Teacher Alienation to School Workplace Characteristics and Career Stages of Teachers* (East Lansing, Mich.: Michigan State U., Institute for Research on Teaching, 1979).

Insight: Characteristics of Maladjusted Teachers in Relation to Student Needs

MASLOW'S HIERARCHY OF NEEDS	MALADJUSTED TEACHER BEHAVIOR
1. Physiological Needs	1. The teacher has rigid, noncompromising times during which students may use the restroom and drinking facilities and leave assigned seats.
2. Safety Needs	2. The teacher's overzealous attempts to have students undertake physical education activities beyond their individual abilities jeopardize their safety.
3. Need for Belonging and Love	3. The teacher rejects students, is unaccepting and unfriendly.
4. Need for Importance, Respect, Self-Esteem, and Independence	4. The teacher is hostile and contemptuous toward students and creates guilt in students by blaming and shaming them in the presence of peers, principal, and/or parents.
5. Need for Information	5. The teacher discourages any questioning or critical thinking in students and appears personally threatened or offended.
6. Need for Understanding	6. The teacher is unsympathetic to students' personal concerns and maintains an impersonal, aloof manner.
7. Need for Beauty	7. The teacher neglects to foster and encourage individual creativity and appreciation for the aesthetic.
8. Need for Self-Actualization	8. The teacher hinders the student's development of a realistic orientation to the world, acceptance of self and others, appreciativeness, humor, and nonconformism as a result of his/her own inhibitions.

From J. Mackiel, "Positive Mental Health for Teachers," in *The Clearing House* 52, no. 7 (March 1979): 309. 1979 by Heldref Publications, a publication of the Helen Dwight Reid Educational Foundation. Reprinted by permission.

Fig. 19.1

schedules that give the teachers little or no time for breaks or rest periods. Additionally, substantial numbers of the teachers cited the current trend toward viewing the teacher and the school as those who should solve all the problems of our society.[10] Vander Zanden reports a significant response which perhaps typifies the frustrations many teachers feel.

> We're asked to assume broader roles, yet we are more and more criticized by the public. Areas once covered by the family and church (such as sex education and moral

---

10. L. Landsmann, "Is Teaching Hazardous to Your Health?" *Today's Education,* vol. 67, 1978, p. 49.

education) are now plopped on the teacher's lap. We're even administering breakfast programs. The same parents that are demanding that we go back to the basics (reading and math) also want us to teach their children discipline, teach them right from wrong. No wonder more and more experienced teachers are leaving the profession. To do all these things without support is demoralizing.[11]

In this same poll, another major area of health concern was weight, diet, and exercise. Teachers seem particularly frustrated with the lunch period, and only twenty-five percent said that they bought lunch in the school cafeteria, with the remaining teachers either bringing their own lunch or skipping lunch altogether. About one-third of the teachers said that the physical environment of the school, particularly the temperature in the classrooms, affected their health negatively.

Another poll taken by the Wall Street Journal had fifty-six percent of the 5,000 teachers responding saying that they suffered physical ailments because of job pressure, and one-fourth of the teachers blamed the job pressure for mental ailments.[12] There is an important distinction here in this particular poll: the teachers said *it was not teaching itself that was so stressful, but rather the discipline problems and the lack of support that brought the most stress and tension to them.*

Kyriacou and Sutcliffe summarized the research on the factors that appear to contribute to teacher stress:

1. Excessive clerical work
2. Supervisory duties
3. Inadequate salary
4. Negative student attitudes
5. Required discipline curtailed teaching time
6. Poor staff relations
7. Inadequate or unsupportive administration
8. Inadequate buildings and equipment
9. Overload; large classes
10. Inadequate training
11. Low status of the profession in society
12. Conflicting demands
13. Lack of parental cooperation.[13]

DEVELOPING AND MAINTAINING GOOD MENTAL HEALTH

Since it so essential for the teacher to maintain good mental health (obviously it has a vital affect on the teacher's performance), we look briefly but

---

11. J.W. Vander Zanden, *Educational Psychology in Theory and Practice* (New York: Random House, 1980), p. 308.
12. *Wall Street Journal,* 4 April 1978.
13. Chris Kyriacou and John Sutcliffe, "Teacher Stress: A Review," *Educational Review* 19, no. 4 (1977):299-305.

importantly at some ways to develop and maintain good mental health. For example, in the case of burnout, the teacher needs to be aware that it does occur, and that it can happen to anyone, *not just to the other person*. The teacher needs to understand that the pressures that come in the teaching-learning process and all of its ramifications cannot in themselves give the teacher burnout. The teacher's attitude toward and view of these pressures can do much to help prevent maladjustment, either temporarily or sometimes permanently. If the teacher is prepared ahead of time to deal with these, those pressures and the results of them will not be so apt to frustrate the teacher, at least to the high degree of intensity that otherwise would be the case.

If there are situations where you feel inadequate, then a positive response to that feeling is simply to go and prepare further in the areas in which you do not feel adequate. In many cases, this may have to wait until summer for a conference or an opportunity to enroll in a class. Be willing to wait, and in the meantime keep the feeling of inadequacy in perspective by knowing that you are going to do something about it as soon as it is reasonable to do so.

Avoid a destructive way of dealing with the pain or pressures, such as heavy drinking, the use of tranquilizers, excessive smoking, or taking it out on other people around you. When you are unaware of what is happening to you because of these pressures, you are most apt to resort to these destructive ways of dealing with them. Strom and Bernard make five brief suggestions which are excellent for avoiding burn-out:

1. Acknowledging that burnout may occur because we allow it to
2. Leaving school work at school and developing other hobbies and concerns
3. Taking a vacation, sick leave, or sabbatical leave, even if income is temporarily reduced
   (Author's note: running away from the environment is never the final answer, but a temporary change of circumstances, if used constructively, can be of great help.)
4. Seeking out opportunities for group counseling
5. Participating in planned therapeutic group discussions[14]

There is no question that teacher burnout is a real and increasingly distressing problem, because of the growing number of pressures related to many and varied factors in the setting of the educational process. But the other side of the story is so often overlooked, the impression is left that teaching is "down the tubes." This is definitely not the case in spite of the many difficulties that all of us in the profession frankly acknowledge. Many of the most satisfied teachers are those who

---

14. Robert B. Strom and Harold W. Bernard, *Educational Psychology* (Monterey, Calif.: Brooks/Cole, 1982), p. 24.

have left the profession, worked at another career, and *returned* to teaching because of their desire to engage in the teaching-learning process with all of its excitement and its joy.[15]

PERSONAL DEVELOPMENT AND THE TEACHING-LEARNING PROCESS

The Insight (fig. 19.2) lists ten commandments for personal development of the Christian teacher. At this point in the chapter as we conclude the personal development section, we would like to reaffirm the necessity for the individual teacher to very deliberately and consciously engage in personal development. That is, the individual needs to keep this in a very high conscious view. Learn to view yourself in positive, appropriate ways.

We know substantial numbers of teachers who, without realizing it, are going about their duties from day to day with a great feeling of inferiority in relation to other teachers, the school administrators, the board of the school, parents—and the tragedy is that these teachers are working under a pressure that is almost unconscious with them, yet affecting them in very serious ways. Perhaps one illustration will make our point here, as typically representative of the importance of personal development in relation to the teaching-learning process. When you go down the hall to your classroom, or if you come to your classroom as soon as you come into the school building each morning, are you thinking of the children or young people as your *enemies* or as your *friends*? It is amazing in samplings we have taken to see how many teachers, many of them without realizing it, view their students as *enemies*. Therefore, they enter the classroom with hostility prevailing, of which they are not even aware, but which vitally affects the morale of the class, the methods by which they teach, and the general quality of the teaching-learning process. Begin to think deliberately and consciously about yourself, and see yourself honestly, share with someone else those areas which you feel you need to share, and do the specific things you can do (such as enrolling in a class), to prepare yourself where you may feel you are not as well prepared as you ought to be. Develop genuine joy and enthusiasm for the teaching-learning process because you have come to know yourself well.

THE PROFESSIONAL DEVELOPMENT OF THE TEACHER

As we begin the second section of this chapter, we remind ourselves that the personal and the professional are very difficult to separate and in fact do have many overlapping areas. However, in this section of the chapter, we are going to be em-

---

15. R.J. Havighurst and B.L. Newgarten, *Society in Education*, 3d ed. (Boston: Allyn and Bacon, 1967); A.T. Jersild and E.A. Lezar, *The Meaning of Psychotherapy in a Teacher's Life and Work*, (New York: Columbia U., New York Teacher's College, 1962). Also Dorothy Moe, "Teacher Burn-out: A Prescription," *Today's Education* 68 (November-December 1979):35-36.

> **Insight: Ten Commandments for Personal Development for the Christian Teacher**
>
> 1. Thou shalt be clear that the God of the Bible is the Ultimate Reality; Thou shalt have no other gods before Me.
> 2. Thou shalt meditate constantly upon the fact that Jesus Christ is the Way, Truth, and Life.
> 3. Thou shalt prepare thyself to be academically excellent in thy field of expertise.
> 4. Thou shalt understand that time, talent, money, and energy are not to be wasted, but are to be used as a good steward of the Lord.
> 5. Thou shalt commit thy way daily unto the Lord, before engaging your students in the teaching-learning process.
> 6. Thou shalt look upon thy students with respect for their dignity as persons made in the image of God, even though all have sinned and come short of the glory of God.
> 7. Thou shalt teach with genuine joy, and discipline with genuine love, that your students may grow in wisdom, stature, and in favor with God and man.
> 8. Thou shalt remember thy body is the temple of the Holy Spirit, and treat it accordingly; that thy mind is to be yielded to the mind of Christ; that thy spirit is to be in submission to the Holy Spirit.
> 9. Thou shalt commit thyself to lifelong personal and professional development, as a teacher called of the Lord.
> 10. Thou shalt undergird thy calling with prayer, the reading of God's Word, and the guidance of the Holy Spirit.

Fig. 19.2

phasizing the significance of professional development and how we relate specifically in the "working" aspects of our calling.

THE SIGNIFICANCE OF LIFELONG PROFESSIONAL DEVELOPMENT

Most teachers today recognize the necessity of constantly upgrading themselves professionally. Most states have requirements for upgrading courses to be taken, with additional credits required at regular intervals. This is true in most other professions today, and it ought to be so in the teaching profession. In a rapidly changing society, it is so necessary that we keep up with new ideas, in order to reflect upon them and to process them through our philosophic approach to the teaching-learning process. But we must be careful not to substitute the taking of courses and the attending of meetings for true professional development. It obviously is not how many credits we have accumulated, nor how many meetings we have attended—given the essential preparation for becoming a teacher—it is what is happening within ourselves and how we apply that in the teaching-learning process that is important in both our personal and professional development.

TEACHERS' EVALUATION CLINIC

The aim of this "clinic" by means of a textbook is simply to help you think through the main areas of your professional relationships. We hope that by listing these and making some suggestions and asking some questions, you will be enabled to do a reasonably effective self-evaluation. Where you see the need for improvement, make plans to engage in bringing about that particular improvement. We have no long questionnaires for you to fill out, because we have found out that either teachers do not want to be bothered with those, or will not take time to complete them, and if they do take the time to complete them they are soon discarded.

Relationship with pupils. It has been fairly well established that the impact of teachers is "the single most potent influence on pupils' behavior and learning."[16] The attitude that children are irresponsible, or foolish, or any other negative attribute, makes for difficult and unproductive classroom interactions. Teachers who on the positive side believe that children are responsible and capable of self-discipline and then approach their pupils with a cheerful and positive attitude find that they produce cooperative fruitful interactions. As you check yourself on this, let us be clear that we are not talking about a "Pollyanna" attitude where everything is fine no matter what. The Christian teacher, for example, believes that all human beings are sinners, and yet this does not cause a Christian teacher to take a negative view of her pupils. For they have the potential of the image of God created in them, and therefore the teacher's privilege is to work with those students to bring about their conversion to Christ and the fullest possible development of their God-given potential.

One study is of particular significance here, in helping to evaluate yourself in relationship to your pupils. The study was done by Sherman and others in 1976 and compared teachers who were more successful in terms of their students' achieving with those who were less successful.[17] It is interesting that the result showed that successful teachers could be young or old, experienced or inexperienced. The practices that characterized successful teachers were: (1) insisting that pupils stay

---

16. K.O. Yap, "Teacher's Education: Teachers' Attitude Toward Children and Learning," *Elementary School Journal* 78 (1977):38.
17. G.J. Sherman, J.E. Brophy, C.M. Evertson, and W.J. Crawford, "Positional Attitudes and Teacher Consistency in Producing Student Learning Games in the Early Elementary Grades," *Journal of School Psychology* 14 (1976):192-201.

in place and work; (2) following a planned schedule; and (3) requiring students to stand while reciting. The beliefs that distinguished the successful teachers were: (1) Except for texts, materials are unimportant. (2) Teachers should spend more time with the class as a whole than with individual pupils. (3) Teachers should urge pupils to do better. (4) After an incorrect response, another pupil should be asked to respond. (5) More should be required of abler pupils. (6) It is the teacher's responsibility to see that supplies are available.

You need to be aware that other studies have been done which would disagree in some respects with the findings of this research, and as you do so remember that the goal is to be an *authoritative* teacher, which means, broadly defined, that you are in charge in your classroom and your pupils know it, and yet as you lead them in the teaching-learning process they participate, and learn, and enjoy the spirit you bring to the process. We stress again that *authoritative* is not *authoritarian*.

Relationship with other teachers. Without any question, this can become a very disturbing area for teacher and student, as well as for the administrator. As professionals, we are not bound to agree with our fellow teachers, but we are bound to respect them and to handle disagreements in professional ways. It is so easy to huddle in a corner of the hallway or some other little nook in the building and talk with an associate about a third teacher in negative fashion. We submit that this is neither professional, nor is it Christian. We suggest that where disagreements occur—and they will—first of all you go to the teacher with whom you disagree and seek to resolve the issue in a quiet and professional way, out of the hearing of students. If that is not successful, the next step is to go to the principal or whomever is designated in the particular situation in your school, and present your side along with the other individual presenting his side, and then reaching a decision to resolve the disagreement. We suggest you be willing to compromise, as long as it does not violate your philosophic integrity or your moral principles.

On the more positive side, there are so many times during the school day when one teacher can be of tremendous help to another, either by a word of encouragement, or by congratulating her on some achievement, or by helping her with a specific task that may have arisen which needs to be done right at that moment. These small gestures accumulate to make very large differences in relationships.

Relationship with the administration. A psychiatrist-consultant reviewed the recorded transcripts of a mental health workshop for teachers some years ago and came up with the following results:

> Administrators who behave in authoritarian ways have a disturbing effect on relations among teachers, creating professional jealousies, hostility, and resentment. In such a climate even teachers who are trying to do their best are afraid to cooperate with the hated administrator lest they be considered "apple-polishers." The pattern of human relationships initiated by the administrator often spreads into the community, especially harassed teachers express their frustrations in the form of anger directed

against the parents, thus making parent/teacher cooperation impossible.

On the positive side, teachers participating in the workshop observed that the kind of interpersonal relations fostered by democratic relationships with administrators made teaching an enriching experience. Administrators should permit teachers to plan with them: sharing in decisions encourages closer working relationships essential to effective administration. Teachers feel the need to be regarded and respected as individuals in their own right. Creativity in teaching depends greatly upon the administrator's respect for individual differences.[18]

We cite this particular study because we are aware that it is very easy to say, "Have a good relationship with your administrator," but sometimes very difficult to put into practice. There are no easy answers at this point, except to encourage those of you who are administrators or planning to be administrators to be aware of how your teachers and students are perceiving you. And for those of you who are teachers or are preparing to be teachers, seek always to maintain 100 percent loyalty to the school and to the administration. If you have honest disagreements, go and voice them to the administrator in a professional manner. If the conflicts cannot ultimately be resolved, then it may be time to look for a position in another school where you will feel your engagement in the teaching-learning process is more in keeping with your philosophic integrity.

Relationships with parents. We reaffirm our position that children belong to the parents, and not to the state. The parents are entrusting their children to the teaching-learning process taking place in the school to which they send their child. Admittedly, many parents are not very concerned about what happens in that teaching-learning process, and others either do not have the time because of other demands (particularly in the single-parent homes), or they use the school as a baby-sitting facility. None of those attitudes should affect the teacher's basic concern to work, as far as it is possible to work within the limits of the teaching-learning process in that particular setting, with the parents in the education of their child.

Some insecure parents become jealous when their children develop a fondness for their teachers; others are upset when their children contradict them and quote the teacher as the authority on the other side. Other parents become angry when a teacher wants to discuss their child's difficulties with them, because they believe that the whole problem of the child, including his discipline and any disruptive behavior, is the responsibility of the school and not theirs as parents. It is amazing how frequently parents who have had difficulties in school when they were youngsters still have negative attitudes toward school and toward teachers.

If the setting of your school permits it (and we are thinking here of some areas where it would be virtually impossible to do so) make a visit to the homes of your children, especially where you observe difficulties in the classroom in terms of the child's behavior. A visit cannot hurt a thing, and it is a good rule of thumb to

---

18. R.J. Margolin, "New Perspectives for Teachers—An Evaluation of a Mental Health Institute," *Mental Hygiene* 37 (1953):394-424.

Insight: Teachers' Perceptions of the Relative Importance of Sixteen Criteria of Teaching Effectiveness

Criteria	Mean Rating*
1. Relationship with class (good rapport)	8.3
2. Willingness to be flexible, to be direct or indirect as situation demands	8.2
3. Effectiveness in controlling class	7.9
4. Capacity to perceive world from students' point of view	7.8
5. Personal adjustment and character	7.7
6. Influence on students' behavior	7.6
7. Knowledge of subject matter and related areas	7.6
8. Ability to personalize teaching	7.6
9. Extent to which verbal behavior in classroom is student-centered	7.3
10. Extent to which inductive (discovery) methods are used	7.0
11. Amount student learns	6.9
12. General knowledge and understanding of educational facts	6.4
13. Civic responsibility (patriotism)	6.2
14. Performance in student teaching	5.7
15. Participation in community and professional activities	4.9
16. Years of teaching experience	3.9

*Rating was done on a nine-point scale, ranging from 9—"extremely important," to 1—"completely unimportant." Any rating over 5, therefore, would indicate that a criterion was perceived as more important than unimportant.

From J. R. Jenkins and R. B. Bausell, "How Teachers View the Effective Teacher: Student Learning Is Not the Top Criteria," *Phi Delta Kappan* 55 (1974): 572-73.

Fig. 19.3

follow. If you feel after the visit that you got nowhere, still you have the satisfaction of having tried. The probabilities are that you have discovered a lot of things about that home which will help you in working with the child in the teaching-learning process. Attend the parent-teacher meetings, and look upon every opportunity to talk with the parents as one that can be helpful to the welfare of the student.

Relationship with the community. Schools do belong to the community (public schools), and because the community is composed of so many varied people and groups, teachers are not going to be able to satisfy everybody. Quite often, the public may be disappointed because there is a fundamental difference between the way they view educational processes and the views held by the teachers. The third Insight box (fig. 19.3) reflects the results of a survey of teacher's opinions which illustrate this problem. The study was conducted in Delaware in 1974, and 264 teachers and administrators were asked to rate, using a nine-point scale, the importance of sixteen criteria for judging teacher effectiveness.

What is particularly of concern, and to the point of our present discussion, is that the criterion most lay people would rate at the top of the list, "amount students learn," is far down the list in eleventh place. Lindgren points out that from the public's point of view, schools exist only to produce learning in students; therefore it follows that the competency of the teacher should be measured in terms of the amount of learning produced.[19] What comes out of all of this frequently is that when the public reads this kind of result from a survey it comes to feel that teachers and administrators are letting it down and the educational system is failing. Teachers usually have set rather high standards for themselves, and when they find themselves the target of community criticism, it is particularly hard to accept. All schools have their advantages and disadvantages in relation to the community relationships. One of the advantages of a private or Christian school in this regard is that the community—those who have established and are operating the school—are much more apt to have basic principles that are very clear and to which everyone associated with the school subscribes. Ordinarily the relationship to the "community" in a private or Christian school is apt to be harmonious.

RELATIONSHIP WITH PROFESSIONAL ORGANIZATIONS AND THE INVOLVEMENT IN PROFESSIONAL TRAINING ACTIVITIES

The matter of teachers and their professional organizations is one of great controversy today. Ordinarily, or perhaps one might say ideally, teachers should be expected to belong to and participate in professional organizations as a matter of their own responsibility and development. At the same time, many of the teachers' organizations have become heavily involved in highly controversial issues, both nationally and in terms of various states. Our position would certainly be to encourage teachers to belong to and participate in professional organizations, but there are issues that can create great conflicts between the individual teacher and the organization because of deep moral convictions. Voluntary prayer in the public schools and tuition tax credits are just two examples of the kinds of issues on which people feel deeply. It is not our purpose to take sides on those issues, but simply to point out that because professional teachers' organizations do take stands on these issues, their stands may create severe conflicts with the conscience of the individual teacher.

Professional teachers' organizations can and have done a great deal to advance the cause of education. Controversies in themselves should not be used as reasons for not belonging to a professional organization, but when this kind of conflict gets to matters of conscience, then it must be left to you as an individual to resolve within your own heart and mind. As the individual gives this kind of matter consideration, it is usually helpful to look at the preponderance of influence of the organization—that is, even though it may stand for some viewpoints with which the individual does not agree, what does it do beyond the controversial issues that can be weighed on the other side of the scales. Again, the process of "synthesizing all of this information without compromising" is the principle we recommend.

19. Lindgren, p. 742.

Certainly, it is the professional obligation of every educator to become aware of the organizations that do exist, what they stand for, what they publish, and to evaluate all of those in relation to one's own professional development.

The training opportunities available to educators today are almost like the sands of the sea, too numerous to count. There are so many areas in which teachers need to become more and more knowledgeable. Various organizations and research groups, including colleges, universities, professional organizations, and private foundations recognize this and seek to provide the kind of updating information that will enable an educator to experience some professional growth through an increase in knowledge, or gaining mastery over some new technique which may be helpful, in addition to the opportunity to share and to converse and to exchange ideas with one's professional colleagues. Depending upon your particular setting and the regulations of your school, you may be able to attend one or more conferences through the year or you may need to relegate those kinds of activities to the summer months. In a time when information is exploding upon the scene, as it is today, it is essential that teachers seize upon every opportunity feasible to gain new information and learn about new techniques and research that apply to the teaching-learning process.

THE COMPETENT TEACHER IN A PLURALISTIC SOCIETY

Regardless of one's particular philosophic approach to the teaching-learning process, or the particular clinical setting in which one engages that process from school day to school day, the teacher must be aware that we do live in a pluralistic society. We need to make a careful distinction here: living in a pluralistic society and being convinced that the school should promote such a society are two entirely different matters. That we live in a pluralistic society, there can be no question. This simply means that we live in a society in which individuals and groups with widely varying points of view are free to speak their convictions, as long as the rights and privileges of their fellow citizens are not impinged upon. It is very difficult, in a society like this one, to be a competent teacher. We have defined competent, you will recall, as being responsibly able to perform one's duties appropriately. But this becomes very difficult when questions such as the following are raised:

1. Is social experience the key to quality experience? Of course John Dewey and those who follow his particular approach will answer yes. There are others who attack Dewey's "life adjustment" viewpoint and argue for firm mental and behavioral discipline.

2. Should schools determine what is learned? Some would argue for standardized subject matter that rescues the learner from triviality and capriciousness. Others believe deeply that an imposed curriculum damages the individual and takes away a basic human right to select one's own path of development.

3. Is religion essential in education? Increasingly, many Americans stand by the view that the original religious foundation has been undermined by the forces of secular humanism. Many others would defend secular humanism's place in education and warn against fundamentalists.

4. The very question itself, Should the schools promote cultural pluralism? is one to which some would answer yes, because they see pluralism as the appropriate social and educational course between the extremes of segregation and assimilation. But there are others who feel just as strongly that pluralism erodes common values and diverts the school's attention from other purposes. And so the questions go on and on—these are but a few examples of highly controversial issues within our multifaceted society, which do indeed affect the teaching-learning process, how the teacher teaches, and what she teaches within the teaching-learning process. It is not easy to be a competent teacher in a pluralistic society.

This means it is of exceeding importance that the teacher be aware of the issues and reflect upon them carefully, and evaluate them in the light of one's philosophic approach to education. It is true as John Milton said, "Where there is much desire to learn, there of necessity will be much arguing."

Hindsight

In this chapter we have talked about the professional and personal development of the teacher. We have stressed the significance of understanding yourself as a person and becoming aware of how other people perceive you. We have talked about teacher maladjustment, including burnout and mental illness. We have made some suggestions for developing and maintaining good mental health, including ten commandments for the Christian teacher's personal development.

We then moved to the area of professional development, pointing out that indeed there are many overlapping areas between the personal and the professional development of the teacher. We used the teacher's evaluation clinic to help you take a look at your own professional relationships with those with whom most commonly you have to deal day by day. We have pointed out the difficulty in being a competent teacher—responsibly able to perform appropriately—in the midst of a pluralistic society.

We add a note here for the Christian teacher, whose philosophic approach makes it both easier and harder to be a competent teacher in the pluralistic society. It is made easier by the fact that the Christian has a definite set of principles, based on the Word of God, by which he or she lives and practices the calling of being a teacher. It is made harder since it can subject the Christian teacher to extreme pressures in some teaching-learning situations because of adherence to those principles as a matter of Christian integrity.

For the Christian teacher in relation to the pluralistic society, we suggest a position of reflective commitment, to which we have alluded before in this text. Christians certainly believe in the freedom of all individuals and groups to express themselves, as long as the rights of other people are not undermined and the essential integrity of our national rights is not treasoned. Christians maintain the integrity of their philosophic approach, their love for the Word of God, and are willing to listen to the ideas of others, and in return expect to have the opportunity to be heard as well. When others express their ideas, Christians filter those ideas through their own philosophic approach, because the Christian's essential difference, as he sees it, is that his ultimate Reality—the God of the Bible—is totally in opposition to the other proposed ultimate reality—matter plus energy shaped by chance. Therefore, for the Christian, man cannot be the measure of all things. God, the ultimate Reality as revealed in His Word, is at the heart of the Christian's life and practice, personally and professionally.

CHALKBOARD CHALLENGES

1. Think about the teaching profession today. Presumably, most of you who read this book are either preparing to go into the teaching profession or you are already in it. Perhaps you've been in it, gone to another occupation, and then returned to it. What improvements do you see needing to be made in order to attract additional qualified people to the teaching profession?

2. List in your teacher's notebook those areas in which you feel you need to improve in terms of your self-understanding. These may be matters of how you feel about yourself, or how you feel about your students, fellow teachers, administrators. List these areas, and then develop a plan to help yourself work on them step by step to achieve the levels you want to achieve.

3. If you are not familiar with all of the teacher organizations, journals, and the opportunities for training and professional upgrading, may we encourage you as soon as possible to become acquainted with the organizations and with the training opportunities, so that you will have the information you need to make your professional decisions about these matters. The journals were listed at the end of chapter 1—not an exhaustive list—but a list that at least can be a starter for you. For the names and addresses of teacher organizations and other professional educational organizations, check with your advisor at your school, or with your librarian, who will be able to give you the information you need. If you are a student, a number of organizations offer special opportunities and discounted membership fees to encourage students to become part of the professional organizations.

4. What do you see as the issues that are controversial for you as you seek to be a competent teacher in our pluralistic society? This is not, incidentally, an issue to be taken lightly. The questions impinging on the teaching-learning process emerging from this particular issue of pluralism are of enormous impact. We encourage you to begin thinking about them, and continue thinking about them, to

increase your repertoire of resources with which to operate in the teaching-learning process in a competent manner.

Want to Know More?

ISSUES AFFECTING TEACHING

A good source of the pros and cons of issues that affect education is the book edited by James William Noll, *Taking Sides: Clashing Views on Controversial Educational Issues* (Guilford, Conn.: Dushkin, 1983).

RESEARCH

A very helpful book is Philip L. Hosford, ed., *Using What We Know About Teaching* (Alexandria, Va.: ASCD, 1984). This is an excellent compendium of research about teaching and how we can put more of the research into the practical operations of the teaching-learning process.

A book that is helpful in so many ways for administrators and teachers, and which condenses the latest research on effective schools and classrooms, is David A. Squires, William G. Hewitt, and John K. Segers, *Effective Schools and Classrooms: A Research Based Perspective* (Alexandria, Va.: ASCD, 1983).

PERSONAL AND PROFESSIONAL DEVELOPMENT

There are a number of excellent books relating to the personal and professional development of the teacher, or containing aspects of those major concerns, from the Christian perspective. Kenneth Gangel and Warren Benson have just recently written a book entitled *Christian Education: Its History and Philosophy* (Chicago: Moody, 1983). They provide an excellent bibliography that will give you many more sources of Christian books and journals in which you will find materials of great help and interest. We also recommend Paul A. Kienel, ed., *The Philosophy of Christian School Education*, Rev. ed. (Whittier, Calif.: ASCI, 1978). This book covers the many areas related to a Christian school, and again contains a bibliography that will be helpful to lead you to further sources.

Many of the major publishers have basic books on the role of the teacher or introduction to teacher education themes, and we suggest that you write to the publishers and ask them for their particular titles in regard to the areas in which you have special interest.

20

Future Changes in the Teaching-Learning Process

CONTENTS

	PAGE
Key Words	487
That's Debatable!	488
Foresight	488
The Three Most Pertinent Trends	490
Education for the Future	493
The Future in the Teaching-Learning Process: Some Methods and Examples	495
The Christian Teacher and the Future Teaching-Learning Process	500
Hindsight	502
Chalkboard Challenges	502
Want to Know More?	503

KEY TERMS

Cross-impact matrix
    A technique which uses the square grid pattern of a matrix to analyze the interrelationship between events and developments
Delphi technique
    Seeks a consensus of experts by having their opinions anonymously filtered through an intermediary
Rehabilitation
    The conviction that we must restructure and rehabilitate our "smokestack" industries, so they can regain strong competitive positions

Retrofitting
> The reeducation of people on a lifelong basis for keeping up with technological changes

Scenario
> A narrative about the future which leads from the present to a specific future time to provoke thinking about an issue or situation

Techno-fix
> The conviction that technology can provide solutions to our problems

Transformationalism
> The conviction there need to be changes in human behavior in order to cope with the future

THAT'S DEBATABLE!
Can Computer-Based Instruction Improve Student Learning?

An analysis of fifty-one studies of computer-based instruction (CBI) shows the following:

1. CBI can improve student learning. The average effect is to raise student test scores from the 50th to the 63rd percentile.
2. Student attitude toward the subject being learned and student ratings of the quality of instruction are only slightly more favorable with CBI. Statistically, the differences are not significant on this item.
3. In contrast, students' attitudes toward computers are strikingly more positive as a result of CBI.
4. Finally, CBI has been reported as saving anywhere from 39 percent to 88 percent of student learning time.

Because of the rapid change in computer technology and classroom use of computers, these findings do not necessarily predict future results.[1]

FORESIGHT

Asked by a school administrator to offer advice on the improvement of English instruction in the schools, Walter Lippmann once wrote:

> Experience that can't be described and communicated in words cannot long be vividly remembered. When you looked at the stars once and remarked that they are grand, and then again only in order to say that the heavens are swell, why not look at the Wrigley Chewing Gum sign on Broadway which is equally grand and swell?

---

1. Resource Information Service (ASCD), *Educational Leadership* 41 (September 1983):21. Reprinted with permission of the Association for Supervision and Curriculum Development. Copyright © 1983 by the Association for Supervision and Curriculum Development. All rights reserved.

Future Changes in the Teaching-Learning Process

Without words to give precision to ideas, the ideas themselves soon become indistinguishable.[2]

In a very real and frustrating kind of way, Walter Lippmann's words express the kind of emotion many people feel when they not only think about all of the possibilities of the future, but read the many suggested solutions for the problems we will be facing. It is frustrating to an author writing a chapter or a book on the future, because a selection must be made out of the reams and reams of materials which have been, and are being, written about the future of our society, our planet, and our universe.

Some of these solutions are "doomsday," and others take on a Buck Rogers nature. As Alvin Toffler has noted: "Every society faces not merely a succession of *probable* futures, but an array of *possible* futures, and a conflict over *preferable* futures. The management of change is the effort to convert certain possibles into probables, in pursuit of agreed on preferables."[3]

What of the teacher and the teaching-learning process in the future? That is the question with which we are concerned as we conclude this textbook on the teaching-learning process. In one sense, this is the most important chapter in the text from the author's standpoint, because "time marches on" and with it come vast changes, whether we like them or not. And the changes are coming with an unbelievable speed in our lifetime. Certainly, as responsible educators, we want to prepare our children in the most excellent fashion possible to meet the almost exploding changes with which they will have to cope.

It is the most important chapter in another sense because it provides an excellent opportunity to indicate how technology fits in with the Christian viewpoint, and the strength of the perspective the Christian viewpoint brings to the teacher in the future teaching-learning process.

In this chapter we will look at two writers whom we consider to be representative of the many experts in the wide number of fields concerned with futuristics. The first is Arthur J. Lewis, professor of education at the University of Florida, on whom we draw for his discussion of the three most pertinent trends as we go toward the twenty-first century. The second is perhaps the best known writer in the field of futuristics and education, Harold Shane, who is currently professor of education at Indiana University in Bloomington. We draw from Shane some of his provocative ideas about education for the future. Then we share some methods and examples of ways in which we can incorporate some techniques into the curriculum concerning the future. Finally, we move to the topic of the Christian teacher and the future teaching-learning process.

---

2. From *Educational Agenda for the 1980s,* by Fred M. Hechinger, Fastback #161, p. 20. © 1981 Phi Delta Kappa Educational Foundation.
3. Alvin Toffler, *Future Shock* (New York: Random House, 1970). Used by permission.

The Three Most Pertinent Trends

The nature of society and education is being transformed very rapidly by technology, the information age, and demographic shifts. So says Arthur J. Lewis, in an article entitled "Education for the Twenty-first Century."[4] By looking at these three trends, we can very rapidly get ourselves into some of the major issues facing all of us in our confrontation with the future.

THE RAPID DEVELOPMENT OF TECHNOLOGY

We need not really dwell long on this, since we hear about it and read about it and discuss it virtually every day of our lives.

This is a time of exponential growth, as evidenced by the world's population figures. In July 1980, the United States Department of HEW and the Council on Environmental Quality submitted a report to President Carter entitled "Global 2000." The report predicts that the world's population will increase by 55 percent to 6.35 billion people over the next two decades.[5] Lewis refers to Platt's article in The Futurist to emphasize that technological development is also growing exponentially.[6] To illustrate this he notes the article in Scientific American: "If the aircraft industry had evolved as spectacularly as the computer industry, a Boeing 767 would cost five hundred dollars today, and it would circle this globe in twenty minutes on five gallons of fuel."[7]

He then cites as another illustration from the New York Times, a description of a communications network between Washington, D.C. and New York City: "A pair of glass fibers as thin as a hair can carry 1300 simultaneous conversations . . . with the laser pulsing 90 million times a second, the entire content of Webster's Unabridged Dictionary could be transmitted through a single fiber in six seconds."[8]

And then, Lewis points out that our look at the future gives us a picture not only of accelerated technological development, but of acceleration itself.

THE INFORMATION AGE

By now, most of us have heard this age designated in this manner, and we are at least generally aware that our entrance into this age is deeply influencing our image of the future, by producing changes in value systems, changes in the way we think, changes in the structures of our society (political, economic, etc.).

---

4. Arthur J. Lewis, "Education for the Twenty-first Century," Educational Leadership 41 (September 1983):9-10.
5. Noted in Robert M. Bjork and Stewart D. Fraser, Population, Education, and Children's Futures (Bloomington, Ind.: Phi Delta Kappa, 1981), p. 31.
6. John Platt, "The Acceleration of Evolution," The Futurist 15 (February 1981):14-23.
7. Hoo-Min D. Toong and Amar Gupta, "Personal Computers," Scientific American 247 (December 1982):87. Copyright © 1982 Scientific American, Inc. Used by permission.
8. Andrew Pollack, "Lighthouse Era is Ushered In," New York Times, 11 February 1983, p. 29. Copyright © 1983 by The New York Times Company. Reprinted by permission.

Lewis cites four significant ways in which this information age differs from the industrial age, and they are worthy of our consideration.

1. The core of the industrial age is powered machinery; the core of the information age is the computer.
2. The industrial age replaced manual work and magnified physical strengths; the information age enables us to replace mental work and magnify mental capabilities.
3. Goods produced in the industrial age are expended; information, the product of the information age, cannot be depleted.
4. Energy—oil, coal, nuclear power—is the driving force in the industrial age; education is the driving force in the information age.

Lewis concludes his discussion of this particular trend by emphasizing that education, which was really a handmaiden in the industrial age, is the *foundation* of the information age.[9]

THE RECENT DEMOGRAPHIC SHIFTS

One of the reasons we chose Arthur Lewis as one of the representatives for this chapter on the future is the inimitable way in which he brings figures together to make his points. In terms of the implications of demographics for education, for example, Lewis cites the fact that the 1957 baby boom (4.3 million) was followed by a baby bust as the fertility rate dropped. Thus, when the 1957 babies begin to retire in 2010, there will be only two active workers paying for the benefits of each retired person. In 1950, that ratio was sixteen to one; today it is approximately three to one.

Another illustration of the consequences of the demographic shifts is the fact that seven million fewer young people will reach working age in the 1990s than in the 1970s. According to Pifer, this fact "places a very high premium on making the most of the much smaller number of Americans now being born . . . human capital formation, always important, has become many times more so because casualties resulting from poor nutrition, poor health care, inferior education, low motivation, and so on simply can no longer be afforded."[10] As Lewis points out, it is very clear that educational programs simply cannot waste human talent—for if they do, they will undermine our society.

Lewis then comments on what these trends mean for the teaching-learning process. There is, of course, no question that one of our national priorities is now to improve the quality of education. We have talked about this extensively in relation to the National Commission on Education's report on excellence and other similar reports. More and more careers are going to be requiring thorough backgrounds in

---

9. Lewis, p. 10.
10. Alan Pifer, "The Report of the President," *Annual Report 1982* (New York: Carnegie Corporation of New York, 1982), p. 6. Used by permission.

computer science, mathematics, and the sciences. If an individual is undereducated, fewer opportunities will be available to that individual. Lewis emphasizes the fact that skills which today are considered high-level (problem-solving, analysis, synthesis, critical thinking, etc.) in the future will become absolutely essential for many workers.

Leonard Silk, quoted by Lewis in his article, tells of the New York stock exchange study concerning Japan. The purpose of that study was to find out why productivity in Japan was so much higher than it is in the United States. The conclusion: "The single most important factor in Japan's extraordinarily high productivity—more important than quality circles, techniques of management, or the partnership between businesses and government—is the high quality of Japanese primary and secondary education.

"The great accomplishment of Japanese primary and secondary education lies not in its creation of a brilliant elite," says this report, "but in producing a high average level of capability in its graduates."[11]

The implication of this finding is that we must avoid the trap of raising standards just for the more able students in our schools. We must have both equality and quality in our educational process. Our expectations for *all* students must be higher.

In concluding his article, Arthur Lewis points to the situation that looking into the future is so complex, it is hard to forecast the problems of the twenty-first century. He says we can anticipate something of the nature of those problems, however. "They will surely be global, and require the integration of knowledge from different fields for their solutions. Increasingly, the first decisions that are made will have to be correct; the harm that may result from a wrong decision could be irreversible. Finally, it will be increasingly important to apply value judgment when weighing solutions to problems."[12] The new technologies—genetic engineering would be an example—have a tremendous impact on human welfare, much more so than did earlier technologies, and therefore value considerations in guiding technological developments are more important than they have ever been.

The final thrust of Lewis's article is that we must not expect technology to solve our social problems in the same way it has solved, and created, so many scientific problems. Lewis points out that that is another kind of trap that allows us to abdicate our personal responsibility for improving society. There are two things, Lewis says, of paramount importance we can do as we engage in the teaching-learning process in relation to the future: (1) We can help the students develop skills of reading, writing, and computing. But those skills have to represent more than mere information. Included must be the development of the ability to

11. Leonard Silk, "A Lesson from Japan," *New York Times*, 17 November 1982, p. 30. Copyright © 1982 by The New York Times Company. Reprinted by permission.
12. Lewis, p. 10.

comprehend information—to analyze it, to synthesize it, and apply it in a value-oriented way. (2) We can encourage students to assume responsibility for their own learning. Says Lewis, "The ultimate goal of education is to shift to the individual the burden of pursuing his or her own education. To cope with emerging global problems, people will need to continue learning throughout their lives. Their survival will depend on it."[13]

EDUCATION FOR THE FUTURE

We turn now to our second representative of education in relation to the future, Harold Shane. Shane is a highly respected scholar in relation to educational futuristics, and the kinds of things he has to say are highly stimulating and make us think carefully about the future and its influences.

WHAT LEADING SCHOLARS SAY

In his book *Educating for a New Millennium,* Shane tells of his interviews with some 132 physicists, chemists, biologists, anthropologists, economists, and other comparable scientists from all over the world.[14] His purpose was to find out what these scholars felt essential for students to know if we are going to survive and live as decent people. Shane reports that *the main concern of the scholars who were interviewed is whether or not human beings can cope fast enough to deal with the problems and changes that threaten them.*[15]

SUGGESTED DIVERSE SOLUTIONS

The wide variety of leading scholars interviewed by Shane came up with widely diverse solutions. Those solutions emerged from the particular point of view each of the scholars held. Some of them took the approach known as "techno-fix"—they believed that technological solutions would provide the answers needed for the problems going into the future. A second group, known as the transformationalists, believe technological solutions by themselves will not be adequate—there will need to be changes in human behavior as well. A third group, whom we will term "rehabilitators" believe it is vital for us to restructure or rehabilitate our smokestack industries—automobile and steel manufacturing—so they can regain a strong competitive position. For any of these approaches, an infusion of high technology was named as absolutely necessary in order to prepare people adequately to meet the problems that will be theirs in the future.

---

13. Ibid.
14. Harold G. Shane, *Educating for a New Millennium* (Bloomington, Ind.: Phi Delta Kappa, 1981).
15. Harold Shane, "On Education in the Future: A Conversation with Harold Shane," *Educational Leadership* 41 (September 1983):11. Used by permission.

A CURRICULUM BRIDGE

In his book *Educational Significance of the Future*, Shane called for fundamental reforms in the schools.[16] Says Shane,

> What we need is a life-long learning continuum beginning with universal nursery education (author's note: a highly controversial issue!), and upgraded experiences for children at age four or five, who are grouped together until they have attained the developmental characteristics of six-year-olds. At age five, six, or seven, and in some cases even eight, children would be grouped with others who had a comparable quality of six-year-oldness. Youngsters at any given time are not the same age in any way except chronologically. We need to figure out some way to reduce the ability spread—even though this means increasing the age spread somewhat in a given group.[17]

And then Shane points out that a learning bridge needs to be built from our current teaching-learning process into the areas that will help to prepare our people for the future. Included in this process is the "retrofitting" of people on a lifelong basis, which means reeducating them periodically in order to keep up with technological changes. And Shane points out if our schools do not meet these new technological needs, some other kinds of agencies will.

Included further in the teaching-learning process ought to be such items as emphasis upon critical listening skills because of the huge amount of auditory and visual input from radio, TV, and the media, which we have to process; instruction that can help us interpret the media—not manipulate, but select the news; a good general education in order to have a better understanding of what is occurring; and top-notch vocational education—which means helping individuals understand not only electronics, but what electronics is doing to our industries and our lifestyles and our educational practices—both in the school and in the home.[18]

THE PARENTS' ROLE

Shane emphasizes that schools must move to establish closer relationships with parents in order to help them with the manner in which children use equipment in the home. Says Shane: "Apparently, there are parents who take some responsibility for TV and other electronic gear in their homes, but there are certainly parents who don't. One of the challenges to education and our society is what to do about this."[19]

It is interesting to note that Shane's emphasis here is on how the children use

---

16. *The Educational Significance of the Future*, by Harold G. Shane, © 1973 by Phi Delta Kappa Educational Foundation. Used by permission.
17. Shane, "On Education in the Future," p. 13. Used by permission.
18. Ibid., p. 12.
19. Ibid.

Future Changes in the Teaching-Learning Process   495

the equipment, but his concern is also with what they see and hear, and ultimately what they learn to prepare them for coping with the future, as a result of the use of that equipment.

OPTIMISM AND PESSIMISM ABOUT THE FUTURE

Shane is optimistic about the future. He believes there is a growing concern on the part of many people who are becoming convinced we have to "make tomorrow work" in the school and in our society. He points out that, in his judgment, many of our young people are more thoughtful and task-oriented than they used to be. "I am talking about a general return to thoughtfulness and a departure from the 'me generation.' This is partly a result of changing parental attitudes, and of growing concerns for the world's future good that are local, national, and international." And Shane continues, "It may be that the times that are being thrust upon us will, in effect, serve to lubricate our educational efforts to achieve the renaissance that the information society demands."[20]

THE FUTURE IN THE TEACHING-LEARNING PROCESS: SOME METHODS AND EXAMPLES

For suggestions as to methodology and examples of actual schools where certain methodology has worked, we turn to a third representative of the futuristics field, Violet Allain. In her book *Futuristics and Education* she sets forth first of all some suggested methods for use in the teaching-learning process to help students develop a more flexible attitude toward the future and to think more imaginatively about it.[21]

METHODS

Scenarios. A scenario is a narrative that describes a possible series of events that might lead to some future state of affairs. It usually describes the events of the curve from the present right up to a specific date in the future, and the purpose of a scenario is to construct a logical sequence of events leading from the present to a future condition. The Insight box (fig. 20.2) contains an example of a scenario and how it might be used.

For younger students, Allain suggests that one of the techniques you might use would be to supply newspaper headlines that might appear in the year 2025 such as: CARS BANNED FROM STREETS AND HIGHWAYS, or NEW LAW SAYS PEOPLE OVER THIRTY-FIVE MUST BE ELIMINATED, or LAST DROP OF GASOLINE SOLD TO THE PRESIDENT OF THE U.S. Then ask the students to write the newpaper article to match the headline.

20. Ibid., p. 13.
21. *Futuristics and Education,* by Violet Allain, © 1979 Phi Delta Kappa Educational Foundation. Used by permission.

Science fiction. Allain points out that the accuracy with which some of our science fiction writers have described our future cannot really be ignored. And it is for this reason, in future-oriented studies, science fiction is recommended as a method and science fiction is used as an example of a possible alternative future, in order to get students to anticipate change more readily. Allain puts stress upon what she calls social science fiction, where the emphasis is on how people cope with the situation in the context of the future. She cites Aldous Huxley's *Brave New World* where embryos are grown artificially so that people can be genetically

---

Insight: Predictions About the Future

Speculation concerning the future and what it has in store for us has always been a favorite subject of discussion for many people. Some predictions have been quite accurate, for example, H. G. Wells's prophesying the emergence of sprawling megalopolises, as well as space exploration. However, some have simply not come true. At the turn of this century a magazine writer, Ray Stannard Baker, predicted, "Automobiles will replace the crashing hoofs, making city streets almost as quiet as a country lane and far less crowded."

Or consider the faulty forecasting involved when King Ferdinand and Queen Isabella organized a committee in 1486 to analyze Columbus's plans to sail west to find a shorter route to the East Indies. In 1490, the committee reported the voyage was impossible because (1) a voyage to Asia would require three years; (2) the Western Ocean is infinite and perhaps unnavigable; (3) if he reached the Antipodes (the land on the other side of the globe from Europe) he could not get back; (4) there are no Antipodes because the greater part of the globe is covered with water, and because St. Augustine says so; (5) of the five zones, only three are habitable; and (6) so many centuries after the creation it was unlikely anyone could find hitherto unknown lands of any value.

Obviously, predictions about the future are not hard to make, but they are fruitless and vain exercises unless we make a serious attempt to look at the future in light of present developments and what the consequences of those present developments logically might lead to. And this is what serious futurists' research attempts to do.

From *Futuristics in Education,* by Violet Allain, p. 15. ©1979 by Phi Delta Kappa Educational Foundation. Used by permission.

Fig. 20.1

> **Insight: A Future Scenario**
>
> In the scenario "Eco-Catastrophe!" Paul Ehrlich forecasts the death of the ocean. "The end of the ocean came late in the summer of 1979, and it came even more rapidly than the biologists had expected. There had even been signs for more than a decade, commencing with the discovery in 1968 that DDT slows down photosynthesis in marine plant life. It was announced in a short paper in a technical journal, *Science,* but to ecologists it smacked of doomsday. They knew that all life in the sea depends on photosynthesis, the chemical process by which green plants bind the sun's energy and make it available to living things. And they knew that DDT and similar chlorinated hydrocarbons had polluted the entire surface of the earth, including the sea." This is the kind of scenario that could be used in the classroom and which could help students to think imaginatively about the future and to explore past and present trends as they are apt to lead to future events.
>
> From Paul Ehrlich, "Eco-Catastrophe!" in Alvin Toffler, ed., *The Futurists* (New York: Random House, 1972). Cited in Allain, p. 24.

Fig. 20.2

designed to fit society's needs, and the fact that there is a culture that is static and uniform. And the reading of that book usually sparks lively discussions of values, politics, and individual freedom and raises the questions about the direction in which our society is heading.[22] Figure 20.3 presents some creative questions for use with science fiction in the classroom as presented by Hollister and Thompson in their book *Grokking the Future.*[23]

Group opinion. Under this kind of technique are polls that can be used to gather information about the next ten, twenty-five, or fifty years from various groups in the community. From these polls the students can get some ideas as to what changes people expect in the future and how aware of these changes and how concerned about them people in various groups may be.

Also under group opinion, Allain suggests the Delphi technique, which seeks a consensus of experts by having their opinions anonymously filtered through an intermediary. This technique can be adapted to the classroom, and how to do this and an example of it are given in detailed fashion in Allain's book. The purpose of the Delphi technique is not to find out what *will* happen, but to provide a fairly reliable indicator of a consensus opinion of what *might* happen.[24]

22. Ibid., p. 27.
23. B.C. Hollister and D.C. Thompson, *Grokking the Future* (Potomac, Md.: Pflaum/Standard, 1973).
24. Allain, p. 29.

> **Insight: Some Questions for the Classroom When Studying Science Fiction**
>
> Economic: What is considered wealth in this society?
> Political: How is order kept in the society?
> Who has the power?
> What sort of leader is considered good?
> What is the author's conception of man: is man basically good? Bad? Trustworthy?
> Social: What classes exist?
> How does one gain and lose status?
> What is the place of the family?
> Religious: What religious beliefs prevail?
> What is the role of a supernatural being?
> How is the religion organized?
> Artistic: Is any allowance made for artistic and aesthetic expression? What kinds of art, music, literature, if any, exist in this society?
> Other cultures: How does the society view other societies? Suspiciously?
> General: How would you like living in this particular society?
> What would you find most distasteful about it?
> What would you find most enjoyable about it?
> What would pose the greatest threat to society? Why?
>
> From Bernard C. Hollister and Dean C. Thompson, *Grokking the Future* (Potomac, Md.: Pflaum/Standard, 1973). (Some of the questions have been omitted for the sake of brevity.)

Fig. 20.3

CROSS-IMPACT MATRIX

This is a technique that uses the square grid pattern of a matrix to analyze the interrelationships between events and developments. "It operates under the assumption that most events and trends are in some way connected with other events and trends. Some versions of this method require complicated mathematical computations, but simpler procedures can also afford one the opportunity of analyzing various forces in terms of their impact on each other. Simply imagine a square with four spaces down and four spaces across. Across the top in spaces two, three, and four you would write a number of factors which you want to deal with and then vertically down the left side in spaces two, three, and four you would write those same factors. Then you simply come down and across the column in order to see how the two factors interact, and you think about them individually, and discuss them as a group or as a class. For example, if one of the factors were "I want to go to college" you come down the grid until you get to where the factor is listed "I want to travel"—as you think about those two factors, you might come up with any number of conclusions or possibilities about them, such as, "If I travel I might not have time to go to college. I can't do both." This is a very simple illustration of the use of the cross-impact matrix. It can be developed into a very sophisticated kind of technique using major problem areas such as population, energy, technology, international relations, life-style.[25] For details on these and other methods, we suggest you read Allain's book *Futuristics and Education*.

SELECTED EXAMPLES

For elementary school level, one of the examples Allain gives in her book is called "Spaceship Earth," and this particular project involved eighty sixth-graders at John Tyler Elementary School in Alexandria, Virginia. "The youngsters transformed their classroom into an imaginary Spaceship Earth and attempted to create an environment in which all their learning needs could be satisfied during an interstellar journey. Among other projects, several students created a planetarium in a tent, the inside of which was covered with star charts and contained a model of the Apollo Twelve capsule."[26]

For an example of a project at the secondary school level, Allain cites as one of several, "Futuristics: Theory and Application." This is a year-long course in the high schools of Richfield and Burnsville, Minnesota, which consists of two major parts: (1) the students are introduced to theoretical futuristics; they study the ideas of futurists and the nature of complex modern society; and (2) they become engaged in an independent project in which each student researches the future of a specific area in which he or she may be interested—an area such as aerospace, the family, genetics.[27]

"Colloquium on the Future" is a course offered at Ball State University in Muncie, Indiana. This covers the subjects of education, nursing, technology, business, and many other areas. The colloquium is concerned with how the images we hold of the future influence our behavior today; how we got here and where we appear to be headed in the future; how our present attitudes may change in the future; and the role of values in determining the future.[28]

Allain concludes her book with several suggestions for implementing futuristics at different levels of education. She stresses that an interdisciplinary approach is recommended in order to help students realize that solutions to future problems are not always found just within one field of study. Her book contains a very brief but very excellent bibliography connected with future studies.

25. Ibid., pp. 30-32.
26. Ibid., p. 38.
27. Ibid., p. 39.
28. Ibid.

The Christian Teacher and the Future Teaching-Learning Process

As the Christian reads the futurists' literature, he is almost bound to have mixed emotions. The Christian realizes that the forces at work in our society are highly significant, for they can be devastating to the lives of human beings. Or they can be turned into forces that are helpful in the daily struggles through which all of us must go.

However, it can be fairly said that because of the Christian's belief in the God of the Bible as the ultimate Reality, the Alpha and the Omega, the Christian has a perspective for the future that differs fom the individual who does not believe in the God of the Bible. The Christian believes without mental reservation that time is in the hands of God, and that includes future time—in fact, it includes both time and eternity. Therefore, while the Christian takes with utmost seriousness the time as God lets it flow to us "one moment at a time" here upon the earth, he likewise sees all of those moments yet to come as being under the ultimate control of the God of creation.

What does this mean, then, for the Christian teacher in the future teaching-learning process? It means, of course, he will bring with him to that process—whatever form it may take—the confidence that he is still under the calling of God to be a teacher. As such, he will be alert to and responsive to technological changes and their impact on the lives of students and others.

Let us look at the situation a bit more closely, as we come to the conclusion of this text.

1. The Christian believes that the universe—the multiverse, if you will—is the Lord's. He is the Ultimate Reality, He is the God of the Bible, He has created all things, He sustains all things, and His purpose will ultimately be fulfilled. This does not mean that the human being has no freedom, but rather, precisely the opposite—the freedom to choose or reject this God of the Bible, who is the Ultimate Reality. We simply call attention one more time to the two possibilities for the origin of life: the God of the Bible or matter-plus-energy-shaped-by-chance (MESC). The Christian believes that is the ultimate choice, and all else flows from that basic choice.

2. Man (in the generic sense) is to have *dominion over* the earth. He is to *subdue* it. This is specifically commanded and spelled out in the book of Genesis. Many of us as Christians see this as the divine order to engage in the technological processes which help us to have dominion over the forces of nature. Therefore, technology is not something from which we hide our faces or try to escape, but we seek to confront it directly and bring it within the will of God. The Christian brings this clear commandment from the Scriptures as he or she enters into the teaching-learning process.

3. Man is the master of things. This third principle emerges directly from the second one. Again, in the book of Genesis, whatever Adam called the things that

were brought to him, or that he saw round about him, was the name they were given. This included the fowls of the air, the fish of the sea, the creatures of the land. Adam was to name and to tame the things of earth.

There is a problem here, however. It is as old as Adam, as current as this present moment, and as futuristic as the farthest reaches of time. If all you have is man as the master of things, if all of the control and the valuing process and the teaching-learning process are measured by man alone, there evolves what we term today *secular humanism*. Secular humanism rejects any supernatural Ultimate Reality, and declares that man is the measure of all things. This opens the way to situational ethics, to the misuse and abuse of technology, and logically leads to a chaotic, hopeless future. It is the next principle that makes all the difference.

4. God is the master of men. Man is to be the master of things, but God is to be the master of men. Everything the Christian does is to be "done as unto the Lord." Every service we perform, every piece of work we do, is a divine service, whether its level of influence is high or low. Therefore, the Christian enters enthusiastically into the world of science and technology, because he believes it is part of the will of God to do so; when he learns something new, it simply adds to his sophistication about how God's universe operates. He then seeks always to put that technology to work within the will of God. The Christian teacher who carries this conviction into the teaching-learning process sees the challenge of the futuristic forces and their possible impact as an exciting implementation of service under the will of God.

5. Until Jesus comes, the Christian is to "occupy." The Christian who understands that the God of the Bible is the Ultimate Reality, in whom all things exist and by whom all things were created, sees all of history and all of creation, including all of the future in relation to that Ultimate Reality. For He is the God who is also the God and Father of our Lord and Savior Jesus Christ, the God who gave His only begotten Son on the cross of Calvary for us, while we were yet sinners. The Christian knows there is only one opportunity for salvation, and that is through the death, burial, and resurrection of Jesus Christ. God, the Ultimate Reality, entered the world of space-time, in order to make possible our reconciliation with Him. And he did this not in an easy way, but came as a little babe, born of the virgin Mary, in the manger at Bethlehem. He was tempted in every way as we are and then suffered beyond all our imagination as the pure Son of God dying on the cross. The God who made all things, who sent His Son to die for our salvation and to resurrect Him from the grave to give us victory over death itself—this God is in charge of time and eternity. Therefore, the Christian's past, present, and future are in the hands of God.

Christian teachers then look upon the teaching-learning process in a twofold manner: (1) Having prepared themselves initially in the best possible manner, and keeping up-to-date as good professionals ought to do in their literary/subject field, they commit themselves, as a calling under God, to provide in the teaching-learning process the very best teaching-learning experience they know how to provide. They want their students to be knowledgeable, literate, thoughtful, and prepared for the present and the future. The Christian classroom, or any other setting where the teaching-learning process is occurring, ought to be the epitome of academic excellence, for it is a stewardship of time, effort, human life, and talent under God.

(2) Christian teachers are interested vitally in the total development of their students—physically, mentally, and spiritually. This is so because each child is made in the image of God. Each child is precious in the sight of the God of all creation. That God is the Ultimate Reality. In response to His calling, Christian teachers view their engagement in the teaching-learning process as their primary service during the "occupation" until Jesus comes. The quality of their service is the measure of the integrity of their response to His calling. What a marvelous and exciting way to occupy and be occupied—spending one's time, talent, and energy, helping Christian students develop into Christian maturity—body, mind, and spirit—under the leadership of the God of the Bible who is as well the Lord of the past, the present, and the future!

Hindsight

There are increasingly larger amounts of futuristic literature being published. It is a matter of critical concern for all of us. In this chapter, we chose representatives of those who write the literature, and presented key points relating to education and the future. These included the three most pertinent trends as Arthur Lewis viewed them; the major concerns of Harold Shane, who is optimistic about the future; and some techniques and examples of how to incorporate futuristic teaching into the curriculum of the school as suggested by Violet Allain.

Our final concern in this chapter was the work of the Christian teacher as it relates to the future of the teaching-learning process. Over the roadway leading from the present to the future, like a sign on the highway pointing the direction, are the words "Occupy until Jesus comes."

Chalkboard Challenges

1. H. G. Wells once commented, "Human history becomes more and more a race between education and catastrophe." Think about this statement in relation to future-oriented education. Can education make any difference? If so, what is that difference or those differences? Jot some of these down in your teacher's notebook for future reference.

2. Critique some of the suggested techniques in this chapter for implementing future-oriented teaching into the curriculum. As a Christian teacher, how could you use them in the teaching-learning process, and do it from a Christian perspective? Can you think of other techniques that you might use for this same kind of purpose? List them in your teacher's notebook for future reference.

3. What differences do you see for the Christian teacher in contrast with the teacher who has no belief in the God of the Bible, in relation to the manner in which the future is viewed? Think carefully. Analyze well. Take time and write these down with precise wording in your teacher's notebook. For example, think about the logic of being a teacher—especially viewing the future in the teaching-learning process—if you had no belief in the supernatural God of the Bible. Would it be worth it? Why?

4. Try your hand at writing a Christian scenario for the future you believe you could really use with a class at the level in which you plan to teach. Then, with proper permission, try this out sometime with your class during your student teaching process. Evaluate how it works. It is one exciting way to help get your students thinking about the Christian future in relation to the teaching-learning process. Depending upon the age level of your class, you may choose to use headlines, or some other particular method, rather than a scenario. If so, make up the headlines you are going to use, and think about the questions you want to raise with your students ahead of time. Listen carefully to their responses as well.

Want to Know More?

HAROLD G. SHANE

Harold G. Shane is one of the outstanding and respected writers about the future and education. We suggest here several of his books, and recommend that as you have the opportunity, you read each of them.

Curriculum Change Toward the Twenty-First Century (Washington, D.C.: National Education Association, 1977).

The Educational Significance of the Future (Bloomington, Ind.: Phi Delta Kappa, 1973).

Educating for a New Millennium (Bloomington, Ind.: Phi Delta Kappa, 1981).

We recommend also "An Interview with Harold Shane," *Educational Leadership* 41 (September 1983):11-13.

EDUCATION IN THE FUTURE

For a discussion of many areas of concern in relation to the future and education, the issue of *Educational Leadership* for September 1983 would make interesting reading. *Educational Leadership* is the journal of the Association for Supervision and Curriculum Development (ASCD), located in Alexandria, Virginia.

A book with a great many common sense ideas about the future is Fred M. Hechinger, *Education Agenda for the 1980s* (Bloomington, Ind.: Phi Delta Kappa, 1981).

Another book of interest in relation to the future is: Robert M. Bjork and

Stewart F. Fraser, *Population, Education, and Children's Futures* (Bloomington, Ind.: Phi Delta Kappa, 1980).

A third book from Phi Delta Kappa, a fastback, is Violet A. Allain, *Futuristics and Education,* 1979.

Two issues of the *Phi Delta Kappan,* one for April 1984, the other for May 1984, contain articles of great interest concerning the future of the teaching-learning process.

THE FUTURE: SUBJECT

Two items by Alvin Toffler, one a book, the other an article, will be of interest to you. The book is entitled *Future Shock* (New York: Random House, 1970). The article is "The Psychology of the Future" in Alvin Toffler, ed., *Learning for Tomorrow* (New York: Vintage, 1974).

You may be interested in reading a two-part series by James Stirewalt, "The Future as an Academic Subject, Part 1," *World Future Society Bulletin* II (January/February 1977):16-20; and "Part 2," II (March/April 1977) 9-14.

Glossary

Ability
: A trained aptitude

Ability grouping
: The practice of organizing classroom groups to put together students of a particular age/grade who have similar standings on measures of achievement and capability

Academic
: Generally a designation of the cognitive aspects of instruction, specifically the formalized school subjects such as the sciences or humanities

Acceleration
: Developmental progress more rapid than the average in any of several possible areas such as mental, physical, social

Accommodation
: The changing of the individual's intellectual structure to fit the new information

Achievement motivation
: A term which refers to individuals for whom success and its visible concomitants are especially important

Achievement test
: Designed to assess the degree to which a student has achieved the objectives of a learning experience, that is, knowledge of the content presented in a course

Actualization
: Stresses the positive nature of behavior and views motivation from the standpoint that we strive to control our environment

Advance organizer (Ausubel)
: Introductory material, usually general and abstract, providing students ahead of time with some structure to aid them in learning the specific information to follow

Affective
: Refers to the way people feel about their perceptions of themselves, other people, and their world

Affective domain
: Includes objectives for developing appreciation, interests, attitudes, values

Alternative school
: Any school other than a typical public school, usually characterized by more flexibility in procedures, a closer relationship among teachers and students, and extended responsibilities for students and faculty; refers to both private schools or to special programs set up within the public school domain; students and staff usually there by choice, so they are sometimes referred to as "choice" schools

Applied behavior analysis
: Application of principles of learning discovered in controlled settings to wider social contexts

Appropriate behavior
: Behavior that is productive and contributes to the teaching-learning process

Aptitude
: Ability before it is trained

Aptitude test
: A measurement device used to estimate the amount of a specific ability, potential, or capacity possessed by an individual in a specific area, for example, artistic aptitude

Assimilation
: The changing of new information to fit the existing intellectual structure of the individual

Attribution
: These explanations of motivative behavior suggest that our inferences about others and ourselves are formed by attributing motives, as we eliminate alternative explanations

Authoritarian approach
: An approach to the teaching-learning process in which the teacher maintains virtually total control without participation in decision-making by the students

Authoritative approach
: An approach to the teaching-learning process characterized by a teacher who is knowledgeable in her subject/literary areas and, while everyone in the

classroom knows the teacher is in charge, nevertheless students have ample opportunities to participate in decision making

Basal reader
A set of graded reading books which provide a developmental sequence of skills and a controlled vocabulary

Basic skills
The minimally required skills in reading, writing, and arithmetic essential to further academic development

Behavior modification
A carefully designed process by which desired behavior outcomes are gradually achieved through the appropriate use of positive reinforcers

"Beta" hypothesis
Practice the wrong response, then relearn the right response

Central tendency
Any of several statistics indicating the typical performance of students; for example, the mean, the median, and the mode

Chaining
The process whereby the individual hooks together a "chain" of small, individual conditioned behaviors to reach a complex skill

Chunking
A technique for holding separate items of information in short term memory by grouping them

Chronological age
A person's "calendar age"; the length of time one has lived; abbreviated "CA"

Classical conditioning (respondent conditioning)
A stimulus is presented to bring forth a response, a new stimulus is presented simultaneously with the old one, and then the old one is dropped, allowing the new one to bring forth the original response (Pavlov)

Classroom climate
The psychological context of the classroom; metaphorically, the classroom's "weather condition" for human development and learning

Classroom management
"Encompasses the provisions and procedures necessary to establish and maintain an environment in which instruction and learning can occur." It includes management of time, space, materials, and guest personnel

Clinical setting
The schoolhouse/classroom environment in which the teacher performs his or her responsibilities

Clinician
The teacher as a person who can perform competently in the teaching-learning process

Cognition
The process by which one comes to know, involving the mental processes of imagination, memory, perception, and reason; also concerned with how a

person takes random stimuli from the environment and then organizes this material into meaningful information
Cognitive development
All events and processes of the human mind
Cognitive domain
Includes objectives for recalling knowledge and developing intellectual skills
Cognitive structure
The student's grasp of the overall pattern of a field of study, emphasizing relationships within the field
Cognitive theories
Concerned primarily that we understand the processes we use when we interpret information about the motivation of our behavior
Cohesiveness
Describes closely-knit social groups that satisfy the needs of their members
Communication skills
Listening, writing, speaking, and the ability to present your ideas in such a manner your listeners will readily understand them
Competent
Responsibly able to perform appropriate duties
Computation skills
The ability to know, understand, and recognize how and when to apply the techniques of mathematics, computers, and statistics to the solutions of real-life problems
Concrete operational stage
The third stage of cognitive development (Piaget), in which logical thought can be applied to specific situations involving actual objects
Confluent
The merging of the affective and cognitive domains in the teaching-learning process
Constructionist
A theoretical approach that sees the child as "constructing" objects by coordinating many schemata; opposed to the idea of the child's simply copying or imitating what he sees in his environment
Continuous development
A term conceptually opposite of "stage deveopment"; children develop gradually and continuously into adults; the child is looked upon as a miniature adult
Corrective classroom management
The appropriate handling of inappropriate behavior in such a manner as to bring minimal disruption to the teaching-learning process and the providing of steps to help prevent such behavior in the future
Creativity
Unusual and useful solutions to problems, or the production of something

Glossary

novel and enjoyable (art, music, etc.)

Criterion-referenced test
A measurement that relates a test performance to specific levels of expected competence

Critical period
A limited period during the child's early years in which a certain type of learning occurs because of neurological development

Cross-impact matrix
A technique which uses the square grid pattern of a matrix to analyze the interrelationship between events and developments

Curriculum
All the academic subjects plus other planned or incidental experiences through which the institutional goals and objectives are to be accomplished

Delphi technique
Seeks a consensus of experts by having their opinions anonymously filtered through an intermediary

Democratic approach
An approach to the teaching-learning process characterized by moderate teacher control, with emphasis on student participation in most of the decision-making

Development
Orderly, directional change (generally associated with age) characterized by increasing differentiation and complex organization

Direct instruction
Instruction in which the teacher does a great deal of the direction as opposed to the open classroom, where discovery learning may be the principal approach

Discipline
As a noun—One aspect of classroom management, defined as the set of appropriate behaviors permitted in the classroom
As a verb—Taking action to correct a student's inappropriate behavior with the goal of restoring the student as one who has appropriate behavior

Discovery learning (Bruner)
The process of confronting children with problems and urging them to seek solutions independently and through group discussions, rather than presenting carefully prearranged and sequenced materials

Dissonance
Better known as "cognitive dissonance," this theory holds that only when cognitions are dissonant (out of harmony) is motivation activated to resolve the dissonance

Distributed practice
Short concentration periods spaced out over time

Drive reduction

The drive to fulfill biological needs motivates or causes behavior

Educational objective
A more or less precise statement of a desired behavior change

Educational psychology
A body of knowledge grounded in psychological research which provides a scientific approach to the teaching-learning process

Educational services professional
A person prepared to work effectively in an educational setting other than the schoolhouse classroom

Educational setting
The particular place/environment in which the teaching-learning process occurs

Effects
Influences, expected or unexpected, that can occur during scientific studies of behavior and can "contaminate" the outcomes

Emotional development
Children's feelings and their affective responses

Emotionally disturbed
Includes two factors: (1) reduced functional abilities in academic pursuits and (2) poor interpersonal relationships; usually progress of these students academically will be very slight until the conflict with which they are battling is resolved

Enactive representation
Associated with infancy and very early childhood, in which children represent past experience through their motor acts (Bruner)

Evaluation
An interpretation of test results which includes comparative-judgmental terms, such as bigger, faster, better

Exceptional children
Children whose behavior deviates from the norm in ways that are maladaptive to the child or society

Extinction
A behavior which has been reinforced weakens or disappears when reinforcement is stopped

Extrinsic motivation
Emphasizes the external goals toward which the activity is directed

Factual level question
A question that requires a factual answer, not requiring a great amount of use of the cognitive processes such as reflecting, reasoning, and the like

Feedback
Initial, medial, or final information on learning given to teachers, students, and parents to facilitate maximal developmental progress

Field theory (Lewin)

Glossary

Stresses that psychological fields are changed in similar fashion as magnetic fields, as positive and negative forces act on human beings

Formal operations stage
: The fourth stage of cognitive development (Piaget), in which logical thought can be applied abstractly, with symbols substituting for objects

Formative evaluation
: Evaluation during instruction to provide corrective feedback for the benefit of both the students and the teacher

Gestalt psychology
: An approach developed largely by early German psychologists, which concentrates on the significance of perceiving stimulation in patterns and relationships

Gifted
: Giftedness is at the opposite end of the continuum of intelligence from mental retardation; these students score two or more standard deviations above the norm on a test of intelligence (from 130 to 160 on the I.Q. scale)

Grade equivalents
: The grade levels which correspond to the mean scores on standardized tests of a normative sample of children at each grade level

Grades
: The symbols, or marks (A, B, C, etc.), given by a teacher to indicate the extent of a student's accomplishment in a particular assignment or course of instruction

Halo effect
: A factor influencing, either positively or negatively, evaluations of products or processes from students known in other ways

"Handles" on your learning
: Features to help you take hold of and understand clearly the meanings of concepts

Hearing impaired
: Hearing impaired students have defects in hearing which limit their ability to take in and process information from their surroundings which has to do with understanding and production of language

Hedonism
: Motivated by pleasure and pain

Homeostasis
: An optimal level exists for various states of the body; and when the body deviates too far from that level, motivational circuits are triggered by the receptors monitoring these states, and behaviors that will bring the body back to its optimal level are begun

Iconic representation
: Associated with the preschool and early elementary years, in which children are able to form visual images of stimuli encountered in their environment,

to retain these images, and to recall them in the absence of the real object or event (Bruner)

Inappropriate behavior
: Behavior that is disruptive, irrelevant, or unproductive in relation to the goals of the teaching-learning process

Incentive
: The goals toward which we strive can in themselves be motivating

Incongruity
: Motivation exists whenever an incongruity occurs between past experience and new information

The Individualized Education Program (IEP)
: Under Public Law 94-142, which took effect in 1977, an IEP must be developed for each exceptional child in the school system

Individualized instruction
: A system that individualizes instruction by designing and programming specific learning tasks so individual learners can progress through the program at their own level of readiness and own learning rate

Information processing theory
: Study of the ways sensory input is transformed, recovered, and used

Inquiry method
: The process of using one's own intellect to gain knowledge by discovering concepts and organizing them into a structure that is personally meaningful

Insight
: For the cognitive theorists, the perception of new relationships by an individual

Instinct
: Genetic programming in the form of instinctive behaviors may become activated when our physical needs reach certain levels

Instructional objectives
: Statement which describes the goals you expect the student to reach when you complete instruction

Intelligence
: The ability of an individual to be aware of and select from his or her environment those certain necessary elements, which when put together in orderly fashion, enable the individual to achieve a desirable goal

Interaction
: Mutual influence between the participants in a defined group

Interference theory
: The theory that previous, future, or coactive current learning may interfere with each other and may cause confusion or forgetting

Intrinsic motivation
: The value or pleasure associated with an activity as opposed to the goal toward which the activity is directed

Glossary

Laissez-faire approach
: An approach to the teaching-learning process in which the teacher exercises minimal controls over the students or classroom activities

Learning
: (1) A change in behavior due to experience
: (2) A change in behavioral repertoire due to experience
: (3) The personal discovery by an individual of his or her relationship to an object, event, process, idea, other persons, God, or self; may or may not be outward behavior that is quantitatively measureable as a result of the inner discovery

Learning disabilities
: Students who have normal intelligence, but are experiencing difficulties in their academic pursuits because of a wide range of perceptual disorders which reflect themselves in disfunctions in language and mathematics; these students usually normal to above normal in intelligence, but have perceptual "short circuits"

Learning society
: Characteristic of our own society, where the explosion of new ideas and techniques has created the need for many people to learn many things

Learning style
: A consistent pattern of behavior with a particular range of individual differences

Life space (Lewin)
: All the elements within the child's psychological environment that influence the child's behavior at a given moment

Long-term memory (LTM)
: Permanent storehouse of information with unlimited capacity

Loss of reinforcement
: A behavior will weaken if its occurrence consistently results in the loss of reinforcers

Mainstreaming
: The practice of bringing exceptional children into the regular classroom for as much time as possible, rather than keeping them in self-contained classrooms; usually, for certain times during the day, the exceptional child will make use of a special *resource room*

Massed practice
: Intensified concentration upon learning material in a short period of time

Mastery learning
: Progress from one learning unit to another should be based upon fully learning each successive task

Maturation
: Changes in behavior, genetically determined, biological in nature, which occur independent of experience

Meaningfulness
: People pursue those objects, events, and experiences that are emotionally important for them

Mediator
: A word or idea, produced by the student himself, to tie together two words, ideas, or objects in a way to make sense out of them

Mental retardation
: Students which are below average in their intellectual functioning (I.Q.)

Metamemory
: Knowledge of how your memory works

Middle school
: The school "between" the elementary and secondary schools; often referred to as "junior high," but grades contained in the middle school vary substantially depending on the philosophy, space availability, and other factors in the local school district; originally developed to meet the special needs of children in this age range

Mnemonic devices
: Special mental "hooks" for helping recall

Modeling
: The presentation of desirable behavior to others in the hope they will imitate it

Morale
: The affective tone of the classroom or school as a result of students' perceptions of major operational characteristics and their relationship to them

Motivation
: A concept used to describe the forces acting on or within a person to explain the initiation, direction, intensity, and persistence of behavior

Multipotentiality
: The highly variable capabilities—physical, mental, and spiritual—which are the result of either genetic inheritance or learning in the individual

National Assessment of Educational Progress (NAEP)
: Set up in 1964 by the Educational Commission of the States to provide information about the knowledge, understanding, skills, attitudes which American children acquire in our public schools

Negative reinforcement
: When a behavior consistently terminates or prevents an unpleasant (aversive) consequence, that behavior will increase in strength

Nonverbal communication
: The giving of a message without using words, such as through the nod of the head, facial expression, the pointing of a finger, and so on

Norm-referenced test
: A measurement that relates a student's performance to group-established norms

Open schedules
: Schedules not circumscribed by tight time requirements, so as to permit students more flexibility in learning

Operant (instrumental) conditioning
: A behavior (response) is expressed and is strengthened or weakened by positive reinforcement, punishment, negative reinforcement, or loss of reinforcement

Operation
: In Piaget's theory, the ability to manipulate concepts internally in increasingly complex ways

Participation chart
: A record of both the quantity and quality of each individual's contributions to a group exchange of idea

Peers
: Those of equal status with whom we interact on a regular basis

Personality
: A person's unique pattern of traits

Philosopher
: The teacher as a person who brings a philosophic perspective—fed by experiences, knowledge, and reflective commitment—to his performance as a clinician in the teaching-learning process

Physical development
: The simple changes in an individual's size and weight, to the gradual quantitative changes that can be charted for other physical and anatomical features

Physical handicaps
: These students are sometimes called orthopedically handicapped; if no other disabilities in addition to the physical disability, then there need be only modifications in terms of physical environment

Positive reinforcer
: Roughly synonymous with "reward." When any behavior is followed by a positive reinforcer, that behavior is strengthened

Preoperational stage
: The second stage of cognitive development (Piaget), in which representation of objects and ideas begins to replace seeing, feeling, touching as a mode of thought

Preschool education
: The education that takes place prior to formal academic instruction

Preventive classroom management
: The organization of the classroom environment to maximize student learning and minimize inappropriate behavior

Private schools
: Schools not in the public domain, financed and operated by private groups for special educational and/or religious purposes

Programmed learning
: The process by which the subject matter is broken up into small steps, so that each student will be reinforced as he or she successfully completes each step

Prosocial behavior
: Refers to "actions that are intended to aid or benefit another person or groups of people without the actor's anticipation of external rewards. Such actions often entail some cost, self sacrifice, or risk on the part of the actor"

Prospective teacher
: The student in the early stages of thinking about a career as a teacher

Psychomotor domain
: Includes objectives for developing manipulative and motor skills

Psychosocial
: The concept referring to the individual's establishing basic orientation to himself and his social world throughout the life cycle

Punishment
: Any consequence which weakens a behavior when it consistently follows that behavior

Realia
: Refers to the objects and activities used to relate classroom teaching to real life

Rehabilitation
: The conviction that we must restructure and rehabilitate our "smokestack" industries, so they can regain strong competitive positions

Reliability
: That quality of a test which indicates its ability to consistently give the same results; does it *consistently* measure whatever it measures?

Remedial teaching
: Specialized instruction aimed at correcting specific learning dysfunctions

Repertoire of responses
: A "stored supply" of information (concepts, skills, techniques, and the like) from which the teacher can draw as they are needed in order to perform competently in the teaching-learning process; educational psychology a major contributor to the repertoire for the teacher

Retrofitting
: The reeducation of people on a lifelong basis for keeping up with technological changes

Role playing
: The assumption of the role of another person by a student for the purpose of helping the student appreciate the feelings and perspectives of the person whose role has been assumed

Scenario
: A narrative about the future which leads from the present to a specific future

Glossary

time to provoke thinking about an issue or situation

Schedules of reinforcement
Fixed-ratio schedule: reward the behavior regularly, based on occurrence of the behavior (for example, every third time it occurs)
Fixed-interval schedule: reward the behavior regularly, based on the passage of time (for example, every two minutes)

Schema
A structurized system of assimilations and accommodations; a behavior pattern

School autonomy
The degree of independence with which a particular school is permitted to operate in relation to its governing body

Schoolhouse environment
All components (people, responsibilities, expectations, smells, etc.) that are found at the schoolhouse and which affect the individuals working there

Self-actualization
The process of discovering, becoming, and developing one's real self and one's full potential

Self-esteem
The worth with which a person perceives himself or herself

Sensorimotor stage
The first level of cognitive development (Piaget), in which the objects of thought are limited to what can be seen, felt, and heard

Sensory register (SR)
Information held briefly for decision on processing

Serial position effect
Tendency to remember more easily items at the beginning and ending of a list

Shaping
Reinforcing behavior by gradual steps into a refined form, by requiring increasingly better approximations of the behavior before providing reinforcement

Short-term memory (STM)
Ordinarily thought of as "working" memory

Simulation games
Games in which the students seek to find solutions; in the process the student is caused to clarify values, perspectives, and feelings

Social
Refers to the child's interaction with other individuals in his environment

Social motivation
Our interaction with other people, which both generates and directs behavior

Socialization
The process through which the child acquires the attitudes and behaviors

considered important and appropriate by the society in which the child lives

Sociobiology
A relatively contemporary and highly controversial science that asserts that man's behavior, like that of all animals, is genetically influenced (it is not that man necessarily behaves like an ape, but that the same mechanism, heredity encoded in genes, operates on both)

Socioeconomic status (SES)
A complex of attributes (occupation, education, income, housing, neighborhood, etc.) used to try to define what people are like

Sociometry
Procedures for describing, measuring, and interpreting group interaction structures

Speech impaired
Speech-impaired students are persons who have disorders of vocal production of such nature that they distract attention from what the individual is trying to say; articulation problems involving omissions, subsitutions, or distortions of speech sounds

Stage development
Periods of development marked by qualitative changes (changes in kind) at the beginning and the end

Standard scores
Scores based on the relationship between the mean and the standard deviation, for example, T scores, z scores, and so forth

Standardized test
A published, formal, ready-made test for teacher use

Stimulus generalization
A reinforcer not only strengthens the original behavior, but by being associated with many behaviors, eventually strengthens any behavior with which it is associated

Stimulus pairing
The function of any stimulus transfers to a previously neutral stimulus, if the two consistently occur together

Summative evaluation
Evaluation at the end of an instructional sequence used to provide a final estimate of student achievement

Symbolic representation
Associated with the later elementary school years, the thought of the child becomes more flexible and abstract due to the child's increasingly complex use of language; words may represent ideas and relationships for which there are no concrete referents (Bruner)

Task analysis
The arranging of skill components in order

Task-oriented
: Instruction designed and implemented with a view to spending a great amount of time on specific tasks

Taxonomy
: A comprehensive scheme for classifying learning objectives

Teacher burnout
: A condition that results from working too hard for too long or enduring too much stress over a short period of time. Symptoms vary from fatigue to depression to quick anger

Teacher competency
: The ability of a teacher to responsibly perform his or her duties appropriately

Teacher morale
: The extent to which teachers experience a sense of general well-being and satisfaction in their job situation

Teacher-made test
: An informal test which is not published, although generally typed and duplicated

Techno-fix
: The conviction that technology can provide solutions to our problems

Textbook "blues"
: The discouraged feelings students frequently experience because they perceive the textbook as boring, drudgery, something they "have to read"

Third force psychology
: Associated with Abraham Maslow and emphasizing "the human being in the process of becoming" rather than as reactive (S-R) or reactive-in-depth (Freud)

Token economy
: A system using tokens, later to be exchange for reinforcers, to control misbehavior and encourage learning

Transductive reasoning
: The child reasons that one event causes a second event when the two are not related; characteristic of preoperational stage in Piaget's theory

Transfer
: What is learned in one situation is helpful to an individual in other situations

Transformationalism
: The conviction that there need to be changes in human behavior in order to cope with the future

"Typical"
: That which occurs in the majority of instances in schools within the framework designated

Unit
: A plan that organizes ideas and knowledge into a meaningful structure for

teaching purposes

Valence (field theory)
: A positive or negative force influencing an individual's behavior

Validity
: The degree to which a measurement procedure truthfully represents that which it is intended to measure; does it *really* measure what it is supposed to?

Values clarification
: The process of looking intensively at one's values so as to become keenly aware of them, thus helping the individual to be able to choose more intelligently

Variability
: Any of several statistics (for example, the range and standard deviation) that indicate the spread of students' scores

Vector (field theory)
: The direction of a valence influencing an individual's behavior

Vicarious learning
: An individual learns by watching a model perform a specific behavior, noting the results, and then imitating whatever behavior brings pleasant consequences

Visual impairment
: Visually impaired students either have a limited field of vision or they have defects of visual acuity

Subject Index

abilities, 374-77
ability grouping in classroom, 314-17
acceleration, 121-24
accommodation, 69, 87
accountability in education, 151
achievement, 359-60
advance organizers, 166
affective educational objectives, 234
age level characteristics, 115-20, 124-25
alternative schools, 40, 62-63
American Federation of Teachers (AFT), 45-46
An Education of Value, 59
anecdotal records, 437-38
anxiety of students, 304-6
apathy in school, 317-18
applied behavior analysis, 92
aptitudes, 374-77
assimilation, 87
Association of Christian Schools International (ACSI), 410
assortment effect, 18
attendance in private schools, 53
attention in sensory register, 257-58
attitudes for learning, 247

attribution, 360-61
audiovisuals, 332
authoritarian teacher, 308-9
authoritative teacher, 309
autonomy of schools, 54

bandwagon effect, 18-19, 241
basic skill instruction, 333-41
behavior and motivation, 351-52
behavior modification, 131, 151-52
behavior studies, difficulties, 17-23
behaviorism, quantitative, 138, 140
behaviorist approach to learning, 75, 77, 92-93, 131-56, 271, 353-54
    curriculum, 151
    freedom and dignity, 153-54
    human nature, 152-53
    human potential, 394
    methodology, 151
    school function, 151-52
    students, 150-51
    teachers, 150
beta hypothesis, 237-38
Bonaker-Yingling Trait List, 438-40
boredom in classroom, 311, 313

central tendency, 441
Chen Course Evaluation Form, 440-41
childhood development, 105-26
Christian approach to learning, 205-25
　critique of, 221-22
　curriculum, 219
　discipline, 294-96
　exceptional students, 404-8
　future trends, 500-2
　human potential, 394-95
　methodology, 219
　philosophy of education, 411
　schools, 219-21
　students, 218
　teachers, 218
　view of cognitive-discovery approach, 176-77
Christian consensus, 207, 209
Christian day school movement, 206, 211
　quality of education, 222-23
Christian Manifesto, 214-15
classical conditioning, 132, 136-37
classroom climate, 299-321
　control, 277-98
　management and student achievement, 282
　methodology, 322-47
　modification for exceptional students, 411-16
　organization, 301
clinician, 3, 28
clustering, 226
coactive interference, 255
cognitive development (Piaget), 85, 108-9
　in elementary school, 119
　in junior-senior high schools, 120
　language in, 175
　in preschool, 116-18
cognitive-discovery approach to learning, 157-82
　Christian view of, 176-77
　curriculum, 170
　methodology, 170, 172-73
　motivation, 356-61
　school function, 173
　students, 170
　teachers, 168-70

cognitive dissonance, 19, 358-59
cognitive educational objectives, 233-34
cognitive strategies, 246-47
cognitive structure (Bruner), 165
cognitive theorists, 271
　view of human potential, 394
College Board, 61-62
Commission for the Visually Handicapped, 404
competition, 191, 243
complex behaviors, 149-50
computer-based instruction (CBI), 19, 330-31, 488
concepts, 246
　teaching of, 344
concrete operational state (Piaget), 86
confluent education, 192-93
connectionism, 136
conscience, 115
consequences, 148-49
consolidation, 167
constructionist, 85
content instruction, 341-45
contracts, teaching, 57-58
creativity in the classroom, 393
cross-impact matrix, 487, 498-99
curriculum, 294
　behaviorist approach, 151
　Christian approach, 219
　cognitive-discovery approach, 170
　humanistic approach, 196-97

death, child's view of, 113
democratic teacher, 309
demographic shifts and education, 491-93
development of children, 105-26
　critical period theories, 88-91
　levels, 23-24
　stages (Erikson), 98, 111
　stages (Freud), 76
　theories, 69-104
direct instruction defined, 41
discipline, 191, 278-82, 296-97
　Christian approach, 294-96
discouragement and students, 306
discovery approach to learning, 157-82
　efficiency of, 174

Subject Index

parental views of teacher, 174
dissonance, 19, 358-59
disuse theory of forgetting, 267
Downs Syndrome, 74
drill method of teaching, 325
drive reduction theory, 353-54

education career salaries, 10-11
education, future trends, 487-504
    goals of, 434-36
    job opportunities, 9-13
educational media, 331-33
educational objectives, cognitive, 233-34
educational psychology, defined, 4, 6, 15-23
    scientific approach, 16-17
Educational Resources Information Center (ERIC), 38
educational services professionals, 12-13
Effective Schools Approach, 62
elementary school characteristics, 119-20
emotional development, 109-12, 185
    in elementary school, 119
    in junior-senior high schools, 120
    in preschool, 118
emotionally disturbed students, 402, 405-6
enactive representation (Bruner), 88
encoding, 261-62
Enlightenment, 205, 211, 223
environment, effect on intelligence, 382-85
    effect on learning, 75, 80, 83-84, 137-40
episodic memories, 260
evaluations, 54
    alternate means, 462-63
    student, 52
exceptional students, 398-417
existentialism, 188-89
experimenter bias effect (EBE), 19

faculty meetings, 58
failure, 191, 198, 242-43
Family Educational Right to Privacy Act, 453
fear in schools, 302-4
fear of failure, 191
feedback of student measurements, 449-63

field of engagement for motivation, 362-64
field theorists, 162-63
films, 332
forces for motivation, 362-64
forgetting, 267-68
formal operational stage (Piaget), 86
free school movement, 198

genetics, and intelligence, 382-86
    and learning, 74, 75, 94
gestalt psychology, 160-63
gifted students, 403, 407-8
goodness of man, 75-76, 222
grade level requirements, 52-53
grades, 452-53
group discussion, 328-29

handicapped students, 401-7
Hawthorne effect, 19-20
hearing impaired students, 402, 404-5
heredity. See genetics.
hierarchy of needs (Maslow), 355-56, 473
human development, 72-73. See also development theories.
human nature, behaviorist view, 152-53
Humanist Manifesto II, 212-13
humanistic approach, 183-204, 206, 243
    curriculum, 196-97
    human potential, 394
    methodology of, 197
    school function, 197-98
    student, 191-95, 200-1
    teacher, 195-96
    values, 199
humanists, 75, 271

iconic representation (Bruner), 88
inappropriate behavior, 292-93
incongruity, 357-58
individualized instruction, 329
information age and education, 490-91
Information Processing Theory, 256-64
inquiry method of learning, 327-38
instructional media, 331-33
instructional objectives, 230-33
instrumental conditioning, 132, 136-37
integrative reconciliation, 167

intellectual learning, 245-46
intelligence, 377-86
    concepts of, 377-79
    crystallized, 378
    environment effects, 382-85
    fluid, 378
    hereditary effects, 382-86
intelligence tests, 379-82
interaction theories, 75, 81
interference theory of learning, 268

journals, professional, 33-37

laissez-faire teacher, 309
language arts instruction, 338-40
language in cognitive learning, 175
lateral transfer of learning, 269
laws of effect, readiness and exercise, 136, 138
learning, 70
    centers, 329-30
    disabilities, 402, 406
    kinds, 244-49
    processes, 25
lecture method of teaching, 324
liberalism, 210
life-long learning, 345-46, 494
listening instruction, 339
loci, 264-66
long-term memory, 259-62

mainstreaming exceptional students, 398-417
management of classroom, 277-98
massed practice, 266
mastery approach to learning, 227, 229-44
materialism, 136
mathematics instruction, 340-41
mean, 441
meaningful learning, 343-44, 361
measurement of student performance, 418-48
media in education, 331-33
median, 441
memorization method of teaching, 325
memory improvement, 264-66
mental health of teacher, 474-76

mental retardation, 403, 406-7
mentor-assisted enrichment projects (MAEP), 407-8
metamemory, 262-64
methodology, 322-47
    behaviorist approach, 151
    Christian approach, 219
    cognitive-discovery approach, 170, 172-73
    drill, 325
    future, 495-500
    humanistic approach, 197
    language arts, 338-40
    lecture, 324
    mathematics, 340-41
    memorization, 325
    preschool, 334-36
    reading, 336-38
    recitation, 325
middle school, defined, 41
mnemonics, 264-66
mode, 441
modeling, 93, 132
models for learning, 146-48, 247
modern math, 158-59, 342-43
molding-unfolding dichotomy, 77-81
moral development, 112-15
    elementary, 119-20
    junior-senior high, 120
    preschool, 118-19
moral reasoning stages (Kohlberg), 114
morale of students, 53, 307
motivation of students, 348-71
    cognitive approaches, 356-61
    developing theoretical framework of, 361-63
    field of engagement, 362-64
    forces inside, 362-64
    forces outside, 363-64
    needs approach to, 354-56
    teacher responsibilities, 365-68
    theoretical approaches, 353-56
motor skills, 247-48
multipotentiality of student, 372-97

National Assessment of Educational Progress (NAEP), 238-40

Subject Index

National Commission on Excellence in Education (1983), 22, 59, 60-61
National Education Association (NEA), 45-46
negative reinforcement, 141
negative transfer, 268
nontraditional education, 12-13
normative research, 83

open classroom, 196-98
open education, 18, 178-79
operant conditioning, 132, 137, 140-44
Our Nation Is at Risk, 22, 59, 60-61
overlearning, 264

pacing of class, 309-10
Paideia Proposal, 59
parent-teacher conferences, 454-57
parents role in education, 316, 494-95
peer pressure, 306-7
percentile scores, 444
permissiveness, 278-82
philosopher-clinician role of teacher, 27-31
philosophy, defined, 27
phonics approach to reading, 337-38
physical development, 105-26
    in elementary school, 119
    in junior-senior high schools, 120
    in preschool, 116
physical environment of classroom, 315, 317-18
physical handicaps, 402, 405
play, 334-35
positive reinforcement, 140-41
positive transfer, 268
positivism, 134
preoperational state (Piaget), 86
preschool, development, 116-19
    education, 334-36
private schools, 53-55
problem-solving method of learning, 327-28
professional development of teacher, 26
    journals, 33-37
    organizations, 482-83
programmed learning, 18, 132, 151
progressive differentiation, 167

progressivism, 187-88
Project Equality, 59
Project Follow Through, 44
project method of learning, 328
Project on Alternatives in Education (PAE), 53
psychomotor educational objectives, 237-38
psychosocial theories of learning, 94-98
Public Law 94-142, 400-1, 408-10
punishment, 132, 141, 143
Pygmalion effect, 20-22, 38-39

quantitative behaviorism, 138, 140

range, 442
readiness, 121-24
reading instruction, 336-38
    basal approach, 337
    individualized approach, 337
    kinesthetic approach, 337
    language-experience approach, 336-37
    phonics approach, 337-38
realia, 333
realism, 134
recitation method of teaching, 325
recognition in sensory register, 257
record keeping by teacher, 55-56
Redefining General Education in the American High School, 59
reinforcement, 140-41
rejection, effect on student, 306-7
reliability of test scores, 444
reorganization theory of forgetting, 267
report cards, 57, 453
representation (Bruner), 87
respondent conditioning, 132
retardation, 403, 406-7
retrieval, 261-62
rote learning, 245, 344
rules of school, 57

safety in schools, 302-4
school boards, 57, 66
school, autonomy, 54
    Christian approach, 219-21

cognitive-discovery approach, 173
social function of, 151-52
without failure, 198
science fiction, 496
scripture, 215-17
seat work, 365-67
secular humanism, 206, 211-12, 215, 223, 501
self-actualization, 95, 97, 192, 197
self-control, 115
self-discipline, 280-81
self-esteem, 41
self-evaluation of student, 368
self-fulfilling prophecy, 21
self-motivation, 173-74
self-understanding of teacher, 469-70
semantic memories, 260-61
sensorimotor state (Piaget), 85-86
sensory register, 256-58
shaping, 132
short-term memory, 258-59
social-emotional development, 109-12
in elementary school, 119
in junior-senior high schools, 120
in preschool, 118
social learning theory (Bandura), 147-50
sociobiology, 71, 81, 93, 104
socioeconomic status (SES), 386-90
SPEC effect, 22
speech, impairment, 401, 404
instruction, 338-39
therapy, 404
spiritual development, 113
stage theories of development, 80, 85-88
Erikson, 98, 111
Freud, 76
standard deviation, 442-43
standardized tests, 419-33
administering, 428-30
evaluating, 430-31
list of, 431-33
measurements of, 421-24
preparation of, 424-28
sources of, 424-25
Stanford-Binet intelligence scale, 379-80
stanines, 444
stimulus pairing, 143-44

stimulus repetition, 144
stimulus-response approach, 153-54
motivation in, 353-54
theory, 136
student evaluations, 52
students, anxiety of, 304-6
behaviorist approach, 150-51
Christian approach, 218
cognitive-discovery approach, 170
discouragement, 306
exceptional, 398-417
expectations of, 286-90
feedback, 449-63
handicapped, 401-7
humanistic view, 191-95, 200-1
motivation, 348-71
multipotentiality of, 372-97
performance measurement, 418-48
rejection, 306-7
self-evaluation, 368
sex difference among, 390-93
Study of High Schools, 50
Study of the American High School, 60
Summerhill, 184, 197-98
symbolic representation (Bruner), 88
systematic instructional design, 249-50

T scores, 444
taxonomy of educational objectives, 227, 233-38
teacher's notebook, 15, 25, 32
teacher, attributes of success, 470
authoritarian, 308-9
authoritative, 309
Christian approach, 218
cognitive-discovery approach, 168-70
competent model, 23-31
contracts, 57-58
democratic, 309
expectations of students, 286-90
humanistic approach, 195-96
laissez-faire, 309
letters to parents, 457-58
maladjustment, 470-74
mental health, 474-76
motivation responsibilities, 365-68
personal development, 26, 469-76

Subject Index

philosopher-clinician role, 27-31
planning, 286-93, 343
professional development, 26, 476-84
record keeping, 55-56
relationship with administration, 479-80
relationship with community, 481-82
relationship with other teachers, 479
relationship with parents, 480-81
relationship with students, 478-79
rule enforcement by, 57
schedule of, 55
self-understanding, 469-70
teaching, adequacy of preparation, 4-6
art of, 39
future changes, 487-504
loads, 52
methods of the future, 495-500
nontraditional education, 12-13
preparation for, 6-9
salaries, 10-11
styles 308-11
techno-fix, 488
technology and education, 490, 492-93
television in education, 332
tenure, 57
test results, interpretation, 441-44
reporting, 451-59

testing, 418-48
abuses of, 462
learning experience of, 458, 461
standardized, 419-33
teacher-made, 433-34
uses of, 459-62
theories of development, 69-104
transductive reasoning, 86
transfer of learning, 268-70
transparencies, 332

ultimate reality, 206, 500-2
unfolding-molding dichotomy, 77-81
unit plan method of learning, 328

validity of test scores, 443
values, humanistic, 199
variability of test scores, 442-43
verbal learning, 245
vertical transfer of learning, 268-69
violence in schools, 303
visual impairment, 401-2, 404
vocational skills, 344-45

Wechsler Scales, 380-81
writing instruction, 339-40

z scores, 444

Person Index

Adler, Mortimer J., 59
Aichhorn, August, 97
Allain, Violet, 495-99
Aristotle, 229
Armbruster, Frank E., 159
Atkinson, J. W., 359-60
Ausubel, David, 166-70

Baker, Ray Stannard, 496
Bandura, Albert, 92-93, 103, 145-50
Barber, Theodore X., 19
Barlett, Frederic, 267
Bartholomew, B. R., 50
Bell, Terrel H., 60
Benson, Warren S., 207
Berry, Sharon R., 403, 404, 406, 407, 410-11
Biehler, R. F., 8, 13, 18
Block, James, 240-41
Bloom, Benjamin S., 89, 229-30, 233-38
Bode, Boyd H., 188
Bower, Gordon, 266
Boyer, Ernest L., 60
Braun, Carl, 21
Bruner, Jerome, 70, 71, 87-88, 103, 160, 165-66, 168, 171-72, 327
Burns, Robert, 240-41
Burt, Cyril, 373-74, 384

Carew, Jean, 91
Carroll, John B., 229
Cattell, Raymond B., 378
Cawelti, Gordon, 59, 60-61
Childs, John L., 188
Combs, Arthur, 189, 202
Comte, Auguste, 134
Cornett, Claudia E., 311, 314
Counts, George S., 188

Dennison, George, 190
Dewey, John, 16, 45, 187, 326-27, 483
Dobson, James, 278, 302
Dopyers, John, 43
Dunlap, Knight, 238

Ehrlich, Paul, 497
Emmer, Edmund T., 282
Erikson, Erik, 76, 81, 84, 94-97, 98, 103, 111
Evertson, Carolyn M., 282

Person Index

Festinger, Leon, 358-59
Freud, Anna, 97
Freud, Sigmund, 76, 78-79, 104, 160, 187

Gagne, Robert, 244-49
Gangel, Kenneth O., 207
Gesell, Arnold, 83, 108, 117-18, 341
Glaser, Robert, 249-50
Glasser, William, 198
Gray, Dennis, 60
Green, Maxine, 327
Gronlund, Norman C., 230-33
Guilford, J. P., 378

Hall, T. Stanley, 117
Hanford, George H., 59
Havighurst, Robert, 89-91, 99, 103
Hechinger, Fred, 63
Highet, Gilbert, 7
Holt, John, 190, 191
Houts, Paul L., 60
Hull, Clark, 138, 140
Hunt, J. McVickers, 88-89, 99, 103, 357-58
Huxley, Aldous, 496

Jackson, Philip, 43, 47-48, 56
James, William B., 16, 376-77
Jensen, Arthur R., 382-86
Jones, Vernon, 281-82

Kail, Robert, 262-64
Kamin, Leon J., 373, 384
Kienel, Paul, 219
Kilpatrick, William H., 188
Klinger, Eric, 361
Knight, George, 134
Kohl, Herbert, 190, 198
Kohlberg, L., 112, 114
Kohler, Wolfgang, 160, 161-62
Kozol, Jonathan, 190, 198

Larrabee, Harold A., 327
Lay, Margaret, 43
Lewin, Kurt, 160, 162
Lewis, Arthur J., 489-93
Lippmann, Walter, 488-89
Lorenz, Conrad, 89

Mager, Robert F., 230-33
Mann, Horace, 42-43, 210
Maslow, Abraham, 81, 84, 94-95, 97, 103, 189, 355-56, 473
McClelland, David, 359-60
McGuffey, William H., 29-30
McLaughlin, Judith B., 59
Morrison, Henry C., 229
Murray, Edward J., 357
Murray, Henry A., 354

Neill, A. S., 197-98

Pavlov, Ivan, 136-37
Penfield, Wilder, 259-60
Perrone, Vito, 178-79
Piaget, Jean, 70, 71, 77, 85-87, 102-3, 109, 112, 160, 163-65, 168, 334, 341, 379
Powell, Arthur G., 60

Rogers, Carl R., 133, 189, 190, 201-2
Rosenthal, Robert, 19, 20-21
Rotter, J. B., 362
Rousseau, Jean Jacques, 186-88
Rugg, Harold, 188

Scarr, Sandra, 386
Schaeffer, Francis, 207-12, 214-15
Schaeffer, Franky, 217-18
Shane, Harold, 489, 493-95
Silk, Leonard, 492
Simpson, Elizabeth Jane, 237
Sizer, Theodore R., 60
Skinner, B. F., 16-17, 103, 133, 140-44, 150, 153, 174-76
Spearman, Charles, 377-78
Stephens, J. M., 9
Stevenson, Harold, 82
Sullivan, Mark, 31

Thales, 228-29
Thorndike, Edward L., 16, 135-38, 447-48
Thurstone, L. L., 378
Toffler, Alvin, 489
Tolving, Endel, 260-61

Veltkamp, James J., 209-10

Washburne, Carleton, 188, 229
Watson, John Broadus, 83-84, 137-40
Wechsler, David, 380
Weinberg, Richard A., 386
Weiner, Bernard, 360-61

Wells, H. G., 496
Westerhoff, John W., III, 31
Wilson, Edward O., 81, 93

Young, Warren, 215